3500+ Objective Chapter-wise Question Bank for CBSE Class 10 SCIENCE & MATHEMATICS

with Case base, A/R & MCQs

Corporate Office

DISHA PUBLICATION

45, 2nd Floor, Maharishi Dayanand Marg,
Corner Market, Malviya Nagar, New Delhi - 110017
Tel : 49842349 / 49842350

Typeset by Disha DTP Team

www.dishapublication.com
Books & ebooks for School & Competitive Exams

www.mylearninggraph.com
Etests for Competitive Exams

Write to us at **feedback_disha@aiets.co.in**

CONTENTS

SCIENCE

MATHEMATICS

Chemical Reactions and Equations

DIRECTIONS : *This section contains multiple choice questions. Each question has four choices (a), (b), (c) and (d) out of which only one is correct.*

1. Which of the following is a decomposition reaction?

    (a) $2HgO \xrightarrow{\text{Heat}} 2Hg + O_2$

    (b) $CaCO_3 \xrightarrow{\text{Heat}} CaO + CO_2$

    (c) $2H_2O \xrightarrow{\text{Electrolysis}} H_2 + O_2$

    (d) All of these

2. On the basis of following features, identify the correct option.
    (i)   This reaction occurs during corrosion.
    (ii) This reaction occurs during respiration.
    (a) Decomposition reaction
    (b) Redox reaction
    (c) Combination reaction
    (d) Endothermic reaction

3. Which of the following is not a physical change?
    (a) Boiling of water to give water vapour.
    (b) Melting of ice to give water.
    (c) Dissolution of salt in water.
    (d) Combustion of Liquefied Petroleum Gas (LPG).

4. Which of the following can be decomposed by the action of light?
    (a) NaCl   (b) KCl
    (c) AgCl   (d) CuCl

5. In which of the following the identity of initial substance remains unchanged?
    (a) Curdling of milk
    (b) Formation of crystals by process of crystallisation
    (c) Fermentation of grapes
    (d) Digestion of food

6. Which of the following reactions involves the combination of two elements?
    (a) $CaO + CO_2 \rightarrow CaCO_3$
    (b) $4Na + O_2 \rightarrow 2Na_2O$

    (c) $SO_2 + \dfrac{1}{2}O_2 \rightarrow SO_3$

    (d) $NH_3 + HCl \rightarrow NH_4Cl$

7. When hydrogen sulphide gas is passed through a blue solution of copper sulphate, a black precipitate of copper sulphide is obtained and the sulphuric acid so formed remains in the solution. The reaction is an example of –
    (a) a combination reaction
    (b) a displacement reaction
    (c) a decomposition reaction
    (d) a double decomposition reaction

8. What happens when copper rod is dipped in iron sulphate solution?
    (a) Copper displaces iron
    (b) Blue colour of copper sulphate solution is obtained
    (c) No reaction takes place
    (d) Reaction is exothermic

9. A student added dilute HCl to a test tube containing zinc granules and made following observations which one is correct?
    (a) The zinc surface became dull and black.
    (b) A gas evolved which burns with a pop sound.
    (c) The solution remained colourless.
    (d) The solution becomes green in colour.

10. A dilute solution of sodium carbonate was added to two test tubes (A) containing dil HCl and (B) containing dilute NaOH. The correct observation was –
    (a) a brown coloured gas liberated in test tube A.
    (b) a brown coloured gas liberated in test tube B.
    (c) a colourless gas liberated in test tube A.
    (d) a colourless gas liberated in test tube B.

11. A balanced chemical equation is in accordance with –
    (a) Avogadro's law
    (b) law of multiple proportion
    (c) law of conservation of mass
    (d) law of gaseous volumes.

12. The equation

    $$Cu + xHNO_3 \rightarrow Cu(NO_3)_2 + yNO_2 + 2H_2O$$

    The values of x and y are –
    (a) 3 and 5   (b) 8 and 6
    (c) 4 and 2   (d) 7 and 1

13. $Zn + H_2SO_4(dil) \longrightarrow ZnSO_4 + H_2\uparrow$

    Above reaction is –
    (a) decomposition reaction
    (b) single displacement reaction
    (c) combination reaction
    (d) synthesis reaction

14. The reaction in which two compounds exchange their ions to form two new compounds is –
    (a) a displacement reaction
    (b) a decomposition reaction
    (c) an isomerization reaction
    (d) a double displacement reaction

15. When the gases sulphur dioxide and hydrogen sulphide mix in the presence of water, the reaction is

    $SO_2 + 2H_2S \rightarrow 2H_2O + 2S$. Here hydrogen sulphide is acting as –
    (a) an oxidising agent   (b) a reducing agent
    (c) a dehydrating agent   (d) a catalyst

16. $CuO + H_2 \rightarrow H_2O + Cu$, reaction is an example of –
    (a) redox reaction   (b) synthesis reaction
    (c) neutralisation   (d) analysis reaction

17. A substance which oxidises itself and reduces other is known as –
    (a) oxidising agent   (b) reducing agent
    (c) both of these   (d) none of these

18. A redox reaction is one in which –
    (a) both the substances are reduced.
    (b) both the substances are oxidised.
    (c) an acid is neutralised by the base.
    (d) one substance is oxidised while the other is reduced.

19. In the following equations :

    $Na_2CO_3 + x\,HCl \rightarrow 2\,NaCl + CO_2 + H_2O$, the value of x is–
    (a) 1   (b) 2
    (c) 3   (d) 4

20. In the equation, $NaOH + HNO_3 \rightarrow NaNO_3 + H_2O$ nitric acid is acting as –
    (a) an oxidising agent   (b) an acid
    (c) a nitrating agent   (d) a dehydrating agent

21. $Fe_2O_3 + 2Al \rightarrow Al_2O_3 + 2Fe$

    The above reaction is an example of a –
    (a) combination reaction
    (b) double displacement reaction
    (c) decomposition reaction
    (d) displacement reaction

22. White silver chloride in sunlight turns to –
    (a) grey   (b) yellow
    (c) remain white   (d) red

23. Black and white photography uses –
    (a) decomposition of silver chloride.
    (b) decomposition of silver bromide.
    (c) both
    (d) none of these

24. When copper powder is heated it gets coated with –
    (a) black copper oxide   (b) yellow copper oxide
    (c) red copper oxide   (d) None of these

25. Combination of phosphorus and oxygen is an example of–
    (a) oxidation   (b) reduction
    (c) rancidity   (d) None of these

26. Rusting of iron is an example of –
    (a) reduction   (b) redox
    (c) oxidation   (d) dissociation

27. Which of the following does not corrode when exposed to the atmosphere?
    (a) Iron   (b) Copper
    (c) Gold   (d) Silver

28. Take about $1.0g\ CaCO_3$ in a test tube. Heat it over a flame, a colourless gas comes out. The reaction is called a
    (a) decomposition reaction
    (b) displacement reaction
    (c) double decomposition reaction
    (d) double displacement reaction

29. Hydrogen sulphide (H_2S) is a strong reducing agent. Which of the following reactions shows its reducing action?
    (a) $Cd(NO_3)_2 + H_2S \longrightarrow CdS + + 2HNO_3$
    (b) $CuSO_4 + H_2S \longrightarrow CuS + H_2SO_4$
    (c) $2FeCl_3 + H_2S \longrightarrow 2FeCl_2 + 2HCl + S$
    (d) $Pb(NO_3)_2 + H_2S \longrightarrow PbS + 2CH_3COOH$

30. $2CuI \rightarrow Cu + CuI_2$, the reaction is –

(a) redox
(b) neutralisation
(c) oxidation
(d) reduction

31. When copper turnings are added to silver nitrate solution, a blue coloured solution is formed after some time. It is because, copper –

(a) displaces silver from the solution
(b) forms a blue coloured complex with $AgNO_3$
(c) is oxidised to Cu^{2+}
(d) is reduced to Cu^{2+}

32. $Zn^{2+}(aq) + 2e^- \rightarrow Zn(s)$. This is –

(a) oxidation
(b) reduction
(c) redox reaction
(d) none of these

33. A substance A reacts with another substance B to produce the product C and a gas D. If a mixture of the gas D and ammonia is passed through an aqueous solution of C, baking soda is formed. The substances A and B are

(a) HCl and NaOH
(b) HCl and Na_2CO_3
(c) Na and HCl
(d) Na_2CO_3 and H_2O

34. Chemically the 'water gas' is

(a) H_2O (gaseous)
(b) $CO_2 + H_2$
(c) $CH_4 + H_2O$
(d) $CO + H_2$

35. The oxidation number of sulphur is –4 in

(a) H_2S
(b) CS_2
(c) Na_2SO_4
(d) Na_2SO_3

36. Identify the endothermic process from the following

(a) Addition of conc. HCl to water
(b) $CH_4(g) + 2O_2(g) \longrightarrow CO_2(g) + 2H_2O(l)$
(c) $H_2O(l) \longrightarrow H_2O(g)$
(d) $CaO(s) + H_2O(l) \longrightarrow Ca(OH)_2(aq)$

37. The schematic diagram is given below

$$\underset{\text{(solid)}}{A} \underset{\text{cool}}{\overset{\text{heat}}{\rightleftarrows}} \underset{\text{(vapour)}}{B} + \underset{\text{(vapour)}}{HCl}$$

A $\xrightarrow{\text{heat}}$ NaOH(aq)

$$\underset{\text{(Gas)}}{C} \xrightarrow{\text{conc. HCl}} D \xrightarrow[\text{shake well}]{H_2O} \underset{\text{(acidic solution)}}{E(aq)}$$

Which of the following is a correct statement ?

(a) A and E are chemically same.
(b) A and D are chemically same.
(c) D and E are chemically same.
(d) C and E are chemically same.

38. The oxidation states of P atom in $POCl_3$, H_2PO_3 and $H_2P_2O_6$, respectively are

(a) $+5, +4, +4$
(b) $+5, +5, +4$
(c) $+4, +4, +5$
(d) $+3, +4, +5$

39. The process of respiration is :

(a) Oxidation reaction which is endothermic
(b) Reduction reaction which is endothermic
(c) Combination reaction which is exothermic
(d) Oxidation reaction which is exothermic

40. Silver articles become black when exposed to air. It is due to the formation of

(a) Silver oxide
(b) Silver nitrate
(c) Silver chloride
(d) Silve sulphide

41. A test tube along with calcium carbonate in it initially weighed 30.08 g. A heating experiment was performed on this test tube till calcium carbonate completely decomposed with evolution of a gas. Loss of weight during this experiment was 4.40 g. What is the weight of the empty test tube in this experiment?

(a) 20.08 g
(b) 21.00 g
(c) 24.50 g
(d) 2.008 g

42. Match chemical reactions given in the List I with the type of chemical reactions given in List II and select the correct answer using the options given below:

List I (Chemical reactions)		List II (Type of Chemical reactions)	
A.	Formation of NH_3 from N_2 and H_2	I.	Decomposition
B.	Calcination of zinc carbonate.	II.	Double displacement
C.	Reaction of aqueous $BaCl_2$ solution with dilute H_2SO_4	III.	Combination
D.	Rancidity of oils	IV.	Redox
		V.	Displacement

(a) A-I, B-V, C-III, D-IV
(b) A-III, B-IV, C-V, D-I
(c) A-IV, B-III, C-V, D-I
(d) A-III, B-I, C-II, D-IV

43.

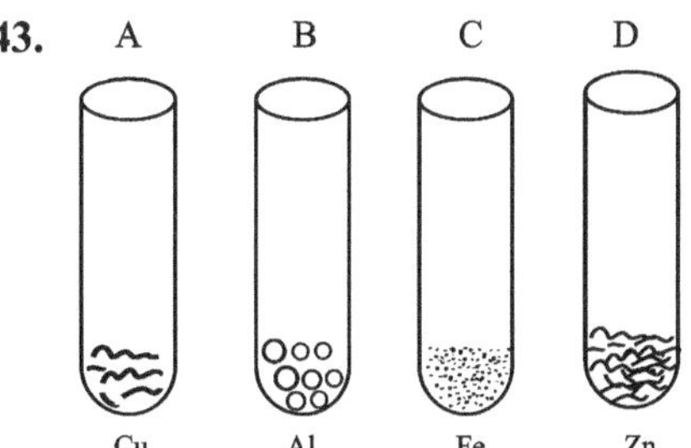

If we added $FeSO_4$ to above four test tubes, in which test tube we observe black residue?

(a) "A" and "B"
(b) "B" and "C"
(c) "A" and "C"
(d) "B" and "D"

≫ Case/Passage Based Questions ≫≫

DIRECTIONS : *Study the given case/passage and answer the following questions.*

Case/Passage - 1

The reaction between MnO_2 with HCl is depicted in the following diagram. It was observed that a gas with bleaching abilities was released . **[From CBSE Question Bank-2021]**

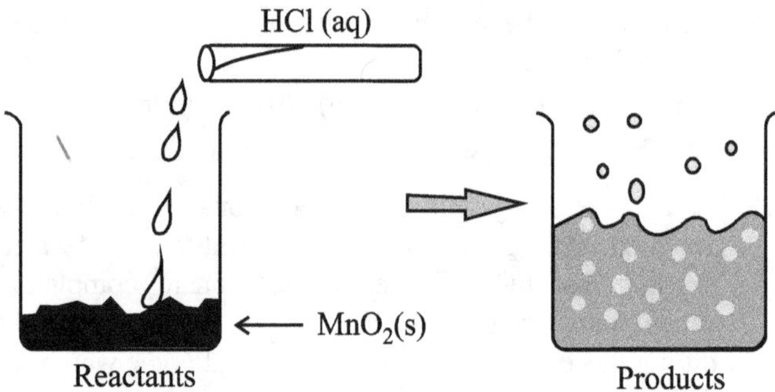

44. The chemical reaction between MnO_2 and HCl is an example of:

(a) displacement reaction

(b) combination reaction

(c) redox reaction

(d) decomposition reaction.

45. Chlorine gas reacts with ______ to form bleaching powder.

(a) dry $Ca(OH)_2$

(b) dil. solution of $Ca(OH)_2$

(c) conc. solution of $Ca(OH)_2$

(d) dry CaO

46. Identify the correct statement from the following:

(a) MnO_2 is getting reduced whereas HCl is getting oxidized

(b) MnO_2 is getting oxidized whereas HCl is getting reduced.

(c) MnO_2 and HCl both are getting reduced.

(d) MnO_2 and HCl both are getting oxidized.

47. In the above discussed reaction, what is the nature of MnO_2?

(a) Acidic oxide   (b) Basic oxide

(c) Neutral oxide   (d) Amphoteric oxide

48. What will happen if we take dry HCl gas instead of aqueous solution of HCl?

(a) Reaction will occur faster.

(b) Reaction will not occur.

(c) Reaction rate will be slow.

(d) Reaction rate will remain the same.

Case/Passage - 2

Chemistry in Automobiles:

For an internal combustion engine to move a vehicle down the road, it must convert the energy stored in the fuel into mechanical energy to drive the wheels. In your car, the distributor and battery provide this starting energy by creating an electrical "spark", which helps in combustion of fuels like gasoline. Below is the reaction depicting complete combustion of gasoline in full supply of air:

[From CBSE Question Bank-2021]

$$2C_8H_{18}(I) + 25O_2(g) \longrightarrow 16 \text{ 'X'} + Y$$

49. Which of the following are the products obtained from the reaction mentioned in the above case?

Product 'X'	Product 'Y'
(a) CO_2	H_2O_2
(b) H_2O	CO
(c) CH_3OH	H_2O
(d) CO_2	H_2O

50. Identify the types of chemical reaction occurring during the combustion of fuel:

(a) Oxidation & Endothermic reaction

(b) Decomposition & Exothermic reaction

(c) Oxidation & Exothermic reaction

(d) Combination & Endothermic reaction

51. On the basis of evolution/absorption of energy, which of the following processes are similar to combustion of fuel?

(i) Photosynthesis in plants

(ii) Respiration in the human body

(iii) Decomposition of vegetable matter

(iv) Decomposition of ferrous sulphate.

(a) (ii) & (iii)   (b) (i) & (ii)

(c) (iii) & (iv)   (d) (ii) & (i)

52. 'A student while walking on the road observed that a cloud of black smoke belched out from the exhaust stack of moving trucks on the road.' Choose the correct reason for the production of black smoke:

(a) Limited supply of air leads to incomplete combustion of fuel.

(b) Rich supply of air leads to complete combustion of fuel.

(c) Rich supply of air leads to a combination reaction.

(d) Limited supply of air leads to complete combustion of fuel.

53. 'Although nitrogen is the most abundant gas in the atmosphere, it does not take part in combustion'. Identify the correct reason for this statement.

(a) Nitrogen is a reactive gas

(b) Nitrogen is an inert gas

(c) Nitrogen is an explosive gas

(d) Only hydrocarbons can take part in combustion

Assertion & Reason

DIRECTIONS : *Each of these questions contains an assertion followed by reason. Read them carefully and answer the question on the basis of following options. You have to select the one that best describes the two statements.*

(a) If both **Assertion** and **Reason** are **correct** and Reason is the **correct explanation** of Assertion.

(b) If both **Assertion** and **Reason** are correct, but Reason is **not the correct explanation** of Assertion.

(c) If **Assertion** is **correct** but **Reason** is **incorrect**.

(d) If **Assertion** is **incorrect** but **Reason** is **correct**.

54. **Assertion :** Chlorine gas react with potassium iodide solution to form potassium chloride and iodine.

    Reason : Chlorine is more reactive than iodine therefore displaces iodine from potassium iodide.

55. **Assertion :** When copper strip is placed in ferrous sulphate solution, colour of the solution changes.

    Reason : Iron is more reactive than copper.

56. **Assertion :** Decomposition of vegetable matter into compost is an endothermic reaction.

    Reason : Heat is required in an endothermic reaction.

57. **Assertion :** Reaction of sodium sulphate with barium chloride is a precipitation reaction.

    Reason : Precipitation reaction produces insoluble salt.

58. **Assertion:** When a mixture of hydrogen and chlorine is placed in sunlight, hydrogen chloride is formed.

    Reason : It is an example of combination reaction.

59. **Assertion :** Stannous chloride gives grey precipitate with mercuric chloride, but stannic chloride does not do so.

    Reason : Stannous chloride is a powerful oxidising agent which oxidises mercuric chloride to mercury.

60. **Assertion :** Corrosion of iron is commonly known as rusting.

    Reason : Corrosion of iron occurs in presence of water and air.

61. **Assertion :** In a reaction

    $$Zn(s) + CuSO_4 (aq) \longrightarrow ZnSO_4 (aq) + Cu(s),$$

    Zn is a reductant but itself get oxidized.

    Reason : In a redox reaction, oxidant is reduced by accepting electrons and reductant is oxidized by losing electrons.

62. **Assertion :** A reducing agent is a substance which can either accept electron.

    Reason : A substance which helps in oxidation is known as reducing agent.

63. **Assertion :** The balancing of chemical equations is based on law of conservation of mass.

    Reason : Total mass of reactants is equal to total mass of products.

Match the Following

DIRECTIONS : *Each question contains statements given in two columns which have to be matched. Statements (A, B, C, D) in column I have to be matched with statements (p, q, r, s) in column II.*

64. Column II gives type of reaction mention in column I, match them correctly.

Column I	Column II
(A) $C + O_2 \rightarrow CO_2$	(p) Displacement
(B) $AgBr \xrightarrow{light} Ag + Br$	(q) Combination
(C) $Zn + CuSO_4 \rightarrow ZnSO_4 + Cu$	(r) Decomposition
(D) $CH_3CH_2OH \xrightarrow{Cu} CH_3CHO + H_2$	(s) Oxidation

65.

Column I	Column II
(A) $KClO_3 \xrightarrow{\Delta}$	(p) O_2
(B) $ZnCO_3 \xrightarrow{\Delta}$	(q) H_2O
(C) $H_2CO_3 \xrightarrow{\Delta}$	(r) CO_2
(D) $C_2H_6 \xrightarrow{\Delta}$	(s) ZnO

	A	B	C	D
(a)	p	s, r	q, r	q, r
(b)	p	q, r	s, r	r, p
(c)	q, r	s, p	p, s	r
(d)	r	q	s	p

Fill in the Blanks

DIRECTIONS : *Complete the following statements with an appropriate word / term to be filled in the blank space(s).*

66. In a .... reaction two or more substances combine to form a new single substance.

67. Reactions in which heat is given out along with the products are called .... reactions.

68. Reactions in which energy is absorbed are known as .... reactions.

69. When an element displaces another element from its compound, a .... reaction occurs.

70. Two different atoms or groups of atoms (ions) are exchanged in .... reactions.

71. Precipitation reactions produce .... salts.

72. Reduction is the .... of oxygen or gain of hydrogen.

73. The digestion of food in the body is an example of .... reaction.

74. The addition of oxygen to a substance is called ....

75. When calcium carbonate is heated, it decomposes to give .... and ....

76. The new substances produced in a reaction are called as ....

True / False

DIRECTIONS : *Read the following statements and write your answer as true or false.*

77. The number of atoms of each element is conserved in any chemical reaction.

78. Oxidation is the loss of electrons from a substance.

79. Reduction is the gain of electrons by a substance.

80. A complete chemical equation represents the reactants, products and their physical states symbolically.

81. A magnesium ribbon burns with a dazzling flame in air (oxygen) and changes into a white substance, magnesium oxide.

82. Rusting is a double decomposition reaction.

83. The reaction between nitrogen and hydrogen to give ammonia is an example of a combination reaction.

84. Action of heat on ferrous sulphate is an example of decomposition reaction.

85. The formation of Cu and H_2O in the reaction of copper oxide with hydrogen is an example of a redox reaction.

ANSWER KEY & SOLUTIONS

1. **(d)** A decomposition reaction is a type of chemical reaction in which a single compound breaks down into two or more elements or new compounds.

2. **(b)** Both are redox reactions. Redox reactions are characterised by the transfer of electrons between chemical species. One species undergoes oxidation while another species undergoes reduction.

3. **(d)** Combustion of liquefied petroleum gas is a chemical change. As it is an irreversible reaction and new products (carbon dioxide and water vapours) are formed during the change. Also, a lot of heat is released during this reaction.

4. **(c)**

5. **(b)** Formation of crystals by process of crystallization.

6. **(b)** Except (b) all other reactions involve compounds.

$$CuSO_4 + H_2S \longrightarrow CuS + H_2SO_4$$
(blue)   (black)
(double decomposition reaction)

7. **(d)**

8. **(c)** Iron is more reactive than copper, hence Cu will not displace iron from iron sulphate, hence no reaction will take place.

9. **(b)** $Zn + 2HCl \longrightarrow ZnCl_2 + H_2$
Hydrogen gas burns with a pop sound.

10. **(c)** $Na_2CO_3 + 2HCl \longrightarrow 2NaCl + H_2O + CO_2$
$Na_2CO_3 + NaOH \longrightarrow$ no reaction

11. **(c)**

12. **(c)** $Cu + 4HNO_3 \longrightarrow Cu(NO_3)_2 + 2NO_2 + 2H_2O$

13. **(b)**   **14.** (d)

15. **(b)** Here H_2S is behaves as a reducing agent and oxidises to H_2O.

16. **(a)**
$$\overset{\text{Oxidation}}{CuO + H_2 \longrightarrow Cu + H_2O}$$
Reduction

17. **(b)**   **18.** (d)

19. **(b)** $Na_2CO_3 + 2HCl \longrightarrow 2NaCl + CO_2 + H_2O$

20. **(b)** The reaction represents a neutralisation reaction in which base (NaOH) reacts with an acid (HNO$_3$) to form salt (NaNO$_3$) and water (H$_2$O).

21. **(d)**

22. **(a)** White silver chloride in sunlight turns to grey.

23. **(b)**

24. **(a)** $2Cu + O_2 \xrightarrow{\Delta} 2CuO$
                 Black

25. **(a)** $4P + 3O_2 \xrightarrow{\text{(Oxidation)}} 2P_2O_3$

$4P + 5O_2 \xrightarrow{\text{(Oxidation)}} 2P_2O_5$

26. **(b)** $2Fe(s) + O_2(g) + 4H^+(aq) \longrightarrow 2Fe^{2+}(aq) + 2H_2O(l)$

27. **(c)** Gold is least reactive hence does not corrode at all.

28. **(a)** $CaCO_3 \xrightarrow{\Delta} CaO + CO_2$

29. **(c)**
$$\overset{\text{Reduction}}{FeCl_3 + H_2S \longrightarrow FeCl_2 + HCl + S}$$
Oxidation

In the given reaction H_2S undergoes oxidation, hence behave as a reducing agent.

30. **(a)**
$$\overset{\text{reduction}}{2\overset{+1}{C}uI \rightarrow \overset{0}{C}u + \overset{+2}{C}uI_2}$$
Oxidation and reduction both
oxidation

occur so the reaction is redo

31. **(a)** Cu is more reactive than Ag.

$\overset{0}{Cu} + 2AgNO_3 \longrightarrow \overset{+1}{C}uNO_3 + 2Ag$

32. **(b)** $\overset{+2}{Zn}(aq) + 2e^- \longrightarrow \overset{0}{Z}n(s)$; reduction

33. **(b)**
$$\underset{\text{(A)}}{HCl} + \underset{\text{(B)}}{Na_2CO_3} \longrightarrow \underset{\text{(C)}}{NaCl(aq)} + \underset{\text{(D)}}{CO_2 + H_2O}$$

$$CO_2 + NH_3 + NaCl(aq) \longrightarrow \underset{\text{Baking soda}}{NaHCO_3} + NH_4Cl$$

Hence A & B are HCl and Na_2CO_3

34. **(d)** Water gas $\rightarrow CO + H_2$

35. **(∗)** Let the oxidation state of S be x

(i) H_2S
$\therefore 2 + x = 0$
    $x = -2$

(ii) CS_2

$4 + 2x = 0 \Rightarrow x = -2$

(iii) Na_2SO_4

$2(+1) + x + 4(-2) = 0$

$2 + x - 8 = 0$

$x = +6$

(iv) Na_2SO_3

$2(+1) + x + 3(-2) = 0$

$2 + x - 6 = 0$

$x = +4$

None of these, option is correct.

36. **(c)** Conversion of liquid to gas is endothermic process.

37. **(b)**

$$(solid)\ \circled{A} \underset{cool}{\overset{heat}{\rightleftharpoons}} \circled{B}\ (vapour) + HCl\ (vapour)$$

$$NH_4Cl \qquad NH_3$$

$heat \mid NaOH\ (aq.)$

$$\circled{C} \xrightarrow{HCl\ (con)} \circled{D}\ NH_4Cl$$

$$NH_3(g)$$

$(shake\ well) \mid H_2O$

$$\circled{E}\ HCl$$

$(acidic\ soln.)$

$A = NH_4Cl;\ D = NH_4Cl$

Hence correct statement is: A and D are chemically same.

38. **(a)** Let the oxidation state of P-atom in $POCl_3$, H_2PO_3 and $H_4P_2O_6$ be x.

(i) $POCl_3$

$x + 1(-2) + 3(-1) = 0$

$x - 2 - 3 = 0$

$x = +5$

(ii) H_2PO_3

$2(1) + x + 3(-2) = 0$

$2 + x - 6 = 0$

$x = +4$

(iii) $H_4P_2O_6$

$4(1) + 2x + 6(-2) = 0$

$4 + 2x - 12 = 0$

$2x = 8$

$x = +4.$

39. **(d)** Respiration is oxidation and exothermic process.

40. **(d)** Layer of silver sulphide deposited on the silver articles when exposed to air.

41. **(a)** On thermal decomposition of calcium carbonate

$$CaCO_3 \xrightarrow{\Delta} CaO + CO_2$$
$$\ \ 100\,g \qquad\qquad 56\,g \quad 44\,g$$

44 g CO_2 is formed from 100 g $CaCO_3$

4.40 g CO is formed from $\dfrac{100}{44} \times 44 = 10$ g $CaCO_3$

If mass of $CaCO_3$ is 10 g, then weight of empty test tube = 30.08 − 10.0 = 20.08 g

42. **(d)** A-III, B-I, C-II, D-IV

43. **(d)** Zn and Al are more reactive than iron, therefore they will displace iron from its salt solution giving black residue, while Cu being less reactive than iron will not able to displace iron from its salt solution.

$$FeSO_4 + 2Al \longrightarrow Al_2(SO_4)_3 + 3Fe$$

$$FeSO_4 + Zn \longrightarrow ZnSO_4 + Fe$$

$$FeSO_4 + Cu \longrightarrow No\ reaction$$

$$FeSO_4 + Fe \longrightarrow No\ reaction$$

44. **(c)** redox reaction

45. **(a)** dry $Ca(OH)_2$

46. **(a)** MnO_2 is getting reduced whereas HCl is getting oxidized

47. **(b)** Basic oxide

48. **(b)** Reaction will not occur

49. **(d)**

50. **(c)**

51. **(a)**

52. **(a)**

53. **(b)**

54. **(a)** Chlorine displaces iodine from potassium iodide solution.

55. **(d)** When copper strip is placed in $FeSO_4$ solution, colour of the solution does not change.

56. **(d)** Decomposition of vegetable matter into compost is an exothermic reaction.

57. **(a)** $Na_2SO_4(aq) + BaCl_2(aq) \longrightarrow$

$$BaSO_4(s) + 2NaCl(aq)$$
$$Precipitate$$

58. **(a)** A combination reaction is a reaction where two or more elements or compounds combine to form a single compound. Hydrogen and chlorine combine to give hydrogen chloride.

59. **(c)**

$$\overset{Reduction}{\overbrace{\underset{+2}{Sn}Cl_2 + 2\underset{+2}{Hg}Cl_2 \longrightarrow \underset{+4}{Sn}Cl_4 + \underset{+1}{Hg_2}Cl_2}}$$

Oxidation (Reducing agent)

$$Hg_2Cl_2 + SnCl_2 \longrightarrow 2Hg + SnCl_4$$

60. **(b)** Corrosion occurs due to oxidation of iron.

Chemical Reactions and Equations

61. (a)

62. (d) A reducing agent is a substance which oxidizes itself but reduces others i.e., looses electrons.

63. (a)

64. A → (q) B → (r)   C → (p)   D → (s)

65. (a)

66. combination

67. exothermic

68. endothermic

69. displacement

70. double displacement

71. insoluble

72. loss

73. Decomposition reaction

74. oxidation

75. CaO (s) and CO_2 (g)

76. products

77. True

78. True

79. True

80. True

81. True

82. False

83. True

84. True

85. True

Acids, Bases and Salts

DIRECTIONS : *This section contains multiple choice questions. Each question has four choices (a), (b), (c) and (d) out of which only one is correct.*

1. During the preparation of hydrogen chloride gas on a humid day, the gas is usually passed through the guard tube containing calcium chloride. The role of calcium chloride taken in the guard tube is to:

   (a) absorb the evolved gas.

   (b) moisten the gas.

   (c) absorb moisture from the gas.

   (d) absorb Cl^- ions from the evolved gas.

2. To protect tooth decay we are advised to brush our teeth regularly. The nature of the tooth paste commonly used is:

   (a) Acidic   (b) Neutral

   (c) Basic   (d) Corrosive

3. Which of the following is not a mineral acid?

   (a) Hydrochloric acid   (b) Citric acid

   (c) Sulphuric acid   (d) Nitric acid

4. Which of the following acid is present in sour milk ?

   (a) glycolic acid   (b) lactic acid

   (c) citric acid   (d) tartaric acid

5. An aqueous solution 'A' turns phenolphthalein solution pink. On addition of an aqueous solution 'B' to 'A', the pink colour disappears. The following statement is true for solution 'A' and 'B'.

   (a) A is strongly basic and B is a weak base.

   (b) A is strongly acidic and B is a weak acid.

   (c) A has pH greater than 7 and B has pH less than 7.

   (d) A has pH less than 7 and B has pH greater than 7.

6. The product of complete neutralization of H_3PO_3 with NaOH is :

   (a) NaH_2PO_3 (b) Na_2HPO_3

   (c) Na_3PO_3 (d) $Na_3(HPO_3)_2$

7. Chemical A is used for water softening to remove temporary hardness. 'A' reacts with sodium carbonate to generate caustic soda. What is 'A'?

   (a) Gypsum   (b) Slaked lime

   (c) Quick lime   (d) Lime stone

8. An aqueous solution turns red litmus solution blue. Excess addition of which of the following solution would reverse the change?

   (a) Baking powder

   (b) Lime

   (c) Ammonium hydroxide solution

   (d) Hydrochloric acid

9. A blue litmus paper was first dipped in dil. HCl and then in dil. NaOH solution. It was observed that the colour of the litmus paper –

   (a) changed to red.

   (b) changed first to red and then to blue.

   (c) changed blue to colourless.

   (d) remains blue in both the solutions.

10. The acid used in making vinegar is –

   (a) formic acid   (b) acetic acid

   (c) sulphuric acid   (d) nitric acid

11. $CuO + (X) \rightarrow CuSO_4 + H_2O$. Here (X) is –

   (a) $CuSO_4$ (b) HCl

   (c) H_2SO_4 (d) HNO_3

12. Reaction of an acid with a base is known as –

   (a) decomposition   (b) combination

   (c) redox reaction   (d) neutralization

13. When CO_2 is passed through lime water, it turns milky. The milkiness in due to formation of –

   (a) $CaCO_3$ (b) $Ca(OH)_2$

   (c) H_2O (d) CO_2

14. Antacids contain –

   (a) weak base   (b) weak acid

   (c) strong base   (d) strong acid

15. $2NaOH + MgSO_4 \longrightarrow$?

   (a) $MgO + Na_2SO_4$ (b) $Mg(OH)_2 + Na_2SO_4$

   (c) $Mg(OH)_2 + Na_2O$ (d) $MgO + Na_2O$

16. Bleaching powder gives smell of chlorine because it –

   (a) is unstable.

   (b) gives chlorine on exposure to atmosphere.

   (c) is a mixture of chlorine and slaked lime.

   (d) contains excess of chlorine.

17. Plaster of paris is made from –

   (a) lime stone   (b) slaked lime

   (c) quick lime   (d) gypsum

18. Chemical formula of baking soda is –

   (a) $MgSO_4$ (b) Na_2CO_3

   (c) $NaHCO_3$ (d) $MgCO_3$

19. Washing soda has the formula –

   (a) $Na_2CO_3.7H_2O$ (b) $Na_2CO_3.10H_2O$

   (c) $Na_2CO_3.H_2O$ (d) Na_2CO_3

20. Plaster of Paris hardens by –

   (a) giving of CO_2

   (b) changing into $CaCO_3$

   (c) combining with water

   (d) giving out water

21. Which of the following is acidic in nature?

   (a) apple juice   (b) soap solution

   (c) slaked lime   (d) lime

22. The reaction of metal with acid results in the formation of–

   (a) only hydrogen gas

   (b) only salt

   (c) both salt and hydrogen gas

   (d) none of these

23. Which of the following acid does not react with metals?

   (a) sulphuric acid   (b) phosphoric acid

   (c) carbonic acid   (d) nitric acid

24. When an oxide of a non–metal reacts with water which of the following is formed?

   (a) Acid   (b) Base

   (c) Salt   (d) None of these

25. 'Alum' is an example of –

   (a) single salt   (b) double salt

   (c) acids   (d) none of these

26. Which of the following statements is correct about an aqueous solution of an acid and of a base?

   (i) Higher the pH, stronger the acid

   (ii) Higher the pH, weaker the acid

   (iii) Lower the pH, stronger the base

   (iv) Lower the pH, weaker the base

   (a) (i) and (iii)   (b) (ii) and (iii)

   (c) (i) and (iv)   (d) (ii) and (iv)

27. A sample of soil is mixed with water and allowed to settle. The clear supernatant solution turns the pH paper yellowish-orange. Which of the following would change the colour of this pH paper to greenish-blue?

   (a) Lemon juice   (b) Vinegar

   (c) Common salt   (d) An antacid

28. Plaster of paris is obtained –

   (a) by adding water to calcium sulphate.

   (b) by adding sulphuric acid to calcium hydroxide.

   (c) by heating gypsum to a very high temperature.

   (d) by heating gypsum to 373 K.

29. What is the term for the positive and negative ions of a compound breaking apart in solution –

   (a) Conglomeration   (b) Oxidation

   (c) Dissociation   (d) None of the Above

30. Of the aqueous solutions listed below, which would be the best conductor of an electric current?

   (a) HCl   (b) H_3PO_4

   (c) HOCl   (d) CH_3COOH

31. Common salt besides being used in kitchen can also be used as the raw material for making

   (i) washing soda   (ii) bleaching powder

   (iii) baking soda   (iv) slaked lime

   (a) (i) and (ii)   (b) (i), (ii) and (iv)

   (c) (i) and (iii)   (d) (i), (iii) and (iv)

32. Which salt can be classified as an acid salt?

   (a) Na_2SO_4 (b) $BiOCl$

   (c) $Pb(OH)Cl$ (d) Na_2HPO_4

33. An element X reacts with dilute H_2SO_4 as well as with NaOH to produce salt and H_2(g). Hence, it may be concluded that:

I.   X is an electropositive element.
II. oxide of X is basic in nature.
III. oxide of X is acidic in nature.
IV. X is an electronegative element.

(a) I, II, III
(b) IV, I, II
(c) III, IV, I
(d) II, III, IV

34. The turmeric solution will turn red by an aqueous solution of -

(a) potassium acetate
(b) copper sulphate
(c) sodium sulphate
(d) ferric chloride

35. The correct order of increasing pH values of the aqueous solutions of baking soda, rock salt, washing soda and slaked lime is

(a) Baking Soda < Rock Salt < Washing Soda < Slaked lime
(b) Rock Salt < Baking Soda < Washing Soda <Slaked lime
(c) Slaked lime < Washing Soda < Rock Salt < Baking Soda
(d) Washing Soda < Baking Soda < Rock Salt < Slaked lime

36. You are provided with aqueous solutions of three salts — A, B and C, 2-3 drops of blue litmus solution, red litmus solution and phenolphthalein were added to each of these solution in separate experiments. The change in colours of different indicators were recorded in the following table:

Sample	With blue litmus solution	With red litmus solution	With phenolphtha-lein solution
A	No change	No change	No change
B	Turns red	No change	No change
C	No change	Turns blue	Turns pink

On the basis of above observations, identify A, B, and C from the following options:

(a) A = NH_4 Cl, B = NaCl, C = CH_3COONa
(b) A = NH_4 Cl, B = CH_3 COONa, C = NaCl
(c) A = NaCl, B = NH_4 Cl, C = CH_3 COONa
(d) A = CH_3 COONa, B = NH_4 Cl, C = NaCl

37. Aqua regia is the mixture of conc. HCl and conc. HNO_3 in the ratio:

(a) 1 : 3
(b) 2 : 3
(c) 3 : 1
(d) 3 : 2

38. The chemical formula of 'Plaster of Paris' is

(a) $CaSO_4 \cdot \frac{1}{2} H_2O$
(b) $CaSO_4 \cdot 2H_2O$
(c) $CaSO_4 \cdot H_2O$
(d) $CaSO_4 \cdot \frac{3}{2} H_2O$

39. A solution turns red litmus blue. Its pH is likely to be –

(a) 2
(b) 4
(c) 5
(d) 10

40. A solution reacts with crushed egg-shells to give a gas that turns lime water milky. The solution contains –

(a) NaCl
(b) HCl
(c) LiCl
(d) KCl

41. 10 mL of a solution of NaOH is found to be completely neutralised by 8 mL of a given solution of HCl. If we take 20 mL of the same solution of NaOH, the amount of HCl solution (the same solution as before) required to neutralise will be –

(a) 4 mL
(b) 8 mL
(c) 12 mL
(d) 16 mL

42. Which of the following type of medicines is used for treating indigestion ?

(a) Antibiotic
(b) Analgesic
(c) Antacid
(d) Antiseptic

43. Which of the following reaction does not results in the evolution of H_2 gas?

(a) dilute sulphuric acid reacts with zinc granules.
(b) dilute hydrochloric acid reacts with magnesium ribbon.
(c) dilute sulphuric acid reacts with aluminium powder.
(d) dilute hydrochloric acid with diute sodium hydroxide solution.

Case/Passage Based Questions

DIRECTIONS : *Study the given case/passage and answer the following questions.*

Case/Passage - 1

Marble's popularity began in ancient Rome and Greece, where white and off-white marble were used to construct a variety of structures, from hand-held sculptures to massive pillars and buildings.

[From CBSE Question Bank-2021]

44. The substance not likely to contain $CaCO_3$ is

(a) Dolomite (b) A marble statue

(c) Calcined gypsum (d) Sea shells.

45. A student added 10g of calcium carbonate in a rigid container, secured it tightly and started to heat it. After some time, an increase in pressure was observed, the pressure reading was then noted at intervals of 5 mins and plotted against time, in a graph as shown below. During which time interval did maximum decomposition took place?

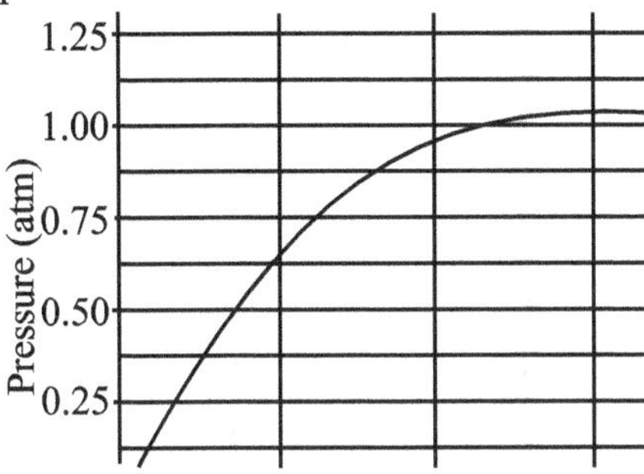

(a) 15-20 min (b) 10-15 min

(c) 5-10 min (d) 0-5 min

46. Gas A, obtained above is a reactant for a very important biochemical process which occurs in the presence of sunlight. Identify the name of the process -

(a) Respiration (b) Photosynthesis

(c) Transpiration (d) Photolysis

47. Marble statues are corroded or stained when they repeatedly come into contact with polluted rain water. Identify the main reason.

(a) decomposition of calcium carbonate to calcium oxide

(b) polluted water is basic in nature hence it reacts with calcium carbonate

(c) polluted water is acidic in nature hence it reacts with calciumcarbonate

(d) calcium carbonate dissolves in water to give calcium hydroxide.

48. Calcium oxide can be reduced to calcium, by heating with sodium metal. Which compound would act as an oxidizing agent in the above process?

(a) sodium (b) sodium oxide

(c) calcium (d) calcium oxide

Case/Passage - 2

Frothing in Yamuna:

The primary reason behind the formation of the toxic foam is high phosphate content in the wastewater because of detergents used in dyeing industries, dhobi ghats and households. Yamuna's pollution level is so bad that parts of it have been labelled 'dead' as there is no oxygen in it for aquatic life to survive.

[From CBSE Question Bank-2021]

49. Predict the pH value of the water of river Yamuna if the reason for froth is high content of detergents dissolved in it.

(a) 10-11 (b) 5-7

(c) 2-5 (d) 7

50. Which of the following statements is correct for the water with detergents dissolved in it?

(a) low concentration of hydroxide ion (OH^-)and high concentration of hydronium ion (H_3O^+)

(b) high concentration of hydroxide ion (OH^-)and low concentration of hydronium ion (H_3O^+)

(c) high concentration of hydroxide ion (OH^-) as well as hydronium ion (H_3O^+)

(d) equal concentration of both hydroxide ion (OH^-) and hydronium ion (H_3O^+).

The table provides the pH value of four solutions P, Q, R and S

Solution	pH value
P	2
Q	9
R	5
S	11

51. Which of the following correctly represents the solutions in increasing order of their hydronium ion concentration?

(a) $P > Q > R > S$ (b) $P > S > Q > R$

(c) $S < Q < R < P$ (d) $S < P < Q < R$

52. High content of phosphate ion in river Yamuna may lead to:

(a) decreased level of dissolved oxygen and increased growth of algae

(b) decreased level of dissolved oxygen and no effect of growth of algae

   (c) increased level of dissolved oxygen and increased growth of algae

   (d) decreased level of dissolved oxygen and decreased growth of algae

53. If a sample of water containing detergents is provided to you, which of the following methods will you adopt to neutralize it?

   (a) Treating the water with baking soda

   (b) Treating the water with vinegar

   (c) Treating the water with caustic soda

   (d) Treating the water with washing soda

≫ Assertion & Reason

DIRECTIONS : *Each of these questions contains an assertion followed by reason. Read them carefully and answer the question on the basis of following options. You have to select the one that best describes the two statements.*

   (a) If both **Assertion** and **Reason** are **correct** and Reason is the **correct explanation** of Assertion.

   (b) If both **Assertion** and **Reason** are correct, but Reason is **not the correct explanation** of Assertion.

   (c) If **Assertion** is **correct** but **Reason** is **incorrect**.

   (d) If **Assertion** is **incorrect** but **Reason** is **correct**.

54. **Assertion :** Aqueous solution of ammonium nitrate turns blue litmus red.

   Reason : Ammonium nitrate is salt of strong acid and strong base.

55. **Assertion :** All alkalis are bases but all bases are not alkali.

   Reason : Water soluble bases are alkali.

56. **Assertion :** Magnesium hydroxide is used as antacid.

   Reason : Magnesium hydroxide is a strong base.

57. **Assertion :** Dry HCl gas does not change the colour of blue litmus paper to red.

   Reason : Dry HCl gas is strongly basic.

58. **Assertion :** Sodium hydrogen carbonate is used in fire extinguisher.

   Reason : Sodium hydrogen carbonate is a mild base.

59. **Assertion :** H_2CO_3 is a strong acid.

   Reason : A strong acid dissociates completely or almost completely in water.

60. **Assertion :** Salts are the products of an acid-base reaction.

   Reason : Salt may be acidic or basic.

61. **Assertion :** On adding H_2SO_4 to water the resulting aqueous solution get corrosive.

   Reason : Hydronium ions are responsible for corrosive action.

≫ Match the Following

DIRECTIONS : *Each question contains statements given in two columns which have to be matched. Statements (A, B, C, D) in column I have to be matched with statements (p, q, r, s) in column II.*

62. Column II gives nature of acids and bases mention in column I, match them correctly.

Column I	Column II
(A) HCl	(p) Strong acid
(B) HCN	(q) Weak acid
(C) NaOH	(r) Weak base
(D) NH_4OH	(s) Strong base

63. Match the salts given in column I with the corresponding acid and base given in column II.

Column I	Column II
(A) KNO_3	(p) Nitric acid, Silver hydroxide
(B) $AgNO_3$	(q) Hydrochloric acid, Magnesium hydroxide
(C) $MgCl_2$	(r) Carbonic acid, Ammonium hydroxide
(D) $(NH_4)_2CO_3$	(s) Nitric acid, Potassium hydroxide

64.

Column I	Column II
(A) $NaHCO_3$	(p) Baking soda
(B) NaOH	(q) Alkaline
(C) $KHSO_4$	(r) Acidic salt
(D) $Ca(OH)_2$	(s) Bitter taste

≫ Fill in the Blanks

DIRECTIONS : *Complete the following statements with an appropriate word / term to be filled in the blank space(s).*

65. Oxy acids contains .... atoms in addition to hydrogen atom.

66. An acid that contains more than one acidic hydrogen atom is called a ....

67. When an acid reacts with a metal, ... gas is evolved and a corresponding .... is formed.

68. When an acid reacts with a metal carbonate or metal hydrogen carbonate, it gives the corresponding salt, ... gas and ....

69. .... is the fixed number of water molecules chemically attached to each formula unit of a salt in its crystalline form.

70. ENO contains .... and is .... in nature.

71. Anhydrous sodium carbonate is commonly known as ....

72. Soda–acid fire extinguisher contains a solution of sodium hydrogen carbonate and ....

73. An alkali reacts with ammonium salts to produce corresponding salt, water and evolve ....

74. $Zn(OH)_2$ is a .... base.

True / False

DIRECTIONS : *Read the following statements and write your answer as true or false.*

75. Acidic nature of a substance is due to the formation of $H^+(aq)$ ions in solution.

76. Mixing concentrated acids or bases with water is a highly endothermic process.

77. Acids and bases neutralise each other to form corresponding salts and water.

78. The colour of caustic soda turns pink when phenolphthalein is added.

79. Hydrogen chloride gas turns the blue litmus red.

80. Sodium hydrogen carbonate is used in fire extinguisher.

81. Washing soda on strong heating gives sodium oxide and carbon dioxide.

82. Plaster of paris is obtained by heating gypsum at 373 K in a kiln.

83. Bleaching powder is used for disinfecting drinking water.

84. Solution of sodium hydrogen carbonate is alkaline in nature.

ANSWER KEY & SOLUTIONS

1. **(c)** Calcium chloride is good dehydrating agent so it is used to absorb moisture from the hydrogen chloride gas.

2. **(c)** The tooth paste commonly used is basic which help in neutralisation of the extra acid formed during tooth decay.

3. **(b)** Citric acid is an example of organic acid or edible acid while HCl, H_2SO_4 and HNO_3 are mineral acids.

4. **(b)** Lactic acid is present in sour milk.

5. **(c)** Aqueous solution of A is basic while that of B is acidic. Therefore A has pH greater than 7 and B has pH less than 7.

6. **(b)** H_3PO_3 is a dibasic acid.

$$H_3PO_3 \rightleftharpoons H^+ + H_2PO_3^-$$

$$H_2PO_3 \rightleftharpoons H^+ + HPO_3^{2-}$$

7. **(b)** Chemical 'A' is calcium hydroxide (slaked lime).

$$Ca(OH)_2 + Na_2CO_3 \longrightarrow 2NaOH + CaCO_3 \downarrow$$

8. **(d)** The given solution is basic in nature when excess of HCl is added, it becomes acidic.

9. **(b)** In acid, blue litmus changes to red and in basic solution red litmus changes to blue. Hence blue litmus first changes its color to red and then to blue.

10. **(b)** 6 - 12% acetic acid is known as vinegar.

11. **(c)** $CuO + H_2SO_4 \longrightarrow CuSO_4 + H_2O$

12. **(d)**

13. **(a)** $Ca(OH)_2 + CO_2 \longrightarrow CaCO_3 + H_2O$

14. **(a)** Antacids are weak bases which are given when a patient is suffering from acidity. These antacids neutralise the acid and give relief to patient.

15. **(b)** $2NaOH + MgSO_4 \longrightarrow Mg(OH)_2 + Na_2SO_4$

16. **(b)**   **17. (d)**   **18. (c)**   **19. (b)**

20. **(c)**   **21. (a)**   **22. (c)**

23. **(c)** Carbonic acid is a weak and so it does not react with metal.

24. **(a)** A non metal oxide forms acid on treatment with water. *e.g.,*

$$CO_2 + H_2O \longrightarrow H_2CO_3$$
(Carbonic acid)

25. **(b)**   **26. (d)**   **27. (d)**   **28. (d)**

29. **(c)** Acids and bases go through a process of dissociation when they are put into solution. They break apart into positively and negatively charged particles.

30. **(a)** HCl is a strong acid.

31. **(c)**

32. **(d)** Because it can furnish H^+ ions in solution.

33. **(a)** Element X can react with both acid and base. It shows that element X is amphoteric in nature and is an electropositive element.

34. **(a)** $CH_3COOK + H_2O \longrightarrow \underset{\text{Strong base}}{KOH} + CH_3COOH$

The solution will be basic in nature so it turns turmeric to red.

35. **(b)** Rock Salt $(NaCl)$ < Baking Soda $(NaHCO_3)$ < Washing Soda (Na_2CO_3) < Slaked lime $(CaCO_3)$

36. **(c)** A neutral salt brings no change with blue litmus solution, red litmus solution and with phenolphthalein solution. An acidic salt turns blue litmus to red and brings no change in red litmus solution as well as in phenolphthalein solution.

Basic salt turns red litmus to blue and also turns phenolphthalein solution pink.

Sample	Solution	With blue litmus solution	With red litmus solution	With phenol-phthalein solution
A	Neutral salt $(NaCl)$	No change	No change	No change
B	Acidic salt (NH_4Cl)	Turns red	No change	No change
C	Basic salt (CH_3COONa)	No change	Turns blue	Turns pink

37. **(c)** Aqua-regia is 3 part conc. HCl and 1 part conc. HNO_3.

38. **(a)** Plaster of paris is calcium sulphate hemihydrate.

39. **(d)** The red litmus solution turns blue in basic solution. The pH of basic solution is more than 7.

40. **(b)** Since the gas produced turns lime water milky so the gas is CO_2. The egg-shell is made of $CaCO_3$ which reacts with an acid (dil. HCl) to produce CO_2.

$$CaCO_3 + 2HCl \longrightarrow CaCl_2 + H_2O + CO_2\uparrow$$

41. **(d)** Since 10 mL of NaOH requires HCl = 8mL

20 mL of NaOH will require HCl $= \dfrac{8}{10} \times 20$ mL

$= 16$ mL

42. **(c)** We use antacids for treating indigestion.

43. **(d)** Zinc + Sulphuric acid $\longrightarrow$

Zinc sulphate + Hydrogen

$$Zn(s) + H_2SO_4(aq) \longrightarrow ZnSO_4(aq) + H_2(g)$$

(b) Magnesium + Hydrochloric acid $\longrightarrow$

Magnesium chloride + Hydrogen

$$Mg(s) + 2HCl(aq) \longrightarrow MgCl_2(aq) + H_2(g)$$

(c) Aluminium + Sulphuric acid $\longrightarrow$

Aluminium sulphate + Hydrogen

$$2Al(s) + 3H_2SO_4(aq) \longrightarrow Al_2(SO_4)_3(aq) + 3H_2(g)$$

(d) dilute Hydrochloric acid + dilute sodium hydroxide

$\longrightarrow$ sodiumchloride + water

$$2HCl + 2NaOH \longrightarrow 2NaCHl + 2H_2O$$

44. **(c)** Calcined gypsum is $CaSO_4 \cdot - H_2O$

45. **(d)** 0-5 min

46. **(b)** Gas is CO_2 which is a important reactant in photosynthesis process.

47. **(c)** polluted water is acidic in nature hence it reacts with calcium carbonate

48. **(d)** calcium oxide

49. **(a)**

50. **(b)**

51. **(c)**

52. **(a)**

53. **(b)**

54. **(c)** Ammonium nitrate is salt of strong acid and weak base.

55. **(a)** Bases generate hydroxide ions in water hence water soluble bases are called alkalis.

56. **(c)** Magnesium hydroxide is a mild base and neutralise the excess acid in the stomach.

57. **(c)** Dry HCl gas does not show acidic character in absence of water. Therefore do not change the colour of blue litmus in dry condition.

58. **(b)** Sodium hydrogen carbonate react with acid present in fire extinguisher to produce carbon dioxide gas.

59. **(d)** H_2CO_3 (carbonic acid) is a weak acid.

60. **(b)**

61. **(a)** Because H_2SO_4 is a strong acid, it readily forms hydronium ions when dissolved in water which are responsible for its corrosive action.

62. A → (p); B → (q); C → (s); D → (r)

63. A → (s); B → (p); C → (q); D → (r)

64. A → (p, q, r); B → (q, s); C → (q, r); D → (q, s)

65. Oxygen   **66.** Polyprotic acid

67. Hydrogen, salt   **68.** Carbon dioxide, water

69. Water of crystallisation

70. Sodium hydrogen carbonate, basic

71. Soda ash   **72.** Sulphuric acid

73. Ammonia   **74.** Diacidic

75. True   **76.** False   **77.** True   **78.** True

79. False   **80.** True   **81.** False   **82.** True

83. True   **84.** True

3 Metals and Non-Metals

DIRECTIONS : *This section contains multiple choice questions. Each question has four choices (a), (b), (c) and (d) out of which only one is correct.*

1. Which of the following metal is liquid at ordinary temperature?
   (a) Aluminium (b) Mercury
   (c) Magnesium (d) Potassium

2. The atomic number of an element Y is 16. The number of electrons in Y^{2-} ion will be:
   (a) 16 (b) 17
   (c) 18 (d) 20

3. Which of the following elements will form basic oxides?
   (a) Barium (b) Aluminium
   (c) Carbon (d) Phosphorus

4. Which one of the following is not correct regarding the electrolytic refining of copper?
   (a) Basic $Cu(OH)_2$ solution is used as cathode.
   (b) Acidified $CuSO_4$ solution is used as electrolyte.
   (c) Impure Cu is taken as cathode
   (d) Cu^{2+} ion gets collected at anode.

5. Which of the following compound is covalent in nature?
   (a) Carbon tetrachloride (b) Ammonium chloride
   (c) Lithium chloride (d) Calcium chloride

6. A student by mistake used a wet gas jar to collect sulphur dioxide. Which one of the following tests of the gas is likely to fail ?
   (a) Odour
   (b) Effect on acidified $K_2Cr_2O_7$ solution
   (c) Solubility test
   (d) None of these

7. Silicon is used in :
   (a) solar energy devices (b) semiconductors
   (c) transistors (d) all of these

8. Which of the following is not a characteristics of metal ?
   (a) Malleable (b) Electropositive nature
   (c) Ductile (d) None of these

9.  $Zn + H_2O$ (Steam) $\longrightarrow A + B$, In the equation A and B are –
   (a) Zn, H only (b) ZnH_2 and O_2
   (c) ZnO_2 & O_2 (d) ZnO & H_2

10. Removal of impurities from ore is known as –
    (a) crushing and grinding (b) concentration of ore
    (c) calcination (d) roasting

11. Froth floatation method is used for the concentration of–
    (a) oxide ores (b) sulphide ores
    (c) sulphate ores (d) halide ores

12. Heating of concentrated ore in absence of air for conversion into oxide ore is known as –
    (a) roasting (b) calcination
    (c) reduction (d) none of these

13. Pure gold is –
    (a) 24 carats (b) 22 carats
    (c) 20 carats (d) 18 carats

14. What is anode mud ?
    (a) Fan of anode
    (b) Metal of anode
    (c) Impurities collected at anode in electrolysis during purification of metals
    (d) All of these

15. Which of the following pairs will give displacement reactions?
    (a) $ZnSO_4$ solution and aluminium metal
    (b) $MgCl_2$ solution and aluminium metal
    (c) $FeSO_4$ solution and silver metal
    (d) $AgNO_3$ solution and copper metal.

16. Which of the following is a chemical method for preventing an iron frying pan from rusting?
    (a) applying grease
    (b) applying paint
    (c) applying a coating of zinc
    (d) all of the above

17. An element reacts with oxygen to give a compound with a high melting point. This compound is also soluble in water. The element is likely to be –
    (a) calcium
    (b) carbon
    (c) silicon
    (d) iron

18. Aluminium does not oxidise readily in air because –
    (a) it is high in the electrochemical series.
    (b) it is low in the electrochemical series.
    (c) the metal does not combine with oxygen.
    (d) the metal is covered with a layer of oxide which does not rub off.

19. The correct order of increasing chemical reactivity is –
    (a) $Zn < Fe < Mg < K$
    (b) $Fe < Mg < Zn < K$
    (c) $Fe < Mg < K < Zn$
    (d) $Fe < Zn < Mg < K$

20. The least malleable is –
    (a) aluminium
    (b) silver
    (c) gold
    (d) carbon

21. The metal that reacts with cold water is –
    (a) mercury
    (b) sodium
    (c) zinc
    (d) tungsten

22. The only metal that is liquid at room temperature is –
    (a) mercury
    (b) sodium
    (c) zinc
    (d) tungsten

23. The process of extraction of metal from its ores, is known as –
    (a) concentration
    (b) calcination
    (c) purification
    (d) metallurgy

24. The compound from which metal is extracted economically is –
    (a) slag
    (b) gangue
    (c) ore
    (d) mineral

25. The process to remove unwanted impurities from the ore is called –
    (a) purification
    (b) calcination
    (c) bassemerisation
    (d) concentration

26. The process to heat the ore in the presence of excess supply of air below its melting point is called –
    (a) roasting
    (b) calcination
    (c) smelting
    (d) liquation

27. Graphite is a/an –
    (a) alloy
    (b) metal
    (c) metalloid
    (d) non-metal

28. One of the constituents of amalgam is –
    (a) aluminium
    (b) copper
    (c) iron
    (d) mercury

29. Which of the following metal reacts with water/steam to produce oxide instead of hydroxide ?
    (a) Sodium
    (b) Potassium
    (c) Calcium
    (d) Magnesium

30. The white phosphorus is stored
    (a) in air
    (b) under water
    (c) under kerosene
    (d) under CS_2

31. Sodium is obtained by the electrolysis of –
    (a) an aqueous solution of sodium chloride
    (b) an aqueous solution of sodium hydroxide
    (c) fused sodium chloride
    (d) fused sodium sulphate

32. In the combined state, zinc is mainly found as –
    (a) chloride
    (b) bromide
    (c) oxide
    (d) sulphide

33. Which of the following is incorrect?
    (a) Chalcocite   –   Copper
    (b) Magnetite   –   Iron
    (c) Calamine   –   Aluminium
    (d) Galena   –   Lead

34. Among Mg, Cu, Fe, Zn the metal that does not produce hydrogen gas in reaction with hydrochloric acid is
    (a) Cu
    (b) Zn
    (c) Mg
    (d) Fe

35. The major products of the following reaction,
    $$ZnS(s) + O_2(g) \xrightarrow{\text{Heat}} \ldots\ldots\ldots are$$
    (a) ZnO and SO_2
    (b) $ZnSO_4$ and SO_3
    (c) $ZnSO_4$ and SO_2
    (d) Zn and SO_2

36. Choose the incorrect pair
    (a) NO - Neutral oxide
    (b) Cl_2O_7 - Acidic oxide
    (c) MgO - Basic Oxide
    (d) P_4O_{10} - Basic oxide

37. Metal present in chloroplast is
    (a) Iron
    (b) Copper
    (c) Magnesium
    (d) Cobalt

38. Magnesium ribbon is rubbed with sand paper before making it to burn. The reason of rubbing the ribbon is to:
(a) remove moisture condensed over the surface of ribbon.
(b) generate heat due to exothermic reaction.
(c) remove magnesium oxide formed over the surface of magnesium.
(d) mix silicon from sand paper (silicon dioxide) with magnesium for lowering ignition temperature of the ribbon.

39. The element that cannot be used as a reducing agent is
(a) carbon
(b) aluminium
(c) sulphur
(d) sodium

40. Al_2O_3 reacts with
(a) only water
(b) only acids
(c) only alkalis
(d) both acids and alkalis

41. Which of the following is an example of neutral oxide?
(a) Fe_2O_3
(b) Al_2O_3
(c) CO
(d) NO_2

42. A metal 'M' of moderate reactivity is present as its sulphide 'X'. On heating in air, 'X' converts into its oxide 'Y' and a gas evolves. On heating 'Y' and 'X' together, the metal 'M' is produced. 'X' and 'Y' respectively are
(a) 'X' cuprous sulphide, 'Y' cuprous oxide
(b) 'X' cupric sulphide, 'Y' cupric oxide
(c) 'X' sodium sulphide, 'Y' sodium oxide
(d) 'X' calcium sulphide, 'Y' calcium oxide

43. Which of the following metals react with conc. sulphuric acid but does not react with a solution of ferrous sulphate?
(a) Cu
(b) Zn
(c) Fe
(d) Mg

44. The formula of phosphate salt of a metal is MPO_4. The formula of its nitrate salt will be
(a) MNO_3
(b) $M(NO_3)_2$
(c) $M_2(NO_3)_3$
(d) $M(NO_3)_3$

45. Solder is an alloy of
(a) Pb and Sn
(b) Zn and Pb
(c) Pb and Zn
(d) Zn and Sn

46. The following observations are given for four metals:
I. Metal H does not react with dilute HCl.
II. Metal K reacts with warm water.
III. Metal L does not react with water but displaces metal H from its aqueous salt solution.
IV. Metal M reacts with cold water.

Choose the correct decreasing order of reactivity of these metals amongst the following:
(a) M > L > H > K
(b) K > M > H > L
(c) M > K > L > H
(d) L > H > K > M

47. ______ gas is evolved when Mn react with very dilute HNO_3
(a) NO_2
(b) H_2
(c) N_2O
(d) NO

48. ____________ alloy is used for welding electrical wires
(a) Solder
(b) Germen silver
(c) Stainless steel
(d) Gun metal

49. Aqueous solution of CsO_2 is :
(a) Basic
(b) Neutral
(c) Acidic
(d) Amphoteric

50. Which of the following will give displacement reactions ?
(a) NaCl solution and copper metal
(b) $MgCl_2$ solution and aluminium metal
(c) $FeSO_4$ solution and silver metal
(d) $AgNO_3$ solution and copper metal

51. Which of the following methods is suitable for preventing an iron frying pan from rusting ?
(a) Applying grease
(b) Applying paint
(c) Applying a coat of zinc
(d) All the above

52. An element can react with oxygen to give a compound with high melting point. This compound is also water soluble. The element is likely to be
(a) Calcium
(b) Carbon
(c) Silicon
(d) Iron

53. Food cans are coated with tin and not with zinc because
(a) zinc is costlier than tin.
(b) zinc has higher melting point than tin.
(c) zinc is more reactive than tin.
(d) zinc is less reactive than tin.

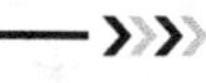

Case/Passage Based Questions

DIRECTIONS : *Study the given case/passage and answer the following questions.*

Case/Passage - 1

Metals are electropositive elements. They can easily lose electrons to form ions. Metals show distinguished physical as well as chemical properties. Generally most of the metals are ductile and malleable with exception such as mercury.

Metals and Non-Metals

These properties make them valuable for commercial as well as domestic uses. Reaction of a metal with water is one of important chemical property. Metals like sodium and potassium reacts with cold water while magnesium reacts with hot water. Metals like aluminium, zinc do not react with hot/cold water but they easily react with steam. When a metal react with hot/cold water the products are metal hydroxide and hydrogen, and when it react with steam, the product are metal oxide and hydrogen. Some metals like sodium, potassium react violently with water.

54. When zinc reacts with steam it produces:
(a) $Zn(OH)_2$
(b) ZnO
(c) O_2
(d) ZnO_2

55. Most ductile metal among the following is:
(a) Au
(b) Ag
(c) Cu
(d) Al

56. During the reaction of calcium with water, pieces of metal start floating due to the formation of:
(a) $Ca(OH)_2$
(b) CO_2
(c) H_2
(d) none of these

57. Consider the reactions:
$$Na(s) + H_2O\ (l) \longrightarrow NaOH\ (aq) + H_2\ (g) \quad ....(i)$$
$$Ca(s) + H_2O\ (l) \longrightarrow Ca(OH)_2(aq) + H_2(g) \quad ....(ii)$$
(a) Reaction (i) is endothermic reaction.
(b) Reaction (ii) is endothermic reaction.
(c) Reaction (ii) is more exothermic than reaction (i).
(d) Reaction (i) is more exothermic than reaction (ii).

58. Metals can be converted into thin sheet by hammering. This property is known as:
(a) Ductility
(b) Sonorous
(c) Malleability
(d) Both (a) and (c)

Case/Passage - 2

Elements can be classified as metals or non-metals on the basis of their properties. The easiest way to start grouping substances is by comparing their physical properties. Metals, in their pure state, have a shining surface. This property is called metallic luster. metals are generally hard. The hardness varies from metal to metal. some metals are used for making cooking vessels.

59. Metals generally are
(a) reducing agents
(b) oxidising agent
(c) both oxidising and reducing agents
(d) None of these

60. The most abundant metal in the earth's crust is -
(a) iron
(b) copper
(c) aluminium
(d) mercury

61. The metal that reacts with cold water is -
(a) mercury
(b) sodium
(c) zinc
(d) tungsten

62. Metal present in chloroplast is
(a) Iron
(b) Copper
(c) Magnesium
(d) Cobalt

63. Which of the following metal(s) catch fire on reaction with water?
(a) Sodium
(b) Potassium
(c) Magnesium
(d) both (a) and (b)

Case/Passage - 3

The huge annual loss due to corrosion is a national waste and should be minimized.

Following are some methods which are helpful to prevent corrosion

(i) Coating the iron surface with paint or oil or grease prevents moist oxygen from coming in contact with the metal and thus effectively prevents rusting of iron.

(ii) Galvanisation : Iron is blasted with fine sand to make the surface rough dipped in molten zinc and then cooled. A thin layer of zinc forms on the iron surface. Since zinc is more reactive than iron, it acts as a sacrificial metal and is preferentially oxidised thus preventing oxidation of iron.

(iii) Electroplating with tin, nickel or chromium also prevents rusting.

(iv) Alloying (mixing iron in its molten state with other metals) prevents rusting. Stainless steel is an alloy of iron with Cr or Ni.

64. The most durable metal plating on iron to protect against corrosion is :
(a) nickel plating
(b) copper plating
(c) tin plating
(d) zinc plating

65. The most convenient method to protect the bottom of ship made of iron is :
(a) coating it with red lead oxide.
(b) white tin plating.
(c) connecting it with Mg block.
(d) connecting it with Pb block.

66. The best way to prevent rusting of iron is :
(a) making it cathode
(b) putting in saline water
(c) both of these
(d) none of these

Case/Passage - 4

Some metals are chemically very reactive, whereas others are less reactive or unreactive. On the basis of vigourness of reactions of various metals with oxygen, water and acids, as well as displacement reactions, the metals have been arranged in a group or series according to their chemical reactivity. The arrangement of metals in a vertical column in the order of decreasing reactivities is called reactivity series of metals (or activity series of metals). In reactivity series, the most reactive metal is placed at the top whereas the least reactive metal is placed at the bottom. As we come down in the series, the chemical reactivity of metals decreases. Since the metals placed at the bottom of the reactivity series (like silver and gold) are less reactive, so they are usually found in free state (native state) in nature.

67. When metal Z is added to dilute HCl solution, there is no evolution of gas. Metal is :
   (a) K (b) Na
   (c) Ag (d) Zn

68. Copper sulphate solution can be safely kept in a container made of :
   (a) aluminium (b) lead
   (c) silver (d) zinc

69. Metal always found in free state is :
   (a) gold (b) silver
   (c) copper (d) sodium

Assertion & Reason

DIRECTIONS : *Each of these questions contains an assertion followed by reason. Read them carefully and answer the question on the basis of following options. You have to select the one that best describes the two statements.*

(a) If both **Assertion** and **Reason** are **correct** and Reason is the **correct explanation** of Assertion.

(b) If both **Assertion** and **Reason** are correct, but Reason is **not the correct explanation** of Assertion.

(c) If **Assertion** is **correct** but **Reason** is **incorrect**.

(d) If **Assertion** is **incorrect** but **Reason** is **correct**.

70. **Assertion:** Metals are electropositive elements.

   Reason: Metals form positive ions by losing electrons.

71. **Assertion:** Electric wires are made up of copper.

   Reason: Non metals are bad conductor of electricity.

72. **Assertion:** Potassium oxide is a basic oxide.

   Reason: Solution of potassium oxide in water turns red litmus blue.

73. **Assertion:** Sodium, potassium and magnesium are never found as free elements in nature.

   Reason: Sodium, potassium and magnesium are reactive elements.

74. **Assertion:** Carbonate ores are changed into oxides by roasting process.

   Reason: It is easier to obtain a metal from its oxides.

75. **Assertion :** Iron is found in the free state in nature.

   Reason : Iron is highly reactive element.

76. **Assertion :** Different metals have different reactivities with water and dilute acids.

   Reason : Reactivity of a metal depends on its position in the reactivity series.

77. **Assertion :** Zinc becomes dull in moist air.

   Reason : Zinc is coated by a thin film of its basic carbonate in moist air.

78. **Assertion :** Zinc is used in the galvanisation of iron.

   Reason : Its coating on iron articles increases their life by protecting them from rusting.

79. **Assertion :** Nitrate ores are rarely available.

   Reason : Bond dissociation energy of nitrogen is very high.

Match the Following

DIRECTIONS : *Each question contains statements given in two columns which have to be matched. Statements (A, B, C, D) in column I have to be matched with statements (p, q, r, s) in column II.*

80.

Column-I	Column-II
(A) CaO	(p) Amphoteric oxide
(B) Al_2O_3	(q) Neutral oxide
(C) SO_2	(r) Basic oxide
(D) H_2O	(s) Acidic oxide

81.

Column-I	Column-II
(A) Iodine	(p) Liquid metal
(B) Diamond	(q) Liquid non-metal
(C) Mercury	(r) Lustrous
(D) Bromine	(s) Hardest substance

82.

Column-I	Column-II
(A) Good conductor of electricity	(p) Hydrogen
(B) Food preservative	(q) Copper
(C) Allotrope of carbon	(r) Nitrogen
(D) Manufacture of ammonia	(s) Graphite

83.

Column-I (Position of the Metal in the Activity Series)	Column - II (Related Reduction Process)
A. The bottom of the series	(p) Electrolysis
B. The top of the series	(q) Reduction by heat alone
C. The lower regions of the series	(r) Found in native state
D. The middle of the series	(s) Reduction using carbon or some other reducing agent

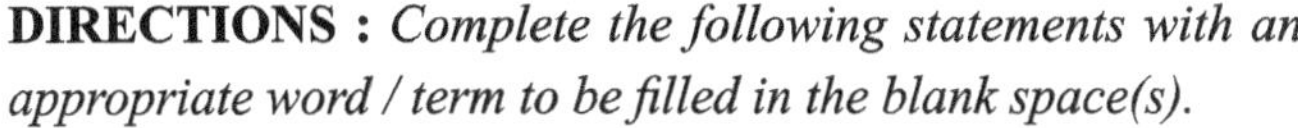

Fill in the Blanks

DIRECTIONS : *Complete the following statements with an appropriate word / term to be filled in the blank space(s).*

84. Metals combine with oxygen to form .... oxides.

85. Metals above hydrogen in the activity series can displace .... from dilute acids.

86. The surface of some metals, such as iron, is corroded when they are exposed to moist air for a long period of time. This phenomenon is known as ....

87. The best conductors of electricity are copper and ....

88. Manganese and .... react with very dilute nitric acid to evolve hydrogen gas.

89. An alloy of any metal with mercury is called .... the electrical conductivity of an alloy is .... than that of pure metals.

90. Stainless steel contains ...., ... and ....

91. Froth floatation process is used for the concentration of .... ores.

92. The method of removing volatile matter from carbonate ores is known as ....

93. Bronze is an alloy of copper and ....

94. The main ore of copper is ....

95. In electrolytic refining, impure metal is used as ....

True / False

DIRECTIONS : *Read the following statements and write your answer as true or false.*

96. Metals can form positive ions by losing electrons to non-metals.

97. Different metals have same reactivities with water and dilute acids.

98. A more reactive metal displaces a less reactive metal from its salt solution.

99. Metals occur in nature only as free elements.

100. Aluminium is the most abundant metal in the earth's crust.

101. Mercury and zinc are purified by liquation method.

102. The presence of carbon in pig iron makes it very soft and malleable.

103. Roasting is done for sulphide ores.

104. Reaction that takes place in aluminothermic process is also known as thermite reaction.

ANSWER KEY & SOLUTIONS

1. **(b)** Mercury is liquid metal at ordinary temperature.

2. **(c)** The number of electrons is Y^{2-} ion $= 16 + 2 = 18$

3. **(a)** Barium will form basic oxide. Aluminium will form amphoteric oxide while carbon and phosphorus will form acidic oxides.

4. **(a)** In the process of electrolytic refining, impure metal is made anode and is connected to the positive terminal of battery. Pure metal is made cathode and is connected to the negative terminal of the battery. Cu^{2+} ions from the solution are deposited on the cathode while Cu from impure anode dissolves into the solution and the impurities settle down below anode as anode mud.

5. **(a)** Carbon tetrachloride is a covalent compound.

6. **(d)** 7. **(d)**

8. **(d)** All are characteristics of metal.

9. **(d)** 10. (b) 11. (b)

12. **(b)** Calcination involves heating of the ore below its fusion temperature in absence of air.

13. **(a)** 14. (c)

15. **(d)** Copper is more reactive than silver hence displaces silver from silver nitrate solution.

16. **(c)**

17. **(a)** $2Ca + O_2 \longrightarrow CaO$ (ionic compound)

$$CaO + H_2O \longrightarrow Ca(OH)_2$$

18. **(d)** 19. (d) 20. (d) 21. (b)

22. **(a)** 23. (d) 24. (c) 25. (d)

26. **(a)** 27. (d) 28. (d) 29. (d)

30. **(b)** 31. (c) 32. (d) 33. (c)

34. **(a)** Cu does not produce hydrogen gas on reaction with hydrochloric acid. Cu is present below hydrogen in reactivity series, i.e. it is less reactive than hydrogen.

35. **(a)** $2ZnS(s) + 3O_2(g) \xrightarrow{\Delta} 2ZnO + 2SO_2$

The sulphide ore is heated in presence of air to produce its oxide form at a temperature below the melting point of the metal. The process is known as roasting.

36. **(d)** Non-metals oxides are acidic in nature.

37. **(c)** In chloroplast Mg is present.

38. **(c)** When magnesium is exposed to air, a layer of oxide is formed on its surface and it gets corroded. So, as to remove the layer, magnesium ribbon is rubbed.

39. **(c)** Sulphur has a tendency to gain electrons. It is a non-metal and cannot be used as reducing agent.

40. **(d)** Al_2O_3 is an amphoteric oxide, so it can react with both acids and alkalis, e.g.

41. **(c)** Fe_2O_3 is basic

Al_2O_3 is amphoteric

CO is neutral

NO_2 is acidic

42. **(a)** $Cu_2S + 3O_2 \longrightarrow 2Cu_2O + 2SO_2$

$2Cu_2O + Cu_2S \longrightarrow 6Cu + SO_2$

X = Cuprous sulphide, Y = Cuprous oxide

43. **(a)** Cu reacts with conc. H_2SO_4 on heating but does not react with $FeSO_4$ as it is less reactive than Fe.

44. **(d)** As $M(NO_3)_3$.

45. **(a)** Solder is an alloy of Pb and Sn.

46. **(c)** Metals below hydrogen in a reactivity series does not react with dilute HCl. Medium reactive metals reacts with warm water and highly reactive metals react with cold water.

As per the given information H, K, L and M can be identified as Cu, Mg, Pb and K/Na respectively. So their reactivity order will be M > K > L > H i.e.

K > Mg > Pb > Cu.

47. **(b)** $Mn + 2HNO_3 \longrightarrow Mn(NO_3)_2 + H_2$.

Hydrogen gas is evolved when Mn reacts with very dilute HNO_3.

48. **(a)** Solder alloy is used for welding electrical wires. The constituents of solder alloy are lead and tin.

49. **(a)** $2CsO_2 + 2H_2O \longrightarrow 2CsOH + H_2O_2 + O_2$

CsO_2 is the oxide of alkali metal. It is a basic oxide. Due to formation of CsOH its aqueous solution is basic.

50. **(d)** Copper will displace silver from silver nitrate solution because copper lies above silver in reactivity series of metals.

51. **(d)** All the above methods are helpful in preventing iron pan from rusting.

52. **(a)** Calcium (Ca) combines with oxygen to form calcium oxide (CaO) which has a high melting point and dissolves in water to form $Ca(OH)_2$.

53. **(c)** Zinc is more reactive than tin (zinc is above tin in reactivity series) so it will react with organic acids (present in food) to form poisonous compounds. To avoid this food cans are coated with tin and not with zinc.

54. **(b)** $Zn(s) + H_2O(g) \longrightarrow ZnO(s) + H_2(g)$

  Steam

55. **(a)** Gold is most ductile metal.

56. **(c)** Hydrogen gas is formed during the reaction which get stick to the surface of the metal and make them float.

57. **(d)** Reaction (i) is more exothermic than reaction (ii).

58. **(c)** Malleability.

59. **(a)** As metals are electropositive in nature and have tendency to lose electrons.

60. **(c)**

61. **(b)** It is because of extremely high reactivity of sodium.

62. **(c)** In chloroplast Mg is present.

63. **(d)** Sodium and potassium both are extremely reactive and react with water so vigorously. The reaction is highly exothermic so the hydrogen evolved will catch fire.

64. **(d)** This is because zinc has higher oxidation potential than Ni, Cu and Sn. The process of coating of iron surface with zinc is known as galvanization. Galvanized iron sheets maintain their lustrue due to the formation of protective layer of basic zinc carbonate.

65. **(c)** To protect the bottom of the ship it is connected with more reactive metal than iron like magnesium. This technique is called cathodic protection.

66. **(a)** Cathodic protection is best method to prevent iron from rusting. In this method iron is made cathode by application of external current.

  Saline water is highly conducting and hence accelerates the formation of rust.

67. **(c)** Ag does not displace hydrogen from acids since it is below hydrogen in activity series.

68. **(c)** Since silver is less reactive than copper it does not react with copper sulphate solution.

69. **(a)** Gold is a noble metal.

70. **(a)** Metals lose electrons to form positive ions therefore they are known as electropositive elements.

71. **(b)** Electric wires are made up of copper metal because metal are good conductor of electricity.

72. **(b)** Potassium is a metal and hence, it forms basic oxide. It turns red litmus blue.

73. **(a)** Sodium, potassium and magnesium are reactive elements and found at the top of the reactivity series. They do not occur in free state.

74. **(d)** Carbonate ores are changed into oxides by calcination process.

75. **(d)**

76. **(a)** The metals placed at the top of the series are most reactive.

77. **(a)**   **78.** (a)

79. **(a)** The bond dissociation energy of N_2 is very high due to presence of triple bond between two nitrogen atoms. Therefore, nitrate ores are rarely available.

80. A → (r); B → (p); C → (s); D → (q)

81. A → (r); B → (s); C → (p); D → (q)

82. A → (q, s); B → (r); C → (s); D → (r, p)

83. A → (r); B → (p); C → (q); D → (s)

84. basic   **85.** hydrogen

86. corrosion   **87.** silver   **88.** magnesium

89. amalgam, less   **90.** iron, chromium, carbon

91. sulphide   **92.** calcination   **93.** tin

94. copper pyrite   **95.** anode

96. True   **97.** False   **98.** True

99. False   **100.** True   **101.** False

102. False   **103.** True   **104.** True

4 Life Processes

DIRECTIONS : *This section contains multiple choice questions. Each question has four choices (a), (b), (c) and (d) out of which only one is correct.*

1. A pacemaker is meant for
   (a) transporting liver.
   (b) transplanting heart.
   (c) initiation of heart beats.
   (d) regulation of blood flow.

2. Root cap has no role in water absorption because:
   (a) It has no direct connection with the vascular system
   (b) It has no cells containing chloroplasts
   (c) It has no root hairs
   (d) It has loosely arranged cells.

3. Veins can be differentiated from arteries because the veins
   (a) have valves
   (b) have hard walls.
   (c) have pure blood in them.
   (d) have thick walls.

4. The function of the glomerulus and Bowman's capsule of the nephron is to
   (a) reabsorb water into the blood.
   (b) eliminate ammonia from the body.
   (c) reabsorb salts and amino acids.
   (d) filter the blood and collect the filtrate.

5. An advantage of excreting nitrogenous wastes in the form of uric acid is that –
   (a) It is less toxic and reduces water loss and the subsequent need for water.
   (b) The formation of uric acid requires a great deal of energy.
   (c) Uric acid is the first metabolic breakdown products of acids.
   (d) Uric acid may be excreted through the lungs.

6. In the following sketch of stomatal apparatus, parts I, II, III and IV were labelled differently by four students. The correct labelling is:

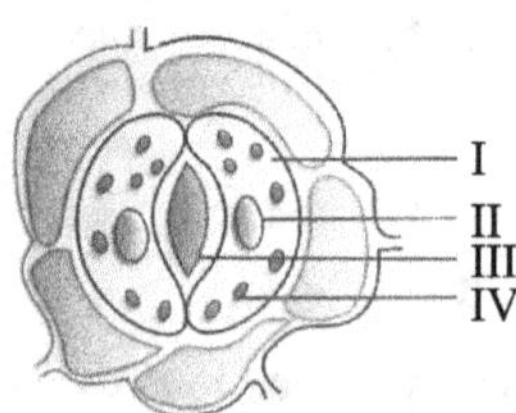

   (a) I-guard cell, II-stoma, III-starch granule, IV-nucleus
   (b) I-cytoplasm II-nucleus, III-stoma, IV-chloroplast
   (c) I-guard cell, II-starch, III-nucleus, IV-stoma
   (d) I-cytoplasm, II-chloroplast, III-stoma, IV-nucleus

7. The correct order of air reaching from atmosphere to the lungs is through
   (a) external nares, larynx, trachea and air sac.
   (b) larynx, trachea, air sac and external nares.
   (c) trachea, air sac, external nares and larynx.
   (d) air sac, trachea, larynx and external nares.

8. The rate at which oxygen moves from the alveoli of our lungs into our blood
   (a) depends on the difference in oxygen concentration between the alveoli and the blood.
   (b) depends on the color of the alveoli.
   (c) depends on the availability of energy to transport gases across the membrane.
   (d) none of the above

9. Major function of contractile vacuole is
   (a) Excretion   (b) Circulation
   (c) Osmoregulation   (d) All of these

10. Heart beat can be initiated by
   (a) Sino-auricular node
   (b) Atrio-ventricular node
   (c) Sodium ion
   (d) Purkinje's fibres

11. Digestion of food in human starts from
    (a) Duodenum
    (b) Small intestine
    (c) Mouth
    (d) Large intestine

12. Large intestine in man mainly carries out
    (a) absorption
    (b) assimilation
    (c) digestion of fats
    (d) digestion of carbohydrates

13. In *Amoeba* the digestion is intracellular because
    (a) *Amoeba* is unicellular
    (b) *Amoeba* is multicellular
    (c) *Amoeba* is found in a pond
    (d) *Amoeba* is a microscopic animal

14. The process of transpiration in plants helps in:
    (a) Opening of stomata
    (b) Absorption of CO_2 from atmosphere
    (c) Upward conduction of water and minerals
    (d) Absorption of O_2 from atmosphere.

15. Erythropoesis may be stimulated by the deficiency of
    (a) Iron
    (b) Oxygen
    (c) Protein
    (d) None of these

16. In the cardiac cycle, diastole is –
    (a) The number of heart beats per minute
    (b) The relaxation period after contraction of the heart
    (c) The forceful pumping action of the heart
    (d) The contraction period after relaxation of the heart.

17. The breakdown of pyruvate to give carbon dioxide, water and energy takes place in
    (a) cytoplasm
    (b) mitochondria
    (c) chloroplast
    (d) nucleus

18. What is the term used when vessels open and let more blood through?
    (a) Vasoconstriction
    (b) Vasodilatation
    (c) Increased permeability
    (d) None of these

19. The chief function of lymph nodes in mammalian body is to
    (a) produce RBCs
    (b) collect and destroy pathogens
    (c) produce a hormone
    (d) destroy the old and worn out red blood cells

20. Select the correct statement?
    (a) Heterotrophs do not synthesise their own food.
    (b) Heterotrophs utilise solar energy for photosynthesis.
    (c) Heterotrophs synthesise their own food.
    (d) Heterotrophs are capable of converting carbon dioxide and water into carbohydrates.

21. In respiration, air passes through
    (a) Pharynx → nasal cavity → larynx → trachea → bronchi → bronchioles
    (b) Nasal cavity → pharynx → larynx → trachea → bronchi → bronchioles
    (c) Larynx → nasal cavity → pharynx → trachea
    (d) Larynx → pharynx → trachea → lungs

22. During deficiency of oxygen in tissues of human beings, pyruvic acid is converted into lactic acid in the
    (a) cytoplasm
    (b) chloroplast
    (c) mitochondria
    (d) golgi body

23. Choose the function of the pancreatic juice from the following?
    (a) Trypsin digests proteins and lipase digests carbohydrates.
    (b) Trypsin digests emulsified fats and lipase proteins.
    (c) Trypsin and lipase digest fats.
    (d) Trypsin digests proteins and lipase emulsify fats.

24. Choose the correct statement that describes arteries.
    (a) They have thick elastic walls, blood flows under high pressure, collect blood from different organs and bring it back to the heart.
    (b) They have thin walls with valves inside, blood flows under low pressure and carry blood away from the heart to various organs of the body.
    (c) They have thick elastic walls, blood flows under low pressure, carry blood from the heart to various organs of the body.
    (d) They have thick elastic walls without valves inside, blood flows under high pressure and carry blood away from the heart to different parts of the body.

25. 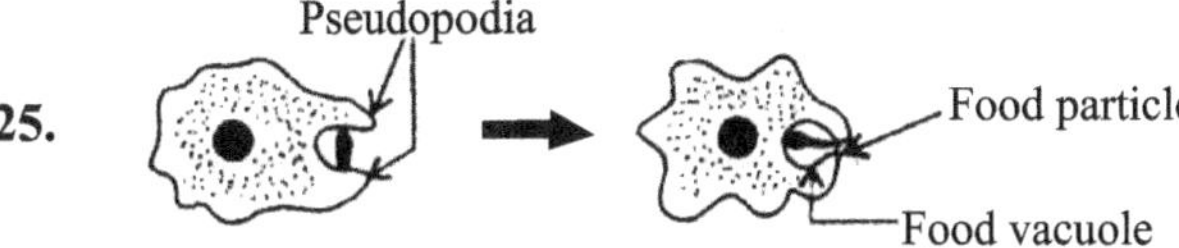

    Which activity is illustrated in the diagram of an *Amoeba* shown above?
    (a) Ingestion
    (b) Digestion
    (c) Egestion
    (d) Assimilation

26. From the given picture of the digestive system, identify the part labelled as gastric gland. 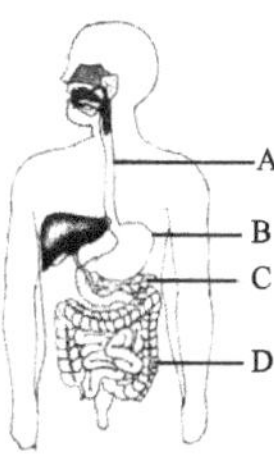

    (a) A
    (b) B
    (c) C
    (d) D

27. The diagram below represents a group of organs in the human body. Urine leaves the urinary bladder by passing through this structure labelled

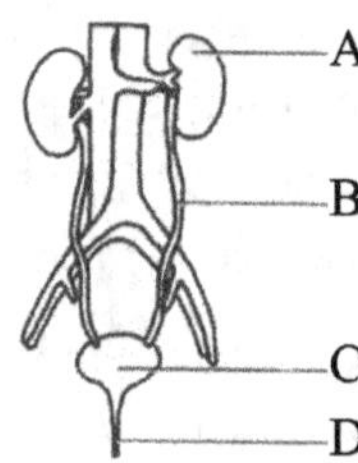

(a) A
(b) B
(c) C
(d) D

28. Given alongside is a sketch of a leaf partially covered with black paper and which is to be used in the experiment to show that light is compulsory for the process of photosynthesis. At the end of the experiment, which one of the leaf parts labelled I, II and III will become black when dipped in iodine solution?

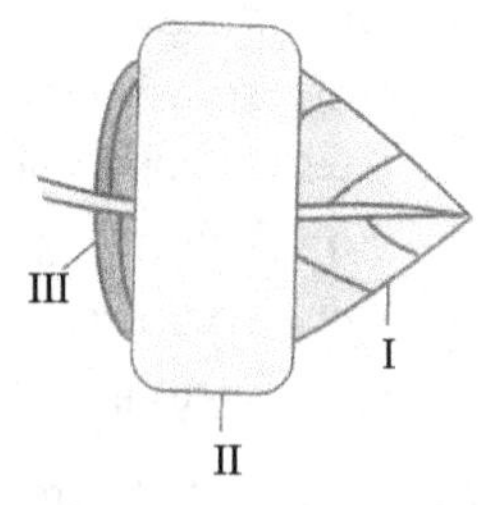

(a) I only
(b) II only
(c) I and III
(d) II and III

29. The phenomenon of normal breathing in a human being comprises.
(a) an active inspiratory and a passive expiratory phase.
(b) a passive inspiratory and an active expiratory phase.
(c) both active inspiratory and expiratory phases.
(d) both passive inspiratory and expiratory phases.

30. Filteration unit of kidney is
(a) ureter
(b) urethra
(c) neuron
(d) nephron

31. A column of water within xylem vessels of tall trees does not break under its weight because of:
(a) Tensile strength of water
(b) Lignification of xylem vessels
(c) Positive root pressure
(d) Dissolved sugars in water

32. Roots play insignificant role in absorption of water in:
(a) *Pistia*
(b) Pea
(c) Wheat
(d) Sunflower

33. Which of the following statements is **not correct?**
(a) Goblet cells are present in the mucosa of intestine and secrete mucus.
(b) Oxyntic cells are present in the mucosa of stomach and secrete HCl.
(c) Acini are present in the pancreas and secrete carboxypeptidase.
(d) Brunner's glands are present in the submucosa of stomach and secrete pepsinogen.

34. Human urine is usually acidic because
(a) excreted plasma proteins are acidic.
(b) potassium and sodium exchange generates acidity.
(c) hydrogen ions are actively secreted into the filtrate.
(d) the sodium transporter exchanges one hydrogen ion for each sodium ion in peritubular capillaries.

35. Which one of the following animals has two separate circulatory pathways?
(a) Lizard
(b) Whale
(c) Shark
(d) Frog

36. Cow has a special stomach as compared to that of a lion in order to
(a) absorb food in better manner.
(b) digest cellulose present in the food.
(c) assimilate food in a better way.
(d) absorb large amount of water.

37. Which of the following is not an enzyme?
(a) Lipase
(b) Amylase
(c) Trypsin
(d) Bilirubin

38. Pancreatic juice contains more than one enzyme. Which among the following combination is correct?
(a) Pepsin and Lipase
(b) Amylase and Pepsin
(c) Pepsin and Trypsin
(d) Trypsin and Lipase

39. Observe the experimental sets [A] & [B].

Observe the test tube A & B. From the list given below, choose the combination of responses of shoot and root that are observed in B.

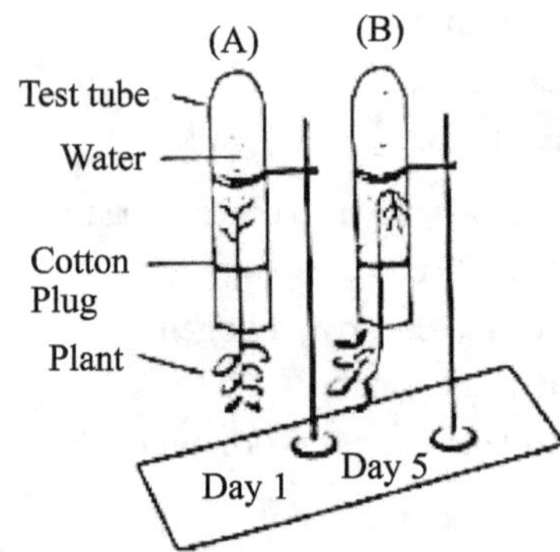

(a) Positive phototropism and positive geotropism
(b) Negative phototropism and positive geotropism
(c) Positive phototropism and negative geotropism
(d) Only negative phototropism

Life Processes

40. Which one of the following organisms respires through the skin?

(a) Blue whale   (b) Salamander

(c) Platypus   (d) Peacock

41. The first enzyme that the food encounters in human digestive system is :

(a) Pepsin   (b) Trypsin

(c) Chymotrypsin   (d) Amylase

42. Red blood corpuscles are formed in

(a) Liver   (b) Kidneys

(c) Small intestine   (d) Bone marrow

43. The Excretory units of Annelids are:

(a) Uniferous tubule   (b) Flame cells

(c) Nephridia   (d) Malpighian tubule

44. Open circulatory system is found in:

(a) Prawn   (b) Snakes

(c) Fish   (d) Man

45. Haemoglobin is dissolved in Plasma of blood in:

(a) Earthworm   (b) Roundworm

(c) Tapeworm   (d) Insects

46. Which one of the following organisms has a cellular respiratory pigment dissolved in plasma and is also a predaceous carnivore and shows matriphagy?

(a) Scorpion   (b) Cockroach

(c) Earthworm   (d) Sea cucumber

47. Glucose is the prime source of energy in our body. However, it is stored in the form of glycogen in the muscle and liver of animals and in the form of starch in plants. As a result, everytime a cell requires glucose, it must hydrolyze glycogen which is an energy consuming process. Why does the cell store glycogen instead of glucose in free form?

(a) Glycogen is more compact and more hydrophilic.

(b) Storage of glucose in free form will consume more ATP.

(c) Glucose in the free form creates more osmotic pressure.

(d) Glucose is highly reactive molecule hence storing in the free form can result in unwanted reactions in the cells.

48. A squirrel was eating a fruit on the ground. Suddenly, it was attacked by a dog. The squirrel rushed to the tree immediately and saved itself from the dangerous attack. What immediate changes are most likely to have taken place in the body of the squirrel?

A. Blood flows to the stomach for rapid digestion.

B. Adrenaline was secreted in the blood by the adrenal glands.

C. Heart beat becomes faster and pumps more blood so that muscles get more oxygen.

D. Adrenocorticotropic hormone is secreted in the blood and blood flows more towards the vital organs.

Select the correct combination of options given below:

(a) A and B   (b) A and C

(c) B and C   (d) C and D

49. Removal of the pancreas impairs the breakdown of

(a) lipids and carbohydrates only

(b) lipids and proteins only

(c) lipids, proteins and carbohydrates

(d) proteins and carbohydrates only

50. Microscopic examination of a blood smear reveals an abnormal increase in the number of granular cells with multiple nuclear lobes. Which one of the following cell Types has increased in number?

(a) Lymphocytes   (b) Monocytes

(c) Neutrophils   (d) Thrombocytes

51. Which one of the following metabolic conversions requires oxygen?

(a) Glucose to pyruvate

(b) Glucose to CO_2 and ethanol

(c) Glucose to lactate

(d) Glucose to CO_2 and H_2O

52. Which one of the following organs is NOT a site for the production of white blood cells?

(a) Bone marrow   (b) Kidney

(c) Liver   (d) Spleen

53. Which of the following process occur only in animals?

(a) Respiration   (b) Nutrition

(c) Nervous control   (d) Hormonal control

54. Tricuspid valve is present in

(a) Right atria and right ventricle

(b) Left atria and left ventricle

(c) Wall of atrium

(d) Wall of vetricle

55. Root pressure is effective way transporting water in xylem. This pressure is generated

(a) In bright sunlight

(b) During night

(c) At very low temperature

(d) In high trees

Case/Passage Based Questions

DIRECTIONS : *Study the given case/passage and answer the following questions.*

Case/Passage - 1

There is a pair of bean-shaped organs P in the human body towards the back, just above the waist. A waste product Q formed by the decomposition of unused proteins in the liver is brought into organ P through blood by an artery R. The numerous tiny filters S present in organ P clean the dirty blood by removing the waste product Q. The clean blood goes into circulation through a vein T. The waste substance Q, other waste salts, and excess water form a yellowish liquid U which goes from organ P into a bag-like structure V through two tubes W. This liquid is then thrown out of the body through a tube X.

56. What is (*i*) organ P, and (*ii*) waste substance Q?

57. Name (*i*) artery R, and (*ii*) vein T.

58. What are tiny filters S known as?

59. Name (*i*) liquid U (*ii*) structure V (*iii*) tubes W, and (*iv*) tube X.

Case/Passage - 2

All living cells require energy for various activities. This energy is available by the breakdown of simple carbohydrates either using oxygen or without using oxygen.

60. Energy in the case of higher plants and animals is obtained by
(a) Breathing
(b) Tissue respiration
(c) Organ respiration
(d) Digestion of food

61. The graph below represents the blood lactic acid concentration of an athlete during a race of 400 m and shows a peak at point D.

Lactic acid production has occurred in the athlete while running in the 400 m race.

Respiration in athletics

The blood of an athlete was tested before, during and after a 400m race:

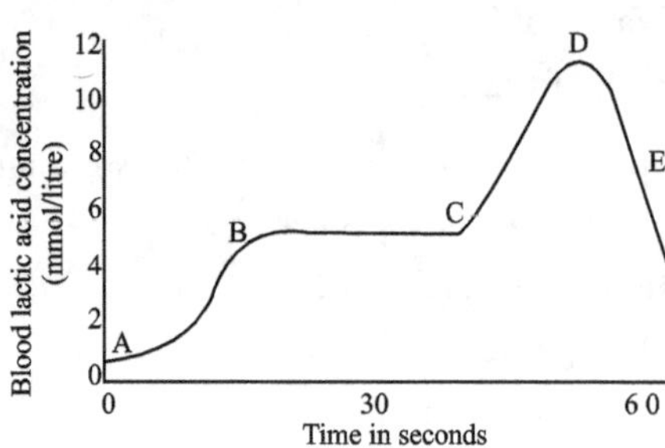

Lactic acid production has occurred in the athlete while running in the 400 m race. Which of the following processes explains this event?

Which of the following processes explains this event?
(a) Aerobic respiration
(b) Anaerobic respiration
(c) Fermentation
(d) Breathing

62. Study the graph below that represents the amount of energy supplied with respect to the time while an athlete is running at full speed.

Choose the correct combination of plots and justification provided in the following table.

	Plot A	Plot B	Justification
(a)	Aerobic	Anaerobic	Amount of energy is low and inconsistent in aerobic and high in anaerobic
(b)	Aerobic	Anaerobic	Amount of energy is high and consistent in aerobic and low in anaerobic
(c)	Anaerobic	Aerobic	Amount of energy is high and consistent in aerobic and low in anaerobic
(d)	Anaerobic	Aerobic	Amount of energy is high and inconsistent in anaerobic and low in aerobic

63. The characteristic processes observed in anaerobic respiration are:
(i) presence of oxygen
(ii) release of carbon dioxide
(iii) release of energy
(iv) release of lactic acid
(a) (i), (ii) only
(b) (i), (ii), (iii) only
(c) (ii), iii), iv) only
(d) (iv) only

64. Study the table below and select the row that has the incorrect information.

		Aerobic	**Anaerobic**
(a)	**Location**	Cytoplasm	Mitochondria
(b)	**End Porduct**	CO_2 and H_2O	Ethanol and CO_2
(c)	**Amount of ATP**	High	Low
(d)	**Oxygen**	Needed	Not needed

>> Assertion & Reason >>>

DIRECTIONS : *Each of these questions contains an assertion followed by reason. Read them carefully and answer the question on the basis of following options. You have to select the one that best describes the two statements.*

(a) If both **Assertion** and **Reason** are **correct** and Reason is the **correct explanation** of Assertion.

(b) If both **Assertion** and **Reason** are correct, but Reason is **not the correct explanation** of Assertion.

(c) If **Assertion** is **correct** but **Reason** is **incorrect**.

(d) If **Assertion** is **incorrect** but **Reason** is **correct**.

65. **Assertion:** Blood of insects is colourless.

Reason: The blood of insect does not play any role in transport of oxygen.

66. **Assertion:** Blood pressure is arterial blood pressure.

Reason: It is measured by sphygmomanometer.

67. **Assertion:** Chloroplast help in photosynthesis.

Reason: Mitochondria have enzymes for dark reaction.

68. **Assertion:** During physiology of excretion, deamination does not take place in liver.

Reason: Deamination is a process to make use of excess of amino acids which can not be incorporated into protoplasm.

69. **Assertion:** Photorespiration decreases net photosynthesis.

Reason: Rate of respiration in dark and light is almost same in all plants.

>> Match the Following >>>

DIRECTIONS : *Each question contains statements given in two columns which have to be matched. Statements (A, B, C, D) in column I have to be matched with statements (p, q, r, s) in column II.*

70.

	Column I		Column II
(A)	Autotrophic	(p)	Leech nutrition
(B)	Heterotrophic nutrition	(q)	*Paramaecium*
(C)	Parasitic nutrition	(r)	Deer
(D)	Digestion in food vaculoes	(s)	Green plant.

71.

	Column I (Animal)		Column II (Respiratory Organ)
(A)	Fish	(p)	Trachea
(B)	Birds	(q)	Gills
(C)	Aquatic	(r)	Lungs
(D)	Earthworm	(s)	Moist cuticle

72.

	Column I		Column II
(A)	Regulation metabolic	(p)	The removal of waste from an organism.
(B)	Reproduction	(q)	The chemical process of oxidizing organic molecules to release energy.
(C)	Respiration	(r)	The replication of an organism.
(D)	Excretion	(s)	The control and coordination of chemical processes within the organism.

73.

	Column I		Column II
(A)	Stomach	(p)	The structure is the site where the chemical breakdown of proteins first occurs.
(B)	Large intestine	(q)	This organ absorbs most of the water from the undigested food.
(C)	Small intestine	(r)	This organ is the section of the alimentary canal where most of the food is absorbed into the blood.
(D)	Liver	(s)	This organ secretes the chemical bile, which is used to emulsify fats.

>> Fill in the Blanks >>>

DIRECTIONS : *Complete the following statements with an appropriate word / term to be filled in the blank space(s).*

74. Ninety percent of the water lost by the plants during transpiration is through the .... of the leaf.

75. The semi-liquid mixture of partially digested food found in the stomach is called ....

76. The .... prevents the entry of food into the respiratory tract.

77. Second heart sound heard as .... is due to closure of .... valves at the beginning of ventricular diastole.

78. Kidney eliminate the excretory waste materials as their aqueous solution, called ....

79. Energy rich compound generated during photosynthesis is ....

80. Pressure in the arteries during ventricular relaxation is called .... pressure.

81. Diffusion is insufficient to meet .... requirement of multicellular organisms like humans.

DIRECTIONS : *Read the following statements and write your answer as true or false.*

82. Translocation is the transportation of the products of photosynthesis.

83. In a general, digestion is simply hydrolysis of complex polymers to monomers.

84. The exchange of nutrients and waste products between the blood and cells occurs within the arteries.

85. Trypsin digests proteins into amino acids.

86. A complete digestive tract consists of an oral and an anal opening.

87. Only the multicellular organisms require transporting mechanisms.

88. Humans have an open circulatory system.

89. Living organisms must maintain a constant internal environment.

90. In humans, the alveoli are the functioning units of external respiration.

91. Circulatory system also performs the function of homeostasis.

92. Essential amino acids cannot be synthesized in human body.

93. Generally gravitational water is utilized by the plants.

94. In photosynthesis, carbon dioxide is given out by diffusion process.

95. Bowman's capsule is found in heart.

ANSWER KEY & SOLUTIONS

1. **(c)**

2. **(c)** Root cap is devoid of root hairs which are instrumental in water absorption by increasing the surface area to speed up osmosis and thus root cap is not involved in the water absorption.

3. **(a)**   4. **(d)**   5. **(a)**   6. **(b)**

7. **(a)** The correct pathway of air: nasal cavities (or oral cavity) > pharynx > trachea > primary bronchi (right & left) > secondary bronchi > tertiary bronchi > bronchioles > alveoli (site of gas exchange).

8. **(a)** During inhalation, there is a greater concentration of oxygen in the alveoli than in the blood of the pulmonary capillaries, so oxygen diffuses from the alveoli into the blood across the capillarics.

9. **(c)**   10. **(a)**

11. **(c)** Digestion begins in the mouth with the secretion of saliva and its digestive enzymes.

12. **(a)** The large intestine, or large bowel, is the last part of the digestive system in vertebrate animals. Its function is to absorb water from the remaining indigestible food matter, and then to pass the useless waste material from the body.

13. **(a)**

14. **(c)** Transpiration is an essential phenomenon. It's pulling action helps in absorption and transportation of water in the plant. It also supplies water for photosynthesis.

15. **(b)**

16. **(b)** Cardiac diastole is the period of the cardiac cycle when, after contraction, the heart relaxes and expands while refilling with blood returning from the circulatory system.

17. **(b)**

18. **(b)** Vasodilation is the widening of your blood vessels. It happens when smooth muscles found in the walls of arteries or large veins relax, allowing the blood vessels to become more open. this leads to an increase in blood flow through your blood vessels as well as a decrease in blood pressure.

19. **(b)**   20. **(a)**   21. **(b)**

22. **(a)** In the absence of oxygen, pyruvic acid is converted into lactic acid in the cytoplasm of the muscle cell.

23. **(d)**   24. **(d)**   25. **(a)**   26. **(b)**

27. **(d)**   28. **(c)**

29. **(a)** During inspiration, muscles of ribs and diaphragm contracts. Hence, it is an active process. During expiration, muscles of ribs and diaphragm relax. Hence, it is a passive process.

30. **(d)** Nephron filter blood in kidney.

31. **(a)** Due to tensile strength of water, a column of water within xylem vessels of tall trees does not break under its weight.

32. **(a)** *Pistia* is a hydrophyte plant where absorption of water by root is not important.

33. **(d)** Duodenum contains Brunner's glands which secrete mucus and digestive juices.

34. **(c)** Urine has acidic nature because hydrogen ions (H^+) are components of an acid which are secreted into the filtrate.

35. **(b)** Whale is a mammal and in mammals, two separate circulatory pathways are found - systemic circulation and pulmonary circulation. Oxygenated and deoxygenated bloods received by the left and right atria respectively pass on to the left and right ventricles. Thus, oxygenated and deoxygenated bloods are not mixed. This is referred to as double circulation.

36. **(b)**

37. **(d)** Bilirubin is yellow compound that occurs in the catabolic pathway which breaks down hence in vertebrates it is not an enzyme. Other options *i.e.,* lipase, amylase, and trypsin are lipid digesting, starch digesting and endopeptidase enzymes respectively.

38. **(d)** Pancreatic juice contains Pancreatic proteases (such as trypsin and chymotrypsin), Pancreatic amylase and Pancreatic lipase.

39. **(a)**

40. **(b)** Salamanders are a group of amphibians typically characterised by a lizard-like appearance with

slender bodies, blunt snouts, short limbs and a tail. Salamanders breath through their skin and the thin membranes in the mouth and throat.

41. (d) The first enzyme that the food encounters in the digestive system is amylase. Digestion begins in the mouth with the secretion of saliva and its digestive enzymes. Saliva contains the digestive enzyme amylase, which works on carbohydrate, starch present in breads, potatoes or pasta to help break them down into simple sugars.

42. (d) Red blood cells are formed in the red bone marrow of bones. Stem cells in the red bone marrow called hemocytoblasts give rise to all of the formed elements in blood.

43. (c) The annelid excretory system is made up of long tubular organs called nephridia. Many species have a pair of nephridia in each segment.

44. (a) Open circulatory system is primarily found in invertebrates, in which the blood flows freely through cavities and there are no vessels to conduct the blood. This type of system is found in animals such as insects and some mollusks (snails, clams).

45. (a) Haemoglobin is found dissolved in the plasma of earthworm because they don't have proper respiratory system. It is dissolved in plasma for the diffusion of gases and other materials.

46. (a) In scorpion, the respiratory pigment is dissolved in plasma and it is also a predaceous carnivore that shows matriphagy, (a process in which an organism feed on its own mother).

47. (c) Glycogen is insoluble thus, storing it as glycogen will not upset the osmotic pressure rather than glucose which is soluble in water. And if cell store it as glucose, it will disturb the osmotic pressure (hypertonic) that will cause the cell to lyse.

48. (3) In this condition, adrenaline is secreated by adrenal gland into the blood stream which increases the heart rate, redistributing blood to the muscles and altering the blood metabolism, so as to maximise blood glucose levels primarily for the brain.

49. (c) The pancreas is a glandular organ. It is the part of the digestive syste, located in the abdomen and produces insulin and other important enzymes and hormones that help break down foods. The enzymes include trypsin and chymotrypsin to digest proteins, amylase to break down carbohydrates and lipase, to break down fats into fatty acids and cholesterol.

50. (c) Granulocytes and agranulocytes are the two types of white blood cells found in blood. Eosinophils, neutrophils and basophils are the granulocytes. Monocytes and lymphocytes are the agranulocytes. If the microscopic examination of a blood smear reveals an abnomal increase in the number of granular cells with multiple nuclear lobes, so out of the given blood cells, neutrophils has increased in number.

51. (d) Aerobic respiration uses oxygen to break down glucose, amino acids and fatty acids and is the main way the body generates adenosine triphosphate (ATP), which supplies energy to the muscles. The products of this process are carbon dioxide and water.

52. (b) In the human adult, the bone marrow produces all of the red blood cells, 60-70 percent of the white cells (i.e., the granulocytes), and all of the platelets. The reticuloendothelial tissues of the spleen, liver, lymph nodes, and other organs produce the monocytes (4-8 percent of the white cells).

53. (c) Nervous control occurs only in animals.

54. (a) Tricuspid valve is present between right atria and right ventricle.

55. (b) During night, root pressure is effectively involved in transport of water through xylem. During day, due to the opening of stomata, transpiration pull becomes the major factor for transporting water in xylem.

56. (a) (i) Kidneys　　(ii) Urea

57. (b) (i) Renal artery　　(ii) Renal vein

58. (c) Nephrons

59. (d) (i) Urine　　(ii) Bladder

　　(iii) Ureters　　(iv) Urethra

60. (b) Tissue respiration

61. (b) Anaerobic respiration

62. (b)

Aerobic	Anaerobic	Amount of energy is high and consistent in aerobic and low in anaerobic

63. (c) (ii), (iii), (iv) only

64. (a) Location Aerobic-Cyloplasm and Anaerobic-Mitochondria

65. (b) The blood of an insect functions differently than the blood of a human. Insect blood, however, does not carry gases and has no haemoglobin which gives red colour to the blood.

66. **(b)** Blood pressure, sometimes called arterial blood pressure, is the pressure exerted by circulating blood upon the walls of blood vessels. Blood pressure is measured by sphygmomanometer.

67. **(c)** Dark reaction occurs in the stroma region of the chloroplast and mitochondria is involved in the synthesis of ATP.

68. **(d)** Deamination takes place in liver during excretion to make excess of amino acids which can not be incorporated into protoplasm.

69. **(c)**

70. **(A) → (s), (B) → (r), (C) → (p), (D) → (q)**

71. **(A) → (q), (B) → (r), (C) → (p), (D) → (s)**

72. **(A) → (s), (B) → (r), (C) → (q), (D) → (p)**

73. **(A) → (p), (B) → (q), (C) → (r), (D) → (s)**

74. stomata   **75.** chyme

76. epiglottis   **77.** Dup/Dubb, semilunar

78. urine   **79.** ATP

80. diastolic   **81.** oxygen

82. True   **83.** True   **84.** False   **85.** True

86. True   **87.** False   **88.** False   **89.** True

90. True   **91.** True   **92.** True   **93.** False

94. False   **95.** False

5 Light-Reflection and Refraction

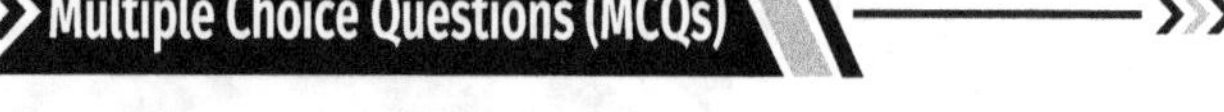

DIRECTIONS : *This section contains multiple choice questions. Each question has four choices (a), (b), (c) and (d) out of which only one is correct.*

1. An object is at a distance of 0.5 m in front of a plane mirror. Distance between the object and image is
   (a) 0.5 m   (b) 1 m
   (c) 0.25 m   (d) 1.5 m

2. Number of images formed when two plane mirrors are inclined at an angle 90° is
   (a) 3   (b) 2
   (c) 4   (d) 5

3. Which one of the following statements is not correct?
   (a) A convex mirror is often used as driving rear-view mirror.
   (b) A convex mirror is often used as a shaving mirror.
   (c) A concave mirror is often used in a search light or a torch.
   (d) A concave mirror is often used as the reflector behind lamp in a projector

4. The relation, $R = 2f$ holds true for :
   (a) concave mirrors only
   (b) convex mirrors only
   (c) all spherical mirrors
   (d) lens as well as for all spherical mirrors.

5. A magnification greater than unity indicates :
   (a) real image
   (b) size of the image is smaller than that of object
   (c) size of the object is smaller than that of image
   (d) size of object is equal to that of image

6. The image formed by a convex mirror
   (a) is always real
   (b) is always virtual
   (c) cannot say
   (d) None of these

7. In case of erect object having inverted image, linear magnification is :
   (a) positive   (b) negative
   (c) zero   (d) no definite sign.

8. If object lies symmetrically and number of images formed are 9, therefore two plane mirrors are kept at an angle of :
   (a) 72°   (b) 40°
   (c) 36°   (d) 50°

9. Reciprocal of focal length of a lens gives the
   (a) power   (b) radius
   (c) magnification   (d) none of these

10. Magnification of a lens is given by
   (a) $\dfrac{\text{image height}}{\text{object height}}$ (b) $\dfrac{1}{\text{Radius}}$
   (c) $\dfrac{1}{\text{focal length}}$ (d) $\dfrac{1}{\text{image distance}}$

11. A man having height 2.5 m. He oberves image of 1m height erect, then mirror used is
   (a) concave   (b) convex
   (c) plane   (d) None of these

12. Where should an object be placed in front of a convex lens to get a real image of the size of the object?
   (a) At the principal focus of the lens
   (b) At twice the focal length
   (c) At infinity
   (d) Between the optical centre of the lens and its principal focus.

13. Find the angle of incidence and angle of reflection from the diagram.

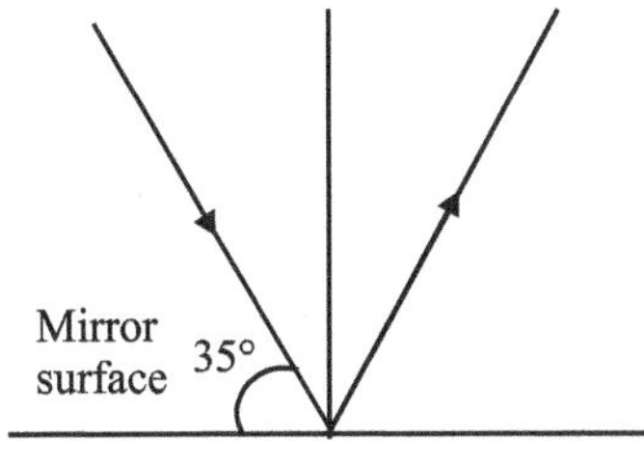

(a) 45°, 40°
(b) 55°, 55°
(c) 60°, 60°
(d) 30°, 30°

14. A spherical mirror and a thin spherical lens have each a focal length of -15 cm. The mirror and the lens are likely to be

(a) both concave.
(b) both convex.
(c) the mirror is concave and the lens is convex.
(d) the mirror is convex, but the lens is concave.

15. Which of the following lenses would you prefer to use while reading small letters found in a dictionary?

(a) A convex lens of focal length 50 cm.
(b) A concave lens of focal length 50 cm.
(c) A convex lens of focal length 5 cm.
(d) A concave lens of focal length 5 cm.

16. An object is situated at a distance of $f/2$ from a convex lens of focal length f. Distance of image will be –

(a) $+ (f/2)$
(b) $+ (f/3)$
(c) $+ (f/4)$
(d) $-f$

17. An object is placed 60 cm in front of a concave mirror. The real image formed by the mirror is located 30 cm in front of the mirror. What is the object's magnification?

(a) $+2$
(b) -2
(c) $+0.5$
(d) -0.5

18. Two plane mirrors are set at right angle and a flower is placed in between the mirrors. The number of images of the flower which will be seen is

(a) One
(b) Two
(c) Three
(d) Four

19. A man is 6.0 ft tall. What is the smallest size plane mirror he can use to see his entire image

(a) 3.0 ft
(b) 6.0 ft
(c) 12 ft
(d) 24 ft

20. An object is placed 60 cm in front of a convex mirror. The virtual image formed by the mirror is located 30 cm behind the mirror. What is the object's magnification

(a) $+2$
(b) -2
(c) $+0.5$
(d) -0.5

21. Light rays A and B fall on optical component X and come out as C and D.

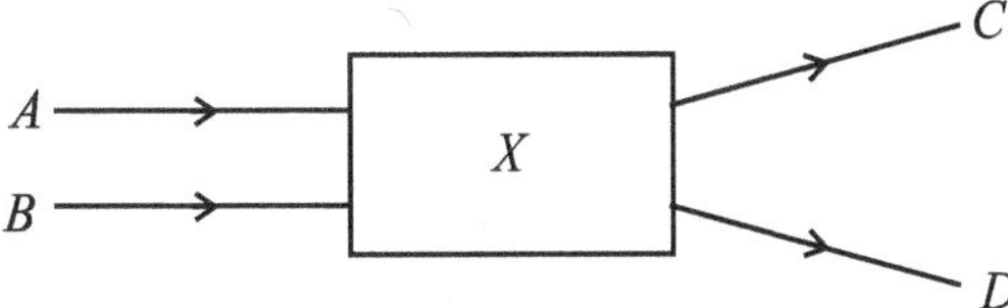

The optical component is a

(a) concave lens
(b) convex lens
(c) convex mirror
(d) prism

22. An object is placed 20.0 cm in front of a concave mirror whose focal length is 25.0 cm. What is the magnification of the object?

(a) $+5.0$
(b) -5.0
(c) $+0.20$
(d) -0.20

23. An object is placed at the radius of curvature of a concave spherical mirror. The image formed by the mirror is

(a) located at the focal point of the mirror.
(b) located between the focal point and the radius of curvature of the mirror.
(c) located at the center of curvature of the mirror.
(d) located out beyond the center of curvature of the mirror.

24. If the refractive indices for water and diamond relative to air are 1.33 and 2.4 respectively, then the refractive index of diamond relative to water is –

(a) 5.5
(b) 1.80
(c) 3.19
(d) None of these

25. There is an equiconvex lens of focal length of 20 cm. If the lens is cut into two equal parts perpendicular to the principle axis, the focal lengths of each part will be

(a) 20 cm
(b) 10 cm
(c) 40 cm
(d) 15 cm

26. An object is placed 20.0 cm in front of a concave mirror whose focal length is 25.0 cm. Where is the image located?

(a) 1.0×10^2 cm in front of the mirror
(b) 1.0×10^2 cm behind the mirror
(c) 5.0×10^1 cm in front of the mirror
(d) 5.0×10^1 cm behind the mirror

27. Which statement best describes the property of light waves illustrated in the diagram below?

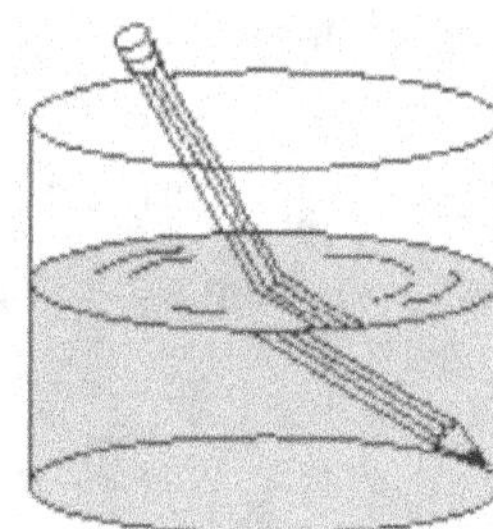

(a) Some materials absorb light waves.
(b) Some materials reflect light waves.
(c) Light waves are refracted by some materials.
(d) Light waves are emitted by some materials.

28. Light waves
(a) require air or another gas to travel through
(b) require an electric field to travel through
(c) require a magnetic field to travel through
(d) can travel through perfect vacuum

29. What are the factors that determine the angle of deviation in a prism?
(a) angle of incidence   (b) wave length
(c) angle of the prism   (d) All the above

30. Morning sun is not so hot as the mid day sun because
(a) Sun is cooler in the morning
(b) Heat rays travel slowly is the morning
(c) It is God gift
(d) The sun's rays travel a longer distance through atmosphere in the morning

31. The layered lens shown below is made of two different transparent materials.

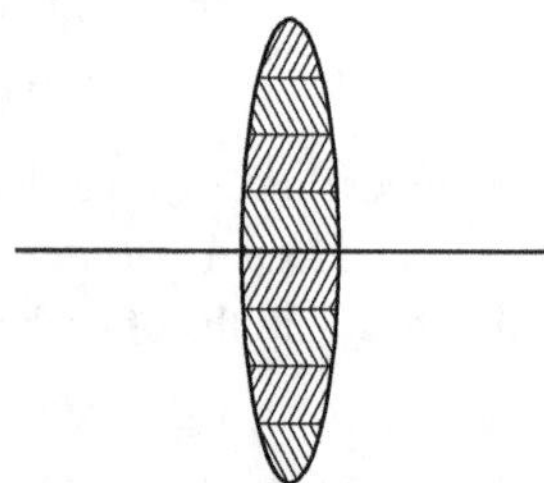

A point object is placed on its axis. The object will form
(a) one image   (b) infinite images
(c) no image   (d) two images

32. An object is placed in front of a concave mirror of focal length 50.0 cm and a real image is formed 75 cm in front of the mirror. How far is the object from the mirror
(a) 25 cm   (b) 30 cm
(c) 150 cm   (d) –150 cm

33. A number of images of a candle flame can be seen in a thick plane mirror. The brightest image is
(a) Fourth   (b) Second
(c) Last   (d) First

34. A ray from air enters water, then through a thick layer of glass placed below water. After passing through glass, it again comes out in air medium. Then final emergent ray will
(a) Bend towards the normal
(b) Suffer lateral displacement
(c) Have the same path as if it had not passed through glass and water.
(d) None of these

35. A concave spherical mirror has a radius of curvature of 100 cm. What is its focal length
(a) 50 cm   (b) 100 cm
(c) 200 cm   (d) 300 cm

36. Light is incident on an air-water interface at an angle of 25° to the normal. What angle does the refracted ray make with the normal
(a) 19°   (b) 34°
(c) 25°   (d) 90°

37. If the speed of light in medium –1 and medium –2 are 2.5×10^8 ms^{-1} and 2×10^8 ms^{-1}, respectively, then the refractive index of medium – 1 with respect to medium – 2 is __________.

(a) $\dfrac{3}{2.5}$ (b) $\dfrac{2}{2.5}$

(c) $\dfrac{2.5}{3}$ (d) $\dfrac{2.5}{2}$

38. Under what conditions does a diverging lens form a virtual image of a real object
(a) Only if $u > f$.
(b) Only if $u < f$.
(c) Only if $u = f$
(d) A diverging lens always forms a virtual image of a real object.

39. A lens produces a enlarged, virtual image. What kind of lens is it?
(a) converging
(b) diverging
(c) It could be either diverging or converging.
(d) None

40. In an experiment to determine the focal length of a concave lens, a student obtained the image of a distant window on the screen. To determine the focal length of the lens, she/he should measure the distance between the

(a) lens and the screen only

(b) lens and the window only

(c) screen and the window only

(d) screen and the lens and also between the screen and the window

41. Ashima looks into the mirror and sees the reflection of the picture behind her.

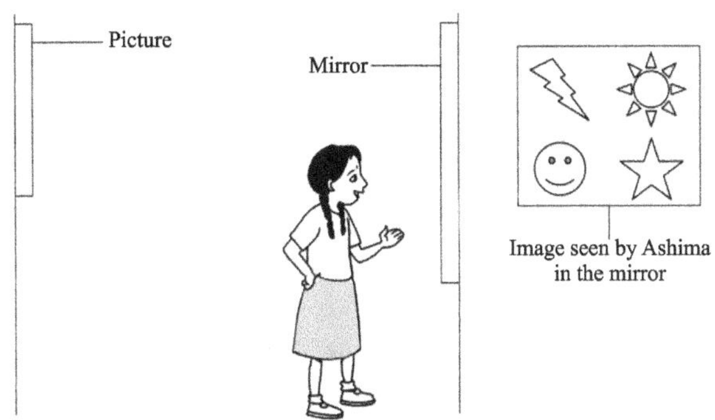

Which of the following is the picture that is behind Ashima?

(a) 

(b) 

(c) 

(d) 

42. On the basis of experiment 'to trace the path of a ray of light passing through a rectangular glass slab' four students arrived at the following interpretations :

I. Angle of incidence is greater than the angle of emergence.

II. Angle of emergence is less than the angle of refraction.

III. Emergent ray is parallel to the incident ray.

IV. Emergent ray is parallel to the refracted ray.

The correct interpretation is that of the student.

(a) I   (b) II

(c) III   (d) IV

43. Light waves

(a) are mechanical waves

(b) are electromagnetic waves

(c) travel with the same velocity in all media

(d) requires a material medium for their propagation

44. Virtual images of object of the same size are formed by

(a) a concave mirror   (b) a convex mirror

(c) a plane mirror   (d) all the above

45. Two plane inclined mirrors form 5 images by multiple reflection. The angle of inclination is

(a) 90°   (b) 60°

(c) 45°   (d) 30°

46. A bright × (cross) mark is made on a sheet of white paper. Over the white paper a rectangular glass-slab of thickness 3 cm is placed. On looking through, the image of the mark appears above the mark. It is below the upper surface of the slab by ($\mu_{glass} = 1.5$)

(a) 2.5 cm   (b) 1.5 cm

(c) 2 cm   (d) 1.75 cm

47. Images formed by an object placed between two plane mirrors whose reflecting surfaces make an angle of 90° with one another lie on a

(a) Straight line   (b) Zig-zag curve

(c) Circle   (d) Ellipse

48. A diver in a swimming pool wants to send a signal to a person lying on the edge of the pool by flashing his water-proof torch

(a) He must direct the beam of light vertically upwards

(b) He must direct the beam horizontally

(c) He must direct the beam at an angle to the vertical which is slightly lesser than the critical angle

(d) He must direct the beam at an angle to the vertical which is slightly greater than the critical angle

49. Two plane mirrors are inclined at an angle θ. A ray of light is incident on one mirror and is then reflected from the other mirror. Then the angle between the first ray and the final ray will be

(a) θ

(b) 2θ

(c) between θ and 2θ

(d) $> 2\theta$

50. A glass slab is placed in the path of a beam of convergent light, then the point of convergence of light

(a) moves towards the glass slab

(b) moves away from the glass slab

(c) remains at the same point

(d) undergoes a lateral shift

51. A real image is formed by a convex mirror when the object is placed at

(a) infinite

(b) between center of curvature and focus

(c) between focus and pole

(d) None of the above

52. A virtual image is formed by a concave mirror when the object is placed between

(a) infinity and center of curvature

(b) center of curvature and focus

(c) focus and the pole

(d) All of the above

53. Which of the following are used in a Kaleidoscope

(a) plane mirrors

(b) concave

(c) convex mirrors

(d) All of the above

54. When a convex lens made up of glass is immersed in water, its focal length

(a) decreases

(b) does not change

(c) increases

(d) None of the above

55. Find out the correct option from the following.

(A) The magnification is positive for all virtual images and is negative for all real images.

(B) The magnification of concave lens and convex mirror is always positive where as the magnification of convex lens and concave mirror can be positive or negative depending on the position of the object before the lens.

(a) Only A is true

(b) Only B is true.

(c) Both A and B are true

(d) Both A and B are false

56. A person standing at some distance from a mirror finds his image erect, virtual and of the same size. Then the mirror is possibly

(a) plane mirror

(b) concave mirror

(c) plane or concave mirror

(d) plane or concave or convex mirror

57. Refraction of light from air to glass and from air to water are shown in figure (i) and (ii) below. The value of the angle in the case of refraction as shown in figure (iii) will be :

(i) 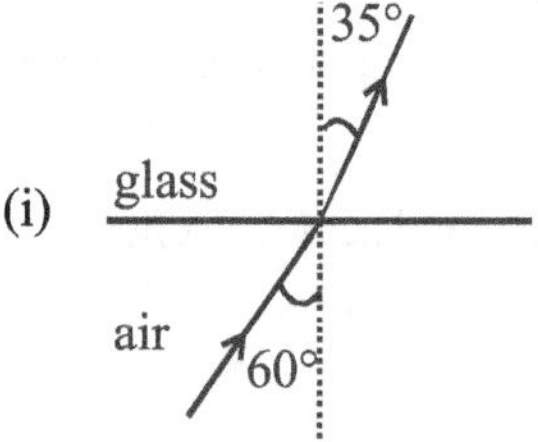

(ii) 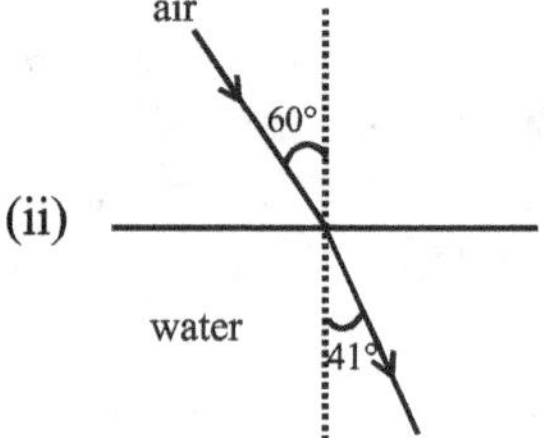

(iii) 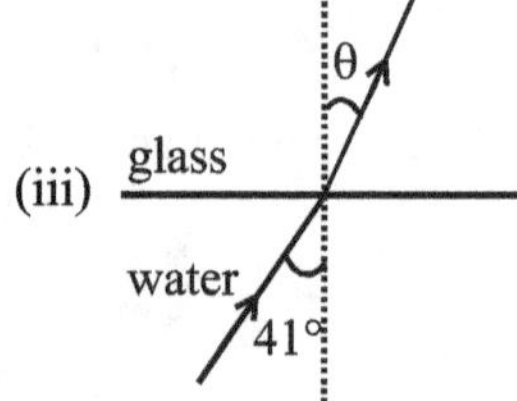

(a) 30°

(b) 35°

(c) 60°

(d) none of the above

58. The focal length of a plane mirror is

(a) positive

(b) negative

(c) zero

(d) infinity

59. Rays from the sun converge at a point 15 cm in front of a concave mirror. Where should an object be placed so that size of its image is equal to the size of the object?

(a) 15 cm in front of the mirror

(b) 30 cm in front of the mirror

(c) between 15 cm and 30 cm in front of the mirror

(d) more than 30 cm in front of the mirror.

60. A convex mirror is used

(a) by a dentist

(b) for shaving

(c) as a rear view mirror in vehicles

(d) as a light reflector for obtaining a parallel beam of light.

61. In case of a concave mirror, when the object is situated at the principal focus, the image formed is

(a) real and inverted

(b) of infinite size

(c) lies at infinity

(d) All of these

62. For an object at infinity, a concave mirror produces an image at its focus which is

(a) enlarged   (b) virtual

(c) erect   (d) real and point sized

63. An inverted image can be seen in a convex mirror,

(a) under no circumstances

(b) when the object is very far from the mirror

(c) when the object is at a distance equal to the radius of curvature of the mirror

(d) when the distance of the object from the mirror is equal to the focal length of the mirror

64. In order to get a diminished virtual image, the object can be placed anywhere in front of a

(a) concave mirror   (b) plane mirror

(c) convex mirror   (d) none of these

65. A full length image of a distant tall building can definitely be seen by using

(a) a concave mirror

(b) a convex mirror

(c) a plane mirror

(d) both concave as well as plane mirror

66. The concave mirrors are used in

(a) reflecting telescopes   (b) magic- lanterns

(c) cinema projectors   (d) All of these

67. Which of the following statements is true?

(a) A convex lens has 4 dioptre power having a focal length 0.25 m

(b) A convex lens has –4 dioptre power having a focal length 0.25 m

(c) A concave lens has 4 dipotre power having a focal length 0.25 m

(d) A concave lens has – 4 dioptre power having a focal length 0.25 m

68. A virtual, erect and magnified image of an object is to be produced with a concave mirror of focal length 12 cm. Which of the following object distance should be chosen for this purpose?

(a) 10 cm   (b) 14 cm

(c) 18 cm   (d) 24 cm

69. A 10 mm long awlpin is placed vertically in front of a concave mirror. A 5 mm long image of the awl pin is formed at 30 cm in front of the mirror. The focal length of this mirror is

(a) – 30 cm   (b) – 20 cm

(c) – 40 cm   (d) – 60 cm

70. The linear magnification for a mirror is the ratio of the size of the image to the size of the object, and is denoted by m. Then, m is equal to (symbols have their usual meanings):

(a) $\dfrac{f}{f-u}$ (b) $\dfrac{f-u}{f}$

(c) $\dfrac{f}{f+v}$ (d) $\dfrac{f+v}{f}$

71. In case of a real and inverted image, the magnification of a mirror is

(a) positive   (b) negative

(c) zero   (d) infinity

72. Magnification produced by a rear view mirror fitted in vehicles

(a) is less than one

(b) is more than one

(c) is equal to one

(d) can be more than or less than one depending upon the position of the object in front of it.

73. The ratio of the sine of angle of incidence to the sine of angle of refraction is called

(a) refractive index

(b) optical density

(c) relative density

(d) none of these

74. When an objects is placed between two mirrors placed inclined to each at an angle 45° Number of images formed are

(a) 3   (b) 5

(c) 7   (d) None of these

75. Foam of soap always appears white as

(a) it contains large hydrocarbon chains.

(b) it absorbs red portion of the visible light

(c) it reflects light of all wavelengths.

(d) it has one hydrophobic end, which is insoluble in water.

76. Two lenses of focal length f_1 and f_2 are kept in contact coaxially. The power of the combination will be

(a) $\dfrac{f_1 f_2}{f_1+f_2}$ (b) $\dfrac{f_1+f_2}{f_1 f_2}$

(c) $\dfrac{f_1 f_2}{f_1-f_2}$ (d) f_1+f_2

77. A mirror is placed at an angle of $30°$ with respect to Y-axis (see figure). A light ray travelling in the negative y-direction strikes the mirror. The direction of the reflected ray is given by the vector

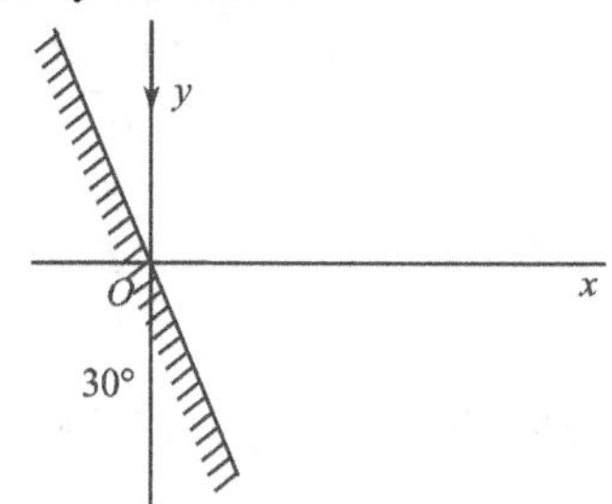

(a) $\hat{i}$

(b) $\hat{i} - \sqrt{3}\hat{j}$

(c) $\sqrt{3}\hat{i} - \hat{j}$

(d) $\hat{i} - 2\hat{j}$

78. A ray of light originates from inside a glass slab and is incident on its inner surface at an angle θ as shown below.

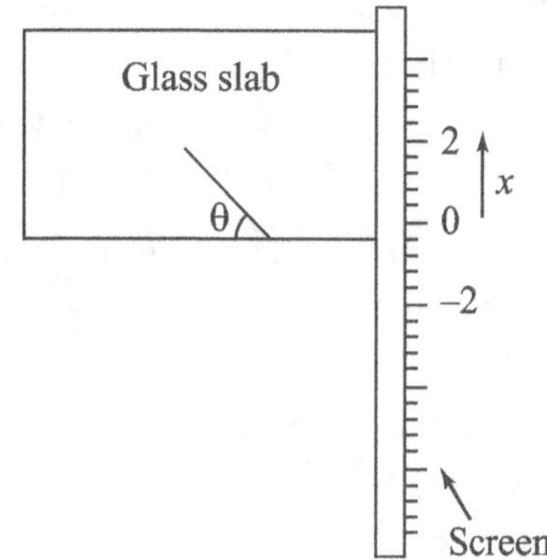

In this experiment, the location x of the spot where the ray hits the screen is recorded. Which of the following correctly shows the plot of variation of x with the angle θ?

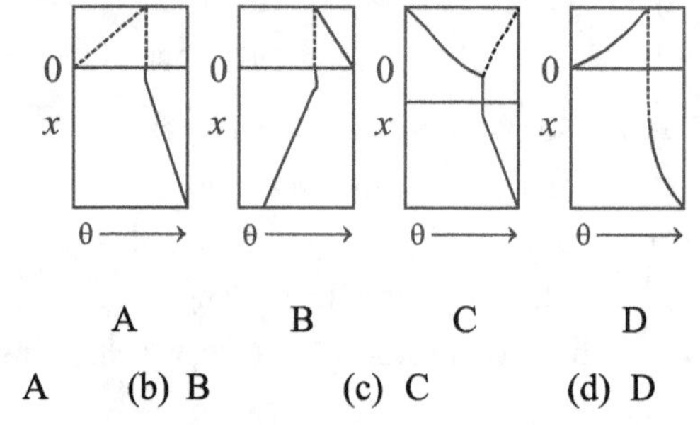

(a) A (b) B (c) C (d) D

79. Two convex lenses A and B each of focal length 30 cm are separated by 30 cm, as shown in the figure. An object O is placed at a distance of 40 cm to the left of lens A.

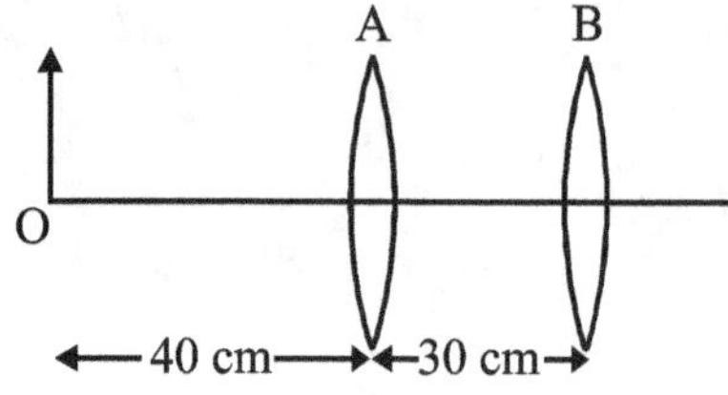

What is the distance of the final image formed by this lens system?

(a) 120 cm to right of lens A

(b) 90 cm to right of lens A

(c) 22.5 cm to right of lens B

(d) 45 cm to right of lens B

80. Two plane mirrors are kept on a horizontal table making an angle θ with each other as shown schematically in the figure. The angle θ is such that any ray of light reflected after striking both the mirrors returns parallel to its incident path. For this to happen, the value of θ should be

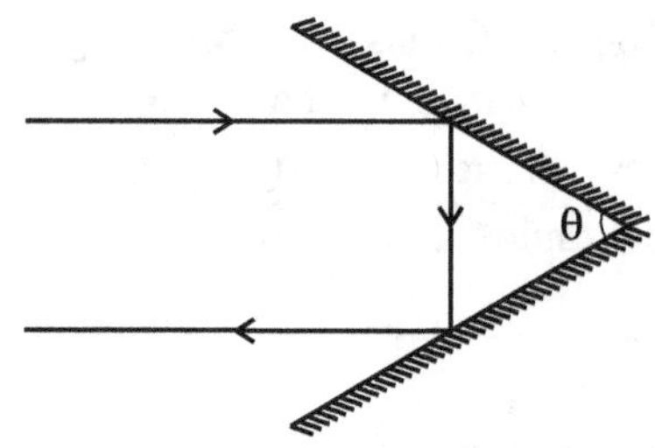

(a) $30°$

(b) $45°$

(c) $60°$

(d) $90°$

81. An object is placed at a distance of 40 cm from a concave mirror of focal length 15 cm. If the object is displaced through a distance of 20 cm towards the mirror, the displacement of the image will be

(a) 30 cm away from the mirror

(b) 36 cm away from the mirror

(c) 36 cm towards the mirror

(d) 30 cm towards the mirror

82. A pin AB of length 2 cm is kept on the axis of a convex lens between 18 cm and 20 cm as shown in figure. Focal length of convex lens is 10 cm. Find magnification produced for the image of the pin.

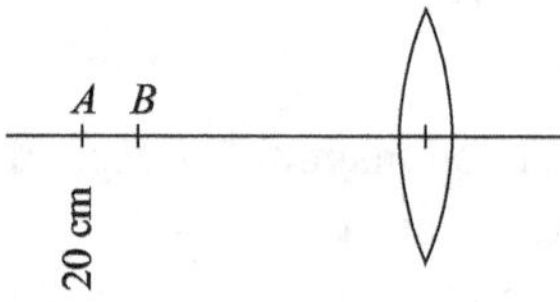

(a) 0.83

(b) 1.00

(c) 1.25

(d) 6.78

83. A concave mirror for face viewing has focal length of 0.4 m. The distance at which you hold the mirror from your face in order to see your image upright with a magnification of 5 is:

(a) 0.24 m

(b) 1.60 m

(c) 0.32 m

(d) 0.16 m

84. A convex lens of focal length 20 cm is cut into two halves. Each of which is placed 0.5 mm and a point object placed at a distance of 30 cm from the lens as shown.

Then the image is at

(a) 60 cm

(b) 30 cm

(c) 70 cm

(d) 50 cm

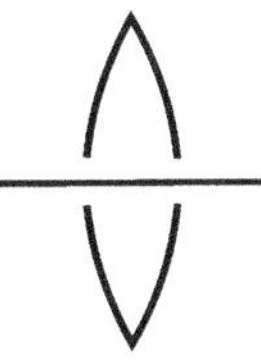

85. Focal length of a lens is 25 cm. In dioptre, power of lens will be

(a) 0.04   (b) 0.4

(c) 4   (d) 2.5

86. When viewed vertically a fish appears to be 4 meter below the surface of the lake. If the index of refraction of water is 1.33, then the true depth of the fish is

(a) 5.32 metres   (b) 3.32 metres

(c) 4.32 metres   (d) 6.32 metres

87. Two thin lenses of focal lengths f_1 and f_2 are placed in contact with each other such that the combination behaves as a glass slab. Then how are f_1 and f_2 related to each other?

(a) $f_1 = \dfrac{1}{f_2}$ (b) $f_2 = -f_1$

(c) $f_1 = f_2$ (d) $f_1 = \sqrt{f_2}$

88. A convex lens of focal length 25 cm receives light from the sun. A diverging lens of focal length – 12 cm is placed 37 cm to the right of the converging lens. Where is the final image located relative to the diverging lens?

(a) 6 cm to the left   (b) 25 cm to the left

(c) At infinity   (d) 12 cm to the right

89. A camera lens focuses light from a 12.0 m tall building located 35.0 m away on film 50.0 mm behind the lens. How tall is the image of the building on the film?

(a) 17.1 mm   (b) 7.00 mm

(c) 2.50 cm   (d) 1.25 mm

90. A hollow lens is made of thin glass and in the shape of a double concave lens. It can be filled with air, water of refractive index 1.33 or CS_2 of refractive index 1.6. It will act as a diverging lens, if it is

(a) filled with air and immersed in water

(b) filled with water and immersed in CS_2

(c) filled with air and immersed in CS_2

(d) filled with CS_2 and immersed in water

91. A diverging lens with magnitude of focal length 25 cm is placed at a distance of 15 cm from a converging lens of magnitude of focal length 20 cm. A beam of parallel light falls on the diverging lens. The final image formed is :

(a) real and at a distance of 40 cm from the divergent lens

(b) real and at a distance of 6 cm from the convergent lens

(c) real and at a distance of 40 cm from convergent lens

(d) virtual and at a distance of 40 cm from convergent lens.

92. A beam of light from a source L is incident normally on a plane mirror fixed at a certain distance x from the source. The beam is reflected back as a spot on a scale placed just above the source L. When the mirror is rotated through a small angle θ, the spot of the light is found to move through a distance y on the scale. The angle θ is given by

(a) $\dfrac{y}{x}$ (b) $\dfrac{x}{2y}$

(c) $\dfrac{x}{y}$ (d) $\dfrac{y}{2x}$

93. A glass beaker is filled with water up to 5 cm. It is kept on top of a 2 cm thick glass slab. When a coin at the bottom of the glass slab is viewed at the normal incidence from above the beaker, its apparent depth from the water surface is d cm. Value of d is close to (the refractive indices of water and glass are 1.33 and 1.5, respectively)

(a) 2.5 cm   (b) 5.1 cm

(c) 3.7 cm   (d) 6.0 cm

94. A convex lens is put 10 cm from a light source and it makes a sharp image on a screen, kept 10 cm from the lens. Now a glass block (refractive index 1.5) of 1.5 cm thickness is placed in contact with the light source. To get the sharp image again, the screen is shifted by a distance d. Then d is:

(a) 1.1 cm away from the lens

(b) 0

(c) 0.55 cm towards the lens

(d) 0.55 cm away from the lens

Case/Passage Based Questions

DIRECTIONS : *Study the given case/passage and answer the following questions.*

Case/Passage - 1

A 5.0 cm tall object is placed perpendicular to the principal axis of a convex lens of focal length 20 cm. The distance of the object from the lens is 30 cm.

95. What is the distance of image from the pole of lens?

(a) $v = 60$ cm   (b) $v = -60$ cm

(c) $v = 30$ cm   (d) $v = -30$ cm

96. What is the power of the used lens?

(a) $+5$ D   (b) -5 D

(c) $+0.5$ D   (d) -0.5 D

Case/Passage - 2

Light travels through a vacuum at a speed $c = 3 \times 10^8$ m/s. It can also travel through many materials, such as air, water and glass. Atoms in the material absorb, reemit and scatter the light, however. Therefore, light travels through the material at a speed that is less than c, the actual speed depending on the nature of the material. To describe the extent to which the speed of light in a material medium differs from that in a vacuum, we use a parameter called the index of refraction (or refractive index).

97. Figure shows a ray of light as it travels from medium A to

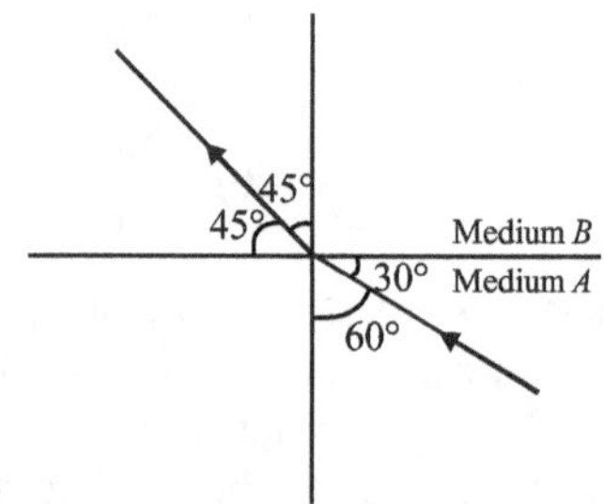

medium B. Retractive index of the medium B relative to medium A is

(a) $\dfrac{\sqrt{3}}{2}$ (b) $\dfrac{\sqrt{2}}{\sqrt{3}}$

(c) $\dfrac{1}{\sqrt{2}}$ (d) $\sqrt{2}$

98. A light ray enters from medium A to medium B as shown

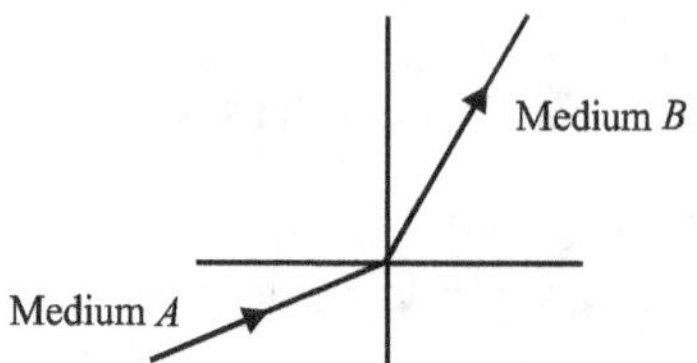

in the figure. The refractive index of medium B relative to A will be

(a) greater than unity   (b) less than unity

(c) equal to unity   (d) zero

99. The path of a ray of light coming from air passing through a rectangular glass slab traced by four students shown as A, B, C and D in the figure. Which one of them is correct?

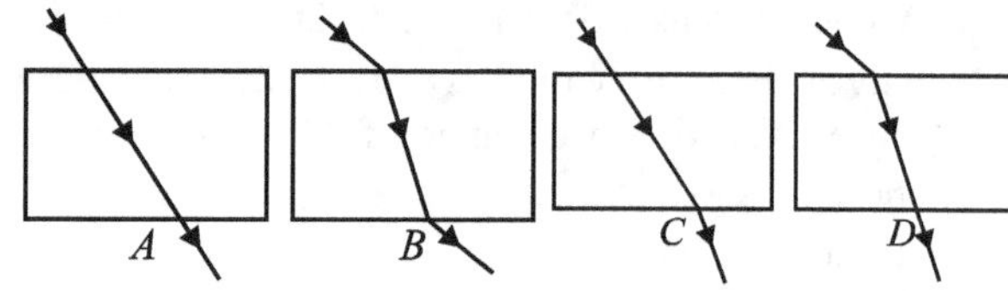

(a) A (b) B

(c) C (d) D

100. You are given water, mustard oil, glycerine and kerosene. In which of these media, a ray of light incident obliquely at same angle would bend the most?

(a) Kerosene   (b) Water

(c) Mustard oil   (d) Glycerine

101. A ray of light is incident in medium 1 on a surface that separates medium 1 from medium 2. Let v_1 and v_2 represent the velocity of light in medium 1 and medium 2 respectively. Also let n_{12} and n_{21} represent the refractive index of medium 1 with respect to medium 2 and refractive index of medium 2 with respect to medium 1, respectively. If i and r denote the angle of incidence and angle of refraction, then-

(a) $\dfrac{\sin i}{\sin r} = n_{21} \dfrac{v_1}{v_2}$ (b) $\dfrac{\sin i}{\sin r} = n_{21} \dfrac{v_2}{v_1}$

(c) $\dfrac{\sin i}{\sin r} = n_{12} \dfrac{v_1}{v_2}$ (d) $\dfrac{\sin i}{\sin r} = n_{12} \dfrac{v_2}{v_1}$

Case/Passage - 3

Inside a substance such as glass or water, light travels more slowly than it does in a vacuum. If c denotes the speed of light in a vacuum and v denotes its speed through some other substance, then $v = c/n$ where n is a constant called the index of refraction.

To good approximation, a substance's index of refraction does not depend on the wavelength of light. For instance, when red and blue light waves enter water, they both slow down by about the same amount. More precise measurements, however, reveal that n varies with wavelength. Table presents some indices of refraction of Custon glass, for different wavelengths of visible light. A nanometer (nm) is 10^{-9} meters. In a vacuum, light travels as $c = 3.0 \times 10^8$ m/s

Table : Indices of refraction of Custon glass

Approximately colour	Wavelength in vacuum (nm)	"Indices n"
yellow	580	1.5
yellow orange	600	1.498
orange	620	1.496
orange red	640	1.494

102. Inside Custon glass

   (a) Orange light travels faster than yellow light

   (b) Yellow light travels faster than orange light

   (c) Orange and Yellow light travels equally fast

   (d) We cannot determine which color of light travels faster

103. For blue-green of wavelength 520 nm, the index of refraction of Custon glass is probably closest to

   (a) 1.49   (b) 1.50

   (c) 1.51   (d) 1.52

104. Which of the following phenomena happens because n varies with wavelength

   (a) A lens focuses light

   (b) A prism breaks sunlight into different colors

   (c) Total internal reflections ensures that light travels down a fiber optic cable

   (d) Light rays entering a pond change direction at the pond's surface

Assertion & Reason

DIRECTIONS : *Each of these questions contains an assertion followed by reason. Read them carefully and answer the question on the basis of following options. You have to select the one that best describes the two statements.*

   (a) If both **Assertion** and **Reason** are **correct** and Reason is the **correct explanation** of Assertion.

   (b) If both **Assertion** and **Reason** are correct, but Reason is **not the correct explanation** of Assertion.

   (c) If **Assertion** is **correct** but **Reason** is **incorrect**.

   (d) If **Assertion** is **incorrect** but **Reason** is **correct**.

105. Assertion : The diameter of convex lens required to form full image of an object is half the height of the object.

   Reason : The smaller diameter lens will give full image of lower intensity.

106. Assertion : The image of a point object situated at the centre of hemispherical lens is also at the centre.
   Reason : For hemisphere Snell's law is not valid.

107. Assertion : A point object is placed at a distance of 26 cm from a convex mirror of focal length 26 cm. The image will not form at infinity.

   Reason : For above given system the equation $\dfrac{1}{u}+\dfrac{1}{v}=\dfrac{1}{f}$ gives $v = \infty$.

108. Assertion : When a concave mirror is held under water, its focal length will increase.

   Reason : The focal length of a concave mirror is independent of the medium in which it is placed.

109. Assertion : A convex mirror is used as a driver's mirror.

   Reason : Because convex mirror's field of view is large and images formed are virtual, erect and diminshed.

110. Assertion : When the object moves with a velocity $\vec{v}$, its image in the plane mirror moves with a velocity of $-2\vec{v}$ with respect to the object.

   Reason : The minimum height of the mirror to be required to see the full image of man of height h is $\dfrac{h}{2}$.

111. Assertion : As the temperature of a medium increases the refractive index decreases.

   Reason : When a ray travels from vacuum to a medium, then μ is known as absolute refractive index of the medium. $(\mu_{vacuum} = 1)$.

112. Assertion : If a spherical mirror is dipped in water, its focal length remains unchanged.

   Reason : A laser light is focused by a converging lens. There will be a significant chromatic aberration.

113. Assertion : A virtual image cannot be projected one screen.

   Reason : Virtual images are formed by actual meeting of rays of light after reflection or refraction.

114. Assertion : Red light travels faster in glass than green light.

   Reason : The refractive index of glass is less for red light than for green light.

115. Assertion : As light travels from one medium to another, the frequency of light does not change.

   Reason : Because frequency is the characteristic of source.

116. Assertion : Light rays retrace their path when their direction is reversed (Law of reversibility of light rays)

   Reason : For the refraction of light, water is denser than air, but for the refraction of sound, water is rarer than air.

117. Assertion : The mirrors used in search lights are parabolic and not concave spherical.

   Reason : Silvered plano convex lens is used in search light.

Match the Following

DIRECTIONS : *Each question contains statements given in two columns which have to be matched. Statements (A, B, C, D) in column I have to be matched with statements (p, q, r, s) in column II.*

118. Match the following :

Column I	Column II
(A) Power of convex mirror	(p) Positive power
(B) Power of concave mirror	(q) Negative power
(C) Power of plane mirror	(r) Zero power
(D) Power of convex lens	(s) Infinite power

119. The graphs given apply to convex lens of focal length f, producing a real image at a distance v from the optical centre when self luminous object is at distance u from the optical centre. The magnitude of magnification is m. Identify the following graphs with the first named quantity being plotted along y-axis.

    Column I   **Column II**

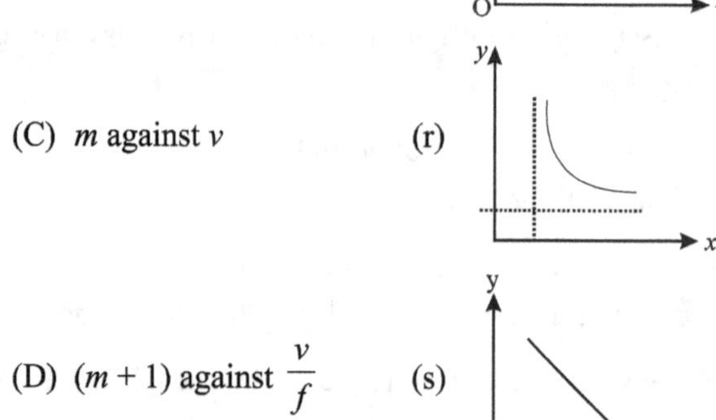

(A) v against u (p)

(B) $\dfrac{1}{v}$ against $\dfrac{1}{u}$ (q)

(C) m against v (r)

(D) $(m + 1)$ against $\dfrac{v}{f}$ (s)

Fill in the Blanks

DIRECTIONS : *Complete the following statements with an appropriate word / term to be filled in the blank space(s).*

120. The power of a convex lens is .... and that of a concave lens is ....

121. Light seems to travel in ....

122. A light ray travelling obliquely from a denser medium to a rarer medium bends .... the normal. A light ray bends .... the normal when it travels obliquely from a rarer to a denser medium.

123. In case of a rectangular glass slab, the refraction takes place at both .... interface and .... interface. The emergent ray is .... to the direction of incident ray.

124. Power of a lens is the reciprocal of its ....

125. The SI unit of power of a lens is ....

126. The angle of incidence is .... to the angle of reflection.

127. The reflecting surface of a spherical mirror may be curved .... or ....

128. The inner surface of the spoon can be approximated to a .... mirror.

129. The centre of the reflecting surface of a spherical mirror is a point called the ....

130. The centre of curvature of a concave mirror lies in .... of it.

131. Line passing through the pole and the centre of curvature of a spherical mirror is called the ....

132. A ray parallel to the principal axis, after reflection, will pass through the ....

133. The dentists use .... mirrors to see large images of the teeth of patients.

134. A transparent material bound by two surfaces, of which one or both surfaces are spherical, forms a ....

135. The degree of .... of light rays achieved by a lens is expressed in terms of its power.

136. An object is placed in front of a spherical mirror. The image is found to be virtual for all positions of the object. The spherical mirror is ....

137. Two immiscible transparent liquids A and B have 1.2 and 1.5 as their refractive indices (with respect to air). The refractive index of B with respect to A is ....

True / False

DIRECTIONS : *Read the following statements and write your answer as true or false.*

138. The reflecting surfaces, of all types, obey the laws of reflection.

139. Light travels in vacuum with an enormous speed of 3×10^8 ms^{-1}.

140. The speed of light is different in different media.

141. The refractive index of a transparent medium is the ratio of the speed of light in vacuum to that in the medium.

142. The incident ray, the normal to the mirror at the point of incidence and the reflected ray, all lie in the same plane.

143. Image formed by a plane mirror is always virtual and erect.

144. The principal focus of a spherical mirror lies midway between the pole and centre of curvature.

145. Convex mirrors enable the driver to view much larger area than would be possible with a plane mirror.

146. A concave lens will always give a virtual, erect and diminished image.

147. A ray of light passing through the optical centre of a lens will emerge without any deviation.

148. The image in a plane mirror lies as far behind the mirror.

149. An object is placed in front of a mirror and an image of it is formed at the object itself. The mirror mentioned in question is a convex mirror.

150. A concave mirror can produce both real and virtual images.

151. Light travels faster in glass than in air.

152. The laws of reflection are valid for plane mirrors and not for spherical mirrors.

153. The mirror formula is valid only if the aperture of the mirror is small.

154. When a ray of light travels from air to water, its speeds up.

155. A lens that is thicker at the middle than at the edges is a diverging lens.

ANSWER KEY & SOLUTIONS

1. **(b)** In plane mirror, object distance = image distance

   ∴ Distance between object and image

   = 0.5 + 0.5 = 1 m

2. **(a)** $n = \dfrac{360°}{90°} = 4$

   so numbe of images is $(n-1) \Rightarrow (4-1) = 3$

3. **(b)** Concave mirror is used as a shaving mirror

4. **(c)** For all spherical mirrors $f = R/2$

5. **(c)** given, $m = \dfrac{\text{Image height}}{\text{object height}} > 1$

   ⇒ Image height > Object height

6. **(b)** Convex mirror always form virtual and erect image.

7. **(b)** 8. **(c)**

9. **(a)** Power $= \dfrac{1}{\text{focal length}}$

10. **(a)** Magnification, $m = \dfrac{\text{Image height}}{\text{Object height}}$

11. **(b)** Diminished, erect image is formed by convex mirror.

12. **(b)** 13. **(b)** 14.   **(a)** 15.   **(c)**

16. **(d)** For a spherical lens $\dfrac{1}{v} - \dfrac{1}{u} = \dfrac{1}{f}$

   For convex lens. $u = -f/2$ and f is $+$ ve

   $\therefore \dfrac{1}{v} = \dfrac{1}{f} + \dfrac{1}{u} = \dfrac{1}{f} + \dfrac{1}{f} = +\dfrac{1}{f} - \dfrac{2}{f} \quad \therefore v = -f$

17. **(d)** 18. **(c)** 19. **(a)** 20. **(c)** 21. **(a)**

22. **(a)** 23. **(c)** 24. **(b)** 25. **(c)** 26. **(b)**

27. **(c)** 28. **(d)** 29. **(d)** 30. **(d)** 31. **(d)**

32. **(d)** 33. **(b)** 34. **(b)** 35. **(a)** 36. **(a)**

37. **(b)** 38. **(d)** 39. **(a)** 40. **(a)** 41. **(b)**

42. **(c)** 43. **(b)** 44. **(c)** 45. **(b)** 46. **(c)**

47. **(c)** 48. **(c)** 49. **(b)** 50. **(b)** 51. **(d)**

52. **(c)** 53. **(a)** 54. **(c)** 55. **(c)** 56. **(a)**

57. **(b)** $_a\mu_g = \dfrac{\sin 60°}{\sin 35°}$ and $_a\mu_w = \dfrac{\sin 60°}{\sin 41°}$

   $\therefore \quad _a\mu_g = \dfrac{_a\mu_g}{_a\mu_w} = \dfrac{\sin 41°}{\sin \theta}$

   or $\left(\dfrac{\sin 60°}{\sin 35°} \Big/ \dfrac{\sin 60°}{\sin 41°}\right) = \dfrac{\sin 41°}{\sin \theta}$

   $\therefore \theta = 35°$

58. **(d)**   59. **(b)**   60. **(c)**   61 **(d)**   62. **(d)**

63. **(a)**   64. **(c)**   65. **(b)**   66. **(d)**   67. **(a)**

68. **(a)**   69. **(b)**   70. **(a)**   71. **(b)**   72. **(a)**

73. **(a)**

74. **(c)** Number of images formed $= \dfrac{360°}{\theta} - 1 = 7$.

75. **(c)**

76. **(b)** $P = P_1 + P_2 \Rightarrow P = \dfrac{1}{f_1} + \dfrac{1}{f_2} \Rightarrow P = \dfrac{f_1 + f_2}{f_1 f_2}$

77. **(c)** According to laws of reflection,

   angle of incidence = angle of reflection

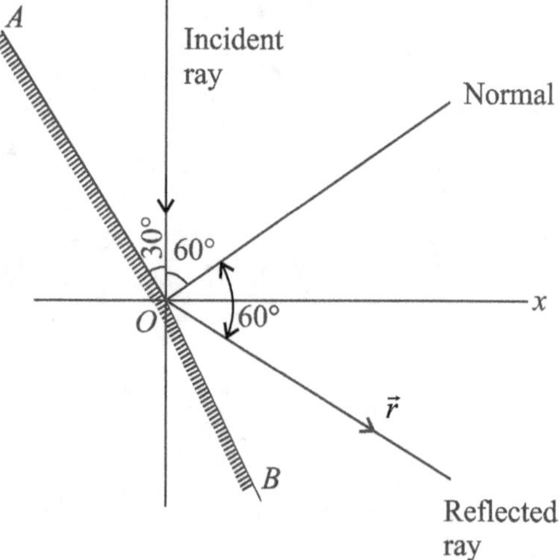

   ∴ if a vector $\vec{r}$ is along the reflected ray, then

   $\vec{r} = \cos 30° \hat{i} - \sin 30 \hat{j}$

   $\vec{r} = \dfrac{\sqrt{3}}{2} \hat{i} - \dfrac{1}{2} \hat{j}$

   $\vec{r} = \sqrt{3} \hat{i} - \hat{j}$

   Hence, the direction of the reflected ray vector is .

   $\sqrt{3} \hat{i} - \hat{j}$

78. **(a)** Angle of incidence, $i = 90° - \theta$, decreases with increase in θ upto angle of incidence $i =$ critical angle reflection takes place so x is positive and beyond the critical angle refraction takes place so x is negative.

Hence graph 'A' correctly depicts variation of x with the angle θ.

79. **(c)** For lens A, $\dfrac{1}{f} = \dfrac{1}{v} - \dfrac{1}{u}$

$\Rightarrow \dfrac{1}{30} = \dfrac{1}{v} - \left(-\dfrac{1}{40}\right)$

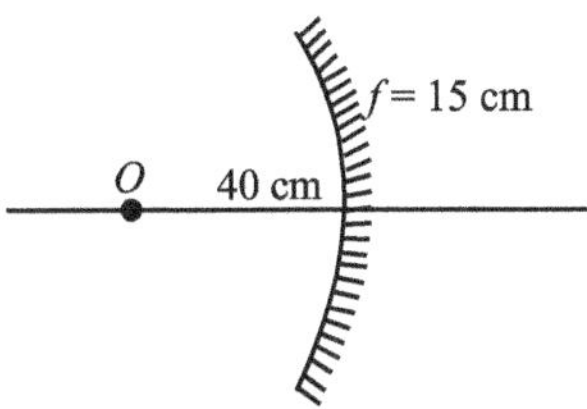

$\Rightarrow \dfrac{1}{30} = \dfrac{1}{v} + \dfrac{1}{40}$

$= \dfrac{4-3}{120} = \dfrac{1}{120}$ or, $v = 120$ cm.

For lens B, $u = 90$ cm $[u = 120 - 30]$

$\dfrac{1}{f} = \dfrac{1}{v} - \dfrac{1}{u} \Rightarrow \dfrac{1}{30} = \dfrac{1}{v} - \dfrac{1}{90}$

$\dfrac{1}{v} = \dfrac{1}{30} + \dfrac{1}{90} = \dfrac{3+1}{90}$

or, $v = 22.5$ cm

Which is positive so that it is 22.5 cm from lens B.

80. **(d)** Two mirrors are inclined at an angle, $\theta = ?$

According to question, emergent ray is parallel to incident ray

$\therefore$ deviation angle $\delta = 180°$

But $\delta = 360° - 2\theta$

or, $360° - 2\theta = 180°$

or, $2\theta = 180°$

$\therefore \theta = 90°$

81. **(b)**

Using mirror formula, $\dfrac{1}{f} = \dfrac{1}{v_1} + \dfrac{1}{u}$

$-\dfrac{1}{15} = \dfrac{1}{v_1} + \dfrac{1}{u} \Rightarrow \dfrac{1}{v_1} = \dfrac{1}{-15} + \dfrac{1}{40}$

$\therefore v_1 = -24$ cm

When object is displaced by 20 cm towards mirror Now, $u_2 = -20$

So, $\dfrac{1}{f} = \dfrac{1}{v_2} + \dfrac{1}{u_2}$

$\dfrac{1}{-15} = \dfrac{1}{v_2} - \dfrac{1}{20} \Rightarrow \dfrac{1}{v_2} = \dfrac{1}{20} - \dfrac{1}{15}$

$\therefore v_2 = -60$ cm

Therefore image shifts away from mirror by $= 60 - 24 = 36$ cm

82. **(c)** For the end B, image distance of end B will be,

$f = 10$ cm

$u_B = -18$ cm

$v_B =$ image distance of end B

As we know,

$\dfrac{1}{f} = \dfrac{1}{v_B} - \dfrac{1}{u_B}$

$\dfrac{1}{v_B} = \dfrac{1}{f} + \dfrac{1}{u_B}$

$\dfrac{1}{v_B} = \dfrac{1}{10} - \dfrac{1}{18} = \dfrac{8}{180}$

$v_B = \dfrac{180}{8} \Rightarrow 22.5$ cm

Similarly, for the end A, image distance of end A will be,

$f = 10$ cm

$u_A = -20$ cm

$v_A =$ image distance of end A

$\dfrac{1}{f} = \dfrac{1}{v_A} - \dfrac{1}{u_A}$

$\dfrac{1}{v_A} = \dfrac{1}{f} + \dfrac{1}{u_A}$

$\dfrac{1}{v_A} = \dfrac{1}{10} - \dfrac{1}{20} = \dfrac{1}{20}$

$v_A = 20$ cm

So, length of image $A'B' = (v_B - v_A)$

$= 22.5 - 20 = 2.5$ cm

So magnification, $m = \dfrac{A'B'}{AB} \Rightarrow \dfrac{2.5}{2} = 1.25$

83. **(c)** $+5 = -\dfrac{v}{u} \Rightarrow v = -5u$

Using $\Rightarrow \dfrac{1}{v} + \dfrac{1}{u} = \dfrac{1}{f} \Rightarrow \dfrac{1}{-5u} + \dfrac{1}{u} = \dfrac{-1}{0.4}$

$\therefore u = -0.32$ m.

84. **(a)** Given,

Object distance, $u = 30$ cm

when a lens is cut along the principle axis into two equal parts focal length remains same for each part.

$\therefore$ Focal length, $f = 20$ cm

using lens formula

$$\frac{1}{f} = \frac{1}{v} - \frac{1}{u}$$

$$Þ \frac{1}{v} = \frac{1}{20} - \frac{1}{30} = \frac{1}{60}$$

$$\Rightarrow v = 60 \text{ cm}$$

85. **(c)** Focal length of a lens, $F = 25$ cm

$$f = 0.25 \text{ m}$$

$$P = \frac{1}{f} = \frac{1}{0.25} = 4D$$

86. **(a)**   **87.** **(b)**   **88.** **(a)**   **89.** **(a)**

90. **(d)** Here $\underset{(1.6)}{\mu_{cs_2}} > \underset{(1.33)}{\mu_{water}} > \underset{(1.0)}{\mu_{air}}$

i.e., CS_2 is denser than water and water is denser than air.

When medium outside a lens is denser than medium of lens, then a concave lens will acts like a convex lens and *vice-versa*.

Hence, lens here acts as a diverging lens when filled with CS_2 and immersed in water.

91. **(c)** As parallel beam incident on diverging lens will form image at focus.

$$\therefore v = -25 \text{ cm}$$

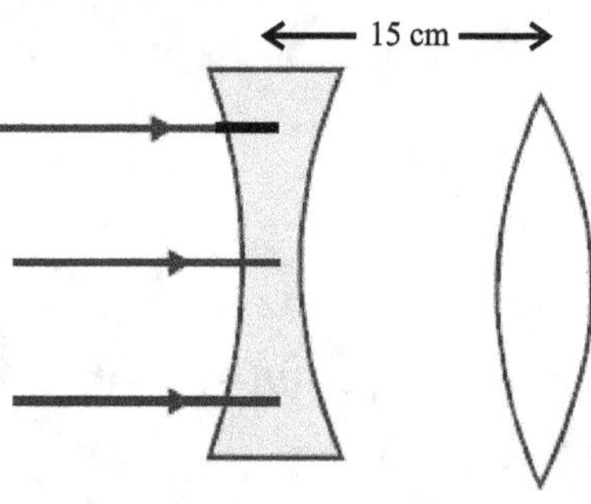

$$f = -25 \text{ } cm \qquad\qquad f = 20 \text{ } cm$$

The image formed by diverging lens is used as an object for converging lens,

So for converging lens $u = -25 - 15 = -40 \text{ } cm$, $f = 20 \text{ } cm$

$\therefore$ Final image formed by converging lens

$$\frac{1}{V} - \frac{1}{-40} = \frac{1}{20}$$

or, $V = 40$ cm from converging lens real and inverted.

92. **(d)** When mirror is rotated by angle θ reflected ray will be rotated by 2θ.

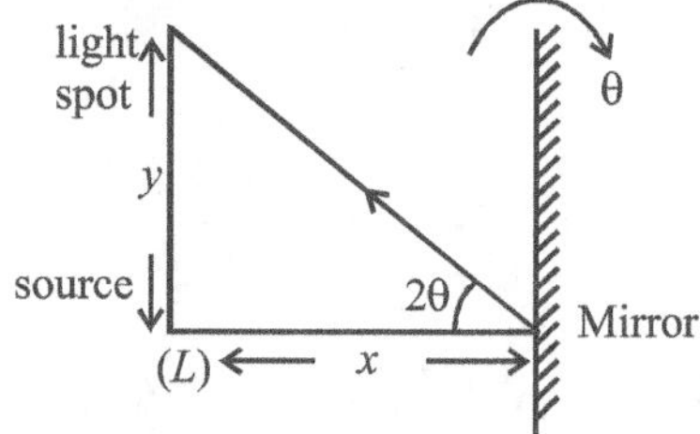

$$\frac{y}{x} = 2\theta \Rightarrow \theta = \frac{y}{2x}$$

93. **(b)** Given: $d_1 = 5$ cm, $\mu_1 = 1.33$

$$d_2 = 2 \text{ cm}, \mu_2 = 1.5$$

d_1 and d_2 are the thickness of slabs of medium with refractive index μ_1 and μ_2, respectively.

using formula, $d = \dfrac{d_1}{\mu_1} + \dfrac{d_2}{\mu_2} + \ldots$

Apparent depth, $d = \dfrac{5}{1.33} + \dfrac{2}{1.5}$

$= 5.088$ cm $= 5.1$ cm

94. **(d)**

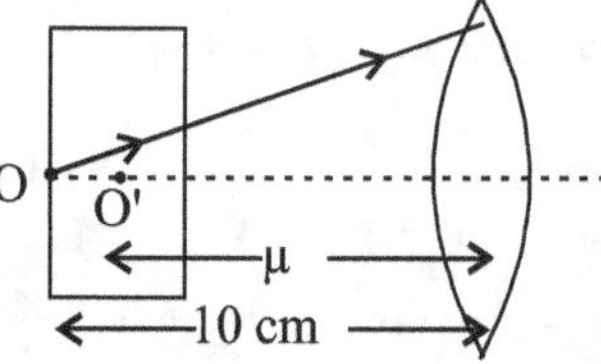

As the object and image distance is same, object is placed at $2f$. Therefore $2f = 10$

or $f = 5$ cm.

Shift due to slab, $d = t\left(1 - \dfrac{1}{\mu}\right)$

in the direction of incident ray

$$\Rightarrow d = 1.5\left(1 - \frac{2}{3}\right) = 0.5 \text{ cm}$$

Now, $u = -9.5$ cm

Again using lens formulas $\dfrac{1}{v} - \dfrac{1}{-9.5} = \dfrac{1}{5}$

$\Rightarrow v = 10.55$ cm

Thus, screen is shifted by a distance $d = 10.55 - 10 = 0.55$ cm away from the lens.

95. (a) Object size $h_0 = 5.0$ cm, $f = 20$ cm,

Object distance $u = -30$ cm

Since, $\dfrac{1}{v} - \dfrac{1}{u} = \dfrac{1}{f}$

$\dfrac{1}{v} = \dfrac{1}{f} + \dfrac{1}{u}$

Then $\dfrac{1}{v} = \dfrac{1}{20} + \dfrac{1}{-30} = \dfrac{1}{60}$

$\therefore\ v = +60$ cm

Positive sign of v shows that image is formed at a distance of 60 cm from the pole to the right of the lens.

Therefore image is real and inverted.

96. (a) Power $= \dfrac{1}{f} = \dfrac{1}{0.2\text{m}} = +5\text{D}$

97. (a) From figure, angle of incidence, $i = 60°$ and angle of refraction, $r = 45°$

Refractive index of the medium B relative to medium A, (from Snell's law)

$$\mu_{BA} = \frac{\sin i}{\sin r} = \frac{\sin 60°}{\sin 45°} = \frac{\left(\dfrac{\sqrt{3}}{2}\right)}{\left(\dfrac{1}{\sqrt{2}}\right)} = \frac{\sqrt{3}}{2}$$

98. (a) Since light rays in the medium B goes towards normal (figure), so it has greater refractive index i.e., denser w.r.t. medium A. Hence, refractive index of medium B relative to medium A is greater than unity.

99. (b) In a rectangular glass slab, the emergent rays are parallel to the direction of the incident ray, as the extent of bending of the ray of light at the opposite parallel faces air-glass and glass-air interface of the rectangular glass slab is equal and opposite.

This is why the ray emerges are parallel to the incident ray.

100. (d) Among the given material kerosene refractive index, $\mu = 1.44$, water $\mu = 1.33$, mustard oil $\mu = 1.46$ and glycerine $\mu = 1.74$. Glycerine is most optically denser. Therefore, ray of light bend most in glycerine.

101. (a) $\dfrac{\sin i}{\sin r} = n_{21} = \dfrac{v_1}{v_2}$

102. (a)   103.   (c)   104. (b)

105. (d) Any size of lens, can form full image, only intensity of image decreases with decrease in size.

106. (c) The rays from centre of hemisphere cut at the centre after refraction - Snell's law is valid in each case of refraction.

107. (d)   108.   (d)   109.   (a)   110.   (b)

111. (b)   112.   (c)

113. (c) Virtual image is formed when the rays of light after reflection or refraction appear to meet at a point.

114. (a)   115.   (a)   116.   (c)   117. (c)

118. (A) → p;   (B) → p;   (C) → r;   (D) → p

119. (A) → r;   (B) → p;   (C) → q;   (D) → s

120. positive, negative.   **121.** straight lines.

122. away from, towards   **123.** air-glass, glass-air, parallel

124. focal length   **125.** dioptre

126. equal   **127.** inwards, outwards.

128. concave   **129.** pole

130. front   **131.** principal axis

132. principal focus   **133.** concave

134. lens.   **135.** convergence or divergence

136. convex   **137.** 5/4

138. True   **139.** True   **140.** True   **141.** True

142. True   **143.** True   **144.** True   **145.** True

146. True   **147.** True   **148.** True   **149.** False

150. True   **151.** False   **152.** False   **153.** True

154. False   **155.** False

6

DIRECTIONS : *This section contains multiple choice questions. Each question has four choices (a), (b), (c) and (d) out of which only one is correct.*

1. The human eye possesses the power of accommodation. This is the power to :
   (a) alter the diameter of the pupil as the intensity of light changes
   (b) distinguish between lights of different colours
   (c) focus objects at different distances
   (d) decide which of the two objects is closer.

2. How does the eye change in order to focus on near or distant objects?
   (a) The lens moves in or out
   (b) The retina moves in or out
   (c) The lens becomes thicker or thinner
   (d) The pupil gets larger or smaller

3. Which of the following changes occur when you walk out of bright sunshine into a poorly lit room?
   (a) The pupil becomes larger
   (b) The lens becomes thicker
   (c) The ciliary muscle relaxes
   (d) The pupil becomes smaller

4. A person got his eyes tested. The optician's prescription for the spectacles reads:

   Left eye : – 3.00 D   Right eye : – 3.50 D

   The person is having a defect of vision called :
   (a) presbyopia   (b) myopia
   (c) astigmatism   (d) hypermetropia

5. A student sitting on the last bench in the class cannot read the writing on the blackboard clearly but he can read the book lying on his desk clearly. Which of the following statement is correct about the student?
   (a) The near point of his eyes has receded away.
   (b) The near point of his eyes has come closer to him.
   (c) The far point of his eyes has receded away.
   (d) The far point of his eyes has come closer to him.

6. A man driving a car can read a distant road sign clearly but finds difficulty in reading the odometer on the dashboard of the car. Which of the following statement is correct about this man?
   (a) The near point of his eyes has receded away.
   (b) The near point of his eyes has come closer to him.
   (c) The far point of his eyes has receded away.
   (d) The far point of his eyes has come closer to him.

7. Which of the following is not caused by the atmospheric refraction of light?
   (a) Twinkling of stars at night
   (b) Sun appearing higher in the sky than it actually is
   (c) Sun becoming visible two minutes before actual sunrise
   (d) Sun appearing red at sunset

8. The sky appears dark to passengers flying at very high altitudes mainly because :   **[CBSE 2020]**
   (a) Scatterings of light is not enough at such heights.
   (b) There is no atmosphere at great heights.
   (c) The size of molecules is smaller than the wavelength of visible light.
   (d) The light gets scattered towards the earth.

9. A near sighted person cannot see distinctly beyond 50 cm from his eye. The power in diopter of spectacle lenses which will enable him to see distant objects clearly is
   (a) +50   (b) –50
   (c) +2   (d) –2

10. The following one is not a primary colour
(a) Yellow　　　　　　(b) Red
(c) Green　　　　　　(d) Blue

11. When a mirror is rotated an angle the reflected ray moves through double that angle, the instrument based on the above principle is
(a) Periscope　　　　　(b) Odometer
(c) Refractometer　　　(d) Sextant

12. In the visible spectrum the colour having the shortest wavelength is
(a) Green　　　　　　(b) Red
(c) Violet　　　　　　(d) Blue

13. The splitting of white light into several colours on passing through a glass prism is due to
(a) refraction　　　　(b) reflection
(c) interference　　　(d) diffraction

14. 1. 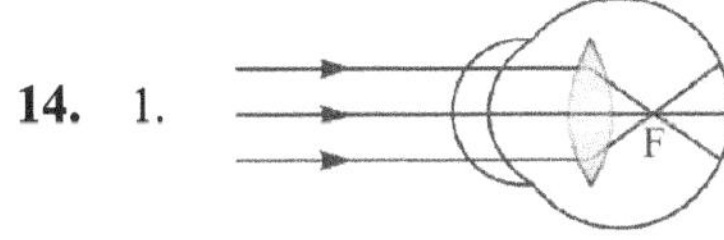

2. 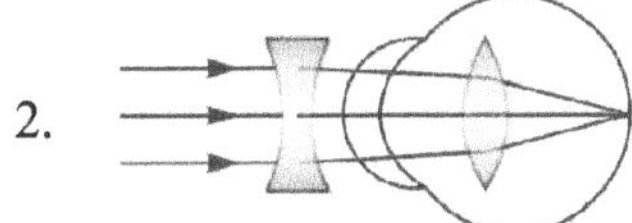

3. 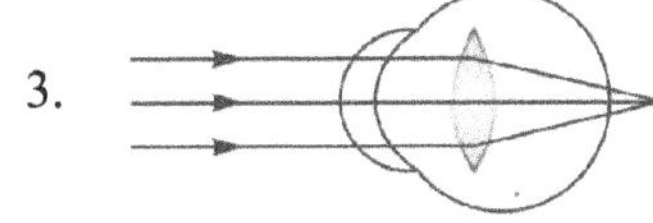

4. 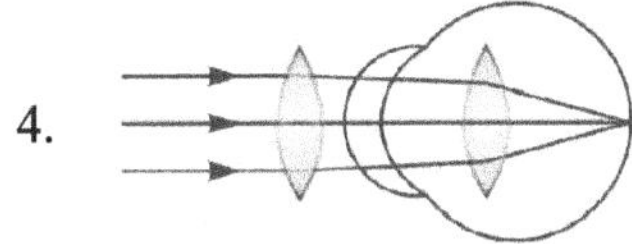

Identify the wrong description of the above figures
(a) 1 represents far-sightedness
(b) 2 correction for short sightedness
(c) 3 represents far sightedness
(d) 4 correction for far-sightedness

15. At sun rise or at sun set the sun appears to be reddish while at mid-day it looks white. This is because
(a) Scattering due to dust particles and air molecules causes this phenomenon
(b) The sun is cooler at sun rise or at sunset
(c) Refraction causes this phenomenon
(d) Diffraction sends red rays to the earth at these times.

16. A person 20 years old cannot see objects clearly which are nearer than 75 cms from his eyes, the disease he is suffering from is

(a) Astigmatism　　　　(b) Myopia
(c) Hypermetropia　　　(d) Presbyopia

17. On entering a glass prism, sun rays are
(a) Deviated but not dispersed
(b) Deviated and dispersed
(c) Dispersed but not deviated
(d) Neither deviated nor dispersed.

18. A piece of cloth looks red in sun light. It is held in the blue portion of a solar spectrum, it will appear
(a) red　　　　　　　(b) black
(c) blue　　　　　　　(d) white

19. To get line spectrum, the substances are excited in their
(a) solid state　　　　(b) molecular state
(c) gaseous state　　　(d) atomic state

20. A student can distinctly see the object upto a distance 15 cm. He wants to see the black board at a distance of 3 m. Focal length and power of lens used respectively will be
(a) $-4.8\ cm, -3.3\ D$　　(b) $-5.8\ cm, -4.3\ D$
(c) $-7.5\ cm, -6.3\ D$　　(d) $-15.8\ cm, -6.3\ D$

21. The pupil of the eye changes in size to adjust for
(a) objects at different distances
(b) objects of different sizes
(c) different colors
(d) different amounts of light

22. What power lens is needed to correct for nearsightedness where the uncorrected far point is 250 cm?
(a) +2.5 diopters　　　(b) –2.5 diopters
(c) + 0.4 diopters　　　(d) –0.4 diopters

23. What power lens is needed to correct for farsightedness where the uncorrected near point is 50 cm?
(a) + 2 diopters　　　(b) – 3 diopters
(c) + 4 diopters　　　(d) – 2 diopters

24. In a room, artificial rain is produced at one end and a strong source of white light is switched on at the other end. To observe the rainbow an observer must
(a) Look anywhere in the room
(b) Look towards the source
(c) Look towards the raindrops
(d) Look in a direction equally inclined to the source of raindrops

25. Astigmatism can be corrected by
(a) Bifocal lenses　　　(b) Cylindrical lenses
(c) Concave lenses　　　(d) Planoconvex lenses

26. The least distance of vision of a longsighted person is 60 cm. By using a spectacle lens, this distance is reduced to 12 cm. The power of the lens is
(a) + 5.0 D　　　　　(b) + (20/3) D
(c) – (10/3) D　　　　(d) + 2.0 D

27. A man can see upto 100 cm of the distant object. The power of the lens required to see far objects will be
    (a) $+0.5\,D$
    (b) $+1.0\,D$
    (c) $+1\,D$
    (d) $-5.0\,D$

28. Dispersion is the term used to describe
    (a) the propagation of light in straight lines
    (b) The splitting of a beam of light into component colours
    (c) The bending of a beam of light when it strikes a mirror
    (d) The change that takes place in white light after passage through red glass.

29. A given ray of light suffers minimum deviation in an equilateral prism P. Additional prisms Q and R of identical shape and material are now added to P as shown in the figure. The ray will suffer
    (a) greater deviatio
    (b) same deviation
    (c) no deviation
    (d) total internal reflection

30. In a glass prism
    (a) Blue light is dispersed more than red light
    (b) Red light is dispersed more than blue light
    (c) Both red light and blue light are equally dispersed
    (d) None of these

31. An optician while testing the eyes finds the vision of a patient to be 6/12. By this he means that
    (a) The person can read the letters of 6 inches from a distance of 12 m
    (b) The person can read the letters of 12 inches from 6 m
    (c) The person can read the letters of 6 m which the normal eye can read from 12 m
    (d) The focal length of eye lens had become half that of the normal eye

32. A person cannot see objects clearly beyond 50 cm. The power of the lens to correct the vision is
    (a) +5 D
    (b) –0.5 D
    (c) –2 D
    (d) +2 D

33. A long sighted person has a minimum distance of distinct vision of 50 cm. He wants to reduce it to 25 cm. He should use a
    (a) Concave lens of focal length 50 cm
    (b) Convex lens of focal length 25 cm
    (c) Convex lens of focal length 50 cm
    (d) Concave lens of focal length 25 cm

34. A long-sighted person cannot see objects clearly at a distance less than 40 cm. from his eye. The power of the lens needed to read an object at 25 cm. is
    (a) -2.5 D
    (b) $+2.5$ D
    (c) -6.25 D
    (d) $+1.5$ D

35. Twinkling of stars is on account of
    (a) Large distance of stars and storms in air
    (b) Small size of stars
    (c) Large size of stars
    (d) Large distance of stars and fluctuations in the density of air.

36. White light is incident at an angle to the surface of a triangular piece of glass. Which color of light deviates most from its original path after leaving the glass?
    (a) red
    (b) orange
    (c) green
    (d) blue

37. The middle vascular coat that darkens the eye chamber and prevents refraction by absorbing the light rays is
    (a) choroid
    (b) sclera
    (c) retina
    (d) cornea

38. When light rays enter the eye, most of the refraction occurs at the
    (a) crystalline lens
    (b) outer surface of the cornea
    (c) iris
    (d) pupil

39. When the light is bright,
    (a) the iris makes the pupil expand
    (b) the iris and the pupil contract
    (c) the iris and the pupil remain as they are
    (d) none of the above

40. The eyelens .... light rays to form real, inverted and highly diminished image on the ....
    (a) converges, retina
    (b) diverges, retina
    (c) converges, pupil
    (d) diverges, pupil

41. The surface of retina has about 125 million light sensitive
    (a) rods only
    (b) cones only
    (c) rods and cones
    (d) neither rods nor cones

42. The 'far point' of a normal human eye is
    (a) 25 cm
    (b) 25 m
    (c) 100 m
    (d) at infinity

43. The property related to the sense of continuity of vision is called
    (a) persistence of vision
    (b) colour blindness
    (c) optical illusion
    (d) none of these

44. When the ciliary muscles are relaxed, the eyelens is .... and distant objects can be seen clearly.

(a) thin (b) thick

(c) inclined (d) none of these

45. While looking at nearby objects, the ciliary muscles .... the eyelens so as to .... its focal length.

(a) contract, increase

(b) contract, decrease

(c) expand, increase

(d) expand, decrease

46. The change in focal length of an eyelens to focus the image of object at varying distances is done by the action of the

(a) pupil (b) ciliary muscles

(c) retina (d) blind spot

47. Which of the following statement is correct?

(a) A person with myopia can see distant objects clearly

(b) A person with hypermetropia can see nearby objects clearly

(c) A person with myopia can see nearby objects clearly

(d) A person with hypermetropia cannot see distant objects clearly

48. A person cannot see distinctly objects kept beyond 2 m. This defect can be corrected by using a lens of power

(a) $+0.5\,D$ (b) $-0.5\,D$

(c) $+0.2\,D$ (d) $-0.2\,D$

49. A beam of light consisting of red, green and blue colours is incident on a right-angled prism as shown. The refractive index of the material of the prism for the above red, green and blue wavelengths are 1.39, 1.44 and 1.47 respectively. The prism will

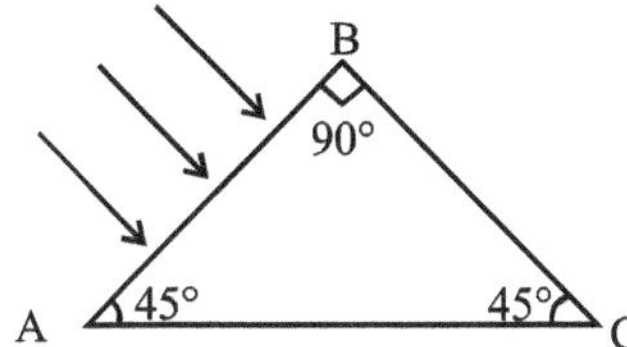

(a) separate part of the red colour from the green and blue colours.

(b) separate part of the blue colour from the red and green colours.

(c) separate all the three colours from one another.

(d) not separate even partially any colour from the other two colours.

50. The rod cells correspond to

(a) the colour of light

(b) the source of light

(c) the intensity of light

(d) none of these

51. Which of the following statements is correct regarding the propagation of light of different colours of white light in air?

(a) Red light moves fastest

(b) Blue light moves faster than green light

(c) All the colours of the white light move with the same speed

(d) Yellow light moves with the mean speed as that of the red and the violet light

52. When a ray passes through a prism,

(a) it goes undeviated

(b) it remains parallel to the base

(c) it bends towards the base

(d) none of the above

53. The clear sky appears blue because

(a) blue light gets absorbed in the atmosphere

(b) ultraviolet radiations are absorbed in the atmosphere

(c) violet and blue lights get scattered more than lights of all other colours by the atmosphere

(d) light of all other colours is scattered more than violet and blue colour lights by the atmosphere

54. At noon the sun appears white as

(a) light is least scattered

(b) all the colours of the white light are scattered away

(c) blue colour is scattered the most

(d) red colour is scattered the most

55. Which of the following phenomena contributes significantly to the reddish appearance of the sun at sunrise or sunset?

(a) Dispersion of light

(b) Scattering of light

(c) Total internal reflection of light

(d) Reflection of light from the earth

56. The bluish colour of water in deep sea is due to

(a) the presence of algae and other plants found in water

(b) reflection of sky in water

(c) scattering of light

(d) absorption of light by the sea

57. A student sitting on the last bench can read the letters written on the blackboard but is not able to read the letters written in his text book. Which of the following statements is correct?

(a) The near point of his eyes has receded away

(b) The near point of his eyes has come closer to him

(c) The far point of his eyes has come closer to him

(d) The far point of his eyes has receded away

58. The danger signals installed at the top of tall buildings are red in colour. These can be easily seen from a distance because among all other colours, the red light

(a) is scattered the most by smoke or fog

(b) is scattered the least by smoke or fog

(c) is absorbed the most by smoke or fog

(d) moves fastest in air

59. A person is suffering from both near sightedness and far sightedness. His spectacles would be made of

(a) two convex lenses with the upper lens having a larger focal length than the lower lens.

(b) two concave lenses with the upper lens having a smaller focal length than the lower lens.

(c) a concave lens as the upper lens and a convex lens as the lower lens

(d) a convex lens as the upper lens and a concave lens as the lower lens

60. The stars twinkle in the night, becauses :

(a) Their emit light intermittently

(b) Their star's atmosphere absorbs light intermittently

(c) The earth's atmosphere absorbs light intermittently

(d) The refractive index of air in atmosphere fluctuates

61. A Red object when seen through a thick blue glass appears:

(a) Green   (b) Violet

(c) Black   (d) Red

62. If a person can see on object clearly when it is placed at 25 cm away from him, he is suffering from :

(a) myopia

(b) hyper metropia

(c) asitgmatism

(d) none of these

63. A person is suffering from some sight problem. From the given diagram say which defect he suffers from?

(a) Myopia

(b) Hypermetropia

(c) Cataract

(d) Astigmatism

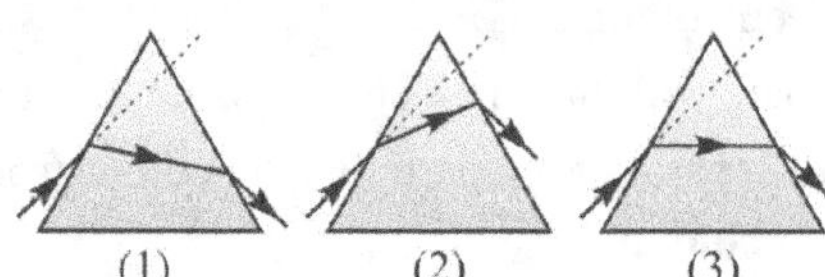

64. To read a poster on a wall, a person with defective vision needs to stand at a distance of 0.4m from the poster. A person with normal vision can read the poster from a distance of 2.0 m. Which one of the following lens may be used to correct the defective vision?

(a) A concave lens of 0.5 D

(b) A concave lens of 1.0 D

(c) A concave lens of 2.0 D

(d) A convex lens of 2.0 D

65. Select the correct statement about rainbow.

(a) We can see a rainbow in the western sky in the late afternoon

(b) The double rainbow has red on the inside and violet in the outside

(c) A rainbow has an arc shape, since the earth is round

(d) A rainbow on the moon is violet on the inside and red on the outside

66. Various optical processes are involved in the formation of a rainbow. Which of the following provides the correct order in time in which these processes occur ?

(a) Refraction, total internal reflection, refraction

(b) Total internal reflection, refraction total internal reflection

(c) Total internal reflection, refraction, refraction

(d) Refraction, total internal reflection, total internal reflection.

67. Pick the wrong answer in the context with rainbow.

(a) When the light rays undergo two internal reflections in a water drop, a secondary rainbow is formed.

(b) The order of colours is reversed in the secondary rainbow.

(c) An observer can see a rainbow when his front is towards the sun.

(d) Rainbow is a combined effect of dispersion, refraction and reflection of sunlight.

68. The reason for using red light in traffic signals to stop vehicles.

(a) Red light has shorter wavelength

(b) Red light has longer wavelength

(c) Red light is very bright and attractive

(d) Red light has highest angle of refraction

69. The figures represent three cases of a ray passing through a prism of angle A. The case corresponding to minimum deviation is

(a) 1   (b) 2

(c) 3   (d) None of these

70. If for a given prism the angle of incidence is changed from 0° to 90°, the angle of deviation

(a) Increases

(b) Decreases

(c) First decreases and then increases

(d) First increases and then decreases

Case/Passage Based Questions

DIRECTIONS : *Study the given case/passage and answer the following questions.*

Case/Passage - 1

Human eye is spherical in shape and has diameter of about 2.5 cm. Sclerotic is a tough, opaque and white substance forming the outermost coating of the eyeball. The front portion is sharply curved and covered by a transparent protective membrane called the 'cornea'. Inner to the sclerotic there is a layer of black tissue called as choroids consisting of a mass of blood vessels, which nourishes the eye. The black colour does not reflect the light and hence rules out the blurring of image by reflection within the eyeball.

Behind the cornea, the space is filled with a liquid called the aqueous humour and behind that a crystalline lens. 'Iris' is a muscular diaphragm lying between the aqueous humour and the crystalline lens. Iris has an adjustable opening in the middle called the pupil of the eye. The pupil appears black because all the light entering is absorbed by the 'retina', which covers the inside of the rear part of the ball. Iris controls the amount of light entering because the retina absorbs nearly all the light, which falls upon it. This is done by varying the aperture of the pupil with the help of the iris. In dim light the iris dilates the pupil so that more light can enter in. When the light is bright the pupil contracts.

The crystalline lens divides the eyeball into two chambers. The chamber between the cornea and the lens is called the anterior chamber filled with a fluid called aqueous humour while the chamber between the lens and the retina is called the posterior chamber which is filled with a transparent gelatinous substance called vitreous humour.

The refractive indices of the cornea, pupil lens and fluid portion of the eye are quite similar. So, when a ray of light enters the eye, it is refracted at the cornea. This refraction produces a real inverted and diminished image of distant objects on the retina.

When the object is kept at different distances then, we may expect the image to be formed at different distances from the lens. It means, it may not form on the retina always.

But in reality it is not so. Image is always formed on the retina. This is possible because the curvature of the crystalline lens is altered by ciliary muscles. When the eye is focused on infinity the muscles are relaxed and the eye lens remains thin. If the object is brought near by, the curvature increases so that the image can be formed on the retina. This property of the eye lens is called accommodation.

71. The change in focal length of an eye lens to focus the image of objects at varying distances is done by the action of ________

(a) pupil   (b) ciliary muscles

(c) retina   (d) blind spot

72. The fluid between the retina and the lens is called ________

(a) aqueous humour

(b) vitreous humour

(c) aqua

(d) humus

73. The part of the eye where optic nerves enter the eye

(a) pupil   (b) ciliary muscles

(c) retina   (d) blind spot

74. The inner back surface of the eyeball is called

(a) pupil   (b) ciliary muscles

(c) retina   (d) blind spot

Case/Passage - 2

The phenomenon of decomposition of the white light into its seven component colours when passing through a prism or through a transparent object delimited by non parallel surfaces is called dispersion of light. A beam of light containing all the visible spectrum of the light is white, because the sum of all the colors generates the white color. The light is decomposed in all the component colours, Violet, Indigo, Blue, Green, Yellow, Orange and Red, called as VIBGYOR. The band of the coloured components of a light beam is called its spectrum. The phenomenon can be explained by thinking that light of different colours (different wavelengths) has different velocities while travelling in a medium $v_m = f\lambda_m$.

Hence, the change in velocity of light observed when the light passes from the air to the glass, depends on the wavelength.

75. A prism *ABC* (with *BC* as base) is placed in different orientations. A narrow beam of white light is incident on the prism as shown in figure. In which of the following cases, after dispersion, the third colour from the top corresponds to the colour of the sky?

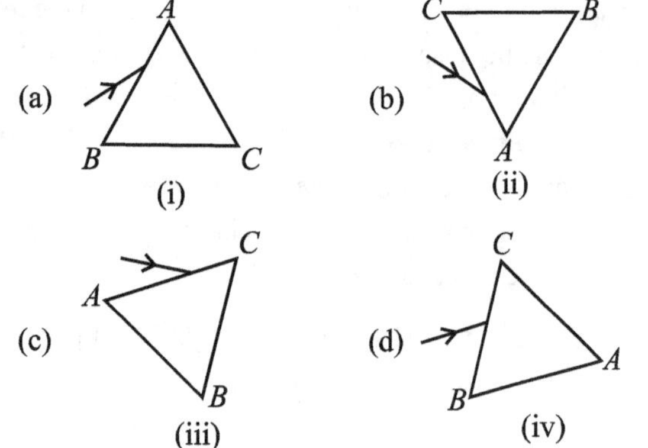

(a) (i)   (b) (ii)   (c) (iii)   (d) (iv)

76. Which of the following statements is correct regarding the propagation of light of different colours of white light in air?
    (a) Red light moves fastest
    (b) Blue light moves faster than green light
    (c) All the colours of the white light move with the same speed
    (d) Yellow light moves with the mean speed as that of the red and the violet light

77. When white light is allowed to pass through a glass prism, which colour deviates the least?
    (a) Violet   (b) Red
    (c) Green   (d) Orange

78. When white light is allowed to pass through a glass prism, which colour deviates the most?
    (a) Indigo   (b) Green
    (c) Red   (d) Violet

79. For a prism material, refractive index is highest for
    (a) Red
    (b) Yellow
    (c) Orange
    (d) Violet Passage Based Questions

Case/Passage - 3

The ciliary muscles of eye control the curvature of the lens in the eye and hence can alter the effective focal length of the system. When the muscles are fully relaxed, the focal length is maximum. When the muscles are strained the curvature of lens increases (that means radius of curvature decreases) and focal length decreases. For a clear vision the image must be on retina. The image distance is therefore fixed for clear vision and it equals the distance of retina from eye-lens. It is about 2.5 cm for a grown-up person.

A person can theoretically have clear vision of objects situated at any large distance from the eye. The smallest distance at which a person can clearly see is related to minimum possible focal length. The ciliary muscles are most strained in this position. For an average grown-up person minimum distance of object should be around 25 cm.

A person suffering for eye defects uses spectacles (Eye glass). The function of lens of spectacles is to form the image of the objects within the range in which person can see clearly. The image of the spectacle-lens becomes object for eye-lens and whose image is formed on retina.

The number of spectacle-lens used for the remedy of eye defect is decided by the power of the lens required and the number of spectacle-lens is equal to the numerical value of the power of lens with sign. For example power of lens required is +3D (converging lens of focal length 100/3 cm) then number of lens will be +3.

For all the calculations required you can use the lens formula and lens maker's formula. Assume that the eye lens is equiconvex lens. Neglect the distance between eye lens and the spectacle lens.

80. Minimum focal length of eye lens of a normal person is
    (a) 25 cm   (b) 2.5 cm
    (c) 25/9 cm   (d) 25/11 cm

81. Maximum focal length of eye lens of normal person is
    (a) 25 cm   (b) 2.5 cm
    (c) 25/9 cm   (d) 25/11 cm

82. A nearsighted man can clearly see object only upto a distance of 100 cm and not beyond this. The number of the spectacles lens necessary for the remedy of this defect will be
    (a) +1 D   (b) – 1 D
    (c) + 3 D   (d) – 3 D

Assertion & Reason

DIRECTIONS : *Each of these questions contains an assertion followed by reason. Read them carefully and answer the question on the basis of following options. You have to select the one that best describes the two statements.*

(a) If both **Assertion** and **Reason** are **correct** and Reason is the **correct explanation** of Assertion.

(b) If both **Assertion** and **Reason** are correct, but Reason is **not the correct explanation** of Assertion.

(c) If **Assertion** is **correct** but **Reason** is **incorrect**.

(d) If **Assertion** is **incorrect** but **Reason** is **correct**.

83. **Assertion :** When ray of light falls on the particles of a colloidal solution, the path of the beam is visible.

Reason : Path of light is visible due to the scattering of light by the colloidal particles.

84. **Assertion :** Sun looks white at noon.

Reason : At noon, the light has to travel longer distance through the atmosphere before reaching the eye of an observer.

85. **Assertion :** When a ray of light passes through a prism, it bends towards the thicker part of the prism.

Reason : An incident ray strikes a prism, undergoes refraction and comes out as an emergent ray.

86. **Assertion:** Myopia is due to the increased converging power of the eye lens.

Reason: Myopia can be corrected by using spectacles made from concave lenses.

87. **Assertion:** The twinkling of stars is due to the fact that refractive index of the earth's atmosphere fluctuates.

Reason: In cold countries, the phenomenon of looming (*i.e.*, ship appears in the sky) takes place, because refractive index of air decreases with height.

88. **Assertion:** When we see an object, the image formed on the retina is real and inverted.

Reason: If the magnification of a system is less than one, then the image formed is inverted.

89. **Assertion:** Rainbow is an example of the dispersion of sunlight by the water droplets.

Reason: Light of shorter wavelength is scattered much more than light of larger wavelength.

Match the Following

DIRECTIONS : *Each question contains statements given in two columns which have to be matched. Statements (A, B, C, D) in column I have to be matched with statements (p, q, r, s) in column II.*

90. Column II gives lens that can be use to correct the defect of vision given in column I, match them correctly.

Column I		Column II
(A) Myopia	(p)	Convex lens
(B) Hypermetropia	(q)	Concave lens
(C) Astigmatism	(r)	Cylindrical lens
(D) Presbyopia	(s)	Bi-focal lens Fill in the Blanks

Fill in the Blanks

DIRECTIONS : *Complete the following statements with an appropriate word / term to be filled in the blank space(s).*

91. The coloured diaphragm between the cornea and the lens is ....

92. The middle point of the iris has a hole, which is called ....

93. The screen on which the image is formed by the lens system of the human eye is called ....

94. For young adult with normal vision, least distance of distinct vision = ...

95. The closest distance at which the eye can focus clearly is called the ....

96. For a normal eye, the range of vision is from ....

97. A person is short-sighted if his eyeball is too ....

98. The eye which cannot simultaneously see with the same distinctness all objects or lines making different inclinations is said to suffer from ....

99. The defect of the eye due to which a person is unable to distinguish between certain colours, known as ....

100. The ability of the eye to focus both near and distant objects, by adjusting its focal length, is called the ....

101. The smallest distance, at which the eye can see objects clearly without strain, is called the .... of the eye.

102. The splitting of white light into its component colours is called ....

103. .... causes the blue colour of sky and the reddening of the Sun at sunrise and sunset.

104. Sunlight comprises .... colours.

True / False

DIRECTIONS : *Read the following statements and write your answer as true or false.*

105. Lens which is used for correcting the presbyopia defect of the eye is concave.

106. The colour that deviates maximum while passing through a glass prism is violet.

107. Water droplets act as tiny prism in the formation of rainbow.

108. The transparent spherical membrane covering the front of the eye is known as cornea.

109. The eye which can see near object clearly is said to suffer from hypermetropia.

110. The eye which cannot see distant objects clearly is said to suffer from myopia.

111. Colour blindness is a genetic disorder which occurs by inheritance.

112. In Myopia the image of distant objects is focused before the retina.

113. Hypermetropia is corrected by using a convex lens of suitable power.

114. A person suffering from myopia cannot see distant objects clearly.

115. The sun looks red at sunset because most of the blue light in sunrays is scattered leaving behind red and yellow lights.

116. Clouds look white because water droplets of clouds scatter all colours of light equally.

117. The sun is visible two minutes before the actual sunrise due to atmospheric refraction.

ANSWER KEY & SOLUTIONS

1. **(c)** The ability of the eye lens to change its shape to focus near and distant objects clearly is called power of accomodation.

2. **(c)** Curvature of eye lens is adjusted with the help of ciliary muscles.

3. **(a)** In poorly lit room or dim light the iris expands the pupil to allow more light to enter the eye.

4. **(b)** **5.** **(d)** **6.** **(a)**

7. **(d)** Near the horizon at sunrise and sunset, most of the blue light and shorter wavelengths are scattered away an hence sun appears red.

8. **(a)** Scattering of light is not enough at such heights.

9. **(d)** **10.** **(a)** **11.** **(d)** **12.** **(c)**

13. **(a)** Dispersion arises because of basic phenomenon refraction.

14. **(a)** **15.** **(a)** **16.** **(c)** **17.** **(b)**

18. **(b)** **19.** **(d)**

20. **(d)** $v = -15$ cm, $u = -300$ cm

As $\dfrac{1}{f} = \dfrac{1}{v} - \dfrac{1}{u}$

$\Rightarrow \dfrac{1}{f} = \dfrac{1}{(-15)} - \dfrac{1}{(-300)} = \dfrac{-19}{300}$

$f = -15.8$ cm $= -0.158$m

Power P $= \dfrac{-100 \times 19}{300} = -6.33$ D

21. **(d)** **22.** **(d)** **23.** **(a)** **24.** **(c)** **25.** **(b)**

26. **(b)** $v = -60$ cm, $u = -12$ cm

$\therefore \dfrac{1}{(-60)} - \dfrac{1}{(-12)} = \dfrac{1}{f}$

$\Rightarrow \dfrac{1}{f} = \dfrac{1}{15} \Rightarrow f = 15$ cm $= \dfrac{15}{100} m$

Power $= \dfrac{100}{15} = \dfrac{20}{3}$ D

27. **(c)** $\dfrac{1}{f} = \dfrac{1}{v} - \dfrac{1}{u}$

Here $u = (-\infty)$

$v = (-100)$

$\dfrac{1}{f} = \dfrac{1}{(-100)} - \dfrac{1}{(-\infty)} = -\dfrac{1}{100}$

$f = -100$ cm $= -1$ m

power $= -1$ D

28. **(b)** **29.** (a) **30.** (a) **31.** (c)

32. **(c)** **33.** (c) **34.** (d) **35.** (d)

36. **(d)** **37.** (a) **38.** (b) **39.** (b)

40. **(a)** **41.** (c) **42.** (d) **43.** (a)

44. **(a)** **45.** (b) **46.** (b) **47.** (c)

48. **(a)**

49. **(a)** Difference in refractive indices of blue and green colour are less so they are seen together and red is seen separate because deviation depends on refractive index.

50. **(c)** **51.** (c) **52.** (c) **53.** (c)

54. **(a)** **55.** (b) **56.** (c) **57.** (a)

58. **(b)**

59. **(c)** **Bifocal lens–** Convex lens (lower part) is used to read books and concave lens (upper part) for viewing distant object.

60. **(d)** As refractive index of air in atmosphere fluctuates, starts twinkle in the night.

61. **(c)** Red object that reflects only red and absorbs any other colour incident upon it.

62. **(a)** Myopia is the defect of eye where person is not able to see f ar off objects and see near by objects clearly.

63. **(a)** In mypoia defect, image formation will take place before the retina.

64. **(c)** $u = 2$ meter, $v = 0.4$ meter, $f = ?$

$\dfrac{1}{f} = \dfrac{1}{-0.4} - \dfrac{1}{(-2)} = \dfrac{-5+1}{2} = \dfrac{-4}{2}$

$\dfrac{1}{f} = \dfrac{-4}{2} = -2$; $P = \dfrac{1}{f} = 2$ D (concave lens)

65. (b) Rainbow is circular because locus of reflected rays reaching eye of observer is a circle not due to roundness of earth.

There is no rainbow on moon as there is no atmosphere.

In case of a primary rainbow, violet colour is on inside and red colour is on outside of arc.

In case of a secondary rainbow, red colour is on inside and violet colour is on outside of arc.

In late afternoon rainbow is visible in east side when light of sun in west side is reflected and refracted by a layer of water droplets.

66. (a) In primary rainbow, two refraction and one TIR

(1) Refraction of incident ray

(2) TIR

(3) Again refraction when rays come out of liquid drops

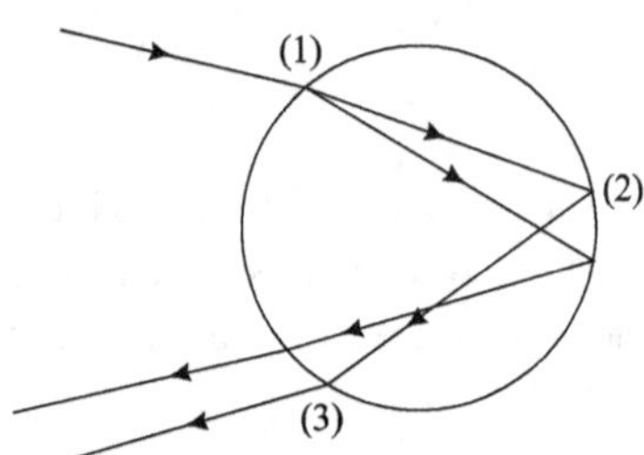

In secondary rainbow, two refraction and two TIR.

67. (c) Rainbow will be observed only when the sun is at the back side of observer.

68. (b) The primary reason why the colour red is used for traffic signals is that red light is scattered the least by air molecules. So, the red light is able to travel the longest distance.

69. (c) In case of minimum deviation, the light ray inside prism becomes parallel to base of the prism.

70. (c)   71. (b)   72. (b)   73. (d)

74. (c)

75. (b) Generally, in case of a prism (i), the formation of spectrum is shown below

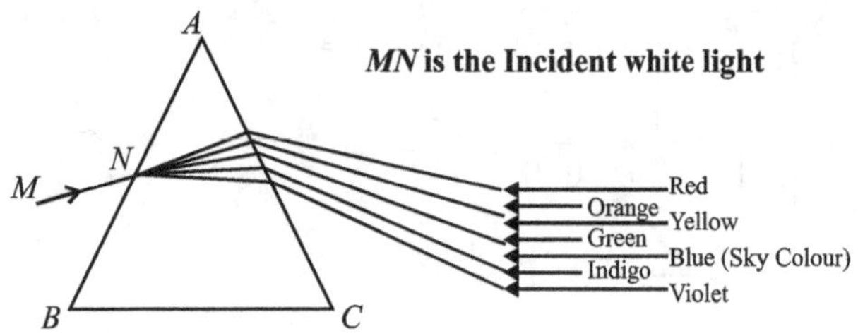

In the above figure, from top the third colour is yellow. But we can see that from bottom the third colour is blue (colour of sky). So, we can obtain the correct situation by inverting the prism. Thus the required orientations can be found in case (ii).

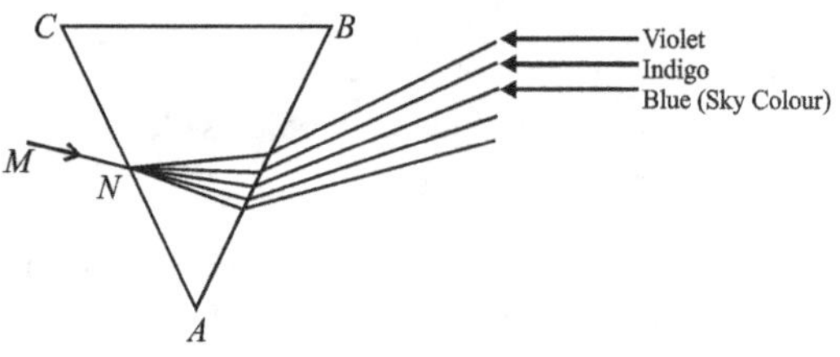

So, option (b) is correct.

76. (c) Speed of light is same for all colours of white light in air but different colours have different wavelengths and frequencies.

77. (b) Red

78. (d) Violet

79. (d) Violet

80. (d)   81. (b)

82. (b) $\dfrac{1}{f} = \dfrac{1}{v} - \dfrac{1}{u}$

Here v = 2.5 (Distance of retina as position of image is fixed)

$u = -x$

$\dfrac{1}{f} = \dfrac{1}{2.5} + \dfrac{1}{x}$

For f_{min} : x is minimum $\dfrac{1}{f_{min}} = \dfrac{1}{2.5} + \dfrac{1}{25}$

For f_{max} : x is maximum $\dfrac{1}{f_{max}} = \dfrac{1}{2.5} + \dfrac{1}{\infty}$

For near sighted man lens should make the image of the object within 100 cm range

For lens u = $-\infty$, v = -100

$\dfrac{1}{f_{lens}} = \dfrac{1}{-100} - \dfrac{1}{-\infty} \Rightarrow P = -1\,D$

83. (a) It is due to phenomenon called Tyndall effect.

84. (c) Sun look white at noon, as light has to travel shorter distance through the atmosphere before reaching the eye of an observer.

85. (b) When a light ray passes through denser medium from a rarer it undergoes refraction.

86. (b) In myopic eye due to the increased converging power of eye lens, the image of a far off object is formed in front of the retina.

87. (b)

88. (c) The image formed on retina is real and inverted. If magnification is less than 1, then diminished image is formed not inverted.

89. (b)

90. (A) → q; (B) → p; (C) → r; (D) → p

91. iris **92.** pupil **93.** retina

94. 25 cm. **95.** near point

96. 25 cm to infinity **97.** long

98. astigmatism. **99.** colour blindness

100. accommodation of the eye.

101. near point **102.** dispersion.

103. Scattering of light **104.** 7

105. False **106.** True **107.** True **108.** True

109. False **110.** True **111.** True **112.** True

113. True **114.** True **115.** True **116.** True

117. True

7 — Carbon and Its Compounds

DIRECTIONS : *This section contains multiple choice questions. Each question has four choices (a), (b), (c) and (d) out of which only one is correct.*

1. The correct name of the given compound is:

   (a) 2, 3-diethyl heptane   (b) 5-ethyl-6-methyl octane

   (c) 4-ethyl-3-methyl octane   (d) 3-methyl-4-ethyl octane

2. Which of the following options is false about a soap?

   (a) The soap solution in water is neutral and can be used to wash all kinds of fabrics.

   (b) Soap forms lather only in soft water.

   (c) Soap is a metallic salt of higher fatty acids.

   (d) Soap cannot be used in slightly acidic medium.

3. Structural formula of benzene is:

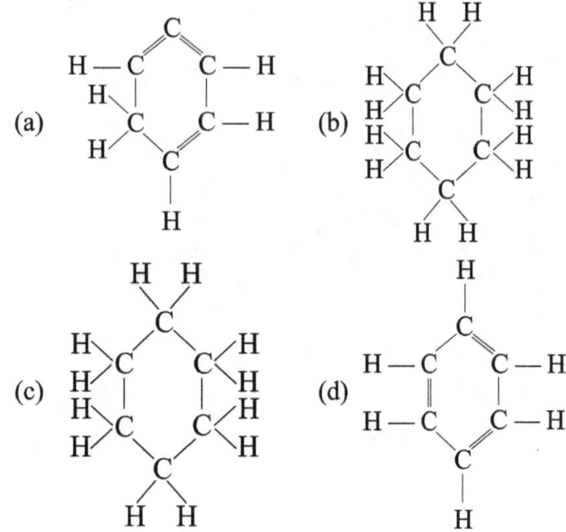

4. What does isomerism explain?

   (a) A difference in molecular formulae.

   (b) A difference in molecular weights.

   (c) A difference in chemical properties and structural formulae.

   (d) A difference in molecular composition.

5. Buckminister fullerene is an allotropic form of

   (a) phosphorus   (b) sulphur

   (c) carbon   (d) tin

6. The number of 4° carbon atoms in 2,2,4,4-tetramethyl pentane is –

   (a) 1   (b) 2

   (c) 3   (d) 4

7. Which is a general formula of alkenes?

   (a) C_nH_{2n+2} (b) C_nH_{2n}

   (c) C_nH_{2n-2} (d) None of these

8. The functional group represent alcohol is –

   (a) $-OH$ (b) $-CHO$

   (c) $-COOH$ (d) $>C=O$

9. Which of the following is the purest form of carbon?

   (a) charcoal   (b) coal

   (c) diamond   (d) graphite

10. Organic compounds will always contain –

    (a) carbon   (b) hydrogen

    (c) nitrogen   (d) sulphur

11. Methane, ethane and propane are said to form a homologous series because all are –

    (a) hydrocarbons

    (b) saturated compounds

    (c) aliphatic compounds

    (d) differ from each other by a CH_2 group

12. When methane is burnt in an excess of air, the products of combustion are –

(a) C and H_2O

(b) CO and H_2O

(c) CO_2 and H_2

(d) CO_2 and H_2O

13. Which of the following gases is called 'marsh gas'?

(a) H_2

(b) CH_4

(c) C_2H_4

(d) C_2H_2

14. The final product of chlorination of methane in the sun light is –

(a) CH_3Cl

(b) CH_2Cl_2

(c) $CHCl_3$

(d) CCl_4

15. The number of oxygen molecules used in the combustion of 1 molecule of ethanol is –

(a) 1

(b) 2

(c) 3

(d) 4

16. General formula of alkyne is –

(a) C_nH_{2n+2}

(b) C_nH_{2n}

(c) C_nH_{2n-2}

(d) C_nH_n

17. When vanaspati oil reacts with hydrogen then it is converted into vanaspati ghee. In this process catalyst used is :

(a) Fe

(b) Mo

(c) V

(d) Ni

18. Observe the following pairs of organic compounds :

(I) C_4H_9OH and $C_5H_{11}OH$

(II) $C_7H_{15}OH$ and $C_5H_{11}OH$

(III) $C_6H_{13}OH$ and C_3H_7OH

Which of these pair is a homologous series according to increasing order of carbon atom?

(a) (III) only

(b) (II) only

(c) (I) only

(d) All of these

19. Carbon exists in the atmosphere in the form of :

(a) carbon monoxide only.

(b) carbon monoxide in traces, and carbon dioxide.

(c) carbon dioxide only.

(d) coal

20. Oils on treating with hydrogen in the presence of palladium or nickel catalyst form fats. This is an example of :

(a) addition reaction

(b) substitution reaction

(c) displacement reaction

(d) oxidation reaction

21. Chlorine reacts with saturated hydrocarbons at room temperature in the

(a) absence of sunlight

(b) presence of sunlight

(c) presence of water

(d) presence of hydrochloric acid

22. Pentane has the molecular formula C_5H_{12}. It has

(a) 5 covalent bonds

(b) 12 covalent bonds

(c) 16 covalent bonds

(d) 17 covalent bonds

23. Carbon forms four covalent bonds by sharing its four valence electrons with four univalent atoms, *e.g.* hydrogen. After the formation of four bonds, carbon attains the electronic configuration of:

(a) helium

(b) neon

(c) argon

(d) krypton

24. Which of the following does not belong to the same homologous series?

(a) CH_4

(b) C_2H_6

(c) C_3H_8

(d) C_4H_8

25. The enzyme involved in the oxidation of ethanol to form vinegar is –

(a) zymase

(b) oxidase

(c) acetobacter

(d) invertase

26. Glacial acetic acid is –

(a) 100% acetic acid free of water

(b) solidified acetic acid

(c) gaseous acetic acid

(d) frozen acetic acid

27. When ethanoic acid is heated with $NaHCO_3$ the gas evolved is –

(a) H_2

(b) CO_2

(c) CH_4

(d) CO

28. During decarboxylation of ethanoic acid with sodalime (NaOH + CaO), CO_2 is removed as –

(a) CO_2

(b) CO

(c) Na_2CO_3

(d) $CaCO_3$

29. When ethanoic acid reacts with ethanol, a sweet smelling product is formed. The functional group in the product is

(a) aldehyde

(b) ketone

(c) alcohol

(d) ester

30. Detergents can lather well in –

(a) soft water

(b) hard water

(c) river water

(d) any one of the above

31. 'Drinking alcohol' is very harmful and it ruins the health. 'Drinking alcohol' stands for –

(a) drinking methyl alcohol

(b) drinking ethyl alcohol

(c) drinking propyl alcohol

(d) drinking isopropyl alcohol

32. The treatment of acetic acid with lithium aluminium hydride produces –

(a) methanol   (b) ethanol

(c) ethanal   (d) methanal

33. The fermentation reactions are carried out in temperature range of –

(a) 20-30°C   (b) 30-40°C

(c) 40-50°C   (d) 50-60°C

34. Soaps are sodium salts of fatty acids. Which of the following fatty acids does not form soap?

(a) butyric acid   (b) oleic acid

(c) palmitic acid   (d) stearic acid

35. The OH group of an alcohol or the —COOH group of a carboxylic acid can be replaced by —Cl using :–

(a) phosphorus pentachloride

(b) hypochlorous acid

(c) chlorine

(d) hydrochloric acid

36. Which compound represents the vinegar?

(a) HCOOH   (b) CH_3CHO

(c) HCHO   (d) CH_3COOH

37. A & B both compounds give H_2 gas with sodium. If A & B react in presence of acid catalyst then they form ethyl acetate. Thus, A & B would be -

(a) CH_3COOH, CH_3OH

(b) HCOOH, CH_3COOH

(c) CH_3COOH, C_2H_5OH

(d) C_3H_7COOH, C_3H_7OH

38. During the cleansing action of soap dirt is surrounded by soap molecules. Soap molecule is like a tadpole which has a head and tail. These head and tail respectively are:

(a) hydrophobic and hydrophilic

(b) hydrophobic and hydrophobic

(c) hydrophilic and hydrophilic

(d) hydrophilic and hydrophobic

39. The total number of electrons and the number of electrons involved in the formation of various bonds present in one molecule of propanal (C_2H_5CHO) are respectively.

(a) 32 and 20   (b) 24 and 20

(c) 24 and 18   (d) 32 and 18

40. The number of structural isomers of the compound having molecular formula C_4H_9Br is

(a) 3   (b) 5

(c) 4   (d) 2

41. A sweet smelling compound formed by reacting acetic acid with ethanol in the presence of hydrochloric acid is

(a) $CH_3COOC_2H_5$ (b) C_2H_5COOH

(c) $C_2H_5COOCH_3$ (d) CH_3OH

42. Percentage of nitrogen in urea (NH_2CONH_2) is

(a) 23.3%   (b) 46.7%

(c) 69.9%   (d) 11.66%

43. The molecular formula of carboxylic acid that differs from the rest is

(a) $C_{13}H_{26}O_2$ (b) $C_2H_4O_2$

(c) $C_9H_{18}O_2$ (d) $C_7H_{12}O_2$

44. During laboratory preparation CH_4 gas is collected by downward displacement of water because

(a) CH_4 is lighter than Air

(b) CH_4 is poisonous gas

(c) It does not dissolve in water

(d) All the above statements are correct

45. Which one of the following statement is incorrect about graphite and diamond ?

(a) Graphite is smooth and slippery.

(b) Diamond is good conductor of heat.

(c) Graphite is a good conductor of electricity.

(d) Physical and chemical properties of graphite and diamond are same.

46. A compound 'X' reacts with a compound 'Y', to produce a colourless and odourless gas. The gas turns lime water milky. When 'X' reacts with methanol in the presence of concentrated H_2SO_4, a sweet smelling substance is produced. The molecular formula of the compound 'X' is –

(a) C_2H_4O (b) $C_2H_4O_2$

(c) C_2H_6O (d) $C_2H_6O_2$

47. The functional groups present in the following compound are –

$$\begin{array}{c} O \\ \| \\ C-OH \\ \\ O-C-CH_3 \\ \| \\ O \end{array}$$

(a) alcohol, ketone and ester

(b) ester and carboxylic acid

(c) carboxylic acid and ketone

(d) ester and alcohol

48. A compound of carbon, hydrogen and nitrogen contains these elements in the ratio of their atomic mass 9 : 1 : 3.5, if its molecular mass is 108 u. What is its molecular formula?

(a) C_2H_2N

(b) C_3H_4N

(c) C_2HN_2

(d) $C_6H_8N_2$

49. How many grams of oxygen gas will be needed for complete combustion of 2 moles of 3rd member of alkyne series ?

(a) 186 g

(b) 256 g

(c) 352 g

(d) 372 g

50. A hydrocarbon 'A' (C_3H_8) on treatment with chlorine in presence of sunlight yielded compound 'B' as major product Reaction of 'B' with aqueous KOH gave 'C' which on treatment with concentrated H_2SO_4 yielded 'D'. Hydrogenation of 'D' gave back 'A'. The sequence of reactions involved in above conversion is:

(a) substitution, substitution, addition, dehydration

(b) substitution, substitution , dehydration, addition

(c) substitution, dehydration, addition, addition

(d) addition, substitution, dehydration, substitution.

51. An organic liquid 'A' with acidified potassium dichromate gave product 'B'. The compound 'B' on heating with methanol in presence of concentrated sulphuric acid formed compound 'C' which on subsequent treatment with sodium hydroxide formed two product 'D' and 'E'. The product 'D' is known to affect the optic nerve causing blindness. Intake of 'D' in very small quantities can cause death. What are compound 'A', 'B', 'C', 'D' and 'E'?

(a) A = Ethanol, B = Ethanoic acid, C = Methanol D = Sodium acetate, E = Methyl ethanoate

(b) A = Ethanol, B = Ethanoic acid, C = Methyl ethanoate D = Methanol, E = Sodium acetate

(c) A = Sodium acetate, B = Ethanoic acid, C = Methyl ethanoate, D = Methanol, E = Ethanol

(d) A = Ethanol, B = Ethanoic acid, C = Methyl ethanoate, D = Sodium acetate, E = Methanol

52. In shaving creams________ is added to prevent rapid drying.

(a) Methanol

(b) Glycerol

(c) Ethanol

(d) Glycol

53. An organic compound A on heating with concentrated H_2SO_4 gave product B and on warming with alkaline $KMnO_4$ gave compound C. Compound A on heating with compound C in presence of concentrated H_2SO_4 formed compound D, which has fruity smell. Identify the compounds A, B, C and D:

(a) A = Alcohol, B = Carboxylic acid, C = Alkene, D = Ester

(b) A = Carboxylic acid, B = Ester, C = Alkene, D = Alcohol

(c) A = Alcohol, B = Alkene, C = Carboxylic acid, D = Ester

(d) A = Alkene, B = Alcohol, C = Ester, D = Carboxylic acid

54. Two organic compounds 'A' and 'B' react with sodium metal and both produce the same gas 'X', but with sodium hydrogen carbonate, only compound B reacts to give a gas 'Y'. Identify 'A', 'B', 'X' and 'Y':

(a) A = Ethylene, B = Ethyl alcohol, X = Carbon dioxide, Y = Hydrogen

(b) A = Ethyl alcohol, B = Acetic acid, X = Hydrogen, Y = Carbon dioxide

(c) A = Methyl alcohol, B = Ethyl alcohol, X = Hydrogen, Y = Carbon dioxide

(d) A = Acetic acid, B = Formic acid, X = Carbon dioxide, Y = Hydrogen

55. Fermentation of sugarcane juice produces

(a) Ethanol

(b) Ethanal

(c) Acetic acid

(d) Gluconic acid

56. Antiknocking compound in gasoline is :

(a) Triethyl lead

(b) Trimethyl lead

(c) Tetramethyl lead

(d) Tetraethyl lead

57. Identify the correct order of boiling points of the following compounds-

(A) $CH_3CH_2CH_2CH_2OH$

(B) $CH_3CH_2CH_2CHO$

(C) $CH_3CH_2CH_2COOH$

(a) (A) > (B) > (C)

(b) (C) > (A) > (B)

(c) (A) > (C) > (B)

(d) (C) > (B) > (A)

58. Ethane with the molecular formula C_2H_6 has :

(a) 6 covalent bonds   (b) 7 covalent bonds

(c) 8 covalent bonds   (d) 9 covalent bonds

59. Butanone is four-carbon compound with the functional group :

(a) carboxylic acid   (b) aldehyde

(c) ketone   (d) alcohol

60. While cooking, if the bottom of the vessel is getting blackened on the outside, it means that :

(a) the food is not cooked completely.

(b) the fuel is not burning completely.

(c) the fuel is wet.

(d) the fuel is burning completely.

Case/Passage Based Questions   »»»

DIRECTIONS : *Study the given case/passage and answer the following questions.*

Case/Passage - 1

A carbon atom attached to one, two, three and four other carbon atoms is called primary, secondary, tertiary and quaternary carbon respectively. Now consider following compound and answer the following questions.

61. In above compound how many carbon atom are primary?

(a) 7   (b) 5

(c) 6   (d) 4

62. In above compound how many carbon atoms are secondary?

(a) 2   (b) 1

(c) 3   (d) 0

63. In above compound which carbon atom is quaternary?

(a) *B*   (b) *D*

(c) *F*   (d) *C*

Case/Passage - 2

Reactions in which an atom or a group of atoms is replaced by some other atom or another group of atoms without causing any change in the structure of the remaining part of the molecule, are called substitution reactions.

All organic compounds containing double or triple bonds give addition reactions, i.e., alkenes, alkynes and aromatic hydrocarbons give addition reactions.

Reactions in which the compounds react with oxygen and form carbon dioxide and water is known as combustion reaction. This process occurs with release of great amount of heat.

64. The reaction

$$CH_4 + Cl_2 \longrightarrow CH_3Cl + HCl \text{ is :}$$

(a) substitution reaction

(b) addition reaction

(c) rearrangement reaction

(d) elimination reaction

65. The reaction $CH_2 = CH_2 + H_2 \longrightarrow CH_3 - CH_3$ is :

(a) substitution reaction

(b) addition reaction

(c) rearrangement reaction

(d) elimination reaction

66. The reaction $C_2H_6 + O_2 \longrightarrow 2CO_2 + 3H_2O$ is :

(a) substitution reaction

(b) rearrangement reaction

(c) addition reaction

(d) combustion reaction

Case/Passage - 3

The given diagram represent an experiment in which a test tube contains 1 mL of ethanol (absolute alcohol) and 1 mL glacial acetic acid along with a few drops of concentrated H_2SO_4. Observe the diagram and answer the following questions.

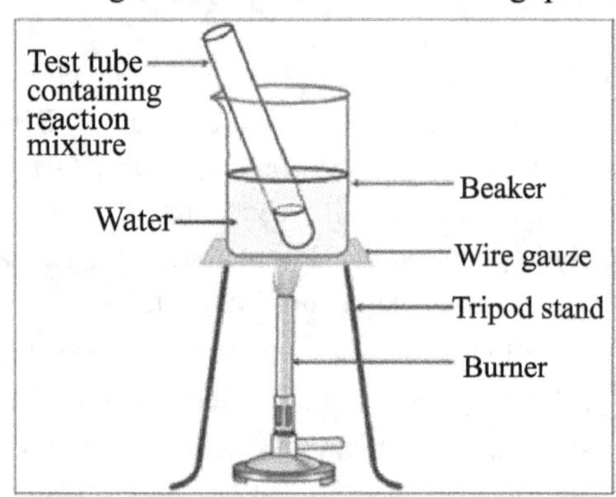

67. Name the type of reaction taking place in this experiment.

68. Write the chemical equation.

69. Why reverse of this reaction is known as saponification reaction?

70. Give two uses of the resulting product.

Case/Passage - 4

Food, clothes, medicines, books, or many of the things are all based on this versatile element carbon. In addition, all living structures are carbon based. The earth's crust has only 0.02% carbon in the form of minerals. The element carbon occurs in different forms in nature with widely varying physical properties. Both diamond and graphite are formed by carbon atoms, the difference lies in the manner in which the carbon atoms are bonded to one another. Carbon has the unique ability to form bonds with other atoms of carbon, giving rise to large molecules. This property is called catenation.

71 From the given alternatives, whose chemical and physical properties are *not* same?

(a) Graphite and Diamond

(b) Phosphorous and Sulphur

(c) Carbon and Hydrogen

(d) Methyl alcohol and Acetic acid

72. Which of the following statements is not correct?

(a) Graphite is much less dense than diamond

(b) Graphite is black and soft

(c) Graphite has low melting point

(d) Graphite feels smooth and slippery

73. Which of the following are isomers?

(a) Butane and isobutene

(b) Ethane and ethene

(c) Propane and propyne

(d) Butane and isobutane

74. Which one of the following is not an allotrope of carbon?

(a) Soot   (b) Graphite

(c) Diamond   (d) Carborundum

75. Pentane has the molecular formula C_5H_{12}. It has

(a) 5 covalent bonds   (b) 12 covalent bonds

(c) 16 covalent bonds   (d) 17 covalent bonds

❯Assertion & Reason

DIRECTIONS : *Each of these questions contains an assertion followed by reason. Read them carefully and answer the question on the basis of following options. You have to select the one that best describes the two statements.*

(a) If both **Assertion** and **Reason** are **correct** and Reason is the **correct explanation** of Assertion.

(b) If both **Assertion** and **Reason** are correct, but Reason is **not the correct explanation** of Assertion.

(c) If **Assertion** is **correct** but **Reason** is **incorrect**.

(d) If **Assertion** is **incorrect** but **Reason** is **correct**.

76. **Assertion:** Ethanoic acid is called as glacial acetic acid.

Reason: On cooling it freezes to form ice-like flakes. They appear like a glaciers.

77. **Assertion :** The correct IUPAC name for the compound

is 2, 4 dimethyl hexane not 3, 5 dimethyl hexane

Reason: When the parent chain has two or more substitutents, numbering must be done in such a way that the sum of the locants on the parent chain is the lowest possible.

78. **Assertion:** Vegetable oil is converted into vegetable ghee by hydrogenation process in presence of nickel catalyst.

Reason: Unsaturated hydrocarbons add hydrogen to give saturated hydrocarbon in presence of a catalyst.

79. **Assertion:** Unsaturated hydrocarbon burns with sooty flame in excess supply of air.

Reason: Saturated hydrocarbon has more carbon content.

80. **Assertion : Following are the members of a homologous series :**

CH3OH, CH3 CH2OH, CH3CH2CH2OH

Reason : A series of compounds with same functional group but differing by – CH2 – unit is called a homologous series.

81. **Assertion :** Diamond and graphite are allotropes of carbon.

Reason : Some elements can have several different structural forms in the same physical state. These differing forms are called allotropes.

82. **Assertion :** Carbon monoxide is extremely poisonous in nature.

Reason : Carbon monoxide is formed by complete combustion of carbon.

83. **Assertion :** Carbon has ability to form long carbon chains.

Reason : Carbon has a unique property to form long straight and branched chains called catenation.

84. **Assertion :** All alcohols have similar chemical properties.

Reason : All alcohols contains similar hydroxy (–OH) functional group.

85. **Assertion :** Hydrogenation converts an oil into a fat, called vegetable ghee.

Reason : Hydrogenation is carried out in presence of a catalyst, usually finely divided nickel.

Match the Following

DIRECTIONS : *Each question contains option given in two columns. options (A, B, C, D) in column I have to be matched with options (p, q, r, s) in column II.*

86.

Column I	Column II
(A) Combustion reaction	(p) $C_3H_8 + Cl_2 \xrightarrow{UV\ light} C_3H_7Cl + HCl$
(B) Oxidation reaction	(q) $CH_2= CH_2 + H_2 \xrightarrow{Ni/Pd} CH_3- CH_3$
(C) Addition reaction	(r) $2CH_4 + O_2(g) \xrightarrow[\text{Molybdenum oxide}]{300\ °C} HCHO + 2H_2O$
(D) Substitution reaction	(s) $C_2H_5OH + 3O_2 \longrightarrow 2CO_2 + 3H_2O$

87.

Column I	Column II
(A) — CHO	(p) Azo compounds
(B) — $CONH_2$	(q) Aldehydes
(C) — NH_2	(r) Acid amides
(D) — N = N —	(s) Amines

88.

Column I	Column II
(A) $CH_2 = CH_2$	(p) Saturated
(B) 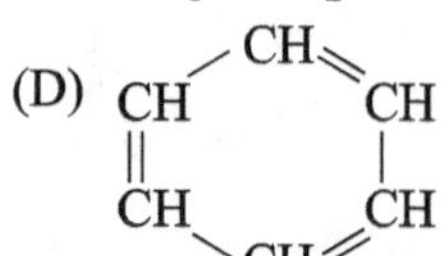	(q) Unsaturated
(C) $CH_3 - CH_2 - CH_3$	(r) Acyclic
(D) (benzene ring structure)	(s) Cyclic

Fill in the Blanks

DIRECTIONS : *Complete the following statements with an appropriate word / term to be filled in the blank space(s).*

89. The ability of carbon to form chains gives rise to a .... series of compounds.

90. Newly discovered allotrope of carbon is ....

91. The soft crystalline form of carbon is ....

92. Next homologue of ethane is ....

93. Valency of carbon in ethylene is ....

94. Ethylene burns in air to form CO_2 and ....

95. The molecular mass of any two adjacent homologues differ by .... amu.

96. The purest form of carbon is ....

97. The general formula of alcohols is ....

98. The functional group present in carboxylic acids is ....

99. Detergents cause .... pollution.

True / False

DIRECTIONS : *Read the following statements and write your answer as true or false.*

100. Carbon is a versatile element.

101. Carbon forms covalent bonds with itself and other elements such as hydrogen, oxygen, sulphur, nitrogen and chlorine.

102. Carbon and its compounds are some of our major sources of fuels.

103. Graphite is a good conductor of electricity.

104. The simplest saturated hydrocarbon is methane.

105. Ethanol is the first member of the alcohol homologous series.

106. Diamond is a good conductor of electricity.

107. Graphite is used in pencils.

108. When hydrocarbons burn in air, carbon dioxide and hydrogen are produced with heat energy.

109. If a hydrocarbon has double or triple covalent bond, it is saturated.

110. Unsaturated hydrocarbons give addition reactions.

111. By hydrogenation, vegetable oils are converted into vanaspati ghee.

112. Invertase and amylase are two enzymes involved in fermentation of ethanol from sugar.

ANSWER KEY & SOLUTIONS

1. **(c)** The name of the compound is 4-ethyl-3-methyl octane.

2. **(a)** The soap solution in water is not neutral and cannot be used to wash all kinds of fabrics.

3. **(c)** Benzene molecule contains alternate single and double bonds. Its formula is C_6H_6.

4. **(c)** Isomers have same molecular formula, molecular weight and molecular composition but different chemical properties and structural formulae because the properties are based on the position of atoms.

5. **(c)**

6. **(b)**

$$CH_3 \overset{\overset{\displaystyle CH_3}{|}}{\underset{\underset{\displaystyle CH_3}{|}}{\overset{4°}{C}}} - CH_2 - \overset{\overset{\displaystyle CH_3}{|}}{\underset{\underset{\displaystyle CH_3}{|}}{\overset{4°}{C}}} - CH_3$$

7. **(b)**

8. **(a)** $-OH \Rightarrow$ alcohol

   $-CHO \Rightarrow$ aldehyde

   $-COOH \Rightarrow$ Carboxylic acid

   $>C=O \Rightarrow$ Ketone

9. **(c)** Diamond is the purest form of carbon.

10. **(a)**

11. **(d)** Methane (CH_4), ethane (C_2H_6) and propane $(CH_3CH_2CH_3)$ differ from each other by CH_2 group. Hence these are said to form a homologous series.

12. **(d)**   13. **(b)**   14. **(d)**

15. **(c)** $C_2H_5OH + 3O_2 \longrightarrow 2CO_2 + 3H_2O$

16. **(c)**

17. **(d)** Catalysts like Pd, Pt or Ni are used in hydrogenation process.

18. **(c)** C_4H_9OH and $C_5H_{11}OH$ represent homologous series in increasing order of C atoms, other two also represent homologous series, but in decreasing order because they differ from each other by a CH_2 group.

    $CH_3CH_2CH_2CH_2OH$, $CH_3CH_2CH_2CH_2CH_2OH$

19. **(b)**   20. **(a)**   21. **(b)**

22. **(c)**

$$H-\overset{\overset{\displaystyle H}{|}}{\underset{\underset{\displaystyle H}{|}}{C}}-\overset{\overset{\displaystyle H}{|}}{\underset{\underset{\displaystyle H}{|}}{C}}-\overset{\overset{\displaystyle H}{|}}{\underset{\underset{\displaystyle H}{|}}{C}}-\overset{\overset{\displaystyle H}{|}}{\underset{\underset{\displaystyle H}{|}}{C}}-\overset{\overset{\displaystyle H}{|}}{\underset{\underset{\displaystyle H}{|}}{C}}-H$$

Pentane has 16 covalent bonds

(12 C – H and 4 C – C bonds)

23. **(b)**   24. **(d)**   25. **(c)**   26. **(a)**

27. **(b)** $\underset{\text{Ethanoic acid}}{CH_3COOH} + NaHCO_3 \longrightarrow$

$$CH_3COONa + H_2O + CO_2$$

28. **(c)**

29. **(d)** $CH_3COOH + CH_3CH_2OH \xrightarrow{\text{acid}} \underset{\text{ester}}{CH_3\overset{\overset{\displaystyle O}{||}}{C}OCH_2CH_3}$

30. **(d)**   31. **(b)**

32. **(b)** $\underset{\text{Acetic acid}}{CH_3COOH} \xrightarrow{\text{LiAlH}_4} \underset{\text{Ethanol}}{CH_3CH_2OH}$

33. **(a)**   34. **(a)**   35. **(a)**   36. **(d)**

37. **(c)**   38. **(d)**

39. **(a)**

$$H-\overset{\overset{\displaystyle H}{|}}{\underset{\underset{\displaystyle H}{|}}{C}}-\overset{\overset{\displaystyle H}{|}}{\underset{\underset{\displaystyle H}{|}}{C}}-\overset{\overset{\displaystyle H}{|}}{C}=O$$

Propanal

Total no. of electrons of C atoms = $3 \times 6 = 18$

Total no. of electrons of O atoms = $1 \times 8 = 8$

Total no. of electorns of H atoms = $6 \times 1 = 6$

Total no. of electrons in one molecule

$= 18 + 8 + 6 = 32$ electrons

Total no. of bonds = 10

Each bond contains $2e^-$. Therefore no. of electrons involved in bonding.

$= 2 \times 10 = 20$ electrons.

40. **(c)** (a) $CH_3CH_2\,CH_2CH_2 - Br$

   1 – Bromobutane

(b) $CH_3 - \underset{\underset{Br}{|}}{CH} - CH_2 - CH_3$

2-Bromobutane

(c) $CH_3 - \underset{\underset{CH_3}{|}}{CH} - CH_2Br$

1-Bromo-2-methyl propane

(d) $CH_3 - \underset{\underset{Br}{|}}{\overset{\overset{CH_3}{|}}{C}} - CH_3$

2-Bromo-2-methyl propane

41. (a) Acetic acid reacts with ethanol in the presence of hydrochloric acid to produce ethyl acetate (ester) which is a sweet smelling compound.

$$\underset{\text{Acetic acid}}{CH_3COOH} + \underset{\text{Ethanol}}{C_2H_5OH} \longrightarrow \underset{\text{Ethyl acetate}}{CH_3COOC_2H_5} + H_2O$$

42. (b) $NH_2CONH_2 \longrightarrow$ Molecular mass = 60

% of N = $(28/60) \times 100 = 46.7\%$

43. (d) $C_{13}H_{26}O_2$, $C_2H_4O_2$, $C_9H_{18}O_2 \longrightarrow$ These acids contains single bond between carbon atoms (C–C). Its general formula is $(C_nH_{2n}O_2)$.

$C_7H_{12}O_2 \longrightarrow$ It contains double bond (C = C). Its general formula is $(C_nH_{2n-2}O_2)$.

44. (c) CH_4 is non-polar compound, so it cannot be dissolved in water.

45. (d) Graphite and diamond show different physical and chemical properties. Diamond is colourless transparent substance. It does not conduct electricity. Graphite is greyish black. It is good conductor of electricity.

46. (b) $X + Y \longrightarrow$ gas (Colourless, odourless)

$$\underset{\text{(Acetic acid)}}{CH_3COOH} + NaHCO_3 \rightarrow CH_3COONa + CO_2\uparrow + H_2O$$

$$CO_2 + \underset{\text{(lime water)}}{Ca(OH)_2} \rightarrow \underset{\text{(Milky water)}}{CaCO_3} + H_2O$$

$$\underset{(X)}{CH_3COOH} + CH_3OH \xrightarrow{H_2SO_4} CH_3COOCH_3 + H_2O$$

Here compound (X) is acetic acid.

47. (b)

48. (d) $C_6H_8N_2$ i.e. $12 \times 6 + 8 \times 1 + 14 \times 2 = 108$ u.

49. (c) $2C_4H_6 + 11O_2 \longrightarrow 8CO_2 + 6H_2O$

For 2 moles of hydrocarbon, 11 moles of O_2 is required

$\therefore$ 11 moles = $11 \times 32 = 352$ g

50. (b) $C_3H_8(A)$ is propane.

(i) $\underset{(A)}{CH_3CH_2CH_3} + Cl_2 \xrightarrow{\text{Sunlight}}$

$\quad \underset{(B)}{CH_3CH_2CH_2Cl} + HCl$ (Substitution)

(ii) $\underset{(B)}{CH_3CH_2CH_2Cl} + $ aq. KOH $\longrightarrow$

$\quad \underset{(C)}{CH_3CH_2CH_2OH} + KCl$ (Substitution)

(iii) $\underset{(C)}{CH_3CH_2CH_2OH} \xrightarrow{\text{conc. } H_2SO_4}$

$\quad \underset{(D)}{CH_3CH= CH_2} + H_2O$ (Dehydration)

(iv) $\underset{(D)}{CH_3CH = CH_2} + H_2 \xrightarrow{Ni/Pt/Pd}$

$\quad \underset{(A)}{CH_3CH_2CH_3}$ (Addition)

51. (b) $\underset{(A)}{CH_3CH_2OH} \xrightarrow[K_2Cr_2O_7]{\text{Acidified}} \underset{(B)}{CH_3COOH}$

$$\underset{(B)}{CH_3COOH} + \underset{(D)}{CH_3OH} \xrightarrow[H_2SO_4]{\text{conc.}} \underset{\substack{\text{Methyl ethanoate}\\(C)}}{CH_3COOCH_3} + H_2O$$

$$\xrightarrow{NaOH}$$

$$\underset{(E)}{CH_3COONa} + \underset{(D)}{CH_3OH}$$

52. (b) Glycerol is added to shaving cream to prevent rapid drying.

53. (c) When ethanol (A) *i.e.* organic compound reacts with conc. H_2SO_4, it forms ethene (B) along with water. When ethanol (A) reacts with alk. $KMnO_4$, it will get oxidised to ethanoic acid (C). Ethanol reacts with ethanoic acid to form an ester called ethyl ethanoate (D), which gives a fruity smell.

$$\underset{(A)}{CH_3CH_2OH} \xrightarrow[443 \text{ K}/\Delta]{\text{Concentrated } H_2SO_4} \underset{(B)}{CH_2 = CH_2} + H_2O$$

$$\xrightarrow[]{\substack{\text{Alkaline}\\KMnO_4} + \text{Heat}}$$

$$\underset{(C)}{CH_3COOH}$$

$$\underset{(A)}{CH_3CH_2OH} + \underset{(C)}{CH_3COOH} \xleftarrow[]{\substack{\text{Concentrated}\\H_2SO_4}} \underset{(D)}{CH_3COOC_2H_5} + H_2O$$

54. **(b)** When alcohol *i.e.* ethanol (A) and acid *i.e.* acetic acid (B) reacts with a sodium metal, then it liberates hydrogen gas (X).

$$2CH_3CH_2OH + 2Na \longrightarrow 2CH_3CH_2\,O\,Na + H_2\uparrow$$

$\qquad$ (A) $\qquad\qquad\qquad\qquad$ (X)

$$2CH_3COOH + 2Na \longrightarrow 2CH_3\,COONa + H_2\uparrow$$

$\qquad$ (B) $\qquad\qquad\qquad\qquad$ (X)

When an acid reacts with carbonates or bicarbonates, it librates CO_2 gas. So, when acitic acid(B) reacts with $NaHCO_3$, it librates CO_2(Y) gas.

$$CH_3COOH + NaHCO_3 \longrightarrow$$

$\qquad$ (B)

$$CH_3\,COO\,Na + H_2O + CO_2\uparrow$$

$\qquad\qquad\qquad\qquad\qquad$ (X)

55. **(a)** Fermentation of sugarcane produces ethanol.

56. **(d)** Antiknocking agent in gasoline is tetraethyl lead (TEL). It raises the octane value of gasoline.

57. **(b)** Carboxylic acid molecule has higher extent of H-bonding than alcohol, therefore order of b.p. is

$$CH_3CH_2CH_2COOH > CH_3CH_2CH_2CH_2OH$$
$$> CH_3CH_2CH_2CH\,O$$

58. **(b)**

$$H - \overset{\displaystyle H}{\underset{\displaystyle H}{C}} - \overset{\displaystyle H}{\underset{\displaystyle H}{C}} - H$$

i.e., it has seven covalent bonds.

(6 C – H bonds and one C – C bond)

59. **(c)** The structure of butanone is

$$CH_3 - CH_2 - \overset{\displaystyle O}{\overset{\|}{C}} - CH_3$$

it has $\diagup\!\!\!C = O$ (ketonic group) as its functional group.

60. **(b)** The fuel is not burning completely, hence produce carbon particles which get deposited on the bottom of vessel.

61. **(b)** $\qquad$ **62. (a)** $\qquad$ **63. (d)**

$$\overset{1^\circ}{CH_3}$$
$$\overset{1^\circ}{CH_3} - \overset{2^\circ}{CH_2} - \overset{2^\circ}{CH_2} - \overset{4^\circ}{\underset{|}{C}} - \overset{3^\circ}{CH} - \overset{1^\circ}{CH_3}$$
$$\underset{\underset{1^\circ}{CH_3}}{|} \quad \underset{\underset{1^\circ}{CH_3}}{|}$$

64. **(a)** $\qquad$ **65. (b)** $\qquad$ **66. (d)**

67. Esterification reaction

68. $CH_3COOH + CH_3–CH_2OH \xrightarrow{\text{Acid}}$

$\quad$ Ethanoic acid $\qquad$ Ethanol

$$CH_3 - \overset{\displaystyle }{\underset{\displaystyle \underset{O}{\|}}{C}} - O - CH_2 - CH_3$$

$\qquad\qquad\qquad$ Ester

69. Reverse reaction is known as saponification reaction because it is used in the prepration of soap.

70. Esters are used in making perfumes and as a flavouring agent.

71. **(d)** Due to presence of different functional groups methyl alcohol and acetic acid. Possess different physical and chemical properties.

72. **(c)**

73. **(d)** Butane and isobutane have same chemical formula but different arrangement of atoms and have different structure.

$$H - \overset{H}{\underset{H}{C}} - \overset{H}{\underset{H}{C}} - \overset{H}{\underset{H}{C}} - \overset{H}{\underset{H}{C}} - H \;,\quad H - \overset{H}{\underset{H}{C}} - \overset{H}{\underset{\underset{H - C - H}{|}}{C}} - \overset{H}{\underset{H}{C}} - H$$

$\qquad\qquad$ (Butane) $\qquad\qquad\qquad\qquad\qquad$ H $\;$ (Isobutane)

74. **(d)** Carborundum is SiC (silicon carbide).

75. **(c)**

$$H - \overset{H}{\underset{H}{C}} - \overset{H}{\underset{H}{C}} - \overset{H}{\underset{H}{C}} - \overset{H}{\underset{H}{C}} - \overset{H}{\underset{H}{C}} - H$$

$\qquad\qquad\qquad$ pentane

76. **(a)** Ethanoic acid is also known as glacial acetic acid.

77. **(a)** The correct IUPAC name for the compound is 2, 4-dimethyl hexane not 3, 5 dimethyl hexane.

78. **(a)**

$$\overset{R}{\underset{R}{\diagdown}} C = C \overset{\diagup R}{\underset{\diagdown R}{}} \xrightarrow[\text{H}_2]{\text{Ni Catalyst}} R - \overset{H}{\underset{R}{C}} - \overset{H}{\underset{R}{C}} - R$$

79. **(c)** Unsaturated hydrocarbon has more carbon content as compare to saturated hydrocarbon of comparable molecular mass.

80. **(a)** CH_3OH, CH_3CH_2OH, $CH_3CH_2CH_2OH$ belongs to same homologous series with – OH functional group and each member is differ by $–CH_2 –$ unit.

81. **(a)** $\qquad$ **82. (c)** $\qquad$ **83. (a)** $\qquad$ **84. (a)**

85. **(b)** Hydrogenation or hardening of oil converted various unsaturated fatty glycerides to saturated glycerides by the addition of hydrogen in the presence of a catalyst, usually finely divided nickel.

86. A – (s), B – (r), C – (q), D – (p)

87. A – (q), B – (r), C – (s), D – (p)

88. A – (q, r), B – (p, s), C – (p, r), D – (q, s)

89. homologous

90. fullerene

91. graphite

92. propane

93. 4

94. water

95. 14

96. diamond

97. $C_nH_{2n+1}OH$

98. –COOH

99. water

100. True	**101.** True	**102.** True
103. True	**104.** True	**105.** False
106. False	**107.** True	**108.** False
109. False	**110.** True	**111.** True
112. False		

Periodic Classification of Elements

DIRECTIONS : *This section contains multiple choice questions. Each question has four choices (a), (b), (c) and (d) out of which only one is correct.*

1. The three elements calcium, strontium and barium form a triad. What is the basis of this grouping?
   - (i) Elements are in the increasing order of their atomic weights.
   - (ii) The atomic weight of the middle element is equal to the average of the atomic weight of extreme elements.
   - (iii) Elements in a triad have similar chemical properties.
   - (a) Only (i) and (ii)
   - (b) Only (ii) and (iii)
   - (c) Only (i) and (iii)
   - (d) (i), (ii) and (iii)

2. Which one of the following elements will form an acidic oxide?
   - (a) An element with atomic number 7
   - (b) An element with atomic number 3
   - (c) An element with atomic number 12
   - (d) None of these

3. On the basis of following features identify correct option.
   - (i) These elements majorly forms acidic oxides.
   - (ii) These elements are majorly non-metals.
   - (a) *s*-block elements
   - (b) *p*-block elements
   - (c) *d*-block elements
   - (d) *f*-block elements

4. Hydrogen has three isotopes ^1H, ^2H and ^3H. On what basis these elements were placed in modern periodic table ?
   - (a) Atomic mass
   - (b) Atomic number
   - (c) Both (a) and (b)
   - (d) None of these

5. An element 'X' is forming an acidic oxide. Its position in modern periodic table will be
   - (a) Group 1 and Period 3
   - (b) Group 2 and Period 3
   - (c) Group 13 and Period 3
   - (d) Group 16 and Period 3

6. If Cl, Br and I, are Dobereiner's triad and the atomic masses of Cl and I are 35.5 and 127 respectively the atomic mass of Br is –
   - (a) 162.5
   - (b) 91.5
   - (c) 81.25
   - (d) 45.625

7. Newland could classify elements only upto –
   - (a) copper
   - (b) chlorine
   - (c) calcium
   - (d) chromium

8. Mendeleev classified elements in –
   - (a) increasing order of atomic groups
   - (b) eight periods and eight groups
   - (c) seven periods and nine groups
   - (d) eight periods and seven groups

9. Noble gases were included in Mendeleev's periodic table in the –
   - (a) 1st group
   - (b) 7th group
   - (c) 8th group
   - (d) none of these

10. The long form of periodic table consists of –
    - (a) seven periods and eight groups
    - (b) seven periods and eighteen groups
    - (c) eight periods and eighteen groups
    - (d) eighteen periods and eight groups

11. In the modern periodic table which of the following does not have appropriate position?
    - (a) Transition elements
    - (b) Inert gases
    - (c) Inner transition elements
    - (d) Halogens

12. An element M has atomic number 9 and atomic mass 17. Its ion will be represented by –
    - (a) M
    - (b) M^{2+}
    - (c) M^-
    - (d) M^{2-}

13. The correct order of first IE of C, N, O, F is –
    (a) $F > O > N > C$
    (b) $C > N > O > F$
    (c) $O > N > F > C$
    (d) $F > N > O > C$

14. Elements belonging to the same group have similar properties because –
    (a) they have similar electronic configuration of the outermost shell.
    (b) their atomic numbers go on increasing as we move down the group.
    (c) all of them are metallic elements.
    (d) none of the above

15. The atoms of elements belonging to the same group of periodic table have the same –
    (a) number of protons
    (b) number of electrons
    (c) number of neutrons
    (d) number of electrons in the outermost shell

16. Which of the following is the correct order of relative size?
    (a) $I^- > I^+ > I$
    (b) $I^- > I > I^+$
    (c) $I > I^+ > I^-$
    (d) $I^+ > I^- > I$

17. The element with the smallest size in the group 13 is –
    (a) beryllium
    (b) carbon
    (c) aluminium
    (d) boron

18. The element present in the 4th period is –
    (a) chlorine
    (b) iodine
    (c) fluorine
    (d) bromine

19. The most metallic element in the fifth period is –
    (a) silver
    (b) rubidium
    (c) gold
    (d) rhodium

20. If the two members of a Dobereiner triad are chlorine and iodine, the third member of this triad is –
    (a) fluorine
    (b) bromine
    (c) sodium
    (d) calcium

21. If the two members of a Dobereiner triad are phosphorus and antimony, the third member of this triad is –
    (a) arsenic
    (b) sulphur
    (c) iodine
    (d) calcium

22. According to Mendeleev periodic law, the properties of elements are periodic function of their –
    (a) atomic masses
    (b) atomic numbers
    (c) atomic volumes
    (d) densities

23. The elements with atomic numbers 2, 10, 18, 36, 54 and 86 are all –
    (a) halogens
    (b) noble gases
    (c) noble metals
    (d) light metals

24. How many periods are there in the long form of the periodic table?
    (a) 6
    (b) 7
    (c) 8
    (d) 9

25. The elements with atomic numbers 3, 11, 19, 37 and 55 belong to
    (a) alkali metals
    (b) alkaline earth metals
    (c) halogens
    (d) noble gases

26. The elements with atomic numbers 9, 17, 35, 53 and 85 belong to
    (a) alkali metals
    (b) alkaline earth metals
    (c) halogens
    (d) noble gases

27. Each transition series contains a total of –
    (a) 2 elements
    (b) 8 elements
    (c) 10 elements
    (d) 18 elements

28. The number of elements in each of the inner transition series are –
    (a) 2
    (b) 8
    (c) 10
    (d) 14

29. The number of elements in the third period of the periodic table are –
    (a) 2
    (b) 8
    (c) 18
    (d) 32

30. The total number of elements in VII A group of the periodic table are –
    (a) 3
    (b) 5
    (c) 7
    (d) 9

31. The total number of elements in the group IB are –
    (a) 3
    (b) 5
    (c) 7
    (d) 9

32. Which of the following elements has the least nonmetallic character?
    (a) fluorine
    (b) chlorine
    (c) bromine
    (d) iodine

33. About how many known elements are there till date?
    (a) 10
    (b) 50
    (c) 118
    (d) 200

34. Elements in the modern periodic table are arranged according to increasing –
    (a) atomic number
    (b) atomic weight
    (c) number of neutrons
    (d) chemical reactivity

35. Which of these things you will not find in the periodic table?

   (a)   element name and symbol

   (b)   atomic weight

   (c)   atomic orbital radius

   (d)   atomic number

36.   Which scientist came up with the concept of a periodic table that included all of the known elements?
   (a)   Joseph Priestly   (b)   Dmitri Mendeleev
   (c)   Antoine Lavoisier   (d)   Albert Einstein

37.   The alkali metals are in which group of the periodic table?
   (a)   Group 1   (b)   Group 2
   (c)   Group 3   (d)   Group 4

38.   As you go down the group, the alkali metals become –
   (a)   brighter   (b)   hotter
   (c)   more reactive   (d)   less reactive

39.   Where are the transition metals in the periodic table?
   (a)   In group 0   (b)   In group 1
   (c)   In group 2   (d)   In a central block

40.   The noble gases are unreactive because
   (a)   they react with sodium.
   (b)   they have a full outer shell of electrons.
   (c)   they have a half outer shell of neutrons.
   (d)   they are too thin.

41.   Which of the following element is not in the liquid state?
   (a)   Hg   (b)   Li
   (c)   Ga   (d)   Br

42.   Which of the following elements does not belongs to alkaline earth metal group?
   (a)   Rb   (b)   Sr
   (c)   Ba   (d)   Ra

43.   Arrange the following in increasing order of their atomic radius : Na, K, Mg, Rb –
   (a) $Mg < K < Na < Rb$ (b) $Mg < Na < K < Rb$
   (c) $Mg < Na < Rb < K$ (d) $Na < K < Rb < Mg$

44.   Which is metalloid?
   (a)   Pb   (b)   Sn
   (c)   Si   (d)   Zn

45.   Which shows variable valency?
   (a) s–block elements   (b) p–block elements
   (c) d–block elements   (d)   Radioactive elements

46.   Dobereiner triads is –
   (a)   Li, K, Rb   (b)   Mg, S, As
   (c)   Cl, Br, I   (d)   P, S, As

47.   Elements in which $4f$ orbitals are progressively filled are called as –
   (a)   transition elements   (b)   lanthanides
   (c)   actinides   (d)   inert gases

48.   Which of the following elements is a lanthanide (Rare–earth element)?
   (a)   cadmium   (b)   californium
   (c)   cerium   (d)   cesium

49.   If the valene shell electronic configuration for an element is ns^2np^5, this element will belong to the group of –
   (a)   alkali metals   (b)   inert metals
   (c)   noble gases   (d)   halogens

50.   If an atom has electronic configuration $1s^2\, 2s^2\, 2p^6\, 3s^2\, 3p^6\, 3d^3\, 4s^2$, it will be placed in –
   (a)   second group   (b)   third group
   (c)   fifth group   (d)   sixth group

51.   On moving from left to right across a period in the table the metallic character –
   (a)   increases
   (b)   decreases
   (c)   remains constant
   (d)   first increases and then decreases

52.   Which of the following is the atomic number of a metal?
   (a)   32   (b)   34
   (c)   36   (d)   38

53.   Which has the maximum atomic radius?
   (a)   Al   (b)   Si
   (c)   P   (d)   Mg

54.   Which one of the following ions has the highest value of ionic radius?
   (a) O^{2-} (b) B^{3+}
   (c) Li^+ (d) F^-

55.   Which one of the following is the smallest in size?
   (a) N^{3-} (b) O^{2-}
   (c) F^- (d) Na^+

56.   The size of the following species increases in the order –
   (a) $Mg^{2+} < Na^+ < F^- < Al$
   (b) $F^- < Al < Na^+ > Mg^{2+}$
   (c) $Al < Mg^{2+} < F^- < Na^+$
   (d) $Na^+ < Al < F^- < Mg^{2+}$

57.   The correct order of radii is –
   (a) $N < Be < B$
   (b) $F^- < O^{2-} < N^{3-}$
   (c) $Na < Li < K$
   (d) $Fe^{3+} < Fe^{2+} < Fe^{4+}$

58. Which of the following is correct regarding ionic radii?
(a) $Ti^{4+} < Mn^{7+}$
(b) $^{35}Cl^- < {}^{37}Cl^-$
(c) $K^+ > Cl^-$
(d) $P^{3+} > P^{5+}$

59. Consider following as a portion of the periodic table from Group No. 13 to 17. Which of the following statements is/are true about the elements shown in it?
I. V., W, Y and Z are less electropositive than X.
II. V, W, X and Y are more .electronegative than Z.
III. Atomic size of Y is greater than that of W.
IV. Atomic size of W is smaller than that of X.

			V	Z
				Y
W				
X				

(a) I, II and III
(b) II and III
(c) I and IV
(d) III and IV

60. Mendeleev's periodic law states that the properties of elements are a periodic function of their
(a) reactivity of elements
(b) atomic size
(c) atomic mass
(d) electronic configuration

61. Chemical symbol of metal tungusten is
(a) W
(b) Xe
(c) Y
(d) Zr

62. Which is incorrect order of size?
(a) $Na > Na^+$
(b) $Na^+ > Mg^{2+}$
(c) $Cl^- > Cl$
(d) $F^- > O^{2-}$

63. The anion O^{2-} is isoelectronic with
(a) F^+
(b) F^-
(c) N^{2-}
(d) N^{+3}

64. A part of the modern periodic table is presented below in which the alphabets represent the symbols of elements.

Group → Period ↓	1	12	14	15	16	17
2				M	Q	V
3	A	J			R	W
4	E		L			T
5	G					X

Consult the above part of the periodic table to predict which of the following is a covalent compound-
(a) RQ_2
(b) AT
(c) JQ
(d) JX_2

65. The maximum number of electrons that can be filled in the shell with the principal quantum number $n = 4$ is
(a) 64
(b) 26
(c) 18
(d) 32

66. The ionic radii of N^{3-}, O^{2-}, F^-, Na^+ follow the decreasing order
(a) $N^{3-} > O^{2-} > F^- > Na^+$
(b) $N^{3-} > Na^+ > O^{2-} > F^-$
(c) $Na^+ > O^{2-} > N^{3-} > F^-$
(d) $O^{2-} > F^- > Na^+ > N^{3-}$

67. Consider the elements A, B, C and D with atomic numbers 6, 7, 14 and 15, respectively. Which of the following statements are correct concerning these elements?
I. D will lose electron more easily than C.
II. C will gain electron more easily than B.
III. The element with highest electronegativity is D.
IV. The element with largest atomic size is C.
(a) I and II
(b) II and III
(c) II and IV
(d) III and IV

68. Which of the following statement can help a chemistry student to predict chemical properties of an element?
I. Position of element in the periodic table
II. Atomic number of the element
III. Number of shells in the atom
IV. Number of electron in the outer most shell
(a) I, II and III
(b) I, II and IV
(c) I, III and IV
(d) II, III and IV

69. The element which normally exist in the liquid state are
(a) Bromine and Iodine
(d) Mercury and chlorine
(c) Iodine and mercury
(d) Bromine and mercury

70. Which gas being filled in weather balloon?
(a) Helium
(b) Neon
(c) Hydrogen
(d) Nitrogen

71. Manya, Kartik, Gurnoor and Sheena had arranged the ions F^-, Na^+, O^{2-} and Mg^{2+} in decreasing orders of their ionic radii.

Manya $- O^{2-} > Mg^{2+} > F^- > Na^+$

Kartik $- Mg^{2+} > Na^+ > O^{2-} > F^-$

Gurnoor $- O^{2-} > F^- > Na^+ > Mg^{2+}$

Sheena $- F^- > Na^+ > O^{2-} > Mg^{2+}$

Who had provided the correct order of their decreasing ionic radii?
(a) Manya
(b) Kartik
(c) Gurnoor
(d) Sheena

72. Consider the elements A, B, C and D with atomic numbers 11, 12, 16 and 17, respectively. Which among the following statements regarding these elements are correct?

  I.   The element C will gain electron more easily than element D.

  II. The element B tends to lose electron more readily than C.

  III. The oxide of A will be least basic while that of D will be most basic.

  IV. The energy required to remove an electron from outermost shell from A will be minimum while that from D will be maximum.

  (a) I and III only
  (b) I and IV only
  (c) II and III only
  (d) II and IV only

73. Which of the following is the correct order of reactivity of metals?

  (a) $Mg > Al > Zn > Fe$

  (b) $Mg > Zn > Fe > Al$

  (c) $Al > Mg > Zn > Fe$

  (d) $Mg > Zn > Al > Fe$

74. The following is the correct decreasing order of the ionic radii-

  (a) $K^+ > Ca^{2+} > S^{2-} > Cl^-$

  (b) $K^+ > Ca^{2+} > Cl^- > S^{2-}$

  (c) $Ca^{2+} > K^+ >> Cl^- > S^{2-}$

  (d) $S^{2-} > Cl^- > K^+ > Ca^{2+}$

75. Electro-negativity of the following elements increase in the order:

  (a) C, N, Si, P
  (b) Si, P, C, N
  (c) P, Si, N, C
  (d) N, Si, C, P

76. Which of the following statements is not a correct statement about the trends when going from left to right across the periods of periodic table.

  (a) The elements become less metallic in nature.

  (b) The number of valence electrons increases.

  (c) The atoms lose their electrons more easily.

  (d) The oxides become more acidic.

77. Element X forms a chloride with the formula XCl_2, which is a solid with a high melting point? X would most likely be in the same group of the periodic table as :

  (a) Na
  (b) Mg
  (c) Al
  (d) Si

DIRECTIONS : *Study the given case/passage and answer the following questions.*

Case/Passage - 1

Metallic Character The ability of an atom to donate electrons and form positive ion (cation) is known as electropositivity or metallic character. Down the group, metallic character increases due to increase in atomic size and across the period, from left to right electropositivity decreases due to decrease in atomic size. Non-Metallic Character The ability of an atom to accept electrons to form a negative ion (anion) is called non-metallic character or electronegativity. The elements having high electro-negativity have a higher tendency to gain electrons and form anion. Down the group, electronegativity decreases due to increase in atomic size and across the period, from left to right electronegativity increases due to decrease in atomic size.

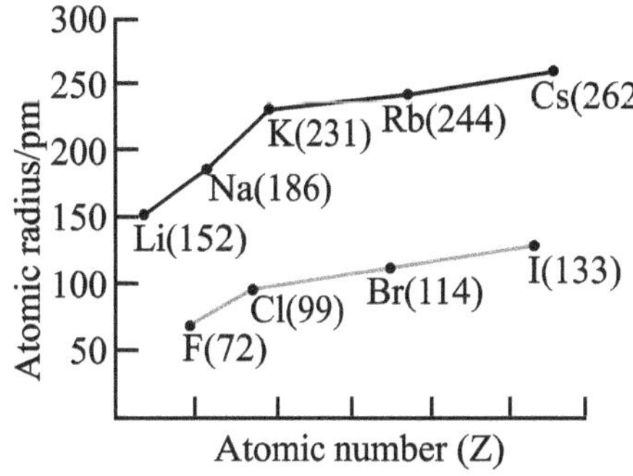

78. Which of the following correctly represents the decreasing order of metallic character of Alkali metals plotted in the graph?   **[CBSE Sample Issued 2021]**

  (a) $Cs > Rb > Li > Na > K$

  (b) $K > Rb > Li > Na > Cs$

  (c) $Cs > Rb > K > Na > Li$

  (d) $Cs > K > Rb > Na > Li$

79. Hydrogen is placed along with Alkali metals in the modern periodic table though it shows non-metallic character

  (a) as Hydrogen has one electron & readily loses electron to form negative ion

  (b) as Hydrogen can easily lose one electron like alkali metals to form positive ion

  (c) as Hydrogen can gain one electron easily like Halogens to form negative ion

  (d) as Hydrogen shows the properties of non-metals

80. Which of the following has highest electronegativity?

  (a) F
  (b) Cl
  (c) Br
  (d) I

81. Identify the reason for the gradual change in electronegativity in halogens down the group.

(a) Electronegativity increases down the group due to decrease in atomic size

(b) Electronegativity decreases down the group due to decrease in tendency to lose electrons

(c) Electronegativity decreases down the group due to increase in atomic radius/ tendency to gain electron decreases

(d) Electronegativity increases down the group due to increase in forces of attractions between nucleus & valence electrons

82. Which of the following reason correctly justifies that "Fluorine (72pm) has smaller atomic radius than Lithium (152pm)"?

(a) F and Li are in the same group. Atomic size increases down the group

(b) F and Li are in the same period. Atomic size increases across the period due to increase in number of shells

(c) F and Li are in the same group. Atomic size decreases down the group

(d) F and Li are in the same period and across the period atomic size/radius decreases from left to right.

Case/Passage - 2

The table given below refers to the elements of the periodic table with atomic number from 3 to 18. These elements are shown by letters. (not by the usual symbols of the elements).

3	4	5	6	7	8	9	10
A	B	C	D	E	F	G	H
11	12	13	14	15	16	17	18
I	J	K	L	M	N	O	P

83. Which of the following are noble gases?

(a) H and P (b) G and O

(c) D and L (d) A and I

84. Which are halogens?

(a) H and L (b) C and M

(c) G and O (d) E and P

85. Which of the following elements have valency 4?

(a) F and N (b) C and K

(c) D and L (d) H and P

Case/Passage - 3

Group VII A elements are strong non-metals because they can easily accept an electron to form an anion whereas group 1 A element are strong metals because they can very easily lose one electron to form cation.

Metals have the tendency to lose their valence electrons and form positive ions, so metallic character is related to the ionisation potential. Elements having low ionisation potential, lose electrons easily. Thus, metallic character generally decreases across a period and increases down a group.

86. The non metallic character on moving along a period –

(a) increases (b) decreases

(c) depends on the period (d) remains the same

87. Group 1 and group 2 elements are considered as strong metals because

(a) they have incomplete octet.

(b) they can easily gain electrons.

(c) they can easily lose electrons.

(d) they form anions.

88. Which of the following is the correct decreasing order of metallic character?

(a) Ca > Sc > Ti > K (b) K > Ca > Sc > Ti

(c) K > Sc > Ca > Ti (d) Ti > Sc > Ca > K

Case/Passage - 4

Question numbers 1 – 3 are based on the periodic table. Study the part of the modern periodic table presented below in which the alphabets represent the symbols of elements and answer the following questions.

Group → Period ↓	1	12	14	15	16	17
2				M	Q	V
3	A	J			R	W
4	E		L			T
5	G					X

89. Consult the above part of the periodic table to predict which of the given combination is a covalent compound: RQ_2, AT, JQ, JX_2.

90. Considering the above part of the periodic table, which of the given element is the most electropositive element?

91. Which of the given element is the most electronegative element?

92. Study the data of the following three categories A, B and C.

Category	Name of the element	Atomic Mass
A	Li	7
	Na	23
	K	39
B	N	14
	P	31
	As	74
C	B	10.8
	Al	27
	Ga	69.7

Periodic Classification of Elements

(i) From the given three categories A, B and C, Pick the one which forms Dobereiner's Triads.

(ii) Why did Mendeleev placed elements of category A, B and C in three different groups?

(iii) Is Newland law of octaves applicable to all the three categories?

Give reason to justify your answer.

Assertion & Reason

DIRECTIONS : *Each of these questions contains an assertion followed by reason. Read them carefully and answer the question on the basis of following options. You have to select the one that best describes the two statements.*

(a) If both **Assertion** and **Reason** are **correct** and Reason is the **correct explanation** of Assertion.

(b) If both **Assertion** and **Reason** are correct, but Reason is **not the correct explanation** of Assertion.

(c) If **Assertion** is **correct** but **Reason** is **incorrect**.

(d) If **Assertion** is **incorrect** but **Reason** is **correct**.

93. **Assertion:** Ionic size of N^{3-} is greater than F^-.

    Reason: N^{3-} and F^- are isoelectronic anions.

94. **Assertion:** Atomic radius of aluminium atom is larger than magnesium atom.

    Reason: Effective nuclear charge increase from magnesium to aluminium.

95. **Assertion:** Oxygen atom is divalent in most of its compounds.

    Reason: Valency is the number of valence electrons present in the outermost shell of its atom.

96. **Assertion:** Silicon, germanium are the metalloids in the modern periodic table.

    Reason: Silicon, germanium has properties of metal as well as non metals.

97. **Assertion:** Bulbs are usually filled with chemically active gases.

    Reason: Nitrogen and argon gases are filled in order to prolong the life of the filament.

98. **Assertion :** Group 1 elements are known as the alkali elements.

    Reason : *s*-orbital can accommodate only two electrons.

99. **Assertion :** Nitrogen has higher ionization energy than that of oxygen.

Reason : Nitrogen has smaller atomic size than that of oxygen.

100. **Assertion :** According to Mendeleev, periodic properties of elements are functions of their atomic number.

    Reason : Atomic number is equal to the number of protons.

101. **Assertion :** Elements in the same vertical column have similar properties.

    Reason : Elements have periodic dependence upon the atomic number.

Match the Following

DIRECTIONS : *Each question contains statements given in two columns which have to be matched. Statements (A, B, C, D) in column I have to be matched with statements (p, q, r, s) in column II.*

102. Column II give period to which an element in column I belongs, match them correctly.

Column I		Column II	
(A)	Hydrogen	(p)	3
(B)	Sodium	(q)	4
(C)	Calcium	(r)	6
(D)	Barium	(s)	1

103. Match the column –

Column I		Column II	
(A)	Element with largest size in second period	(p)	boron
(B)	Element with smallest size in group 13	(q)	fluorine
(C)	Element with maximum non-metallic character.	(r)	bromine
(D)	Element with smallest size in fourth period	(s)	lithium

104.

Column I		Column II	
(A)	*s*-block elements	(p)	Alkali metals
(B)	*p*-block elements	(q)	Alkaline earth metals
(C)	Representative elements	(r)	Halogens
(D)	High ionisation energy	(s)	Noble gases

Fill in the Blanks

DIRECTIONS : *Complete the following statements with an appropriate word / term to be filled in the blank space(s).*

105. The law of triads was given by ....

106. According to modern periodic law, the elements are arranged in the periodic table in the order of their increasing ....

107. Elements with eight electrons in their outermost energy shell are called ....

108. If two elements have the same number of valence electrons, then they belong to the same .... of the periodic table.

109. The elements in groups 1, 2 and 13 to 18 are known as .... elements.

110. The valency of an atom is equal to its ....

111. The atomic size in a period .... from left to right.

112. Dobereiner grouped the elements into triads and Newlands gave the ....

113. Mendeleev arranged the elements in increasing order of their .... and according to their .... properties.

114. Mendeleev predicted the existence of some yet to be discovered elements on the basis of .... in his periodic table.

115. Elements in the modern periodic table are arranged in ...... vertical columns called .... and .... horizontal rows called ....

True / False

DIRECTIONS : *Read the following statements and write your answer as true or false.*

116. As nuclear charge increases, atomic orbitals become smaller and more stable.

117. As number of shells increases, atomic orbitals become larger and less stable.

118. Atomic radii decrease from left to right across a row of the periodic table.

119. Atomic radii increase from top to bottom down a column of the periodic table.

120. Fluorine has highest electron affinity in the periodic table.

121. Noble gases are placed extremely left in the periodic table.

122. Magnesium is more metallic in nature than sodium.

123. The number of shells increases in a given period from left to right in the periodic table.

124. The elements silicon, germanium and arsenic are called metalloids.

125. Elements are classified on the basis of similarities in their properties.

126. Rows in the periodic table are called periods.

127. The columns of the periodic table are called groups.

128. You will find metals on the extreme right side of the periodic table.

129. Although the order of elements is based on atomic number, vertical families share similar chemical properties.

ANSWER KEY & SOLUTIONS

1. **(d)** Dobereiner noticed that strontium had similar chemical properties as that of calcium and barium and its atomic weight fell midway between the two. Hence, elements like calcium, strontium and barium form a triad based on the given characteristics.

2. **(a)** Non-metals form acidic oxides. Element with atomic number 7 (electronic configuration 2, 5) is non-metal (N) and hence will form an acidic oxide, other elements Li(3) and Mg(12) are metals and hence form basic oxides.

3. **(b)** *p*-block elements majorly forms acidic oxides and are non-metals.

4. **(b)** On the basis of atomic number, elements were placed in the modern periodic table.

5. **(d)** Elements of group 16 and period 3 are non metals. Non metals generally form acidic oxides. Elements of group 1 and 2 form basic oxides while elements of group 13 form amphoteric oxides.

6. **(c)** According to Dobereneir's triad the atomic mass of Br will be average of the atomic masses of Cl & I

   $$\text{Atomic mass of Br} = \frac{35.5 + 127}{2} = 81.25$$

7. **(c)** 　　8. **(c)** 　　9. **(d)** 　　10. **(b)**

11. **(c)**

12. **(c)** The element is halogen and has one electron less than inert gas configuration, hence its ion can be represented as M^- ion.

13. **(d)** In a period, the value of ionisation potential increases from left to right with breaks where the atoms have stable configurations hence the correct order will be

    $$F > N > O > C$$

14. **(a)** 　　15. **(d)** 　　16. **(b)** 　　17. **(d)**

18. **(d)** On moving along a period atomic radii decreases.

19. **(b)** The metallic character decreases as we move from left, to right in a period.

20. **(b)** 　　21. **(a)** 　　22. **(a)** 　　23. **(b)**

24. **(b)** 　　25. **(a)** 　　26. **(c)** 　　27. **(c)**

28. **(d)** 　　29. **(b)**

30. **(b)** The VII A group has 5 elements.

    F, Cl, Br, I and At

31. **(a)** Group I B contain Cu, Ag and Au.

32. **(d)** Non-metallic character decreases in a group from top to bottom, hence iodine will be least non-metallic.

33. **(c)** There are about 118 known elements listed in the periodic table.

34. **(a)** The elements of the modern periodic table are organized according to increasing atomic number. The atomic number represents the number of electrons which is equal to number of protons in a neutral atom.

35. **(c)** You will not get information about the atomic radius of an atom. Periodic table will have the atomic number, atomic weight, name, and symbol for each element.

36. **(b)** Dmitri Mendeleev is credited with designing the modern periodic table.

37. **(a)** 　　38. **(c)** 　　39. **(d)** 　　40. **(b)**

41. **(b)** 　　42. **(a)** 　　43. **(b)** 　　44. **(c)**

45. **(c)** 　　46. **(c)** 　　47. **(b)** 　　48. **(c)**

49. **(d)** 　　50. **(c)** 　　51. **(b)**

52. **(d)** 38 is the atomic no. of stronium (Sr) which is *s*-block element and all elements of *s*-block are metals.

53. **(d)** Mg, as we move across the period atomic radius decreases.

54. **(a)** O^{2-} has the highest value of ionic radii as this can be explained on the basis of Z/e $\left\{\dfrac{\text{Nuclear charge}}{\text{No. of electrons}}\right\}$

    When Z/e ratio increases, the size decreases and when Z/e ratio decreases, size increases.

55. **(d)** $Na^+ < F^- < O^{2-} < N^{3-}$

    All are isoelectronic, effective nuclear charge is highest for Na^+ so it has smallest size.

56. **(a)** $Mg^{2+} < Na^+ < F^- < Al$

    F^- has bigger size than Mg^{2+} and Na^+

57. **(b)** Ionic radii decreases significantly from left to right in a period among representative elements.

58. **(d)** Nuclear charge per electron is greater in P^{5+}. Therefore, its size is smaller.

59. **(c)** Electropositive nature increases from top to bottom in a group and decrease along a period. Therefore X is most electropositive.

Atomic size decreases along a period and increases down the group. Therefore W < X.

60. **(c)** Mendeleev's periodic law states that the physical and chemical properties of the elements are a periodic function of their atomic mass.

61. **(a)** Tungsten → W

62. **(d)** Size of F^- is less than O^{2-}

63. **(b)** Anion O^{2-} has 10 electrons.

Anion F^- has 10 electrons.

64. **(a)** R and Q are members of Group 16th which is non metallic having O, S, Se, Te etc. These are characterised by showing the formation of covalent bond.

65. **(d)** The maximum number of electrons that can be filled in the shell with principle quantum number$(n) = 2n^2$.

Maximum number of electrons $= 2(4)^2 = 32$

66. **(a)** Increase in positive charge decrease the ionic radii of cation while increase in negative charge increases the ionic size of anion. So $N^{3-} > O^{2-} > F^- > Na^+$.

67. **(c)**

68. **(b)** Position, atomic number and number of electrons in the outermost shell of an element predicts its chemical properties.

69. **(d)** Bromine and mercury exist in the liquid state.

70. **(a)** Helium is filled in weather balloon.

71. **(c)** The ions F^-, Na^+, O^{2-} and Mg^{2+} are isoelectronic species having same electronic configuration but their nuclear charges differ from each other because of their difference in the number of protons in the nucleus. With increase in the number of protons in the nucleus, the electrons are more attracted towards nucleus thereby causing the decrease in ionic radius. Therefore, the given ions are

F^- : no. of proton = 9 and no. of electron = 10

Na^+ : no. of proton = 11 and no. of electron = 10

O^{2-} : no. of proton = 8 and no. of electron = 10

Mg^{2+} : no. of proton = 12 and no. of electron = 10

72. **(d)**

Atomic Number	Element	Electronic configuration
A(11)	Na	2, 8, 1
B(12)	Mg	2, 8, 2
C(16)	S	2, 8, 6
D(17)	Cl	2, 8, 7

From the above table it is clear that:

(a) Chlorine (D) will gain electrons more easily than sulphur (C).

(b) The oxide of sodium (A) which is an alkali metal, will be the most basic while that of chlorine (D) which is a halogen, will be the most acidic.

73. **(a)** The correct order of reactivity is as follows.

$Mg > Al > Zn > Fe$

Alkali metals and alkaline earth metals are very reactive elements in the periodic table and reactivity decreases on moving from left to right in the periodic table.

74. **(d)** Among the isoelectronic species greater the ratio larger will be the ionic radii, hence the order is

$S^{2-} > Cl^- > K^+ > Ca^{2+}$

75. **(b)** Electro-negativity increases on moving left to right in the periodic table, while it decreases on moving down the group.

The correct order of E.N. is

$Si < P < C < N$

(1.8) (2.1) (2.5) (3.0)

76. **(c)** As we move from left to right in a period no. of shells remains same whereas one more electron is added thus the size of atom decreases and hence the valence electron becomes more and more near to the nucleus and hold of nucleus on valence electron increases, due to this, the tendency of an atom to lose valence electron decreases.

77. **(b)** X forms XCl_2 suggests that X is in +2 state in XCl_2. Therefore X would most like be in gp 2 of periodic table.

78. **(c)** $Cs > Rb > K > Na > Li$

79. **(b)** As Hydrogen can easily lose one electrion like alkali metals to form positive ion

80. **(a)** F

81. **(c)** Electronegativity decreases down the group due to increase in atomic radius/ tendency to gain election decreases.

82. **(d)** F and Li are in the same period and across the period atomic size/radius decreases from left to right.

83. **(a)** H and P have complete octet.

84. **(c)** G and O

Both have 7 electrons in their outermost shell.

85. **(c)** Both have four electrons in their outermost shell.

86. **(a)**   **87. (c)**

88. **(b)** On moving along a period metallic character decreases.

89. R and Q are members of group 16th having elements, O, S, Se, Te etc. RQ_2 is characterised by showing the formation of covalent bond.

90. Element 'G' is the most electropositive element.

91. Element 'V' is the most electronegative element

92. (i) Dobereiner's Triads is **A**.

(ii) Mendeleev placed elements of category A,B and C in three different groups because they have different physical and chemical properties.

(iii) No, Newland's Law of octaves is not applicable for all three categories.

Because the **law of octaves** states that every eighth element has similar properties when the elements are arranged in the increasing order of their atomic masses.

93. **(b)** N^{3-} and F^- are isoelectronic anions. N^{3-} has only seven protons and F^- has nine. Therefore, N^{3-} has larger ionic size.

94. **(d)** Atomic radius of aluminium atom is smaller than magnesium atom because of increased effective nuclear charge.

95. **(c)** Valency of an element is determined by the number of valence electrons present in the outermost shell of its atom.

96. **(a)** Silicon and germanium are among the metalloids in the modern periodic table.

97. **(d)** Bulbs are usually filled with chemically inactive gases. Nitrogen and argon gases are inactive and are filled in order to prolong the life of the filament.

98. **(b)** Group I elements are known as alkali metals as the hydroxides of these metals are soluble in water and these solutions are highly alkaline in nature.

99. **(c)** Nitrogen has higher ionisation energy as it has stable half filled electronic configuration.

100. **(d)** According to Mendeleev, periodic properties of elements is a function of their atomic masses.

101. **(b)**

102. A → (s); B → (p); C → (q); D → (r)

103. A → (s); B → (p); C → (q); D → (r)

104. A → (p, q); B → (r, s); C → (p, q, r); D → (r, s)

105. Dobereiner   **106.** atomic number

107. noble gases   **108.** group

109. main group   **110.** combining capacity

111. decreases   **112.** law of octaves

113. atomic masses, chemical   **114.** gaps

115. 18, groups, 7, periods

116. True   **117.** True   **118.** True

119. True   **120.** False

121. False

Noble gases are placed extremely right in the periodic table.

122. False   **123.** False

The number of shells remain same in a given period.

124. True   **125.** True

126. True

Rows in the periodic table are called periods. The columns of the periodic table are called groups.

127. True

128. False

Inert gases are found on the far right of the periodic table. Halogens are in the second group form the right. Metals of all types are found around the left. Transition metal are found in the middle side of the periodic table.

129. True

9 How Do Organisms Reproduce

DIRECTIONS : *This section contains multiple choice questions. Each question has four choices (a), (b), (c) and (d) out of which only one is correct.*

1. The vegetative reproduction in sweet potato is done by –
   (a) stem
   (b) leaf
   (c) root
   (d) flower

2. Menstrual cycle is generally of
   (a) 21 days
   (b) 28 days
   (c) 38 days
   (d) 40 days

3. Tunica albuginea is the covering around
   (a) ovary
   (b) testes
   (c) kidney
   (d) heart

4. Example of external fertilization is
   (a) fish and frog
   (b) frog and monkey
   (c) dog and goat
   (d) goat and fish

5. Plants of desired qualities are produced by:
   (a) Cutting
   (b) Grafting
   (c) Layering
   (d) Any one of (a), (b),(c)

6. Budding and fission are processes used by
   (a) diocious species.
   (b) hermaphroditic organisms.
   (c) organisms requiring new gene combinations for each generation.
   (d) asexually reproducing species.

7. Ovulation in mammals is caused by:
   (a) FSH and TSH
   (b) FSH and LH
   (c) FSH and LTH
   (d) LTH and LH

8. Gemmule formation in sponges is helpful in:
   (a) Parthenogenesis
   (b) Sexual reproduction
   (c) Only dissemination
   (d) Asexual reproduction

9. In mammals, the testes lie in scrotal sacs due to
   (a) presence of urinary bladder.
   (b) presence of rectum.
   (c) long vas-deferens.
   (d) requirement of low temperature for spermatogenesis.

10. The following figure represents :

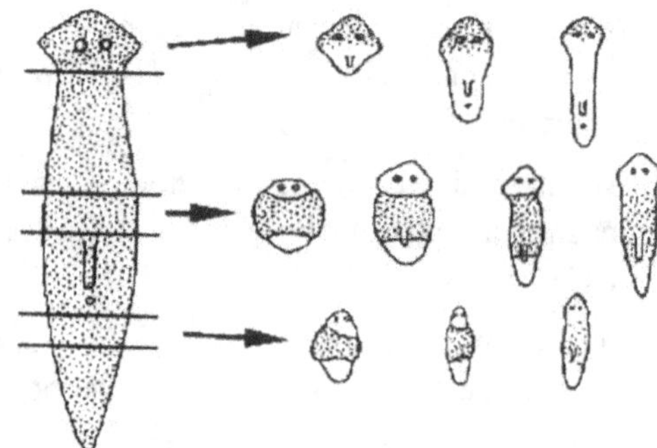

   (a) Budding in *Hydra*
   (b) Budding in *Planaria*
   (c) Regeneration in *Planaria*
   (d) Regeneration in *Hydra*

11. The correct sequence of reproductive stages seen in flowering plants is
   (a) gametes, zygote, embryo, seedling
   (b) zygote, gametes, embryo, seedling
   (c) seedling, embryo, zygote, gametes
   (d) gametes, embryo, zygote, seedling

12.

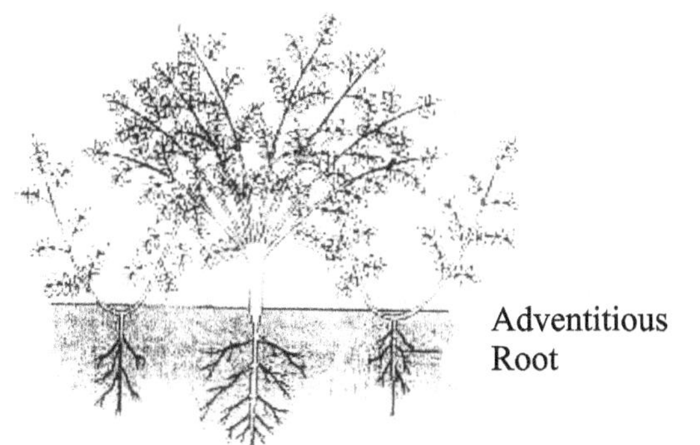

The figure shown above illustrates which method of vegetative propagation?

(a) Bud formation

(b) Grafting

(c) Layering

(d) Spore formation

13. In figure, the parts A, B and C are sequentially:

(a) cotyledon, plumule and radicle

(b) plumule, radicle and cotyledon

(c) plumule, cotyledon and radicle

(d) radicle, cotyledon and plumule

14. The diagrams below represent the reproductive systems in the human male and female.

Male

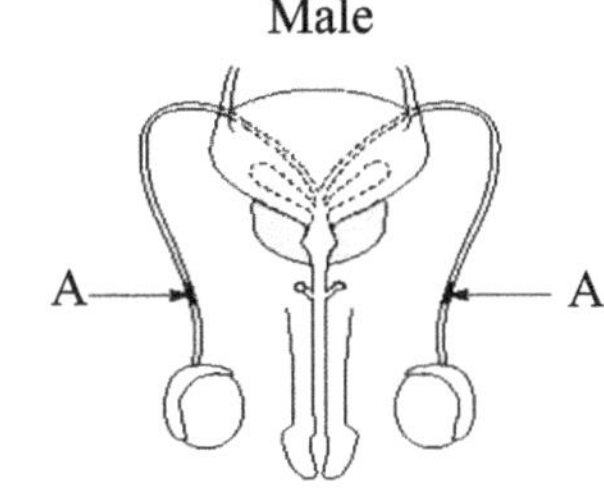

Female

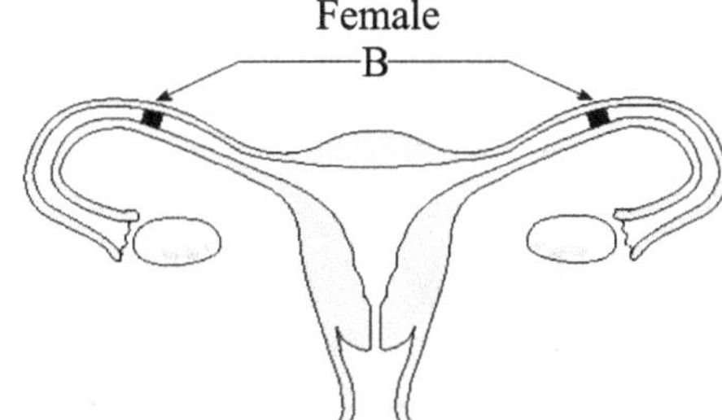

The blockages shown at A and B would most likely interfere with the ability to

(a) transport gametes

(b) produce mature gametes

(c) eliminate waste products through the urethra

(d) express secondary sex characteristics

15. Vegetative propagation is possible by

(a) Root   (b) Stem

(c) Leaves   (d) All of these

16. Ovaries produce

(a) oestrogen and progesterone

(b) oestrogen only

(c) progesterone only

(d) testosterone

17. Site of fertilization in mammals is

(a) ovary   (b) uterus

(c) vagina   (d) fallopian tube

18. Fertilization does not occur in which part?

(a) fallopian tube   (b) ampulla

(c) oviduct   (d) vagina

19. Seminiferous tubules are composed of

(a) Spermatogonia   (b) Glandular epithelium

(c) Sensory epithelium   (d) Germinal epithelium

20. Cowper's glands are found in

(a) male mammals   (b) female mammals

(c) male amphibians   (d) female amphibians

21. Progesterone is secreted by

(a) corpus luteum   (b) thyroid

(c) thymus   (d) testes

22. The general method of asexual reproduction, in yeast fungus is –

(a) by spores   (b) by budding

(c) binary fission   (d) gemma

23. Oral-contraceptives prevent the

(a) fertilization

(b) ovulation

(c) implantation

(d) entrance of sperms in vagina

24. The process of development of organism like itself is called

(a) budding   (b) flowering

(c) reproduction   (d) none of the above

25. Which of the following organisms do not depend on reproduction to exchange genetic information?

(a) animals   (b) plants

(c) bacteria   (d) fungi

26. Like animals, plants produce
    (a) many more sperm than eggs.
    (b) a few more sperm than eggs.
    (c) equal numbers of sperm and eggs.
    (d) fewer sperm than eggs.

27. The asexual process replaced by the sexual method is known as:
    (a) Semigany
    (b) Amphimixis
    (c) Apospory
    (d) Apomixis

28. The cyclic period of sexual activity in non-human female mammals is called
    (a) Menstruation
    (b) Luteinization
    (c) Oogenesis
    (d) Oestrous cycle

29. Characters transmitted from parents to offspring are present in
    (a) cytoplasm
    (b) ribosome
    (c) golgi bodies
    (d) genes

30. In sweet potato, vegetative propagation takes place by
    (a) Root
    (b) Stem
    (c) Leaves
    (d) Fruit

31. If a starfish is cut into pieces, each piece grow into a complete animal. The process is called
    (a) regeneration
    (b) reproduction
    (c) healing of wounds
    (d) growth

32. In the figure of budding in Yeast, structures a, b, c and d should be labelled respectively as

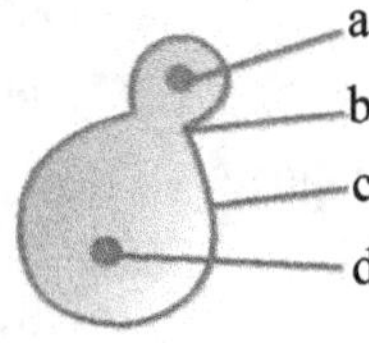

    (a) Nucleus of bud, bud, Yeast, nucleus
    (b) Dividing nucleus of bud, bud, Yeast, nucleus
    (c) Nucleus of bud, bud, Yeast, dividing nucleus of yeast
    (d) Dividing nucleus of Yeast, Yeast, bud, nucleus of bud.

33. The nutritive medium for the ejaculated sperms is given by
    (a) Seminal fluid
    (b) Vaginal fluid
    (c) Uterine lining
    (d) Fallopian tube

34. If both ovaries are removed from a rat, then which hormone is decreased in blood
    (a) Oxytocin
    (b) Oestrogen
    (c) Prolactin
    (d) Gonadotrophin

35. Which part of the ovary in mammals acts as an endocrine gland after ovulation ?
    (a) Vitelline membrane
    (b) Graafian follicles
    (c) Stroma
    (d) Germinal epithelium

36. In budding,
    (a) Outgrowth develops earlier than nuclear division
    (b) Nucleus divides earlier than development of outgrowth
    (c) Both occur simultaneously
    (d) There is no fixed sequence

37. A student upon observing a permanent slide of binary fission in *Amoeba* drew the following diagram. Identify the fault in the diagram:

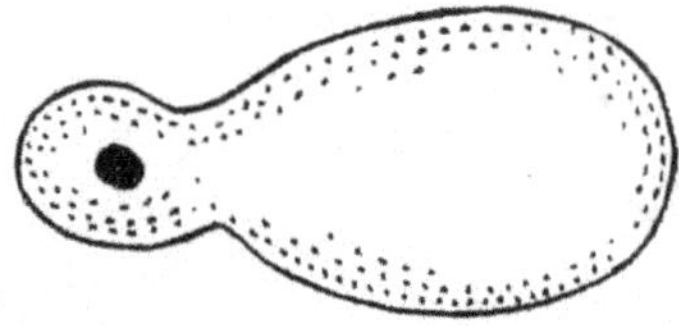

    (a) Size of daughter cell to be formed is not appropriate.
    (b) Constriction has appeared before nuclear division.
    (c) Constriction is not equally deep on the either side.
    (d) None of the above

38. In the process of binary fission:
    (a) Cytoplasm divides first followed by division of nucleus
    (b) Nucleus divides first followed by division of cytoplasm
    (c) Both nucleus and cytoplasm divide simultaneously
    (d) Cell protrudes followed by division of nucleus

39. Given below are stages of binary fission in *Amoeba*. Which one out of the following would you select as correct sequence of these stages?

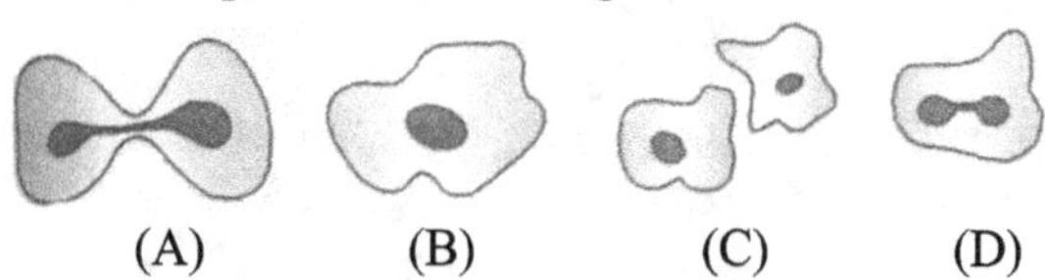

    (a) A, B, C, D
    (b) A, C, A, B
    (c) B, D, A, C
    (d) C, A, D, B

40. **(A):** Vigrous contraction of the uterus at the end of pregnancy causes expulsion.
    (B): The stimulatory reflex between the uterine contraction and oxytocin results in weakening contractions.
    (a) Both the statements (A) and (B) are correct
    (b) Statement (A) is correct but (B) is incorrect.
    (c) Both the statements (A) and (B) are incorrect
    (d) Statement(B) is correct but (A) is incorrect.

41. **(A):** The middle piece is called as power house of the sperm.

   (B): The numerous mitochondria coiled around axial filament produce energy for the movement of the tail.

   (a) Both the statements (A) and (B) are correct

   (b) Statement (A) is correct but (B) is incorrect.

   (c) Both the statements (A) and (B) are incorrect

   (d) Statement(B) is correct but (A) is incorrect.

42. Which of the following cells during gametogenesis is normally dipoid?

   (a) Spermatid   (b) Spermatogonia

   (c) Secondary polar body   (d) Primary polar body

43. In human females, meiosis II is not complete until?

   (a) Fertilisation   (b) Uterine implantation

   (c) Birth   (d) Puberty

44. The human embryo gets nutrition from the mother blood with the help of a special organ called

   (a) Zygote   (b) Ovary

   (c) Oviduct   (d) Placenta

45. The source of mammalian hormone 'relaxin' is

   (a) ovary   (b) stomach

   (c) intestine   (d) pancreas

46. Grafting in monocot plants is not possible because they have

   (a) Parallel venation

   (b) Have only one cotyledon

   (c) Have cambium

   (d) Have scattered vascular bundles

47. In the flowering plants sexual reproduction involves several events beginning with the bud and ending in a fruit. These events are arranged in four different combinations. Select the combination that has the correct sequence of events.

   (a) Embryo, zygote, gametes, fertilization.

   (b) Gametes, fertilization, zygote, embryo.

   (c) Fertilization, zygote, gametes, embryo.

   (d) Gametes, zygote, embryo, fertilization.

48. "Double fertilization" is a complex mechanism of flowering plants that is also unique to angiosperms. Choose the most appropriate statement from the options listed below that explains this phenomenon.

   (a) Fertilization in two flowers of the same plant forming endosperms.

   (b) Two male gametes fertilize two eggs inside the ovule as a result the ovary gives rise to bigger fruits.

   (c) Two fertilizations occur in a flower-one fertilization results in the formation of a diploid zygote and the second fertilization results in the formation of a triploid endosperm.

   (d) Two pollen grains sending two pollen tubes inside the ovary, resulting in the formation of two seeds inside the fruit.

49. During oogenesis in mammals, the second meiotic division occurs

   (a) before fertilisation

   (b) after implantation

   (c) before ovulation

   (d) after fertilisation

50. The correct route that sperm follows when it releases from the testis of a mammal:

   (a) Vas deferens → Epididymis → Urethra

   (b) Urethra → Epididymis → Vas deferens

   (c) Epididymis → Urethra → Vas deferens

   (d) Epididymis → Vas deferens → Urethra

51. Which of the following is not a part of the female reproductive system in human beings?

   (a) Ovary   (b) Uterus

   (c) Vas deferens   (d) Fallopian tube

52. The anther contains

   (a) sepals   (b) ovules

   (c) carpel   (d) pollen grains

Case/Passage Based Questions

DIRECTIONS : *Study the given case/passage and answer the following questions.*

Case/Passage - 1

When the branches of a plant growing in the field are pulled towards the ground and a part of them is covered with moist soil (leaving the tips of the branches exposed above the ground), then after sometime new roots develop from the parts of branches buried in the soil. On cutting these branches from the parent plant, new plants are produced from the cut parts of branches which had developed roots.

53. What is this method of propagation of plants known as?

54. What type of branches should a plant have to be able to be propagated by this method?

55. Name any two plants which are grown for their flowers and propagated by this method.

56. Name any two plants which are grown for their fruits and propagated by this method.

57. Name one plant which gets propagated by this method naturally by forming runners (soft horizontal stems running above the ground).

Case/Passage - 2

When an insect sits on the flower of a plant then some particles, present on the top of little stalks in the flower get stick to its body hair. When this insect now sits on the flower of another similar plant, then particles attached to the hair of insect are shifted to top of a flask-shaped organ at the centre of a flower. This particle grows a long tube B from the top of flask-shaped organ through which C moves down and reaches the bottom of the flask-shaped organ. Here C fuses with the nucleus of D, present in structure E.

The fusion of C and D forms a new cell F which grows and develops into a seed of the plant.

58. What are these particles? Name the process by which these particles are transfered from one flower to other flower of another similar plant.

59. What is the name of tube B?

60. What is C which moves down through the tube B?

61. Name D and E.

62. What is F?

Case/Passage - 3

The male reproductive system consists of portions which produce the germ-cells and other portions that deliver the germ-cells to the site of fertilisation. The formation of germ-cells or sperms takes place in the testes. These are located outside the abdominal cavity in scrotum because sperm formation requires a lower temperature than the normal body temperature. We have discussed the role of the testes in the secretion of the hormone, testosterone, in the previous chapter. In addition to regulating the formation of sperms, testosterone brings about changes in appearance seen in boys at the time of puberty. The sperms formed are delivered through the vas deferens which unites with a tube coming from the urinary bladder. The urethra thus forms a common passage for both the sperms and urine. Along the path of the vas deferens, glands like the prostate and the seminal vesicles add their secretions so that the sperms are now in a fluid which makes their transport easier and this fluid also provides nutrition. The sperms are tiny bodies that consist of mainly genetic material and a long tail that helps them to move towards the female germ-cell.

63. The seminiferous tubules of the testes are lined by the germinal epithelium consisting of

(a) spermatids

(b) cells of Sertoli

(c) spermatogonium

(d) spermatocytes

64. The seminiferous tubules of the testes are lined by the germinal epithelium consisting of

(a) sertoli cells

(b) cells of germinal epithelium

(c) cells of Leydig or interstitial cells

(d) secondary spermatocytes

65. Another name for Bulbourethral gland is

(a) Meibomian gland

(b) Prostate gland

(c) Perineal gland

(d) Cowper's gland

66. In man, Cryptorchidism is the condition when

(a) testes do not descent into the scrotum

(b) there are two testes in each scrotum

(c) testis degenerates in the scrotum

(d) testis enlarges in the scrotum

67. Which of these is an accessory reproductive gland in male mammals

(a) Inguinal gland

(b) Prostate gland

(c) Mushroom-shaped gland

(d) Gastric gland

≫ Assertion & Reason ⟶ ≫≫

DIRECTIONS : *Each of these questions contains an assertion followed by reason. Read them carefully and answer the question on the basis of following options. You have to select the one that best describes the two statements.*

(a) If both **Assertion** and **Reason** are **correct** and Reason is the **correct explanation** of Assertion.

(b) If both **Assertion** and **Reason** are correct, but Reason is **not the correct explanation** of Assertion.

(c) If **Assertion** is **correct** but **Reason** is **incorrect**.

(d) If **Assertion** is **incorrect** but **Reason** is **correct**.

68. **Assertion:** Asexual reproduction is also called blastogenesis.

Reason: In asexual reproduction, there is no formation and fusion of gametes.

69. **Assertion:** *Amoeba* shows multiple fission during unfavourable conditions.

Reason: Chances of survival are less during unfavourable conditions.

How Do Organisms Reproduce

70. Assertion: Urethra in human male acts as urinogenital canal.

Reason: Urethra carries only urine while sperms are carried by vasa deferentia only.

71. Assertion: In morula stage, cells divide without increase in size.

Reason: Zona pellucida remain undivided till cleavage is complete.

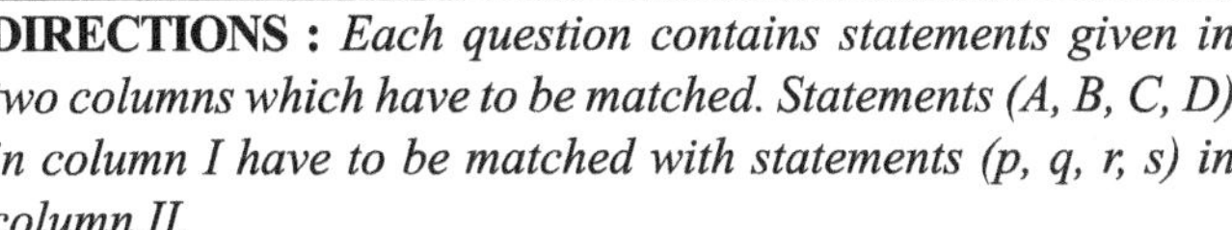

Match the Following

DIRECTIONS : *Each question contains statements given in two columns which have to be matched. Statements (A, B, C, D) in column I have to be matched with statements (p, q, r, s) in column II.*

72.

	Column A		Column B
(A)	Animals which give birth to young one	(p)	*Hydra*
(B)	Animal which produces bud	(q)	*Planaria*
(C)	An animal which shows regeneration	(r)	Placenta
(D)	Provides nutrition to the developing embryo from the mother	(s)	Cross-pollination
(E)	The pollen transferred from one flower to another flower of other plant	(t)	Germination
(F)	The process in which embryo develops into seedling	(u)	Viviparous
(G)	Fertilised egg in humans gets implanted in	(v)	Menstruation
(H)	When egg in humans is not fertilised, what happens?	(w)	Uterus

73.

	Column A		Column B
(A)	Seminal vesicle	(p)	Latex sheath
(B)	Urinogenital duct	(q)	Semen plasma
(C)	Condom	(r)	Protozoan
(D)	Trichomoniasis	(s)	Corpus spongiosum

Fill in the Blanks

DIRECTIONS : *Complete the following statements with an appropriate word / term to be filled in the blank space(s).*

74. In many invertebrate organisms, both sexes are found in the same individual. This is called ....

75. During the birth process, the pituitary hormone .... signals the uterus to contract.

76. A technique to produce genetically alike individuals from a single cell is known as ....

77. Budding is a common method of asexual reproduction in yeast and ....

78. In ...., vegetative propagation occurs by leaves.

79. Surgically when fallopian tube is removed or ligated, it is called ....

80. An egg cell of a plant is contained in an .... present in an ovary.

81. Transfer of pollen from one flower to stigma of another flower of same species is termed ....

82. Ovaries are also responsible for the production of hormone called ....

83. Plants raised by vegetative propagation bear early .... and ....

84. Future shoot hidden in a seed is called ....

85. The gametes are formed in most of the multicellular organisms by a process of cell division called ....

86. The two parts tied together during grafting are called .... and ....

87. Simply break up into smaller pieces upon maturation is found in ....

True / False

DIRECTIONS : *Read the following statements and write your answer as true or false.*

88. Basic event in reproduction is creation of DNA copy.

89. Copper–T is a contraceptive device used by women.

90. At the time of birth, a baby girl has thousands of immature eggs.

91. Sperms mature at a temperature higher than that of human body.

92. The only function of the testes is to produce sperm.

93. Animal development is limited to the period prior to bird hatching.

94. Onset of menstruation is termed as menopause.

95. In *Spirogyra*, asexual reproduction takes place by fragmentation.

96. Vegetative propagation by leaves occurs in sweet potato.

97. Transfer of male gametes to the stigma of flower is called pollination.

98. In mammals including man, fertilization takes place externally.

99. The ovulation takes place 10-12 days after the start of menstruation.

100. In human-beings, male can produce sperms upto the age of 45-50 years.

101. In fission, many bacteria and protozoa simply divide into two or more daughter cells.

102. Plants that produce asexually do not produce flower.

103. Placenta is the name of a vital connection between mother and embryo.

104. The male germ-cell produced by pollen grain contains half the amount of DNA as compared to the other body cells of the plant.

105. Vegetative propagation produces plants that are genetically similar to the parent plant.

106. Regeneration is the same as reproduction.

107. Before cell division copying of DNA is not essential.

108. Sexually transmitted diseases can be prevented by using condoms.

109. Plants produced by vegetative propagation are genetically similar to the parent plant.

110. Sexual reproduction does not lead to variation in a population.

111. The ovary of a flower grows into a fruit.

ANSWER KEY & SOLUTIONS

1. **(c)** Sweet potato is an example of vegetative propagation by roots. Sweet potato bears adventitious buds. When it is planted in the soil, new plants are produced from the roots.

2. **(b)**

3. **(b)** *Tunica albuginea* (testicles) is a layer of connective tissue which covers the testicles.

4. **(a)** External fertilization is a mode of reproduction in which a male sperm fertilizes a female egg outside of the female body. Example: fish and frog.

5. **(b)** Grafting is a horticultural technique used to join parts from two or more plants so that they appear to grow as a single plant. It is often used to combine the desirable or advantageous characteristics of two different plants.

6. **(d)**   7. **(b)**   8. **(d)**   9. **(d)**

10. **(c)**   11. **(a)**   12. **(c)**   13. **(c)**

14. **(a)**   15. **(d)**   16. **(a)**   17. **(d)**

18. **(d)**

19. **(d)** The germinal epithelium is the innermost layer of the testicle. It is also known as the wall of the seminiferous tubule within the testes.

20. **(a)** The Cowper's glands (or bulbourethral glands) are a pair of exocrine glands in the mammals (male reproductive system). They produce thick clear mucus prior to ejaculation that drains into the spongy urethra.

21. **(a)** The corpus luteum secretes progesterone, which is a steroid hormone responsible for the changes occur in the endometrium (its development) and its maintenance.

22. **(b)**

23. **(b)** The birth control pill works by stopping sperm from joining with an egg (which is called fertilization). The hormones in the pill stop ovulation. No ovulation means there's no egg hanging around for sperm to fertilize, so pregnancy can't happen.

24. **(a)**

25. **(c)** Bacteria have three mechanism for genetic information transfer without undergoing reproduction *i.e.,* transformation, transduction and conjugation.

26. **(a)**   27. **(d)**

28. **(d)** Oestrus cycle is the period in the sexual cycle of female mammals, except the higher primates, during which they are in heat *i.e.,* ready to accept a male and to mate.

29. **(d)**   30. **(a)**

31. **(a)** Regeneration means the regrowth of a damaged or missing organ part from the remaining tissue. Starfish exhibit regeneration.

32. **(a)**   33. **(a)**   34. **(b)**   35. **(b)**

36. **(a)**   37. **(b)**   38. **(b)**   39. **(c)**

40. **(c)** Vigorous contraction of the uterus at the end of pregnancy causes parturition. Parturition is induced by a complex neuroendocrine mechanism. The signals for parturition originate from the fully developed foetus and the placenta which induce mild uterine contractions called foetal ejection reflex.

41. **(a)** The middle piece of human contains mitochondria coiled a round the axial filament called mitochondrial spiral. They provide energy for the movement of the sperm. So it is called as the 'power house of the sperm'.

42. **(b)** Spermatogonia are diploid male germ cells which undergo meiosis to form sperms.

43. **(a)** Meiosis II does not complete untill fertilisation occurs in females (in human being). If fertilisation takes place, it results in a fertilized mature ovum and second polar body.

44. **(d)** It is a connecting link between mother and developing foetus, which provides nutrients and removes the waste from baby's blood.

45. **(a)** Relaxin is produced in the corpus luteum, the placenta and the uterus in females as well as in other reproductive structures, this varies by species. It also promotes the development of mammary glands in pregnant mammals.

46. **(d)** Grafting in monocot plants is not possible because they have scattered Vascular Bundles.

47. **(b)**

48. **(c)** In double fertilization, one male gamete fuses with the egg and results in the formation of a diploid

zygote and this process is called fertilization. The other male gamete fuses with the two polar nuclei to form a triploid endosperm. This process is called triple fusion. After fertilisation, the fertilized ovule forms the seed while the tissues of the ovary become the fruit.

49. (d) A primary oocyte begins the first meiotic division, but then arrests until later in life when it will finish this division in a developing follicle. This results in a secondary oocyte, which will complete meiosis if it is fertilized. So, the second meiotic division occurs after fertilisation.

50. (d) The sperm releases from the testis, enters into epididymis which leads to vas deferens. Then sperms are transferred into the urethra.

51. (c) Ovary, uterus and fallopian tube are the part of female reproductive system but vas deferens is a part of male reproductive system in human beings. The sperms are delivered through the vas deferens which unites with a tube coming from the urinary bladder.

52. (d) Stamens are the male reproductive parts of flowers. A stamen consists of an anther (which produces pollen) and a filament.

53. (a) Layering

54. (b) Slender branches (Thin branches)

55. (c) Jasmine and China rose

56. (d) Lemon and Guava

57. (e) Strawberry

58. (a) These particles are known as pollen grains; cross pollination

59. (b) Pollen-tube

60. (c) C is male gamete.

61. (d) D is female gamete (ovum or egg); E is ovule

62. (e) F is fertilised egg (zygote).

63. (b)   **64. (a)**   **65. (d)**   **66. (a)**

67. (b)

68. (b) Development of the offspring from reproductive units, such as buds or fragments, in asexual reproduction is called blastogenesis. In asexual reproduction, only one parent is involved, so also called uniparental reproduction.

69. (a)

70. (c) The urethra is the tube that allows urine to pass out of the body. In men, it's a long tube that runs through the penis. It also carries semen in men.

71. (a)

72. (A) → (u), (B) → (p), (C) → (q), (D) → (r), (E) → (s), (F) → (t), (G) → (w), (H) → (v)

73. (A) → (q), (B) → (s), (C) → (p), (D) → (r)

74. hermaphroditism   **75.** oxytocin

76. cloning   **77.** *Hydra*

78. *Bryophyllum*   **79.** tubectomy

80. ovule   **81.** cross-pollination

82. oestrogen/progesterone

83. flowers, fruits   **84.** plumule

85. meiosis   **86.** stock, scion

87. *Spirogyra*

88. True   **89.** True   **90.** True   **91.** False

92. False   **93** False   **94.** False   **95.** True

96. False   **97.** True   **98.** False   **99.** True

100. False   **101.** True   **102.** False   **103** True

104. True   **105.** True   **106.** False   **107.** False

108. True   **109.** True   **110.** False   **111.** True

10 Heredity and Evolution

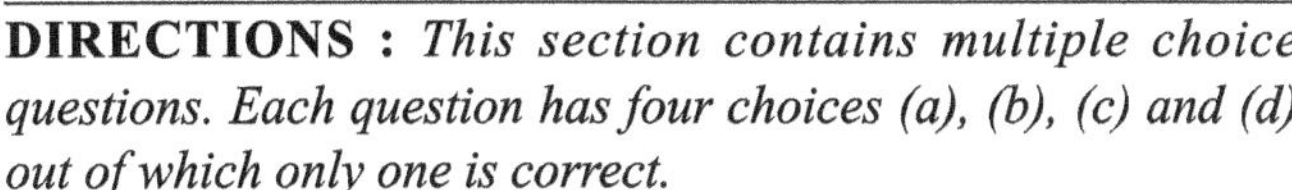

DIRECTIONS : *This section contains multiple choice questions. Each question has four choices (a), (b), (c) and (d) out of which only one is correct.*

1. A pair of contrasting characters is called
   (a) phenotype   (b) genotype
   (c) allele   (d) gene

2. An allele is said to be dominant if
   (a) it is expressed only in heterozygous combination.
   (b) it is expressed only in homozygous combination.
   (c) it is expressed in both homozygous and heterozygous condition.
   (d) it is expressed only in second generation.

3. Which of the following is a test cross?
   (a) TT × tt   (b) Tt × tt
   (c) Tt × TT   (d) tt × tt

4. Which is the example of homologous organs?
   (a) Forelimbs of man and wings of bird
   (b) Wings of birds and wings of insects
   (c) Vermiform appendix and nictitating membrane
   (d) *Archaeopteryx* and *Balanoglossus*

5. Which of the following features do humans lack that other primates have ?
   (a) Forward-facing eyes
   (b) Short snouts
   (c) Flexible shoulder and elbow joints
   (d) Opposable big toes

6. A pure tall plant can be differentiated from a hybrid tall plant:
   (a) By measuring length of plant
   (b) By spraying gibberellins
   (c) If all plants are tall after self-pollination
   (d) If all plants are dwarf after self-pollination

7. In fruit flies wild-type colour is red and is dominant to white eye colour. Because this eye colour is located on the:
   (a) Y chromosome only.   (b) autosome only.
   (c) X and Y chromosomes   (d) X chromosome only.

8. The diagram below represents a portion of a nucleic acid molecule.

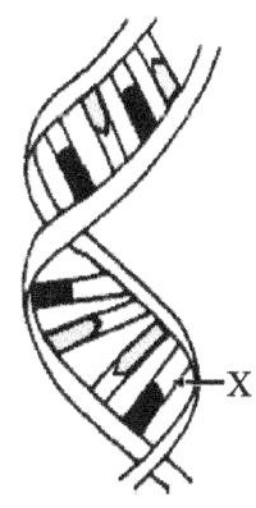

The part indicated by arrow X could be
   (a) adenine   (b) ribose
   (c) deoxyribose   (d) phosphate

9. Mendel's concept of segregation implies that the two members of an allelic pair of genes –
   (a) are distributed to separate gametes
   (b) may contaminate one another
   (c) are segregated in pairs
   (d) are linked

10.

The figure above shows :
   (a) A bird sitting on a tree
   (b) Connection between Birds and Reptiles
   (c) Connection between Pisces and Aves
   (d) All of the above

11. If a homozygous red-flowered plant is crossed with a homozygous white-flowered plant, the offspring would be:
    (a) Half red-flowered   (b) Half white-flowered
    (c) All red-flowered   (d) Half pink-flowered

12. Which of the following would stop evolution by natural selection from occurring?
    (a) If humans became extinct because of a disease epidemic.
    (b) If a thermonuclear war killed most living organisms and changed the environment drastically.
    (c) If ozone depletion led to increased ultraviolet radiation, which caused many new mutations.
    (d) If all individuals in a population were genetically identical, and there was no genetic recombination, sexual reproduction, or mutation.

13. If the fossil of an organism is found in the deeper layers of earth, then we can predict that:
    (a) The extinction of organism has occurred recently.
    (b) The extinction of organism has occurred thousands of year ago.
    (c) The fossil position in the layers of earth is not related to its time of extinction.
    (d) Time of extinction cannot be determined.

14. A Mendelian experiment consisted of breeding tall pea plants bearing violet flowers with short pea plants bearing white flowers. The progeny all bore violet flowers, but almost half of them were short. This suggests that the genetic make-up of the tall parent can be depicted as:
    (a) TTWW   (b) TTww
    (c) TtWW   (d) TtWw

15. Normal maize has starchy seed which remain smooth when dry. A mutant form has sugary seed which go crinkled when dry. When a mutant was crossed with a normal plant, an F_1 was produced which had smooth seeds. What would be the relative ratios of the different seed types, if the F_1 was allowed to self
    (a) 1 smooth : 3 sugary   (b) 3 smooth : 1 sugary
    (c) 1 smooth : 1 sugary   (d) All sugary

16. Mendel formulated some laws which are known as
    (a) Laws of germplasm
    (b) Laws of origin of species
    (c) Laws of recapitulation
    (d) Laws of inheritance

17. Vestigial organs are:
    (a) Primitive organs
    (b) Primordial organs
    (c) Organs reduced due to disuse
    (d) Organs marked only in embryonic stage

18. Who out of the following was of the strong opinion that acquired characteristics are inherited:
    (a) Lamarck   (b) Lysenko
    (c) Mendel   (d) Huxley

19. Guanine pairs with:
    (a) Adenine   (b) Cytokine
    (c) Thymine   (d) None of the above

20. Chemically a nucleotide has a:
    (a) Pentose group   (b) Nitrogenous base
    (c) Phosphate group   (d) All of these

21. Which of the following rediscovered the Mendel's work?
    (a) Correns   (b) De Vries
    (c) Tschermark   (d) All of these

22. Mendel's law of segregation is based on separation of alleles during:
    (a) Gametes formation
    (b) Seed formation
    (c) Pollination
    (d) Embryonic development

23. Mendel formulated the law of purity of gametes on the basis of :
    (a) Dihybrid cross   (b) Monohybrid cross
    (c) Back cross   (d) Test cross

24. The earliest living organisms were:
    (a) Multicellular   (b) Eukaryotes
    (c) Prokaryotes   (d) None of these

25. Sudden inheritable change is called:
    (a) Recombination   (b) Mutation
    (c) National selection   (d) Segregation

26. When one gene pair hides the effect of the other unit, this phenomenon is referred as –
    (a) Dominance   (b) Mutation
    (c) Epistasis   (d) None of these

27. The genotype of offspring formed from Tt × tt will be –
    (a) TT and tt   (b) Tt and tt
    (c) only tt   (d) only TT

28. A complete set of chromosomes inherited as a unit from one parent, is known as:
    (a) Karyotype   (b) Gene pool
    (c) Genome   (d) Genotype

29. Which of the following is Heterozygous?
    (a) TTRR   (b) ttrr
    (c) TT   (d) Tt

30. An experiment to prove that organic compounds were the basis of life, was performed by:
    (a) Oparin   (b) Miller
    (c) Melvin   (d) Fox

31. The idea of "Survival of fittest" was given by:

(a) Darwin (b) Herbert Spencer

(c) Germplasm RNA (d) Somatic DNA

32. If two parents have the genotypes AA × aa, the probability of having an aa genotype in the F, generation is –

(a) 25 percent (b) 50 percent

(c) 75 percent (d) None of these

33. Heredity deals with the study of

(a) resemblances and differences between the parents and offsprings.

(b) resemblances between the parents and offsprings.

(c) differences between the parents and offspring.

(d) none of the above

34. The given figure shows bones in the forelimbs of three mammals.

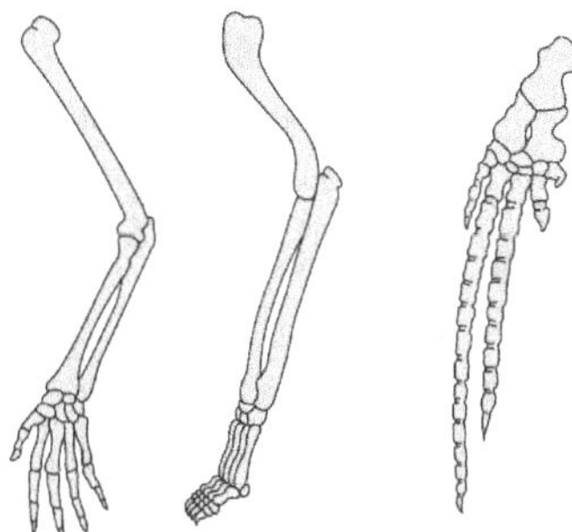

For these mammals, the number, position, and shape of the bones must likely indicates that they may have

(a) developed in a common environment.

(b) developed from the same earlier species.

(c) identical genetic makeup.

(d) identical methods of obtaining food.

35. A male child will be born if

(a) father is healthy

(b) mother is well fed during pregnancy

(c) genetic composition of child has XY set of chromosomes

(d) genetic composition of child has XX set of chromosomes.

36. According to the evolutionary theory, formation of a new species is generally due to

(a) sudden creation by nature.

(b) accumulation of variations over several generations.

(c) clones formed during asexual reproduction.

(d) movement of individuals from one habitat to another.

37. Which of the following is dominant character according to the Mendel?

(a) Dwarf plant and yellow fruit

(b) Terminal fruit and wrinkled seed

(c) White testa and yellow pericarp

(d) Green coloured pod and rounded seed

38. From heredity point of view, which marriage is not suitable?

(a) Man Rh (–) and Woman Rh (+)

(b) Both Rh (+)

(c) Both Rh (–)

(d) Man Rh (+) and Woman Rh (–)

39. Which of the following are fossils?

(a) Pollen grains buried in the bottom of a peat bog.

(b) The petrified cast of a clam's burrow.

(c) The impression of clam shell made in mud, preserved in mudstone.

(d) All of the above.

40. Which of the following evolutionary mechanisms acts to slow down or prevent the evolution of reproductive isolation?

(a) Natural selection (b) Gene flow

(c) Mutation (d) Genetic drift

41. In natural selection,

(a) the genetic composition of the population changes at random over time.

(b) new mutations are generated over time.

(c) all individuals in a population are equally likely to contribute offspring to the next generation.

(d) individuals that possess particular inherited characters survive and reproduce at a higher rate than other individuals.

42. A heterozygous red-eyed female *Drosophila* mated with a white-eyed male would produce

(a) red-eyed females and white-eyed males in the F_1

(b) white-eyed females and red-eyed males in the F_1

(c) half red and half white-eyed females and all white eyed males in the F_1

(d) half red and half white-eyed females as well as males in the F_1

43. Sex-linked disorders such as color blindness and haemophilia are

(a) caused by genes on the X chromosome

(b) caused by genes on the autosome

(c) caused by genes on the Y chromosome

(d) expressed only in men

44. The smallest unit that can evolve is a:

(a) Species (b) Genotype

(c) Gene (d) Population

45. Both prokaryotic and eukaryotic fossils are found in:

(a) Azoic   (b) Coenozic

(c) Proterozoic   (d) Archaeozoic

46. **(A):** Genes pass from one generation to another.

(B): The unit of inheritance is genes.

(a) Statement (A) and (B) both are correct.

(b) Statement (A) is correct but (B) is incorrect.

(c) Statement (A) is incorrect but (B) is correct

(d) Statement (A) and (B) both are incorrect.

47. The given figure shows an example of:

(a) Homologous organs   (b) Convergent evolution

(c) Divergent evolution   (d) Both (a) and (c)

48. Which of the following statements best describe the theory of natural selection?

(a) All organisms are equally suited to their environment.

(b) Random selection will determine which organisms survive.

(c) Organisms better adapted to their environment have greater reproductive success.

(d) Organisms that produce the most offspring are better suited to their environment.

49. **(A):** Mendel was successful in his hybridisation.

(B): Garden pea was proved as ideal experimental material.

(a) Statement (A) and (B) both are correct.

(b) Statement (A) is correct but (B) is incorrect.

(c) Statement (A) is incorrect but (B) is correct

(d) Statement (A) and (B) both are incorrect.

50. Match the following columns and select the correct answer from the codes given below.

Column-I		Column-II
A. Non-parental gene exchange	I.	Crossing over
B. Non-sister chromatids	II.	X and Y
C. Sex chromosome	III.	Autosome-linked disease
D. Thalassaemia	IV.	Recombination

(a) A – IV; B – I; C – II; D – III

(b) A – II; B – I; C – IV; D – III

(c) A – II; B – IV; C – III; D – I

(d) A – II; B – IV; C – I; D – III

51. In order to find out different types of gametes produced by a pea plant having the genotype AaBb, it should be crossed to a plant with the genotype:

(a) AABB   (b) AaBb

(c) aabb   (d) aaBB

52. **(A):** A good example of multiple alleles is ABO blood group system.

(B): When I^A and I^B alleles are present together in ABO blood group system, they both express their own types.

(a) Statement (A) and (B) both are correct.

(b) Statement (A) is correct but (B) is incorrect.

(c) Statement (A) is incorrect but (B) is correct

(d) Statement (A) and (B) both are incorrect.

53. Suppose that in sheep, a dominant allele (B) produces black hair and a recessive allele (b) produces white hair. If you saw a black sheep, you would be able to identify

(a) its phenotype for hair colour.

(b) its genotype for hair colour.

(c) the genotypes for only one of its parents.

(d) the genotypes for both of its parents.

54. Refer the given statements and select the **correct** option.

(i) Percentage of homozygous dominant individuals obtained by selfing Aa individuals is 25%.

(ii) Types of genetically different gametes produced by genotype AABbcc are 2.

(iii) Phenotypic ratio of monohybrid F_2 progeny in case of *Mirabilis jalapa* is 3 : 1.

(a) All the statements are correct.

(b) Statements (i) and (ii) are true, but statement (iii) is false.

(c) Statements (i) and (iii) are true, but statement (ii) is false.

(d) Statements (ii) and (iii) are true, but statement (i) is false.

55. In a case of mammalian coat color, the principal gene identified is 'C' which codes for a tyrosinase enzyme. In case of rabbits four different phenotypes are observed *Full Color > Chinchilla > Himalayan > Albino* (in order of the expression of gene 'C' and its alleles). In a progeny obtained after crossing two rabbits, the percentages of *Chinchilla, Himalayan* and *Albino* rabbits were 50, 25 and 25 respectively. What must have been the genotypes of the parent rabbits?

(a) $C^{ch}C^{ch}$ X $C^{ch}c$ (b) $C^{ch}C^h$ X $C^{ch}c$

(c) $C^{ch}c$ X C^hc (d) C^hC^h X $C^{ch}C^{ch}$

56. The gene for hemophilia is present on X chromosome. If a hemophilic male marries a normal female, the probability of their son being hemophilic is

(a) nil   (b) 25%

(c) 50%   (d) 100%

57. In the experiment conducted by Mendel, RRyy (round green) and rrYY (wrinkled, yellow) seeds of pea plant were used. In the F_2 generation 240 progeny were produced, out of which 15 progeny had specific characteristics. What were the characteristics?

    (a) round and green   (b) round and yellow

    (c) wrinkle and yellow   (d) wrinkle and green

58. A breeder crossed a pure bred tall plant having white flowers to a pure bred short plant having blue flowers. He obtained 202 F_1 progeny and found that they are all tall having white flowers. Upon selfing these F_1 plants, he obtained a progeny of 2160 plants. Approximately, how many of these are likely to be short and having blue flowers?

    (a) 1215   (b) 405

    (c) 540   (d) 135

59. Varieties of vegetables such as cabbage, broccoli and cauliflower have been produced from a wild cabbage species. Such process of producing new varieties of living organisms is called

    (a) Natural selection   (b) Artificial selection

    (c) Speciation   (d) Genetic drift

60. Which of the following are pairs of analogous organs?

    (I) Forelimbs of horse – Wings of bat

    (II) Wings of bat –Wings of butterfly

    (III) Forelimbs of horse – Wings of butterfly

    (IV) Wings of bird – Wings of bat

    (a) (I) and (II)   (b) (II) and (IV)

    (c) (III) and (IV)   (d) (II) and (III)

61. Of the periods listed below, which one is the earliest period when ostracoderms, the jawless and finless fishes, appeared?

    (a) Devonian period   (b) Cambrian period

    (c) Carboniferous period   (d) Silurian period

62. Which one of the following options lists the primary energy source(s) for all forms of life on the earth?

    (a) Light, inorganic substances

    (b) Inorganic substances, organic substances

    (c) Light, organic substances

    (d) N_2, CO_2

63. Four important events given below may have led to the origin of life on the earth.

    (A) Formation of amino acids and nucleotides

    (B) Availability of water

    (C) Organization of Cells

    (D) Formation of complex molecules

    (a) A, B, C and D   (b) B, A, D and C

    (b) A, D, B and C   (d) B, C, A and D

64. Which of the following carry hereditary characters to the off spring in the organism?

    (a) Ribosome   (b) Chromosome

    (c) Plasma   (d) Lysosome

65. If the genotypes determining the blood groups of a couple are $I^A I^O$ and $I^A I^B$, then the probability of their first child having type O blood is:

    (a) 0   (b) 0.25

    (c) 0.50   (d) 0.75

66. A cross was carried out between two individuals heterozygous for two pairs of genes. Assuming segregation and independent assortment, the number of different genotypes and phenotypes obtained respectively would be:

    (a) 4 and 9   (b) 6 and 3

    (c) 9 and 4   (d) 11 and 4

67. A plant with red coloured flowers is crossed with a plant having white flowers. The red and white colour of the flower is controlled by a single gene. Red is dominant over white. The F^1 progeny is self-pollinated and the flower colour in F_2 is observed. Given the above information, what is the expected phenotypic ratio of plants with different flower colours?

    (a) All plants with red flowers

    (b) Red : white in the ratio of 3 : 1

    (c) Pink : white in the ratio of 3 : 1

    (d) Red : pink : white in a ratio of 1 : 2 : 1

68. Which one of the following is a correct statement about primates evolution?

    (a) Chimpanzees and gorillas evolved from macaques

    (b) Humans and chimpanzees evolved from gorillas

    (c) Humans, chimpanzees and gorillas evolved from a common ancestor

    (d) Humans and gorillas evolved from chimpanzees

69. The gene for the genetic disease "Haemophilia" is present on the 'X' chromosome. If a haemophilic male marries a normal female, what would be the probability of their son being haemophilic.

    (a) 50%   (b) 100%

    (c) Nil   (d) 3 : 1

70. A Mendelian experiment consisted of breeding tall pea plants bearing violet flowers with short pea plants bearing white flowers. The progeny all bear violet flowers, but almost half of them were short. This suggests that the genetic make-up of the tall parent can be depicted as

    (a) TTWW   (b) TTww

    (c) TtWW   (d) TtWw

71. An example of homologous organs is
    (a) our teeth and elepahant's tusks
    (b) our arm and a dog's fore-leg
    (c) potato and runners of grass.
    (d) all of the above.

Case/Passage Based Questions

DIRECTIONS : *Study the given case/passage and answer the following questions.*

Case/Passage - 1

72. Question number (a) - (d) are based on the images (A) and (B) given below. Study them and answer the following questions.

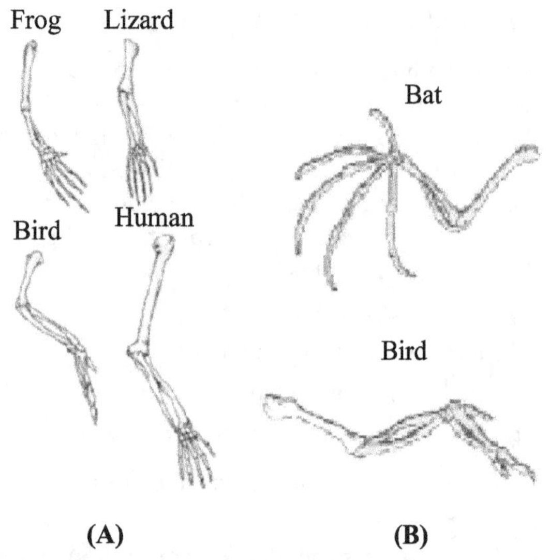

    (a) What term can be used for the structure given in image A?
    (b) What term can be used for the structure given in image B?
    (c) Which image shows a common ancestry?
    (d) Which image has a common function but different origin?

73. A person first crossed pure-breed pea plants having round-yellow seeds with pure-breed pea plants having wrinkled-green seeds and found that only A-B type of seeds were produced in the F_1 generation. When F_1 generation pea plants having A-B type of seeds were cross-breed by self-pollination, then in addition to the original round-yellow and wrinkled-green seeds, two new varieties A-D and C-B type of seeds were also obtained.

    (a) What are A-B type of seeds?
    (b) State whether A and B are dominant traits or recessive traits.
    (c) What are A-D type of seeds?
    (d) What are C-B type of seeds?

    (e) Out of A-B and A-D types of seeds, which one will be produced in (i) minimum numbers, and (ii) maximum numbers, in the F_2 generation?

Case/Passage - 2

Most human chromosomes have a maternal and a paternal copy, and we have 22 such pairs. But one pair, called the sex chromosomes, is odd in not always being a perfect pair. Women have a perfect pair of sex chromosomes, both called X. But men have a mismatched pair in which one is a normal-sized X while the other is a short one called Y. So women are XX, while men are XY.

74. If a normal cell of human body contains 46 pairs of chromosomes then the numbers of chromosomes in a sex cell of a human being is most likely to be:
    (a) 60　　　　　　(b) 23
    (c) 22　　　　　　(d) 40

75. Which of the following determines the sex of a child?
    (a) The length of the mother's pregnancy
    (b) The length of time between ovulation and copulation
    (c) The presence of an X chromosome in an ovum
    (d) The presence of a Y chromosome in a sperm

76. In human males, all the chromosomes are paired perfectly except one. These unpaired chromosomes are:
    (a) Large chromosome　　(b) Small chromosome
    (c) Y chromosome　　　　(d) X chromosome

77. The process where characteristics are transmitted from parent to offsprings is called:
    (a) Variation　　　　(b) Heredity
    (c) Gene　　　　　　(d) Allele
    (e) None of the above

78 Who have a perfect pair of sex chromosomes?
    (a) Girls only
    (b) Boys only
    (c) Both girls and boys
    (d) It depends on many other factors

Assertion & Reason

DIRECTIONS : *Each of these questions contains an assertion followed by reason. Read them carefully and answer the question on the basis of following options. You have to select the one that best describes the two statements.*

(a) If both **Assertion** and **Reason** are **correct** and Reason is the **correct explanation** of Assertion.

(b) If both **Assertion** and **Reason** are correct, but Reason is **not the correct explanation** of Assertion.

(c) If **Assertion** is **correct** but **Reason** is **incorrect**.

(d) If **Assertion** is **incorrect** but **Reason** is **correct**.

79. Assertion: Chromosomes are known as hereditary vehicles.

Reason: The chromosomes are capable of self-reproduction and maintaining morphological and physiological properties through successive generations.

80. Assertion: Ear muscles of external ear in man are poorly developed.

Reason: These muscles are useful which move external ear freely to detect sound efficiently.

81. Assertion: Although living organism always arise from other living organism, life should certainly have had a beginning.

Reason: The study of the conditions and the mechanisms involved in the creation of most primitive living structures on earth is actually the problem of origin of life.

82. Assertion: The establishment of reproductive isolations in an event of biological significance.

Reason: In the absence of reproductive isolation species can merge back into single population.

83. Assertion: DNA fingerprinting is a method in which polymerase chain reaction followed by DNA probe is used.

Reason: A DNA fingerprint is inherited and therefore, resembles that of parents.

84. Assertion: The birds have large, light spongy bones with air sacs.

Reason : These adaptations help them during flight.

85. Assertion: We have lost all the direct evidence of origin of life.

Reason: The persons responsible for protecting evidences were not skilled.

86. Assertion: Among the primates, chimpanzee is the closest relative of the present day humans.

Reason: The banding pattern in the autosome numbers 3 and 6 of man and chimpanzee is remarkably similar.

87. Assertion: Human ancestors never used their tails and so the tail expressing gene has disappeared in them.

Reason: Lamarck's theory of evolution is popularly called theory of continuity of germplasm.

88. Assertion: The genetic complement of an organism is called genotype.

Reason: Genotype is the type of hereditary properties of an organism.

DIRECTIONS : *Each question contains statements given in two columns which have to be matched. Statements (A, B, C, D) in column I have to be matched with statements (p, q, r, s) in column II.*

89. Match the genetic cross of the parents on the left with the genotypes of the offspring most likely to be produced from that cross on the right.

	Column I		Column II
(A)	BB × bb	(p)	100% BB
(B)	Bb × Bb	(q)	100% bb
(C)	BB × BB	(r)	25% BB, 50%Bb, 25%bb
(D)	bb × bb	(s)	100% Bb

90. Match the physical evidence of evolution with the best description of that particular type of evidence.

	Column I		Column II
(A)	Fossils	(p)	Comparing similarities and differences between amino acid sequences in two organisms.
(B)	Embryology	(q)	Comparing and contrasting cell structures found within an organism.
(C)	Cytology	(r)	The remains of dead organisms that are studied.
(D)	DNA evidence	(s)	Comparisons of the early development stages of an organism.

91.

	Column A		Column B
(A)	Genetic changes	(p)	Homologous organ
(B)	Independent assortment	(q)	Fossil
(C)	Natural selection	(r)	Analogous organ
(D)	Dihybrid ratio	(s)	XY
(E)	Male human beings	(t)	9 : 3 : 3 : 1
(F)	Wing of a bat and a wing of a bird	(u)	Darwin
(G)	Remnant of ancient animals	(v)	Mendel
(H)	Arm of a man and wing of a bird	(w)	DNA copying

Fill in the Blanks

DIRECTIONS : *Complete the following statements with an appropriate word / term to be filled in the blank space(s).*

92. Mendel performed his experiments on ....

93. According to modern concept, Mendel's factor is called a ....

94. Mendelian factors or genes as well as chromosomes are present in ....

95. The traits which express themselves in F_1 generation are called ....

96. The phenotypic ratio between tall and dwarf is ....

97. The phenotypic ratio in dihybrid cross is ....

98. There are .... pairs of chromosomes in human.

99. The offspring can be of two types with XX and .... chromosomes.

100. The traits which are acquired by an organism during its lifetime are called ....

101. Transmission of traits from one generation to the next generation is called ....

102. .... traits are unable to express in a hybrid.

103. Two types of nucleic acids are DNA and ....

104. Chromosome consists of a DNA molecule and ....

105. If tall plant contains TT gene then dwarf plant contains ....

106. Mendel choose .... characters in Pea for his experiments.

107. Broccoli has been developed from .... cabbage through artificial selection.

108. .... speciation occurs in geographically separated populations.

109. The first organisms were .... and not autotrophs.

100. The study of fossils, a branch of biology called .... was founded by Goerges Cuiver.

111. The age of fossil is usually determined by analysing the .... present in the rock from which fossil is recovered.

112. Theory of natural selection was proposed by ....

113. Wind of bat and wing of bird are the example of the .... organs.

114. Forelimbs of frog and lizard are the example of the .... organs.

True / False

DIRECTIONS : *Read the following statements and write your answer as true or false.*

115. Mouth parts of insects show divergent evolution.

116. Life can originate on earth from pre-existing life only.

117. The atmosphere of the primitive earth was reducing.

118. Variations arising during the process of reproduction cannot be inherited.

119. Sex is determined by different factors in various species.

120. Changes in the non-reproductive tissues caused by environmental factors are inheritable.

121. Exchange of genetic material takes place in asexual reproduction.

122. A cross between a true tall and pure dwarf pea plant resulted in production of all tall plants because tallness is the dominant trait.

123. Reduction in weight of an organism due to nutrition is genetically controlled.

124. New species may be formed if DNA undergoes significant changes or chromosome number changes in the gametes.

125. Both the parents contribute DNA equally to the offspring.

126. Sex of the child is determined by the type of ovum provided by the mother.

127. A recessive trait can also be common as blood group O.

128. Attached ear lobe is recessive trait.

129. Charles Darwin discovered the law of independent assortment.

ANSWER KEY & SOLUTIONS

1. **(c)**

2. **(c)** An allele is dominant if it is expressed in both homozygous and heterozygous states. Dominant alleles expresses itself in the homozygous as well as heterozygous condition. It is denoted by capital letter.

3. **(b)** A test cross involves mating of an unknown genotypic individual with a known homozygous recessive.

4. **(a)**   5. **(d)**

6. **(c)** Pure breeding varieties are the one that carries same allele for a particular character and pass the trait without change from one generation to next upon selfing. For example, pure breeding tall (TT) plant carries two copies of "T" allele and selfing of these plants produce a uniform progeny of tall plants only. Hybrids are the one which carries contrasting allele of a particular gene.

7. **(a)** In fruit flies, the wild-type eye color is red (XW) and is dominant to white eye color. Because this eye-color gene is located on the X chromosome only. Males are said to be hemizygous, because they have only one allele for any X-linked characteristic.

8. **(a)** The part indicated by arrow 'X' is adenine.

Nitrogenous bases:

3'   5'

Adenine
Thymine
Guanine
Cytosine

Base pair

Sugar-phosphate backbone

3'   5'

9. **(a)** The law of segregation states that the two alleles of a single trait will separate randomly, meaning that there is a 50% either allele will end up in either gamete.

10. **(b)**   11. **(c)**   12. **(d)**   13. **(b)**

14. **(c)** The genetic make-up of the tall parent can be depicted as TtWW Since all the progeny bore violet flowers, it means that the tall plant having violet flowers has WW genotype for violet flower colour. Since the progeny is both tall and short, the parent plant was not a pure tall plant. Its genotype must be Tt. Therefore, the cross involved is:

TtWw × ttww

↓

TtWw – ttww

Therefore, half the progeny is tall, but all of them have violet flowers.

15. **(c)** Suppose the genotype of a normal plant with smooth seeds is SS and that of wrinkled seeds is ss. For a cross between SS and ss, all the offsprings produced will have genotype Ss (smooth seeds). If the F1 with smooth seeds Ss is allowed to self, then 3 smooth and 1 maize plant with wrinkled seeds will be formed.

Genotypes: Ss (smooth seeds) × Ss (smooth seeds)

Gametes	S	s
S	SS	Ss
s	Ss	ss

As is evident from Punnette square, 3 plants with smooth seeds and 1 with wrinkled seeds are formed.

16. **(d)**   17. **(c)**   18. **(a)**   19 **(b)**

20. **(d)** A nucleotide is made up of three parts: a phosphate group, a 5-carbon sugar, and a nitrogenous base. The four nitrogenous bases in DNA are adenine, cytosine, guanine and thymine.

21. **(d)**

22. **(a)** According to Mendel's monohybrid cross, during gamete formation, the alleles for each gene segregate from each other so that each gamete carries only one allele for each gene. It is called Law of Segregation.

23. **(b)**

24. **(c)** The first living things on Earth, single-celled micro-organisms or microbes lacking a cell nucleus or cell membrane known as prokaryotes, seem to have first appeared on Earth almost four billion years ago, just a few hundred million years after the formation of the Earth itself.

25. **(b)**

26. **(c)** Epistasis is the phenomenon wherein the effect of one gene (locus) is dependent on the presence of one or more 'modifier genes', *i.e.,* the genetic background.

27. **(b)**   **28. (c)**

29. **(d)** Heterozygous means that an organism has two different alleles of a gene. Thus Tt is heterozygous.

30. **(b)**   **31. (a)**   **32. (d)**   **33. (a)**

34. **(b)** The given figures show the forelimbs of three mammals which indicate the homology among themselves. Homologous organs are those organs which are dissimilar in shape, size and function but their origin, basic plan and development are similar. Such differences are due to divergent evolution or adaptation for varied conditions.

35. **(c)**   **36. (b)**

37. **(d)** In peas, the dominant seed shape is round and the recessive is wrinkled (w). The dominant trait for pod color is green and recessive is yellow (y).

38. **(d)**

39. **(d)** A fossil is the mineralized partial or complete form of an organism, or of an organism's activity, that has been preserved as a cast, impression or mold. Thus all the given options are the examples of fossils.

40. **(b)** Gene flow is the movement of genes from one population to another population. It helps to prevent the genetic evolution of reproductive isolation.

41. **(d)**   **42. (d)**

43. **(a)** There are several disorders that are caused by abnormal sex-linked traits. A common Y-linked disorder is male infertility. In addition to hemophilia, other X-linked recessive disorders include color blindness, muscular dystrophy etc.

44. **(d)** A population is the smallest unit of living organisms that can undergo evolution.

45. **(d)**

46. **(c)** Chromosomes carry gene that passes on the traits of parents to the offspring during genetic recombination.

47. **(d)** The given figure of *Bougainvillea* and *Cucurbita* shows an example of homologous organ or divergent evolution. Homologous organs are those organs which are dissimilar in shape, size and function but their origin, basic plan and development are similar. Other examples in animals are forelimbs of frog, reptile, birds and mammals. Such differences are due to divergent evolution or adaptation for varied conditions.

48. **(c)** The theory of natural selection states that those individuals that are better adapted to their environment will have greater reproductive success.

49. **(a)** Mendel choose garden pea as plant material for his experiments, since it had the following advantages:

(i)   Well defined characters.

(ii) Bisexual flowers.

(iii) Predominantly self-fertilisation.

(iv) Easy hybridisation.

Besides these features, garden pea, being self-fertilised, had pure lines due to natural self fertilisation for a number of years. Therefore, any variety used was pure for the characters it carried. Mendel's success was mainly based on the fact that he considered a single character at one time.

50. **(a)** Crossing over takes place only between non-sister chromatids.

51. **(c)** In order to find out the gamete or the genotype of an unknown individual, scientists perform a test cross. In test cross, the individual in question is crossed with the homozygous recessive parent.

52. **(a)** ABO system consists of four blood groups-A, B, AB and O. ABO blood groups are controlled by gene I. The gene has three alleles I^A, I^B and i. This phenomenon is known as multiple allelism. I^A and I^B are completely dominant over i. When I^A and I^B are present together, they both express themselves and produce AB blood group. This phenomenon is known as co-dominance.

53. **(a)** Black is the phenotype of the sheep. Without further information, you cannot identify the genotype of a black sheep because it could be either BB or Bb. The possible genotypes of the parents of a black sheep could be BB × BB, BB × Bb, Bb × bb, or Bb × Bb.

54. **(b)**

55. **(c)** Here :

Genotype of Full Colour - $C^{ch}C^{ch}$

Genotype of Chinchilla - $C^{ch}C^{h}$ or $C^{ch}c$

Genotype of Himalayan - $C^{h}C^{h}$ or $C^{h}c$

Genotype of Albino - cc

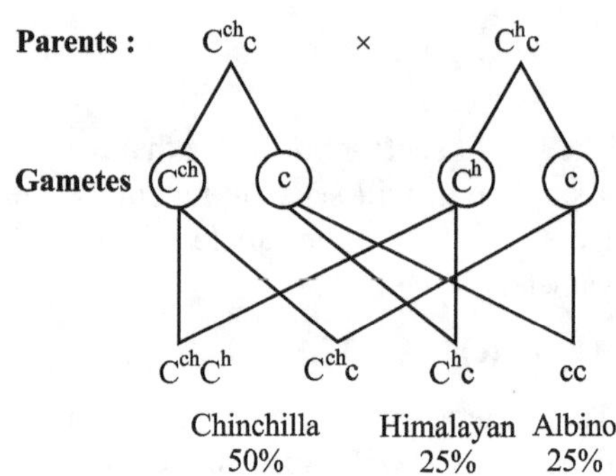

56. (a)

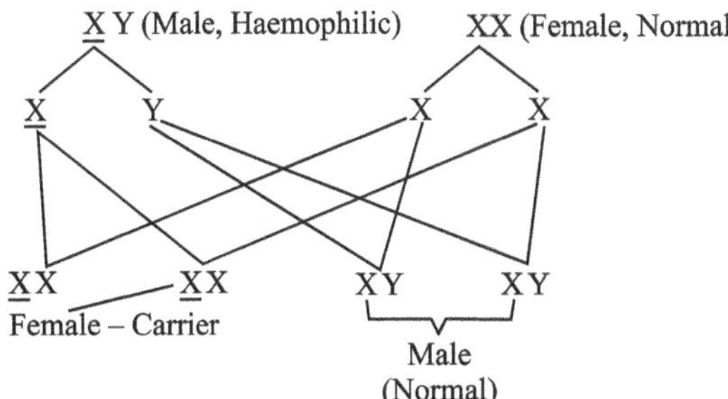

Since all the male progeny will get the X chromosome form their mother, they will all be normal.

57. (d)

58. (d) According to dihybrid phenotypic ratio

$9 : 3 : 3 : 1$,

TW — 9	Tw — 3
tW – 3	tw – 1

The total number of short and blue flowered plants is

$$\frac{1}{16} \times 2130 = \frac{1080}{8} = 135$$

59. (b) Artificial selection is characterized by intentional reproduction of an organism having desirable traits. It is also called as selective breeding.

60. (b) Analogous organs are such organs which show anatomically different structures but doing similar functions. Example : wings of a bat and wings of a pigeon.

61. (b)   **62. (a)**   **63. (b)**

64. (b) Chromosomes carry genes, which are the hereditary characters to the offspring.

65. (a) The genotypes of offspring of parents having $I^A I^O$ and $I^A I^B$ blood groups are:

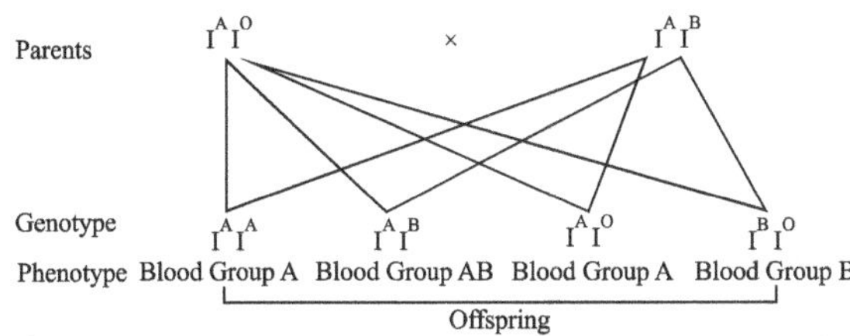

From the above cross, it is shown that none of the offspring will be of blood group O.

∴ The probability of their first child having type O blood is zero.

66. (c) In the given question, both parents are heterozygous for two pairs of genes. This means the cross is a dihybrid cross.

Let us assume a dihybrid cross,

Pure breeding – Yellow round × Wrinkled green
traits   seeds   seeds
(YYRR)   (yyrr)

F_1 – Yellow round seeds
(YyRr)

Gametes

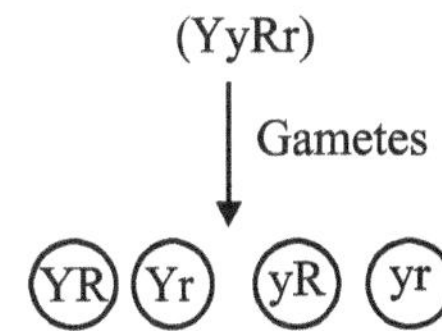

♀ \ ♂	YR	Yr	yR	yr
YR	YYRR yellow round	YYRr yellow round	YyRR yellow round	YyRr yellow round
Yr	YYRr yellow round	Yyrr yellow wrinkled	YyRr yellow round	Yyrr yellow wrinkled
yR	YyRR yellow round	YyRr yellow round	yyRR green round	yyRr green round
yr	YyRr yellow round	Yyrr yellow wrinkled	yyRr green round	yyrr green wrinkled

The genotype ratio is $1 : 2 : 1 : 2 : 4 : 2 : 1 : 2 : 1$

The phenotypic ratio is $9 : 3 : 3 : 1$

∴ The number of different genotypes and phenotypes obtained would be 9 and 4, respectively.

67. (b) Phenotypic ratio can be determined by doing a test cross and identifying the frequency of a trait or trait combinations that will be expressed based on the genotypes of the offspring.

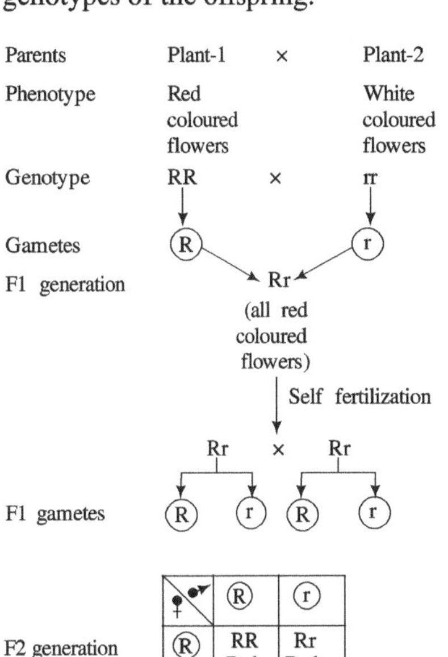

F2 ♀ \ ♂	R	r
R	RR Red	Rr Red
r	RR Red	rr white

Phenotype :   Red : White
              3 : 1

68. **(c)** According to the new genetic research-when combined with known fossils-the lineage that led to humans, chimps, and gorillas evolved from a common ancestor about 10 million years ago.

69. **(c)**

Parents: X^hY ×   XX

Haemophilic man   Normal female

♀ \ ♂	X^h	Y
X	X^hX	XY
X	X^hX	XY

70. **(c)** Since, all the progeny bore violet flowers, it implies that the tall plant with violet flowers has genotype 'WW' for violet flower colour. Since, the progeny obtained is both tall and short, the parent plant was not a pure tall plant and bears genes that determine short height of the plant. Therefore, the genotype of the plant with respect to height would be 'Tt'. So, if a cross is carried out between tall parent with violet flowers (TtWW) and short parent with white flowers (ttww), the progeny obtained is TtWw (8) : ttWw (4) : ttWw(4). All the progeny bear violet flowers but half of them are tall and half are short.

71. **(d)** Homologous organ have same origin but different functions like each of the organ above. Our teeth and elephant's tusks, our arm and a dog's fore-leg and potato and runners of grass are the examples of homologous organs.

72. **(a)** Homologous organs

(b) Analogous organs

(c) Image A shows common ancestry

(d) Image B *i.e.,* analogous organs have a different origin but common functions.

73. **(a)** Round yellow

(b) A (round) and B (yellow) are dominant traits

(c) Round-green

(d) Wrinkled-yellow

(e) (i) A–D (ii) A–B

74. **(b)**   **75.** **(d)**   **76.** **(c)**   **77.** **(b)**

78 **(a)**   **79.** **(a)**

80. **(c)** Ear muscles of external ear in man are poorly developed. These muscles are useless which move external ear freely and these muscles are called vestigial organs.

81. **(a)**   **82.** **(a)**

83. **(a)** There is an inheritable quality to fingerprints. Pattern types are often genetically inherited, but the individual details that make a fingerprint unique are not.

84. **(a)** Birds have very light, honeycombed or hollow bones which help them to minimise the pull of gravity, mostly by reducing body weight.

85. **(c)**

86. **(a)** The banding pattern seen on stained chromosomes from humans and chimpanzee show striking similarities which indicates that they have evolutionary relationships (cytogenetic evidence).

87. **(c)** According to Lamarck's theory, continuous disuse of organs make them weak. The theory of continuity of germplasm was given by Weismann.

88. **(a)** Genotype of the organism include all dominant and recessive characters.

89. (A) → (s), (B) → (r), (C) → (p), (D) → (q)

90. (A) → (r), (B) → (s), (C) → (q), (D) → (p)

91. (A) → (w), (B) → (v), (C) → (u), (D) → (t), (E) → (s), (F) → (r), (G) → (q), (H) → (p)

92. garden pea   **93.** gene

94. pairs   **95.** dominant

96. 3 : 1   **97.** 9 : 3 : 3 : 1

98. 23   **99.** XY

100. acquired traits   **101.** heredity

102. recessive   **103.** RNA

104. protein   **105.** tt

106. Seven   **107.** Wild

108. Allopatric   **109.** heterotrophs

110. paleontology   **111.** radioactive materials

112. Darwin   **113.** analogous

114. homologous

115. True   **116.** True   **117.** True   **118.** False

119. True   **120.** False   **121.** False   **122.** True

123. False   **124.** True   **125.** True   **126.** False

127. True   **128.** True   **129.** False

11 Electricity

DIRECTIONS : *This section contains multiple choice questions. Each question has four choices (a), (b), (c) and (d) out of which only one is correct.*

1. The charge of 150 coulomb flows through a wire in one minute. What is the electric current flowing through it?
   (a) 2.5 A
   (b) 3.5 A
   (c) 4.5 A
   (d) 5.5 A

2. Find the current I flown in the circuit
   (a) 0.05 A
   (b) 5 A
   (c) 50 A
   (d) 500 A

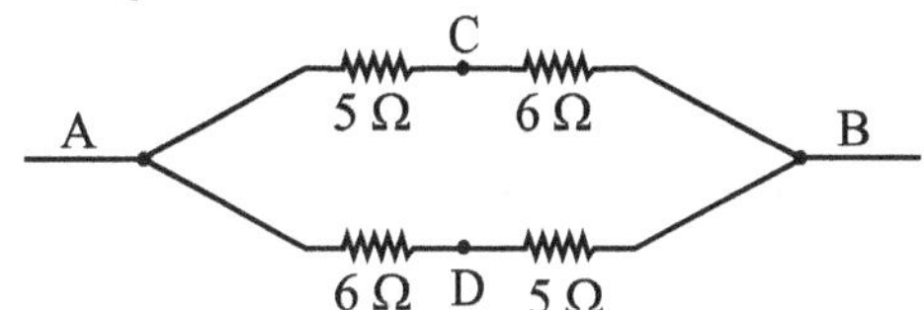

3. A current of 10 A flows through a conductor for 2 minutes. What is the amount of charge passed through the conductor?
   (a) 1200 C
   (b) 150 C
   (c) 18 C
   (d) 1.8 C

4. A current of 10 A flows through a conductor for 2 minutes. Find the total number of electrons flowing through the conductor.
   (a) 75×10^{20}
   (b) 70×10^{15}
   (c) 60×10^{15}
   (d) 11×10^{12}

5. A metal wire 80 cm long and 1.00 mm² in cross-section has a resistance of 0.92 ohm. It's resistivity is:
   (a) 0.000 115 ohm m
   (b) 0.0 115 ohm m
   (c) 1.15 ohm m
   (d) None of these

6. 1 Ampere is equivalent to:
   (a) $\dfrac{1\,\text{coulomb}}{1\,\text{sec}}$
   (b) $\dfrac{1\,\text{volt}}{1\,\text{sec}}$
   (c) $\dfrac{1\,\text{volt meter}}{1\,\text{sec}}$
   (d) None

7. Device used to measure electric current is:
   (a) Ammeter
   (b) Voltmeter
   (c) Galvanometer
   (d) Generator

8. Reciprocal of resistance is called:
   (a) Inductance
   (b) Conductance
   (c) Resistivity
   (d) None of these

9. Find the equivalent resistance between A and B of following circuit:

   (a) $\dfrac{6}{2}\,\Omega$
   (b) $\dfrac{5}{2}\,\Omega$
   (c) $\dfrac{11}{2}\,\Omega$
   (d) $\dfrac{1}{2}\,\Omega$

10. The maximum resistance which can be made using four resistors each of resistance $\dfrac{1}{2}\,\Omega$ is **[CBSE 2020]**
    (a) 2Ω
    (b) 1 Ω
    (c) 2.5 Ω
    (d) S Ω

11. A current of 1 A is drawn by a filament of an electric bulb. Number of electrons passing through a cross section of the filament in 16 seconds would be roughly
    (a) 10^{20}
    (b) 10^{16}
    (c) 10^{18}
    (d) 10^{23}

12. The proper representation of series combination of cells (Figure) obtaining maximum potential is

(iii) 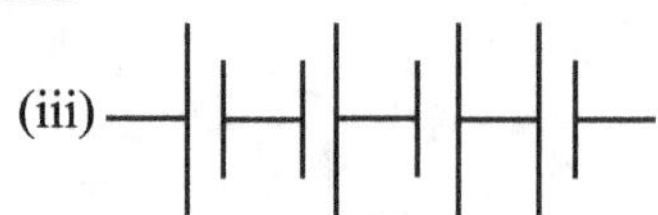

(iv) 

(a) (i)
(b) (ii)
(c) (iii)
(d) (iv)

13. A cylindrical conductor of length l and uniform area of crosssection A has resistance R. Another conductor of length $2l$ and resistance R of the same material has area of cross section **[CBSE 2020]**

(a) $A/2$
(b) $3A/2$
(c) $2A$
(d) $3A$

14. If 'i' is the current flowing through a conductor of resistance 'R' for time 't'. then the heat produced (Q) is given by

(a) $\dfrac{i^2R}{t}$
(b) $\dfrac{iR^2}{t}$
(c) i^2Rt
(d) iRt^2

15. An electric kettle consumes 1 kW of electric power when operated at 220 V. A fuse wire of what rating must be used for it?

(a) 1 A
(b) 2 A
(c) 4 A
(d) 5 A

16. A cylindrical rod is reformed to twice its length with no change in its volume. If the resistance of the rod was R, the new resistance will be

(a) R
(b) $2R$
(c) $4R$
(d) $8R$

17. What is the current through a 5.0 ohm resistor if the voltage across it is $10V$

(a) zero
(b) $0.50\,A$
(c) $2.0\,A$
(d) 5.0 A

18. The length of a wire is doubled and the radius is doubled. By what factor does the resistance change

(a) 4 times as large
(b) twice as large
(c) unchanged
(d) half as large

19. Resistance of a metallic conductor depends on ________.

(a) its length
(b) its area of cross section
(c) its temperature
(d) All the above

20. A 24V potential difference is applied across a parallel combination of four 6 ohm resistor. The current in each resistor is

(a) 1 A
(b) 4 A
(c) 16 A
(d) 36 A

21. Three resistances of 2Ω, 3Ω and 5Ω are connected in parallel to a 10V battery of negligible internal resistance. The potential difference across the 3Ω resistance will be

(a) 2 V
(b) 3 V
(c) 5 V
(d) 10 V

22. Two unequal resistances are connected in parallel. Which of the following statement is true

(a) current in same in both
(b) current is larger in higher resistance
(c) voltage-drop is same across both
(d) voltage-drop is lower in lower resistance

23. You are given n identical wires, each of resistance R. When these are connected in parallel, the equivalent resistance is X. When these will be connected in series, then the equivalent resistance will be

(a) X/n^2
(b) n^2X
(c) X/n
(d) nX

24. A piece of wire of resistance R is cut into five equal parts. These parts are then connected in parallel. If the equivalent resistance of this combination is R', then the ratio R/R' is

(a) 1/25
(b) 1/5
(c) 5
(d) 25

25. 2 ampere current is flowing through a conductor from a 10 volt emf source then resistance of conductor is

(a) 20 Ω
(b) 5 Ω
(c) 12 Ω
(d) 8 Ω

26. Charge on an electron is 1.6×10^{-19} coulomb. Number of electrons passing through the wire per second on flowing of 1 ampere current through the wire will be

(a) 0.625×10^{-19}
(b) 1.6×10^{-19}
(c) 1.6×10^{-19}
(d) 0.625×10^{19}

27. 20 coulomb charge is flowing in 0.5 second from a point in an electric circuit then value of electric current in amperes will be

(a) 10
(b) 40
(c) 0.005
(d) 0.05

28. In this circuit, the value of I_2 is

(a) 0.2 A
(b) 0.3 A
(c) 0.4 A
(d) 0.6 A

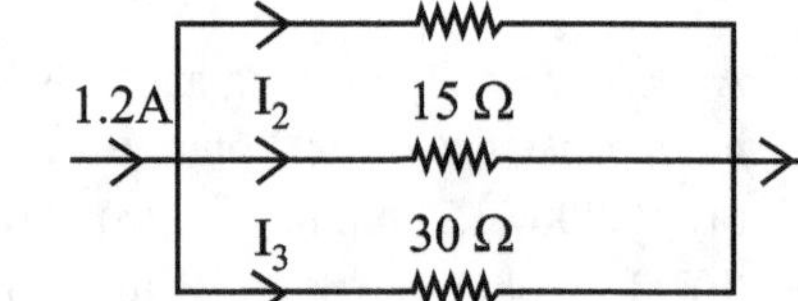

29. A letter 'A' is constructed of a uniform wire of resistance 1 ohm per cm. The sides of the letter are 20 cm and the cross piece in the middle is 10 cm long. The resistance between the ends of the legs will be

(a) 32.4 ohm
(b) 28.7 ohm
(c) 26.7 ohm
(d) 24.7 ohm

30. A wire of resistance R is cut into ten equal parts which are then joined in parallel. The new resistance is
(a) 0.01 R
(b) 0.1 R
(c) 10 R
(d) 100 R

31. If a wire is stretched to make its length three times, its resistance will become
(a) three times
(b) one-third
(c) nine times
(d) one-ninth

32. The resistivity of a wire depends on
(a) length
(b) area of cross-section
(c) material
(d) All the above

33. The effective resistance between the points A and B in the figure is
(a) 5 Ω
(b) 2 Ω
(c) 3 Ω
(d) 4 Ω

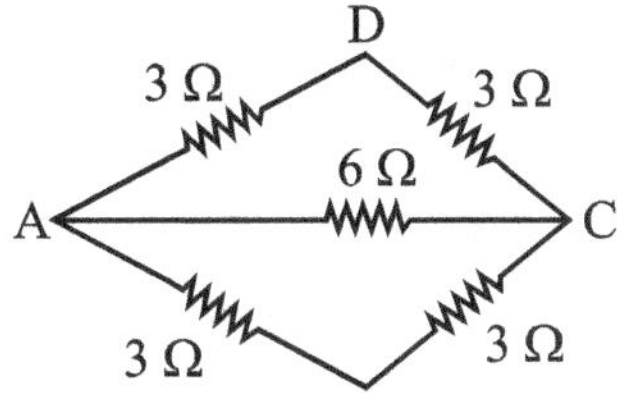

34. In the circuits shown below the ammeter A reads 4 amp. and the voltmeter V reads 20 volts. The value of the resistance R is

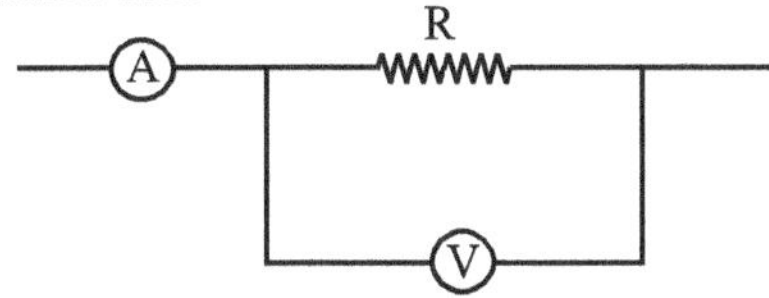

(a) slightly more than 5 ohms
(b) slightly less than 5 ohms
(c) exactly 5 ohms
(d) None of the above

35. Three resistors are connected to form the sides of a triangle ABC as shown below.

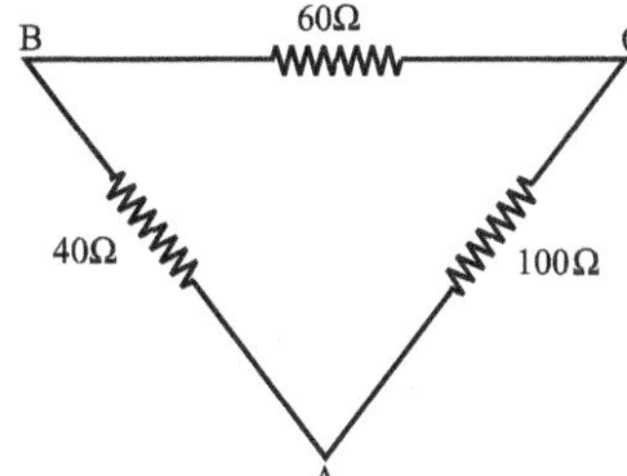

The resistance of side AB is 40 ohms, of side BC 60 ohms and of side CA 100 ohms. The effective resistance between the point A and B in ohms is
(a) 50
(b) 64
(c) 32
(d) 100

36. If one micro-amp. current is flowing in a wire, the number of electrons which pass from one end of the wire to the other end in one second is
(a) 6.25×10^{12}
(b) 6.25×10^{15}
(c) 6.25×10^{18}
(d) 6.25×10^{19}

37. The unit for specific resistance is
(a) ohm × second
(b) ohm × m
(c) ohm
(d) ohm/cm

38. If the temperature of a conductor is increased, its resistance will
(a) not increase
(b) increase
(c) decrease
(d) change according to the whether

39. The equivalent resistance between points a and b of a network shown in the figure is given by
(a) $\dfrac{3}{4}R$
(b) $\dfrac{4}{3}R$
(c) $\dfrac{5}{4}R$
(d) $\dfrac{4}{5}R$

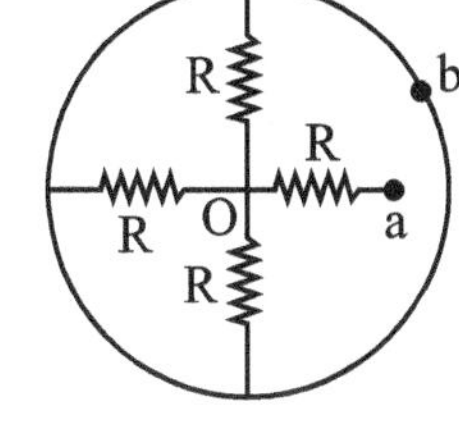

40. Two wires of resistance R_1 and R_2 are joined in parallel. The equivalent resistance of the combination is
(a) $R_1R_2/(R_1 + R_2)$
(b) $(R_1 + R_2)$
(c) $R_1 \times R_2$
(d) R_1/R_2

41. In the given circuit, the potential of the point E is
(a) Zero
(b) -8 V
(c) $-4/3$ V
(d) $4/3$ V

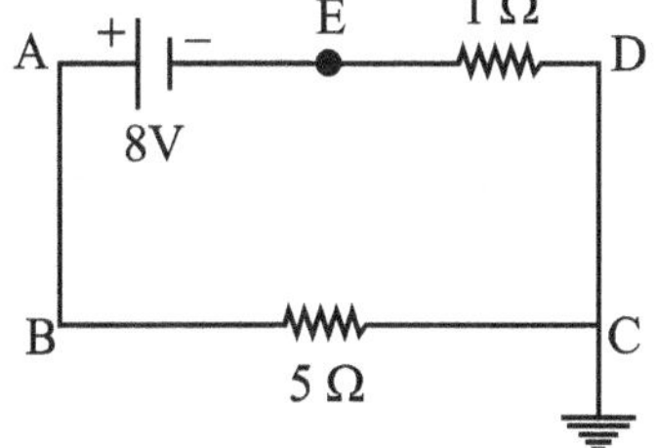

42. The resistance of a thin wire in comparison of a thick wire of the same material
(a) is low
(b) is equal
(c) depends upon the metal of the wire
(d) is high

43. If the specific resistance of a wire of length l and radius r is k then resistance is
(a) $k\pi r^2/l$
(b) $\pi r^2/lk$
(c) $kl/\pi r^2$
(d) k/lr^2

44. If a charge of 1.6×10^{-19} coulomb flows per second through any cross section of any conductor, the current constitute will be
(a) 2.56×10^{-19} A
(b) 6.25×10^{-19} A
(c) 1.6×10^{-19} A
(d) 3.2×10^{-19} A

45. The number of electrons flowing per second through any cross section of wire, if it carries a current of one ampere, will be
(a) 2.5×10^{18} (b) 6.25×10^{18}
(c) 12.5×10^{18} (d) 5×10^{18}

46. The number of electron passing through a heater wire in one minute, if it carries a current of 8 ampere, will be
(a) 2×10^{20} (b) 2×10^{21}
(c) 3×10^{20} (d) 3×10^{21}

47. The heat produced in a wire of resistance 'x' when a current 'y' flow through it in time 'z' is given by
(a) $x^2 \times y \times z$ (b) $y \times z^2 \times x$
(c) $x \times z \times y^2$ (d) $y \times z \times x$

48. In a wire of length 4m and diameter 6mm, a current of 120 ampere is passed. The potential difference across the wire is found to be 18 volt. The resistance of wire will be
(a) 0.15 ohm   (b) 0.25 ohm
(c) 6.660 ohm   (d) None of the these

49. The resistance of an incandescent lamp is
(a) greater when switched off
(b) smaller when switched on
(c) grater when switched on
(d) Same whether it is switched off or switched on

50. If resistance of a wire formed by 1.cc of copper be 2.46Ω. The diameter of wire is 0.32 mm, then the specific resistance of wire will be
(a) 1.59×10^{-6} ohm. cm   (b) 2.32×10^{-6} ohm. cm
(c) 3.59×10^{-6} ohm. cm   (d) 1.59×10^{-8} ohm. cm

51. A given piece of wire length ℓ, cross sectional area A and resistance R is stretched uniformly to a wire of length 2ℓ. The new resistance will be
(a) 2 R   (b) 4 R
(c) R/2   (d) Remains unchanged

52. A given piece of wire of length ℓ, radius r and resistance R is stretched uniformly to a wire of radius $(r/2)$. The new resistances will be
(a) 2 R   (b) 4 R
(c) 8 R   (d) 16 R

53. There are two wires of the same length and of the same material and radial r and $2r$. The ratio of their specific resistance is
(a) 1 : 2   (b) 1 : 1
(c) 1 : 4   (d) 4 : 1

54. Specific resistance of a wire depends on the
(a) length of the wire
(b) area of cross-section of the wire
(c) resistance of the wire
(d) material of the wire

55. The resistance of some substances become zero at very low temperature, then these substances are called
(a) good conductors   (b) super conductors
(c) bad conductors   (d) semi conductors

56. The resistance of wire is 20Ω. The wire is stretched to three time its length. Then the resistance will now be
(a) $6.67\ \Omega$ (b) $60\ \Omega$
(c) $120\ \Omega$ (d) $180\ \Omega$

57. When the resistance of copper wire is $0.1\ \Omega$ and the radius is 1 mm, then the length of the wire is (specific resistance of copper is 3.14×10^{-8} ohm $\times$ m)
(a) 10 cm   (b) 10 m
(c) 100 m   (d) 100 cm

58. When the resistance wire is passed through a die the cross-section area decreases by 1%, the change in resistance of the wire is
(a) 1% decrease   (b) 1% increase
(c) 2% decrease   (d) 2% increase

59. The lowest resistance which can be obtained by connecting 10 resistors each of $\dfrac{1}{10}$ ohm is
(a) $\dfrac{1}{250}\Omega$ (b) $\dfrac{1}{200}\Omega$
(c) $\dfrac{1}{100}\Omega$ (d) $\dfrac{1}{10}\Omega$

60. The resistance $4R, 16R, 64R, ...\infty$ are connected in series, their resultant will be
(a) 0   (b) ∞
(c) 4/3 R   (d) 3/4 R

61. Resistance R, 2R, 4R, 8R .... ∞ are connected in parallel. Their resultant resistance will be
(a) R   (b) R/2
(c) 0   (d) ∞

62. The equivalent resistance between points X and Y is

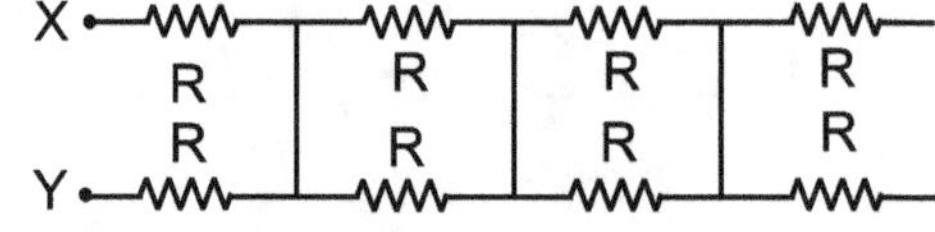

(a) R   (b) 2R
(c) R/2   (d) 4 R

63. The equivalent resistance between points A and B is

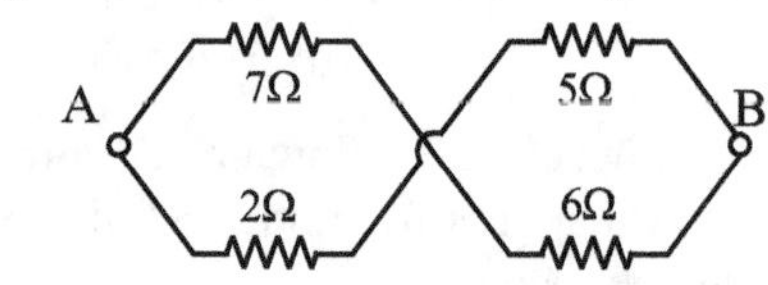

(a) 4Ω (b) $4.5\ \Omega$
(c) $2\ \Omega$ (d) $20\ \Omega$

64. Three resistances 4Ω each of are connected in the form of an equilateral triangle. The effective resistance between two corners is
(a) 8Ω (b) 12Ω
(c) 3/8 Ω (d) 8/3 Ω

65. Two wires of same metal have the same length but their cross-sections area in the ratio 3 : 1. They are joined in series. The resistance of the thicker wire is 10Ω. The total resistance of the combination will be
(a) 40 Ω (b) 40/3 Ω
(c) 5/2 Ω (d) 100 Ω

66. A certain piece of silver of given mass is to be made like a wire. Which of the following combination of length (L) and the area of cross-sectional (A) will lead to the smallest resistance
(a) L and A
(b) 2L and A/2
(c) L/2 and 2A
(d) Any of the above, because volume of silver remains same

67. A certain wire has a resistance R. The resistance of another wire identical with the first except having twice of its diameter is
(a) 2 R (b) 0.25 R
(c) 4 R (d) 0.5 R

68. What length of the wire of specific resistance 48×10^{-8} Ω-m is needed to make a resistance of 4.2 Ω (diameter of wire = 0.4 mm)
(a) 4.1 m (b) 3.1 m
(c) 2.1 m (d) 1.1 m

69. The resistance of an ideal voltmeter is
(a) zero (b) very low
(c) very large (d) Infinite

70. Masses of 3 wires of same metal are in the ratio 1 : 2 : 3 and their lengths are in the ratio 3 : 2 : 1. The electrical resistances are in ratio
(a) 1 : 4 : 9 (b) 9 : 4 : 1
(c) 1 : 2 : 3 (d) 27 : 6 : 1

71. We have two wires A and B of same mass and same material. The diameter of the wire A is half of that B. If the resistance of wire A is 24 ohm then the resistance of wire B will be
(a) 12 ohm (b) 3.0 ohm
(c) 1.5 ohm (d) None of the above

72. The electric resistance of a certain wire of iron is R. If its length and radius are both doubled, then
(a) The resistance will be doubled and the specific resistance will be halved
(b) The resistance will be halved and the specific resistance will remain unchanged
(c) The resistance will be halved and the specific resistance will be doubled
(d) The resistance and the specific resistance, will both remain unchanged

73. When a wire of uniform cross-section a, length ℓ and resistance R is bent into a complete circle, resistance between any two of diametrically opposite points will be
(a) $R/4$ (b) $R/8$
(c) $4R$ (d) $R/2$

74. A solenoid is at potential difference 60V and current flows through it is 15 ampere, then the resistance of coil will be
(a) 4 Ω (b) 8 Ω
(c) 0.25 Ω (d) 2 Ω

75. A strip of copper and another of germanium are cooled from room temperature to 80 K. The resistance of
(a) Each of these increases
(b) Each of these decreases
(c) Copper strip increases and that of germanium decreases
(d) Copper strip decreases and that of germanium increases

76. In the circuit shown in the figure, the current through

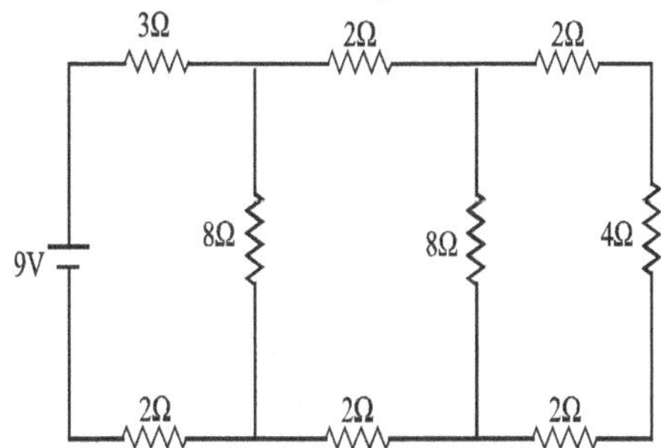

(a) the 3Ω resistor is 0.50A
(b) the 3Ω resistor is 0.25A
(c) the 4Ω resistor is 0.50A
(d) the 4Ω resistor is 0.25A

77. Two electric lamps each of 100 watts 220V are connected in series to a supply of 220 volts. The power consumed would be –
(a) 100 watts (b) 200 watts
(c) 25 watts (d) 50 watts

78. If it takes 8 minutes to boil a quantity of water electrically, how long will it take to boil the same quantity of water using the same heating coil but with the current doubled
(a) 32 minutes (b) 16 minutes
(c) 4 minutes (d) 2 minutes

79. An electric bulb is filled with
(a) hydrogen (b) oxygen and hydrogen
(c) ammonia (d) nitrogen and argon

80. When current is passed through an electric bulb, its filament glows, but the wire leading current to the bulb does not glow because
(a) less current flows in the leading wire as compared to that in the filament
(b) the leading wire has more resistance than the filament
(c) the leading wire has less resistance than the filament
(d) filament has coating of fluorescent material over it

81. Which of the following terms does not represent electrical power in a circuit?
(a) I^2R
(b) IR^2
(c) VI
(d) V^2/R

82. The power dissipated in the circuit shown in the figure is 30 watts. The value of R is
(a) $20\,\Omega$
(b) $15\,\Omega$
(c) $10\,\Omega$
(d) $30\,\Omega$

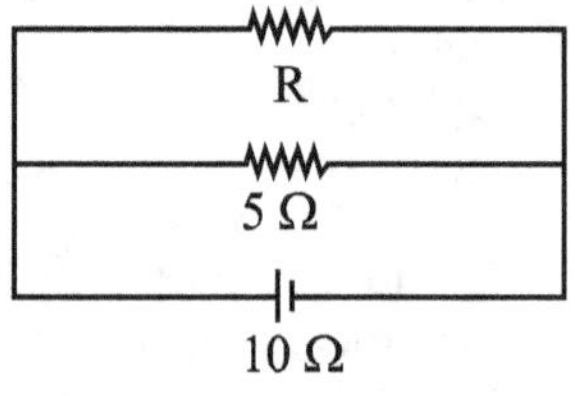

83. The filament of an electric bulb is of tungsten because
(a) Its resistance is negligible
(b) It is cheaper
(c) Its melting point is high
(d) Filament is easily made

84. When the current passes through the filament, it gets heated to incandescence and give light while the connecting wires are not heated because
(a) The connecting wires are good conductor of heat while the filament is bad conductor
(b) The connecting wires are of low resistance while the filament is of high resistance
(c) The density of connecting wires is less than that of the filament
(d) The connecting wires are bad conductor of heat while the filament is good conductor

85. Which one of the following heater element is used in electric press
(a) copper wire
(b) nichrome wire
(c) lead wire
(d) iron wire

86. What should be the characteristic of fuse wire?
(a) High melting point, high specific resistance
(b) Low melting point, low specific resistance
(c) High melting point, low specific resistance
(d) Low melting point, high specific resistance

87. The heating element of an electric heater should be made with a material, which should have
(a) high specific resistance and high melting point
(b) high specific resistance and low melting point
(c) low specific resistance and low melting point
(d) low specific resistance and high melting point

88. Resistance of conductor is doubled keeping the potential difference across it constant. The rate of generation of heat will
(a) become one fourth
(b) be halved
(c) be doubled
(d) become four times

89. A current I passes through a wire of length l, radius r and resistivity ρ. The rate of heat generated is
(a) $\dfrac{I^2\rho\ell}{r}$
(b) $\dfrac{I^2\rho\ell}{\pi r^2}$
(c) $\dfrac{I^2\rho\ell}{\pi r}$
(d) none of these

90. The resistance R_1 and R_2 are joined in parallel and a current is passed so that the amount of heat liberated is H_1 and H_2 respectively. The ratio H_1/H_2 has the value
(a) R_2/R_1
(b) R_1/R_2
(c) R_1^2/R_2^2
(d) R_2^2/R_1^2

91. Power dissipated across the $8\,\Omega$ resistor in the circuit shown here is 2 watt. The power dissipated in watt units across the $3\,\Omega$ resistor is
(a) 1.0
(b) 0.5
(c) 3.0
(d) 2.0

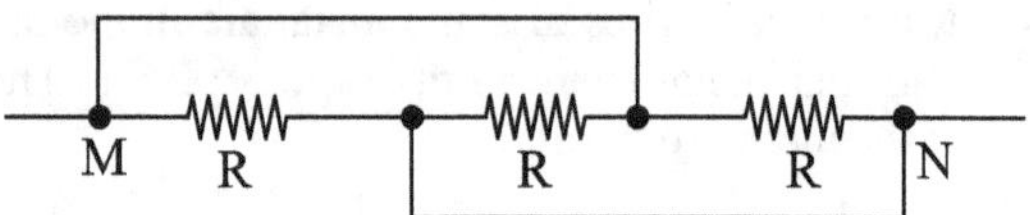

92. In house electrical circuits the fuse wire for safety should be of
(a) High resistance – high melting point
(b) Low resistance – high melting point
(c) Low resistance – low melting point
(d) High resistance – low melting point

93. What is the equivalent resistance of the following arrangement between M and N
(a) R/2
(b) R/3
(c) R/4
(d) R/6

94. If a wire of resistance $1\,\Omega$ is stretched to double its length, then resistance will be
(a) $\dfrac{1}{2}\,\Omega$
(b) $2\,\Omega$
(c) $\dfrac{1}{4}\,\Omega$
(d) $4\,\Omega$

95. Across a metallic conductor of non-uniform cross section a constant potential difference is applied. The quantity which remains constant along the conductor is :
(a) current
(b) drift velocity
(c) electric field
(d) current density

96. In the circuit diagram shown below, V_A and V_B are the potentials at points A and B respectively. Then, $V_A - V_B$ is

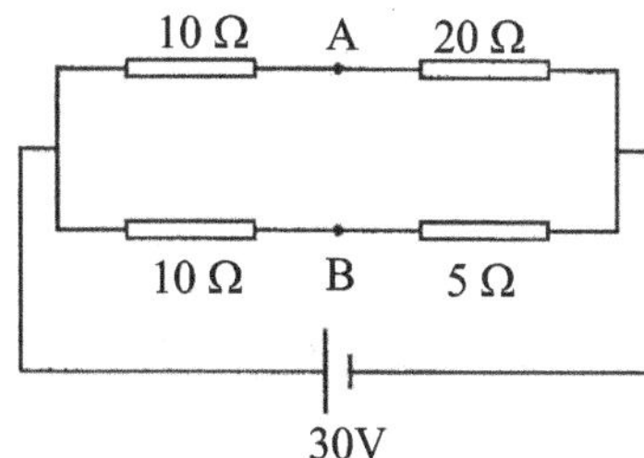

(a) −10 V   (b) −20 V

(c) 0 V   (d) 10 V

97. The diameter of a wire is reduced to one-fifth of its original value by stretching it. If its initial resistance is R, what would be its resistance after reduction of the diameter?

(a) $\dfrac{R}{625}$ (b) $\dfrac{R}{25}$

(c) 25 R   (d) 625 R

98. A heater coil is cut into two equal parts and only one part is used in the heater, the heat generated now will be

(a) doubled   (b) four times

(c) one fourth   (d) halved

99. The resistance of a wire is R. After melting it is remouled such that its area of cross section becomes n times its initial area of cross section. It new resistance will be

(a) nR   (b) $\dfrac{R}{n}$

(c) n^2R (d) $\dfrac{R}{n^2}$

100. The resistance of a wire is 'R' ohm. If it is melted and stretched to 'n' times its original length, its new resistance will be :

(a) $\dfrac{R}{n}$ (b) n^2R

(c) $\dfrac{R}{n^2}$ (d) nR

101. Three electric bulbs of rating 40 W – 200 V; 50 W – 200 V and 100 W – 200 V are connected in series to a 600 V supply. What is likely to happen as the supply is switched on?

(a) Only 50 W bulb will fuse

(b) Both 40 W and 50 W bulbs will fuse.

(c) All the three bulbs will emit light with their rated powers.

(d) 100 W bulb will emit light of maximum intensity.

102. In the circuit given, the ratio of work done by the battery to maintain the current between point A and B to the work done for the whole circuit is

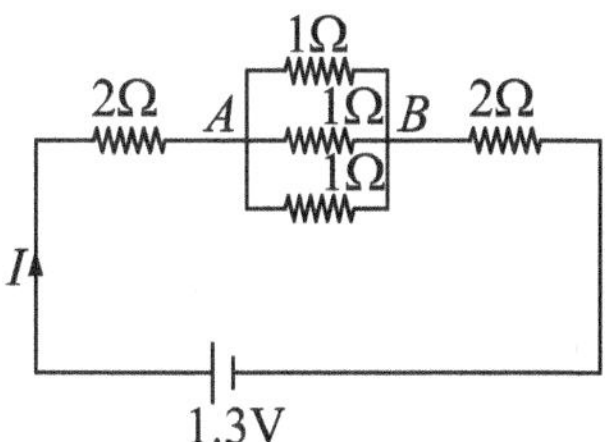

(a) $\dfrac{1}{117}$ (b) $\dfrac{1}{13}$

(c) $\dfrac{1}{12}$ (d) 1

103. What is the current supplied by the battery in the circuit shown below? Each resistance used in circuit is of 1 kΩ and potential difference V_{AB}= 8V

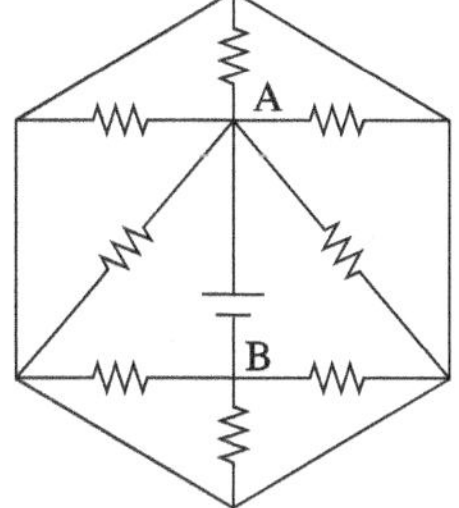

(a) 64 mA

(b) 15 mA

(c) 9.87 mA

(d) 1 mA

104. A wire of resistance R is bent to form a square ABCD as shown in the figure. The effective resistance between E and C is: (E is mid-point of arm CD)

(a) R   (b) $\dfrac{7}{64}R$

(c) $\dfrac{3}{4}R$ (d) $\dfrac{1}{16}R$

105. Which of the following acts as a circuit protection device?

(a) conductor   (b) inductor

(c) switch   (d) fuse

106. If the ammeter in the given circuit reads 2 A, What is the value of resistence R (the resistance of ammeter is negligible).

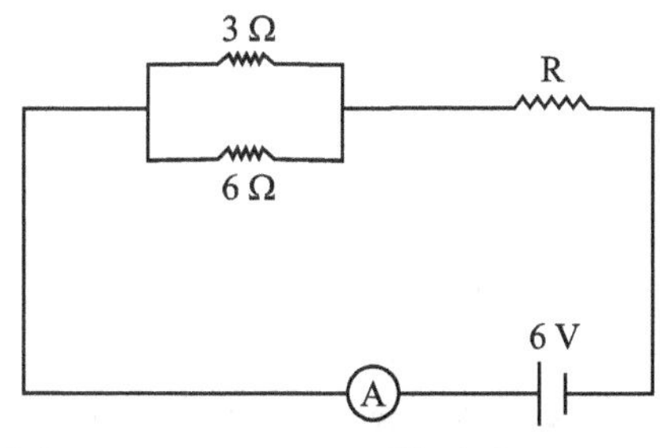

(a) 1 Ω   (b) 2 Ω

(c) 3 Ω   (d) 4 Ω

107. A circuit to verify Ohm's law uses ammeter and voltmeter in series or parallel connected correctly to the resistor. In the circuit :
   (a) ammeter is always used in parallel and voltmeter is series
   (b) Both ammeter and voltmeter must be connected in parallel
   (c) ammeter is always connected in series and voltmeter in parallel
   (d) Both, ammeter and voltmeter must be connected in series

108. An electric bulb is rated 220V and 100W. When it is operated on 110V, the power consumed will be
   (a) 100W   (b) 75W
   (c) 50W   (d) 25W

109. From a power station, the power is transmitted at a very high voltage because –
   (a) it is generated only at high voltage
   (b) it is cheaper to produce electricity at high voltage
   (c) electricity at high voltage is less dangerous
   (d) there is less loss of energy in transmission at high voltage

110. Two electric bulbs rated P_1 watt V volts and P_2 watt V volts are connected in parallel and applied across V volts. The total power (in watts) will be
   (a) $P_1 + P_2$ (b) $\sqrt{P_1 P_2}$

   (c) $\dfrac{P_1 P_2}{P_1 + P_2}$ (d) $\dfrac{P_1 + P_2}{P_1 P_2}$

111. In the circuit, wire 1 is of negligible resistance. Then,

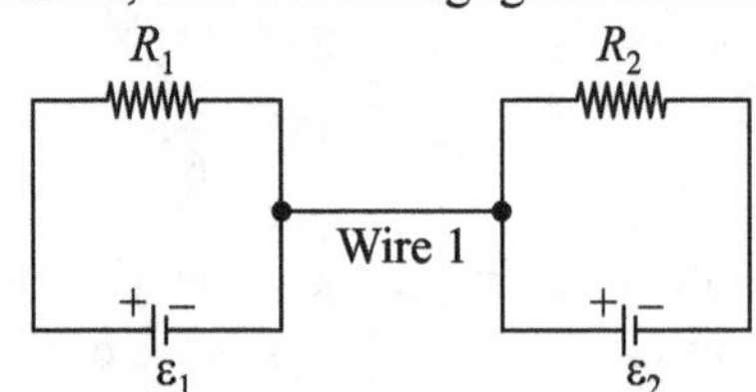

   (a) current will flow through wire 1, if $\varepsilon_1 \neq \varepsilon_2$

   (b) current will flow through wire 1, if $\dfrac{\varepsilon_1}{R_1} \neq \dfrac{\varepsilon_2}{R_2}$

   (c) current will flow through wire 1, if

   $$\dfrac{\varepsilon_1 + \varepsilon_2}{(R_1 + R_2)} \neq \dfrac{\varepsilon_1 - \varepsilon_2}{(R_1 - R_2)}$$

   (d) no current will flow through wire 1

112. In the circuit shown below, a student performing Ohm's law experiment accidently puts the voltmeter and the ammeter as shown in the circuit below. The reading in the voltmeter will be close to

   (a) 0 V
   (b) 4.8 V
   (c) 6.0 V
   (d) 1.2 V

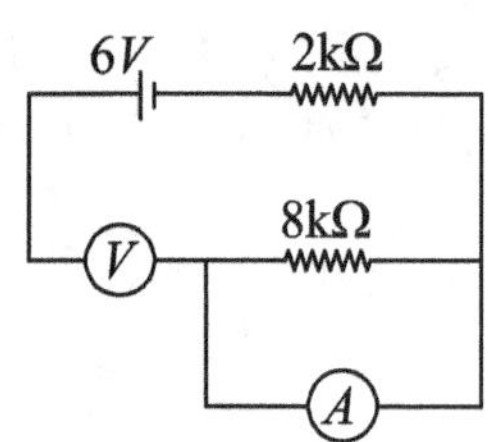

113. A student in a town in India, where the price per unit (1 unit = 1 kW-hr) of electricity is ₹5.00, purchases a 1 kVA UPS (uninterrupted power supply) battery. A day before the exam, 10 friends arrive to the student's home with their laptops and all connect their laptops to the UPS. Assume that each laptop has a constant power requirement of 90 W. Consider the following statements
   I   All the 10 laptops can be powered by the UPS if connected directly.
   II   All the 10 laptops can be powered if connected using an extension box with a 3A fuse.
   III   If all the 10 friends use the laptop for 5 hours, then the cost of the consumed electricity is about ₹22.50.

   Select the correct option with the true statements.
   (a) I only   (b) I and II only
   (c) I and III only   (d) II and III only

114. A copper wire is stretched to make it 0.5% longer. The percentage change in its electrical resistance if its volume remains unchanged is:
   (a) 2.0%   (b) 2.5%
   (c) 1.0%   (d) 0.5%

115. Six similar bulbs are connected as shown in the figure with a DC source of emf E, and zero internal resistance.

The ratio of power consumption by the bulbs when (i) all are glowing and (ii) in the situation when two from section A and one from section B are glowing, will be:

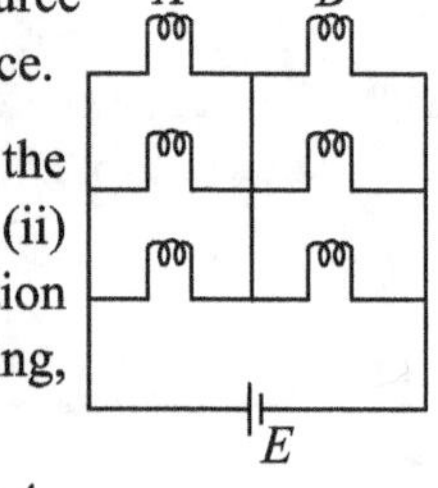

   (a) 4 : 9   (b) 9 : 4
   (c) 1 : 2   (d) 2 : 1

≫ Case/Passage Based Questions ≫≫≫

DIRECTIONS : *Study the given case/passage and answer the following questions.*

Case/Passage - 1

Two tungston lamps with resistances R_1 and R_2 respectively at full incandescence are connected first in parallel and then in series, in a lighting circuit of negaligible internal resistance. It is given that: $R_1 > R_2$.

116. Which lamp will glow more brightly when they are connected in parallel?

(a) Bulb having lower resistance

(b) Bulb having higher resistance

(c) Both the bulbs

(d) None of the two bulbs

117. If the lamp of resistance R_1 now burns out, how will the illumination produced change?

(a) Net illumination will increase

(b) Net illumination will decrease

(c) Net illumination will remain same

(d) Net illumination will reduced to zero

118. Which lamp will glow more brightly when they are connected in series?

(a) Bulb having lower resistance

(b) Bulb having higher resistance

(c) Both the bulbs

(d) None of the two bulbs

119. If the lamp of resistance R_2 now burns out and the lamp of resistance R_1 alone is plugged in, will the illumination increase or decrease?

(a) Illumination will remain same

(b) Illumination will increase

(c) Illumination will decrease

(d) None

120. Would physically bending a supply wire cause any change in the illumination?

(a) Illumination will remain same

(b) Illumination will increase

(c) Illumination will decrease

(d) It is not possible to predict from the given datas

Case/Passage - 2

The rate at which electric energy is dissipated or consumed in an electric circuit. This is termed as electric power,

$$P = IV, \text{According to Ohm's law } V = IR$$

We can express the power dissipated in the alternative forms

$$P = I^2 R = \frac{V^2}{R}$$

If 100W – 220V is written on the bulb then it means that the bulb will consume 100 joule in one second if used at the potential difference of 220 volts. The value of electricity consumed in houses is decided on the basis of the total electric energy used. Electric power tells us about the electric energy used per second not the total electric energy.

The total energy used in a circuit = power of the electric circuit × time.

121. Which of the following terms does not represent electrical power in a circuit?

(a) I^2R (b) IR^2

(c) VI   (d) V^2/R

122. An electric bulb is rated 220V and 100W. When it is operated on 110V, the power consumed will be–

(a) 100 W   (b) 75 W

(c) 50 W   (d) 25 W

123. Two conducting wires of the same material and of equal lengths and equal diameters are first connected in sereis and then in parallel in an electric circuit. The ratio of heat produced in series and in parallel combinations would be–

(a) 1 : 2   (b) 2 : 1

(c) 1 : 4   (d) 4 : 1

124. In an electrical circuit three incandescent bulbs. A, B and C of rating 40 W, 60 W and 100 W, respectively are connected in parallel to an electric source. Which of the following is likely to happen regarding their brightness?

(a) Brightness of all the bulbs will be the same

(b) Brightness of bulb A will be the maximum

(c) Brightness of bulb B will be more than that of A

(d) Brightness of bulb C will be less than that of B

125. In an electrical circuit, two resistors of 2Ω and 4Ω respectively are connected in series to a 6V battery. The heat dissipated by the 4Ω resistor in 5s will be

(a) 5 J   (b) 10 J

(c) 20 J   (d) 30 J

Case/Passage - 3

Answer the following questions based on the given circuit.

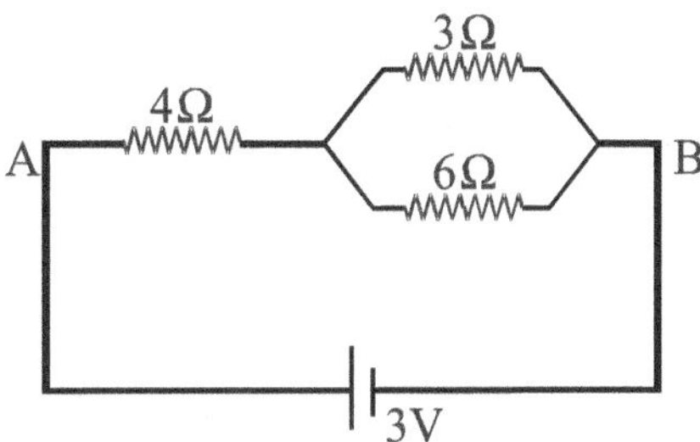

126. The potential drop across the 3Ω resistor is

(a) 1 V   (b) 1.5 V

(c) 2 V   (d) 3 V

127. The equivalent resistance between points A and B is

(a) 7Ω (b) 6Ω

(c) 13Ω (d) 5Ω

128. The current flowing through in the given circuit is

(a) 0.5 A   (b) 1.5 A

(c) 6 A   (d) 3 A

Case/Passage - 4

Answer the following questions based on the given circuit.

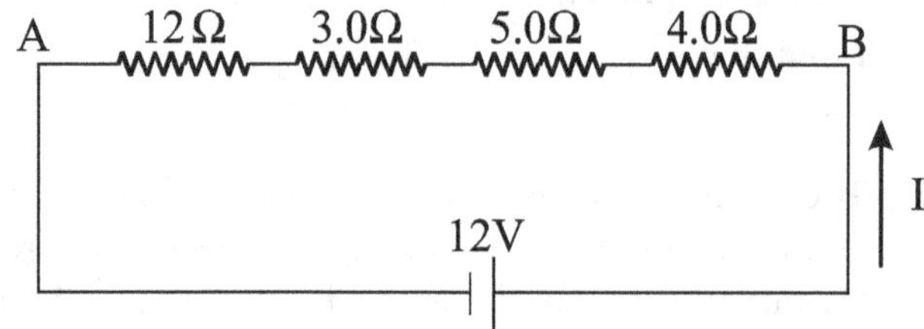

129. The equivalent resistance between points A and B, is

(a) 12 Ω   (b) 36 Ω

(c) 32 Ω   (d) 24 Ω

130. The current through each resistor is

(a) 1 A   (b) 2.3 A

(c) 0.5 A   (d) 0.75 A

131. The potential drop across the 12Ω resistor is

(a) 12 V   (b) 6 V

(c) 8 V   (d) 0.5 V

Case/Passage - 5

Answer the following questions based on the given circuit.

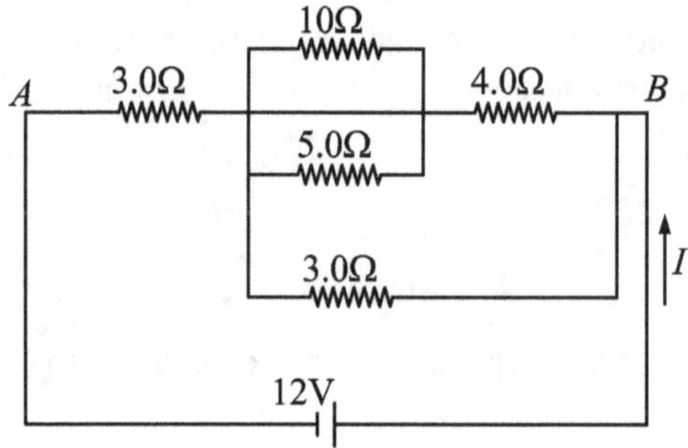

132. The equivalent resistance between points A and B

(a) 6.2 Ω   (b) 5.1 Ω

(c) 13.33 Ω   (d) 1.33 Ω

133. The current through the battery is

(a) 2.33 A   (b) 3.12 A

(c) 4.16 A   (d) 5.19 A

134. The current through the 4.0 ohm resistor is

(a) 5.6 A   (b) 0.98 A

(c) 0.35 A   (d) 0.68 A

Case/Passage - 6

Answer the following questions based on the given circuit.

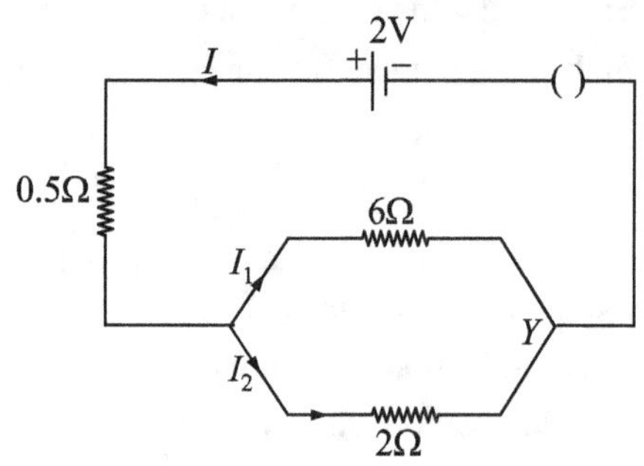

135. The total resistance of the circuit is

(a) 2 Ω   (b) 4 Ω

(c) 1.5 Ω   (d) 0.5 Ω

136. The current flowing through 0.5Ω resistor is

(a) 1 A   (b) 1.5 A

(c) 3 A   (d) 2.5 A

137. The current flowing through 6Ω resistor is

(a) 0.50 A   (b) 0.75 A

(c) 0.80 A   (d) 0.25

≫ Assertion & Reason   ≫≫

DIRECTIONS : *Each of these questions contains an assertion followed by reason. Read them carefully and answer the question on the basis of following options. You have to select the one that best describes the two statements.*

(a) If both **Assertion** and **Reason** are **correct** and Reason is the **correct explanation** of Assertion.

(b) If both **Assertion** and **Reason** are correct, but Reason is **not the correct explanation** of Assertion.

(c) If **Assertion** is **correct** but **Reason** is **incorrect**.

(d) If **Assertion** is **incorrect** but **Reason** is **correct**.

138. Assertion : Fuse wire must have high resistance and low melting point.

Reason : Fuse is used for very small current flow only.

139. Assertion : Alloys are commonly used in electrical heating devices like electric iron and heater.

Reason : Resistivity of an alloy is generally higher than that of its constituent metals but the alloys have low melting points than their constituent metals.

140. Assertion : In a simple battery circuit, the point of lowest potential is negative terminal of the battery.

Reason : The current flows towards the point of higher potential as it flows in such a circuit from the negative to positive terminal.

141. **Assertion :** The equation $V = Ri$ can be applied to those conducting devices which do not obey Ohm's law.

Reason : V = Ri is a statement of Ohm's law.

142. **Assertion :** All electric devices shown in the circuit are ideal. The reading of each of ammeter (A) and voltmeter (V) is zero.

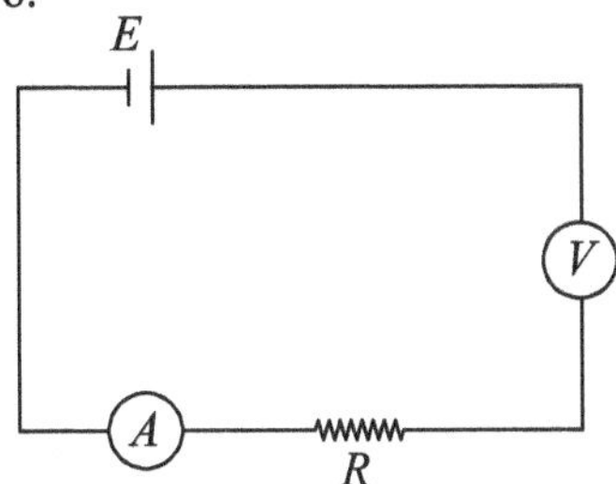

Reason : An ideal voltmeter draws almost no current due to very large resistance, and hence (A) will read zero.

143. **Assertion :** If ρ_1 and ρ_2 be the resistivities of the materials of two resistors of resistances R_1 and R_2 respectively and $R_1 > R_2$, then $\rho_1 > \rho_2$.

Reason : The resistance $R = \rho\dfrac{\ell}{A} \Rightarrow \rho_1 > \rho_2$ if $R_1 > R_2$

144. **Assertion :** Insulators do not allow flow of current through themselves.
Reason : They have no free-charge carriers.

145. **Assertion :** Positive charge inside the cell always goes from positive terminal to the negative terminal.
Reason : Positive charge inside the cell may go from negative terminal to the positive terminal.

146. **Assertion :** Wire A is thin in comparison to wire B of same material and same length then resistance of wire A is greater than resistance of wire B.
Reason : Resistivity of wire A is greater than resistivity of wire B.

147. **Assertion :** Resistivity of material may change with temperature.
Reason : Resistivity is a material property & independent on temperature.

148. **Assertion :** When current through a bulb decreases by 0.5%, the glow of bulb decreases by 1%.
Reason : Glow (Power) which is directly proportional to square of current.

149. **Assertion :** Long distance power transmission is done at high voltage.
Reason : At high voltage supply power losses are less.

150. **Assertion :** Resistance of 50W bulb is greater than that of 100 W.
Reason : Resistance of bulb is inversely proportional to rated power.

151. **Assertion :** A resistor of resistance R is connected to an ideal battery. If the value of R is decreased, the power dissipated in the circuit will increase.

Reason : The power dissipated in the circuit is directly proportional to the resistance of the circuit.

DIRECTIONS : *Each question contains statements given in two columns which have to be matched. Statements (A, B, C, D) in column I have to be matched with statements (p, q, r, s) in column II.*

152.

Column I		Column II
(A) Ohm	(p)	$\dfrac{\rho L}{A}$
(B) Resistance	(q)	$\dfrac{1 \text{ volt}}{1 \text{ ampere}}$
(C) Resistivity	(r)	zero resistance
(D) Super conductor	(s)	ohm-meter

153. Column II gives name of material use for device given in column I

Column I	Column II
(A) Resistance of resistance box	(p) tungsten
(B) Fuse wire	(q) maganin
(C) Bulb	(r) tin-lead alloy
(D) Insulator	(s) glass

DIRECTIONS : *Complete the following statements with an appropriate word / term to be filled in the blank space(s).*

154. The rate of flow of electric charge is called ....

155. If there is no current, a voltmeter connected across a resistor will register.................... voltage.

156. Combined resistance is the sum of separate resistances provided that the various conductors are connected in ....

157. In a parallel circuit, each circuit element has the same ....

158. Copper is a preferred material for making wire because of its low........................

159. The S.I. unit of electric current is ....

160. .... is a property that resists the flow of electrons in a conductor.

161. The S.I. unit of resistance is ....

162. The potential difference across the ends of a resistor is .... to the current through it, provided its .... remains the same.

163. The resistance of a conductor depends directly on its ...., inversely on its ...., and also directly proportioned on the .... of the conductor.

164. 1 volt × 1 coulomb = ...

165. Potential difference is a .... quantity.

166. The resistance of a semiconductor .... with increase in temp.

167. The S.I. unit of resistivity is ....

168. Physical quantity represented by coulomb per second is ....

169. Two resistances of 2 Ω each are connected in parallel. The equivalent resistance is ....

170. The resistance of a wire is .... proportional to the square of its radius.

171. Kilowatt is the unit of electrical .... but kilowatt-hour is the unit of electrical ....

172. Energy spent in kilowatt-hour

$$\frac{\text{volt} \times .... \times ....}{1000}$$

173. A fuse is a short piece of wire of high .... and low ....

174. Fuse wire has a .... melting point and is made of an alloy of ....and .... If the current in a circuit rises too high, the fuse wire ....

175. A fuse is connected in .... to the .... wire.

176. Electric energy is produced by the .... of charges.

177. Energy converted per unit charge is measured with an instrument called a ....

178. The electrical energy dissipated in a resistor is given by $W = ...$

179. The unit of power is ....

180. One watt of power is consumed when 1 A of current flows at a potential difference of ....

181. 1 kW h = ...

182. The alloy which is used for making the filament of bulbs is ....

183. Power transmission is carried out at high........................ and low ....

184. Rate at which electric work is done is called ....

DIRECTIONS : *Read the following statements and write your answer as true or false.*

185. The quantity of charge flowing through a point multiplied by time is a current.

186. The resistivity of all pure metals increases with the rise in temperature.

187. Ohm's law is a relation between the power used in a circuit to the current and the potential difference.

188. Direction of current is taken opposite to the direction of flow of electrons.

189. The equivalent resistance of several resistors in series is equal to the sum of their individual resistances.

190. In parallel combination, the reciprocal of equivalent resistance is the sum of the reciprocal of individual resistance.

191. The series arrangement is used for domestic circuits.

192. The reciprocal of resistance is called specific resistance.

193. Resistivity is measured in ohm-metre.

194. The resistance of a wire is directly proportional to length.

195. The resistance of a wire is directly proportional to area.

196. The resistivity of alloys decreases with the rise in temp.

197. The filament resistance of glowing bulb is greater, to its resistance when it is not glowing.

198. The commercial unit of electrical energy is kilowatt-hour (kWh).

199. Pure tungsten has high resistivity and a high melting point (nearly 3000°C).

200. When a metallic conductor is heated the atoms in the metal vibrate with greater amplitude and frequency.

201. One kilowatt is equal to 10 horse power.

202. Fuse is a thin wire which melts and breaks the electric circuit due to only high voltage.

ANSWER KEY & SOLUTIONS

1. **(a)** $Q = 150$ C, $t = 60$ sec so, $I = \dfrac{Q}{t} = \dfrac{150}{60} = 2.5\,A$

2. **(a)** $V = IR \Rightarrow I = \dfrac{V}{R} = \dfrac{1.5V}{30\Omega} = 0.05\,A$

3. **(a)** $Q = I \times t \Rightarrow Q = 10\,A \times (2 \times 60\ \text{sec}) = 1200$ C

4. **(a)** Charge on one electron $e = -1.6 \times 10^{-19}$ C

So, number of electrons flown

$$n = \dfrac{Q}{e} = \dfrac{10 \times 2 \times 60}{1.6 \times 10^{-19}} = 75 \times 10^{20}$$

5. **(a)** $R = \rho \dfrac{l}{A} \Rightarrow \rho = R\dfrac{A}{l} = 0.000115\,\Omega\,m$

6. **(a)**   **7.** (a)   **8.** (b)

9. **(c)** $R_{\text{equivalent}} = \dfrac{(5+6)}{2} = \dfrac{11}{2}\Omega$

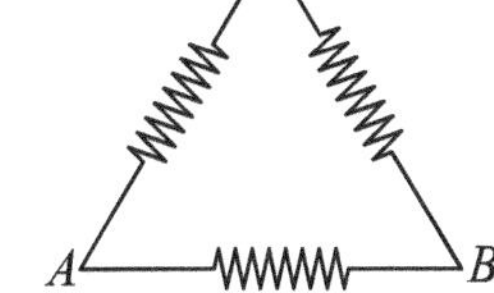

64. **(d)** $R_{AB} = \dfrac{(4+4) \times 4}{4+4+4} = \dfrac{8}{3}\Omega$

65. **(a)** Same metal means same specific resistance

$$\dfrac{R_1}{R_2} = \dfrac{A_2}{A_1} = \dfrac{1}{3} \quad \Rightarrow \quad R_2 = 3R_1 = 3 \times 10 = 30\ \Omega$$

$$R = R_1 + R_2 = 40\ \Omega$$

66. **(c)** $R \propto \dfrac{\ell}{A}$. Hence minimum for option (c)

67. **(b)** $R \propto \dfrac{1}{A} \propto \dfrac{1}{r^2}$. Hence $\dfrac{1}{4}^{\text{th}}$

68. **(d)** $R = \dfrac{\rho\ell}{A}$; $\ell = \dfrac{RA}{\rho} = \dfrac{4.2 \times \pi \left(\dfrac{0.4}{2} \times 10^{-3}\right)^2}{4.8 \times 10^{-8}} = 1.1m$

69. **(c)** Ideal voltmeter should not draw any current flow source hence its resistance $= \infty$.

Practically infinite resistance is not possible, but ideal voltmeter is possible with the help of potentiometer that you will learn in higher classes.

10. **(a)** To get the maximum resistance, all four resistors should be connected in series,

$$\therefore R = \dfrac{1}{2}\Omega + \dfrac{1}{2}\Omega + \dfrac{1}{2}\Omega + \dfrac{1}{2}\Omega = 2\Omega$$

70. **(d)** $R = \dfrac{\rho\ell}{A} = \dfrac{d\rho\ell^2}{m}$; $R \propto \dfrac{\ell^2}{m}$

$$\left[V = A\ell, d = \dfrac{m}{V} = \dfrac{m}{A\ell} \Rightarrow A = \dfrac{m}{d\ell}\right]$$

$$R_1 : R_2 : R_3 \equiv \dfrac{9}{1} : \dfrac{4}{2} : \dfrac{1}{3} \equiv 9 : 2 : \dfrac{1}{3} = 27 : 6 : 1$$

11. (a)	**12.** (a)	**13.** (c)	**14.** (c)
15. (d)	**16.** (c)	**17.** (c)	**18.** (d)
19. (d)	**20.** (b)	**21.** (d)	**22.** (c)
23. (b)	**24.** (d)	**25.** (b)	**26.** (d)
27. (b)	**28.** (c)	**29.** (c)	**30.** (b)
31. (c)	**32.** (c)	**33.** (b)	**34.** (a)
35. (c)	**36.** (b)	**37.** (b)	**38.** (b)
39. (b)	**40.** (a)	**41.** (c)	**42.** (d)
43. (c)	**44.** (c)	**45.** (b)	**46.** (d)
47. (a)	**48.** (a)	**49.** (c)	**50.** (a)
51. (b)	**52.** (d)	**53.** (b)	**54.** (d)
55. (b)	**56.** (d)	**57.** (b)	**58.** (d)
59. (b)	**60.** (b)	**61.** (b)	**62.** (b)
63. (b)			

71. **(c)** Same material $\rightarrow$ same density, specific resistance as they are material property.

$$R = \dfrac{\rho\ell}{A} = \dfrac{\rho V}{A^2} = \dfrac{\rho m}{dA^2}$$

$$R \propto \dfrac{1}{A^2} \propto \dfrac{1}{r^4}$$

$$\dfrac{R_A}{R_B} = \dfrac{r_B^4}{r_A^4} = 2^4 = 16 \Rightarrow R_B = \dfrac{24}{16} = 1.5\Omega$$

72. **(b)** $R = \dfrac{\rho\ell}{A} = \dfrac{\rho\ell}{\pi r^2}$

$$R' = \dfrac{\rho 2\ell}{\pi(2r)^2} = \dfrac{R}{4}$$

Specific resistance will remain same as it is a material property but remember it depends on temperature.

73. (a) Two resistance ($R/2$) will be in parallel, hence

$R_{eq} = R/4$

74. (a) $V = i \times R$; $R = 60/15 = 4\ \Omega$

75. (d) Copper is a conductor while germanium is a semi-conductor. Resistance of temperature decreases with temperature while that of semi-conductor increases hence resistance of copper strip decreases and that of germanium increases.

76. (d) 2Ω, 4Ω, 2Ω on right side are in series resultant parallel to 8Ω then in series with 2Ω, 2Ω then in parallel with 8Ω, then in series with 3Ω, 2Ω. Thus, $R_{eq} = 9$ ohm.

$i = 9/9 = 1$ amp flow from battery.

Passing through 3Ω it will divide into equal parts (1/2 amp) in 8Ω (near to cell) and remaining section then again divide into equal parts (1/4 amp) in 8Ω (middle one) and remaining section hence 1/4 amp. passes through 4Ω.

77. (d)   **78. (d)**   **79. (d)**

80. (c)   **81. (b)**   **82. (c)**   **83. (c)**

84. (b)   **85. (a)**

86. (d) Fuse wire should be such that it melts immediatley when strong current flows through the circuit. The same is possible if its melting point is low and resistivity is high.

87. (a) A heating wire should be such that it produces more heat when current is passed through it and also does not melt. It will be so if it has high specific resistance and high melting point.

88. (b) The rate of generation of heat, for a given potential difference is, $P = V^2 / R$

89. (b) The rate of heat generation

$= I^2 R = I^2 (\rho \ell / \rho r^2)$.

90. (a) Heat produced, $H = V^2\, t\, /R$ i.e., $H \propto 1/R$

so $H_1/H_2 = R_2 / R_1$.

91. (c) Power $= V \cdot I = I^2 R$

$i_2 = \sqrt{\dfrac{\text{Power}}{R}} = \sqrt{\dfrac{2}{8}} = \sqrt{\dfrac{1}{4}} = \dfrac{1}{2}\,\text{A}$

Potential over $8\Omega = Ri_2 = 8 \times \dfrac{1}{2} = 4V$

This is the potential over parallel branch. So,

$i_1 = \dfrac{4}{4} = 1\,\text{A}$

Power of $3\Omega = i_1^2 R = 1 \times 1 \times 3 = 3\text{W}$

92. (d) In house electrical circuits the fuse wire for safety should be of high resistance and low melting point.

93. (b) An the three resistors are connected in parallel

$\dfrac{1}{R_{eq}} = \dfrac{1}{R} + \dfrac{1}{R} + \dfrac{1}{R} \Rightarrow \dfrac{1}{R_{eq}} = \dfrac{3}{R}\ R_{eq} = \dfrac{R}{3}$

94. (d) Resistance $(R) = \dfrac{\rho L}{A}$

Length is stretched to double

$L' = 2L$

Area $A' = \dfrac{A}{2}$ $\therefore R' = \dfrac{\rho \times 2L}{\dfrac{A}{2}}$

$R' = 4\dfrac{\rho L}{A} \Rightarrow R' = 4R$

$R = 1\Omega$ $\therefore$ New Resistance, $R' = 4\Omega$

95. (a) Here, metallic conductor can be considered as the combination of various conductors connected in series. And in series combination current remains same.

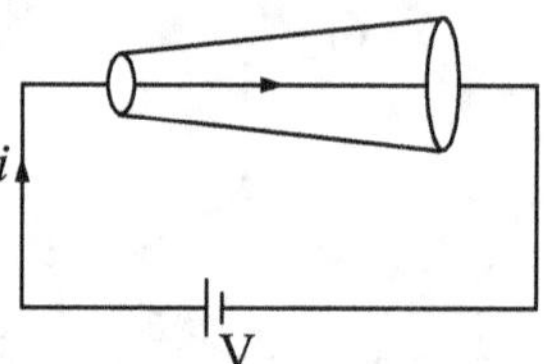

96. (d) $\because$ 10Ω and 20Ω are in series $= (10 + 20)\Omega = 30\Omega$ and 10Ω and 5Ω are in series $= (10 + 5)\Omega = 15\Omega$

$R_{eff} = \dfrac{30 \times 15}{15 + 30} = \dfrac{450}{45} = 10\Omega$

So the total current $I = \dfrac{V}{R} = \dfrac{30}{10} = 3$ Ampere

In branch CA current $= 1A$

In branch CB current $= 2A$

$\therefore V_C - V_A = 10$ Volt ....(i)

$\&\ V_C - V_B = 20$ Volt ....(ii)

Subtracting (i) from (ii), $V_A - V_B = 10$ volt.

97. (d) Let the Diameter of wire $= \dfrac{d}{5}$

Radius will be $= \dfrac{r}{5}$

Changed Area will be $= A = \pi r^2$

$= \pi \left(\dfrac{r}{5}\right)^2 = \dfrac{\pi r^2}{25} \Rightarrow A = \dfrac{\pi r^2}{25} \Rightarrow 25A = \pi r^2$

Hence stretched length will be = 25 l

Change resistance $(R) = \dfrac{\rho\,\ell}{A} = \dfrac{\rho(25\ell)}{A/25} = 625\,R$

98. (a) Resistance of the heater be R.

New resistance of heater is R/2

Initial power $= \dfrac{V^2}{R}$ Final power $= \dfrac{V^2}{R/2} = 2\dfrac{V^2}{R}$

$\therefore$ Heat generated is doubled.

99. (d) $R = \dfrac{\rho\ell}{A}$; New area $= nA$ $\therefore$ New length $= \dfrac{\ell}{n}$

$\Rightarrow$ $R' = \dfrac{\rho\ell}{n^2 A} = \dfrac{R}{n^2}$

100. (b) We know that, $R = \dfrac{\rho\ell}{A}$

or $R = \dfrac{\rho\ell^2}{\text{Volume}} \Rightarrow R \propto \ell^2$

According to question $\ell_2 = n\ell_1$

$\dfrac{R_2}{R_1} = \dfrac{n^2 l_1^2}{l_1^2}$

or, $\dfrac{R_2}{R_1} = n^2$

$\Rightarrow$ $R_2 = n^2 R_1$

101. (b) Resistance of 40 W – 200 V, 50 W – 200 V,

100 W – 200 V are respectively.

$R_{40} = \dfrac{V^2}{P_{40}} = \dfrac{200\times 200}{40} = 1000\ \Omega$

$R_{50} = 800\ \Omega$ and $R_{100} = 400\ \Omega$

$I = \dfrac{600}{1000+800+400} = \dfrac{600}{2200} = 0.2727\ \text{A}$

$I_{40} = \dfrac{P_1}{V} = \dfrac{40}{200} = 0.2\ \text{A}$

$I_{50} = \dfrac{P_2}{V} = \dfrac{50}{200} = \dfrac{5}{20} = 0.25\ \text{A}$

$I_{100} = \dfrac{P_3}{V} = \dfrac{100}{200} = 0.5\ \text{A}$

Clearly, 0.2 A & 0.25 A < 0.27 A hence both 40 W and 50 W bulbs will fuse.

102. (b) After simplifying the given circuit, we get,

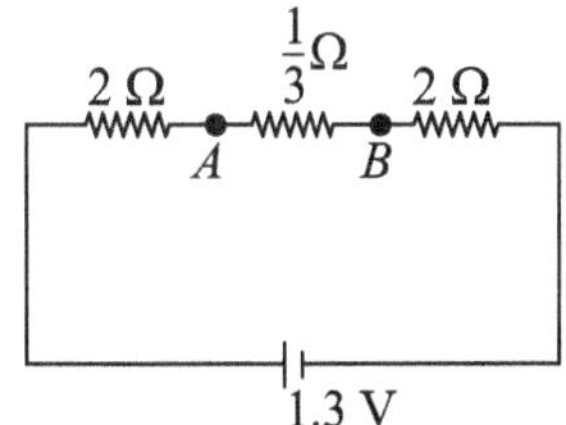

$R_{AB} = \dfrac{1}{3}\Omega$

Then equivalent resistance across the battery,

$R_{eq} = 2 + \dfrac{1}{3} + 2 = \dfrac{13}{3}\Omega$

So current in circuit, $I = \dfrac{V}{R_{eq}} \Rightarrow \dfrac{1.3}{13}\times 3$ amp

$I = \dfrac{3}{10}$ amp

Power dissipated across arm AB,

$P_{AB} = I^2 \times R_{AB} = \left(\dfrac{3}{10}\right)^2 \times \dfrac{1}{3}$

$P_{AB} = \dfrac{3}{100} = 0.03$ Watt

Total power dissipated in circuit,

$P_{ckt} = I^2 \times R_{eq} = \left(\dfrac{3}{10}\right)^2 \times \dfrac{13}{3}$

$P_{ckt} = \dfrac{39}{100} = 0.39$ watt

Ratio of power across A and B to total power = Ratio of work done across A and B to total circuit

$\because$ $W = P \times t$

So, $\dfrac{P_{AB}}{P_{ckt}} = \dfrac{W_{AB}}{W_{ckt}} = \dfrac{0.03}{0.39} = \dfrac{1}{13}$

103. (b) After simplifying the given circuit, we get

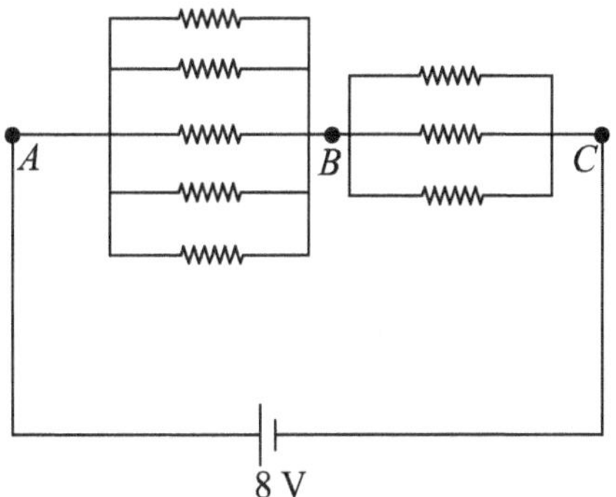

Resistance between arm AB, $R_{\text{net }AB} = \dfrac{1}{5}k\Omega = \dfrac{1000}{5}\Omega$

Resistance between arm BC, $R_{net\,BC} = \dfrac{1}{3}k\Omega = \dfrac{1000}{3}\Omega$

So, $R_{net} = R_{net\,AB} + R_{net\,BC}$

We get, $R_{net} = \dfrac{1000}{5} + \dfrac{1000}{3}$

$R_{net} = \dfrac{8000}{15}\Omega$

According to ohm's law, $V = IR$

$I = \dfrac{8 \times 15}{8000} = 15mA$

104. (b) Here $R_{DA} = R_{AB} = R_{BC} = R/4$

and $R_{DE} = R_{EC} = R/8$

Now $R_{ED}, R_{DA}, R_{AB}, R_{BC}$ are in series.

$\therefore R_s = \dfrac{R}{8} + \dfrac{R}{4} + \dfrac{R}{4} + \dfrac{R}{4} = \dfrac{R + 2R + 2R + 2R}{8} = \dfrac{7R}{8}$

$\therefore R_{eq} = \dfrac{\left(\dfrac{7R}{8}\right)\left(\dfrac{R}{8}\right)}{R} = \dfrac{7R}{64}$

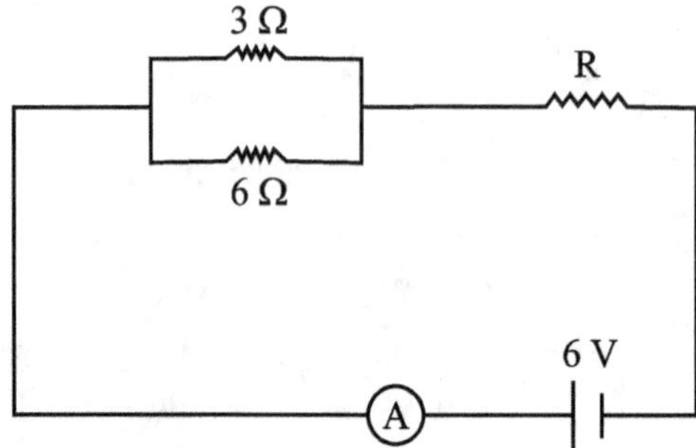

105. (d) Fuse is an safety device that operates to provide over current protection of an electrical circuit. A fuse is mainly a metal wire that melts when too much current flows through it due to low melting point and protects electric appliances.

106. (a) $I = 2\,A$

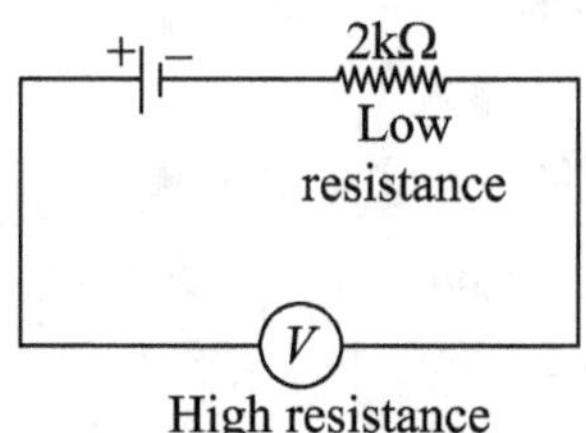

Two resistance are in parallel,

$\dfrac{1}{R_1} = \dfrac{1}{3} + \dfrac{1}{6} = \dfrac{2+1}{6} = \dfrac{3}{6} = \dfrac{1}{2}$

$\therefore R_1 = 2\Omega \qquad \text{...(i)}$

$R_{eq} = \dfrac{\text{Voltage}}{\text{Current}}$

$R_{eq} = \dfrac{6\,V}{2\,A} = 3\,\Omega \qquad \text{...(ii)}$

where unknown resistance R, from (i) and (ii)

$R = 3\,\Omega - 2\,\Omega$

$R = 1\,\Omega$

107. (c) **Ammeter :** In series connection, the same current flows through all the components. It aims at measuring the current flowing through the circuit and hence, it is connected in series.

Voltmeter : A voltmeter measures voltage change between two points in a circuit. So we have to place the voltmeter in parallel with the circuit component.

108. (d) **109. (d)**

110. (a) In parallel combination, total power $P = P_1 + P_2$

111. (d) Current leaving the cell must be equal to current going into the cell.

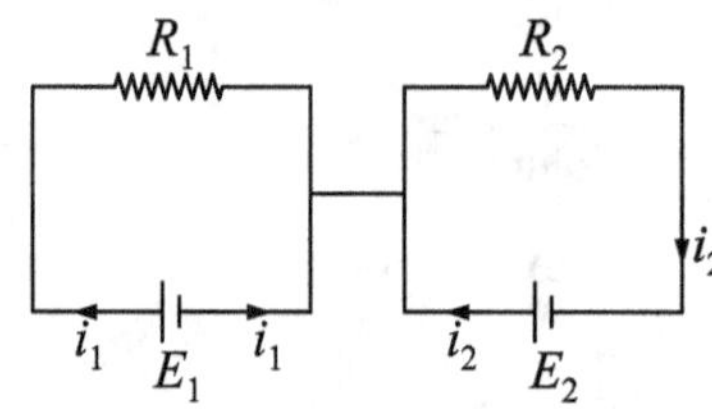

For any value of E or R current going from first loop to second loop must be zero.

Hence, there is no current through the wire 1.

112. (c) The resistance of ammeter is very low and resistance of voltmeter is very high. When ammeter is put in parallel to 8kΩ resistor, nearly whole of current goes through the ammeter.

The equivalent circuit is as follows

Hence, maximum potential drop occurs in the voltmeter.

So, reading of voltmeter is nearly 6 V.

113. (c) Power delivered by the UPS battery is 1kVA i.e. 1000 V.A = 1000W

When all the laptops connected directly to UPS then total power requirement

$90 \times 10 = 900W,$

So battery (UPS) can provide power to all laptops.

If all laptops are used for 5 hours, then cost of electricity consumed as the cost of electricity is ₹5.00 per unit.

$$= \frac{900 \times 5 \times 3600}{3.6 \times 10^6} \times 5 = 22.5$$

114. (c) Resistance, $R = \dfrac{\rho \ell}{A}$

$$R = \rho \frac{\ell}{A} \times \frac{\ell}{\ell} = \frac{\rho \ell^2}{V}$$

$[\because \quad \text{Volume (V)} = A\ell]$

Since resistivity and volume remains constant therefore % change in resistance

$$\frac{\Delta R}{R} = \frac{2\Delta \ell}{\ell} = 2 \times (0.5) = 1\%$$

115. (b) When all bulbs are glowing

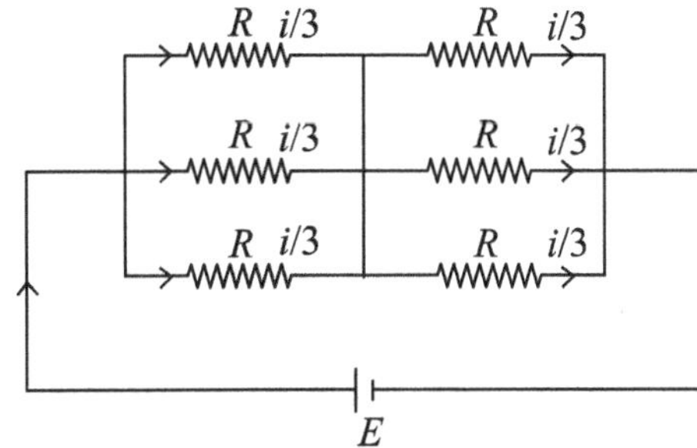

$$R_{eq} = \frac{R}{3} + \frac{R}{3} = \frac{2R}{3}$$

$$\text{Power } (P_i) = \frac{E^2}{R_{eq}} = \frac{3E^2}{2R} \qquad \ldots(i)$$

When two from section A and one from section B are glowing, then

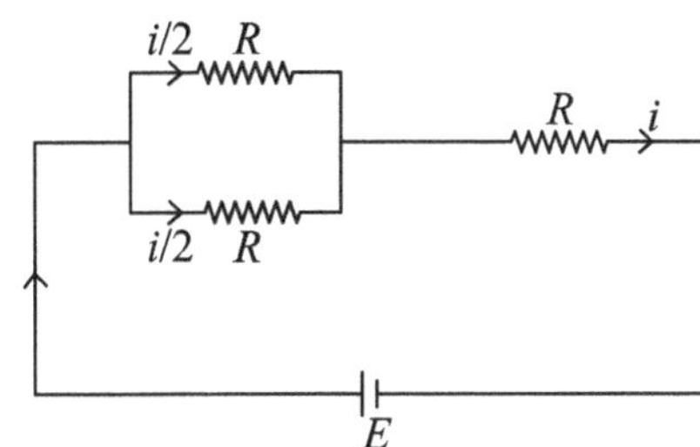

$$R_{eq} = \frac{R}{2} + R = \frac{3R}{2}$$

$$\text{Power } (P_f) = \frac{2E^2}{3R} \qquad \ldots(ii)$$

Dividing equation (i) by (ii) we get

$$\frac{P_i}{P_f} = \frac{3E^2}{2R} \frac{3R}{2E^2} = 9 : 4$$

116. (a) When the lamps are connected in parallel, then potential difference V across each lamp will be same and will be equal to potential necessary for full brightness of each bulb. Because illumination produced by a lamp is proportional to electric power consumed in it, and power consumed,

$$P_1 = \frac{V^2}{R_1} < \frac{V^2}{R_2} = P_2$$

Hence, illumination produced by 2nd bulb will be higher than produced by 1st bulb, i.e., bulb having lower resistance will shine more brightly.

117. (b) When R_1 burns out, then power is dissipated in R_2 only. Because internal resistance is quite low in lighting circuit, potential difference is still equal to V, hence, power dissipated in 2nd lamp, i.e.,

$$\frac{V^2}{R_2} < \left(\frac{V^2}{R_1} + \frac{V^2}{R_2} \right)$$

i.e., net power consumed initially. In other words, net illumination will now decrease.

118. (b) When two lamps are connected in series, the potential difference across each lamp will be different but current I flowing through each lamp will be same.

Hence, $P_1 = I^2 R_1 > I^2 R_2 = P_2$

i.e., illumination produced by 1st lamp will be higher as compared to that produced by 2nd lamp, i.e., lamp having higher resistance will glow more brightly.

119. (b) When lamp of resistance R_2 burns out and only lamp of resistance R_1 is connected in the circuit then current flowing the circuit will change. Let new current be I'. Because potential difference still remains same (due to low internal resistance), hence

$$I' R_1 = I (R_1 + R_2)$$

$$\text{or } I' = \frac{I(R_1 + R_2)}{R_1}$$

If P' is the power consumed, then

$$P' = I'^2 R_1 = I^2 \frac{(R_1 + R_2)(R_1 + R_2)}{R_1}$$

When both the lamps were present then total power consumed was given by:

$$P_S = P_1 + P_2 = I^2 (R_1 + R_2), \text{ i.e., } P' > P_S$$

i.e., illumination gets increased when only one bulb is used.

120. (a) If a water pipe is given bend at some points, then it definitely reduces the flow of water in the pipe but this is not true in case of an electric current flowing in a conductor because electric current is established in a conductor due to drift motion of electrons in it along the line of the potential gradient. Hence, illumination is not affected due to bending along the length of supply wires.

121. (b) $P = VI = V^2/R = I^2R$

122. (d) $P = \dfrac{V^2}{R} \Rightarrow R = \dfrac{V^2}{P} = \dfrac{220 \times 220}{100} = 484\ \Omega$

$$P = \dfrac{V^2}{R} = \dfrac{110 \times 110}{484} = 25W$$

123. (c) $R_S = R_1 + R_2 = R + R = 2R$

$$\dfrac{1}{R_P} = \dfrac{1}{R_1} + \dfrac{1}{R_2} = \dfrac{1}{R} + \dfrac{1}{R} = \dfrac{2}{R}$$

$$R_P = R/2$$

$$\dfrac{H_1}{H_2} = \dfrac{V^2}{R_S}\dfrac{R_P}{V^2} = \dfrac{R_P}{R_S} = \dfrac{R}{2 \times 2R} = \dfrac{1}{4} = 1:4.$$

124. (c) The bulb with the highest wattage glows with maximum brightness. Brightness of bulb B (100 W) is maximum.

Correct order of brightness will be,

Bulb of 100 W > Bulb of 60 W > Bulb of 40 W.

125. (c) Given, resistors, $R_1 = 2\Omega$ and $R_2 = 4\Omega$

Voltgage, $V = 6$ V

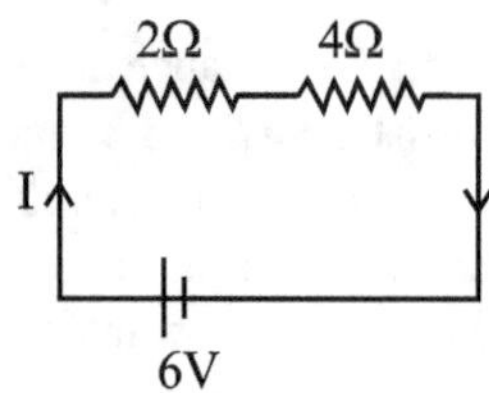

Equivalent Resistance,

$= R_1 + R_2 = 2 + 4 = 6\Omega$ [Series combination]

Current, $I = \dfrac{V}{R} = \dfrac{6}{6} = 1A.$

Heat dissipated in 4Ω Resistor

$= I^2Rt = 1 \times 4 \times 5 = 20$ J

$[\quad I = 1A, R = 4\Omega, t = 5\ \text{sec.}]$

126. (b) Equivalent resistance of 3Ω and 6Ω $= \dfrac{3 \times 6}{3+6} = 2\Omega$

as they are in parallel they have same p.d.

$$i = \dfrac{3}{6} = \dfrac{1}{2}$$

P.D. across $3\Omega = \dfrac{1}{2} \times 3 = 1.5$ volt

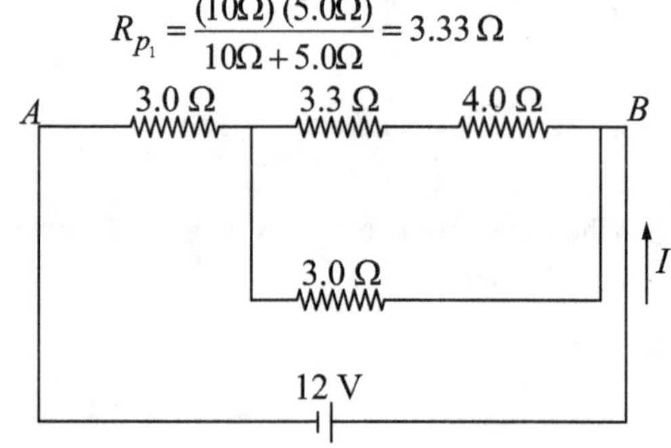

127. (b)   **128. (a)**

129. (d) Given : $R_1 = 12\Omega$, $R_2 = 3.0\Omega$, $R_3 = 5.0\Omega$, $R_4 = 4.0\Omega$, All four resistors are in series combination, so

$R_s = R_1 + R_2 + R_3 + R_4$

$= 12\Omega + 3.0\Omega + 5.0\Omega + 4.0\Omega = 24\Omega$

130. (c) The current through all resistors in series is the same

$$I = \dfrac{V}{R} = \dfrac{V}{R_s} = \dfrac{12V}{24\Omega} = 0.50\ A$$

131. (b) Potential drop across, 12Ω resistor

$V = IR = 12\Omega\ (0.5A)$

or $V = 6V$

132. (b) Here we have a variety of series-parallel combinations.

We follow the general procedures outlined in the text.

The 10 Ω and the 5.0 Ω are in parallel

$$R_{P_1} = \dfrac{(10\Omega)\ (5.0\Omega)}{10\Omega + 5.0\Omega} = 3.33\ \Omega$$

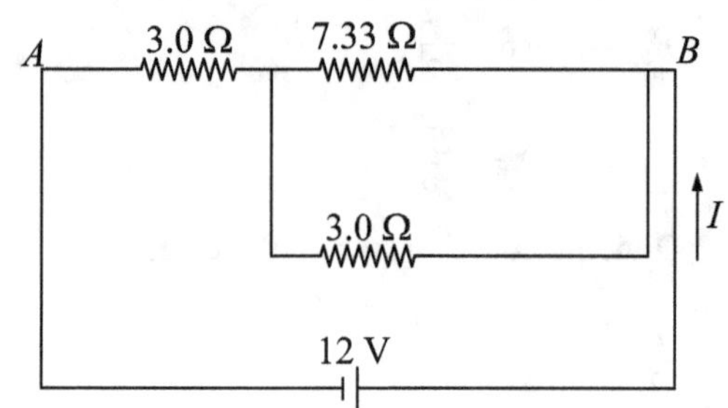

(i) The circuit reduces to figure (a)

Now the 3.33 Ω and the 4.0 Ω are in series.

$$R_{s_1} = 3.33\Omega + 4.0\Omega = 7.33\Omega$$

The circuit reduces to figure (ii)

(ii) The 7.33 Ω and the 3.0 Ω are in parallel.

$$R_{p_2} = \frac{(7.33\Omega)\,(3.0\Omega)}{7.33\Omega + 3.0\Omega} = 2.13\Omega$$

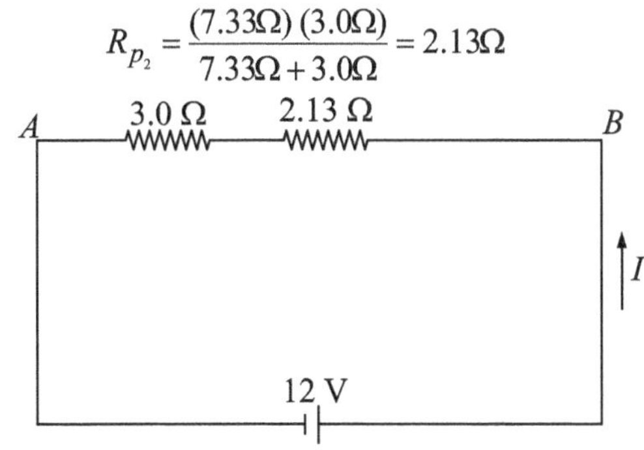

(iii) The circuit reduces to figure (iii).

Finally, the 2.13 Ω and the 3.0 Ω are in series.

$$R = R_{s_2} = 2.13\Omega + 3.0\Omega = 5.13\ \Omega = 5.1\Omega$$

(iv) The circuit reduces to figure (iv).

133. (a) From Ohm's law, $I = \dfrac{V}{R} = \dfrac{12V}{5.13\Omega} = 2.33A = 2.3A$

134. (d) To find the current through the 4.0 ohm resistor, we need to expand the combinations.

In figure (iii), the current through the 2.13 Ω and 3.0 Ω is the same as the total current, 2.33 A.

The voltage across the 2.13 Ω is then $V_{2.13}$ = (2.13 Ω) (2.33 A) = 4.96 V.

In figure (ii), the voltage across the 7.33 Ω and 3.0 Ω is the same as that across the 2.13 Ω, 4.96V.

So, the current through the 7.33 Ω is

$$I_{7.33} = \frac{4.96V}{7.33\Omega} = 0.677A$$

In figure (i), the current through the 3.33 Ω and the 4.0 Ω is the same as the current through the 7.33 Ω

Therefore, $I_{4.0} = 0.68$ A.

135. (a) E.m.f. of the battery = $2V$

Effective resistance of the parallel resistors is given by R_1.

$$\frac{1}{R_1} = \frac{1}{6} + \frac{1}{2} = \frac{1+3}{6} = \frac{4}{6} = \frac{2}{3} \quad \Rightarrow \quad R_1 = \frac{3}{2} = 1.5\Omega$$

Total resistance of the circuit, $R = 1.5 + 0.5 = 2\Omega$

136. (a) Main current $I = \dfrac{V}{R} = \dfrac{2}{2} = 1A$

Current flowing through 0.5Ω resistor = $1A$

137. (d) P.D. across the junctions :

$$V_1 = IR_1 = 1 \times 1.5 = 1.5V$$

Hence current I_1, flowing through 6Ω resistor

$$I_1 = \frac{V_1}{6} = \frac{1.5}{6} = 0.25\ A$$

138. (c)

139. (c) Alloys are used in electrical heating device because they have high resistivity or resistance as compared to pure metals and high melting point.

140. (c) It is clear that in a battery circuit, the point of lowest potential is the negative terminal of battery.

and current flows from higher potential to lower potential.

141. (c) It is common error to say that V = Ri is a statement of Ohm's law. The essence of Ohm's law is that the value of R is independent of the value of V. The equation $V = Ri$ is used for finding resistance of all conducting devices, whether they obey Ohm's law or not.

142. (d) (A) will read zero but (V) will read E

143. (d) ρ is the characteristic of the material of resistors. It does not depend on the length and cross-sectional area of resistors. But R depends on the length and the cross-sectional are of the resistor.

So, R_1 may be greater than R_2 even when $\rho_1 \le \rho_2$.

144. (a)   **145. (d)**

146. (c) Resistivity is a material property.

147. (c) $\rho = \rho_0(1 + \alpha\Delta T)$

148. (b) Glow = Power $(P) = I^2R$

$$\therefore \quad \frac{dP}{P} = 2\left(\frac{dI}{I}\right) = 2 \times 0.5 = 1\%$$

149. (a) Power loss = $i^2R = \left(\dfrac{P}{V}\right)^2 R$

$[P = \text{Transmitted power}]$

150. (b) $P = \dfrac{V^2}{R}$; $R \propto \dfrac{1}{P}$ (same rated voltage)

151. (c) Here, $P = \dfrac{E^2}{R}$, so $P \propto R$ only when I is constant.

Here I increases as R is decreased. Hence the reason is wrong.

152. (A) → (q); (B) → (p); (C) → (s); (D) → (r)

153. (A) → q; (B) → r; (C) → p; (D) → s

154. electric current

155. zero

156. series

157. potential difference

158. resistivity

159. ampere

160. Resistance

161. ohm (Ω)

162. directly proportional, temperature

163. length, area of cross-section, resistivity

164. joule

165. Scalar

166. decreases

167. ohm-meter

168. electric current

169. 1 Ω

170. inversely.

171. power, energy

172. ampere, hour

173. resistance, melting point

174. low, lead, tin, melts

175. series, live

176. separation

177. voltmeter

178. $V \times I \times t$

179. watt (W)

180. 1 V

181. 3,600,000 J

182. Tungsten

183. voltage, current

184. electric power

185. False

186. True

187. False

188. True

189. True

190. True

191. False

192. False

193. True

194. True

195. False

196. False

197. True

198. True

199. True

200. True

201. False

202. False

12 Magnetic Effects of Electric Current

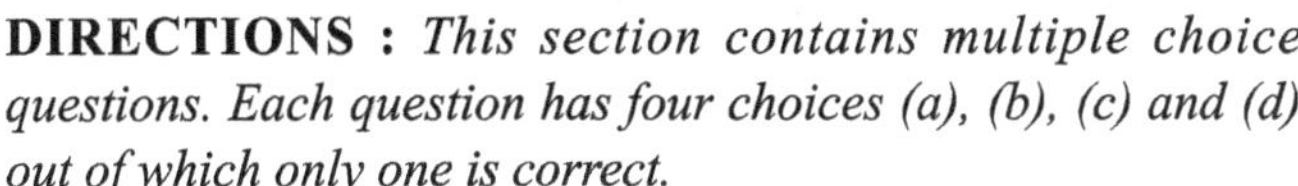

» Multiple Choice Questions (MCQs)

DIRECTIONS : *This section contains multiple choice questions. Each question has four choices (a), (b), (c) and (d) out of which only one is correct.*

1. A magnet attracts:
   (a) plastics   (b) carbon
   (c) aluminium   (d) iron and steel

2. A plotting compass is placed near the south pole of a bar magnet. The pointer of plotting compass will:
   (a) point away from the south pole
   (b) point parallel to the south pole
   (c) point towards the south pole
   (d) point at right angles to the south pole

3. Which of the following statements is incorrect regarding magnetic field lines?
   (a) The direction of magnetic field at a point is taken to be the direction in which the north pole of a magnetic compass needle points.
   (b) Magnetic field lines are closed curves
   (c) If magnetic field lines are parallel and equidistant, they represent zero field strength
   (d) Relative strength of magnetic field is shown by the degree of closeness of the field lines

4. The magnetic field lines in the middle of the current carrying solenoid are
   (a) circles
   (b) spirals
   (c) parallel to the axis of the tube
   (d) perpendicular to the axis of the tube

5. The front face of a circular wire carrying current behaves like a north pole, The direction of current in this face of the circular wire is:
   (a) clockwise   (b) downwards
   (c) anticlockwise   (d) upwards

6. The most suitable material for making the core of an electromagnet is:
   (a) soft iron   (b) brass
   (c) aluminium   (d) steel

7. In an electric motor, the direction of current in the coil changes once in each:
   (a) two rotations   (b) one rotation
   (c) half rotation   (d) one-fourth rotation

8. An electron beam enters a magnetic field at right angles to it as shown in the Figure.

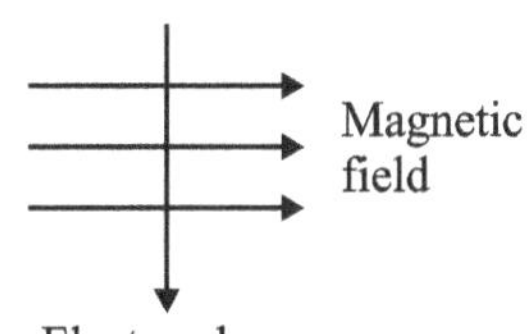

   The direction of force acting on the electron beam will be:
   (a) to the left   (b) to the right
   (c) into the page   (d) out of the page

9. The force experienced by a current-carrying conductor placed in a magnetic field is the largest when the angle between the conductor and the magnetic field is:
   (a) $45°$ (b) $60°$
   (c) $90°$ (d) $180°$

10. The force exerted on a current-carrying wire placed in a magnetic field is zero when the angle between the wire and the direction of magnetic field is:
    (a) $45°$ (b) $60°$
    (c) $90°$ (d) $180°$

11. A circular loop placed in a plane perpendicular to the plane of paper carries a current when the key is ON.

The current as seen from points A and B (in the plane of paper and on the axis of the coil) is anti clockwise and clockwise respectively. The magnetic field lines point from B to A. The N-pole of the resultant magnet is on the face close to

(a) A

(b) B

(c) A if the current is small, and B if the current is large

(d) B if the current is small and A if the current is large

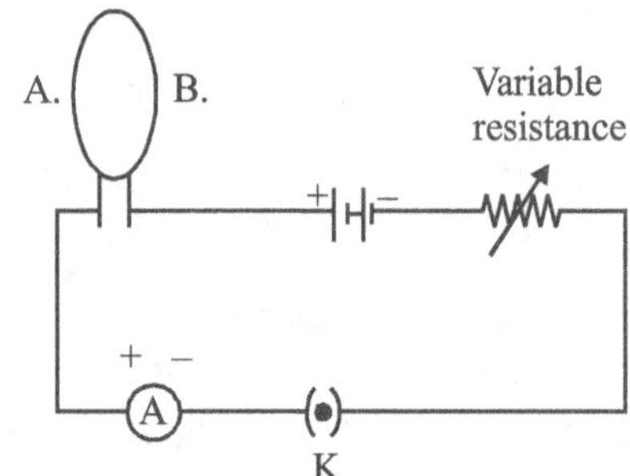

12. A small magnet is placed perpendicular to a uniform magnet field. The forces acting on the magnet will result in

(a) Rotational motion

(b) Translatory motion

(c) No motion at all

(d) Translational and rotational motion both

13. Which one of the following substances is the magnetic substances?

(a) Mercury   (b) Iron

(c) Gold   (d) Silver

14. Magnetic lines do not intersect on one-another because

(a) they are at a distance

(b) they are in the same direction

(c) they are parallel to another

(d) at the point of intersection there will be two direction of the magnetic force which is impossible

15. By removing the inducing magnet, the induced magnetism is

(a) Finished after some time

(b) Finished just after

(c) Not finished for a long time

(d) Not changed

16. A current carrying wire in the neighbour hood produces

(a) no field

(b) electric and magnetic fields

(c) electric field only

(d) magnetic field only

17. The magnetic lines of force, inside a current carrying solenoid, are

(a) along the axis and are parallel to each other

(b) perpendicular to the axis and equidistance from each other

(c) circular and they do not intersect each other

(d) circular at the ends but they are parallel to the axis inside the solenoid.

18. Which of the following determines the direction of magnetic field due to a current carrying conductor?

(a) Faraday's laws of electromagnetic induction

(b) Fleming's left-hand rule

(c) Lenz's rule

(d) Maxwell's cork screw rule

19. Along the direction of current carrying wire, the value of magnetic field is

(a) zero

(b) infinity

(c) depends on the length of the wire

(d) uncertain

20. The value of magnetic field due to a small element of current carrying conductor at a distance r and lying on the plane perpendicular to the element of conductor is

(a) zero

(b) maximum

(c) inversely proportional to the current

(d) none of the above

21. The value of intensity of magnetic field at a point due to a current carrying conductor depends

(a) Only on the value of current

(b) Only on a small part of length of conductor

(c) On angle between the line joining the given point to the mid point of small length and the distance between the small length and the given point

(d) On all of the above

22. The direction of magnetic lines of forces close to a straight conductor carrying current will be

(a) along the length of the conductor

(b) radially outward

(c) circular in a plane perpendicular to the conductor

(d) helical

23. When an electron beam is moving in a magnetic field, then the work done is equal to the

(a) charge of electron

(b) magnetic field

(c) product of electronic charge and the magnetic field

(d) zero

24. A current carrying loop lying in a magnetic field behaves like a.
(a) A magnetic dipole
(b) magnetic pole
(c) magnetic material
(d) non-magnetic material

25. Two identical coaxial circular loops carry a current i each circulating in the same direction. If the loops approach each other, you will observe that
(a) the current in each increases,
(b) the current in each decreases,
(c) the current in each remains the same,
(d) the current in one increases whereas that in the other decreases

26. An induced e.m.f. is produced when a magnet is plunged into a coil. The strength of the induced e.m.f. is independent of
(a) the strength of the magnet
(b) number of turns of coil
(c) the resistivity of the wire of the coil
(d) speed with which the magnet is moved

27. The laws of electromagnetic induction have been used in the construction of a
(a) galvanometer   (b) voltmeter
(c) electric motor   (d) generator

28. Direction of induced e.m.f. is determined by -
(a) Fleming's left hand rule
(b) Fleming's right hand rule
(c) Maxwell's rule
(d) Ampere's rule of swimming

29. The phenomenon of electromagnetic induction is –
(a) the process of charging a body.
(b) the process of generating magnetic field due to a current passing through a coil.
(c) producing induced current in a coil due to relative motion between a magnet and the coil.
(d) the process of rotating a coil of an electric motor.

30. The device used for producing electric current is called a
(a) generator   (b) galvanometer
(c) ammeter   (d) motor

31. In an electric motor, conversion takes place of
(a) Chemical energy into electrical energy
(b) Electrical energy into mechanical energy
(c) Electrical energy into light
(d) Electrical energy into chemical energy

32. The current in a generator armature is AC because
(a) the magnetic field reverses at intervals
(b) the current in the field coils is AC
(c) the rotation of the armature causes the field through it to reverse
(d) the commutator feeds current into it in opposite directions every half cycle

33. The current in the armature of a motor is reversed every half cycle due to the action of a(n)
(a) armature   (b) field coil
(c) brush   (d) commutator.

34. In an electric motor, the energy transformation is
(a) from electrical to chemical
(b) from chemical to light
(c) from mechanical to electrical
(d) from electrical to mechanical

35. The direction of induced current is obtained by
(a) Fleming's left hand rule
(b) Maxwell's cork-screw rule
(c) Ampere's rule
(d) Fleming's right hand rule

36. A metal sheet is placed in a variable magnetic field which is increasing from zero to maximum. Induced current flows in the directions as shown in figure. The direction of magnetic field will be -
(a) normal to the paper, inwards
(b) normal to the paper, outwards
(c) from east to west
(d) from north to south

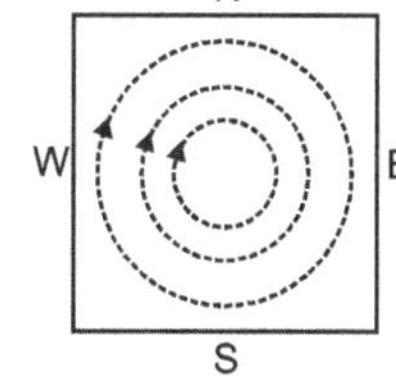

37. A magnet NS is placed along the axis of a circular coil. The magnet is moved away from the coil. The induced current in the coil is:
(a) Zero
(b) Clockwise
(c) Anti-clockwise
(d) None of these

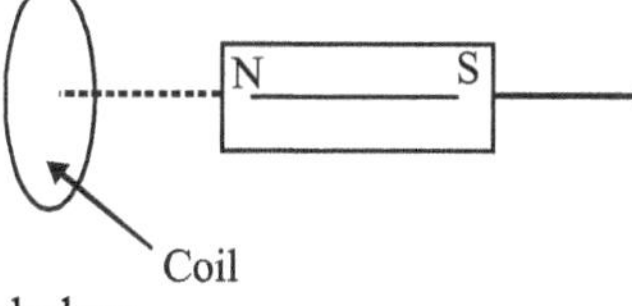

38. Four situations are given below-
I.   An infinitely long wire carrying current
II. A rectangular loop carrying current
III. A solenoid of finite length carrying current
IV. A circular loop carrying current.

In which of the above cases will the magnetic field produced be like that of a bar magnet?
(a) I   (b) I and III
(c) Only III   (d) Only IV

39. The similar magnets of steel are .... than the magnets of soft iron

    (a) stronger   (b) of equal strength

    (c) weaker   (d) none of the above

40. A bar of soft iron is placed flat on the table. A bar magnet is taken and its south pole is placed on one end of the bar of soft iron. The magnet is held almost vertically. The bar is stroked from one end to the other with magnet. On the other end of the bar, magnet is lifted and again placed on the first end and the bar is again stroked. The end of the bar where the magnet is lifted will be

    (a) south pole

    (b) no pole

    (c) south and north both type

    (d) north pole

41. When a bar magnet is broken into two pieces?

    (a) we will have a single pole on each piece

    (b) each piece will have two like poles

    (c) each piece will have two unlike poles

    (d) each piece will be lose magnetism

42. The permanent magnets are kept with soft iron pieces at ends as keepers

    (a) to magnetise the soft iron pieces

    (b) to increase the strength of the magnets

    (c) to avoid self demagnetisation

    (d) for physical safety of the magnets

43. Whenever the magnetic flux linked with a coil changes, an induced e.m.f. is produced in the circuit. The e.m.f. lasts

    (a) for a short time

    (b) for a long time

    (c) for ever

    (d) so long as the change in flux takes place

44. A magnet is moved towards a coil (i) quickly (ii) slowly, then the induced e.m.f. is

    (a) larger in case (i)

    (b) smaller in case (i)

    (c) equal in both the cases

    (d) larger or smaller depending upon the radius of the coil

45. The laws of electromagnetic induction have been used in the construction of a

    (a) galvanometer   (b) voltmeter

    (c) electric motor   (d) generator

46. The diagram below shows two circular loops of wire (A and B) centred on and perpendicular to the X-axis and oriented with their planes parallel to each other. The Y-axis passes vertically through loop A (dashed line). There is a current I_B in loop B as shown in the diagram. Possible actions which we might perform on loop A are

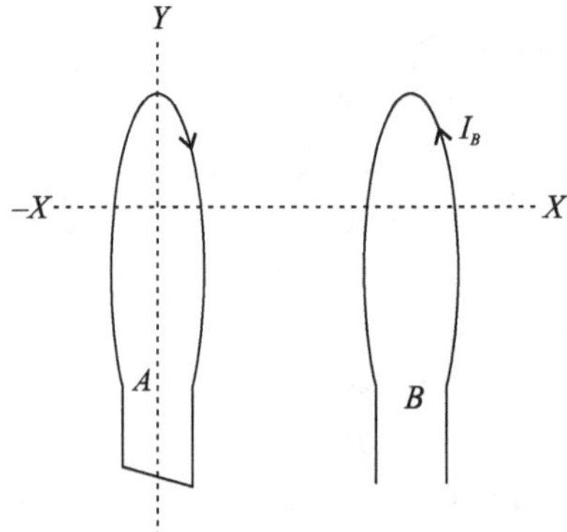

    (I) move A to the right along X-axis closer to B

    (II) move A to the left along X-axis away from B

    (III) as viewed from above, rotate A clockwise about Y-axis

    (IV) as viewed from above, rotate A anti-clockwise about y-axis

Which of the actions will induce a current in A only in the direction shown?

    (a) Only (I)   (b) Only (II)

    (c) Only (I) and (IV)   (d) Only (II) and (III)

47. An electron move with velocity v in a uniform magnetic field B. The magnetic force experienced by the electron is

    (a) Always zero

    (b) Never zero

    (c) Zero if v is perpendicular to B

    (d) Zero if v is parallel to B

DIRECTIONS : *Study the given case/passage and answer the following questions.*

Case/Passage - 1

A solenoid is a long helical coil of wire through which a current is run in order to create a magnetic field. The magnetic field of the solenoid is the superposition of the fields due to the current through each coil. It is nearly uniform inside the solenoid and close to zero outside and is similar to the field of a bar magnet having a north pole at one end and a south pole at the other depending upon the direction of current flow. The magnetic field produced in the solenoid is dependent on a few factors such as, the current in the coil, number of turns per unit length etc. The following graph is obtained by a researcher while doing an experiment to see the variation of the magnetic field with respect to the current in the solenoid. The unit of magnetic field as given in the graph attached is in milli-Tesla (mT) and the current is given in Ampere.

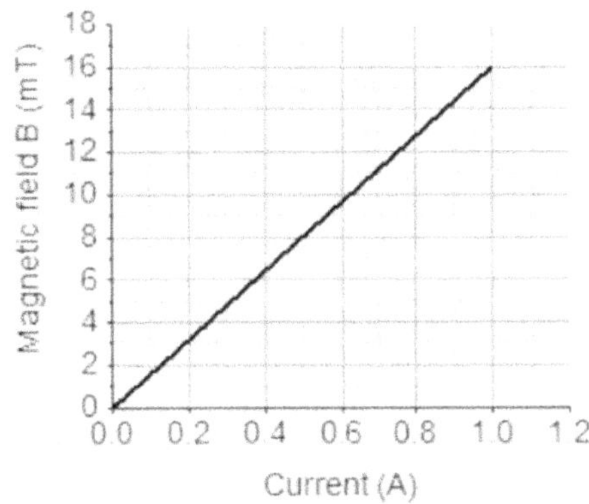

48. What type of energy conversion is observed in a linear solenoid?
   (a) Mechanical to Magnetic
   (b) Electrical to Magnetic
   (c) Electrical to Mechanical
   (d) Magnetic to Mechanical

49. What will happen if a soft iron bar is placed inside the solenoid?
   (a) The bar will be electrocuted resulting in short-circuit.
   (b) The bar will be magnetised as long as there is current in the circuit.
   (c) The bar will be magnetised permanently.
   (d) The bar will not be affected by any means.

50. The magnetic field lines produced inside the solenoid are similar to that of …
   (a) a bar magnet 10
   (b) a straight current carrying conductor
   (c) a circular current carrying loop
   (d) electromagnet of any shape

51. After analysing the graph a student writes the following statements.
   I. The magnetic field produced by the solenoid is inversely proportional to the current.
   II. The magnetic field produced by the solenoid is directly proportional to the current.
   III. The magnetic field produced by the solenoid is directly proportional to square of the current.
   IV. The magnetic field produced by the solenoid is independent of the current.

   Choose from the following which of the following would be the correct statement(s).

   (a) Only IV
   (b) I and III and IV
   (c) I and II
   (d) Only II

52. From the graph deduce which of the following statements is correct.
   (a) For a current of 0.8A the magnetic field is 13 mT
   (b) For larger currents, the magnetic field increases non-linearly.
   (c) For a current of 0.8A the magnetic field is 1.3 mT
   (d) There is not enough information to find the magnetic field corresponding to 0.8A current.

Case/Passage - 2

For a conductor of length L carrying a current of I in a field B the force experienced by the conductor $\vec{F} = I\,\vec{L} \times \vec{B}$

If the current-carrying conductor in the form of a loop of any arbitrary shape is placed in a uniform field, then, $\vec{F} = 0$ i.e., the net magnetic force on a current loop in a uniform magnetic field is always zero. Here it must be kept in mind that in this situation different parts of the loop may experience elemental force due to which the loop may be under tension or may experience a torque.

Direction of force can be determined by fleming's left hand rule, right hand palm rule or screw rule.

53. The direction of induced current is obtained by
   (a) Fleming's left hand rule
   (b) Maxwell's cork-screw rule
   (c) Ampere's rule
   (d) Fleming's right hand rule

54. An electron moving with uniform velocity in x-direction enters a region of uniform magnetic field along y-direction. Which of the following physical quantity(ies) is (are) non-zero and remain constant?
   I. Velocity of the electron
   II. Magnitude of the momentum of the electron.
   III. Force on the electron.
   IV. The kinetic energy of electron.

   (a) Only I and II.
   (b) Only III and IV.
   (c) All four
   (d) Only II and IV.

55. Which of the following can produce a magnetic field?
   (a) Electric charges at rest
   (b) Electric charges in motion
   (c) Only by permanent magnets
   (d) Electric charges whether at rest or in motion

56. A wire is lying horizontally in the north-south direction and there is a horizontal magnetic field pointing towards the east. Some positive charges in the wire move north and an equal number of negative charges move south. The direction of force on the wire will be

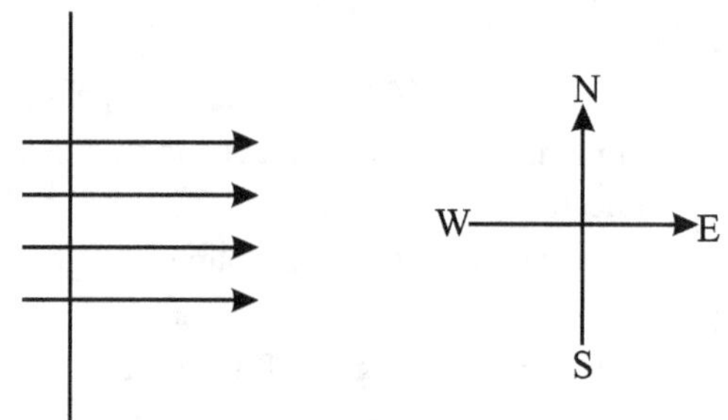

(a) east

(b) down, into the page

(c) up, out of the page

(d) west

57. Four situations are given below-

I. An infinitely long wire carrying current

II. A rectangular loop carrying current

III. A solenoid of finite length carrying current

IV. A circular loop carrying current.

In which of the above cases will the magnetic field produced be like that of a bar magnet?

(a) I   (b) I and III

(c) Only III   (d) Only IV

Case/Passage - 3

The strength of the magnetic field produced by a current-carrying circular coil (or circular wire) depends on (i) Current flowing through the coil. (ii) Radius of the circular coil. (iii) Number of turns of wire in the circular coil.

58. A long horizontal power line is carrying a current of 100 A in the east-west direction. The direction of magnetic field at a point 1.0 m below it is

(a) south to north

(b) north to south

(c) east to west

(d) west to east

59. What type of curve we get, between magnetic field and distance along the axis of a current carrying circular coil?

(a) Straight   (b) Circular

(c) Parabolic   (d) None of these

60. If a current carrying straight conductor is placed is east-west direction, then the direction of the force experienced by the conductor due to earth's magnetic field is:

(a) downward   (b) upward

(c) east-west   (d) west east

Assertion & Reason 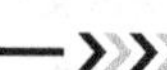

DIRECTIONS : *Each of these questions contains an assertion followed by reason. Read them carefully and answer the question on the basis of following options. You have to select the one that best describes the two statements.*

(a) If both **Assertion** and **Reason** are **correct** and Reason is the **correct explanation** of Assertion.

(b) If both **Assertion** and **Reason** are correct, but Reason is **not the correct explanation** of Assertion.

(c) If **Assertion** is **correct** but **Reason** is **incorrect**.

(d) If **Assertion** is **incorrect** but **Reason** is **correct**.

61. **Assertion :** Magnetic field interacts with a moving charge and not with a stationary charge.

Reason : A moving charge produces a magnetic field.

62. **Assertion :** No net force acts on a rectangular coil carrying a steady current when suspended freely in a uniform magnetic field.

Reason : Force on coil in magnetic field is always non-zero.

63. **Assertion :** Force experienced by moving charge will be maximum if direction of velocity of charge is perpendicular to applied magnetic field.

Reason : Force on moving charge is independent of direction of applied magnetic field.

64. **Assertion :** There is no change in the energy of a charged particle moving in a magnetic field although a magnetic force is acting on it.

Reason : Work done by centripetal force is always zero.

65. **Assertion :** In a conductor, free electrons keep on moving but no magnetic force acts on a conductor in a magnetic field.

Reason: Force on free electrons due to magnetic field always acts perpendicular to its direction of motion.

66. **Assertion :** A proton moves horizontally towards a vertical long conductor having an upward electric current. It will deflect vertically downward.

Reason : Seeing the proton and the conductor from the side of the proton, the magnetic field at the site of the proton will be towards right. Hence the force $\vec{F} = q\vec{v} \times \vec{B}$ will deflect the proton vertically downward.

67. **Assertion :** A spark occurs between the poles of a switch when the switch is opened.

Reason : Current flowing in the conductor produces magnetic field.

Match the Following

DIRECTIONS : *Each question contains statements given in two columns which have to be matched. Statements (A, B, C, D) in column I have to be matched with statements (p, q, r, s) in column II.*

68.

	Column I		Column II
(A)	An electric motor works on	(p)	to a battery
(B)	An electric motor is also	(q)	direct current
(C)	A commutator is used to	(r)	reverse the direction of flow of current.
(D)	Commutator rings are connected	(s)	known as DC MOTOR

69. Equal currents i flow in two wires along x and y axis as shown. Match the following :

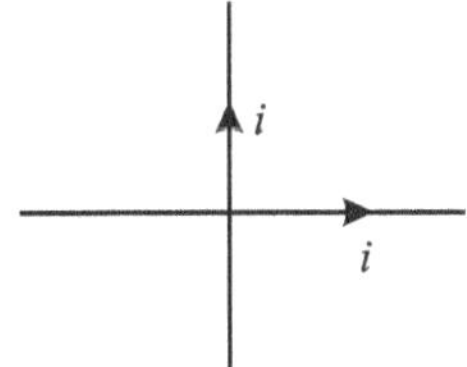

	Column I		Column II
(A)	Magnetic field in first quadrant	(p)	inwards
(B)	Magnetic field in second quadrant	(q)	outwards
(C)	Magnetic field in third quadrant	(r)	may be inwards or outwards
(D)	Magnetic field in fourth quadrant		

Fill in the Blanks

DIRECTIONS : *Complete the following statements with an appropriate word / term to be filled in the blank space(s).*

70. A compass needle is a .... magnet.

71. Field lines are used to represent a ....

72. Field lines are shown closer together where the magnetic field is ....

73. A metallic wire carrying an electric current has associated with it a .... field.

74. The field lines about the wire consist of a series of concentric circles whose direction is given by the .... rule.

75. The magnetic lines of force are the lines drawn in a magnetic field along which a .... pole would move.

76. An electric current can be used for making temporary magnets known as ....

77. The unit of magnetic field is ....

78. The N-pole of a compass points to the .... pole of a permanent magnet.

79. The force that a magnetic field exerts on a current is always perpendicular to the .... and to the ....

80. In a magnetic field pointing away from you, an electron traveling to the right will experience a force in the .... direction.

81. Magnetic fields are produced by ....

82. You are looking into a solenoid, at its S-pole, along its axis. From your view point, the direction of the current in the solenoid is ....

83. Crowding the wires of a solenoid more closely together will .... the strength of the field inside it.

84. Magnetic field lines emerge from the .... pole of a solenoid or a permanent magnet.

85. You are looking down the axis of a solenoid, and the current from your position is clockwise. The end of the solenoid facing you is a .... pole.

86. A generator converts mechanical energy into .... energy. It works on the basis of ....

87. In our houses we receive AC electric power of .... with a frequency of ....

88. The frequency for A.C. (alternating current) in USA is ....

89. The armature in a motor rotates within a(n) .... field.

90. To produce DC, the output of a generator must be fed through a (n) ....

91. In any generator, the current in the armature is of the .... type.

92. In an AC generator, maximum number of lines of force pass through the coil when the angle between the plane of coil and lines of force is ....

True / False

DIRECTIONS : *Read the following statements and write your answer as true or false.*

93. A magnetic field exists in the region surrounding a magnet, in which the force of the magnet can be detected.

94. The pattern of the magnetic field around a conductor due to an electric current flowing through it depends on the shape of the conductor.

95. A current-carrying conductor when placed in a magnetic field always experiences a force.

96. The direction of force on a current carrying conductor placed in a magnetic field can be reversed by reversing the direction of current flowing in the conductor.

97. The direction of force on a current carrying conductor placed in a magnetic field cannot be reversed by reversing the direction of magnetic field.

98. Two magnetic lines of force never intersect each other.

99. The field lines inside the infinite solenoid are in the form of parallel straight lines.

100. An electric generator works on the principle of electromagnetic induction.

101. In a DC electric motor a pair of split rings is used as commutator.

102. The magnitude of induced current can be increased by decreasing the speed of rotation of coil.

ANSWER KEY & SOLUTIONS

1. **(d)** Magnet attracts iron and steel

2. **(c)**

3. **(c)** If magnetic field lines are parallel and equidistant then it represents uniform magnetic field.

4. **(c)**   5. **(c)**

6. **(a)** Soft iron is the most suitable material for making the core of an electromagnet

7. **(c)** The direction of current changes in each half rotation in an electric motor.

8. **(c)**   9. **(c)**   10. **(d)**   11. **(a)**   12. **(a)**

13. **(b)**   14. **(d)**   15. **(b)**   16. **(d)**   17. **(a)**

18. **(d)**   19. **(a)**   20. **(b)**   21. **(d)**   22. **(c)**

23. **(d)**   24. **(a)**   25. **(b)**   26. **(c)**   27. **(d)**

28. **(b)**   29. **(c)**   30. **(a)**   31. **(b)**   32. **(c)**

33. **(d)**   34. **(d)**   35. **(d)**   36. **(b)**

37. **(b)** The induced current in coil is in clockwise direction when N pole of powerful magnet is moved to right.

38. **(c)** A long coil of finite length of wire carrying current consisting of closely packed loops is called solenoid whose magnetic field resembles that of a bar magnet.

39. **(c)**   40. **(d)**   41. **(c)**   42. **(c)**   43. **(d)**

44. **(a)**   45. **(d)**

46. **(a)** In loop shown current is anti-clockwise.

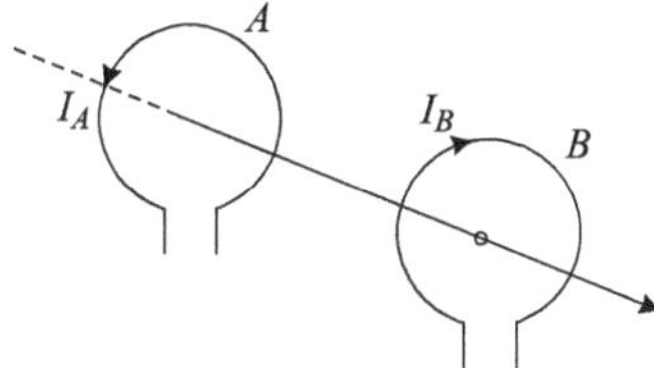

So to induce a anti-clockwise current in A, flux going into A must be increased and by bringing A closer to B, we get a anti-clockwise current in A. This is in accordance with Lenz's law.

47. **(d)** We know, Lorentz Force

$$F = q v B \sin \theta$$

where θ is angle between the direction s of v and B.

Case-I, If $\theta = 0°$

$\therefore$ F = 0

Case-II, If $\theta = 90°$

$\therefore$ F = $q v B \neq 0$

48. **(c)** Electrical to Mechanical

49. **(b)** The bar will be magnetised as long as there is current in the circuit.

50. **(a)** A bar magnet

51. **(d)** Only II

52. **(a)** For a current of 0.8 A the magnetic field is 13 mT

53. **(d)** Fleming's right hand rule.

54. **(d)** Velocity and force change due to change in direction but magnitude of PE and KE of electron remain constant speed is constant.

55. **(b)** Magnetic field (B) is produced by moving charge.

56. **(b)** According to Fleming's left hand rule the direction of force on the wire will be down into the page.

57. **(c)** A long coil of finite length of wire carrying current consisting of closely packed loops is called solenoid whose magnetic field resembles that of a bar magnet.

58. **(b)**   59. **(d)**   60. **(a)**

61. **(a)** A moving charge experiences a force in magnetic field. It is because of interaction of two magnetic fields, one which is produced due to motion charge and other in which charge is moving.

62. **(c)** Force acting on each pair of the opposite sides of the coil are equal.

63. **(c)** Force on moving charge will be maximum if direction of velocity of charge is perpendicular to direction of magnetic field

64. **(a)** Magnetic force is always perpendicular to the direction of motion of charged particle, i.e., work done on the charge particle moving on a circular path in magnetic field is zero.

65. **(c)** In a conductor, the average velocity of electrons is zero. Hence no current flows through the conductor. Hence, no force acts on this conductor.

66. (a)   67. (b)

68. (A) → q, (B) → s,   (C) → r,   (D) → p

69. (A) → r, (B) → q,   (C) → r,   (D) → p

70. small

71. magnetic field

72. greater.

73. magnetic

74. right-hand

75. north magnetic

76. electromagnets

77. tesla

78. South

79. field, current

80. downward

81. currents

82. clockwise

83. increase

84. North

85. south

86. electrical, electromagnetic induction.

87. 220 V, 50 Hz.

88. 60 Hz

89. magnetic

90. commutator

91. A.C

92. 90 degree

93. True   94. True   95. False   96. True

97. False   98. True   99. True   100. True

101. True   102. False

13 — Our Environment

DIRECTIONS : *This section contains multiple choice questions. Each question has four choices (a), (b), (c) and (d) out of which only one is correct.*

1. An example of a producer in the aquatic food web would be:
   - (a) Duckweed
   - (b) Ducks
   - (c) Fish
   - (d) Insects

2. Which one is recyclable waste?
   - (a) Paper
   - (b) Torn clothes
   - (c) Metallic and plastic discards
   - (d) All the above

3. Which of the following does not form part of particulate matter?
   - (a) Dust
   - (b) Fly ash
   - (c) Aerosols
   - (d) Nitric oxide

4. Which of the following are environment-friendly practices?
   - (a) Carrying cloth-bags to put purchases in while shopping
   - (b) Switching off unnecessary lights and fans
   - (c) Walking to school instead of getting your mother to drop you on her scooter
   - (d) All of the above

5. Habitat together with functions of species constitute:
   - (a) Trophic level
   - (b) Boundary
   - (c) Topography
   - (d) Niche

6. Plants are killed in winter by frost:
   - (a) Because of dessication and mechanical damage to the tissue.
   - (b) Because no photosynthesis take place at such a low temperature.
   - (c) Because respiration ceases at such low temperature.
   - (d) Because there is no transpiration.

7. In order to maintain proper ecological balance
   - (a) the existing forests would be cleared and new ones should be planted.
   - (b) some quick growing annuals should be planted if a tree must be cut for other uses.
   - (c) tree must be cut whenever necessary because the underground part performs the useful purpose.
   - (d) a tree should be planted in place of one to be cut.

8. It is said, the Tajmahal may be destroyed due to
   - (a) Flood in Yamuna river
   - (b) Decomposition of marble as a result of high temperature
   - (c) Air pollutants released from oil refinery of Mathura
   - (d) All the above

9. In an ecosystem, the function of the producers is to
   - (a) convert organic compounds into inorganic compounds.
   - (b) trap solar energy and convert it into chemical energy.
   - (c) utilize chemical energy.
   - (d) release energy.

10. Free services provided to humans by ecosystems include
    - (a) control of atmospheric carbon dioxide concentration.
    - (b) prevention of soil erosion.
    - (c) filtering of pollutants from water and air.
    - (d) all of the above

11. Carcinogenic chemicals produced during recycling of plastics and polythene is/are
    - (a) formaldehyde
    - (b) polycyclic aromatic compounds
    - (c) vinyl chloride
    - (d) dioxins and furans

12. Organisms of a higher trophic level which feed on several types of organisms belonging to a lower trophic level constitute the
    (a) food web
    (b) ecological pyramid
    (c) ecosystem
    (d) food chain

13. A decrease in the grass population will most immediately decrease the available energy for the
    (a) mouse
    (b) snake
    (c) hawk
    (d) frog

14. Why do scientists think that human-induced global warming will be more harmful to plants and animals than were past, natural climate fluctuations ?
    (a) Because temperatures will change faster
    (b) Because the temperature changes will be larger
    (c) Because species now are less adaptable than species in the past
    (d) Because ecosystems are now more complicated than they used to be

15. Each step in a food chain is called a
    (a) trophic level.
    (b) consumer level.
    (c) food web.
    (d) producer.

16. As a biologist, if you become very interested in the study of the interaction of organisms with each other and the environment your subspeciality would be
    (a) Zoology
    (b) Ecology
    (c) Botany
    (d) Herpetology

17. The last chain of food is
    (a) producers
    (b) decomposers
    (c) parasites
    (d) none of these

18. Trophic levels are formed by –
    (a) only plants
    (b) only animals
    (c) only carnivores
    (d) organisms linked in food chain

19. The part of earth comprising water is called an
    (a) atmosphere
    (b) hydrosphere
    (c) lithosphere
    (d) none of the above

20. The maximum energy is stored at following tropical level in any ecosystem
    (a) Producers
    (b) Herbivores
    (c) Carnivores
    (d) Top carnivores

21. Pyramids of energy are
    (a) always upright
    (b) always inverted
    (c) mostly upright
    (d) mostly inverted

22. Individuals of any species at a place form
    (a) biotic community
    (b) ecosystem
    (c) population
    (d) biome

23. City garbage can be used to produce
    (a) sewage sludge
    (b) useful articles
    (c) biogas and manure
    (d) all of the above.

24. Acid rain is the downpour of
    (a) carbon dioxide in rain
    (b) dust in rain
    (c) sulphur dioxide in rain
    (d) oxygen in rain

25. Select the most dangerous pollutant
    (a) CO
    (b) SO_2
    (c) NO_2
    (d) CO_2

26. Ozone layer is essential because it absorbs most of the
    (a) infrared radiations
    (b) heat
    (c) solar radiation
    (d) ultraviolet-radiation

27. The biotic and abiotic components interacting with each other in a pond form
    (a) a community
    (b) a population
    (c) an ecosystem
    (d) a biome

28. Environment consists of
    (a) land, air, water
    (b) light, temperature and rainfall
    (c) plants, animals and microbes
    (d) All the above.

29. Carnivores represent
    (a) primary consumers
    (b) secondary and tertiary consumers
    (c) reducers
    (d) zooplankton.

30. World environment day is celebrated on
    (a) 15th March
    (b) 15th April
    (c) 4th May
    (d) 5th June

31. Flow of energy in an ecosystem is always
    (a) unidirectional
    (b) bidirectional
    (c) multi-directional
    (d) no specific direction

32. Which of the following is a biodegradable waste?

(a) Radioactive wastes   (b) Aluminium cans

(c) DDT   (d) Cattle dung

33. For corrosion of metals, there should be

(a) Exposed surface of metal

(b) Moisture

(c) Air

(d) All these

34. Sun gives radiations in the form of

(a) Infra-red radiation   (b) Visible light

(c) Ultra-violet   (d) All these

35. In an ecosystem green plants are known as

(a) primary consumers   (b) secondary consumers

(c) producers   (d) tertiary consumers

36. Carbon monoxide is a pollutant because

(a) It reacts with O_2

(b) It inhibits glycolysis

(c) Reacts with haemoglobin

(d) Makes nervous system inactive

37. The presence of which of the following pollutants in the atmosphere has caused damage to Taj Mahal?

(a) CO_2

(b) SO_2

(c) Pb particles

(d) Radioactive disintegrations

38. Which of the following does not affect ozone layer?

(a) Cl_2 (b) CH_3Cl

(c) NO   (d) $CFCl_3$

39. Which one is present in maximum number in an ecosystem?

(a) Herbivores   (b) Carnivores

(c) Producers   (d) Omnivores.

40. The percentage of solar radiation absorbed by all the green plants for the process of photosynthesis is about

(a) 1%   (b) 5%

(c) 8%   (d) 10%

41. Decrease in number of trees may cause

(a) increase in rainfall

(b) decrease in rainfall

(c) increase in temperature

(d) conservation of nutrients in soil

42. Rag pickers remove

(a) plastic, polythene, paper and metal wastes

(b) rags, cardboard, glass articles

(c) both (a) and (b)

(d) food articles.

43. As energy is passed from one trophic level to another, the amount of usable energy

(a) increases

(b) decreases

(c) remains the same

(d) energy is not passed from one trophic level to another

44. In the biosphere, which of the following is the ultimate source of energy?

(a) Carbon   (b) Water

(c) Sunlight   (d) Nitrogen

45. Sulphur dioxide affects

(a) Haemoglobin of blood   (b) Arteries

(c) Alveoli of lungs   (d) Nerves

46. Pyramid of energy in a forest ecosystem is

(a) Always inverted

(b) Always upright

(c) Both upright and inverted depending on ecosystem

(d) First upright then inverted

47. CO_2 absorbs some of the .... that radiates from the surface of earth to space

(a) ozone   (b) heat

(c) ultraviolet light   (d) smog

48. Human-caused changes to the nitrogen cycle are expected to result in

(a) an increase in acid rain.

(b) an increase in the loss of species from ecosystems.

(c) higher concentrations of a greenhouse gas.

(d) all of the above

49. The biological process by which carbon is returned to its reservoir is

(a) photosynthesis   (b) denitrification

(c) carbon fixation   (d) cellular respiration

50. Which of the following constitute a food-chain?

(a) grass, wheat and mango

(b) grass, goat and human

(c) goat, cow and elephant

(d) grass, fish and goat

51. As a black widow spider consumes her mate, what is the lowest trophic level she could be occupying

(a) third (b) first

(c) second (d) fourth

52. Among the most dangerous non-biodegradable waste is

(a) cow-dung (b) plastic articles

(c) garbage (d) radioactive waste

53. In an ecosystem, the 10% of energy is transferred from one trophic level to the next in the form of

(a) heat energy (b) light energy

(c) chemical energy (d) mechanical energy

54. Organisation involved in formulating programmes for protecting environment is:

(a) WHO (b) UNDP

(c) UNEP (d) UNICEF

55. In every food chain green plants are

(a) decomposers (b) producers

(c) consumers (d) None of the above.

56. The decomposers in an ecosystem

(a) convert inorganic material, to simpler forms.

(b) convert organic material to inorganic forms.

(c) convert inorganic materials into organic compounds.

(d) do not break-down organic compounds.

57. If a grasshopper is eaten by a frog, then the energy transfer will be from

(a) producer to decomposer

(b) producer to primary consumer

(c) primary consumer to secondary consumer

(d) secondary consumer to primary consumer

58. The diagram below shows a food pyramid.

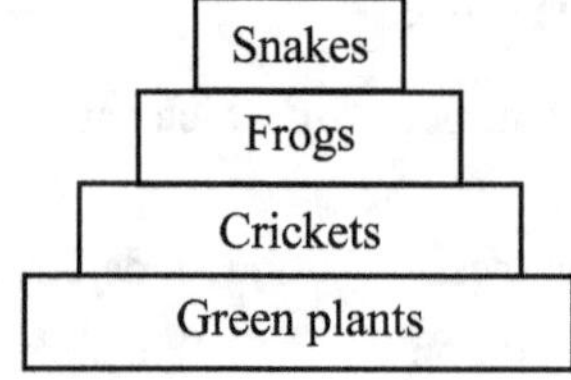

Which level of the food pyramid contains consumers with the least biomass?

(a) snakes (b) frogs

(c) crickets (d) green plants

59. Which two of the following statements regarding food chains are **correct**?

(i) Removal of 80% tigers resulted in increased growth of vegetation.

(ii) Removal of most carnivores resulted in increased population of deer.

(iii) Length of food chain is limited to 3 – 4 trophic levels due to energy loss.

(iv) Length of food chain may vary from 2 – 3 trophic levels.

(a) (i) and (iv) (b) (i) and (ii)

(c) (ii) and (iii) (d) (iii) and (iv)

60. Match the terms given in column-I with their definition given in column-II and choose the correct option.

Column - I	Column - II
A. Food chain	I. An organism that eats meat.
B. Food web	II. An organism that eats plants.
C. Heterotrophs	III. An organism that makes its food from light or chemical energy.
D. Autotrophs	IV. An organism that gets its energy by eating other organisms.
E. Carnivore	V. The sequence of organisms of who eats whom in a biological community.
F. Herbivore	VI. The network of all the interrelated food chains in a biological community.

(a) A – V; B – VI; C – IV; D – III; E – I; F – II

(b) A – VI; B – IV; C – III; D – I; E – II; F – V

(c) A – III; B – I; C – II; D – V; E – VI; F – IV

(d) A – II, B – V; C – VI; D – IV; E – III; F – I

61. Assertion: Pond ecosystem is upright in the pyramid of number.

Reason: Phytoplanktons are maximum and secondary consumers are lesser in number.

(a) Statement (A) and (B) both are correct.

(b) Statement (A) is correct but (B) is incorrect.

(c) Statement (A) and (B) both are incorrect.

(d) Statement (A) is incorrect but (B) is correct.

62. Which of the following ecological pyramid is never inverted?

(a) Pyramid of number in forest ecosystem

(b) Pyramid of biomass in pond ecosystem

(c) Pyramid of energy in parasitic food chain

(d) Pyramid of biomass in parasitic food chain

63. Match column - I with column - II and select the correct answer using the codes given below.

	Column - I		Column - II
A.	Phosphorus	I.	Atmosphere
B.	Carbon	II.	Producers
C.	Goat	III.	Rock
D.	Grasses	IV.	T2

(a) A – III; B – II; C – IV; D – I
(b) A – III; B – I; C – IV; D – II
(c) A – I; B – III; C – II; D – IV
(d) A – II; B – III; C – IV; D – I

64. Which of the following pair is **incorrectly** matched ?

(a) Autotrophs – Fungi

(b) Primary consumers – Zooplankton

(c) Secondary consumers – Fishes

(d) Decomposers – Fungi

65. Abundance of coliform bacteria in a water body is indicative of pollution from

(a) petroleum refinery   (b) metal smelter

(c) fertilizer factory   (d) domestic sewage

66. Prolonged exposure to the fumes released by incomplete combustion of coal may cause death of a human because of

(a) inhalation of unburnt carbon particles.

(b) continuous exposure to high temperature.

(c) increased level of carbon monoxide.

(d) increased level of carbon dioxide.

67. Which among grass, goat, tiger and vulture in a food chain, will have the maximum concentration of harmful chemicals in its body due to contamination of pesticides in the soil?

(a) Grass since it grows in the contaminated soil

(b) Goat since it eats the grass

(c) Tiger since it feeds on the goat which feeds on the grass

(d) Vulture since it eats the tiger, which in turn eats the goat, which eats the grass

68. Which of the following is an result of biological magnification?

(a) Top level predators may be harmed by toxic chemicals in environment.

(b) Increase in carbon dioxide

(c) The green-house effect will be most significance at the poles

(d) Energy is lost at each trophic level of a food chain

69. What is the main reason for increase in temperature in a glass house?

(a) Sunlight is completely absorbed by plants in the glass house

(b) Radiation fails to escape from the glass house completely

(c) Plant do not utilize sunlight in a glass house

(d) Plants produce heat inside the glass house

70. Read the following statements carefully.

(I) Energy transfer in the biotic world always proceeds from the autotrophs.

(II) Energy flow is unidirectional.

(III) Energy availability is maximum at the tertiary level.

(IV) There is loss of energy from one trophic level to the other.

Select the relevant statements for the forest ecosystem

(a) I, II and IV   (b) I, II and III

(c) I, III and IV   (d) II, III and IV

71. In a highly pesticide polluted pond. Which of the following aquatic organisms will have the maximum amount of pesticide per gram of body mass?

(a) Lotus   (b) Fishes

(c) *Spirogyra*   (d) Zooplanktons

72. DDT is non-biodegradable chemical when it enters food chain it gets accumulated in each trophic level. This phenomenon is called as -

(a) Eutrophication

(b) Chemical amplification

(c) Biomagnification

(d) Chemical magnification

73. The following diagram shows a simple version of energy flow through food web.

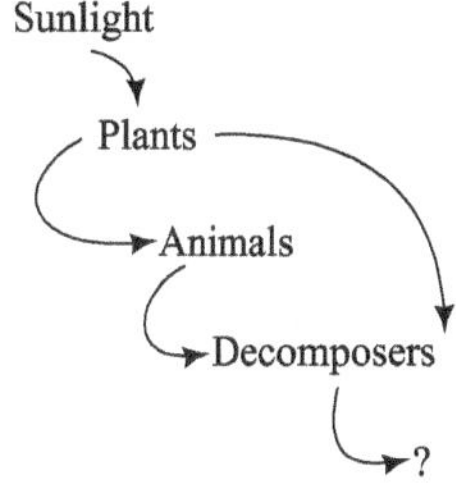

What happens to energy having the decomposers?

(a) It is used by the decomposers itself.

(b) It is reflected from the surface of earth.

(c) It is lost as heat

(d) It is used in natural biocomposting

74. Which of the following groups contain only biodegradable items ?

(a) Grass, flowers and leather

(b) Grass, wood and plastic

(c) Fruit-peels, cake and lime-juice

(d) Cake, wood and grass

75. Which of the following constitute a food-chain?

(a) Grass, wheat and mango

(b) Grass, goat and human

(c) Goat, cow and elephant

(d) Grass, fish and goat

76. Which of the following are environment-friendly practices?

(a) Carrying cloth-bags to put purchases in while shopping.

(b) Switching off unnecessary lights and fans.

(c) Walking to school instead of getting your mother to drop you on her scooter.

(d) All of the above.

77. Organisms which synthesise carbohydrates from inorganic compounds using radiant energy are called

(a) decomposers   (b) producers

(c) herbivores   (d) carnivores

78. Which of the statement is incorrect?

(a) All green plants and blue-green algae are producers.

(b) Green plants get their food from organic compounds.

(c) Producers prepare their own food from inorganic compounds.

(d) Plants convert solar energy into chemical energy.

79. Which of the following limits the number of trophic levels in a food chain?

(a) Decrease in energy at higher trophic levels.

(b) Deficient food supply.

(c) Polluted air.

(d) Water.

80. In the given diagram, the various trophic levels are shown in a pyramid. At which trophic level is maximum energy available?

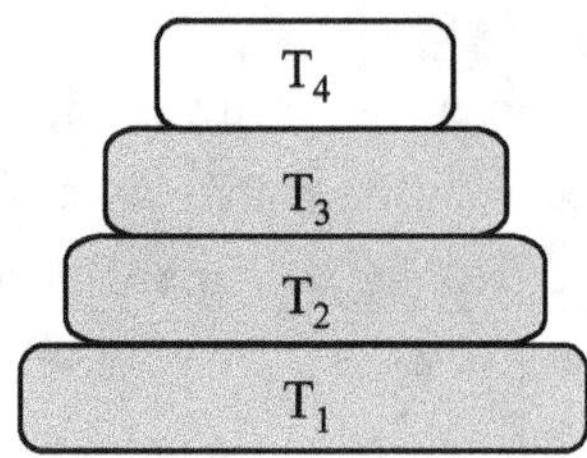

(a) T_4 (b) T_2

(c) T_1 (d) T_3

81. What will happen if deer is missing in the food chain given below?

Grass → Deer → Tiger

(a) The population of tiger increases.

(b) The population of grass decreases.

(c) Tiger will start eating grass.

(d) The population of tiger decreases and the population of grass increases.

Case/Passage Based Questions

DIRECTIONS : *Study the given case/passage and answer the following questions.*

Case/Passage - 1

Food chains are very important for the survival of most species. When only one element is removed from the food chain it can result in extinction of a species in some cases. The foundation of the food chain consists of primary producers.

Primary producers, or autotrophs, can use either solar energy or chemical energy to create complex organic compounds, whereas species at higher trophic levels cannot and so must consume producers or other life that itself consumes producers. Because the sun's light is necessary for photosynthesis, most life could not exist if the sun disappeared. Even so, it has recently been discovered that there are some forms of life, chemotrophs, that appear to gain all their metabolic energy from chemosythesis driven by hydrothermal vents, thus showing that some life may not require solar energy to thrive.

[From CBSE Question Bank-2021]

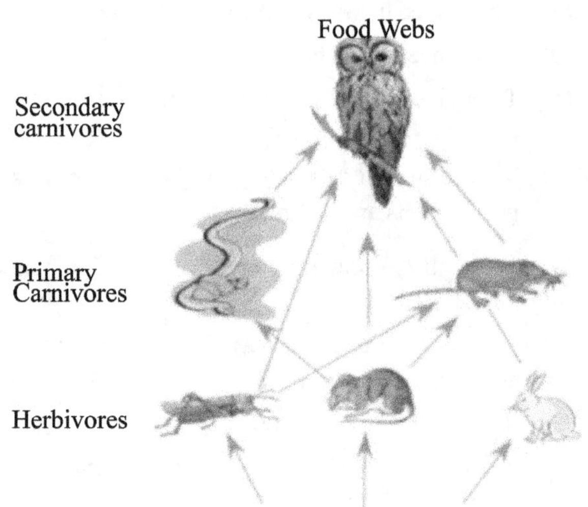

82. If 10,000 J solar energy falls on green plants in a terrestrial ecosystem, what percentage of solar energy will be converted into food energy?

(a) 10,000 J

(b) 100 J

(c) 1000 J

(d) It will depend on the type of the terrestrial plant.

83. If Ravi is consuming curd/yogurt for lunch, which trophic level in a food chain he should be considered as occupying ?

(a) First trophic level   (b) Second trophic level

(c) Third trophic level   (d) Fourth trophic level

84. The decomposers are not included in the food chain.The correct reason for the same is because decomposers:

(a) Act at every trophic level of the food chain

(b) Do not breakdown organic compounds

(c) Convert organic material to inorganic forms

(d) Release enzymes outside their body to convert organic material to inorganic forms

85. Matter and energy are two fundamental inputs of an ecosystem. Movement of

(a) Energy is bidirectional and matter is repeatedly circulating.

(b) Energy is repeatedly circulation and matter is unidirectional.

(c) Energy is unidirectional and matter is repeatedly circulating.

(d) Energy is multidirectional and matter is bidirectional.

86. Which of the following limits the number of trophic levels in a food chain?

(a) Decrease in energy at higher trophic levels

(b) Less availability of food

(c) Polluted air

(d) Water

Case/Passage - 2

The diagram below shows a food web from the sea shore

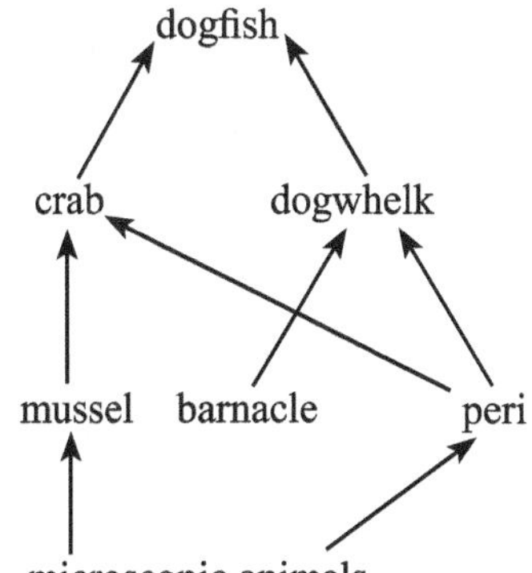

[From CBSE Question Bank-2021]

87. The mussel can be described as

(a) Producer   (b) Primary consumer

(c) Secondary consumer   (d) decomposer

88. Which trophic level is incorrectly defined?

(a) Carnivores – secondary or tertiary consumers

(b) Decomposers – microbial heterotrophs

(c) Herbivores – primary consumers

(d) Omnivores – molds, yeast and mushrooms

89. The given figure best represents:

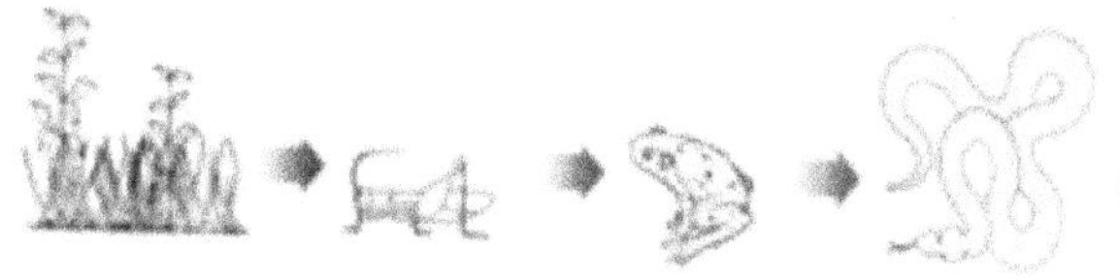

(a) Grassland food chain   (b) Parasitic food chain

(c) Forest food chain   (d) Aquatic food chain

90. Why do all food chains start with plants?

(a) Because plants are easily grown

(b) Because plants are nutritious

(c) Because plants can produce its own energy

(d) Because plants do not require energy

91. In the food web, what two organisms are competing for food?

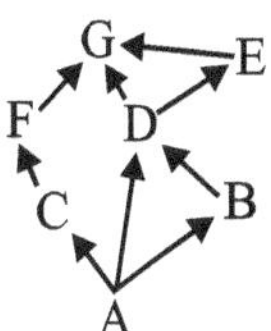

(a) A and B   (c) A and C

(b) D and F   (d) B and D

92. Consider the following statements concerning food chains:

(i) Removal of 80% tigers from an area resulted in greatly increased growth of vegetation

(ii) Removal of most of the carnivores resulted in an increased population of herbivores.

(iii) The length of the food chains is generally limited to 3 – 4 trophic levels due to energy loss

(iv) The length of the food chains may vary from 2 to 8 trophic levels

Which two of the above statements are correct?

(a) (i), (iv)   (b) (i), (ii)

(c) (ii), (iii)   (d) (iii), (iv)

93. Which of the following group of organisms are not included in ecological food chain?

(a) Carnivores   (b) Saprophytes

(c) Herbivores   (d) Predators

Case/Passage - 3

Biosphere is a global ecosystem composed of living organisms and abiotic factors from which they derive energy and nutrients. And ecosystem is defined as structural and functional unit of the biosphere comprising of living and non-living environment that interact by means of food chains and chemical cycles resulting in energy flow, biotic diversity and material cycling to form a stable, self-supporting system

[From CBSE Question Bank-2021]

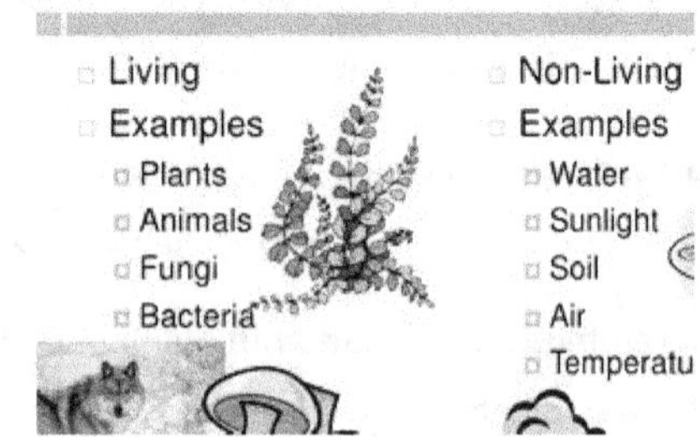

94. Which trophic level is incorrectly defined?

(a) Carnivores – secondary or tertiary consumers

(b) Decomposers – microbial heterotrophs

(c) Herbivores – primary consumers

(d) Omnivores – molds, yeast and mushrooms

The diagram below shows a food web from the sea shore

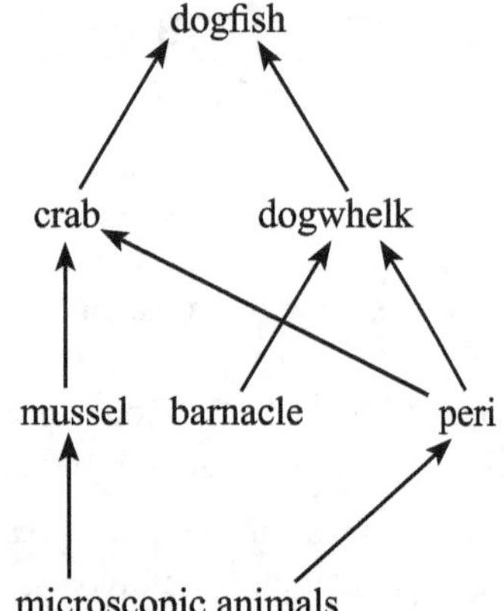

95. The mussel can be described as

(a) Producer

(b) Primary consumer

(c) Secondary consumer

(d) decomposer

96. The given figure best represents:

(a) Grassland food chain   (b) Parasitic food chain

(c) Forest food chain   (d) Aquatic food chain

Assertion & Reason

DIRECTIONS : *Each of these questions contains an assertion followed by reason. Read them carefully and answer the question on the basis of following options. You have to select the one that best describes the two statements.*

(a) If both **Assertion** and **Reason** are **correct** and Reason is the **correct explanation** of Assertion.

(b) If both **Assertion** and **Reason** are correct, but Reason is **not the correct explanation** of Assertion.

(c) If **Assertion** is **correct** but **Reason** is **incorrect**.

(d) If **Assertion** is **incorrect** but **Reason** is **correct**.

97. **Assertion:** In an ecosystem, the function of producers is to convert organic compounds into inorganic compounds.
Reason: Green plants, the producers, transduce solar energy.

98. **Assertion:** Ecology is study of relationship between living organisms and their environment.

Reason: The biotic community and non-living environment of an area function together to form an ecosystem.

99. **Assertion:** Animals adopt different strategies to survive in hostile environment.

Reason: Praying mantis is green in colour which merges with plant foliage.

100. **Assertion:** Abiotic component of an ecosystem involves cycling of material and flow of energy.

Reason: This is essential to keep biotic factors alive.

101. **Assertion:** The crown fires are most destructive as they burn the tree top.

Reason: Due to crown fire, the temperature of that area may rise upto 700°C.

102. **Assertion:** Trophic levels are formed by only plants.

Reason: Food chains and webs are formed due to linked organisms on the basis of their nutrition.

103. Assertion: A network of food chains existing together in an ecosystem is known as food web.

Reason: An animal like kite cannot be a part of a food web.

104. Assertion: Supersonic jets cause pollution as they thin out ozone.

Reason: Depletion of ozone cause green house effect.

105. Assertion: Tropical rain forests are disappearing fast from developing countries such as India.

Reason: No value is attached to these forests because these are poor in biodiversity.

Match the Following

DIRECTIONS : *Each question contains options given in two columns which have to be matched. options (A, B, C, D) in column I have to be matched with options (p, q, r, s) in column II.*

106.

Column I	Column II
(A) Grass	(p) Primary carnivore
(B) Grasshopper	(q) Secondary carnivore
(C) Frog	(r) Producer
(D) Hawk	(s) Primary consumer

107.

Column A	Column B
(A) Third trophic level	(p) Ozone
(B) Accumulation of pesticides at higher trophic level	(q) CFCs
(C) Green plants	(r) Herbivore
(D) Flow of energy in an ecosystem	(s) Biomagnification
(E) Consists of 3 atoms of oxygen	(t) Decomposers
(F) Main cause of depletion of ozone layer	(u) Producers
(G) Second trophic level	(v) Unidirectional
(H) Break-down of dead organic compounds	(w) Carnivores

Fill in the Blanks

DIRECTIONS : *Complete the following statements with an appropriate word / term to be filled in the blank space(s).*

108. Climate refers to the prevailing .... conditions.

109. The total amount of .... per unit time produced in an ecosystem is called the gross primary productivity.

110. The hierarchies within a food web are called .... levels.

111. Without the .... in a food web many chemicals would not be recycled.

112. Decrease in ozone in stratosphere is linked to release of synthetic chemicals like ....

113. The .... make the energy from sunlight available to the rest of the ecosystem.

114. The use of chemicals like CFCs has endangered the .... layer.

115. The waste we generate may be .... or ....

116. All the interacting organisms in an area together with the non-living constituents of the environment form an ....

117. Gardens and crop fields are example of .... ecosystem.

118. The decomposers comprising micro-organisms like .... and ....

119. The energy flows from .... to the heterotrophs and decomposers.

120. The flow of energy is always .... in food chains.

121. The interlocking pattern of various food chains is referred as ....

122. The disposal of the waste we generate is causing serious ....problems.

123. The various populations of living organisms in an area together form .... community.

124. All the ecosystems taken together in a geographical area form a bigger unit known as ....

125. Hydrosphere, lithosphere and atmosphere along with living organism form ....

126. The plants trap .... energy and convert it into .... energy.

127. The energy available at each successive trophic level is ....of the previous level.

128. Nitrogen-fixing bacteria live in nodules on the roots of .... plants.

129. Nitrates and nitrites present in the soil are changed into ....by micro-organisms.

130. The increased nitrogen in rivers and lakes boosts the growth of .... and other phytoplankton at the cost of other aquatic organisms.

≫ True / False

DIRECTIONS : *Read the following statements and write your answer as true or false.*

---

131. Non-biodegradable articles are the ones which cannot be digested.

132. Ozone is formed in stratosphere by action of ultraviolet radiations on oxygen.

133. Earth is kept warm due to green house flux.

134. Biodegradable wastes should be separated and kept in blue colour bins for garbage collectors.

135. Blue green algae are producers.

136. The reproduction and other activities of living organisms are affected by the abiotic components of ecosystem.

137. Specific enzymes are needed for the break-down of a particular substance.

138. The materials like plastics are not acted upon by physical process.

139. Secondary consumers in a food chain are always carnivores.

140. Carbon dioxide causes depletion of ozone layer thereby allowing more UV-radiations to reach the earth.

141. Organisms can make organic compounds from inorganic substances by using the radiant energy of the sun in the presence of chlorophyll.

142. Ecology is the scientific study of the interaction of organisms with each other and the environment.

143. The abiotic components of the environment are the living factors.

144. The amount of usable energy remains constant as it is passed from one trophic level to another.

145. The energy within an ecosystem is fixed and never changes.

146. Human population and technology are having a destructive impact on the biosphere.

ANSWER KEY & SOLUTIONS

1. (a)	**2.** (d)	**3.** (d)	**4.** (d)
5. (d)	**6.** (a)	**7.** (d)	**8.** (c)
9. (b)	**10.** (d)	**11.** (d)	**12.** (a)
13. (a)	**14.** (a)	**15.** (a)	**16.** (b)
17. (b)	**18.** (d)	**19.** (b)	**20.** (a)
21. (a)	**22.** (c)	**23.** (c)	**24.** (c)
25. (a)	**26.** (d)	**27.** (c)	**28.** (d)
29. (b)	**30.** (d)	**31.** (a)	**32.** (d)
33. (d)	**34.** (d)	**35.** (c)	**36.** (c)
37. (b)	**38.** (a)	**39.** (c)	**40.** (a)
41. (c)	**42.** (c)	**43.** (b)	**44.** (c)
45. (c)	**46.** (b)	**47.** (b)	**48.** (d)
49. (d)	**50.** (b)	**51.** (d)	**52.** (d)
53. (c)	**54.** (c)	**55.** (b)	**56.** (b)
57. (c)	**58.** (c)		

59. (c) Statement (ii) and (iii), regarding food chain, are correct.

60. (a)

61. (a) In the graphical representation pyramid of number shows the arrangement of number of individuals (population size) of different trophic levels in a food chain in an ecosystem.

The pyramid of pond ecosystem is upright, because the base of this pyramid is occupied by the maximum number of phytoplanktons (autotrophs) and number of individuals which gradually decreases towards the primary and secondary consumers side respectively.

62. (c) **63.** (b)

64. (a) Fungi is not autotrophic. Autotrophs are producers which make their own food through the process of photosynthesis.

65. (d) Domestic sewage contains faecal matter, having coliform bacteria E. coli. If a water body has coliform bacteria, it indicates pollution from domestic sewage.

66. (c) Incomplete combustion of coal produces carbon monoxide which is highly toxic and can cause death of human.

67. (d) The increase in concentration of harmful chemical substance like pesticides in the body of living organisms at each trophic level of a food chain is called biological magnification. The organism which occurs at the highest trophic level in the food chain will have the maximum concentration of harmful chemicals in its body. Since vulture occupies the top level as it eats the tiger, which in turn eats the goat, which eats the grass in the food chain. So, it will have the maximum concentration of harmful chemicals in its body.

68. (a) The accumulation of harmful chemicals with an increase in trophical level is known as biological magnification.

69. (b) This process can be seen in green house effect. Infra-red radiations fails to escape from glass house. As a result temperature rises in a glass house.

70. (a) **71.** (b)

72. (c) The phenomenon of accumulation of non-biodegradable chemicals, e.g., DDT, in a food chain at each trophic level is called biomagnifaction.

73. (d) Decomposers are present at the final level in a food web. They breakdown dead and decaying organic matter (plants and animals) and convert into nutrients in the soil. They naturally increase the decomposition process and therefore used in natural biocomposting.

74. (c) and (d) The term biodegradable is used to describe materials that decompose through the actions of bacteria, fungi, and other living organisms. Temperature and sunlight may also play roles in the decomposition of biodegradable plastics and other substances.

Example: human and animal excreta, plant products like rubber, paper, wood, leaves, cotton, and wool, dead remains of living organisms, kitchen waste, agricultural waste.

75. (b) Food chain is a linear sequence of organisms which starts from producer organism and ends with decomposer species. In the given group, grass is a producer, goat is a herbivore and human is top carnivore.

76. **(d)** Eco-friendly products promote green living that helps to conserve energy and also prevent air, water and noise pollution. They prove to be a boon for the environment and also prevent human health from deterioration.

77. **(b)** Organisms which synthesise carbohydrates from inorganic compounds using radiant energy are called producers e.g., all green plants. The producers make the energy from sunlight available to the rest of the ecosystem.

Organisms which consume the food produced, either directly from producers or indirectly by feeding on other consumers are the consumers.

Microorganisms which break-down the complex organic substances into simple inorganic substances used by plants are called decomposers.

Carnivores and herbivores are types of consumers.

78. **(b)** Producers capture the solar energy and convert it into chemical energy. All green plants and certain blue-green algae which can produce food by photosynthesis come under this category and are called the producer.

79. **(a)** There is a loss of energy as we go from one trophic level to the next, this limits the number of trophic levels in a food-chain.

80. **(c)**   81. **(d)**

82. **(b)** 100 J

83. **(c)** Third Trophic level

84. **(a)** Act at every trophic level of the food chain

85. **(c)** Energy is unidirectional and matter is repeatedly circulating

86. **(a)** Decrease in energy at higher trophic level

87. **(c)** Secondary consumer

88. **(d)** Omnivores – molds, yeast and mushrooms

89. **(a)** Grassland food chain

90. **(c)** Because plants can produce its own energy

91. **(d)** B and D

92. **(c)** (ii), (iii)

93. **(b)** Saprophytes

94. **(d)** Omnivores – molds, yeast and mushrooms

95. **(c)** Secondary consumer

96. **(a)** Grassland food chain

97. **(a)** 98. **(a)**

99. **(a)** Animals blend with the surroundings or background to remain unnoticed for protection and aggression.

100. **(a)** 101. **(a)**   102. **(d)**

103. **(c)** In the food web, different food chains are interconnected. Each chain consists of different trophic levels *i.e.*, producers, consumers and detrivores. So, kite can also be a part of food web.

104. **(a)**

105. **(c)** Tropical rain forests have disappeared mainly due to man's activities. Due to over population in countries like India, rain forests are cut to make place available for man to live and build houses. To build buildings and factories man has incessantly cut down trees. This has caused the depletion of rain forests.

106. (A) → r (B) → s (C) → p (D) → q

107. (A) → (w), (B) → (s), (C) → (u), (D) → (v), (E) → (p), (F) → (q), (G) → (r), (H) → (t)

108. weather   109. organic material

110. trophic   111. decomposers

112. Chorofluorocarbons   113. producers

114. ozone

115. biodegradable, non-biodegradable.

116. ecosystem   117. artificial

118. bacteria, fungi   119. autotrophs

120. unidirectional   121. food web

122. environmental   123. biotic

124. biome   125. biosphere

126. light, chemical   127. 10%

128. leguminious   129. ammonia

130. algae

131. True   132. True   133. True   134. False

135. True   136. True   137. True   138. False

139. True   140. False   141. True   142. True

143. False   144. False   145. False   146. True

MATHEMATICS
TERM I & TERM II

Real Numbers

DIRECTIONS : *This section contains multiple choice questions. Each question has 4 choices (a), (b), (c) and (d) out of which only one is correct.*

1. What is the largest number that divides 70 and 125, leaving remainders 5 and 8 respectively?
   (a) 13   (b) 9
   (c) 3   (d) 585

2. What is the largest number that divides 245 and 1029, leaving remainder 5 in each case?
   (a) 15   (b) 16
   (c) 9   (d) 5

3. A class of 20 boys and 15 girls is divided into n groups so that each group has x boys and y girls. Values of x, y and n respectively are
   (a) 3, 4 and 8   (b) 4, 3 and 6
   (c) 4, 3 and 7   (d) 7, 4 and 3

4. If p, q are two consecutive natural numbers, then H.C.F. (p, q) is
   (a) p (b) q
   (c) 1   (d) pq

5. Given that L.C.M. $(91, 26) = 182$, then H.C.F. $(91, 26)$ is
   (a) 13   (b) 26
   (c) 17   (d) 9

6. Which of the following statement is true?
   (a) Every point on the number line represents a rational number.
   (b) Irrational numbers cannot be represented by points on the number line.
   (c) $\dfrac{22}{7}$ is a rational number.
   (d) None of these.

7. The sum of exponents of prime factors in the prime-factorisation of 196 is
   (a) 3   (b) 4
   (c) 5   (d) 2

8. When 2^{256} is divided by 17, then remainder would be
   (a) 1   (b) 16
   (c) 14   (d) None of these

9. The sum of three non-zero prime numbers is 100. One of them exceeds the other by 36. Then, the largest number is
   (a) 73   (b) 91
   (c) 67   (d) 57

10. The rational number of the form $\dfrac{p}{q}$, $q \neq 0$, p and q are positive integers , which represents $0.1\overline{34}$ i.e., $(0.1343434....)$ is
   (a) $\dfrac{134}{999}$ (b) $\dfrac{134}{990}$
   (c) $\dfrac{133}{999}$ (d) $\dfrac{133}{990}$

11. The least number which is a perfect square and is divisible by each of 16, 20 and 24 is
   (a) 240   (b) 1600
   (c) 2400   (d) 3600

12. If n is an even natural number, then the largest natural number by which $n (n + 1) (n + 2)$ is divisible is
   (a) 6   (b) 8
   (c) 12   (d) 24

13. The least number which when divided by 15, leaves a remainder of 5, when divided by 25, leaves a remainder of 15 and when divided by 35, leaves a remainder of 25, is
   (a) 515   (b) 525
   (c) 1040   (d) 1050

14. The number $3^{13} - 3^{10}$ is divisible by

(a) 2 and 3

(b) 3 and 10

(c) 2, 3 and 10

(d) 2, 3 and 13

15. A number lies between 300 and 400. If the number is added to the number formed by reversing the digits, the sum is 888 and if the unit's digit and the ten's digit change places, the new number exceeds the original number by 9. Then, the number is

(a) 339   (b) 341

(c) 378   (d) 345

16. Which of the following will have a terminating decimal expansion?

(a) $\dfrac{77}{210}$ (b) $\dfrac{23}{30}$

(c) $\dfrac{125}{441}$ (d) $\dfrac{23}{8}$

17. I. The L.C.M. of x and 18 is 36.

II. The H.C.F. of x and 18 is 2.

What is the number x ?

(a) 1   (b) 2

(c) 3   (d) 4

18. If $a = 2^3 \times 3$, $b = 2 \times 3 \times 5$, $c = 3^n \times 5$ and

L.C.M. $(a, b, c) = 2^3 \times 3^2 \times 5$, then $n =$

(a) 1   (b) 2

(c) 3   (d) 4

19. If p_1 and p_2 are two odd prime numbers such that $p_1 > p_2$, then $p_1^2 - p_2^2$ is

(a) an even number

(b) an odd number

(c) an odd prime number

(d) a prime number

20. When a natural number x is divided by 5, the remainder is 2. When a natural number y is divided by 5, the remainder is 4. The remainder is z when x + y is divided by 5. The value of $\dfrac{2z - 5}{3}$ is

(a) −1   (b) 1

(c) −2   (d) 2

21. The largest non-negative integer k such that 24^k divides 13! is

(a) 2   (b) 3

(c) 4   (d) 5

22. On dividing a natural number by 13, the remainder is 3 and on dividing the same number by 21, the remainder is 11. If the number lies between 500 and 600, then the remainder on dividing the number by 19 is

(a) 4   (b) 6

(c) 9   (d) 13

23. Let $a_1, a_2, ..., a_{100}$ be non-zero real numbers such that $a_1 + a_2 + ... + a_{100} = 0$

Then,

(a) $\displaystyle\sum_{i=1}^{100} a_i 2^{a_i} > 0$ and $\displaystyle\sum_{i=1}^{100} a_i 2^{-a_i} < 0$

(b) $\displaystyle\sum_{i=1}^{100} a_i 2^{a_i} \geq 0$ and $\displaystyle\sum_{i=1}^{100} a_i 2^{-a_i} \geq 0$

(c) $\displaystyle\sum_{i=1}^{100} a_i 2^{a_i} \leq 0$ and $\displaystyle\sum_{i=1}^{100} a_i 2^{-a_i} \leq 0$

(d) The sign of $\displaystyle\sum_{i=1}^{100} a_i 2^{a_i}$ or $\displaystyle\sum_{i=1}^{100} a_i 2^{-a_i}$ depends on the choice of a_i's

24. The value of $0.2\overline{35}$ is :

(a) $\dfrac{233}{900}$ (b) $\dfrac{233}{990}$

(c) $\dfrac{235}{999}$ (d) $\dfrac{235}{990}$

25. Consider the following statements: For any integer n,

I. $n^2 + 3$ is never divisible by 17.

II. $n^2 + 4$ is never divisible by 17.

Then,

(a) both I and II are true

(b) both I and II are false

(c) I is false and II is true

(d) I is true and II is false

26. Given that $\dfrac{1}{7} = 0.\overline{142857}$, which is a repeating decimal having six different digits. If x is the sum of such first three positive integers n such that $\dfrac{1}{n} = 0.\overline{abcdef}$, where a, b, c, d, e and f are different digits, then the value of x is

(a) 20   (b) 21

(c) 41   (d) 42

27. If $m = n^2 - n$, where n is an integer, then $m^2 - 2m$ is divisible by

(a) 20   (b) 24

(c) 30   (d) 16

28. The unit digit in the expression $55^{725} + 73^{5810} + 22^{853}$ is

(a) 0   (b) 4

(c) 5   (d) 6

29. For some integer m, every even integer is of the form

(a) m (b) $m + 1$

(c) $2m$ (d) $2m + 1$

30. For some integer q, every odd integer is of the form

(a) q (b) $q + 1$

(c) $2q$ (d) $2q + 1$

31. The decimal expansion of the rational number $\dfrac{33}{2^2.5}$ will terminate after

(a) one decimal place

(b) two decimal places

(c) three decimal places

(d) more than 3 decimal places

32. Product of two co-prime numbers is 117. Their L.C.M. should be

(a) 1

(b) 117

(c) equal to their H.C.F.

(d) Lies between 1 to 117

33. Which of the following statement(s) is/are always true?

(a) The sum of two distinct irrational numbers is rational.

(b) The rationalising factor of a number is unique.

(c) Every irrational number is a surd.

(d) None of these

34. Which of the following statement(s) is/are not correct?

(a) $\dfrac{7^3}{5^4}$ is a non-terminating repeating decimal.

(b) If $a = 2 + \sqrt{3}$ and $b = \sqrt{2} - \sqrt{3}$, then $a + b$ is irrational.

(c) If 19 divides a^3, then 19 divides a, where a is a positive integer.

(d) Product of L.C.M. and H.C.F. of 25 and 625 is 15625.

35. The product of unit digit in $(7^{95} - 3^{58})$ and $(7^{95} + 3^{58})$ is

(a) 8

(b) lies between 3 and 7

(c) 6

(d) lies between 3 and 6

36. Which of the following statement(s) is/are not correct?

(a) Every integer is a rational number.

(b) The sum of a rational number and an irrational number is an irrational number.

(c) Every real number is rational.

(d) Every point on a number line is associated with a real number.

37. Which of the following statement(s) is/are not correct?

(a) There are infinitely many even primes.

(b) Let 'a' be a positive integer and p be a prime number such that a^2 is divisible by p, then a is divisible by p.

(c) Every positive integer different from 1 can be expressed as a product of non-negative power of 2 and an odd number.

(d) If 'p' is a positive prime, then $\sqrt{p}$ is an irrational number.

❯ Case/Passage Based Questions

DIRECTIONS : *Study the given Case/Passage and answer the following questions.*

Case/Passage-I

To enhance the reading skills of grade X students, the school nominates you and two of your friends to set up a class library. There are two sections-section A and section B of grade X. There are 32 students in section A and 36 students in section B.

[From CBSE Question Bank-2021]

38. What is the minimum number of books you will acquire for the class library, so that they can be distributed equally among students of Section A or Section B?

(a) 144   (b) 128   (c) 288   (d) 272

39. If the product of two positive integers is equal to the product of their HCF and LCM is true then, the HCF (32, 36) is

(a) 2   (b) 4   (c) 6   (d) 8

40. 36 can be expressed as a product of its primes as

(a) $2^2 \times 3^2$ (b) $2^1 \times 3^3$

(c) $2^3 \times 3^1$ (d) $2^0 \times 3^0$

41. $7 \times 11 \times 13 \times 15 + 15$ is a

(a) Prime number

(b) Composite number

(c) Neither prime nor composite

(d) None of the above

42. If p and q are positive integers such that $p = ab^2$ and $q = a^2b$, where a, b are prime numbers, then the LCM (p, q) is
    (a) ab   (b) a^2b^2 (c) a^3b^2 (d) a^3b^3

Case/Passage-II

A seminar is being conducted by an Educational Organisation, where the participants will be educators of different subjects. The number of participants in Hindi, English and Mathematics are 60, 84 and 108 respectively.

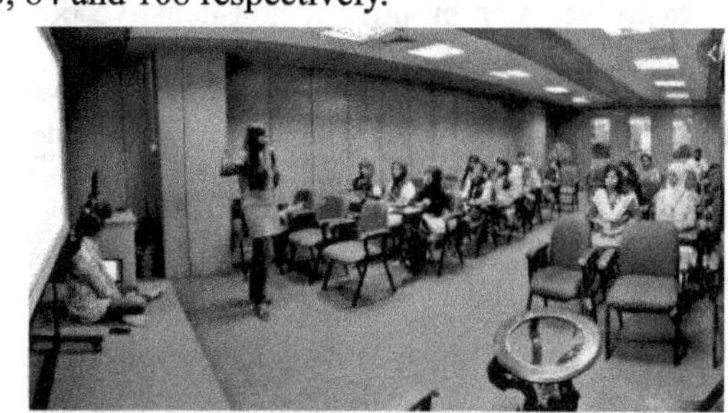

[From CBSE Question Bank-2021]

43. In each room the same number of participants are to be seated and all of them being in the same subject, hence maximum number participants that can accommodated in each room are
    (a) 14   (b) 12   (c) 16   (d) 18

44. What is the minimum number of rooms required during the event?
    (a) 11   (b) 31   (c) 41   (d) 21

45. The LCM of 60, 84 and 108 is
    (a) 3780   (b) 3680   (c) 4780   (d) 4680

46. The product of HCF and LCM of 60,84 and 108 is
    (a) 55360   (b) 35360   (c) 45500   (d) 45360

47. 108 can be expressed as a product of its primes as
    (a) $2^3 \times 3^2$ (b) $2^3 \times 3^3$
    (c) $2^2 \times 3^2$ (d) $2^2 \times 3^3$

Case/Passage-III

A Mathematics exhibition is being conducted in your school and one of your friends is making a model of a factor tree. He has some difficulty and asks for your help in completing a quiz for the audience.

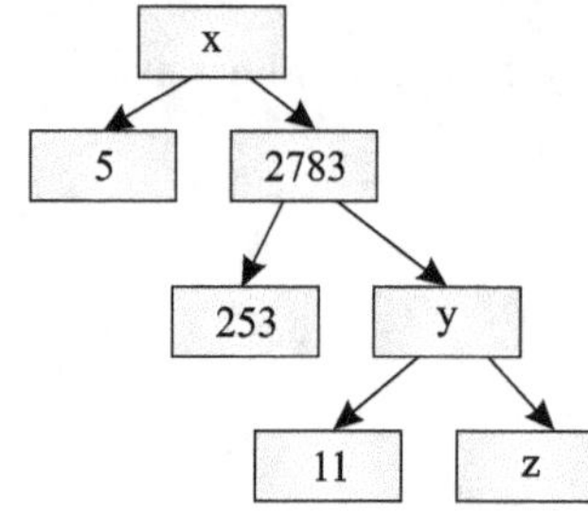

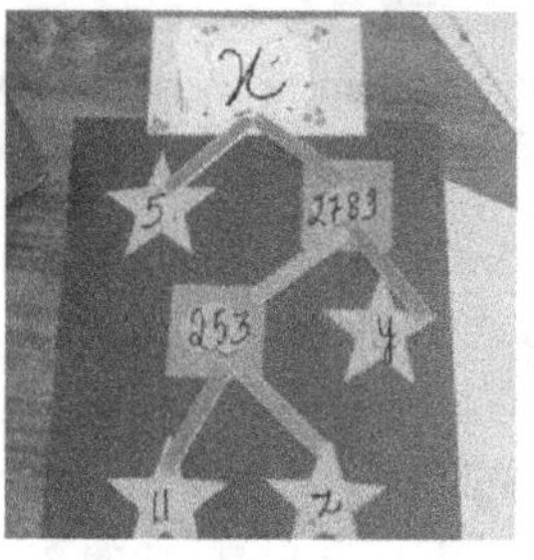

[From CBSE Question Bank-2021]

Observe the following factor tree and answer the following:

48. What will be the value of x?
    (a) 15005   (b) 13915
    (c) 56920   (d) 17429

49. What will be the value of y?
    (a) 23   (b) 22   (c) 11   (d) 19

50. What will be the value of z?
    (a) 22   (b) 23   (c) 17   (d) 19

51. According to Fundamental Theorem of Arithmetic 13915 is a
    (a) Composite number
    (b) Prime number
    (c) Neither prime nor composite
    (d) Even number

52. The prime factorisation of 13915 is
    (a) $5 \times 11^3 \times 13^2$ (b) $5 \times 11^3 \times 23^2$
    (c) $5 \times 11^2 \times 23$ (d) $5 \times 11^2 \times 13^2$

Assertion & Reason 

DIRECTIONS : *Each of these questions contains an Assertion followed by Reason. Read them carefully and answer the question on the basis of following options. You have to select the one that best describes the two statements.*

(a) If both **Assertion** and **Reason** are **correct** and Reason is the **correct explanation** of Assertion.

(b) If both **Assertion** and **Reason** are correct, but Reason is **not the correct explanation** of Assertion.

(c) If **Assertion** is **correct** but **Reason** is **incorrect**.

(d) If **Assertion** is **incorrect** but **Reason** is **correct**.

53. **Assertion :** $\dfrac{13}{3125}$ is a terminating decimal fraction.

    Reason : If $q = 2^n \cdot 5^m$ where n, m are non-negative integers, then $\dfrac{p}{q}$ is a terminating decimal fraction.

54. **Assertion :** Denominator of 34.12345. When expressed in the form $\dfrac{p}{q}$, $q \neq 0$, is of the form $2^m \times 5^n$, where m, n are non-negative integers.

    Reason : 34.12345 is a terminating decimal fraction.

55. **Assertion :** The H.C.F. of two numbers is 16 and their product is 3072. Then, their L.C.M = 162.

    Reason : If a, b are two positive integers, then H.C.F $\times$ L.C.M. $= a \times b$.

56. **Assertion :** 2 is a rational number.

Reason : The square roots of all positive integers are irrationals.

57. **Assertion :** If L.C.M. $\{p, q\}$ = 30 and H.C.F $\{p, q\}$ = 5, then $p.q$ = 150.

Reason : L.C.M. of (a, b) × H.C.F of (a, b) = $a.b$.

58. **Assertion :** $n^2 - n$ is divisible by 2 for every positive integer.

Reason : $\sqrt{2}$ is not a rational number.

59. **Assertion :** $n^2 + n$ is divisible by 2 for every positive integer n.

Reason : If x and y are odd positive integers, from $x^2 + y^2$ is divisible by 4.

Match the Following

DIRECTIONS : *Each question contains statements given in two columns which have to be matched. Statements (A, B, C, D) in column-I have to be matched with statements (p, q, r, s) in column-II.*

60.

Column-I	Column-II
(A) Irrational number is always	(p) rational number
(B) Rational number is always	(q) irrational number
(C) $\sqrt[3]{6}$ is not a	(r) non-terminating, non-repeating
(D) $2\sqrt{2}$ is an	(s) terminating decimal

61.

Column-I	Column-II
(A) H.C.F of the smallest composite number and the smallest prime number	(p) 6
(B) H.C.F of 336 and 54	(q) 5
(C) H.C.F of 475 and 495	(r) 2

62.

Column-I	Column-II
(A) $\dfrac{551}{2^3 \times 5^6 \times 7^9}$	(p) a prime number
(B) Product of $\left(\sqrt{5} - \sqrt{3}\right)$ and $\left(\sqrt{5} + \sqrt{3}\right)$ is	(q) is an irrational number
(C) $\sqrt{5} - 4$	(r) is a terminating decimal representation
(D) $\dfrac{422}{2^3 \times 5^4}$	(s) is a non-terminating but repeating decimal representation

Fill in the Blanks

DIRECTIONS : *Complete the following statements with an appropriate word / term to be filled in the blank space(s).*

63. $\sqrt{5}$ is a/ an .... number.

64. $\dfrac{1}{\sqrt{2}}$ is a/ an .... number.

65. The exponent of 2 in the prime factorisation of 144, is ....

66. $7\sqrt{5}$ is a/ an .... number.

67. $6 + \sqrt{2}$ is a/ an .... number.

68. An .... is a series of well defined steps which gives a procedure for solving a type of problem.

69. An........... is a proven statement used for proving another statement.

70. L.C.M. of 96 and 404 is ....

71. H.C.F. of 6, 72 and 120 is ....

72. 156 as a product of its prime factors ....

73. $\dfrac{35}{50}$ is a .... decimal expansion.

True / False

DIRECTIONS : *Read the following statements and write your answer as true or false.*

74. Given positive integers a and b, there exist whole numbers q and r satisfying $a = bq + r$, $0 \le r < b$.

75. Every composite number can be expressed (factorised) as a product of primes and this factorisation is unique, apart from the order in which the prime factors occur.

76. $\sqrt{2}$ and $\sqrt{3}$ are irrational numbers.

77. If $x = p/q$ be a rational number, such that the prime factorisation of q is of the form $2^n 5^m$, where n, m are non-negative integers. Then x has a decimal expansion which is terminating.

78. Any positive odd integer is of the form $6q + 1$ or $6q + 3$ or $6q + 5$, where q is some integer.

79. The quotient of two integers is always a rational number.

80. 1/0 is not rational.

81. The number of irrational numbers between 15 and 18 is infinite.

82. Every fraction is a rational number.

ANSWER KEY & SOLUTIONS

1. **(a)** Required number = H.C.F. $\{(70-5), (125-8)\}$
    = H.C.F. $(65, 117) = 13$.

2. **(b)** Required number = H.C.F.$\{(245-5), (1029-5)\}$
    = H.C.F. $(240, 1024) = 16$.

3. **(c)** H.C.F. of 20 and 15 = 5

    So, 5 students are in each group.

    $\therefore \quad n = \dfrac{20+15}{5} = \dfrac{35}{5} = 7$

    Hence, x = 4, y = 3 and n = 7

4. **(c)** 1

5. **(a)** H.C.F. $(91, 126) = \dfrac{91 \times 126}{\text{L.C.M.}(91, 126)} = \dfrac{91 \times 126}{182} = 13$

6. **(d)** All the given statements are false.

7. **(b)** $196 = 2^2 \cdot 7^2$, sum of exponents $= 2 + 2 = 4$

8. **(a)** When 2^{256} is divided by 17 then, $\dfrac{2^{256}}{2^4 + 1} = \dfrac{(2^4)^{64}}{(2^4 + 1)}$

    By remainder theorem when $f(x)$ is divided by $x + a$ the remainder $= f(-a)$

    Here, $f(a) = (2^4)^{64}$ and $x = 2^4$ and $a = 1$

    $\therefore$ Remainder $= f(-1) = (-1)^{64} = 1$

9. **(c)** Since, the sum of all the three prime numbrs is 100.

    Then, there are two cases

    Case 1: All the three numbers should be even because 100 is an even number. But this case is not possible as there is only one even prime.

    Case 2 : One prime is even and other two primes are odd.

    Since, 2 is only even prime, so it must be one of three primes.

    Let p and $p + 36$ be the other two primes.

    Then, according to question

    $2 + p + (p + 36) = 100; 2p + 38 = 100$

    $2p = 100 - 38 = 62; p = \dfrac{62}{2} = 31$

    So, all the three primes are 2, 31 and 67.

    Hence, largest prime number is 67.

10. **(d)** $0.1\overline{34} = \dfrac{134-1}{990} = \dfrac{133}{990}$

11. **(d)** The L.C.M. of 16, 20 and 24 is 240. The least multiple of 240 that is a perfect square is 3600 and also we can easily eliminate choices (a) and (c) since they are not perfect number. Hence, the required least number which is also a perfect square is 3600 which is divisible by each of 16, 20 and 24.

12. **(d)** Out of n and $n + 2$, one is divisible by 2 and the other by 4, hence $n(n + 2)$ is divisible by 8. Also n, $n + 1$, $n + 2$ are three consecutive numbers, hence one of them is divisible by 3. Hence, $n(n + 1)(n + 2)$ must be divisible by 24. This will be true for any even number n.

13. **(a)** The number divisible by 15, 25 and 35 = L.C.M. $(15, 25, 35) = 525$

    Since, the number is short by 10 for complete division by 15, 25 and 35.

    Hence, the required least number $= 525 - 10 = 515$.

14. **(d)** $3^{13} - 3^{10} = 3^{10}(3^3 - 1) = 3^{10}(26) = 2 \times 13 \times 3^{10}$

    Hence, $3^{13} - 3^{10}$ is divisible by 2, 3 and 13.

15. **(d)** Sum is 888 $\Rightarrow$ unit's digit should add up to 8. This is possible only for option (d) as "3" + "5" = "8".

16. **(d)**

17. **(d)** L.C.M $\times$ H.C.F = First number $\times$ second number

    Hence, required number $= \dfrac{36 \times 2}{18} = 4$.

18. **(b)** Value of $n = 2$.

19. **(a)** Since, p_1 and p_2 are odd primes and sum of two odd number is an even number.

    So, $p_1 + p_2$ is an even number.

    Since, multiple of even number is always even.

    Therefore, $(p_1 + p_2)(p_1 - p_2)$ is even

    Hence, $p_1^2 - p_2^2 = (p_1 + p_2)(p_1 - p_2)$ is an even number.

20. **(a)** Since, x is divided by 5, the remainder is 2

    therefore x = 5m + 2

    similarly, y = 5n + 4 consider x + y = 5(m + n) + 6

    = 5(m + n) + 5 + 1 = 5(m + n + 1) + 1

    But given that when x + y is divided by 5, the remainder is z

    $\therefore \quad z = 1$

    Now, $\quad \dfrac{2z - 5}{3} = \dfrac{2(1) - 5}{3} = -1$

21. **(b)** We know that

$13! = 2 \times 3 \times 4 \times 5 \times 6 \times 7 \times 8 \times 9 \times 10 \times 11 \times 12 \times 13$

$= 2^{10} \times 3^5 \times 5^2 \times 7 \times 11 \times 13 \Rightarrow 24^k = (2^3 \times 3)^k$

where k is largest non-negative integer

When 13! is an divided by 24^k, we get

$$\frac{2^{10} \times 3^5 \times 5^2 \times 7 \times 11 \times 13}{2^{3k} \cdot 3^k}$$

$= 2^{10-3k} \cdot 3^{5-k} \cdot 5^2 \times 7 \times 11 \times 13$

$\therefore \quad 10 - 3k$ is integer.

Then, maximum value of $k = 3$.

22. **(a)** **Given:** The natural number, when divided by 13 leaves remainder 3

The natural number, when divided by 21 leaves remainder 11

So, $13 - 3 = 21 - 11 = 10 = k$

Now, LCM $(13, 21) = 273$

But the number lies between 500 and 600

$\therefore \quad 2\,\text{LCM}\,(13, 21) - k = 546 - 10 = 536$

$536 = 19 \times 8 + 4 \quad \therefore \quad$ remainder $= 4$

23. **(a)** Let $a_1, a_2, a_3, ..., a_{100}$ be non-zero real number and

$a_1 + a_2 + a_3 + ... + a_{100} = 0$

$a_i \cdot 2^{a_i} > a_i$ and $a_i \cdot 2^{-a_i} < a_i$

$\therefore \quad \displaystyle\sum_{i=1}^{100} a_1 \cdot 2^{a_i} > \sum_{i=1}^{100} a_i$ and $\displaystyle\sum_{i=1}^{100} a_1 \cdot 2^{-a_i} < \sum_{i=1}^{100} a_i$

$\Rightarrow \quad \displaystyle\sum_{i=1}^{100} a_1 \cdot 2^{a_i} > 0$ and $\displaystyle\sum_{i=1}^{100} a_1 \cdot 2^{-a_i} < 0$

Hence, option (a) is correct.

24. **(c)** Let $x = 0.\overline{235}$ ...(i)

$1000x = 235.\overline{235}$ ...(ii)

Subtract (i) from (ii), $999x = 235 \Rightarrow x = \dfrac{235}{999}$

25. **(d)** Let us consider that $n^2 + 3$ is divisible by 17

$\therefore \quad n^2 + 3 = 17K \quad [K \in N]$

$\Rightarrow n^2 = 17K - 3 \Rightarrow n^2 = 3(17m - 1) \quad [\because K = 3m]$

$3(17m - 1)$ is a perfect square, which is not possible.

$\therefore \quad n^2 + 3$ is never divisible by 17.

In, $n^2 + 4$, put $n = 9$

So, $(9)^2 + 4 = 81 + 4 = 85$ which is divisible by 17.

$\therefore$ I is true and II is false.

26. **(c)** $\dfrac{1}{7} = 0.\overline{142857}$

The second positive integer whose reciprocal have six different repeating decimals is

$\dfrac{1}{13} = 0.\overline{076923}$

And the third positive integer whose reciprocal have six different repeating decimals is

$\dfrac{1}{21} = 0.\overline{047619}$

Therefore, the values of x are 7, 13, 21

Hence, the required sum is $= 7 + 13 + 21 = 41$

27. **(b)** $\because \quad m = n^2 - n = n(n - 1)$

Now, $m^2 - 2m = m(m - 2)$

$= n(n - 1)(n^2 - n - 2) = n(n - 1)(n - 2)(n + 1)$

Since we know that product of any four consecutive integers is always divisible by 24.

$\therefore \quad m^2 - 2m$ is divisible by 24.

28. **(d)** For given numbers,

$(55)^{725}$, unit digit $= 5$; $(73)^{5810}$, unit digit $= 9$

$(22)^{853}$, unit digit $= 2$

Unit digit in the expression

$55^{725} + 735^{810} + 22^{853}$ is 6

29. **(c)** **30.** **(d)** **31.** **(b)**

32. **(b)** Since, H.C.F. of co-prime number is 1.

$\therefore$ Product of two co-prime numbers is equal to their L.C.M. So, L.C.M. $= 117$

33. **(d)**

34. **(a)**

35. **(a)** Unit digit in $(7^{95}) =$ Unit digit in $[(7^4)^{23} \times 7^3]$

$=$ Unit digit in 7^3 (as unit digit in $7^4 = 1$)

$=$ Unit digit in 343

Unit digit in $3^{58} =$ Unit digit in $(3^4)^4 \times 3^2$

 [as unit digit $3^4 = 1$]

$=$ Unit digit is 9

So, unit digit in $(7^{95} - 3^{58})$

$=$ Unit digit in $(343 - 9) =$ Unit digit in $334 = 4$

Unit digit in $(7^{95} + 3^{58}) =$ Unit digit in $(343 + 9)$

$=$ Unit digit in 352 $= 2$

So, the product is $4 \times 2 = 8$

36. **(c)**

37. **(a)**

38. **(c)** For getting least number of books, taking LCM of 32, 36

4	32, 36
8	8, 9
9	1, 9
	1, 1

$\Rightarrow$ $4 \times 8 \times 9 = 288$

39. **(b)** HCF of 32, 36 is

4	32, 36
	8, 9

$= 4$

40. **(a)** 36 is expressed as prime
$36 = 2 \times 2 \times 3 \times 3 = 2^2 \times 3^2$

41. **(b)** $7 \times 11 \times 13 \times 15 + 15$
$\Rightarrow$ $15 (7 \times 11 \times 13 + 1)$
so given no. is a composite number.

42. **(b)** Given a, b are prime number. So
LCM of p, q, where $p = ab^2$, $q = a^2b$
$p = a \times b \times b$
$q = a \times b \times a$
$a \times b \times b \times a \Rightarrow a^2b^2$

43. **(b)** For maximum number of participants, taking HCF of 60, 84 and 108

12	60, 84, 108
	5, 7, 9

$= 12$

44. **(d)** Minimum number of rooms required are
$5 + 7 + 9 = 21$

45. **(a)** LCM of 60, 84, 108 is
$12 \times 5 \times 7 \times 9 = 3780$

46. **(d)** Product is $= 12 \times 3780 = 45360$

47. **(d)** $108 = 2 \times 2 \times 3 \times 3 \times 3 = 2^2 \times 3^3$

48. **(b)** $x = 5 \times 2783 = 13915$

49. **(c)** $y = 253\overline{)2783}(= 11$

50. **(b)** $z = 11\overline{)253}(= 23$

51. **(a)** Composite number having more than 2 factors.

52. **(c)** Prime factorisation of 13915 =

5	13915
11	2783
11	253
23	23
	1

$\Rightarrow$ $5 \times 11 \times 11 \times 23$
$\Rightarrow$ $5 \times 11^2 \times 23$

53. **(a)** Reason is correct.

Since, the factors of the denominator 3125 is of the form $2^0 \times 5^5$.

$\therefore$ $\dfrac{13}{3125}$ is a terminating decimal

Since, assertion follows from reason.

54. **(a)** Reason is clearly true.

Again, $34.12345 = \dfrac{3412345}{100000} = \dfrac{682469}{20000} = \dfrac{682469}{2^5 \times 5^4}$

Its denominator is of the form $2^m \times 5^n$, where

$m = 5$, $n = 4$ are non-negative integers

$\therefore$ Assertion is true. Since, reason gives assertion

$\therefore$ (a) holds.

55. **(d)** Here, reason is true [standard result]

Assertion is false. $\because \dfrac{3072}{16} = 192 \neq 162$

56. **(c)** Here, reason is not true.

$\because \sqrt{4} = \pm 2$, which is not an irrational number.

$\therefore$ Reason does not hold. Clearly, assertion is true.

57. **(a)**   **58.** **(b)**   **59.** **(a)**

60. (A) $\to$ (r) [$\because$ $12 = 3 \times 4$ $\therefore$ it is a composite number]

(B) $\to$ (s)   [$\because$ g.c.d. between 2 and 7 = 1]

(C) $\to$ (p)   [$\because$ 2 is a prime number]

(D) $\to$ (q) [$\because$ $\sqrt{2}$ is not a rational number]

61. (A) $\to$ (r); (B) $\to$ (p); (C) $\to$ (q)

62. (A) $\to$ (s); (B) $\to$ (p); (C) $\to$ (q); (D) $\to$ (r)

63. irrational   **64.** irrational

65. 4   **66.** irrational

67. irrational   **68.** algorithm

69. lemma   **70.** 9696

71. 6   **72.** $2^2 \times 3 \times 13$

73. terminating

74. True   **75.** True

76. True   **77.** True

78. True   **79.** False

80. True   **81.** True

82. True

Polynomials

DIRECTIONS : *This section contains multiple choice questions. Each question has 4 choices (a), (b), (c) and (d) out of which only one is correct.*

1. If the zeroes of the polynomial $f(x) = k^2x^2 - 17x + k + 2$, $(k > 0)$ are reciprocal of each other than value of k is

   (a) 2   (b) –1

   (c) –2   (d) 1

2. If one zero of the quadratic polynomial

   $2x^2 - 8x - m$ is $\dfrac{5}{2}$, then the other zero is

   (a) $\dfrac{2}{3}$ (b) $-\dfrac{2}{3}$

   (c) $\dfrac{3}{2}$ (d) $\dfrac{-15}{2}$

3. Let $p(y) = y^4 - 3y^2 + 2y + 5$, then the remainder when $p(y)$ is divided by $(y - 1)$.

   (a) 2   (b) 3

   (c) –5   (d) 5

4. If the polynomials $ax^3 + 4x^2 + 3x - 4$ and $x^3 - 4x + a$ leave same remainder when divided by $(x - 3)$, find the value of a.

   (a) –1   (b) 1

   (c) $\dfrac{1}{2}$ (d) $-\dfrac{1}{2}$

5. Let $f(x) = x^2 - 27x + 196$. If $f(a) = a$, then what is the value of a.

   (a) 7   (b) 14

   (c) 21   (d) 6

6. If $f(x) = 2x^3 - 6x + 4x - 5$ and $g(x) = 3x^2 - 9$, then the value of $f(1) + g(-2)$ is

   (a) –3   (b) –2

   (c) 3   (d) 2

7. Factor of the polynomial $x^3 - 3x^2 - 10x + 24$ are:

   (a) $(x - 2)(x + 3)(x - 4)$

   (b) $(x + 2)(x + 3)(x + 4)$

   (c) $(x + 2)(x - 3)(x - 4)$

   (d) $(x - 2)(x - 3)(x - 4)$

8. The zeroes of the polynomial are

   $p(x) = x^2 - 10x - 75$

   (a) 5, – 15   (b) 5, 15

   (c) 15, – 5   (d) – 5, – 15

9. If a and b are zeroes of the polynomial

   $2t^2 - 4t + 3$, then the value of $a^2b + ab^2$ is :

   (a) $\dfrac{3}{4}$ (b) 2

   (c) 3   (d) 4

10. The zeroes of the polynomial $x^2 - 3x - m(m + 3)$ are

    (a) $m, m + 3$ (b) $-m, m + 3$

    (c) $m, -(m + 3)$ (d) $-m, -(m + 3)$

11. The value of x, for which the polynomials $x^2 - 1$ and $x^2 - 2x + 1$ vanish simultaneously, is

    (a) 2   (b) –2

    (c) –1   (d) 1

12. If $x = 0.\overline{7}$, then $2x$ is

    (a) $1.\overline{4}$ (b) $1.\overline{5}$

    (c) $1.\overline{54}$ (d) $1.\overline{45}$

13. Lowest value of $x^2 + 4x + 2$ is

   (a) 0   (b) –2

   (c) 2   (d) 4

14. If $a^3 - 3a^2b + 3ab^2 - b^3$ is divided by $(a - b)$, then the remainder is

   (a) $a^2 - ab + b^2$

   (b) $a^2 + ab + b^2$

   (c) 1

   (d) 0

15. A quadratic polynomial when divided by $x + 2$ leaves a remainder of 1 and when divided by $x - 1$, leaves a remainder of 4. What will be the remainder if it is divided by $(x + 2)(x - 1)$?

   (a) 1   (b) 4

   (c) $x + 3$ (d) $x - 3$

16. If the polynomials $ax^3 + 4x^2 + 3x - 4$ and $x^3 - 4x + a$ leave the same remainder when divided by $x - 3$, then the value of a is

   (a) 1   (b) –1

   (c) 19/14   (d) –5/14

17. If the value of a quadratic polynomial p(x) is 0 only at x = –1 and p(–2) = 2, then the value of p(2) is

   (a) 18   (b) 9

   (c) 6   (d) 3

18. If $x^2 - 4$ is the factor of $2x^3 + k_1x^2 + k_2x + 12$, where k_1, k_2 are constant, then the value of $k_1 + k_2$ is

   (a) 11   (b) 5

   (c) –11   (d) –5

19. If $x = 3 + 3^{2/3} + 3^{1/3}$, then the value of $x^3 - 9x^2 + 18x - 12$ is

   (a) 1   (b) 0

   (c) –1   (d) 2

20. Let $P(x)$ be a polynomial of degree 3 and $P(n) = \dfrac{1}{2}$ for $n = 1, 2, 3, 4$. Then the value of $P(5)$ is

   (a) 0   (b) $\dfrac{1}{5}$

   (c) $-\dfrac{2}{5}$ (d) $\dfrac{3}{5}$

21. The polynomial, $f(x) = (x - 1)^2 + (x - 2)^2 + (x - 3)^2 + (x - 4)^2$ has minimum value, when $x =$ ....

   (a) 40   (b) 20

   (c) 10   (d) 2.5

22. If one zero of the quadratic polynomial $x^2 + 3x + k$ is 2, then the value of k is

   (a) 10   (b) –10

   (c) 5   (d) –5

23. If one of the zeroes of the quadratic polynomial $(k - 1)x^2 + kx + 1$ is –3, then the value of k is

   (a) $\dfrac{4}{3}$ (b) $\dfrac{-4}{3}$

   (c) $\dfrac{2}{3}$ (d) $\dfrac{-2}{3}$

24. The zeroes of the quadratic polynomial $x^2 + 99x + 127$ are

   (a) both positive

   (b) both negative

   (c) one positive and one negative

   (d) both equal

25. Which of the following given options is/are correct?

   (a) $\dfrac{2}{x} + 3$ is a polynomial

   (b) $\sqrt{x} + 5$ is a polynomial

   (c) $\dfrac{2}{3x - 4}$ is a polynomial

   (d) $\sqrt{5}x^2 + \dfrac{1}{2}x + \dfrac{3}{7}$ is a polynomial

26. Which of the following given options is/are correct?

   (a) Degree of a zero polynomial is '0'.

   (b) Degree of a zero polynomial is not defined.

   (c) Degree of a constant polynomial is not defined.

   (d) A polynomial of degree n must have n zeroes.

27. Which of the following is/are a polynomial?

   (a) $x^2 + \dfrac{1}{x}$

   (b) $2x^2 - 3\sqrt{x} + 1$

   (c) $x^3 - 3x + 1$

   (d) $2x^{\frac{3}{2}} - 5x$

Polynomials

28. Which of the following is/are not graph of a quadratic polynomial ?

(a) 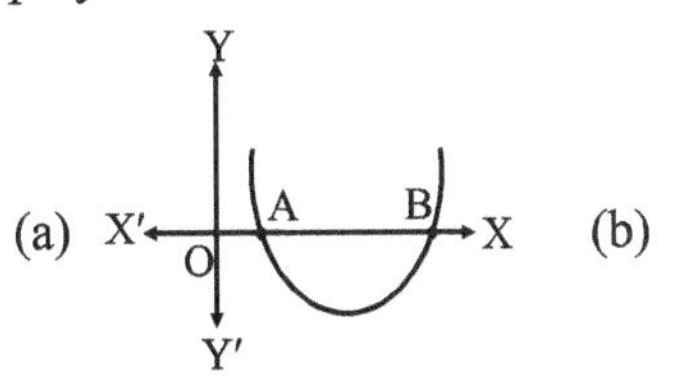

(b) 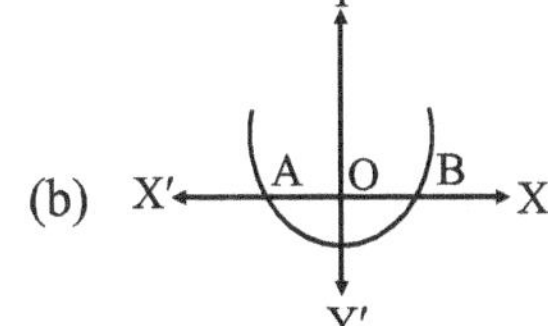

(c) 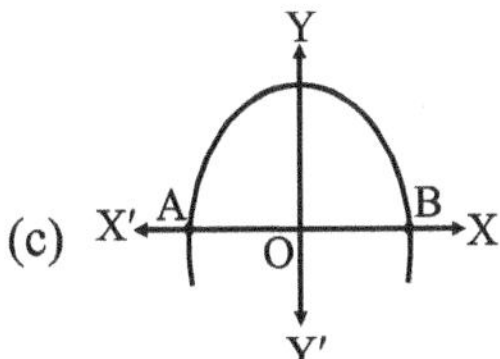

(d) 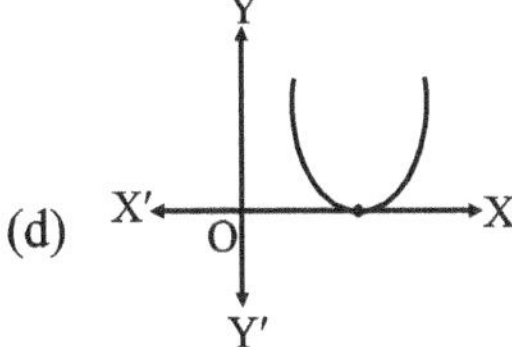

› Case/Passage Based Questions   ›››

DIRECTIONS : *Study the given Case/Passage and answer the following questions.*

Case/Passage-I

The below picture are few natural examples of parabolic shape which is represented by a quadratic polynomial. A parabolic arch is an arch in the shape of a parabola. In structures, their curve represents an efficient method of load, and so can be found in bridges and in architecture in a variety of forms.

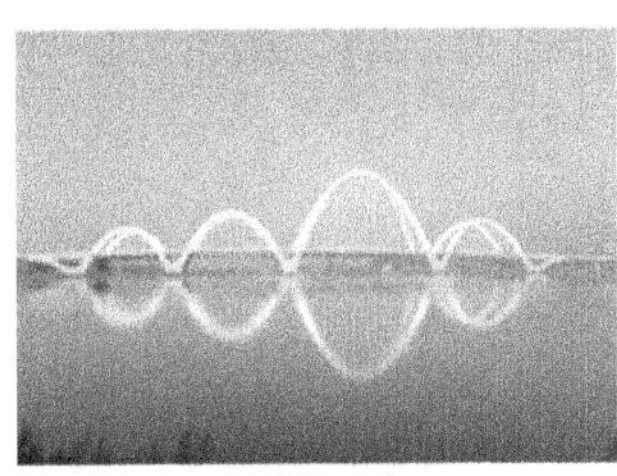
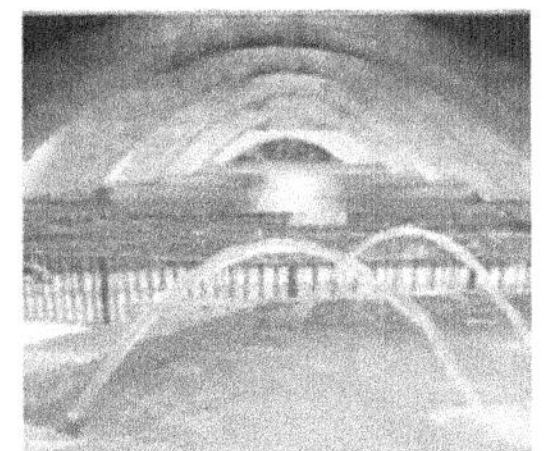

[From CBSE Question Bank-2021]

29. In the standard form of quadratic polynomial, $ax^2 + bx + c$, a, b and c are

(a) All are real numbers.

(b) All are rational numbers.

(c) 'a' is a non zero real number and b and c are any real numbers.

(d) All are integers.

30. If the roots of the quadratic polynomial are equal, where the discriminant $D = b^2 - 4ac$, then

(a) $D > 0$ (b) $D < 0$

(c) $D \geq 0$ (d) $D = 0$

31. If α and $\dfrac{1}{\alpha}$ are the zeroes of the quadratic polynomial $2x^2 - x + 8k$, then k is

(a) 4   (b) $\dfrac{1}{4}$

(c) $\dfrac{-1}{4}$ (d) 2

32. The graph of $x^2 + 1 = 0$

(a) Intersects x-axis at two distinct points.

(b) Touches x-axis at a point.

(c) Neither touches nor intersects x-axis.

(d) Either touches or intersects x-axis.

33. If the sum of the roots is –p and product of the roots is $-\dfrac{1}{p}$, then the quadratic polynomial is

(a) $k\left(-px^2 + \dfrac{x}{p} + 1\right)$ (b) $k\left(px^2 - \dfrac{x}{p} - 1\right)$

(c) $k\left(x^2 + px - \dfrac{1}{p}\right)$ (d) $k\left(x^2 - px + \dfrac{1}{p}\right)$

Case/Passage-II

An asana is a body posture, originally and still a general term for a sitting meditation pose, and later extended in hatha yoga and modern yoga as exercise, to any type of pose or position, adding reclining, standing, inverted, twisting, and balancing poses. In the figure, one can observe that poses can be related to representation of quadratic polynomial.

TRIKONASANA

ADHOMUKHA SAVASANA   ADHO MUKHA SVANA

[From CBSE Question Bank-2021]

34. The shape of the poses shown is

(a) Spiral   (b) Ellipse

(c) Linear   (d) Parabola

35. The graph of parabola opens downwards, if__________.

(a) $a \geq 0$ (b) $a = 0$

(c) $a < 0$ (d) $a > 0$

36. In the graph, how many zeroes are there for the polynomial?

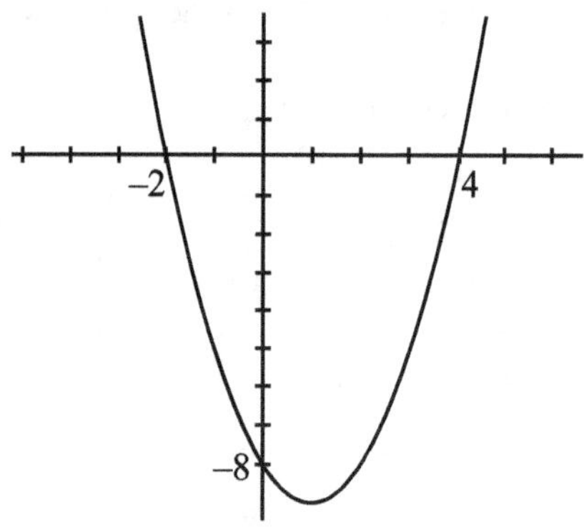

(a) 0   (b) 1

(c) 2   (d) 3

37. The two zeroes in the above shown graph are

(a) 2, 4   (b) −2, 4

(c) −8, 4   (d) 2, −8

38. The zeroes of the quadratic polynomial $4\sqrt{3}x^2 + 5x - 2\sqrt{3}$ are

(a) $\dfrac{2}{\sqrt{3}}, \dfrac{\sqrt{3}}{4}$ (b) $-\dfrac{2}{\sqrt{3}}, \dfrac{\sqrt{3}}{4}$

(c) $\dfrac{2}{\sqrt{3}}, -\dfrac{\sqrt{3}}{4}$ (d) $-\dfrac{2}{\sqrt{3}}, -\dfrac{\sqrt{3}}{4}$

Case/Passage-III

Basketball and soccer are played with a spherical ball. Even though an athlete dribbles the ball in both sports, a basketball player uses his hands and a soccer player uses his feet. Usually, soccer is played outdoors on a large field and basketball is played indoor on a court made out of wood. The projectile (path traced) of soccer ball and basketball are in the form of parabola representing quadratic polynomial.

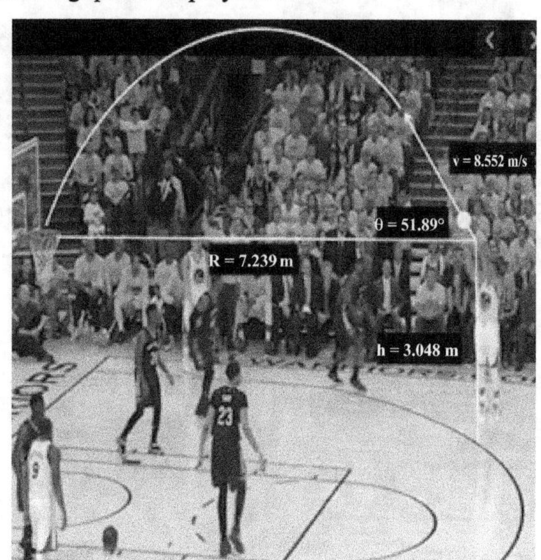

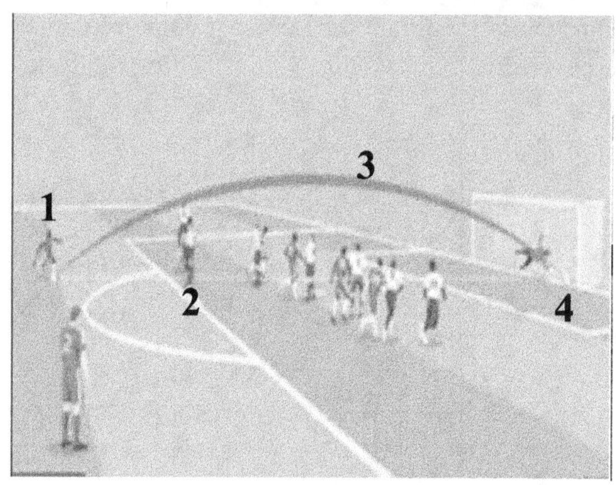

[From CBSE Question Bank-2021]

39. The shape of the path traced shown is

(a) Spiral   (b) Ellipse   (c) Linear   (d) Parabola

40. The graph of parabola opens upwards, if __________.

(a) a = 0   (b) a < 0   (c) a > 0   (d) a ≥ 0

41. Observe the following graph and answer

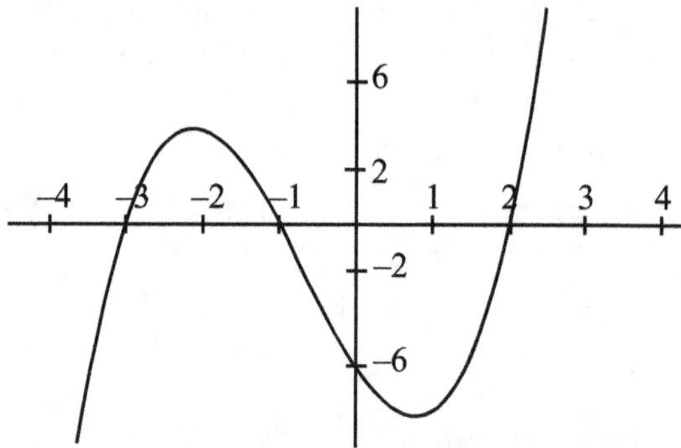

In the above graph, how many zeroes are there for the polynomial?

(a) 0   (b) 1   (c) 2   (d) 3

42. The three zeroes in the above shown graph are

(a) 2, 3, −1   (b) −2, 3, 1

(c) −3, −1, 2   (d) −2, −3, −1

43. What will be the expression of the polynomial?

(a) $x^3 + 2x^2 - 5x - 6$ (b) $x^3 + 2x^2 - 5x + 6$

(c) $x^3 + 2x^2 + 5x - 6$ (d) $x^3 + 2x^2 + 5x + 6$

»Assertion & Reason

DIRECTIONS : *Each of these questions contains an Assertion followed by Reason. Read them carefully and answer the question on the basis of following options. You have to select the one that best describes the two statements.*

Polynomials

(a) If both **Assertion** and **Reason** are **correct** and Reason is the **correct explanation** of Assertion.

(b) If both **Assertion** and **Reason** are correct, but Reason is **not the correct explanation** of Assertion.

(c) If **Assertion** is **correct** but **Reason** is **incorrect**.

(d) If **Assertion** is **incorrect** but **Reason** is **correct**.

44. **Assertion :** If one zero of polynomial $p(x) = (k^2 + 4) x^2 + 13x + 4k$ is reciprocal of other, then $k = 2$.

Reason : If $(x - \alpha)$ is a factor of $p(x)$, then $p(\alpha) = 0$ i.e. α is a zero of $p(x)$.

45. **Assertion :** $x^3 + x$ has only one real zero.

Reason : A polynomial of nth degree must have n real zeroes.

46. **Assertion :** Degree of a zero polynomial is not defined.

Reason : Degree of a non-zero constant polynomial is '0'.

47. **Assertion :** Zeroes of $f(x) = x^2 - 4x - 5$ are $5, -1$.

Reason : The polynomial whose zeroes are $2 + \sqrt{3}, 2 - \sqrt{3}$ is $x^2 - 4x + 7$.

48. **Assertion :** $x^2 + 4x - 5$ has two zeroes.

Reason : A quadratic polynomial can have at the most two zeroes.

Match the Following

DIRECTIONS : *Each question contains statements given in two columns which have to be matched. Statements (A, B, C, D) in column-I have to be matched with statements (p, q, r, s) in column-II.*

49.

Column-I (Zeroes)	Column-II (Quadratic polynomial)
(A) 3 and –5	(p) $x^2 - 25$
(B) $5 + \sqrt{2}$ and $5 - \sqrt{2}$	(q) $x^2 + 2x - 15$
(C) – 9 and 1/9	(r) $x^2 + (80/9)x - 1$
(D) 5 and – 5	(s) $x^2 - 10x + 21$

50.

Column-I (Polynomials)	Column-II (Zeroes)
(A) $4 - x^2$	(p) 7
(B) $x^3 - 2x^2$	(q) –2
(C) $6x^2 - 3 - 7x$	(r) 3/2
(D) $-x + 7$	(s) 0

Fill in the Blanks

DIRECTIONS : *Complete the following statements with an appropriate word / term to be filled in the blank space(s).*

51. Polynomials of degrees 1, 2 and 3 are called ...., ... and .... polynomials respectively.

52. The zeroes of a polynomial $p(x)$ are precisely the x-coordinates of the points, where the graph of $y = p(x)$ intersects the ....-axis.

53. A quadratic polynomial can have at most 2 zeroes and a cubic polynomial can have at most .... zeroes.

54. If α and β are the zeroes of the quadratic polynomial $ax^2 + bx + c$, then $\alpha + \beta = \dfrac{-b}{......}$ & $\alpha\beta = \dfrac{c}{.....}$

55. Zero of a polynomial is always ....

56. A polynomial of degree n has at the most .... zeroes.

True / False

DIRECTIONS : *Read the following statements and write your answer as true or false.*

57. Sum of zeroes of quadratic polynomial $= -\dfrac{(\text{coefficient of } x)}{(\text{coefficient of } x^2)}$

58. $\dfrac{1}{\sqrt{5}} x^{\frac{1}{2}} + 1$ is a polynomial

59. $\dfrac{6\sqrt{x} + x^{\frac{3}{2}}}{\sqrt{x}}$ is a polynomial, $x \neq 0$

60. Product of zeroes of quadratic polynomial $= -\dfrac{\text{constant term}}{(\text{coefficient of } x^2)}$

61. A polynomial cannot have more than one zero.

62. The degree of the sum of two polynomials each of degree 5 is always 5.

63. $3, -1, 1/3$ are the zeroes of the cubic polynomial $p(x) = 3x^3 - 5x^2 - 11x - 3$.

64. Zeroes of quadratic polynomial $x^2 + 7x + 10$ are 2 and –5

65. Sum of zeroes of $2x^2 - 8x + 6$ is – 4

ANSWER KEY & SOLUTIONS

1. **(a)** Since zeroes are reciprocal of each other, so product of the roots will be 1, so $\dfrac{k+2}{k^2} = 1$,

$k^2 - k - 2 = 0 \Rightarrow (k-2)(k+1) = 0$

$k = 2, k = -1$, Since $k > 0$ $\therefore$ $k = 2$

2. **(c)** Let α, β be two zeroes of $2x^2 - 8x - m$, where $a = \dfrac{5}{2}$.

$\therefore$ $a + b = \dfrac{(-\text{Coefficient of } x)}{\text{Coefficient of } x^2}$

$\Rightarrow$ $\dfrac{5}{2} + b = \dfrac{8}{2}$

$\Rightarrow$ $b = \dfrac{8}{2} - \dfrac{5}{2} = \dfrac{3}{2}$.

3. **(d)** Substitute $y = 1$

4. **(a)** Substitute $x = 3$ in polynomial $ax^3 + 4x^2 + 3x - 4$ and $x^3 - 4x + a$ to obtain remainder and equate.

$a(3)^3 + 4(3)^2 + 3(3) - 4 = (3)^3 - 4(3) + a \Rightarrow a = -1$

5. **(b)** Equate value of polynomial at $x = a$ with a

$a^2 - 27a + 196 = a \Rightarrow a^2 - 28a + 196 = 0 \Rightarrow a = 14$

6. **(b)** Substitute $x = 1$ in $f(x)$ and $x = -2$ in $g(x)$, and add

$f(1) = 2(1) - 6(1) + 4(1) - 5 = -5 \Rightarrow g(-2) = 3(4) - 9 = 3$

$f(1) + g(-2) = -2$

7. **(a)** $x^3 - 3x^2 - 10x + 24$

$\because$ Last term = (product of roots)

$\therefore$ Factorising $24 = 2 \times 4 \times 3$

Also sum of roots must be "3"

$\therefore$ Possible factors are $(2, 4, -3)$

$\therefore$ Factorization of $x^3 - 3x^2 - 10x + 24$

$= (x - 2)(x + 3)(x - 4)$

8. **(c)** We have, $p(x) = x^2 - 10x - 75 = x^2 - 15x + 5x - 75$

$= x(x - 15) + 5(x - 15) = (x - 15)(x + 5)$

$\therefore$ $p(x) = (x - 15)(x + 5)$

So, $p(x) = 0$ when $x = 15$ or $x = -5$. Therefore required zeroes are 15 and -5.

9. **(c)** We have, sum of zeroes

$= a + b = -\dfrac{(-4)}{2} = 2$

Product of zeroes $= ab = \dfrac{3}{2}$

$\therefore$ $a^2b + ab^2 = ab(a + b) = \dfrac{3}{2} \times 2 = 3$

10. **(b)** $x^2 - (m+3)x + mx - m(m+3) = 0$

$\Rightarrow$ $x[x - (m+3)] + m[x - (m+3)] = 0$

$\Rightarrow$ $(x + m)[x - (m+3)] = 0$

$\therefore$ $x + m = 0$ | $x - (m+3) = 0$

$x = -m$ | $x = m + 3$

11. **(d)** The expressions $(x-1)(x+1)$ and $(x-1)(x-1)$ which vanish if $x = 1$.

12. **(b)** $10x = 7.\overline{7}$ or $x = 0.\overline{7}$

Subtracting, $9x = 7$ $\therefore$ $x = \dfrac{7}{9}$

$2x = \dfrac{14}{9} = 1.555......... = 1.\overline{5}$

13. **(b)** $x^2 + 4x + 2 = (x^2 + 4x + 2) - 2 = (x + 2)^2 - 2$

Lowest value $= -2$ when $x + 2 = 0$

14. **(d)** Put $a = b$ in given polynomial. Remainder comes to be 0.

15. **(c)**

16. **(b)** $P(x) = ax^3 + 4x^2 + 3x - 4$

$P(3) = 27a + 36 + 9 - 4 = 27a + 41$

$P(x) = x^3 - 4x + a; P(3) = 27 - 12 + a = 15 + a$

$\therefore$ $27a + 41 = 15 + a \Rightarrow a = -1$

17. **(a)** $x = -1$ is the root of the quadratic polynomial $p(x)$

So, quadratic polynomial $p(x) = k(x + 1)^2$

$p(-2) = k(-2 + 1)^2 = 2 \Rightarrow k = 2$ $\therefore$ $p(x) = 2(x + 1)^2$

Also, $p(2) = 2(2 + 1)^2 = 2 \times 3 \times 3 = 18$

18. (c) $x^2 - 4 = (x - 2)(x + 2)$ are the factors

$\therefore x = 2, -2$ are roots of polynomial

$\therefore$ at $x = 2$; $P(2) = 2(2)^3 + k_1(2)^2 + k_2(2) + 12 = 0$

$\Rightarrow 16 + 4k_1 + 2k_2 + 12 = 0 \Rightarrow 2k_1 + k^2 = -14$ ...(i)

at $x = 2$; $P(-2) = 2(-2)^3 + k_1(-2)^2 + k_2(-2) + 12 = 0$

$\Rightarrow -16 + 4k_1 - 2k_2 + 12 = 0$

$\Rightarrow 2k_1 - k_2 = 2$ ...(ii)

From (i) & (ii), $k_1 = -3$ $\therefore$ $k_1 + k_2 = -11$

19. (b) $x = 3 + 3^{2/3} + 3^{1/3}$

$(x - 3)^3 = \left(3^{\frac{2}{3}} + 3^{\frac{1}{3}} \right)^3$

$x^3 - 27 - 9x^2 + 27x = 3^2 + 3 + 3 \times 3^{2/3} \times 3^{1/3} (3^{2/3} + 3^{1/3})$

$x^3 - 27 - 9x^2 + 27x - 9 - 3 = 9(x - 3)$

$x^3 - 39 - 9x^2 + 27x - 9x + 27 = 0$

$x^3 - 9x^2 + 18x - 12 = 0$

20. (a) $P(x)$ is a polynomial of degree 3.

and $P(n) = \dfrac{1}{n} \Rightarrow n \, P(n) - 1 = 0$

$n(P(n))$ is a polynomial of degree 4

$\therefore n \, P(n) - 1 = k(n - 1)(n - 2)(n - 3)(n - 4)$

For $n = 0$; $-1 = 24 k \Rightarrow k = \dfrac{-1}{24}$

For $n = 5$; $5 \times P(5) - 1 = \dfrac{-1}{24}(4)(3)(2)(1)$

$\Rightarrow 5 \cdot P(5) - 1 = -1 \Rightarrow P(5) = 0$

21. (d) $f(x) = (x - 1)^2 + (x - 2)^2 + (x - 3)^2 + (x - 4)^2$

$= 4\left(x - \dfrac{5}{2} \right)^2 + 5$

$f(x)$ is minimum at $x = \dfrac{5}{2} = 2.5$

22. (b) Since, 2 is the zero of $x^2 + 3x + k$,

$\therefore$ $(2)^2 + 3(2) + k = 0 \Rightarrow k + 10 = 0 \Rightarrow k = -10$

23. (a) Since -3 is the zero of $(k - 1)x^2 + kx + 1$,

$\therefore$ $(k - 1)(-3)^2 + k(-3) + 1 = 0$

$\Rightarrow 9k - 9 - 3k + 1 = 0 \Rightarrow 6k - 8 = 0 \Rightarrow k = \dfrac{4}{3}$

24. (b) Coefficient of all the terms are positive. So, both roots will be negative.

25. (d) In (a) power of x is -1 i.e. negative

$\therefore$ (a) is not true.

In (b) power of $x = \dfrac{1}{2}$, not an integer. $\therefore$ (b) is not true

In (c) Here also power of x is not an integer $\therefore$ (c) is not true

(d) holds [$\because$ all the powers of x are non-negative integers.]

26. (b)

(a) is not true [By def.]

(b) holds

[$\because$ degree of a zero polynomial is not defined]

(c) is not true

[$\because$ degree of a constant polynomial is '0']

(d) is not true

[$\because$ a polynomial of degree n has at most n zeroes].

27. (c)

(a) $x^2 + \dfrac{1}{x} = x^2 + x^{-1}$ is not a polynomial since the exponent of variable in 2nd term is negative

(b) $2x^2 - 3\sqrt{x} + 1 = 2x^2 - 3x^{\frac{1}{2}} + 1$ is not a polynomial, since the exponent of variable in 2nd term is a rational number.

(c) $x^3 - 3x + 1$ is a polynomial.

(d) $2x^{\frac{3}{2}} - 5x$ is also not a polynomial, since the exponents of variable in 1st term is a rational number

Hence, (a), (b) and (d) is not a polynomial.

28. (d)

(a) It is quadratic polynomial

[$\because$ the graph meets the x-axis in two points]

(b) It is a quadratic polynomial

[$\because$ the graph meets the x-axis in two points]

(c) It is a quadratic polynomial

[$\because$ the graph meets the x-axis in two points]

(d) It is a not quadratic polynomial

[$\because$ the graph meets the x-axis in one point]

29. **(c)** $a \neq 0$, a, b, c are real numbers

30. **(d)** For roots are equal

$$b^2 - 4ac = 0$$

or $\quad D = 0$

31. **(b)** For value of k,

$$\alpha . \frac{1}{\alpha} = \frac{c}{a} \quad \text{(Product of roots} = \frac{c}{a} \text{)}$$

$$1 = \frac{8k}{2}$$

or $\quad k = \dfrac{1}{4}$

32. **(c)** For $x^2 + 1 = 0$

roots are not real.

So, graph of $x^2 + 1 = 0$, neither touches nor intersects x-axis.

33. **(c)** We know, for a quadratic polynomial

$$k(x^2 - (\text{Sum of roots}) \, x + \text{Product of roots})$$

$$k(x^2 - (-p) + (-1/p))$$

$$k \, (x^2 + p - 1/p)$$

34. **(d)** Parabola.

35. **(c)** $a < 0$, Graphs look like

open downwards

36. **(c)** According to graph, there are two zeros

one at (-2) and 2nd at 4, -2, 4

37. **(b)** $-2, 4$

38. **(b)** For zeros $D = \dfrac{-b \pm \sqrt{b^2 - 4ac}}{2a}$

Here, $a = 4\sqrt{3}, b = 5, c = -2\sqrt{3}$

$$= \frac{-5 \pm \sqrt{25 + 4 \times 4\sqrt{3} \times 2\sqrt{3}}}{8\sqrt{3}} = \frac{-5 \pm 11}{8\sqrt{3}}$$

$$\Rightarrow \frac{-2}{\sqrt{3}}, \frac{\sqrt{3}}{4}$$

39. **(d)** Parabola

40. **(c)** If $a > 0$, Graph of parabola looks like

41. **(d)** Here graph cuts x-axis at 3 points

so it has three zeros.

42. **(c)** Observing the graph we find $-3, -1, 2$ as zeros.

43. **(a)** Given zeros are $-3, -1, 2$, then

Expression is $(x - (-3)) \, (x - (-1)) \, (x - 2)$

$$= (x + 3)(x + 1)(x - 2)$$

$$= x^3 + 2x^2 - 5x - 6$$

$x^3 - (\text{Sum of zeros})x^2 + (\text{Sum of zeros taking two at a time})x - (\text{Product of zeros})$

$$x^3 - (-3 - 1 + 2) \, x^2 + ((-3)(-1) + (-1)(2) + (2)(-3))x$$
$$- (-3)(-1)(2)$$

$$x^3 + 2x^2 + (3 - 2 - 6)x - 6$$

$$x^3 + 2x^2 - 5x - 6$$

44. **(b)** Reason is true.

Let $\alpha, \dfrac{1}{\alpha}$ be the zeroes of $p(x)$, then

$$\alpha . \frac{1}{\alpha} = \frac{4k}{k^2 + 4} \Rightarrow 1 = \frac{4k}{k^2 + 4}$$

$$\therefore \quad k^2 - 4k + 4 = 0$$

$$\Rightarrow (k - 2)^2 = 0 \; \therefore \; k = 2$$

$\therefore$ Assertion is true.

Since, reason is not correct explanation for assertion.

45. **(c)** Reason is false [$\therefore$ a polynomial of nth degree has at most x zeroes.]

Again, $x^3 + x = x \, (x^2 + 1)$

which has only one real zero $(x = 0)$

$$[\because x^2 + 1 \neq 0 \text{ for all } x \in R]$$

$\therefore$ Assertion is true.

46. **(b)**

47. **(c)**

48. **(d)**

49. (A) $\rightarrow$ q; (B) $\rightarrow$ s; (C) $\rightarrow$ r; (D) $\rightarrow$ p

50. (A) $\rightarrow$ q ; (B) $\rightarrow$ s ; (C) $\rightarrow$ r ; (D) $\rightarrow$ p

(A) $4 - x^2 = 0 \Rightarrow x = \pm 2$

(B) $x^3 - 2x^2 = 0 \Rightarrow x^2(x - 2) = 0$

$x = 0$ or $x = 2$

(C) $6x^2 - 7x - 3 = 0 \Rightarrow 6x^2 - 9x + 2x - 3 = 0$

$3x(2x - 3) + 1(2x - 3) = 0 \Rightarrow (3x + 1) \, (2x - 3) = 0$

$x = 3/2$ or $x = -1/3$

(D) $x = 7$

51. linear, quadratic, cubic

52. x

53. 3

54. a, a

Polynomials

55. zero

56. n

57. True

58. False, because the exponent of the variable is not a whole number.

59. True, because $\dfrac{6\sqrt{x}+x^{\frac{3}{2}}}{\sqrt{x}} = 6+x,$ which is a polynomial.

60. False

61. False, a polynomial can have any number of zeroes. It depends upon the degree of the polynomial.

62. False, $x^5 + 1$ and $-x^5 + 2x + 3$ are two polynomials of degree 5 but the degree of the sum of the two polynomials is 1.

63. True, $p(3) = 0, p(-1) = 0, \ p\left(\dfrac{1}{3}\right) = 0$

64. False

65. False, sum of zeroes $= \dfrac{\text{Coefficient of } x}{\text{Coefficient of } x^2} = \dfrac{-(-8)}{2} = 4$

3 — Pair of Linear Equations in Two Variables

DIRECTIONS : *This section contains multiple choice questions. Each question has 4 choices (a), (b), (c) and (d) out of which only one is correct.*

1. For which value of p, will the lines represented by the following pair of linear equations be parallel

$3x - y - 5 = 0$

$6x - 2y - p = 0$

(a) all real values except 10

(b) 10

(c) 5/2

(d) 1/2

2. For what values of k will the following pair of linear equations have infinitely many solutions?

$kx + 3y - (k - 3) = 0$

$12x + ky - k = 0$

(a) $k = 4$ (b) $k = 3$

(c) $k = 6$ (d) $k = 2$

3. Which of the following is true if following pair of linear equations has unique solution?

$3x - 2y = -8$

$(2m - 5)x + 7y - 6 = 0$

(a) $m = \dfrac{11}{4}$ (b) $m = -\dfrac{11}{4}$

(c) $m \neq -\dfrac{11}{4}$ (d) $m \neq \dfrac{11}{4}$

4. The perimeter of a rectangle is 40 cm. The ratio of its sides is 2 : 3. Find its length and breadth.

(a) $l = 10$ cm, b = 8 cm   (b) $l = 12$ cm, b = 8 cm

(c) $l = 12$ m, b = 8 m   (d) $l = 40$ m, b = 30 m

5. Which of the following is the other name for a pair of linear equations in two variables?

(a) Consistent equations   (b) Simultaneous equations

(c) Inconsistent equations (d) Dependent equations

6. The difference between two numbers is 26 and one number is three times the other. Find them.

(a) 39, 13   (b) 41, 67

(c) 96, 70   (d) 52, 26

7. Sanjay starts his job with a certain monthly salary and earns a fixed increment every year. If his salary was ₹ 4500 after four years of service and ₹ 5400 after 10 years, find his initial salary and annual increment.

(a) 4000, 200   (b) 3900, 150

(c) 4500, 100   (d) 3800, 250

8. The pair of linear equations $x + 2y = 5$ and $3x + 12y = 10$ has

(a) unique solution

(b) no solution

(c) more than two solutions

(d) infinitely many solutions

9. ₹ 49 was divided among 150 children. Each girl got 50 paise and each boy got 25 paise. How many boys were there?

(a) 100   (b) 102

(c) 104   (d) 105

10. If the sum of the ages (in years) of a father and his son is 65 and twice the difference of their ages (in years) is 50, what is the age of the father?

(a) 45 years   (b) 40 years

(c) 50 years   (d) 55 years

11. The value of k for which the system of linear equations $x + 2y = 3$, $5x + ky + 7 = 0$ is inconsistent is

(a) $-\dfrac{14}{3}$ (b) $\dfrac{2}{5}$

(c) 5   (d) 10

12. A can do a piece of work in 24 days. If B is 60% more efficient than A, then the number of days required by B to do the twice as large as the earlier work is
    (a) 24
    (b) 36
    (c) 15
    (d) 30

13. X's salary is half that of Y's. If X got a 50% rise in his salary and Y got 25% rise in his salary, then the percentage increase in combined salaries of both is
    (a) 30
    (b) $33\dfrac{1}{3}$
    (c) $37\dfrac{1}{2}$
    (d) 75

14. The points $(7, 2)$ and $(-1, 0)$ lie on a line
    (a) $7y = 3x - 7$
    (b) $4y = x + 1$
    (c) $y = 7x + 7$
    (d) $x = 4y + 1$

15. At present ages of a father and his son are in the ratio 7 : 3, and they will be in the ratio 2 : 1 after 10 years. Then the present age of father (in years) is
    (a) 42
    (b) 56
    (c) 70
    (d) 77

16. A fraction becomes 4 when 1 is added to both the numerator and denominator and it becomes 7 when 1 is subtracted from both the numerator and denominator. The numerator of the given fraction is
    (a) 2
    (b) 3
    (c) 5
    (d) 15

17. A motor boat takes 2 hours to travel a distance 9 km down the current and it takes 6 hours to travel the same distance against the current. The speed of the boat in still water and that of the current (in km/hour) respectively are
    (a) 3, 1.5
    (b) 3, 2
    (c) 3.5, 2.5
    (d) 3, 1

18. The 2 digit number which becomes (5/6)th of itself when its digits are reversed. The difference in the digits of the number being 1, then the two digits number is
    (a) 45
    (b) 54
    (c) 36
    (d) None of these

19. x and y are 2 different digits. If the sum of the two digit numbers formed by using both the digits is a perfect square, then value of $x + y$ is
    (a) 10
    (b) 11
    (c) 12
    (d) 13

20. If $3x + 4y : x + 2y = 9 : 4$, then $3x + 5y : 3x - y$ is equal to
    (a) 4 : 1
    (b) 1 : 4
    (c) 7 : 1
    (d) 1 : 7

21. In a number of two digits, unit's digit is twice the tens digit. If 36 be added to the number, the digits are reversed. The number is
    (a) 36
    (b) 63
    (c) 48
    (d) 84

22. A man can row a boat in still water at the rate of 6 km per hour. If the stream flows at the rate of 2 km/hr, he takes half the time going downstream than going upstream the same distance. His average speed for upstream and down stream trip is
    (a) 6 km/hr
    (b) 16/3 km/hr
    (c) Insufficient data to arrive at the answer
    (d) none of the above

23. A boat travels with a speed of 15 km/hr in still water. In a river flowing at 5 km/hr, the boat travels some distance downstream and then returns. The ratio of average speed to the speed in still water is
    (a) 8 : 3
    (b) 3 : 8
    (c) 8 : 9
    (d) 9 : 8

24. x and y are two non-negative numbers such that $2x + y = 10$. The sum of the maximum and minimum values of $(x + y)$ is
    (a) 6
    (b) 9
    (c) 10
    (d) 15

25. The average incomes of the people in two villages are P and Q respectively. Assume that $P \neq Q$. A person moves from the first village to the second village. The new average incomes are P' and Q' respectively. Which of the following is not possible?
    (a) $P' > P$ and $Q' > Q$
    (b) $P' > P$ and $Q' < Q$
    (c) $P' = P$ and $Q' = Q$
    (d) $P' < P$ and $Q' < Q$

26. The graphs of the equations $x - y = 2$ and $kx + y = 3$, where k is a constant, intersect at the point (x, y) in the first quadrant, if and only if k is
    (a) equal to -1
    (b) greater than -1
    (c) less than 3/2
    (d) lying between -1 and 3/2

27. For what value of p, the following pair of linear equations in two variables will have infinitely many solutions ?
    $$px + 3y - (p - 3) = 0, \quad 12x + py - p = 0$$
    (a) 6
    (b) -6
    (c) 0
    (d) 2

28. In a classroom, one-fifth of the boys leave the class and the ratio of the remaining boys to girls is 2 : 3. If further 44 girls leave the class, then the ratio of boys to girls is 5 : 2. How many more boys should leave the class so that the number of boys equals that of girls?

    (a) 16 (b) 24
    (c) 30 (d) 36

29. The equations $\dfrac{1}{x}+\dfrac{1}{y}=15$ and $\dfrac{1}{x}-\dfrac{1}{y}=5$ are such that $ax = 1$ and $by = 1$. The values of 'a' and 'b' respectively are

    (a) 10, 5   (b) 10, –5
    (c) –5, 10 (d) 5, 10

30. Consider the following two statements:

    I. Any pair of consistent linear equations in two variables must have a unique solution.

    II. There do not exist two consecutive integers, the sum of whose squares is 365.

    Then,

    (a) both I and II are true   (b) both I and II are false
    (c) I is true and II is false (d) I is false and II is true

31. In village Madhubani 8 women and 12 girls can paint a large mural in 10 hours. 6 women and 8 girls can paint it in 14 hours. The number of hours taken by 7 women and 14 girls to paint the mural is

    (a) 10 (b) 15
    (c) 20 (d) 35

32. A boat takes 3 hours to travel 30 km downstream and takes 5 hours to return to the same spot upstream. Find the speed of the boat in still water. (km/hr)

    (a) 10 km/hr (b) 8 km/hr
    (c) 6 km/hr   (d) 5 km/hr

33. The pair of equations $5x - 15y = 8$ and $3x - 9y = \dfrac{24}{5}$ has

    (a) one solutio
    (b) two solutions
    (c) infinitely many solutions
    (d) no solution

34. The sum of the digits of a two-digit number is 9. If 27 is added to it, the digits of the number get reversed. The number is

    (a) 25 (b) 72
    (c) 63 (d) 36

35. The value of c for which the pair of equations $cx - y = 2$ and $6x + 2y = 3$ will have infinitely many solutions is

    (a) 3   (b) – 3
    (c) – 12 (d) no value

36. If $x = a, y = b$ is the solution of the equations $x - y = 2$ and $x + y = 4$, then the values of a and b are, respectively.

    (a) 3 and 5   (b) 5 and 3
    (c) 3 and 1   (d) – 1 and – 3

37. I. If $x - y = xy = 1 - x - y$, then $x + y$ is $\dfrac{5}{3}$

    II. The system of equations $3x + 2y = a$ and $5x + by = 4$ has infinitely many solutions for x and y, then $a = 4, b = 3$

    III. If $\dfrac{x}{a}+\dfrac{y}{b}=2$ and $ax - by = a^2 - b^2$, then $x = a, y = b$

    Which is true?

    (a) I only   (b) II only
    (c) III only (d) None of these.

38. I.   If $3x - 5y = -1$ and $x - y = -1$, then $x = -2, y = -1$

    II. $2x + 3y = 9, 3x + 4y = 5 \Rightarrow x = -21, y = 17$

    III. $\dfrac{2x}{a}+\dfrac{y}{b}=2, \dfrac{x}{a}-\dfrac{y}{b}=4 \Rightarrow x = 2a, y = 2b$

    Which is true?

    (a) I   (b) II
    (c) III (d) None of these

39. If a pair of linear equations is inconsistent, then the lines will be

    (a) parallel   (b) always coincident
    (c) intersecting (d) coincident

40. For what values of k, do the equations $3x - y + 8 = 0$ and $6x - ky = -16$ represent coincident lines?

    (a) solution of $3k - 9 = 0$ (b) solution of $2k - 8 = 0$
    (c) 2 (d) 3

⟫ Case/Passage Based Questions

DIRECTIONS : *Study the given Case/Passage and answer the following questions.*

Case/Passage-I

A test consists of 'True' or 'False' questions. One mark is awarded for every correct answer while 1/4 mark is deducted for every wrong answer. A student knew answers to some of the questions. Rest of the questions he attempted by guessing. He answered 120 questions and got 90 marks.

Type of Question	Marks given for correct answer	Marks deducted for wrong answer
True/False	1	0.25

[From CBSE Question Bank-2021]

41. If answer to all questions he attempted by guessing were wrong, then how many questions did he answer correctly?

42. How many questions did he guess?

43. If answer to all questions he attempted by guessing were wrong and answered 80 correctly, then how many marks he got?

44. If answer to all questions he attempted by guessing were wrong, then how many questions answered correctly to score 95 marks?

Case/Passage-II

Amit is planning to buy a house and the layout is given below. The design and the measurement has been made such that areas of two bedrooms and kitchen together is 95 sq.m.

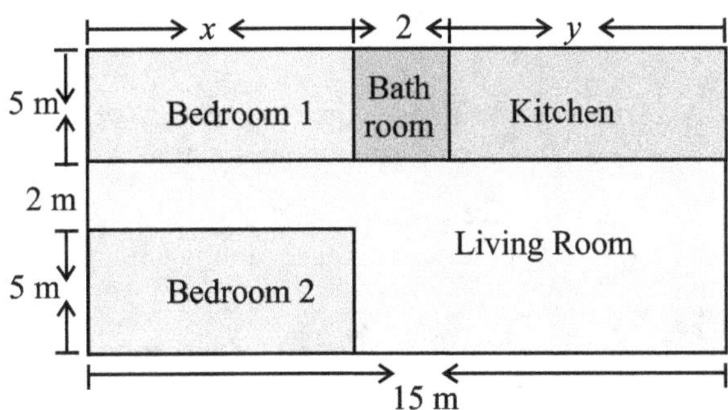

[From CBSE Question Bank-2021]

Based on the above information, answer the following questions:

45. Form the pair of linear equations in two variables from this situation.

46. Find the length of the outer boundary of the layout.

47. Find the area of each bedroom and kitchen in the layout.

48. Find the area of living room in the layout.

49. Find the cost of laying tiles in kitchen at the rate of ₹ 50 per sq.m

Case/Passage-III

It is common that Governments revise travel fares from time to time based on various factors such as inflation (a general increase in prices and fall in the purchasing value of money) on different types of vehicles like auto, rickshaws, taxis, radio cab etc. The auto charges in a city comprise of a fixed charge together with the charge for the distance covered. Study the following situations.

Name of the city	Distance travelled (km)	Amount paid (₹)
City A	10	75
	15	110
City B	8	91
	14	145

Situation 1: In city A, for a journey of 10 km, the charge paid is ₹ 75 and for a journey of 15 km, the charge paid is ₹ 110.
Situation 2: In a city B, for a journey of 8 km, the charge paid is ₹ 91 and for a journey of 14km, the charge paid is ₹ 145.

[From CBSE Question Bank-2021]

Refer situation 1

50. If the fixed charges of auto rickshaw be ₹ x and the running charges be ₹ y km/hr, the pair of linear equations representing the situation is

(a) $x + 10y = 110, x + 15y = 75$

(b) $x + 10y = 75, x + 15y = 110$

(c) $10x + y = 110, 15x + y = 75$

(d) $10x + y = 75, 15x + y = 110$

51. A person travels a distance of 50km. The amount he has to pay is

(a) ₹ 155 (b) ₹ 255 (c) ₹ 355 (d) ₹ 455

Refer situation 2

52. What will a person have to pay for travelling a distance of 30km?

(a) ₹ 185 (b) ₹ 289 (c) ₹ 275 (d) ₹ 305

53. The graph of lines representing the conditions are: (situation 2)

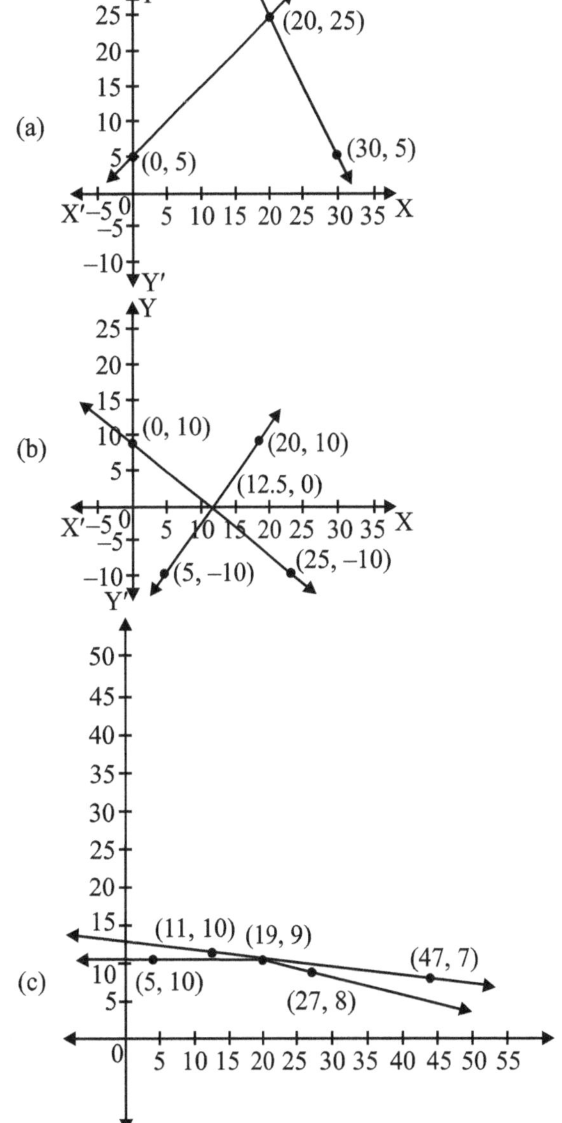

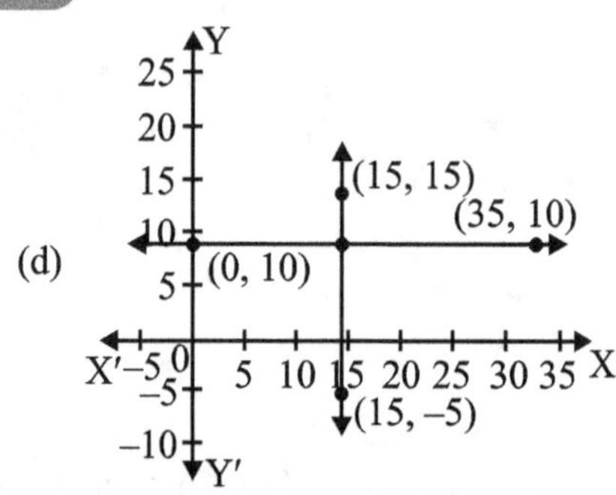

Assertion & Reason

DIRECTIONS : *Each of these questions contains an Assertion followed by Reason. Read them carefully and answer the question on the basis of following options. You have to select the one that best describes the two statements.*

(a)   If both **Assertion** and **Reason** are **correct** and Reason is the **correct explanation** of Assertion.

(b)   If both **Assertion** and **Reason** are correct, but Reason is **not the correct explanation** of Assertion.

(c)   If **Assertion** is **correct** but **Reason** is **incorrect**.

(d)   If **Assertion** is **incorrect** but **Reason** is **correct**.

54.   Assertion : $3x + 4y + 5 = 0$ and $6x + ky + 9 = 0$ represent parallel lines if $k = 8$

Reason : $a_1x + b_1y + c_1 = 0$ and $a_2x + b_2y + c_2 = 0$

represent parallel lines if $\dfrac{a_1}{a_2} = \dfrac{b_1}{b_2} \neq \dfrac{c_1}{c_2}$

55.   Assertion : $x + y - 4 = 0$ and $2x + ky - 3 = 0$ has no solution if $k = 2$

Reason : $a_1x + b_1y + c_1 = 0$ and $a_2x + b_2y + c_2 = 0$ are

consistent if $\dfrac{a_1}{a_2} \neq \dfrac{b_1}{b_2}$

56.   Assertion : If the system of equations $2x + 3y = 7$ and $2ax + (a + b)y = 28$ has infinitely many solutions, then $2a - b = 0$

Reason : The system of equations $3x - 5y = 9$ and $6x - 10y = 8$ has a unique solution.

57.   Assertion : If the pair of lines are coincident, then we say that pair of lines is consistent and it has a unique solution.

Reason : If the pair of lines are parallel, then the pair has no solution and is called inconsistent pair of equations.

58.   Assertion : If $kx - y - 2 = 0$ and $6x - 2y - 3 = 0$ are inconsistent, then $k = 3$

Reason : $a_1x + b_1y + c_1 = 0$ and $a_2x + b_2y + c_2 = 0$ are

inconsistent if $\dfrac{a_1}{a_2} = \dfrac{b_1}{b_2} \neq \dfrac{c_1}{c_2}$

59.   Assertion : $3x - 4y = 7$ and $6x - 8y = k$ have infinite number of solution if $k = 14$

Reason : $a_1x + b_1y + c_1 = 0$ and $a_2x + b_2y + c_2 = 0$ have

a unique solution if $\dfrac{a_1}{a_2} \neq \dfrac{b_1}{b_2}$

60.   Assertion : The linear equations $x - 2y - 3 = 0$ and $3x + 4y - 20 = 0$ have exactly one solution

Reason : The linear equations $2x + 3y - 9 = 0$ and $4x + 6y - 18 = 0$ have a unique solution

Match the Following

DIRECTIONS : *Each question contains statements given in two columns which have to be matched. Statements (A, B, C, D) in column-I have to be matched with statements (p, q, r, s) in column-II.*

61.   Column-II give value of x and y for pair of equation given in Column-I.

Column-I	Column-II
(A) $2x + y = 8$, $x + 6y = 15$	(p) (3, 4)
(B) $5x + 3y = 35$, $2x + 4y = 28$	(q) (1/14, 1/6)
(C) $\dfrac{1}{7x} + \dfrac{1}{6y} = 3$, $\dfrac{1}{2x} - \dfrac{1}{3y} = 5$	(r) (4, 5)
(D) $15x + 4y = 61$ $\\ 4x + 15y = 72$	(s) (3, 2)

62.

Column-I	Column-II
(A) $5y - 4x = 14$, $y - 2x = 1$	(p) Infinite solutions
(B) $6x - 3y + 10 = 0$, $2x - y + 9 = 0$	(q) Consistent
(C) $3x - 2y = 4$, $9x - 6y = 12$	(r) No solution
(D) $2x - 3y = 8$, $4x - 6y = 9$	(s) Inconsistent

63.

Column-I	Column-II
(A) No solution	(p) $5x - 15y = 8$, $3x - 9y = \dfrac{24}{5}$
(B) Infinitely many solutions	(q) $2x + 4y = 10$, $3x + 6y = 12$
(C) Unique solution	(r) $x + y = 6$, $x - y = 2$
(D) Integral solution	(s) $2x + y = 6$, $4x - 2y - 2 = 0$

❯ Fill in the Blanks

❯ True / False

DIRECTIONS : *Complete the following statements with an appropriate word / term to be filled in the blank space(s).*

DIRECTIONS : *Read the following statements and write your answer as true or false.*

64. If the lines intersect at a point, then that point gives the unique solution of the two equations. In this case, the pair of equations is ....

65. If the lines are parallel, then the pair of equations has no solution. In this case, the pair of equations is ....

66. Two distinct natural numbers are such that the sum of one number and twice the other number is 6. The two numbers are ....

67. If $p + q = k$, $p - q = n$ and $k > n$, then q is .... (positive/negative).

68. Sum of the ages of X and Y, 12 years, ago, was 48 years and sum of the ages of X and Y, 12 years hence will be 96 years. Present age of X is ....

69. The number of common solutions for the system of linear equations $5x + 4y + 6 = 0$ and $10x + 8y = 12$ is ....

70. If $2x + 3y = 5$ and $3x + 2y = 10$, then $x - y =$ ....

71. If $\dfrac{1}{x} + \dfrac{1}{y} = k$ and $\dfrac{1}{x} - \dfrac{1}{y} = k$, then the value of y is ....

72. If a pair of linear equations is given by $a_1 x + b_1 y + c_1 = 0$ and $a_2 x + b_2 y + c_2 = 0$ and $\dfrac{a_1}{a_2} \neq \dfrac{b_1}{b_2}$. In this case, the pair of linear equations is consistent.

73. If a pair of linear equations is given by $a_1 x + b_1 y + c_1 = 0$ and $a_2 x + b_2 y + c_2 = 0$ and $\dfrac{a_1}{a_2} = \dfrac{b_1}{b_2} \neq \dfrac{c_1}{c_2}$. In this case, the pair of linear equations is consistent.

74. If a pair of linear equations is given by $a_1 x + b_1 y + c_1 = 0$ and $a_2 x + b_2 y + c_2 = 0$ and $\dfrac{a_1}{a_2} = \dfrac{b_1}{b_2} = \dfrac{c_1}{c_2}$. In this case, the pair of linear equations is consistent.

75. $3x - y = 3$, $9x - 3y = 9$ has infinite solution.

76. $\sqrt{2}x + \sqrt{3}y = 0$, $\sqrt{3}x - \sqrt{8}y = 0$ has no solution.

77. $3x + 2y = 5$, $2x - 3y = 7$ are consistent pair of equation.

78. In a $\triangle ABC$, $\angle C = 3 \angle B = 2 (\angle A + \angle B)$, then angles are $20°, 40°, 100°$.

ANSWER KEY & SOLUTIONS

1. (a) If the lines are parallel, then

$$\frac{a_1}{a_2} = \frac{b_1}{b_2} \neq \frac{c_1}{c_2}$$

Here, $a_1 = 3$, $b_1 = -1$, $c_1 = -5$,

$$a_2 = 6, b_2 = -2, c_2 = -p$$

$$\Rightarrow \quad \frac{3}{6} = \frac{-1}{-2} \neq \frac{-5}{-p} \qquad \ldots \text{(i)}$$

Taking II and III part of equation (i), we get

$$\Rightarrow \quad \frac{1}{2} \neq \frac{-5}{-p} \quad \Rightarrow \quad -p \neq -10 \quad \Rightarrow \quad p \neq 10$$

So, option (a) is correct.

2. (c) Here, $\dfrac{a_1}{a_2} = \dfrac{k}{12}$, $\dfrac{b_1}{b_2} = \dfrac{3}{k}$, $\dfrac{c_1}{c_2} = \dfrac{k-3}{k}$

For a pair of linear equations to have infinitely many solutions:

$$\frac{a_1}{a_2} = \frac{b_1}{b_2} = \frac{c_1}{c_2}$$

So, we have $\dfrac{k}{12} = \dfrac{3}{k} = \dfrac{k-3}{k}$ or $\dfrac{k}{12} = \dfrac{3}{k}$ which gives

$k^2 = 36$ i.e., $k = \pm 6$

Also, $\dfrac{3}{k} = \dfrac{k-3}{k}$ gives $3k = k^2 - 3k$, i.e., $6k = k^2$,

which means $k = 0$ or $k = 6$.

Therefore, the value of k that satisfies both the conditions, is $k = 6$. For this value, the pair of linear equations has infinitely many solutions.

3. (c) For a pair of linear equations having unique solution

$$\frac{a_1}{a_2} \neq \frac{b_1}{b_2} \Rightarrow \frac{3}{2m-5} \neq \frac{-2}{7}$$

or $-4m + 10 \neq 21$

or $-4m \neq 11$

or $m \neq -\dfrac{11}{4}$

4. (b) Let length and breadth be x cm and y cm respectively. According to problem,

$$2(x+y) = 40 \qquad \ldots \text{(i)}$$

and $\dfrac{y}{x} = \dfrac{2}{3} \qquad \ldots \text{(ii)}$

on solving, $x = 12$, $y = 8$

∴ length = 12 cm and breadth = 8cm.

5. (b) The pair of linear equations in two variables is also known as simultaneous equations.

6. (a) Let the two numbers be x and $y\,(x > y)$. Then,

$$x - y = 26 \qquad \ldots \text{(i)}$$
$$x = 3y \qquad \ldots \text{(ii)}$$

Substituting value of x from equation (ii) in (i)

$3y - y = 26 \Rightarrow 2y = 26 \Rightarrow y = 13$

Substituting value of y in equation (ii), $x = 3 \times 13 = 39$

Thus, two numbers are 13 and 39.

7. (b) Let the annual increment be ₹ y and initial salary be ₹ x

∴ $\quad x + 4y = 4500 \qquad \ldots \text{(i)}$

and $\quad x + 10y = 5400 \qquad \ldots \text{(ii)}$

Solving eqs. (i) and (ii), we get

$x = 3900$ and $y = 150$

∴ Initial salary = ₹ 3900

and increment = ₹ 150

8. (a) The pair of linear equations are

$x + 2y - 5 = 0$ and

$3x + 12y - 10 = 0$

Here, $a_1 = 1$, $b_1 = 2$, $c_1 = -5$

and $a_2 = 3$, $b_2 = 12$,

$c_2 = -10$. Now, $\dfrac{a_1}{a_2} = \dfrac{1}{3}, \dfrac{b_1}{b_2} = \dfrac{2}{12} = \dfrac{1}{6}$.

As $\dfrac{a_1}{a_2} \neq \dfrac{b_1}{b_2}$

So, pair of equations has a unique solution.

9. (c) Let the no. of girls be 'x' and the no. of boys be 'y'. Given, $0.50x + 0.25y = 49$

and $x + y = 150 \qquad \ldots \text{(i)}$

$$\Rightarrow \quad \frac{x}{2} + \frac{x}{4} = 49 \qquad \ldots \text{(ii)}$$

From (i) & (ii), $x = 46$, $y = 104$

Hence, number of boys $(y) = 104$

10. (a) Let the age of father be 'x' years and the age of son be 'y' years

According to question, $x + y = 65 \qquad \ldots \text{(i)}$

and $2(x - y) = 50 \Rightarrow x - y = 25$ ...(ii)

Adding eqs. (i) and (ii), we get, $2x = 90 \Rightarrow x = 45$

Hence, the age of father = 45 years

11. **(d)** $\dfrac{1}{5} = \dfrac{2}{k} \neq \dfrac{-3}{7}$ $\qquad \left[\begin{array}{l} \because \text{ For inconsistent} \\[4pt] \dfrac{a_1}{a_2} = \dfrac{b_1}{b_2} \neq \dfrac{c_1}{c_2} \end{array} \right]$

$\Rightarrow \quad k = 10$

12. **(d)** Work ratio of $A : B = 100 : 160$ or $5 : 8$

$\therefore$ time ratio $= 8 : 5$ or $24 : 15$

If A takes 24 days, B takes 15 days. Hence, B takes 30 days to do double the work.

13. **(b)** Let salary of Y be $= A$ and of X is $= \dfrac{A}{2}$

$\therefore$ Total salary of X and $Y = \dfrac{3A}{2}$ ... (i)

Let X' and Y' be the new salary after increment, then we get

$X' = \dfrac{3A}{4}$ and $Y' = \dfrac{5A}{4} \Rightarrow X' + Y' = 2A$ ... (ii)

$\therefore$ Required percentage increase $= \dfrac{\left(\dfrac{2A - 3A}{2}\right) \times 100}{\dfrac{3A}{2}}$

[from (i) & (ii) eqns.]

$= \dfrac{1}{3} \times 100 \Rightarrow 33\dfrac{1}{3}\%$

14. **(b)** The point satisfy the line $4y = x + 1$

15. **(c)** Let the ages of father and son be $7x, 3x$

After 10 years,

$\therefore (7x + 10) : (3x + 10) = 2 : 1$ or $x = 10$

$\therefore$ Age of the father is $7x$ i.e. 70 years.

16. **(d)** Let the fraction be $\dfrac{x}{y}$

According to given conditions,

$\dfrac{x + 1}{y + 1} = 4$ ... (i)

and $\dfrac{x - 1}{y - 1} = 7$ ... (ii)

Solving (i) and (ii), we have $x = 15$, $y = 3$

i.e. numbers = 15

17. **(a)** Let speed of boat in still water $= x$ km/hr

and speed of stream $= y$ km/hr

According to question,

time $(t_1) = \dfrac{9}{x + y} = 2$ (for down = rate) ... (i)

and time $(t_2) = \dfrac{9}{x - y} = 6$ (for up = rate) ... (ii)

Solving equations (i) & (ii), we get

$x = 3$ km/hr and $y = 1.5$ km/hr

Speed of the boat = 3 km/hr

Speed of the current = 1.5 km/hr

18. **(b)** If the two digits are x and y, then the number is $10x + y$.

Given that, $\dfrac{5}{6}(10x + y) = 10y + x$. Solving it,

we get $44x + 55y \Rightarrow \dfrac{x}{y} = \dfrac{5}{4}$.

Also $x - y = 1$. Solving them, we get $x = 5$ and $y = 4$. Therefore, number is 54.

19. **(b)** The numbers that can be formed are xy and yx. Hence $(10x + y) + (10y + x) = 11(x + y)$. If this is a perfect square then $x + y = 11$.

20. **(c)** $\dfrac{3x + 4y}{x + 2y} = \dfrac{9}{4}$

$\Rightarrow 4(3x + 4y) = 9(x + 2y)$

Hence, $12x + 16y = 9x + 18y$ or $3x = 2y$

$\therefore x = \dfrac{2}{3}y$.

Substitute $x = \dfrac{2}{3}y$ in the required expression.

i.e. $3x + 5y : 3x - y$

$= 3\left(\dfrac{2}{3}y\right) + 5y : 3\left(\dfrac{2}{3}y\right) - y$

$= 2y + 5y : 2y - y$

$= 7y : y = 7 : 1$

21. **(c)** Let unit's digit : x, tens digit : y

then $x = 2y$, number $= 10y + x$

Also $10y + x + 36 = 10x + y$

$\therefore 9x - 9y = 36$ or $x - y = 4$

Solve, $x = 2y$, $x - y = 4$

Substitute $x = 2y$ in $x - y = 4$

we get, $2y - y = 4 \Rightarrow y = 4$

and $x = 8$

So, the number $= 10y + x = 48$

22. **(b)** Upstream speed = 4 km/hr and time = x hrs.

Downstream speed = 8 km/hr and

time taken = $x/2$ hrs.

Hence average speed $= \dfrac{4x + 8 \times x/2}{x + x/2} = \dfrac{16}{3}$ km/hr.

23. (c) Let distance $= d$,

Time taken upstream $= \dfrac{d}{15-5} = \dfrac{d}{10}$

Time taken downstream $= \dfrac{d}{15+5} = \dfrac{d}{20}$

Hence, average speed

$= \dfrac{2d}{\dfrac{d}{10} + \dfrac{d}{20}} = \dfrac{2d \times 20}{3d} = \dfrac{40}{3}$ km/hr

Ratio $= \dfrac{40}{3} : 15 = 40 : 45 = 8 : 9$

24. (d) Given $2x + y = 10$

on adding y both sides, we get, $2x + y + y = 10 + y$

$\Rightarrow \quad 2(x + y) = 10 + y \ \Rightarrow\ x + y = 5 + \dfrac{y}{2}$

Now, $(x + y)_{max}$ when y is maximum & maximum value of y will be 10. ($\because y = 10 - 2x$)

So $(x + y)_{max} = 5 + 5 = 10$ & $(x + y)_{min}$ when y $= 0$

$\therefore \quad$ minimum value of $x + y = 5$

So, sum of $(x + y)_{max}$ & $(x + y)$min $= 15$

25. (c) Let the number of people in first and second village be x and y respectively.

According to given condition,

average income of x people $= P$ and

average income of y people $= Q$, where $P \neq Q$

$\therefore \quad$ Total income of people in two villages are Px and Qy respectively.

When, one person moves from first village to second village.

Then, number of people in first village $= x - 1$ and in second village $= y + 1$.

New average income $= P'$ and Q'

(Total income $=$ no. of persons $\times$ average income)

$\therefore \quad$ Total income $= P'(x - 1)$ and $Q'(y + 1)$

Total income in both cases are same

$\therefore \quad Px + Qy = P'(x - 1) + Q'(y + 1)$

$\Rightarrow \quad Px - P'(x - 1) = Q'(y + 1) - Qy$

$\Rightarrow \quad x(P - P') + P' = y(Q' - Q) + Q'$

$\therefore \quad P' \neq P$ and $Q' \neq Q$

Hence, option (c) is not possible.

26. (d) $x - y = 2$ .... (i)

$kx + y = 3$ .... (ii)

Adding (i) and (ii), we have

$kx + x = 5 \ \Rightarrow\ x(k + 1) = 5 \ \Rightarrow\ x = \dfrac{5}{k+1}$

Putting the value of x in equation (i), we have

$\dfrac{5}{k+1} - y = 2$

$\Rightarrow \dfrac{5}{k+1} - 2 = y \Rightarrow \dfrac{5 - 2k - 2}{k+1} = y \Rightarrow y = \dfrac{3 - 2k}{k+1}$

y should be positive as they intersect in 1st quadrant

Therefore, $y > 0$

$\dfrac{3 - 2k}{k+1} > 0 \Rightarrow \dfrac{2k - 3}{k+1} < 0$

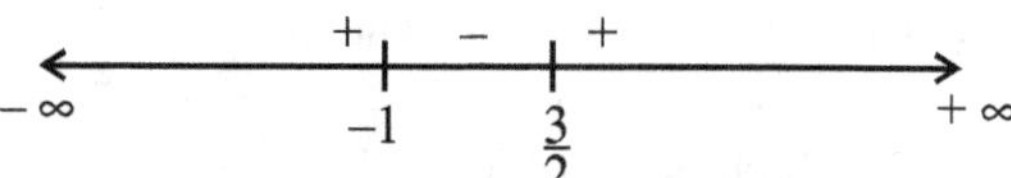

$\therefore \quad k$ should lie between $- 1$ and 3/2

27. (a) Condition for infinite many solutions.

$\dfrac{p}{12} = \dfrac{3}{p} = \dfrac{p-3}{p} \left\{ \dfrac{a_1}{a_2} = \dfrac{b_1}{b_2} = \dfrac{c_1}{c_2} \right\}$

$p^2 = 36 ; p =$ {From I and II}

$p^2 - 3p = 3p$ {From II and III}

$p = 6$

$\therefore \quad p = 6$

28. (b) Let the number of boys and girls in classroom is x and y.

According to question

$\dfrac{x - x/5}{y} = \dfrac{2}{3} \Rightarrow \dfrac{4x}{5y} = \dfrac{2}{3} \ \Rightarrow\ \dfrac{x}{y} = \dfrac{5}{6}$ ...(i)

Also, $\dfrac{x - x/5}{y - 44} = \dfrac{5}{2} \Rightarrow \dfrac{4x}{5(y - 44)} = \dfrac{5}{2}$

$\Rightarrow 8x = 25y - 1100$ ...(ii)

From Eqs. (i) and (ii), we get, $x = 50, y = 60$

Let n number of boy leaves the class so number of boys and number of girls become equal.

$\therefore 50 - 10 - n = 60 - 44$

$n = 40 - 16 = 24$

29. (a) $x = \dfrac{1}{10} \Rightarrow a = 10$ and $y = \dfrac{1}{5} \Rightarrow b = 5$

30. (b) (I) Statement I is false. Consistent Linear equations may have unique or infinite solutions.

(II) Statement or is also false

$\therefore \quad Q\ 13^2 + 14^2 = 365$

31. (a) Let one woman can paint a large mural in W hours and one girl can paint it in G hours

According to question,

$$\frac{8}{W}+\frac{12}{G}=\frac{1}{10} \Rightarrow \frac{2}{W}+\frac{3}{G}=\frac{1}{40} \qquad ...(i)$$

Also, $\frac{6}{W}+\frac{8}{G}=\frac{1}{14} \Rightarrow \frac{3}{W}+\frac{4}{G}=\frac{1}{28} \qquad ...(ii)$

On solving equation (i) and (ii), we get

$W = 140$ and $G = 280$

Now, $\frac{7}{140}+\frac{14}{280}=\frac{1}{\text{Time taken}}=\frac{1}{t}(\text{say})$

$\Rightarrow \frac{1}{t}=\frac{1}{20}+\frac{1}{20} \Rightarrow t = 10$ hours

32. (b) Let speed of boat in still water be x km/hr
and speed of stream be y km/hr

$$\frac{30}{x+y}=3 \quad \Rightarrow \quad x+y=10 \qquad ...(i)$$

$$\frac{30}{x-y}=5 \quad \Rightarrow \quad x-y=6 \qquad ...(ii)$$

From solving equations (i) and (ii)

$x + y = 10$

$-x - y = 6$

$\underline{\quad + \qquad - \quad}$

$2y = 4 \qquad y = 2$ km/hr. and

$x = 8$ km/hr

33. (c) $\dfrac{a_1}{a_2}=\dfrac{b_1}{b_2}=\dfrac{c_1}{c_2}=\dfrac{5}{3}$

34. (d) Let x & y be the unit and tenth digits respectively of a two digit number. Then,

$x + y = 9$ ($\because$ Given) $\qquad ... (i)$

and according to given condition,

$10x + y = 10y + x + 27$

$\Rightarrow 9x - 9y = 27$

$\Rightarrow x - y = 3 \qquad ... (ii)$

On adding (i) & (ii)

$2x = 12 \Rightarrow x = 6$

Hence, from equation (i),

$6 + y = 9 \Rightarrow y = 3$

So number will be $10 \times 3 + 6 = 36$

35. (d) For solution to be infinite, $\dfrac{-c}{6}=\dfrac{-1}{2}=\dfrac{-2}{-3}$ must satisfy.

but $\dfrac{-1}{2} \neq \dfrac{2}{3}$, so, infinite solution don't exist, for given equations.

36. (c) On adding both the equations, we get $x = 3, y = 1$

37. (c) | **38. (a)** | **39. (a)**

40. (c) For coincident lines, $\dfrac{3}{6}=\dfrac{-1}{-k}=\dfrac{8}{16}$

$\dfrac{1}{2}=\dfrac{1}{k} \Rightarrow k = 2$

Sol. (41-44):

Let x be number of known questions and y be number of questions cheating by the student.

Here, $x + y = 120$

$x - \dfrac{1}{4}y = 90$

On solving these two equations

We have, $x = 96$ and $y = 24$

41. No. of correct questions are 96

42. He guessed 24 questions.

43. Marks $= 80 - \dfrac{1}{4}$ of $40 = 70$

44. Here, $x + y = 120 \qquad ...(i)$

$x - \dfrac{1}{4}y = 95 \qquad ...(ii)$

On solving (i) & (ii) $x = 100$

45. Given area of two bedrooms and a kitchen is 95 sq m.

$2 \times$ Area of bedroom + Area of kitchen $= 95$

$2 \times 5x + 5y = 95$

or $2x + y = 19 \qquad ...(i)$

and $x + 2 + y = 15$

or $x + y = 13 \qquad ...(ii)$

46. Length of outer boundary $= 12 + 15 + 12 + 15 = 54$ m

47. On solving $x + y = 13$

$2x + y = 19$

$x = 6m, y = 7m$

Area of a bedroom $= 5x = 5 \times 6 = 30$ sq m

Area of kitchen $= 5y = 5 \times 7 = 35$ sq m

48. Area of living room $= 9 \times 5 + 2 \times 15 = 75$ sq m

49. Total cost of laying tiles in the kitchen $= ₹\ 50 \times 35 = ₹\ 1750$

50. (b) Given, fixed charges of auto rickshaw be ₹ x and running charges be ₹ y km/hr, so representing situation 1

$x + 10y = 75$

$x + 15y = 110$

51. (c) On solving $x + 10y = 75$

$x + 15y = 110$

we get $x = 5$ km,

$y = ₹\ 7$/km

Charges to go 50 km.

$x + 50y = 5 + 50 \times 7 = ₹\ 355$

52. **(b)** To cover 30 km distance,

$x + 30y = 19 + 30 \times 9 = 289$

53. **(c)**

54. **(a)** Reason is true.

In assertion, given lines represent parallel lines if

$\dfrac{3}{6} = \dfrac{4}{k} \neq \dfrac{5}{9} \Rightarrow k = \dfrac{6 \times 4}{3} = 8$ ∴ Reason is also true

Also, reason is the correct explanation for assertion.

55. **(b)** Reason is true.

For assertion, given equation has no solution if

$\dfrac{1}{2} = \dfrac{1}{k} \neq \dfrac{-4}{-3}$ i.e. $\dfrac{4}{3} \Rightarrow k = 2\left[\dfrac{1}{2} \neq \dfrac{4}{3} \text{holds}\right]$

∴ Assertion is true.

Reason does not give result of assertion.

56. **(c)** Assertion: given system of equations has infinitely many solutions if

$\dfrac{2}{2a} = \dfrac{3}{a+b} = \dfrac{-7}{-28}$

i.e. $\dfrac{1}{4} \Rightarrow \dfrac{1}{a} = \dfrac{3}{a+b} = \dfrac{1}{4} \Rightarrow 3a = a+b \Rightarrow 2a - b = 0$

Also clearly $a = 4$, and $a + b = 12 \Rightarrow b = 8$

∴ $2a - b = 8 - 8 = 0$

∴ Assertion is true

But reason is false ∵ $\dfrac{3}{6} = \dfrac{-5}{-10}$

$$[\because 3(-10) = (-5)(6) = -30]$$

For unique solution if $a_1 x + b_2 y + c_2 = 0$, then $\dfrac{a_1}{a_2} \neq \dfrac{b_1}{b_2}$

57. **(d)** Assertion is clearly false.

[∵ If the lines are coincident, then it has infinite number of solutions]

Reason is clearly true.

58. **(a)**   **59.** **(b)**   **60.** **(c)**

61. (A) → (s); (B) → (r); (C) → (q); (D) → (p)

62. (A) → (q); (B) → (s); (C) → (p); (D) → (r)

63. (A) → (q); (B) → (p); (C) → (s); (D) → (r)

64. consistent   **65.** inconsistent.

66. 4 and 1   **67.** positive

68. Cannot be determined   **69.** zero

70. 5   **71.** Does not exist

72. True   **73.** False   **74.** True

75. True   **76.** False   **77.** True

78. False

Coordinate Geometry

DIRECTIONS : *This section contains multiple choice questions. Each question has 4 choices (a), (b), (c) and (d) out of which only one is correct.*

1. If P = (2, 5), Q = (x, –7) and PQ = 13, what is the value of 'x'?

(a) 5   (b 3

(c) –3   (d) –5

2. The points (a, b), (a^1, b^1) and $(a – a^1, b – b^1)$ are collinear if

(a) $ab = a^1 b^1$ (b) $ab^1 = a^1 b$

(c) $a = b$ (d) $a^1 = b^1$

3. If $\left(\dfrac{a}{3}, 4\right)$ is the midpoint of the line segment joining A(–6, 5) and B(–2, 3), then what is the value of 'a'?

(a) –4   (b) –12

(c) 12   (d) –6

4. If the mid point of the line joining (3, 4) and (k, 7) is (x, y) and 2x + 2y + 1 = 0. Find the value of k.

(a) 10   (b) –15

(c) 15   (d) –10

5. In what ratio is the line segment joining the points (3, 5) & (–4, 2) divided by y–axis?

(a) 3 : 2   (b) 3 : 4

(c) 2 : 3   (d) 4 : 3

6. In what ratio does the point (–2, 3) divide the line-segment joining the points (–3, 5) and (4, –9) ?

(a) 2 : 3   (b) 1 : 6

(c) 6 : 1   (d) 2 : 1

7. If P (x , y) is any point on the line joining the points A $(a, 0)$ and B $(0, b)$, then

(a) $\dfrac{x}{b} + \dfrac{y}{a} = 1$ (b) $\dfrac{x}{a} - \dfrac{y}{b} = 1$

(c) $\dfrac{x}{a} + \dfrac{y}{b} = 1$ (d) $\dfrac{x}{b} - \dfrac{y}{a} = 1$

8. The perimeter of a triangle with vertices (0, 4), (0, 0) and (3, 0) is

(a) 5   (b) 12

(c) 11   (d) $7 + \sqrt{5}$

9. The point P on x-axis equidistant from the points A(–1, 0) and B(5, 0) is

(a) (2, 0)   (b) (0, 2)

(c) (3, 0)   (d) (2, 2)

10. The coordinates of the point which is reflection of point (–3, 5) in x-axis are

(a) (3, 5)   (b) (3, –5)

(c) (–3, –5)   (d) (–3, 5)

11. If the point P(6, 2) divides the line segment joining A(6, 5) and B(4, y) in the ratio 3 : 1, then the value of y is

(a) 4   (b) 3   (c) 2   (d) 1

12. P, Q, R are three collinear points. The coordinates of P and R are (3, 4) and (11, 10) respectively and PQ is equal to 2.5 units. Coordinates of Q are

(a) (5, 11/2)   (b) (11, 5/2)

(c) (5, –11/2)   (d) (–5, 11/2)

13. C is the mid-point of PQ, if P is (4, x), C is (y, –1) and Q is (–2, 4), then x and y respectively are

(a) – 6 and 1   (b) – 6 and 2

(c) 6 and – 1   (d) 6 and – 2

14. The ratio in which the point $(2, y)$ divides the join of $(-4, 3)$ and $(6, 3)$ and hence the value of y is

(a) $2 : 3, y = 3$ (b) $3 : 2, y = 4$

(c) $3 : 2, y = 3$ (d) $3 : 2, y = 2$

15. Ratio in which the line $3x + 4y = 7$ divides the line segment joining the points $(1, 2)$ and $(-2, 1)$ is

(a) $3 : 5$ (b) $4 : 6$

(c) $4 : 9$ (d) None of these

16. The point on the X-axis which is equidistant from the points $A(-2, 3)$ and $B(5, 4)$ is

(a) $(0, 2)$ (b) $(2, 0)$

(c) $(3, 0)$ (d) $(-2, 0)$

17. The point which divides the line joining the points $A\,(1, 2)$ and $B\,(-1, 1)$ internally in the ratio $1 : 2$ is

(a) $\left(\dfrac{-1}{3}, \dfrac{5}{3}\right)$ (b) $\left(\dfrac{1}{3}, \dfrac{5}{3}\right)$

(c) $(-1, 5)$ (d) $(1, 5)$

18. The centroid of the triangle whose vertices are $(3, -7)$, $(-8, 6)$ and $(5, 10)$ is

(a) $(0, 9)$ (b) $(0, 3)$

(c) $(1, 3)$ (d) $(3, 5)$

19. The points $A\,(-4, -1)$, $B\,(-2, -4)$, $C\,(4, 0)$ and $D\,(2, 3)$ are the vertices of a

(a) Parallelogram   (b) Rectangle

(c) Rhombus   (d) Square

20. If the point $P\,(p, q)$ is equidistant from the points $A\,(a + b, b - a)$ and $B\,(a - b, a + b)$, then

(a) $ap = by$ (b) $bp = ay$

(c) $ap + bq = 0$ (d) $bp + aq = 0$

21. The distances of a point from the x-axis and the y-axis are 5 and 4 respectively. The coordinates of the point can be

(a) $(5, 4)$ (b) $(5, 0)$

(c) $(0, 4)$ (d) $(4, 5)$

22. If the points $(a, 0)$, $(0, b)$ and $(1, 1)$ are collinear then which of the following is true :

(a) $\dfrac{1}{a} + \dfrac{1}{b} = 2$ (b) $\dfrac{1}{a} - \dfrac{1}{b} = 1$

(c) $\dfrac{1}{a} - \dfrac{1}{b} = 2$ (d) $\dfrac{1}{a} + \dfrac{1}{b} = 1$

23. P is a point on the graph of $y = 5x + 3$. The coordinates of a point Q are $(3, -2)$. If M is the mid point of PQ, then M must lie on the line represented by

(a) $y = 5x + 1$ (b) $y = 5x - 7$

(c) $y = \dfrac{5}{2}x - \dfrac{7}{2}$ (d) $y = \dfrac{5}{2}x + \dfrac{1}{2}$

24. A line l passing through the origin makes an angle θ with positive direction of x-axis such that $\sin\theta = \dfrac{3}{5}$. The coordinates of the point, which lies in the fourth quadrant at a unit distance from the origin and on perpendicular to l, are

(a) $\left(\dfrac{3}{5}, \dfrac{4}{5}\right)$ (b) $\left(\dfrac{4}{5}, \dfrac{3}{5}\right)$

(c) $(3, -4)$ (d) $(4, -3)$

25. The centre of the circle passing through the ponts $(6, -6)$, $(3, -7)$ and $(3, 3)$ is

(a) $(3, 2)$ (b) $(-3, -2)$

(c) $(3, -2)$ (d) $(-3, 2)$

26. A circle passes through the vertices of a triangle ABC. If the vertices are $A(-2, 5)$, $B(-2, -3)$, $C(2, -3)$, then the centre of the circle is

(a) $(0, 0)$ (b) $(0, 1)$

(c) $(-2, 1)$ (d) $(0, -3)$

27. Which of the following points is 10 units from the origin?

(a) $(-6, 8)$ (b) $(-4, 2)$

(c) $(-6, 5)$ (d) $(6, 4)$

28. The distance between which of the following two points is 2 units?

(a) $(-2, -3)$ and $(-2, -4)$ (b) $(0, 4)$ and $(0, 6)$

(c) $(7, 2)$ and $(6, 2)$ (d) $(4, -3)$ and $(2, 3)$

29. Which of the following is / are not correct ?

Three points will form :

(a) an equilateral triangle, if all the three sides are equal.

(b) an isosceles triangle, if any two sides are equal.

(c) a collinear or a line, if sum of two sides is equal to third side.

(d) a rhombus, if all the four sides are equal.

30. Which of the following is / are correct?

Four points will form :

(a) a rectangle, if opposite sides and diagonals are not equal.

(b) a parallelogram, if opposite sides are not equal.

(c) a square, if all the four sides and diagonals are equal.

(d) a right angle triangle, if sum of squares of any two sides is equal to square of third largest side.

Coordinate Geometry

Case/Passage Based Questions

DIRECTIONS : *Study the given Case/Passage and answer the following questions.*

Case/Passage-I

In order to conduct Sports Day activities in your School, lines have been drawn with chalk powder at a distance of 1 m each, in a rectangular shaped ground ABCD, 100 flowerpots have been placed at a distance of 1 m from each other along AD, as shown in given figure below. Niharika runs 1/4 th the distance AD on the 2nd line and posts a green flag. Preet runs 1/5 th distance AD on the eighth line and posts a red flag.

[From CBSE Question Bank 2021]

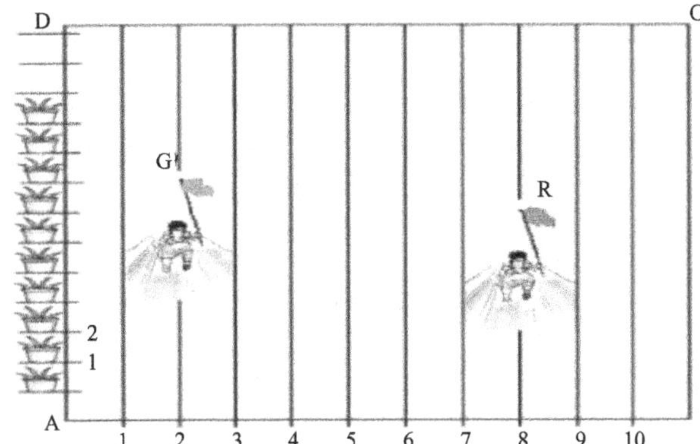

31. Find the position of green flag

   (a) (2, 25)   (b) (2, 0.25)

   (c) (25, 2)   (d) (0, –25)

32. Find the position of red flag

   (a) (8, 0)   (b) (20, 8)

   (c) (8, 20)   (d) (8, 0.2)

33. What is the distance between both the flags?

   (a) $\sqrt{41}$ (b) $\sqrt{11}$

   (c) $\sqrt{61}$ (d) $\sqrt{51}$

34. If Rashmi has to post a blue flag exactly halfway between the line segment joining the two flags, where should she post her flag?

   (a) (5, 22.5)   (b) (10, 22)

   (c) (2, 8.5)   (d) (2.5, 20)

35. If Joy has to post a flag at one-fourth distance from green flag ,in the line segment joining the green and red flags, then where should he post his flag?

   (a) (3.5, 24)   (b) (0.5, 12.5)

   (c) (2.25, 8.5)   (d) (25, 20)

Assertion & Reason

DIRECTIONS : *Each of these questions contains an Assertion followed by Reason. Read them carefully and answer the question on the basis of following options. You have to select the one that best describes the two statements.*

  (a) If both **Assertion** and **Reason** are **correct** and Reason is the **correct explanation** of Assertion.

  (b) If both **Assertion** and **Reason** are correct, but Reason is **not the correct explanation** of Assertion.

  (c) If **Assertion** is **correct** but **Reason** is **incorrect**.

  (d) If **Assertion** is **incorrect** but **Reason** is **correct**.

36. **Assertion :** If $A(2a, 4a)$ and $B(2a, 6a)$ are two vertices of an equilateral triangle ABC then, the vertex C is given by $(2a + a\sqrt{3}, 5a)$.

   Reason : In equilateral triangle, all the coordinates of three vertices can be rational.

37. **Assertion :** The points $(k, 2 - 2k)$, $(-k+1, 2k)$ and $(-4 - k, 6 - 2k)$ are collinear if $k = \dfrac{1}{2}$.

   Reason : Three points A, B and C are collinear in same straight line, if $AB + BC = AC$.

38. **Assertion :** Mid-point of a line segment divides line in the ratio 1 : 1.

   Reason : If area of triangle is zero that means points are collinear.

Match the Following

DIRECTIONS : *Each question contains statements given in two columns which have to be matched. Statements (A, B, C, D) in column-I have to be matched with statements (p, q, r, s) in column-II.*

39. Column-II gives distance between pair of points given in Column-I

Column-I	Column-II
(A) (–5, 7), (–1, 3)	(p) $\sqrt{17}$
(B) (5, 6), (1, 3)	(q) $\sqrt{8}$
(C) $(\sqrt{3}+1,1), (0,\sqrt{3})$	(r) $\sqrt{6}$
(D) (0,0) $(-\sqrt{3},\sqrt{3})$	(s) $4\sqrt{2}$

40. Column-II gives the coordinates of the point P that divides the line segment joining the points given in Column-I.

Column-I	Column-II
(A) A (–1, 3) and B (5, –6) internally in the ratio 1 : 2	(p) (7, 3)
(B) A (–2, 1) and B (1, 4) internally in the ratio 2 : 1	(q) (0, 3)
(C) A (–1, 7) and B (4, –3) internally in the ratio 2 : 3	(r) (1, 3)
(D) A (4, –3) and B (8, 5) internally in the ratio 3 : 1	(s) (1, 0)

≫ Fill in the Blanks ⟫⟫

DIRECTIONS : *Complete the following statements with an appropriate word / term to be filled in the blank space(s).*

41. Points (3, 2), (–2, –3) and (2, 3) form a .... triangle.

42. If $x - y = 2$, then point (x, y) is equidistant from (7, 1) and (.........)

43. Distance between (2, 3) and (4, 1) is ....

44. Points (1, 5), (2, 3) and (– 2, – 11) are ....

45. (5, – 2) (6, 4) and (7, – 2) are the vertices of an .... triangle.

46. Point on the X-axis which is equidistant from (2, –5) and (–2, 9) is ....

47. Point (– 4, 6) divide the line segment joining the points A(– 6, 10) and B(3, – 8) in the ratio ....

48. (1, 2), (4, y), (x, 6) and (3, 5) are the vertices of a parallelogram taken in order, then the value of x and y are ....

49. Relation between x and y if the points (x, y), (1, 2) and (7, 0) are collinear is ....

50. The distance of the point (x^1, y^1) from the origin is ....

≫ True / False ⟫⟫

DIRECTIONS : *Read the following statements and write your answer as true or false.*

51. The distance between P (x_1, y_1) and Q (x_2, y_2) is
$$\sqrt{(x_2 + x_1)^2 + (y_2 + y_1)^2}$$

52. The coordinates of the point P(x, y) which divides the line segment joining the points A(x_1, y_1) and B(x_2, y_2) internally in the ratio $m_1 : m_2$ are
$$\left(\frac{m_1 x_2 - m_2 x_1}{m_1 + m_2}, \frac{m_1 y_2 - m_2 y_1}{m_1 + m_2} \right)$$

53. The mid-point of the line segment joining the points P (x_1, y_1) and Q (x_2, y_2) is $\left(\dfrac{x_1 + x_2}{2}, \dfrac{y_1 + y_2}{2} \right)$.

54. Points (1, 7), (4, 2), (–1, –1) and (– 4, 4) are the vertices of a square.

55. Coordinates of the point which divides the join of (–1, 7) and (4, –3) in the ratio 2 : 3 is (1, 3).

56. Ratio in which the line segment joining the points (– 3, 10) and (6, – 8) is divided by (– 1, 6) is 3 : 7.

57. The ratio in which the point (3, 5) divides the join of (1, 3) and (4, 6) is 2 : 1.

58. The distance of the point (5, 3) from the X-axis is 5 units

59. The distance of a point (2, 3) from Y-axis is y-units.

ANSWER KEY & SOLUTIONS

1. **(c)** $PQ = 13 \Rightarrow PQ^2 = 169$

$\Rightarrow (x-2)^2 + (-7-5)^2 = 169$

$\Rightarrow x^2 - 4x + 4 + 144 = 169$

$\Rightarrow x^2 - 4x - 21 = 0$

$\Rightarrow x^2 - 7x + 3x - 21 = 0$

$\Rightarrow (x-7)(x+3) = 0$

$\Rightarrow x = 7, -3$

2. **(b)** We have,

$a(b_1 - b + b_1) + a_1(b - b_1 - b) + (a - a_1)(b - a_1)(b - b_1) = 0$

$\Rightarrow 2ab_1 - ab - a_1b_1 + ab - ab_1 - a_1b + a_1b_1 = 0$

$\Rightarrow ab_1 - a_1b = 0$

$\Rightarrow ab_1 = a_1b.$

3. **(b)** Coordinates of mid-point are given by

$$\left(\frac{x_1 + x_2}{2}, \frac{y_1 + y_2}{2} \right)$$

Here, coordinates of mid-point are $\left(\frac{a}{3}, 4 \right)$

So, $\dfrac{a}{3} = \dfrac{-6-2}{2}$

$\therefore \quad a = -12$

4. **(b)** Since (x, y) is midpoint of $(3, 4)$ and $(k, 7)$

$\therefore \quad x = \dfrac{3+k}{2}$ and $y = \dfrac{4+7}{2}$

Also $2x + 2y + 1 = 0$ putting values we get

$3 + k + 4 + 7 + 1 = 0$

$\Rightarrow k + 15 = 0 \Rightarrow k = -15$

5. **(b)** Let the required ratio be $K : 1$

$\therefore$ The coordinates of the required point on the y-axis is

$x = \dfrac{K(-4) + 3(1)}{K+1}$; $y = \dfrac{K(2) + 5(1)}{K+1}$

Since, it lies on y-axis

$\therefore$ Its x-cordinates $= 0$

$\therefore \dfrac{-4K+3}{K+1} = 0 \Rightarrow -4K + 3 = 0$

$\Rightarrow K = \dfrac{3}{4}$

$\Rightarrow$ Required ratio $= \dfrac{3}{4} : 1$

$\therefore$ ratio $= 3 : 4$

6. **(b)** Suppose the required ratio is $m_1 : m_2$

Then, using the section formula, we get

$-2 = \dfrac{m_1(4) + m_2(-3)}{m_1 + m_2}$

$\Rightarrow -2m_1 - 2m_2 = 4m_1 - 3m_2$

$\Rightarrow m_2 = 6m_1 \Rightarrow m_1 : m_2 = 1 : 6$

7. **(c)** As the point $P(x, y)$ lies on the line joining the points $A(a, 0)$ and $B(0, b)$, the points A, B and P are collinear

$\Rightarrow a(b-y) + 0(y-0) + x(0-b) = 0$

$\Rightarrow ab - ay - bx = 0 \Rightarrow bx + ay = ab$

$\Rightarrow \dfrac{x}{a} + \dfrac{y}{b} = 1$

8. **(b)** $A(0, 4), B(0, 0), C(3, 0)$

$AB = \sqrt{(0-0)^2 + (0-4)^2} = 4$

$BC = \sqrt{(3-0)^2 + (0-0)^2} = 3$

$CA = \sqrt{(0-3)^2 + (4-0)^2} = 5$

$AB + BC + CA = 12$

9. **(a)** $P(x, 0) = \left(\dfrac{5-1}{2}, 0 \right) = (2, 0)$

$[\because$ A and B both lies on x-axis$]$

Three or more points lies in same line are called collinear.

10. **(c)** For reflection of a point with respect to x-axis change sign of y-coordinate and with respect to y-axis change sign of x-coordinate.

11. **(d)** $P(6, 2) = \left(\dfrac{4 \times 3 + 1 \times 6}{3+1}, \dfrac{3 \times y + 1 \times 5}{3+1} \right)$

$\because \quad 6 \ne \dfrac{18}{4}$ (Question is wrong)

$2 = \dfrac{3y+5}{4} \quad \Rightarrow \quad 3y + 5 = 8$

$3y = 3 \quad \Rightarrow \quad y = 1$

12. **(a)**

13. **(a)** Since, $C(y, -1)$ is the mid-point of $P(4, x)$ and $Q(-2, 4)$.

$$
\begin{array}{ccc}
P & C & Q \\
\times & | & \times \\
(4, x) & (y_1, -1) & (-2, 4)
\end{array}
$$

We have, $\dfrac{4-2}{2} = y$ and $\dfrac{4+x}{2} = -1$

$\therefore \ y = 1$ and $x = -6$

14. **(c)** Let the required ratio be $k : 1$

Then, $2 = \dfrac{6k - 4(1)}{k+1}$ or $k = \dfrac{3}{2}$

$\therefore$ The required ratio is $\dfrac{3}{2} : 1$ or $3 : 2$

Also, $y = \dfrac{3(3) + 2(3)}{3+2} = 3$

15. **(c)** $-\dfrac{3(1) + 4(2) - 7}{3(-2) + 4(1) - 7} = -\dfrac{4}{-9} = \dfrac{4}{9}$

16. **(b)** Let $P(x, 0)$ be a point on X-axis such that $AP = BP$

$\Rightarrow \ AP^2 = BP^2$

$\Rightarrow \ (x+2)^2 + (0-3)^2 = (x-5)^2 + (0+4)^2$

$\Rightarrow \ x^2 + 4x + 4 + 9 = x^2 - 10x + 25 + 16$

$\Rightarrow \ 14x = 28 \Rightarrow x = 2$

Hence, required point is $(2, 0)$.

17. **(b)**

18. **(b)** Centroid is $\left(\dfrac{x_1 + x_2 + x_3}{3}, \dfrac{y_1 + y_2 + y_3}{3} \right)$

i.e. $\left(\dfrac{3 + (-8) + 5}{3}, \dfrac{-7 + 6 + 10}{3} \right) = \left(\dfrac{0}{3}, \dfrac{9}{3} \right) = (0, 3)$

19. **(b)**

20. **(b)**

21. **(d)**

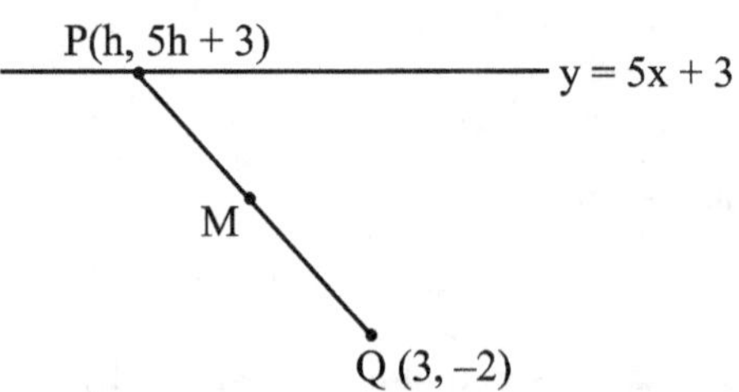

22. **(d)** As $(a, 0)$, $(0, b)$ and $(1, 1)$ are collinear

$\therefore \ a(b-1) + 0(1-0) + 1(0-b) = 0$

$ab - a - b = 0$

$ab = a + b$

$1 = \dfrac{1}{a} + \dfrac{1}{b}$

23. **(b)** Let coordinate of point p be $(h, 5h + 3)$

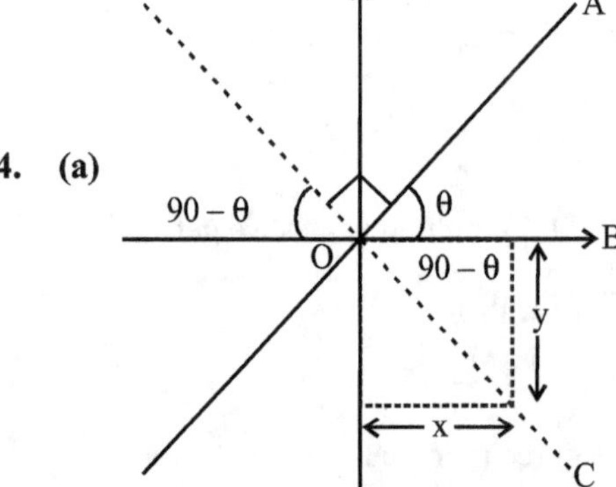

Since, M is the mid-point of PQ, therefore by mid-point formula, we have $M = \left(\dfrac{h+3}{2}, \dfrac{5h+3-2}{2} \right)$.

Clearly by observing the options, we can say that M must lie on the line

$y = 5x - 7$

24. **(a)**

$\angle AOB = \theta$

$\because \ CO \perp OA$

$\therefore$ $\angle BOC = (90° - \theta)$

$$\sin\theta = \frac{3}{5}; \quad \cos\theta = \frac{4}{5} \quad \left[\because \cos\theta = \sqrt{1-\sin^2\theta}\right]$$

Now, $\sin(90° - \theta) = \dfrac{-y}{1}$

$\Rightarrow y = -\cos\theta \Rightarrow y = \dfrac{-4}{5}$

$\cos(90° - \theta) = \dfrac{x}{1} \Rightarrow x = \sin\theta, \; x = \dfrac{3}{5}$

25. **(c)** $(x-6)^2 + (y+6)^2 = (x-3)^2 + (y+7)^2$ ...(i)

Also, $(x-3)^2 + (y-3)^2 = (x-3)^2 + (y+7)^2$

$y^2 - 6y + 9 = y^2 + 14y + 49$

$-20y = 40 \Rightarrow y = -2$

Putting $y = -2$ in equation (i), we have

$(x-6)^2 + (4)^2 = (x-3)^2 + (5)^2$

$x^2 - 12x + 36 + 16 = x^2 - 6x + 9 + 25$

$-6x = -18 \Rightarrow x = 3$

26. **(b)**

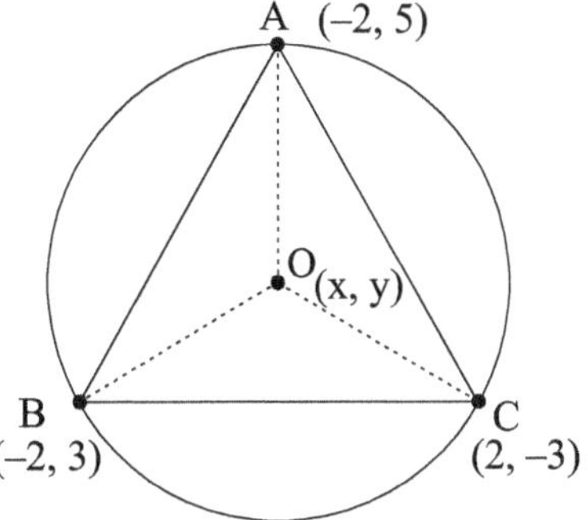

Let O(x, y) is the centre of the given circle.

Join OA, OB & OC.

$\because$ OA = OB = OC

$\therefore$ OA^2 = OB^2

$\Rightarrow \sqrt{(x+2)^2 + (y-5)^2} = \sqrt{(x+2)^2 + (y+3)^2}$

$\Rightarrow x^2 + 4 + 4x + y^2 + 25 - 10y = x^2 + 4 + 4x + y^2 + 9 + 6x$

$\Rightarrow 16y = 16 \Rightarrow y = 1$

Again: OB^2 = OC^2

$\Rightarrow \sqrt{(x+2)^2 + (y+3)^2} = \sqrt{(x-2)^2 + (y+3)^2}$

$\Rightarrow x^2 + 4 + 4x + (y+3)^2 = x^2 + 4 - 4x + (y+3)^2$

$\Rightarrow 8x = 0 \Rightarrow x = 0$

$\therefore$ centre of the circle is (0, 1).

27. **(a)**

28. **(b)**

29. **(d)** All the statements given in option 'a', 'b' and 'c' are correct.

30. **(c)**

31. **(a)** $(2, 25)$ $\left[\because x = 2, y = \dfrac{1}{4} \times 100 = 25\right]$

32. **(c)** $(8, 20)$ $\left[\because x = 8, y = \dfrac{1}{5} \times 100 = 20\right]$

33. **(c)** $\sqrt{(8-2)^2 + (25-20)^2} = \sqrt{36+25} = \sqrt{61}$

34. **(a)** $\left(\dfrac{8+2}{2}, \dfrac{25+20}{2}\right) = (5, 22.5)$

35. **(a)** $\left(\dfrac{2+5}{2}, \dfrac{25+22.5}{2}\right) = (3.5, 24)$

36. **(c)** Let $A(x_1, y_1)$, $B(x_2, y_2)$ & $C(x_3, y_3)$ are all rational coordinates of a triangle ABC.

$$\text{ar}(\Delta ABC) = \frac{1}{2}\begin{vmatrix} x_1 & y_1 & 1 \\ x_2 & y_2 & 1 \\ x_3 & y_3 & 1 \end{vmatrix}$$

$$= \frac{\sqrt{3}}{4}\left[(x_1 - x_2)_2 + (y_1 - y_2)_2\right]$$

LHS = rational, RHS = irrational

Hence, (x_1, y_1) (x_2, y_2) & (x_3, y_3) cannot be all rational.

37. **(a)** Both assertion and reason are correct. Reason is correct explanation of assertion.

38. **(b)** Both statements are individually correct.

39. (A) $\to$ (s); (B) $\to$ (p); (C) $\to$ (q); (D) $\to$ (r)

40. (A) $\to$ (s); (B) $\to$ (q); (C) $\to$ (r); (D) $\to$ (p)

41. right angle

42. (3, 5)

43. $2\sqrt{2}$

44. Non-collinear

45. isosceles

46. $(-7, 0)$

47. $2 : 7$

48. $(6, 3)$

49. $x + 3y = 7$

50. $\sqrt{x_1^2 + y_1^2}$

51. False

52. False

53. True

54. True

55. True

56. False

57. True

58. False

59. False

5 — Triangles

DIRECTIONS : *This section contains multiple choice questions. Each question has 4 choices (a), (b), (c) and (d) out of which only one is correct*

1. In the given figure, AD is the bisector of $\angle A$. If BD = 4 cm, DC = 3 cm and AB = 6 cm, determine AC

   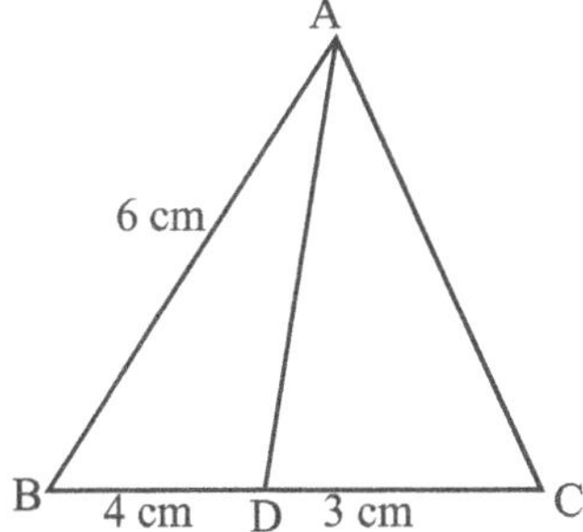

   (a) 4.5 cm   (b) 3.5 cm

   (c) 4.8 cm   (d) 3.2 cm

2. $\triangle ABC$ is an isosceles triangle right angled at B. Similar triangles ACD and ABE are constructed on sides AC and AB. Ratio between the areas of $\triangle ABE$ and $\triangle ACD$ is

   (a) 1 : 4   (b) 2 : 1

   (c) 1 : 2   (d) 4 : 3

3. Two isosceles triangles have their corresponding angles equal and their areas are in the ratio 25 : 36. The ratio of their corresponding height is

   (a) 25 : 35   (b) 36 : 25

   (c) 5 : 6   (d) 6 : 5

4. In $\triangle ABC$, $\dfrac{AB}{AC} = \dfrac{BD}{DC}$, $\angle B = 70°$ and $\angle C = 50°$. Then, $\angle BAD = \underline{\hspace{2cm}}$.

   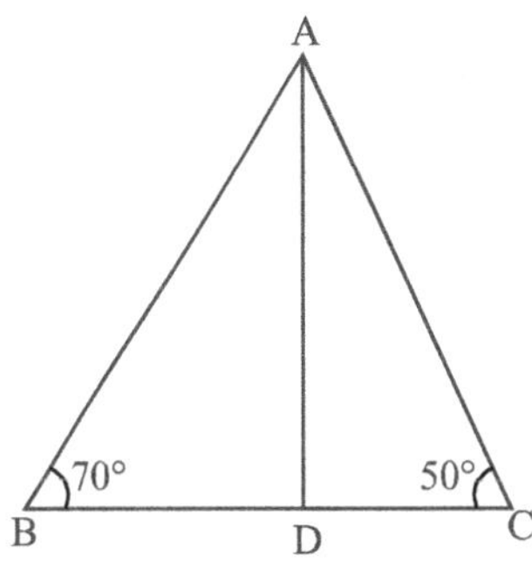

   (a) 30°   (b) 40°

   (c) 50°   (d) 45°

5. If $\triangle ABC \sim \triangle DEF$ such that BC = 2.1 cm and EF = 2.8 cm. If the area of triangle DEF is 16 cm^2, then the area of triangle ABC (in sq. cm) is

   (a) 9   (b) 12

   (c) 8   (d) 13

6. From the given figure, then length of the sides AB and BD.

   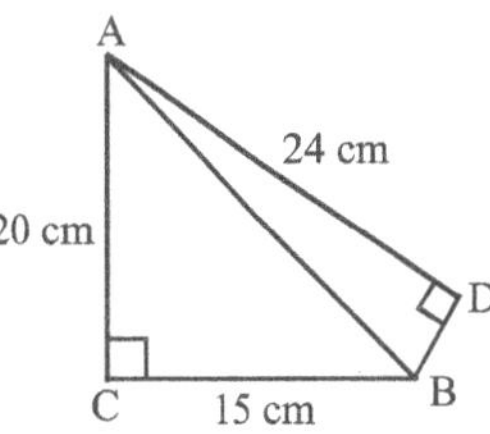

   (a) 25 cm and 7 cm   (b) 25 cm and 17 cm

   (c) 7 cm and 15 cm   (d) 18 cm and 7 cm

7. The diagonal BD of a parallelogram ABCD intersects the segment AE at the point F, where E is any point on the side BC. Then

   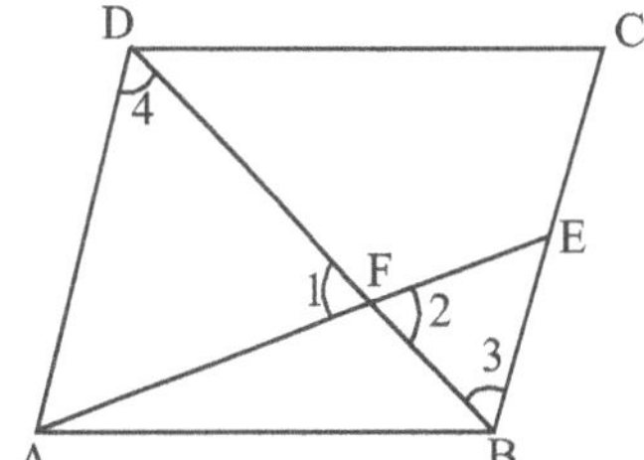

(a) $\dfrac{EF}{FA} = \dfrac{FB}{AB}$ (b) $DF \times EF = FB \times FA$

(c) $DF \times EF = (FB)^2$ (d) None of these

8. ABC is an isosceles triangle in which AB = AC = 10 cm, BC = 12 cm. PQRS is a rectangle inside the isosceles triangle. Given PQ = SR = y cm and PS = QR = $2x$ cm, then x =

(a) $6 - \dfrac{3y}{4}$ (b) $6 + 6y$

(c) $6 + \dfrac{4y}{3}$ (d) $\dfrac{7x + 8y}{4}$

9. If ABC and EBC are two equilateral triangles such that D is mid-point of BC, then the ratio of the areas of triangles ABC and BDE is

(a) $2 : 1$ (b) $1 : 2$ (c) $1 : 4$ (d) $4 : 1$

10. Given $\triangle ABC \sim \triangle DEF$, if $AB = 2DE$ and area of $\triangle ABC$ is 56 cm^2, find the area of $\triangle DEF$.

(a) 14 sq.cm   (b) 5 sq.cm

(c) 18 sq.cm   (d) 56 sq.cm

11. The area of a right angled triangle is 40 sq. cm. and its perimeter is 40 cm. The length of its hypotenuse is

(a) 16 cm   (b) 18 cm

(c) 17 cm   (d) Data insufficient

12. In the given figure, P and Q are points on the sides AB and AC respectively of a triangle ABC. PQ is parallel to BC and divides the triangle ABC into 2 parts, equal in area. The ratio of $PA : AB$ =

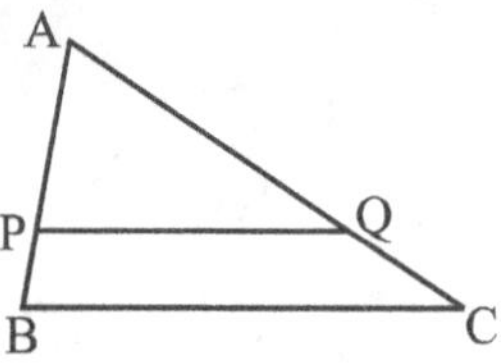

(a) $1 : 1$ (b) $(\sqrt{2} - 1) : \sqrt{2}$

(c) $1 : \sqrt{2}$ (d) $(\sqrt{2} - 1) : 1$

13. It is given that $\triangle ABC \sim \triangle PQR$ with $\dfrac{BC}{QR} = \dfrac{1}{3}$. Then $\dfrac{ar(\triangle PQR)}{ar(\triangle ABC)}$ is equal to

(a) 9   (b) 3   (c) $\dfrac{1}{3}$ (d) $\dfrac{1}{9}$

14. The area of a right angled isosceles triangle whose hypotenuse is equal to 270 m is-

(a) 19000 m^2 (b) 18225 m^2

(c) 17256 m^2 (d) 18325 m^2

15. The perimeters of two similar triangles ABC and PQR are respectively 36 cm and 24 cm. If $PQ = 10$ cm, then AB =

(a) 10 cm   (b) 20 cm

(c) 25 cm   (d) 15 cm

16. In the given figure, $DE \parallel BC$. The value of EC is

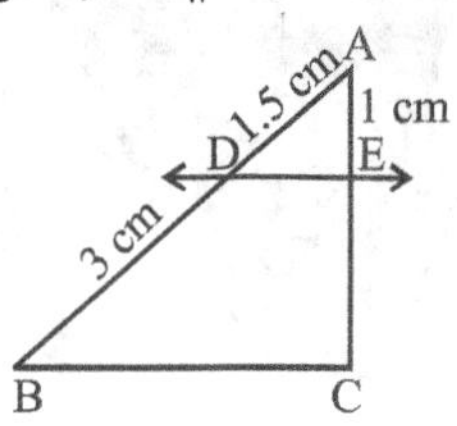

(a) 1.5 cm   (b) 3 cm

(c) 2 cm   (d) 1 cm

17. In the given figure, express x in terms of a, b and c.

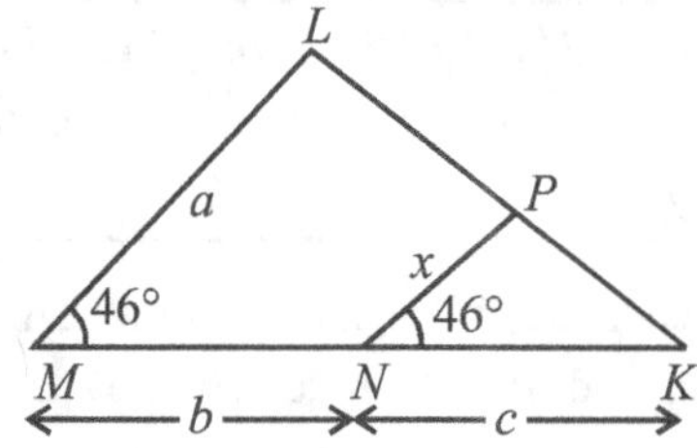

(a) $x = \dfrac{ab}{a + b}$ (b) $x = \dfrac{ac}{b + c}$

(c) $x = \dfrac{bc}{b + c}$ (d) $x = \dfrac{ac}{a + c}$

18. Which of the following statement is false?

(a) All isosceles triangles are similar.

(b) All quadrilateral triangles are similar.

(c) All circles are similar.

(d) None of the above

19. If $\triangle ABC \sim \triangle APQ$ and ar $(\triangle APQ) = 4$ ar $(\triangle ABC)$, then the ratio of BC to PQ is

(a) $2 : 1$ (b) $1 : 2$

(c) $1 : 4$ (d) $4 : 1$

20. The areas of two similar triangles ABC and PQR are in the ratio 9 : 16. If $BC = 4.5$ cm, then the length of QR is

(a) 4 cm   (b) 4.5 cm

(c) 3 cm   (d) 6 cm

21. The length of the side of a square whose diagonal is 16 cm, is

(a) $8\sqrt{2}$ cm   (b) $2\sqrt{8}$ cm

(c) $4\sqrt{2}$ cm   (d) $2\sqrt{2}$ cm

22. $\triangle ABC$ is an equilateral triangle with each side of length $2p$. If $AD \perp BC$, then the value of AD is

(a) $\sqrt{3}$ (b) $\sqrt{3}\,p$

(c) $2p$ (d) $4p$

23. The areas of two similar triangles are 81 cm^2 and 49 cm^2 respectively, then the ratio of their corresponding medians is

(a) 7 : 9 (b) 9 : 81

(c) 9 : 7 (d) 81 : 7

24. In the figure, ABC is a triangle in which AD bisects $\angle A$, AC = BC, $\angle B = 72°$ and CD = 1cm. Length of BD (in cm) is

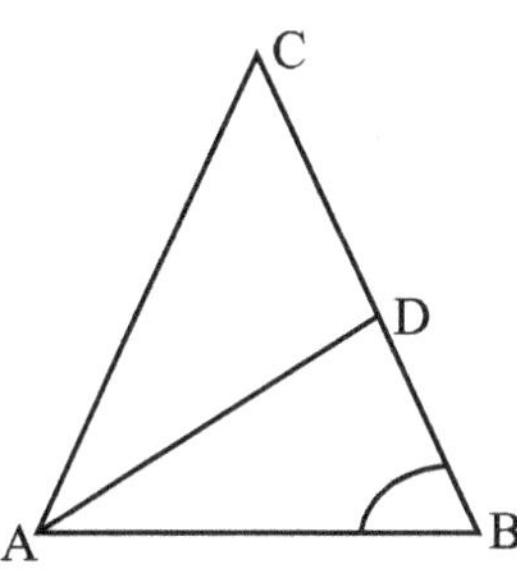

(a) 1 (b) $\dfrac{1}{2}$

(c) $\dfrac{\sqrt{5}-1}{2}$ (d) $\dfrac{\sqrt{3}+1}{2}$

25. Let P be an interior point of a $\triangle ABC$. Let Q and R be the reflections of P in AB and AC, respectively. If Q, A, R are collinear, then $\angle A$ equals

(a) 30° (b) 60°

(c) 90° (d) 120°

26. Let ABC be a triangle and M be a point on side AC closer to vertex C than A. Let N be a point on side AB such that MN is parallel to BC and let P be a point on side BC such that MP is parallel to AB. If the area of the quadrilateral $BNMP$ is equal to $\dfrac{5}{18}$ of the area of $\triangle ABC$, then the ratio AM/MC equals

(a) 5 (b) 6

(c) $\dfrac{18}{5}$ (d) $\dfrac{15}{2}$

27. In $\triangle ABC$, AB = AC, P and Q are points on AC and AB respectively such that BC = BP = PQ = AQ. Then, $\angle AQP$ is equal to (use $\pi =180°$)

(a) $\dfrac{2\pi}{7}$ (b) $\dfrac{3\pi}{7}$

(c) $\dfrac{4\pi}{7}$ (d) $\dfrac{5\pi}{7}$

28. Consider a $\triangle PQR$ in which the relation $QR^2 + PR^2 = 5\ PQ^2$ holds. Let G be the points of intersection of medians PM and QN. Then $\angle QGM$ is always

(a) less than 45°

(b) obtuse

(c) a right angle

(d) acute and larger than 45°

29. Let D be a point on the side BC of a triangle ABC such that $\angle ADC = \angle BAC$. If $AC = 21$ cm, then the side of an equilateral triangle whose area is equal to the area of the rectangle with sides BC and DC is

(a) $14 \times 3^{1/2}$ (b) $42 \times 3^{-1/2}$

(c) $14 \times 3^{3/4}$ (d) $42 \times 3^{1/2}$

30. In a triangle ABC, $\angle BAC = 90°$; AD is the altitude from A on to BC. Draw DE perpendicular to AC and DF perpendicular to AB. Suppose $AB = 15$ and $BC = 25$. Then the length of EF is

(a) 12 (b) 10

(c) $5\sqrt{3}$ (d) $5\sqrt{5}$

31. If $\triangle ABC$ is an equilateral triangle such that $AD \perp BC$, then $AD^2 =$

A. $\dfrac{3a^2}{4}$ B. $\dfrac{3a^2}{2}$

C. $\dfrac{3}{4}BC^2$ D. $\dfrac{\sqrt{3}}{2}a$

(a) A and C (b) A

(c) D (d) B and C

32. Which among the following is/are correct?

(a) The ratios of the areas of two similar triangles is equal to the ratio of their corresponding sides.

(b) The areas of two similar triangles are in the ratio of the corresponding altitudes.

(c) The ratio of area of two similar triangles are in the ratio of the corresponding medians.

(d) If the areas of two similar triangles are equal, then the triangles are congruent.

33. Which among the following is/are correct?

(I) If the altitudes of two similar triangles are in the ratio 2 : 1, then the ratio of their areas is 4 : 1.

(II) $PQ \parallel BC$ and $AP : PB = 1 : 2$.

Then, $\dfrac{\text{area}\,(\triangle APQ)}{\text{area}\,(\triangle ABC)} = \dfrac{1}{4}$

(III) The areas of two similar triangles are respectively 9cm^2 and 16cm^2. The ratio of their corresponding sides is 3 : 16.

(a) I (b) II

(c) III (d) None of these

34. In a right angled triangle $\triangle ABC$, length of two sides are 8cm and 6cm, then which among the given statements is/are correct?

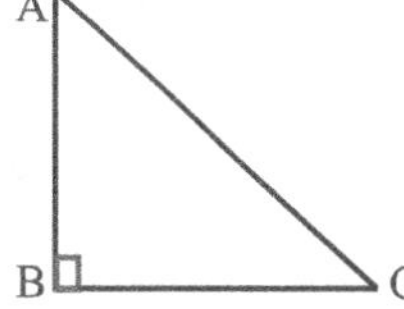

(a) Length of greatest side is 10cm

(b) $\angle ACB = 45°$

(c) $\angle BAC = 45°$

(d) Pythagoras theorem is not applicable here.

35. Two triangles are similar if
   (a) their corresponding angles are equal.
   (b) their corresponding sides are equal.
   (c) both are right triangle.
   (d) None of the above

36. Which of the following is/are not correct?
   (a) If the diagonals of a quadrilateral divide each other proportionally, then it is a trapezium.
   (b) The line segments joining the mid-points of the adjacent sides of a quadrilateral form a parallelogram.
   (c) If corresponding sides of two similar triangles are in the ratio 4 : 5, then corresponding medians of the triangles must be in the ratio 4 : 5.
   (d) None of the above

» Case/Passage Based Questions » » »

DIRECTIONS : *Study the given Case/Passage and answer the following questions.*

Case/Passage-I

Vijay is trying to find the average height of a tower near his house. He is using the properties of similar triangles. The height of Vijay's house if 20m when Vijay's house casts a shadow 10m long on the ground. At the same time, the tower casts a shadow 50m long on the ground and the house of Ajay casts 20m shadow on the ground.   **[From CBSE Question Bank-2021]**

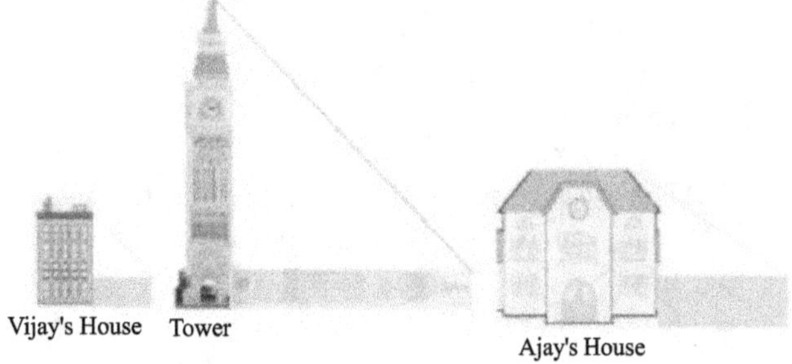

37. What is the height of the tower?
   (a) 20m   (b) 50m
   (c) 100m   (d) 200m

38. What will be the length of the shadow of the tower when Vijay's house casts a shadow of 12m?
   (a) 75m   (b) 50m
   (c) 45m   (d) 60m

39. What is the height of Ajay's house?
   (a) 30m   (b) 40m
   (c) 50m   (d) 20m

40. When the tower casts a shadow of 40m, same time what will be the length of the shadow of Ajay's house?
   (a) 16m   (b) 32m
   (c) 20m   (d) 8m

41. When the tower casts a shadow of 40m, same time what will be the length of the shadow of Vijay's house?
   (a) 15m   (b) 32m
   (c) 16m   (d) 8m

Case/Passage-II

Rohan wants to measure the distance of a pond during the visit to his native. He marks points A and B on the opposite edges of a pond as shown in the figure below. To find the distance between the points, he makes a right-angled triangle using rope connecting B with another point C are a distance of 12m, connecting C to point D at a distance of 40m from point C and the connecting D to the point A which is are a distance of 30m from D such the $\angle ADC = 90°$.

[From CBSE Question Bank-2021]

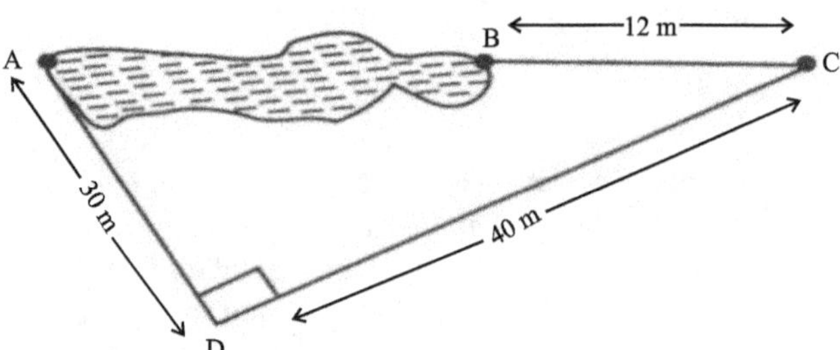

42. Which property of geometry will be used to find the distance AC?
   (a) Similarity of triangles   (b) Thales Theorem
   (c) Pythagoras Theorem   (d) Area of similar triangles

43. What is the distance AC?
   (a) 50m   (b) 12m
   (c) 100m   (d) 70m

44. Which is the following does not form a Pythagoras triplet?
   (a) (7, 24, 25)   (b) (15, 8, 17)
   (c) (5, 12, 13)   (d) (21, 20, 28)

45. Find the length AB?
   (a) 12m   (b) 38m
   (c) 50m   (d) 100m

46. Find the length of the rope used.
   (a) 120m   (b) 70m
   (c) 82m   (d) 22m

Assertion & Reason

DIRECTIONS : *Each of these questions contains an Assertion followed by reason. Read them carefully and answer the question on the basis of following options. You have to select the one that best describes the two statements.*

(a) If both **Assertion** and **Reason** are **correct** and Reason is the **correct explanation** of Assertion.

(b) If both **Assertion** and **Reason** are correct, but Reason is **not the correct explanation** of Assertion.

(c) If **Assertion** is **correct** but **Reason** is **incorrect**.

(d) If **Assertion** is **incorrect** but **Reason** is **correct**.

47. **Assertion :** If in a $\triangle ABC$, a line $DE \parallel BC$, intersects AB in D and AC in E, then $\dfrac{AB}{AD} = \dfrac{AC}{AE}$.

Reason : If a line is drawn parallel to one side of a triangle intersecting the other two sides, then the other two sides are divided in the same ratio.

48. **Assertion :** ABC is an isosceles, right triangle, right angled at C. Then $AB^2 = 3AC^2$.

Reason : In an isosceles triangle ABC if $AC = BC$ and $AB^2 = 2AC^2$, then $\angle C = 90°$.

49. **Assertion :** ABC and DEF are two similar triangles such that $BC = 4$ cm, $EF = 5$ cm and area of $\triangle ABC = 64$ cm^2, then area of $\triangle DEF = 100$ cm^2.

Reason : The areas of two similar triangles are in the ratio of the squares of the corresponding altitudes.

Match the Following

DIRECTIONS : *Each question contains statements given in two columns which have to be matched. Statements (A, B, C, D) in column-I have to be matched with statements (p, q, r, s) in column-II.*

50. If in a $\triangle$ ABC, DE $\parallel$ BC and intersects AB in D and AC in E, then.

	Column-I		**Column-II**
(A)	$\dfrac{AD}{DB}$	(p)	$\dfrac{AC}{AE}$
(B)	$\dfrac{AB}{AD}$	(q)	$\dfrac{AE}{EC}$
(C)	$\dfrac{DB}{AB}$	(r)	$\dfrac{AE}{AC}$
(D)	$\dfrac{AD}{AB}$	(s)	$\dfrac{EC}{AC}$

51. In figure, the line segment XY is parallel to the side AC of $\triangle ABC$ and it divides the triangle into two parts of equal areas, then,

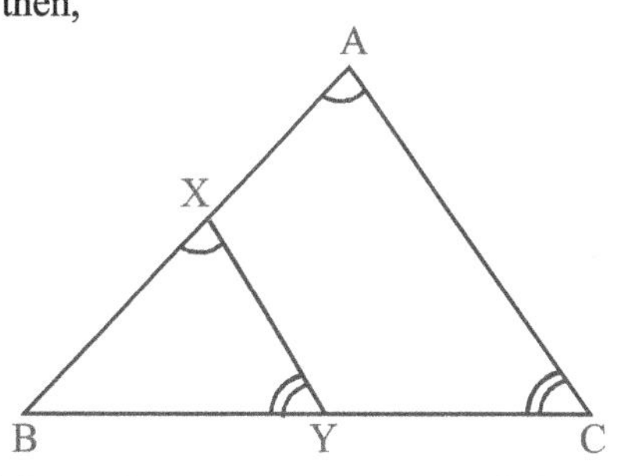

	Column-I		**Column-II**
(A)	$AB : XB$	(p)	$\sqrt{2} : 1$
(B)	ar $(\triangle ABC)$: ar $(\triangle XBY)$	(q)	$2 : 1$
(C)	$AX : AB$	(r)	$(\sqrt{2} - 1)^2 : \sqrt{2}$
(D)	$\angle X : \angle A$	(s)	$1 : 1$

52.

	Column-I		**Column-II**
(A)	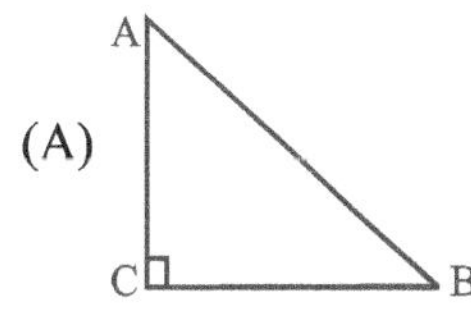 ABC is an isosceles right angled triangle. $AB^2 = ?$	(p)	$36 : 49$
(B)	$\triangle ABC \sim \triangle DEF$, such that $AB = 1.2$ cm and $DE = 1.4$ cm $\dfrac{\text{area}(\triangle ABC)}{\text{area}(\triangle DEF)} = ?$	(q)	$AB^2 = 2AC^2$
(C)	$\triangle ABC \sim \triangle APQ$ and $\dfrac{\text{area}(\triangle APQ)}{\text{area}(\triangle ABC)} = \dfrac{36}{49}$ $\dfrac{BC}{PQ} = ?$	(r)	$36 : 49$
(D)	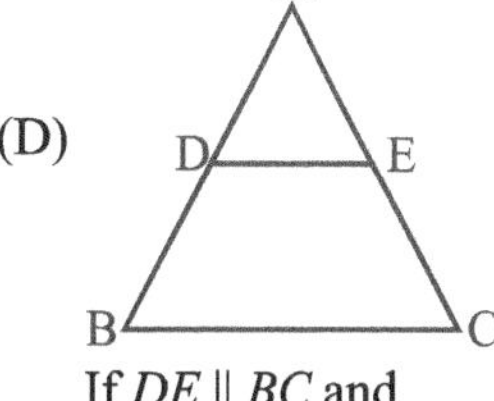 If $DE \parallel BC$ and $\dfrac{AD}{DB} = \dfrac{6}{7}$ then, $\dfrac{AE^2}{EC^2} = ?$	(s)	$6 : 7$

≫ Fill in the Blanks

DIRECTIONS : *Complete the following statements with an appropriate word / term to be filled in the blank space(s).*

53. All circles are ....

54. All squares are ....

55. All .... triangles are similar.

56. Two polygons of the same number of sides are similar, if their corresponding angles are .... and their corresponding sides are in the same ....

57. If a line is drawn parallel to one side of a triangle to intersect the other two sides in distinct points, then the other two sides are divided in the .... ratio.

58. If a line divides any two sides of a triangle in the same ratio, then the line is parallel to the .... side.

59. All congruent figures are similar but the similar figures need .... be congruent.

60. Two polygons of the same number of sides are similar, if all the corresponding angles are ....

61. The diagonals of a quadrilateral $ABCD$ intersect each other at the point O such that $\dfrac{AO}{BO} = \dfrac{CO}{DO}$. $ABCD$ is a ....

62. A line drawn through the mid-point of one side of a triangle parallel to another side bisects the .... side.

63. Line joining the mid-points of any two sides of a triangle is .... to the third side.

64. In fig., MN ∥ BC and AM : MB = 1 : 2, then

$$\dfrac{\text{ar}(\triangle\text{AMN})}{\text{ar}(\triangle\text{ABC})} = \dots\dots\dots$$

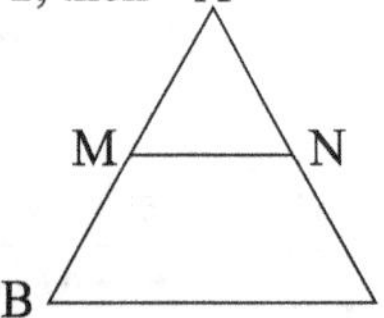

65. In $\triangle$ABC, AB = $6\sqrt{3}$ m, AC = 12 cm and BC = 6 cm, then ∠B = ...

OR

Two triangles are similar if their corresponding sides are ....

≫ True / False

DIRECTIONS : *Read the following statements and write your answer as true or false.*

66. Two figures having the same shape but not necessarily the same size are called similar figures.

67. All the congruent figures are similar but the converse is not true.

68. If in two triangles, corresponding angles are equal, then their corresponding sides are in the same ratio and hence the two triangles are similar.

69. If in two triangles, two angles of one triangle are respectively equal to the two angles of the other triangle, then the two triangles are similar.

70. If in two triangles, corresponding sides are in the same ratio, then their corresponding angles are equal and hence the triangles are similar.

71. If one angle of a triangle is equal to one angle of another triangle and the sides including these angles are in the same ratio (proportional), then the triangles are similar.

72. The ratio of the areas of two similar triangles is equal to the square of the ratio of their corresponding sides.

73. In a right triangle, the square of the hypotenuse is equal to the sum of the squares of the other two sides.

74. If, in a triangle, square of one side is equal to the sum of the squares of the other two sides, then the angle opposite the first side is a right angle.

75. Diagonals AC and BD of a trapezium $ABCD$ with $AB \parallel DC$ intersect each other at the point O, $\dfrac{OA}{OC} = \dfrac{OB}{OD}$.

ANSWER KEY & SOLUTIONS

1. **(a)** It is given that AD is the bisector of $\angle A$.

$$\frac{AB}{AC} = \frac{BD}{DC} \Rightarrow AC = \frac{6 \times 3}{4} = 4.5 \text{ cm}$$

2. **(c)**

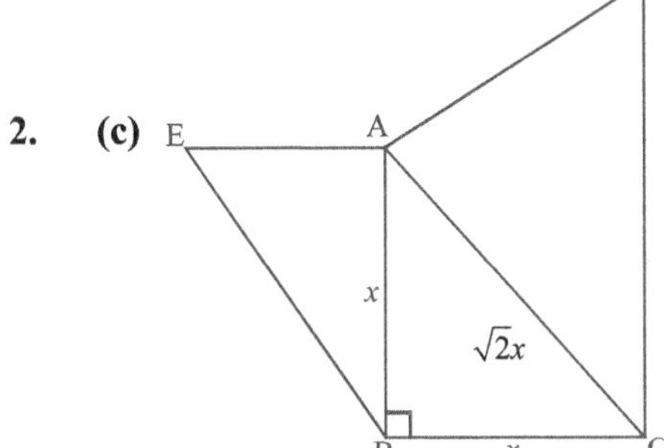

Let $AB = BC = x$.

Since, $\triangle ABC$ is right-angled with $\angle B = 90°$

$\therefore \quad AC^2 = AB^2 + BC^2 = x^2 + x^2 = 2x^2$

$\Rightarrow \quad AC = \sqrt{2}x$

Since, $\triangle ABE \sim \triangle ACD$

$\therefore \quad \dfrac{\text{Area}(\triangle ABE)}{\text{Area}(\triangle ACD)} = \dfrac{AB^2}{AC^2} = \dfrac{x^2}{2x^2} = \dfrac{1}{2}.$

Thus, $\dfrac{\text{Area}(\triangle ABE)}{\text{Area}(\triangle ACD)} = \dfrac{1}{2}$

Thus, required ratio is $1 : 2$.

3. **(c)** Here, the two triangles are similar.

Ratio of areas of two similar triangles is equal to the ratio of squares of their corresponding altitudes.

So, $\dfrac{h_1^2}{h_2^2} = \dfrac{25}{36}$

$\therefore \quad \dfrac{h_1}{h_2} = \dfrac{5}{6}$

4. **(a)** In $\triangle ABC$, $\angle A = 180° - (70° + 50°) = 60°$.

$\dfrac{BD}{DC} = \dfrac{AB}{AC}$. It means AD is the bisector of $\angle A$.

$\therefore \quad \angle BAD = \dfrac{1}{2} \times 60° = 30°$

5. **(a)** $\dfrac{\text{ar}(\triangle ABC)}{\text{ar}(\triangle DEF)} = \dfrac{BC^2}{EF^2}$

$\Rightarrow \text{ar}(\triangle ABC) = \left(\dfrac{2.1}{2.8}\right)^2 \times \text{ar}(\triangle DEF) = 9\text{cm}^2$

6. **(a)** From the right angled $\triangle ACB$,

$AB^2 = AC^2 + CB^2$

$= (20)^2 + (15)^2 = 400 + 225 = 625$

$\therefore \quad AB = \sqrt{625} = 25\text{cm}$

Again, from right angled $\triangle ABD$

$AB^2 = AD^2 + BD^2$

$\Rightarrow 625 = (24)^2 + (BD)^2$

$\Rightarrow \quad (BD)^2 = 625 - 576 = 49$

$\Rightarrow \quad BD = 7 \text{ cm}$

7. **(a)** In $\triangle AFD$ & $\triangle FEB$,

$\angle 1 = \angle 2$ (V.O.A)

$\angle 3 = \angle 4$ (Alternate angle)

$\therefore \triangle FBE \sim \triangle FDA$

So, $\dfrac{EF}{FA} = \dfrac{FB}{DF}$

8. **(a)** In $\triangle ABC$, $AB = AC$

Draw $AL \perp BC$,

then L is the mid-point of BC

Using Pythagoras theorem in $\triangle ABL$, we get

$AL = 8\text{cm}$

Also, $\triangle BPS \cong \triangle CQR$,

$\therefore BS = RC$

$SL = LR = x \text{ cm}$

$\therefore BS = CR = 6 - x$

In $\triangle ABL$, $PS \parallel AL$

$\therefore \quad \dfrac{PS}{AL} = \dfrac{BS}{BL} \Rightarrow \dfrac{y}{8} = \dfrac{6-x}{6}$

or $x = 6 - \dfrac{3}{4}y$

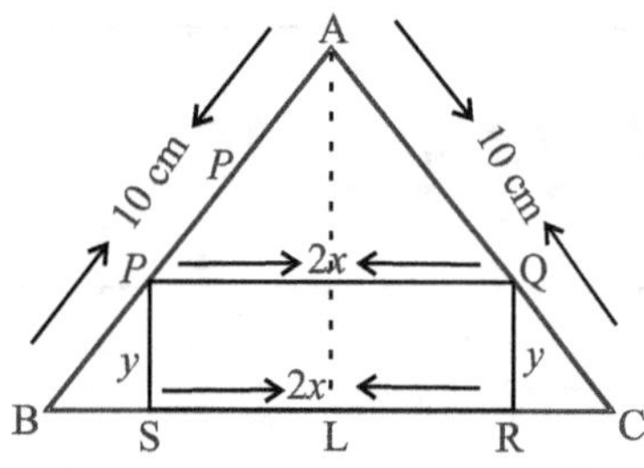

9. **(d)** All equilateral triangles are similar

$\therefore \quad \Delta ABC \sim \Delta EBD$

$\Rightarrow \quad \dfrac{\text{Area of } \Delta ABC}{\text{Area of } \Delta BDE} = \dfrac{BC^2}{BD^2}$

D is mid-point of BC

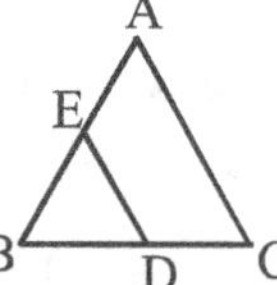

$\therefore BC = 2BD = \dfrac{(2BD)^2}{BD^2} = \dfrac{4}{1}$

$\Rightarrow \quad$ Area (ΔABC) : Area $(\Delta BDE) = 4 : 1$

10. **(a)** Given, $AB = 2DE$ and $\Delta ABC \sim \Delta DEF$

Hence, $\dfrac{\text{area}(\Delta ABC)}{\text{area}(\Delta DEF)} = \dfrac{AB^2}{DE^2}$

or $\dfrac{56}{\text{area}(\Delta DEF)} = \dfrac{4DE^2}{DE^2} = 4 \quad [\because AB = 2DE]$

area $(\Delta DEF) = \dfrac{56}{4} = 14\,\text{sq.cm.}$

11. **(b)**

12. **(c)** As PQ is parallel to $BC \Rightarrow \Delta ABC \sim \Delta APQ$

$\Rightarrow \quad \dfrac{\text{Area of } \Delta ABC}{\text{Area of } \Delta APQ} = \dfrac{2}{1}$

Ratio of sides $= \dfrac{AB}{AP} = \dfrac{\sqrt{2}}{1} \quad \therefore \text{AP} : \text{AB} = 1 : \sqrt{2}$

13. **(a)** Since, $\Delta ABC \sim \Delta PQR$

$\therefore \dfrac{\text{ar}(\Delta PQR)}{\text{ar}(\Delta ABC)} = \dfrac{PR^2}{AC^2} = \dfrac{QR^2}{BC^2} = \dfrac{9}{1} \left[\because \dfrac{QR}{BC} = \dfrac{3}{1} \right] = 9$

14. **(b)** Hypotenuse = 270m

$\Rightarrow$ Hypotenuse^2 = Side^2 + Side^2 = 2 Side^2

$\Rightarrow$ Side^2 = $(270)^2/2$ = 72900/2 = 36450

or Side = 190.91m

$\Rightarrow$ Required area = 1/2 × 190.91 × 190.91

$= 36446.6/2 = 18225 \text{ m}^2$ (approx).

15. **(d)** $\because \dfrac{\text{Perimeter of } \Delta ABC}{\text{Perimeter of } \Delta PQR} = \dfrac{AB}{PQ} = \dfrac{BC}{QR} = \dfrac{AC}{PR}$

16. **(c)** Since, $DE \parallel BC \quad \therefore \Delta ADE \sim \Delta ABC$

$\therefore \dfrac{AD}{DB} = \dfrac{AE}{EC} \Rightarrow \dfrac{1.5}{3} = \dfrac{1}{EC} \Rightarrow EC = 2 \text{ cm}$

17. **(b)** In ΔKPN and ΔKLM, we have

$\angle KNP = \angle KML = 46°$

$\angle K = \angle K \qquad\qquad$ (Common)

$\therefore \quad \Delta KNP \sim \Delta KLM$ (By $A\,A$ criterion of similarity)

$\Rightarrow \dfrac{KN}{KM} = \dfrac{NP}{ML} \Rightarrow \dfrac{c}{b+c} = \dfrac{x}{a}$

18. **(a)** Statement given in option (a) is false.

19. **(b)** Since, $\Delta ABC \sim \Delta APQ$

$\therefore \dfrac{\text{ar}(\Delta ABC)}{\text{ar}(\Delta APQ)} = \dfrac{BC^2}{PQ^2}$

$\Rightarrow \dfrac{\text{ar}(\Delta ABC)}{4 \cdot \text{ar}(\Delta ABC)} = \dfrac{BC^2}{PQ^2} \Rightarrow \left(\dfrac{BC}{PQ} \right)^2 = \dfrac{1}{4}$

$\Rightarrow \dfrac{BC}{PQ} = \dfrac{1}{2}$

20. **(d)** Since, $\Delta ABC \sim \Delta PQR$

$\therefore \dfrac{\text{ar}(\Delta ABC)}{\text{ar}(\Delta PQR)} = \dfrac{BC^2}{QR^2} \Rightarrow \dfrac{9}{16} = \dfrac{(4.5)^2}{QR^2}$

$\Rightarrow QR^2 = \dfrac{16 \times (4.5)^2}{9} \Rightarrow QR = 6 \text{ cm}$

21. **(a)** Let side of a square = x cm

$\therefore$ By Pythagoras theorem, $x^2 + x^2 = (16)^2 = 256$

$\Rightarrow 2x^2 = 256 \Rightarrow x^2 = 128 \Rightarrow x = 8\sqrt{2}$ cm.

22. **(b)** Given an equilateral triangle ABC in which

$AB = BC = CA = 2p$

and $AD \perp BC$.

$\therefore \quad$ In ΔADB,

$AB^2 = AD^2 + BD^2$

(By Pythagoras theorem)

$\Rightarrow (2p)^2 = AD^2 + p^2 \Rightarrow AD^2 = \sqrt{3}\, p.$

23. **(c)** Given, area of two similar triangles,

$A_1 = 81 \text{cm}^2 , A_2 = 49 \text{ cm}^2$

Ratio of corresponding medians $= \sqrt{\dfrac{A_1}{A_2}} = \sqrt{\dfrac{81}{49}} = \dfrac{9}{7}$

24. (c) Let BD = x cm

Since AC = BC, therefore $\triangle ABC$ is an isoscele triangle.

$\Rightarrow \quad \angle B = \angle CAB = 72°$

Since AD bisects $\angle A$

$\therefore \quad \angle DAB = 36°$ so, In $\triangle ADB$, $\angle ADB = 72°$

$\Rightarrow \quad \triangle ADB$ is an isoscele triangle

$\therefore \quad AB = AD = 1cm$

$\Rightarrow \quad AB = 1$ cm

Similarly, $\triangle ADC$ is also an isoscele triangle.

$\therefore \quad AD = CD \Rightarrow AD = 1$ cm

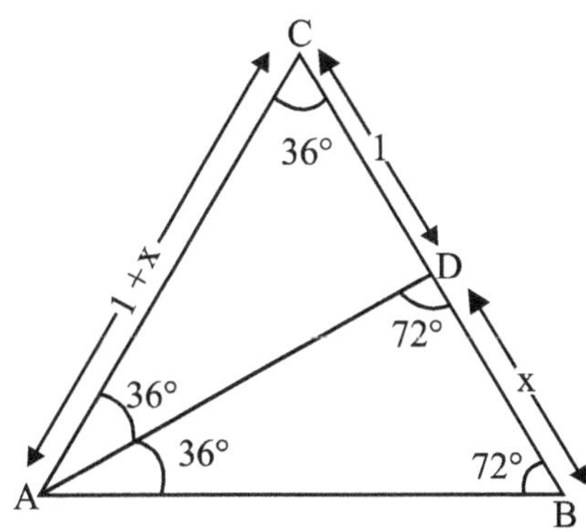

Now $\dfrac{AC}{AB} = \dfrac{CD}{BD}$

$\Rightarrow \quad \dfrac{1+x}{1} = \dfrac{1}{x} \quad \Rightarrow \quad x + x^2 - 1 = 0$

$\Rightarrow \quad x = \dfrac{-1 \pm \sqrt{(1)^2 - 4(1)(-1)}}{2} = \dfrac{-1 \pm \sqrt{5}}{2}$

$BD = \dfrac{\sqrt{5} - 1}{2}$

25. (c) Here, *ABC* is a triangle & *P* be interior point of a $\triangle ABC$, *Q* and *R* be the reflections of *P* in *AB* and *AC*, respectively.

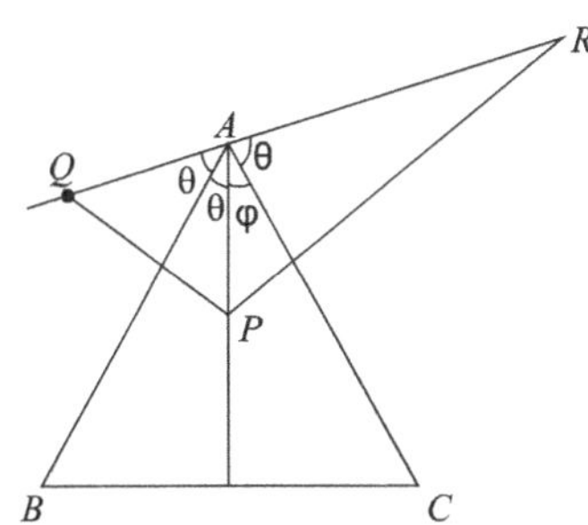

As *QAR* are collinear

$\therefore \quad \angle QAR = 180°$

Q is reflection of *P* on *AB*

$\therefore \quad \angle QAB = \angle BAP$

R is reflection of *P* on *AC*

$\therefore \quad \angle RAC = \angle CAP$

$\angle QAR = 180°$

$\therefore \quad 2\angle BAP + 2\angle CAP = 180°$

$\angle BAP + \angle CAP = 90° \quad \Rightarrow \quad \angle BAC = 90°$

26. (a) $\triangle ABC \sim \triangle ANM$

$\therefore \quad \dfrac{\text{Area of } \triangle ABC}{\text{Area of } \triangle ANM} = \dfrac{AC^2}{AM^2} \qquad \text{...(i)}$

$\triangle ABC \sim \triangle MPC$

$\therefore \quad \dfrac{\text{Area of } \triangle ABC}{\text{Area of } \triangle MPC} = \dfrac{AC^2}{MC^2} \qquad \text{...(ii)}$

From Eqs. (i) and (ii,) we get

$\dfrac{\text{Area of } \triangle ANM}{\text{Area of } \triangle MPC} = \dfrac{AM^2}{MC^2}$

$\dfrac{\text{Area of } \triangle ANM + \text{Area of } \triangle MPC}{\text{Area of } \triangle MPC} = \dfrac{AM^2 + MC^2}{MC^2}$

Now, Area of $\triangle ANM$ + Area of $\triangle MPC$

= Area of $\triangle ABC$ – Area of $BNMP$

Using Area of $BNMP = \dfrac{5}{18}$ of area of $\triangle ABC$

$\therefore \quad \dfrac{13}{18} \dfrac{(\text{Area of } \triangle ABC)}{(\text{Area of } \triangle MPC)} = \dfrac{AM^2 + MC^2}{MC^2} \qquad \text{...(iii)}$

From Eq. (iii), $\dfrac{13}{18}\left(\dfrac{AC^2}{MC^2}\right) = \dfrac{AM^2 + MC^2}{MC^2}$

$\Rightarrow \quad 13\,(AM + MC)^2 = 18\,(AM^2 + MC^2)$

$\Rightarrow \quad \dfrac{AM}{MC} = 5, \dfrac{1}{5}$. Hence, option (a) is correct.

27. (d)

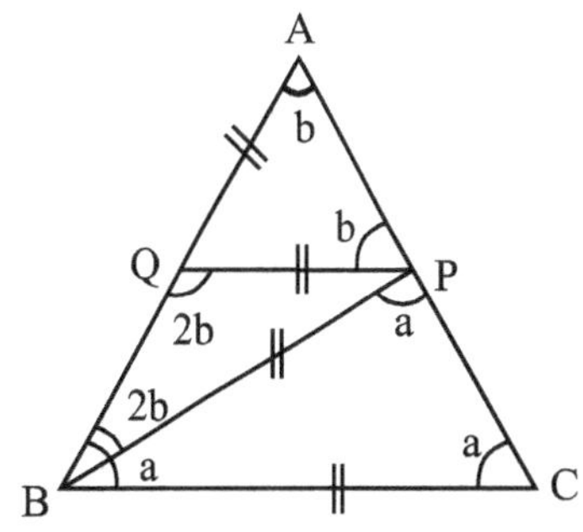

In $\triangle ABC$

$AB = AC$

$\Rightarrow \quad \angle C = \angle B \Rightarrow \angle B = \angle C = a$

By angle sum properly in ΔABC,

$b + a + a = 180$

$\Rightarrow b + 2a = 180°$ ...(i)

In ΔQPB

$\Rightarrow \angle QPB = 180 - 4b$

Since 'APC' is a straight line

$\Rightarrow 180 - 4b + a + b = 180$

$\Rightarrow a = 3b$ ...(ii)

From equations (i) & (ii)

$b + 2(3b) = 180 \Rightarrow b = \dfrac{180}{7}$

$\angle AQP = 180° - 2\left(\dfrac{180}{7}\right) = \dfrac{5}{7}\pi$

28. (c) Let ΔPQR

Given, $QR^2 + PR^2 = 5PQ^2$

Median PM and QN intersect at G.

$\Rightarrow PN = NR = \dfrac{1}{2}PR$ &

$QM = MR = \dfrac{1}{2}QR$

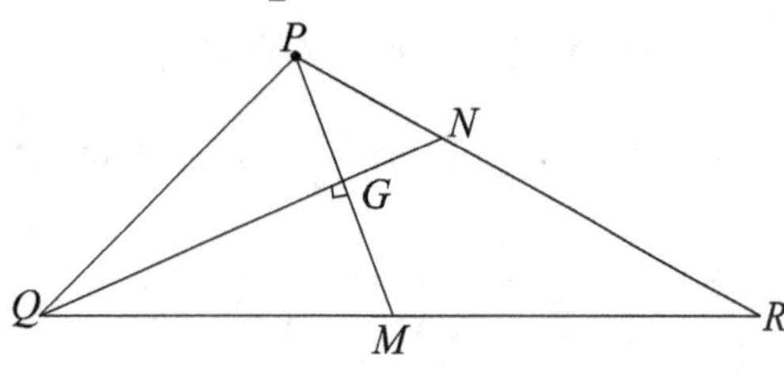

$QG = \dfrac{2}{3}QN, GM = \dfrac{1}{3}PM$

$\Rightarrow QG^2 + GM^2 = \left(\dfrac{2}{3}QN\right)^2 + \left(\dfrac{1}{3}PM\right)^2$

$= \dfrac{4}{9}QN^2 + \dfrac{1}{9}PM^2$

$= \dfrac{4}{9}\left(\dfrac{2PQ^2 + 2QR^2 - PR^2}{4}\right)$

$+ \dfrac{1}{9}\left(\dfrac{2PQ^2 + 2PR^2 - QR^2}{4}\right)$

$= \dfrac{1}{9}\left[\dfrac{\begin{array}{c}8PQ^2 + 8QR^2 - 4PR^2 \\ +2PQ^2 + 2PR^2 - QR^2\end{array}}{4}\right]$

$= \dfrac{1}{9}\left[\dfrac{10PQ^2 + 7QR^2 - 2PR^2}{4}\right]$

$= \dfrac{1}{9}\left[\dfrac{2QR^2 + 7QR^2}{4}\right] = \dfrac{1}{4}QR^2 = QM^2$

$QG^2 + GM^2 = QM^2 \qquad \therefore \angle QGM = 90°$

29. (c) $\because \angle BAC = \angle ADC$ (given)

$\angle C = \angle C$ (common)

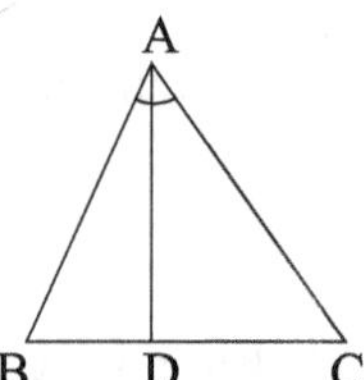

$\therefore \Delta ABC \sim \Delta DAC$ (by AA similarity criterion)

$\Rightarrow \dfrac{BC}{AC} = \dfrac{AC}{DC} \Rightarrow BC \times DC = AC^2$

$\Rightarrow BC \times DC = (21)^2$ = area of rectangle with sides BC & DC

Now, Area of equilateral triangle = area of rectangle

$\Rightarrow \dfrac{\sqrt{3}}{4}(\text{side})^2 = (21)^2 \Rightarrow \text{Side} = 14 \times 3^{3/4}$

30. (a) Here, BAC is a right angle triangle

$AB = 15$ & $BC = 25$

$\therefore AC = \sqrt{BC^2 - AB^2} = 20$

Area of $\Delta ABC = \dfrac{1}{2}BC.AD$

$= \dfrac{1}{2}AB.AC$

$\Rightarrow BC.AD = AB.AC$

$\Rightarrow 25(AD) = 15(20) \qquad \Rightarrow AD = 12$

$\because AEDF$ is rectangle then, $AD = EF = 12$

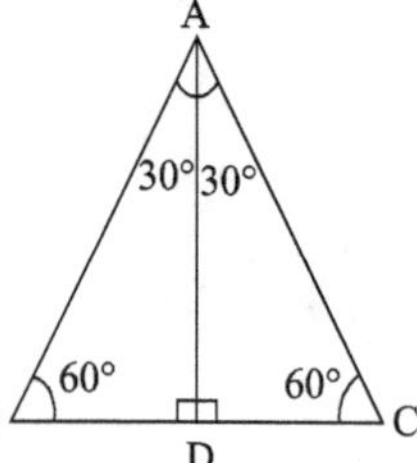

31. (a) We know that height of an equilateral triangle $\dfrac{\sqrt{3}}{2}a$, where a is the side of equilateral triangle

$\therefore AD^2 = \dfrac{3}{4}a^2 = \dfrac{3}{4}BC^2$

32. (d)   **33. (a)**   **34. (a)**

35. (a) (By definition of similar triangles).

36. (d) All the statements given in option (a, b, c) are correct.

Sol. (37-41)

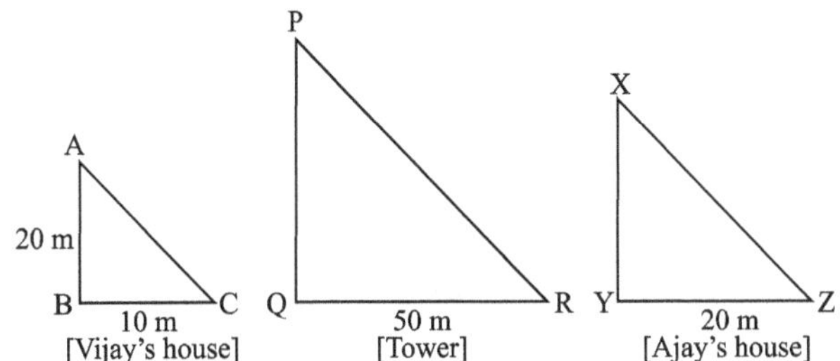

37. (c) $\because \triangle ABC \sim \triangle PQR$

$\therefore \dfrac{AB}{PQ} = \dfrac{BC}{QR} \Rightarrow \dfrac{20}{PQ} = \dfrac{10}{50}$

$\Rightarrow PQ = 100$

$\therefore$ Height of the tower $= 100$ m

38. (d) Let $BC = 12$ m and $PQ = 100$ m

$\dfrac{AB}{PQ} = \dfrac{BC}{QR} \Rightarrow \dfrac{20}{100} = \dfrac{12}{QR}$

$\Rightarrow QR = 60$

39. (b) $\because \triangle ABC \sim \triangle XYZ$

$\therefore \dfrac{AB}{XY} = \dfrac{BC}{YZ} \Rightarrow \dfrac{20}{XY} = \dfrac{10}{20}$

$\Rightarrow XY = 40$

40. (a) Let $QR = 40$ m, $PQ = 100$ m and $XY = 40$ m

$\therefore \dfrac{PQ}{XY} = \dfrac{QR}{YZ} \Rightarrow \dfrac{100}{40} = \dfrac{40}{YZ}$

$\Rightarrow YZ = 16$ m.

41. (d) Let $QR = 40$m, $PQ = 100$m and $AB = 20$ m

$\because \dfrac{AB}{PQ} = \dfrac{BC}{QR} \Rightarrow \dfrac{20}{100} = \dfrac{BC}{40}$

$\Rightarrow BC = 8$ m.

42. (c) Pythagoras theorem

43. (a) $AC^2 = 30^2 + 40^2 = 2500 \Rightarrow AC = 50$m

44. (d) $(21, 20, 28) \because 28^2 \neq (21)^2 + (20)^2$

45. (b) $AB = 50 - 12 = 38$m

46. (c) 82m

47. (a) Reason is true. [This is Thale's Theorem]

For Assertion

Since $DE \parallel BC$ $\therefore$ by Thale's Theorem

$\dfrac{AD}{DB} = \dfrac{AE}{EC} \Rightarrow \dfrac{DB}{AD} = \dfrac{EC}{AE}$

$\Rightarrow 1 + \dfrac{DB}{AD} = 1 + \dfrac{EC}{AE}$

$\Rightarrow \dfrac{AD + DB}{AD} = \dfrac{AE + EC}{AE}$

$\Rightarrow \dfrac{AB}{AD} = \dfrac{AC}{AE}$

$\therefore$ Assertion is true.

Since reason gives Assertion.

48. (d) In right angled $\triangle ABC$,

$AB^2 = AC^2 + BC^2$ (By Pythagorus Theorem)

$= AC^2 + AC^2$ $[\because BC = AC]$

$= 2AC^2$

$\therefore AB^2 = 2AC^2$

$\therefore$ Assertion is false.

Again since

$AB^2 = 2AC^2 = AC^2 + AC^2$

$= AC^2 + BC^2$ $(\because AC = BC$ given$)$

$\therefore \angle C = 90°$ (By converse of Pythagoras Theorem)

$\therefore$ Reason is true.

49. (b) Reason is true [standard result]

For Assertion, since $\triangle ABC \sim \triangle DEF$

$\therefore \dfrac{\text{area}(\triangle ABC)}{\text{area}(\triangle DEF)} = \dfrac{BC^2}{EF^2} = \dfrac{(4)^2}{(5)^2} = \dfrac{16}{25}$

($\because$ ratio of areas of two similar $\triangle s$ is equal to the ratio of the squares of corresponding sides)

$\therefore \dfrac{64}{\text{area}(\triangle DEF)} = \dfrac{16}{25} \Rightarrow \text{area}(\triangle DEF) = \dfrac{64 \times 25}{16}$

$= 4 \times 25 = 100$ cm^2

$\therefore$ Assertion is true. But reason is not the correct explanation for assertion.

50. (A) $\rightarrow$ q; (B) $\rightarrow$ p; (C) $\rightarrow$ s; (D) $\rightarrow$ r

51. (A) $\rightarrow$ p; (B) $\rightarrow$ q; (C) $\rightarrow$ r; (D) $\rightarrow$ s

52. (A) $\rightarrow$ q; (B) $\rightarrow$ p; (C) $\rightarrow$ s; (D) $\rightarrow$ r

(A) $AB^2 = AC^2 + BC^2$

Since, $\triangle ABC$ is an isosceles right angled triangle.

$\therefore AC = BC$

Now, $AB^2 = AC^2 + AC^2 = 2AC^2$

(B) $\dfrac{\text{area}(\Delta ABC)}{\text{area}(\Delta DEF)} = \dfrac{(AB)^2}{(DE)^2} = \dfrac{(1.2)^2}{(1.4)^2} = \dfrac{1.44}{1.96}$

$\qquad = \dfrac{36}{49} = \dfrac{(36 \times 2)}{(49 \times 2)} = \dfrac{72}{98}$

(C) $\dfrac{\text{area}(\Delta APQ)}{\text{area}(\Delta ABC)} = \dfrac{(BC)^2}{(PQ)^2} = \dfrac{36}{49} = \dfrac{BC}{PQ} = \dfrac{6}{7}$

(D) $\because DE \parallel BC \quad \therefore \dfrac{AD}{DB} = \dfrac{AE}{EC} = \dfrac{6}{7}$

53. similar   **54.** similar   **55.** equilateral

56. equal , ratio   **57.** same   **58.** third   **59.** not

60. equal   **61.** trapezium   **62.** third

63. parallel

64. $\left[\dfrac{1}{9}\right]$

$\qquad \dfrac{AM}{AB} = \dfrac{AM}{AM + BM} = \dfrac{1}{1+2} = \dfrac{1}{3}$

$\qquad \therefore \dfrac{\text{ar}(\Delta AMN)}{\text{ar}(\Delta ABC)} = \left(\dfrac{AM}{AB}\right)^2 = \left(\dfrac{1}{3}\right)^2 = \dfrac{1}{9}$

65. $[90°]$

$\qquad \because \quad AB^2 + BC^2 = 108 + 36 = 144 = AC^2$

So, AC is hypotenuse and $\angle B = 90°$.

OR

[Proportional]

66. True   **67.** True   **68.** True   **69.** True

70. True   **71.** True   **72.** True   **73.** True

74. True   **75.** True

6 — Introduction to Trigonometry

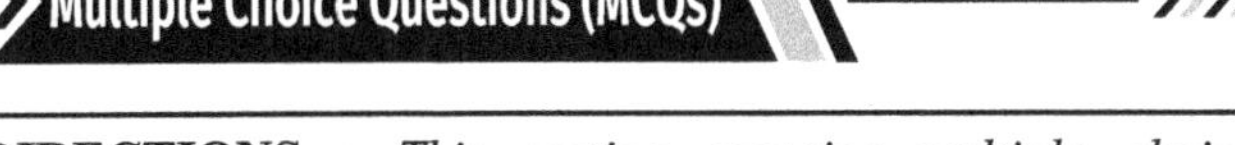

DIRECTIONS : *This section contains multiple choice questions. Each question has 4 choices (a), (b), (c) and (d) out of which ONLY ONE is correct.*

1. If $(\sec^2\theta)(1 + \sin\theta)(1 - \sin\theta) = k$, then find the value of k.
   - (a) $\sin\theta$
   - (b) $\sec\theta$
   - (c) 1
   - (d) $\cot\theta$

2. If $\cot\theta = \left(\dfrac{15}{8}\right)$, then evaluate $\dfrac{(2 + 2\sin\theta)(1 - \sin\theta)}{(1 + \cos\theta)(2 - 2\cos\theta)}$
   - (a) 1
   - (b) $\dfrac{225}{64}$
   - (c) $\dfrac{156}{7}$
   - (d) -1

3. If $x = a\,(\operatorname{cosec}\theta + \cot\theta)$ and $y = \dfrac{b(1 - \cos\theta)}{\sin\theta}$, then $xy =$
   - (a) $\dfrac{a^2 + b^2}{a^2 - b^2}$
   - (b) $a^2 - b^2$
   - (c) ab
   - (d) $\dfrac{a}{b}$

4. If $p\sin\theta + q\cos\theta = a$ and $p\cos\theta - q\sin\theta = b$, then $\dfrac{p + a}{q + b} + \dfrac{q - b}{p - a} =$
   - (a) 1
   - (b) $a^2 + b^2$
   - (c) 0
   - (d) 2

5. If $x = r\sin A\cos C$, $y = r\sin A\sin C$, $z = r\cos A$, then
   - (a) $r^2 = x^2 + y^2 + z^2$
   - (b) $r^2 = 2xy$
   - (c) $r^2 = x + y + z$
   - (d) $r^2 = y^2 + z^2 + 2xy$

6. If $\tan^2\theta = 1 - a^2$, then the value of $\sec\theta + \tan^3\theta\operatorname{cosec}\theta$ is
   - (a) $(2 - a^2)$
   - (b) $(2 - a^2)^{1/2}$
   - (c) $(2 - a^2)^{2/3}$
   - (d) $(2 - a^2)^{3/2}$

7. If $x = a\cos^2\theta + b\sin^2\theta$, then $(x - a)(b - x)$ is equal to
   - (a) $(a - b)\sin\theta\cos\theta$
   - (b) $(a - b)^2\sin^2\theta\cos^2\theta$
   - (c) $(a - b)^2\sin\theta\cos\theta$
   - (d) $(a - b)\sin^2\theta\cos^2\theta$

8. If $\cos A = \dfrac{3}{5}$, find the value of $9\cot^2 A - 1$.
   - (a) 1
   - (b) $\dfrac{16}{65}$
   - (c) $\dfrac{65}{16}$
   - (d) 0

9. $\cos 1°\cdot\cos 2°\cdot\cos 3° \ldots\ldots \cos 179°$ is equal to
   - (a) -1
   - (b) 0
   - (c) 1
   - (d) $1/\sqrt{2}$

10. $\sin^2\theta + \operatorname{cosec}^2\theta$ is always
    - (a) greater than 1
    - (b) less than 1
    - (c) greater than or equal to 2
    - (d) equal to 2

11. If $x = p\sec\theta$ and $y = q\tan\theta$, then
    - (a) $x^2 - y^2 = p^2 q^2$
    - (b) $x^2 q^2 - y^2 p^2 = pq$
    - (c) $x^2 q^2 - y^2 p^2 = \dfrac{1}{p^2 q^2}$
    - (d) $x^2 q^2 - y^2 p^2 = p^2 q^2$

12. If $b\tan\theta = a$, the value of $\dfrac{a\sin\theta - b\cos\theta}{a\sin\theta + b\cos\theta}$ is
    - (a) $\dfrac{a - b}{a^2 + b^2}$
    - (b) $\dfrac{a + b}{a^2 + b^2}$
    - (c) $\dfrac{a^2 + b^2}{a^2 - b^2}$
    - (d) $\dfrac{a^2 - b^2}{a^2 + b^2}$

13. $(\cos^4 A - \sin^4 A)$ is equal to
    - (a) $1 - 2\cos^2 A$
    - (b) $2\sin^2 A - 1$
    - (c) $\sin^2 A - \cos^2 A$
    - (d) $2\cos^2 A - 1$

14. If $\tan\theta = \dfrac{a\sin\phi}{1-a\cos\phi}$ and $\tan\phi = \dfrac{b\sin\theta}{1-b\cos\theta}$, then $\dfrac{a}{b} =$

(a) $\dfrac{\sin\theta}{1-\cos\theta}$ (b) $\dfrac{\sin\theta}{1-\cos\phi}$

(c) $\dfrac{\sin\phi}{\sin\theta}$ (d) $\dfrac{\sin\theta}{\sin\phi}$

15. If $\operatorname{cosec} x - \cot x = \dfrac{1}{3}$, where $x \neq 0$, then the value of $\cos^2 x - \sin^2 x$ is

(a) $\dfrac{16}{25}$ (b) $\dfrac{9}{25}$

(c) $\dfrac{8}{25}$ (d) $\dfrac{7}{25}$

16. If $\operatorname{cosec} x + \sin x = a$ and $\sec x + \cos x = b$, then

(a) $(a^2 b)^{\frac{2}{3}} + (ab^2)^{\frac{2}{3}} = 1$

(b) $(ab^2)^{\frac{2}{3}} + (a^2 b^2)^{\frac{2}{3}} = 1$

(c) $a^2 + b^2 = 1$

(d) $b^2 - a^2 = 1$

17. If $\tan^2\theta = 1 - e^2$, then the value of $\sec\theta + \tan^3\theta\,\operatorname{cosec}\theta$ is equal to

(a) $(1 - e^2)^{1/2}$ (b) $(2 - e^2)^{1/2}$

(c) $(2 - e^2)^{3/2}$ (d) $(1 - e^2)^{3/2}$

18. If $\sin\theta + \sin^3\theta = \cos^2\theta$, then the value of $\cos^6\theta - 4\cos^4\theta + 8\cos^2\theta$ is

(a) 1   (b) 4
(c) 2   (d) 0

19. If $\operatorname{cosec} A + \cot A = \dfrac{11}{2}$, then $\tan A$

(a) $\dfrac{21}{22}$ (b) $\dfrac{15}{16}$

(c) $\dfrac{44}{117}$ (d) $\dfrac{11}{117}$

20. $\dfrac{2\tan 30^\circ}{1 + \tan^2 30^\circ}$ is equal to

(a) $\sin 30^\circ$ (b) $\cos 60^\circ$

(c) $\dfrac{1}{2}$ (d) $\dfrac{\sqrt{3}}{2}$

21. $\dfrac{\sin\theta - 2\sin^3\theta}{2\cos^3\theta - \cos\theta}$ is equal to

(a) $\sec\theta$ (b) $\tan\theta$

(c) $\sqrt{\sec\theta - 1}$ (d) $\cot\theta$

22. If $\dfrac{\cos\theta}{1-\sin\theta} + \dfrac{\cos\theta}{1+\sin\theta} = 4$, then

(a) $\cos\theta = \dfrac{\sqrt{3}}{2}$ (b) $\sin\theta = \dfrac{1}{2}$

(c) $\theta = 60^\circ$ (d) $\tan\theta = \dfrac{1}{\sqrt{3}}$

23. $\dfrac{\tan\theta - \cot\theta}{\sin\theta\cos\theta}$ is equal to

(a) $\sec^2\theta + \operatorname{cosec}^2\theta$ (b) $\cot^2\theta - \tan^2\theta$
(c) $\cos^2\theta - \sin^2\theta$ (d) $\tan^2\theta - \cot^2\theta$

24. $\dfrac{2\tan 30^\circ}{1 + \tan^2 30^\circ} =$

(a) $\sin 60^\circ$ (b) $\cos 60^\circ$
(c) $\tan 60^\circ$ (d) $\sin 30^\circ$

25. $\dfrac{1 - \tan^2 45^\circ}{1 + \tan^2 45^\circ} =$

(a) $\tan 90^\circ$ (b) 1
(c) $\sin 45^\circ$ (d) 0

26. $\sin 2A = 2\sin A$ is true when $A =$
(a) 0° (b) 30°
(c) 45° (d) 60°

27. $\dfrac{2\tan 30^\circ}{1 - \tan^2 30^\circ} =$

(a) $\cos 60^\circ$ (b) $\sin 60^\circ$
(c) $\tan 60^\circ$ (d) $\sin 30^\circ$

28. $9\sec^2 A - 9\tan^2 A =$
(a) 1   (b) 9
(c) 8   (d) 0

29. $(1 + \tan\theta + \sec\theta)(1 + \cot\theta - \operatorname{cosec}\theta) =$
(a) 0   (b) 1
(c) 2   (d) -1

30. $(\sec A + \tan A)(1 - \sin A) =$
(a) $\sec A$ (b) $\sin A$
(c) $\operatorname{cosec} A$ (d) $\cos A$

31. $\dfrac{1 + \tan^2 A}{1 + \cot^2 A} = L$

(a) $\sec^2 A$ (b) -1
(c) $\cot^2 A$ (d) $\tan^2 A$

32. The value of $(\sin 30^\circ + \cos 30^\circ) - (\sin 60^\circ + \cos 60^\circ)$ is
(a) -1 (b) 0
(c) 1   (d) 2

33. The value of $\dfrac{\tan 30°}{\cot 60°}$ is

(a) $\dfrac{1}{\sqrt{2}}$ (b) $\dfrac{1}{\sqrt{3}}$

(c) $\sqrt{3}$ (d) 1

34. The value of $(\sin 45° + \cos 45°)$ is

(a) $\dfrac{1}{\sqrt{2}}$ (b) $\sqrt{2}$

(c) $\dfrac{\sqrt{3}}{2}$ (d) 1

35. Given that $\sin \theta = \dfrac{a}{b}$, then $\cos \theta$ is equal to

(a) $\dfrac{b}{\sqrt{b^2 - a^2}}$ (b) $\dfrac{b}{a}$

(c) $\dfrac{\sqrt{b^2 - a^2}}{b}$ (d) $\dfrac{a}{\sqrt{b^2 - a^2}}$

36. If $\sin A + \sin^2 A = 1$, then the value of the expression $(\cos^2 A + \cos^4 A)$ is

(a) 1 (b) $\dfrac{1}{2}$

(c) 2 (d) 3

37. If $\sin (A + B) = \dfrac{\sqrt{3}}{2}$ and $\sin 2B = \dfrac{1}{2}$, then

(a) $\tan B = 1$ (b) $B = 30°$

(c) $B = 45°$ (d) $\cos A = \dfrac{1}{2}$

DIRECTIONS : *Study the given Case/Passage and answer the following questions.*

Case/Passage

In $\triangle ABC$, right angled at B

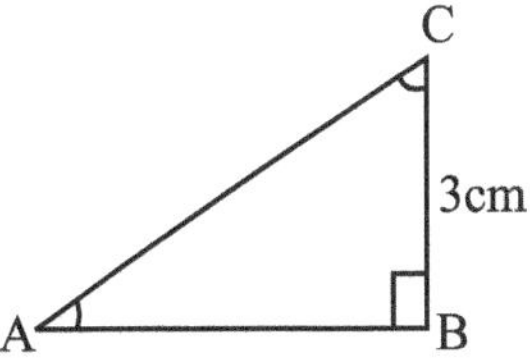

$AB + AC = 9$ cm and $BC = 3$cm.

38. The value of cot C is

[From CBSE Question Bank-2021]

(a) $\dfrac{3}{4}$ (b) $\dfrac{1}{4}$

(c) $\dfrac{5}{4}$ (d) None of these

39. The value of sec C is

(a) $\dfrac{4}{3}$ (b) $\dfrac{5}{3}$

(c) $\dfrac{1}{3}$ (d) None of these

40. $\sin^2 C + \cos^2 C =$

(a) 0 (b) 1

(c) -1 (d) None of these

DIRECTIONS : *Each of these questions contains an Assertion followed by reason. Read them carefully and answer the question on the basis of following options. You have to select the one that best describes the two statements.*

(a) If both **Assertion** and **Reason** are **correct** and Reason is the **correct explanation** of Assertion.

(b) If both **Assertion** and **Reason** are correct, but Reason is **not the correct explanation** of Assertion.

(c) If **Assertion** is **correct** but **Reason** is **incorrect**.

(d) If **Assertion** is **incorrect** but **Reason** is **correct**.

41. **Assertion:** In a right angled triangle, if $\tan \theta = \dfrac{3}{4}$, the greatest side of the triangle is 5 units.

Reason: (greatest side)^2 = (hypotenuse)^2 = (perpendicular)^2 + (base)^2.

42. **Assertion :** In a right angled triangle, if $\cos \theta = \dfrac{1}{2}$ and $\sin \theta = \dfrac{\sqrt{3}}{2}$, then $\tan \theta = \sqrt{3}$

Reason: $\tan \theta = \dfrac{\sin \theta}{\cos \theta}$

DIRECTIONS : *Each question contains statements given in two columns which have to be matched. Statements (A, B, C, D) in column-I have to be matched with statements (p, q, r, s) in column-II.*

43. In $\triangle ABC$, $\angle B = 90°$, $AB = 3$ cm and $BC = 4$ cm, then match the column.

Column-I	**Column-II**
(A) $\sin C$	(p) 3/5
(B) $\cos C$	(q) 4/5
(C) $\tan A$	(r) 5/3
(D) $\sec A$	(s) 4/3

44.

Column-I		Column-II
(A) $\dfrac{\cos A}{1+\sin A}+\dfrac{1+\sin A}{\cos A}$	(p)	$\operatorname{cosec} A + \cot A$
(B) $\dfrac{\cos A-\sin A+1}{\cos A+\sin A-1}$	(q)	$2 \sec A$
(C) $\sqrt{\dfrac{1+\sin A}{1-\sin A}}$	(r)	$\sec A + \tan A$
(D) $\dfrac{\sin^2 A}{1-\cos A}$	(s)	$\dfrac{1+\sec A}{\sec A}$

45. If $\sin A = \dfrac{7}{25}$, then

Column-I		Column-II
(A) $\cos A$	(p)	$24/25$
(B) $\tan A$	(q)	$7/24$
(C) $\operatorname{cosec} A$	(r)	$25/7$
(D) $\sec A$	(s)	$25/24$

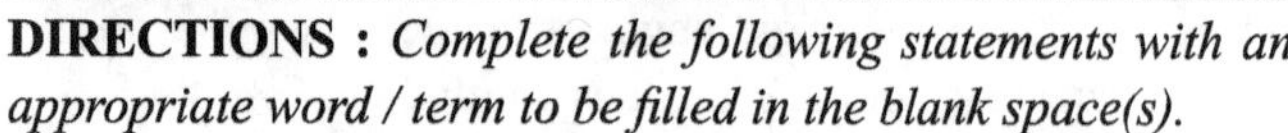

≫ Fill in the Blanks

DIRECTIONS : *Complete the following statements with an appropriate word / term to be filled in the blank space(s).*

46. The value of $\sin A$ or $\cos A$ never exceeds ......

47. $\sin^2 A + \cos^2 A =$ ....

48. If $\tan A = 4/3$, then $\sin A$ ....

49. In a right trianlge ABC, right angled at B, if $\tan A = 1$, $\sin A \cos A =$ ....

50. In $\Delta\,ABC$, right-angled at B, $AB = 24$ cm, $BC = 7$ cm. $\sin A =$ ....

51. If $15 \cot A = 8$, $\sec A =$ ....

52. In $\Delta\,PQR$, right-angled at Q, $PR + QR = 25$ cm and $PQ = 5$ cm. The value of $\tan P$ is ....

53. $\sin 60° \cos 30° + \sin 30° \cos 60° =$ ....

54. $2 \tan^2 45° + 3 \cos^2 30° - \sin^2 60° =$ ....

55. $\dfrac{\cos 45°}{\sec 30° + \operatorname{cosec} 30°} =$ ....

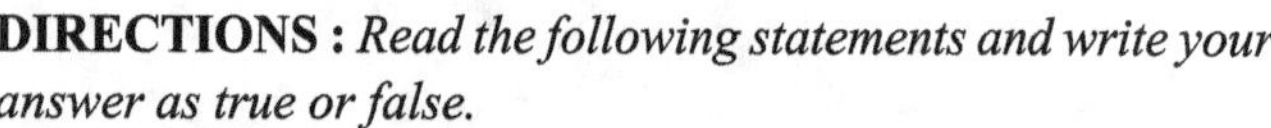

≫ True / False

DIRECTIONS : *Read the following statements and write your answer as true or false.*

56. The value of $\tan A$ is always less than 1.

57. $\sec A = 12/5$, for some value of angle A.

58. $\cos A$ is the abbreviation used for the cosecant of angle A.

59. $\cot A$ is the product of cot and A.

60. $\sin \theta = \dfrac{4}{3}$, for some angle θ.

61. $\sin (A + B) = \sin A + \sin B$.

62. $\cot A$ is not defined for $A = 0°$.

63. If $\angle B$ and $\angle Q$ are acute angles such that $\sin B = \sin Q$, then $\angle B \neq \angle Q$.

ANSWER KEY & SOLUTIONS

1. **(c)** $\sec^2\theta\,(1+\sin\theta)\,(1-\sin\theta)=k$

$$\left(\frac{1}{\cos^2\theta}\right)(1-\sin^2\theta)=k$$

$$\Rightarrow\left(\frac{1}{\cos^2\theta}\right)(\cos^2\theta)=k\Rightarrow 1=k.$$

2. **(b)** $\dfrac{(2+2\sin\theta)\,(1-\sin\theta)}{(1+\cos\theta)\,(2-2\cos\theta)}=\dfrac{2(1+\sin\theta)\,(1-\sin\theta)}{(1+\cos\theta)\,(2)\,(1-\cos\theta)}$

$$=\frac{2(1-\sin^2\theta)}{2(1-\cos^2\theta)}=\frac{2\cos^2\theta}{2\sin^2\theta}=\cot^2\theta=\left(\frac{15}{8}\right)^2=\frac{225}{64}$$

3. **(c)** We have, $x=a\,(\text{cosec }\theta+\cot\theta)$

$$\Rightarrow\frac{x}{a}=(\text{cosec }\theta+\cot\theta)\qquad\qquad\ldots(1)$$

and $y=b\left(\dfrac{1-\cos\theta}{\sin\theta}\right)\Rightarrow\dfrac{y}{b}=\dfrac{1}{\sin\theta}-\dfrac{\cos\theta}{\sin\theta}$

$$\Rightarrow\frac{y}{b}=\text{cosec }\theta-\cot\theta\qquad\qquad\ldots(2)$$

$$\Rightarrow\frac{x}{a}\times\frac{y}{b}=(\text{cosec }\theta+\cot\theta)\,(\text{cosec }\theta-\cot\theta)$$

$$\Rightarrow\frac{xy}{ab}=(\text{cosec}^2\theta-\cot^2\theta)\ \ \therefore\ xy=ab$$

4. **(c)** By squaring and adding both the given equations, we get

$p^2\,(\sin^2\theta+\cos^2\theta)+q^2\,(\cos^2\theta+\sin^2\theta)$
$=a^2+b^2$

$$\Rightarrow\ p^2+q^2-a^2-b^2=0$$

$$\Rightarrow\ (p-a)\,(p+a)+(q-b)\,(q+b)=0$$

$$\Rightarrow\ \frac{p+a}{q+b}+\frac{q-b}{p-a}=0$$

5. **(a)** $x=r\sin A\cos C,\ y=r\sin A\sin C,\ z=r\cos A$

$x^2+y^2+z^2=r^2\sin^2 A\cos^2 C+r^2\sin^2 A\sin^2 C+r^2\cos^2 A$

$$=\left(r^2\sin^2 A\right)\left(\cos^2 C+\sin^2 C\right)+r^2\cos^2 A$$

$$=r^2\sin^2 A(1)+r^2\cos^2 A=r^2(\sin^2 A+\cos^2 A)=r^2$$

6. **(d)** $\sec\theta+\tan^3\theta\,\text{cosec }\theta$

$$=\sec\theta+\frac{\sin\theta}{\cos\theta}\tan^2\theta\,\text{cosec }\theta=\sec\theta\,(1+\tan^2\theta)$$

$$=(1+\tan^2\theta)^{3/2}=[1+(1-a^2)]^{3/2}$$

7. **(b)** $x-a=b\sin^2\theta-a\sin^2\theta=(b-a)\sin^2\theta$

$b-x=b\cos^2\theta-a\cos^2\theta=(b-a)\cos^2\theta$

$\therefore\ (x-a)\,(b-x)=(b-a)^2\sin^2\theta\cos^2\theta$

$=(a-b)^2\sin^2\theta\cos^2\theta$

8. **(c)** $\cos A=\dfrac{3}{5}\Rightarrow\sin A=\sqrt{1-\dfrac{9}{25}}=\dfrac{4}{5}$

Consider,

$$9\cot^2 A-1=\frac{9\cos^2 A}{\sin^2 A}-1=\frac{9\cos^2 A-\sin^2 A}{\sin^2 A}$$

$$=\frac{9\left(\dfrac{9}{25}\right)-\left(\dfrac{16}{25}\right)}{\dfrac{16}{25}}=\frac{(81-16)}{25}\times\frac{25}{16}=\frac{65}{16}$$

9. **(b)**   **10.** **(c)**

11. **(d)** We know that $\sec^2\theta-\tan^2\theta=1$ and $\sec\theta=\dfrac{x}{p},$

$\tan\theta=\dfrac{y}{q}$

$$\therefore\ x^2q^2-p^2y^2=p^2q^2$$

12. **(d)** Given, $\tan\theta=\dfrac{a}{b}$

$$\therefore\quad\frac{a\sin\theta-b\cos\theta}{a\sin\theta+b\cos\theta}=\frac{a\tan\theta-b}{a\tan\theta+b}=\frac{a^2-b^2}{a^2+b^2}$$

13. **(d)** $(\cos^4 A-\sin^4 A)=(\cos^2 A)^2-(\sin^2 A)^2$

$$=(\cos^2 A-\sin^2 A)(\cos^2 A+\sin^2 A)$$

$$=(\cos^2 A-\sin^2 A)(1)=\cos^2 A-(1-\cos^2 A)$$

$$=2\cos^2 A-1$$

14. **(d)** We have, $\tan\theta=\dfrac{a\sin\phi}{1-a\cos\phi}$

$$\Rightarrow\cot\theta=\frac{1}{a\sin\phi}-\cot\phi\Rightarrow\cot\theta+\cot\phi=\frac{1}{a\sin\phi}\ \ldots(i)$$

and $\tan\phi=\dfrac{b\sin\theta}{1-b\cos\theta}$

$$\Rightarrow\cot\phi=\frac{1}{b\sin\theta}-\cot\theta$$

$$\Rightarrow \cot\phi + \cot\theta = \frac{1}{b\sin\theta} \qquad \ldots(ii)$$

From (i) and (ii), we have

$$\frac{1}{a\sin\phi} \quad \frac{1}{b\sin\theta} \Rightarrow \frac{a}{b} = \frac{\sin\theta}{\sin\phi}$$

15. **(d)** Let $\operatorname{cosec} x - \cot x = \dfrac{1}{3}$

$$\Rightarrow \quad \frac{1}{\sin x} - \frac{\cos x}{\sin x} = \frac{1}{3}$$

$$\Rightarrow \quad \frac{1-\cos x}{\sin x} = \frac{1}{3} \Rightarrow \frac{2\sin^2\frac{x}{2}}{2\sin\frac{x}{2}\cos\frac{x}{2}} = \frac{1}{3}$$

$$\Rightarrow \quad \tan\frac{x}{2} = \frac{1}{3}$$

Consider

$$\tan x = \frac{2\tan\frac{x}{2}}{1-\tan^2\frac{x}{2}} = \frac{\frac{2}{3}}{1-\frac{1}{9}} = \frac{3}{4}$$

Thus $\sin x = \dfrac{3}{5},\ \cos x = \dfrac{4}{5}$

$$\therefore \quad \cos^2 x - \sin^2 x = \frac{16}{25} - \frac{9}{25} = \frac{7}{25}$$

16. **(a)** $\operatorname{cosec} x - \sin x = a$ & $\sec x - \cos x = b$

$$\operatorname{cosec} x - \frac{1}{\operatorname{cosec} x} = a \ \& \ \sec x - \frac{1}{\sec x} = b$$

$$\Rightarrow \quad \frac{\operatorname{cosec}^2 x - 1}{\operatorname{cosec} x} = a \ \& \ \frac{\sec^2 x - 1}{\sec x} = b$$

$$\Rightarrow \quad \frac{\cot^2 x}{\operatorname{cosec} x} = a \ \& \ \frac{\tan^2 x}{\sec x} = b$$

$$\frac{\cos^2 x}{\sin x} = a \ \& \ \frac{\sin^2 x}{\cos x} = b$$

Now, $a^2 b = \dfrac{\cos^4 x}{\sin^2 x}\cdot\dfrac{\sin^2 x}{\cos x} = \cos^3 x$

$$\Rightarrow \quad \cos x = (a^2 b)^{1/3} \Rightarrow \cos^2 x = (a^2 b)^{2/3}$$

Similarly, $\sin^2 x = (ab^2)^{2/3}$

We know that, $\sin^2 x + \cos^2 x = 1$

$$\Rightarrow \quad (ab^2)^{2/3} + (a^2 b)^{2/3} = 1$$

17. **(c)** $\because \tan^2\theta = 1 - e^2$

$$\Rightarrow \sec\theta = \sqrt{1+\tan^2\theta} = \sqrt{1+1-e^2}$$

$$\Rightarrow \sec\theta = \sqrt{2-e^2} \qquad \ldots(i)$$

$$\therefore \sec\theta + \tan^3\theta\,\operatorname{cosec}\theta = \frac{1}{\cos\theta} + \tan^2\theta.\frac{\sin\theta}{\cos\theta}.\frac{1}{\sin\theta}$$

$$= \frac{1}{\cos\theta}(1+\tan^2\theta) = \frac{\sec^2\theta}{\cos\theta} = \sec^3\theta = (2-e^2)^{3/2} \quad \text{[from (i)]}$$

18. **(b)** $\sin\theta + \sin^3\theta = \cos^2\theta$

$$\sin\theta(1+1-\cos^2\theta) = \cos^2\theta$$

$$\Rightarrow \quad \sin^2\theta(2-\cos^2\theta)^2 = \cos^4\theta$$

$$\Rightarrow \quad (1-\cos^2\theta)(4+\cos^4\theta - 4\cos^2\theta) = \cos^4\theta$$

$$\Rightarrow \quad 4+\cos^4\theta - 4\cos^2\theta - 4\cos^2\theta - \cos^6\theta + 4\cos^4\theta = \cos^4\theta$$

$$\Rightarrow \quad \cos^6\theta - 4\cos^4\theta + 8\cos^2\theta = 4$$

19. **(c)**

20. **(d)** We have, $\dfrac{2\tan 30°}{1+\tan^2 30°}$

$$= \frac{2\times\frac{1}{\sqrt3}}{1+\left(\frac{1}{\sqrt3}\right)^2} = \frac{\frac{2}{\sqrt3}}{1+\frac{1}{3}} = \frac{2\times 3}{\sqrt3\times 4} = \frac{\sqrt3}{2}$$

Alternate method:

$$\left(\text{Using identity, } \sin 2A = \frac{2\tan A}{1+\tan^2 A}\right)$$

$$\sin 60° = \frac{2\tan 30°}{1+\tan^2 30°} = \frac{\sqrt3}{2}$$

21. **(b)** We have,

$$\frac{\sin\theta - 2\sin^3\theta}{2\cos^3\theta - \cos\theta} = \frac{\sin\theta(1-2\sin^2\theta)}{\cos\theta(2\cos^2\theta - 1)}$$

$$= \tan\theta\left[\frac{1-2(1-\cos^2\theta)}{2\cos^2\theta - 1}\right] = \tan\theta\left[\frac{(2\cos^2\theta - 1)}{2\cos^2\theta - 1}\right]$$

$$= \tan\theta$$

22. **(c)** We have, $\dfrac{\cos\theta}{1-\sin\theta} + \dfrac{\cos\theta}{1+\sin\theta} = 4$

$$\Rightarrow \cos\theta\left(\frac{1+\sin\theta+1-\sin\theta}{1-\sin^2\theta}\right) = 4$$

$$\Rightarrow \frac{2\cos\theta}{\cos^2\theta} = 4 \Rightarrow \cos\theta = \frac{1}{2} \Rightarrow \theta = 60°$$

23. **(d)** We have, $\dfrac{\tan\theta - \cot\theta}{\sin\theta\cos\theta}$

$$= \frac{\tan\theta}{\sin\theta\cos\theta} - \frac{\cot\theta}{\sin\theta\cos\theta}$$

$$= \frac{\sin\theta}{\cos\theta\sin\theta\cos\theta} - \frac{\cos\theta}{\sin\theta\cos\theta\cos\theta}$$

$$= \frac{1}{\cos^2\theta} - \frac{1}{\sin^2\theta} = \sec^2\theta - \mathrm{cosec}^2\theta$$

$$= 1 + \tan^2\theta - 1 - \cot^2\theta = \tan^2\theta - \cot^2\theta$$

24. **(a)** $\dfrac{2\tan 30°}{1 + \tan^2 30°} = \dfrac{2\left(\dfrac{1}{\sqrt{3}}\right)}{1 + \left(\dfrac{1}{\sqrt{3}}\right)^2}$

$$= \frac{\dfrac{2}{\sqrt{3}}}{1 + \dfrac{1}{3}} = \frac{2}{\sqrt{3}} \times \frac{3}{4} = \frac{\sqrt{3}}{2} = \sin 60°.$$

25. **(d)** $\dfrac{1 - \tan^2 45°}{1 + \tan^2 45°} = \dfrac{1 - (1)^2}{1 + (1)^2} = 0.$

26. **(a)** Here, when A = 0°

LHS = sin 2 A = sin 0° = 0

and   RHS = 2 sin A = 2 sin 0° = 2 × 0 = 0

In the other options, we will find that

LHS ≠ RHS

27. **(c)** $\dfrac{2\tan 30°}{1 - \tan^2 30°} = \dfrac{2\left(\dfrac{1}{\sqrt{3}}\right)}{1 - \left(\dfrac{1}{\sqrt{3}}\right)^2}$

$$= \frac{\dfrac{2}{\sqrt{3}}}{1 - \dfrac{1}{3}} = \frac{2}{\sqrt{3}} \times \frac{3}{2} = \sqrt{3} = \tan 60°.$$

28. **(b)** $9\sec^2 A - 9\tan^2 A = 9(\sec^2 A - \tan^2 A)$
$= 9 \times 1 = 9.$

29. **(c)** $(1 + \tan\theta + \sec\theta)(1 + \cot\theta - \mathrm{cosec}\,\theta)$

$$= \left\{1 + \frac{\sin\theta}{\cos\theta} + \frac{1}{\cos\theta}\right\} \times \left\{1 + \frac{\cos\theta}{\sin\theta} - \frac{1}{\sin\theta}\right\}$$

$$= \frac{\{(\cos\theta + \sin\theta) + 1\} \times \{(\cos\theta + \sin\theta) - 1\}}{\cos\theta \times \sin\theta}$$

$$= \frac{(\cos\theta + \sin\theta)^2 - (1)^2}{\cos\theta \times \sin\theta} \quad \{\because (a+b)(a-b) = a^2 - b^2\}$$

$$= \frac{1 + 2\cos\theta\sin\theta - 1}{\cos\theta \times \sin\theta} = 2.$$

30. **(d)** $(\sec A + \tan A)(1 - \sin A)$

$$= \left(\frac{1}{\cos A} + \frac{\sin A}{\cos A}\right) \times (1 - \sin A)$$

$$= \frac{(1 + \sin A)(1 - \sin A)}{\cos A}$$

$$= \frac{1 - \sin^2 A}{\cos A} = \frac{\cos^2 A}{\cos A} \qquad (\because \cos^2 A = 1 - \sin^2 A)$$

$$= \cos A.$$

31. **(d)** $\dfrac{1 + \tan^2 A}{1 + \cot^2 A} = \dfrac{(\sec^2 A - \tan^2 A) + \tan^2 A}{(\mathrm{cosec}^2 A - \cot^2 A) + \cot^2 A}$

$$= \frac{\sec^2 A}{\mathrm{cosec}^2 A} = \frac{\sin^2 A}{\cos^2 A} = \left(\frac{\sin A}{\cos A}\right)^2 = \tan^2 A.$$

32. **(b)** $(\sin 30° + \cos 30°) - (\sin 60° + \cos 60°)$

$$= \left(\frac{1}{2} + \frac{\sqrt{3}}{2}\right) - \left(\frac{1}{2} + \frac{\sqrt{3}}{2}\right) = 0$$

33. **(d)** $\dfrac{\tan 30°}{\cot 60°} = \dfrac{\dfrac{1}{\sqrt{3}}}{\dfrac{1}{\sqrt{3}}} = 1$

34. **(b)** $\sin 45° + \cos 45° = \dfrac{1}{\sqrt{2}} + \dfrac{1}{\sqrt{2}} = \dfrac{2}{\sqrt{2}} = \sqrt{2}$

(on rationalizing)

35. **(c)** $\cos\theta = \sqrt{1 - \sin^2\theta} = \sqrt{1 - \dfrac{a^2}{b^2}} = \dfrac{\sqrt{b^2 - a^2}}{b}$

36. **(a)** Given, $\sin A + \sin^2 A = 1$

$\Rightarrow \sin A = 1 - \sin^2 A = \cos^2 A$

Consider, $\cos^2 A + \cos^4 A = \sin A + (\sin A)^2 = 1$

37. **(c)** We have, $\sin(A + B) = \dfrac{\sqrt{3}}{2}$

$\Rightarrow A + B = 60°$ ...(i)

and $2B = 30° \therefore B = 15°$

Putting B in (i), we get

$A + 15° = 60° \Rightarrow A = 45°$

Sol. (38–40):

In $\triangle ABC$, by Pythagoras theorem,
$AC^2 = AB^2 + BC^2 \Rightarrow AB = 4$ cm.
$AC = 5$ cm.

38. **(a)** $\cot C = \dfrac{BC}{AB} = \dfrac{3}{4}$

39. **(b)** $\sec C = \dfrac{AC}{BC} = \dfrac{5}{3}$

40. **(b)** $\sin C = \dfrac{4}{5}, \ \cos C = \dfrac{3}{5}$

$$\text{L.H.S} = \sin^2 C + \cos^2 C = \left(\frac{4}{5}\right)^2 + \left(\frac{3}{5}\right)^2$$

$$= \frac{16+9}{25} = 1 = \text{R.H.S}$$

41. **(a)** Both Assertion and Reason are correct and Reason is the correct explanation of the assertion.

greatest side $= \sqrt{(3)^2 + (4)^2} = 5$ units.

42. **(a)** Both assertion and reason are correct and reason is the correct explanation of the assertion.

$$\tan\theta = \frac{\sqrt{3}}{2} \times 2 = \sqrt{3}.$$

43. (A) $\rightarrow$ p; (B) $\rightarrow$ q; (C) $\rightarrow$ s; (D) $\rightarrow$ r

44. (A) $\rightarrow$ q; (B) $\rightarrow$ p; (C) $\rightarrow$ r; (D) $\rightarrow$ s

45. (A) $\rightarrow$ p; (B) $\rightarrow$ q; (C) $\rightarrow$ r; (D) $\rightarrow$ s

46. 1   **47.** 1   **48.** 4/5

49. $\dfrac{1}{2}$ **50.** 7/25   **51.** 17/8

52. 12/5   **53.** 1

54. $\dfrac{7}{2}$ **55.** $\dfrac{3(\sqrt{3}-1)}{4}$

56. False   **57.** True   **58.** False

59. False   **60.** False   **61.** False

62. True   **63.** False

7 — Areas Related to Circles

DIRECTIONS : *This section contains multiple choice questions. Each question has 4 choices (a), (b), (c) and (d) out of which only one is correct.*

1. Find area of minor segment made by a chord which subtends right-angle at the centre of a circle of radius 10 cm.
   - (a) 24.5 cm^2
   - (b) 25.5 cm^2
   - (c) 24.5 cm^2
   - (d) 28.5 cm^2

2. The figure shows two concentric circles with centre O and radii 3.5 m and 7 m. If $\angle BOA = 40°$, find the area of the shaded region.

   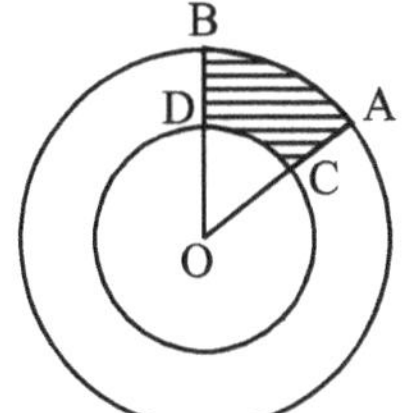

   - (a) $\dfrac{77}{6}$ cm^2
   - (b) $\dfrac{76}{5}$
   - (c) $\dfrac{73}{6}$
   - (d) None of these

3. A drain cover is made from a square metal plate of side 40 cm having 441 holes of diameter 1 cm each drilled in it. Find the area of the remaining square plate.
   - (a) 1250.5 cm^2
   - (b) 1253.5 cm^2
   - (c) 1240.2 cm^2
   - (d) 1260.2 cm^2

4. The figure given shows two identical semi-circles cut out from a piece of coloured paper.

   Find the area of the remaining piece of paper (Use $\pi = \dfrac{22}{7}$)

   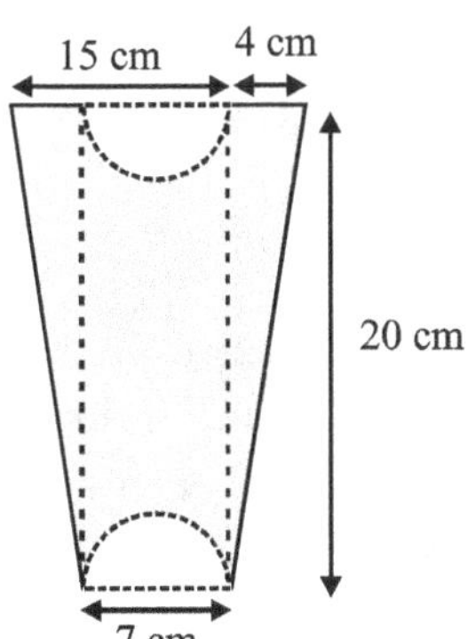

   - (a) 296.1 cm^2
   - (b) 265.4 cm^2
   - (c) 221.5 cm^2
   - (d) 201.7 cm^2

5. Mrs. Vidya bought a piece of cloth as shown in the figure. The portion of the cloth that is not coloured consists of 6 identical semi-circles.

   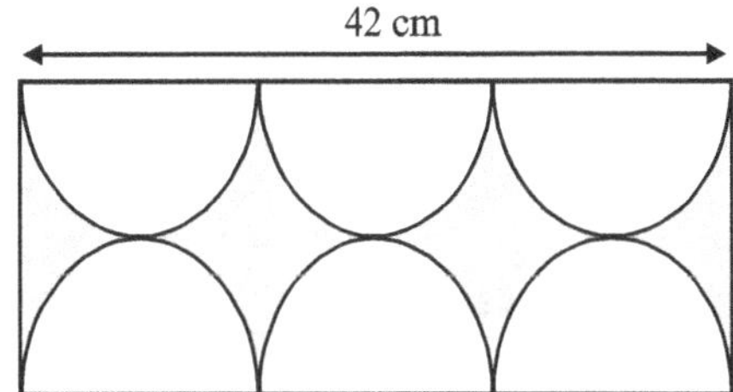

   Find the area of the coloured portion.
   - (a) 144 cm^2
   - (b) 126 cm^2
   - (c) 195 cm^2
   - (d) 243 cm^2

6. The figure given shows a rectangle with a semi-circle and 2 identical quadrants inside it.

   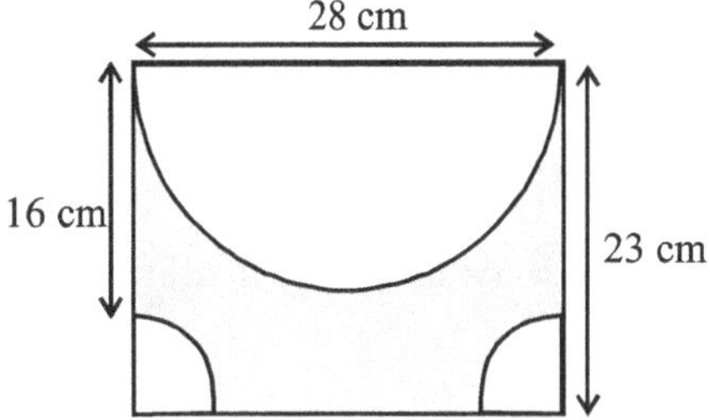

   What is the shaded area of the figure? (Use $\pi = \dfrac{22}{7}$)
   - (a) 363 cm^2
   - (b) 259 cm^2
   - (c) 305 cm^2
   - (d) 216 cm^2

7. The perimeter of a sector of a circle with central angle 90° is 25 cm. Then the area of the minor segment of the circle is.
   - (a) 14 cm^2
   - (b) 16 cm^2
   - (c) 18 cm^2
   - (d) 24 cm^2

8. The sum of the areas of two circles, which touch each other externally, is 153 π. If the sum of their radii is 15, then the ratio of the larger to the smaller radius is
   - (a) 4 : 1
   - (b) 2 : 1
   - (c) 3 : 1
   - (d) None of these

9. A race track is in the form of a ring whose inner and outer circumference are 437m and 503m respectively. The area of the track is

(a) 66 sq. cm   (b) 4935 sq. cm

(c) 9870 sq. cm   (d) None of these

10. If the sum of the circumferences of two circles with diameters d_1 and d_2 is equal to the circumference of a circle of diameter d, then

(a) $d_1^2 + d_2^2 = d^2$ (b) $d_1 + d_2 = d$

(c) $d_1 + d_2 > d$ (d) $d_1 + d_2 < d$

11. In the adjoining figure, $OABC$ is a square of side 7 cm. OAC is a quadrant of a circle with O as centre. The area of the shaded region is

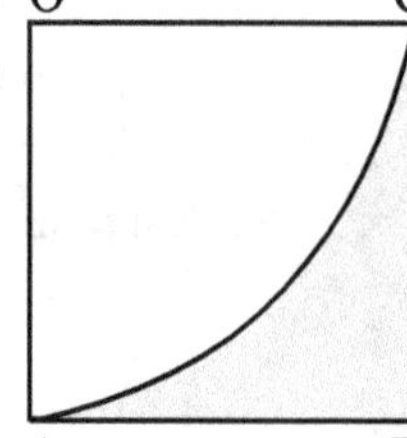

(a) 10.5 cm^2

(b) 38.5 cm^2

(c) 49 cm^2

(d) 11.5 cm^2

12. The area of a circular ring formed by two concentric circles whose radii are 5.7 cm and 4.3 cm respectively is

(Take $\pi = 3.1416$)

(a) 43.98 sq.cm   (b) 53.67 sq. cm

(c) 47.24 sq.cm   (d) 38.54 sq.cm

13. A sector is cut from a circular sheet of radius 100 cm, the angle of the sector being 240°. If another circle of the area same as the sector is formed, then radius of the new circle is

(a) 79.5 cm   (b) 81.6 cm

(c) 83.4 cm   (d) 88.5 cm

14. The area of a sector of angle p (in degrees) of a circle with radius R is

(a) $\dfrac{p}{360°} \times 2\pi R$ (b) $\dfrac{p}{180°} \times \pi R^2$

(c) $\dfrac{p}{720°} \times 2\pi R$ (d) $\dfrac{p}{720°} \times 2\pi R^2$

15. If the sector of a circle of diameter 10 cm subtends an angle of 144° at the centre, then the length of the arc of the sector is

(a) 2π cm   (b) 4π cm

(c) 5π cm   (d) 6π cm

16. The figure below shows two concentric circles with centre O. $PQRS$ is a square inscribed in the outer circle. It also circumscribes the inner circle, touching it at point B, C, D and A. The ratio of the perimeter of the outer circle to that of polygon $ABCD$ is

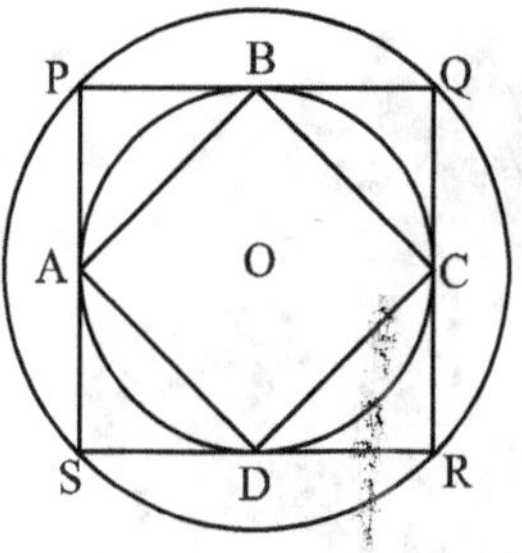

(a) $\dfrac{\pi}{4}$ (b) $\dfrac{3\pi}{2}$

(c) $\dfrac{\pi}{2}$ (d) π

17. If a circular grass lawn of 35m in radius has a path 7m wide running around it on the outside, then the area of the path is

(a) 1450 m^2 (b) 1576 m^2

(c) 1694 m^2 (d) 3368 m^2

18. In the adjoining figure, $OACB$ is a quadrant of a circle of radius 7 cm. The perimeter of the quadrant is

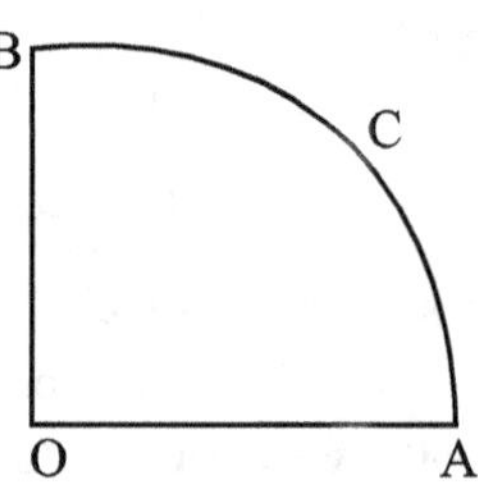

(a) 11 cm   (b) 18 cm

(c) 25 cm   (d) 36 cm

19. If the circumference of a circle increases from 4π to 8π, then its area is

(a) halved   (b) doubled

(c) tripled   (d) quadrupled

20. If the radius of a circle is diminished by 10%, then its area is diminished by

(a) 10%   (b) 19%

(c) 36%   (d) 20%

21. If the perimeter of a semi-circular protractor is 36 cm, then its diameter is

(a) 10 cm   (b) 14 cm

(c) 12 cm   (d) 16 cm

22. The area of a circular path of uniform width 'd' surrounding a circular region of radius 'r' is

(a) $\pi d(2r + d)$ (b) $\pi(2r + d)\,r$

(c) $\pi(d + r)d$ (d) $\pi(d + r)r$

Areas Related to Circles

23. If Anish is moving along the boundary of a triangular field of sides 35 m, 53 m and 66 m and you are moving along the boundary of a circular field whose area is double the area of the triangular field, then the radius of the circular field is (Take $\pi = \dfrac{22}{7}$)

(a) $14\sqrt{3}$ m (b) $3\sqrt{14}$ m (c) $28\sqrt{3}$ m (d) $7\sqrt{3}$ m

24. If the area of a square inscribed in a semicircle is 2cm^2, then the area of the square inscribed in a full circle of the same radius is ______

(a) 5 cm^2 (b) 10 cm^2 (c) $5\sqrt{2}$ cm^2 (d) 25 cm^2

25. Suppose we have two circles of radius 2 each in the plane such that the distance between their centers is $2\sqrt{3}$. The area of the region common to both circles lies between

(a) 0.5 and 0.6   (b) 0.65 and 0.7

(c) 0.7 and 0.75   (d) 0.8 and 0.9

26. A circle is inscribed in a right angled triangle of perimeter 7π . Then the ratio of numerical values of circumference of the circle to the area of the right angled triangle is

(a) $4 : 7$ (b) $3 : 7$ (c) $2 : 7$ (d) $1 : 7$

27. How much time the minute hand of a clock will take to describe an angle of $\dfrac{2\pi}{3}$ radians?

(a) 15 minutes   (b) 20 minutes

(c) 10 minutes   (d) 25 minutes

28. If the radius of a circle is $\dfrac{7}{\sqrt{\pi}}$ cm, then the area of the circle is equal to

(a) $\dfrac{49}{\pi}$ cm^2 (b) π cm^2

(c) 154 cm^2 (d) 49 cm^2

29. If the ratio of the areas of the two circles is 25 : 16, then the ratio of their circumferences is

(a) $\dfrac{25}{16}$ (b) $\dfrac{4}{5}$ (c) $\dfrac{5}{4}$ (d) $\dfrac{500}{625}$

30. If the sector of a circle of diameter 14cm subtends an angle of 30° at the centre, then its area is

(a) 49π (b) $\dfrac{49\pi}{12}$ (c) $\dfrac{242}{3\pi}$ (d) $\dfrac{121}{\pi}$

31. Which of the following is/are not correct?

(a) Area of a circle with radius 6 cm, if angle of sector is 60°, is $\dfrac{132}{14}$ cm^2.

(b) If a chord of circle of radius 14 cm makes an angle of 60° at the centre of the circle, then area of major sector is 512.87 cm^2.

(c) The ratio between the circumference and area of a circle of radius 5 cm is 2 : 5.

(d) Area of a circle whose radius is 6 cm, when the length of the arc is 22 cm, is 66 cm^2.

32. Which of the following statement is/are not correct?

(a) A chord divides the interior of a circle into two parts.

(b) An arc of a circle whose length is less than that of a semicircle of the same circle is a called a minor arc.

(c) Circles having the same centre but different radii are called concentric circles.

(d) A line segment joining any two points of a circle is called an arc.

33. Tick the correct answer in the following and justify your choice. If the perimeter and the area of a circle are numerically equal, then the radius of the circle is

(a) 2 units   (b) π units

(c) 4 units   (d) 7 units

34. If θ is the angle (in degree) of a sector of a circle of radius r, then, area of the sector is

(a) $\dfrac{\pi r^2 \theta}{360°}$ (b) $\dfrac{\pi r^2 \theta}{180°}$

(c) $\dfrac{2\pi r \theta}{360°}$ (d) $\dfrac{2\pi r \theta}{180°}$

35. If the sum of the areas of two circles with radii R_1 and R_2 is equal to the area of a circle of radius R, then

(a) $R_1 + R_2 = R$ (b) $R_1^2 + R_2^2 = R^2$

(c) $R_1 + R_2 < R$ (d) $R_1^2 + R_2^2 < R^2$

36. It is proposed to build a single circular park equal in area to the sum of areas of two circular parks of diameters 16 m and 12 m in a locality. The radius of the new park would be

(a) 10 m   (b) 15 m   (c) 20 m   (d) 24 m

▶ Case/Passage Based Questions ▶▶▶

DIRECTIONS : *Study the given Case/Passage and answer the following questions.*

Case/Passage-I

Pookalam is the flower bed or flower pattern designed during Onam in Kerala. It is similar as Rangoli in North India and Kolam in Tamil Nadu.

During the festival of Onam, your school is planning to conduct a Pookalam competition. Your friend who is a partner in competition , suggests two designs given below.

Observe these carefully. **[From CBSE Question Bank-2021]**

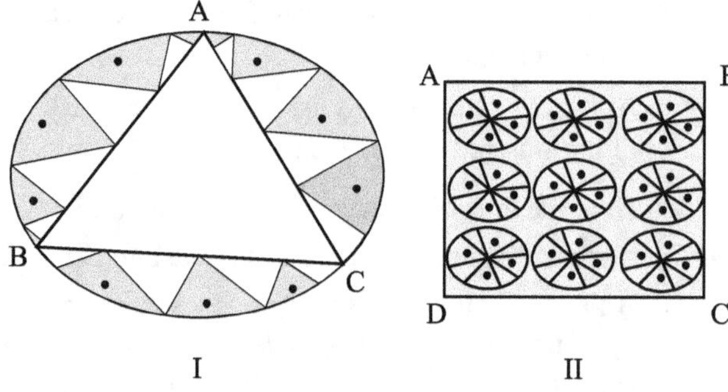

I   II

Design I: This design is made with a circle of radius 32cm leaving equilateral triangle ABC in the middle as shown in the given figure.

Design II: This Pookalam is made with 9 circular design each of radius 7cm.

Refer Design I:

37. The side of equilateral triangle is
   - (a) $12\sqrt{3}$ cm
   - (b) $32\sqrt{3}$ cm
   - (c) 48 cm
   - (d) 64 cm

38. The altitude of the equilateral triangle is
   - (a) 8 cm
   - (b) 12 cm
   - (c) 48 cm
   - (d) 52 cm

Refer Design II:

39. The area of square is
   - (a) 1264 cm^2
   - (b) 1764 cm^2
   - (c) 1830 cm^2
   - (d) 1944 cm^2

40. Area of each circular design is
   - (a) 124 cm^2
   - (b) 132 cm^2
   - (c) 144 cm^2
   - (d) 154 cm^2

41. Area of the remaining portion of the square ABCD is
   - (a) 378 cm^2
   - (b) 260 cm^2
   - (c) 340 cm^2
   - (d) 278 cm^2

Case/Passage-II

A brooch is a small piece of jewellery which has a pin at the back so it can be fastened on a dress, blouse or coat.

Designs of some brooch are shown below. Observe them carefully.   **[From CBSE Question Bank-2021]**

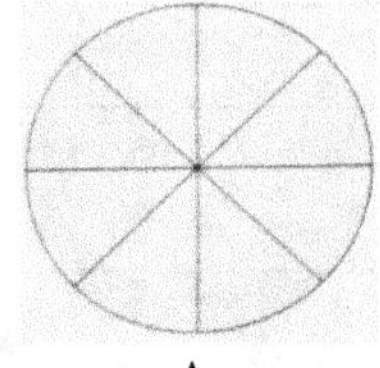 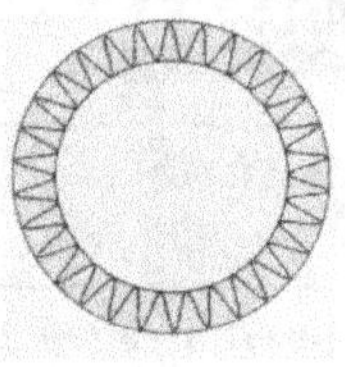 

A   B

Design A: Brooch A is made with silver wire in the form of a circle with diameter 28mm. The wire used for making 4 diameters which divide the circle into 8 equal parts.

Design B: Brooch b is made two colours-Gold and silver. Outer part is made with Gold. The circumference of silver part is 44mm and the gold part is 3mm wide everywhere.

Refer to Design A

42. The total length of silver wire required is
   - (a) 180 mm
   - (b) 200 mm
   - (c) 250 mm
   - (d) 280 mm

43. The area of each sector of the brooch is
   - (a) 44 mm^2
   - (b) 52 mm^2
   - (c) 77 mm^2
   - (d) 68 mm^2

Refer to Design B

44. The circumference of outer part (golden) is
   - (a) 48.49 mm
   - (b) 82.2 mm
   - (c) 72.50 mm
   - (d) 62.86 mm

45. The difference of areas of golden and silver parts is
   - (a) 18 π
   - (b) 44 π
   - (c) 51 π
   - (d) 64 π

46. A boy is playing with brooch B. He makes revolution with it along its edge. How many complete revolutions must it take to cover 80 π mm ?
   - (a) 2
   - (b) 3
   - (c) 4
   - (d) 5

❯Assertion & Reason 

DIRECTIONS : *Each of these questions contains an Assertion followed by Reason. Read them carefully and answer the question on the basis of following options. You have to select the one that best describes the two statements.*

(a) If both **Assertion** and **Reason** are **correct** and Reason is the **correct explanation** of Assertion.

(b) If both **Assertion** and **Reason** are correct, but Reason is **not the correct explanation** of Assertion.

(c) If **Assertion** is **correct** but **Reason** is **incorrect**.

(d) If **Assertion** is **incorrect** but **Reason** is **correct**.

47. **Assertion :** If the circumference of a circle is 176 cm, then its radius is 28 cm.

   Reason : Circumference = $2\pi \times$ radius.

48. **Assertion :** If the outer and inner diameter of a circular path is 10m and 6m, then area of the path is 16π m^2.

   Reason : If R and r be the radius of outer and inner circular path respectively then area of path = $\pi (R^2 - r^2)$.

49. **Assertion :** If a wire of length 22 cm is bent in the shape of a circle, then area of the circle so formed is 40 cm^2.

   Reason : Circumference of the circle = length of the wire.

Match the Following

DIRECTIONS : *Each question contains statements given in two columns which have to be matched. Statements (A, B, C, D) in column-I have to be matched with statements (p, q, r, s) in column-II.*

50. For circle shown, match the column.

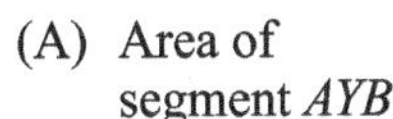

Column-I		Column-II
(A) Area of segment AYB	(p)	$\dfrac{441}{4}\sqrt{3}$
(B) Area of sector $OAYB$	(q)	$\dfrac{21}{4}(88-21\sqrt{3})$
(C) Area of Δ OAB	(r)	462
(D) OM	(s)	$21/2$

51. Two circular flower beds have been shown on two sides of a square lawn $ABCD$ of side 56m. If the centre of each circular flowered bed is the point of intersection O of the diagonals of the square lawn, then match the column.

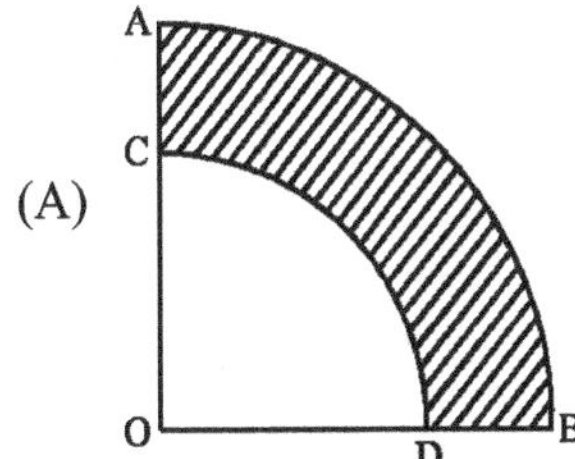

Column-I		Column-II
(A) Area of ΔOAB	(p)	4032
(B) Area of flower bed	(q)	784
(C) Area of sector OAB	(r)	448
(D) Total area	(s)	1232

52.

Column - I		Column - II
(A) Circumference	(p)	$2r+\dfrac{\theta}{360°}\times 2\pi r$
(B) Area of a quadrant	(q)	$\dfrac{\theta}{360°}\times \pi r^2$
(C) Length of the arc of the sector	(r)	$\dfrac{\pi r^2}{4}$
(D) Perimeter of the sector	(s)	$\dfrac{\theta}{360°}\times 2\pi r$
(E) Area of the sector	(t)	$2\pi r$

53.

Column-I		Column-II
(A) 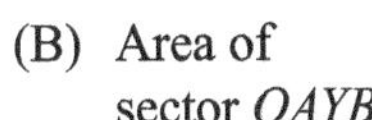	(p)	$30\ \text{cm}^2$

$OA = 26\text{m}, OC = 23\text{m}.$
Area of shaded region = ?

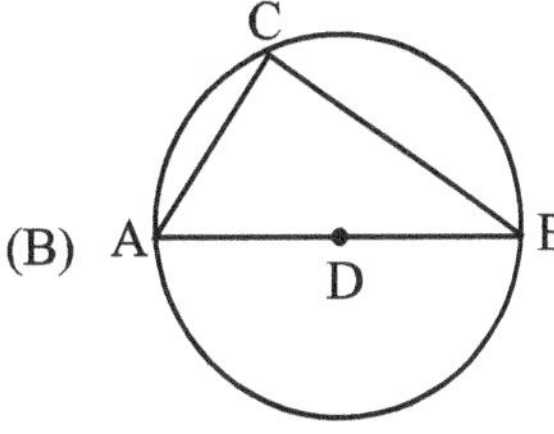

$AD = 6.5$ cm, $CA = 5$ cm.
Area of ΔABC = ?

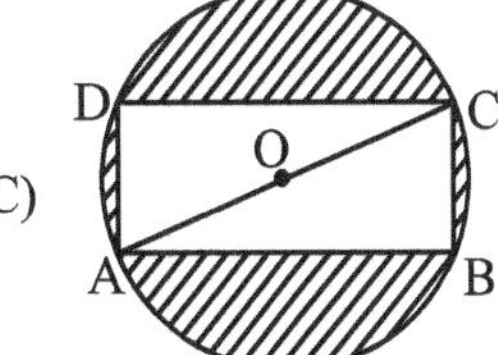

$BC = 6$ cm, $AB = 8$ cm.
Area of the shaded region = ?

	(q)	$115\ \text{m}^2$
	(r)	$114.7\ \text{cm}^2$
	(s)	$30.57\ \text{cm}^2$

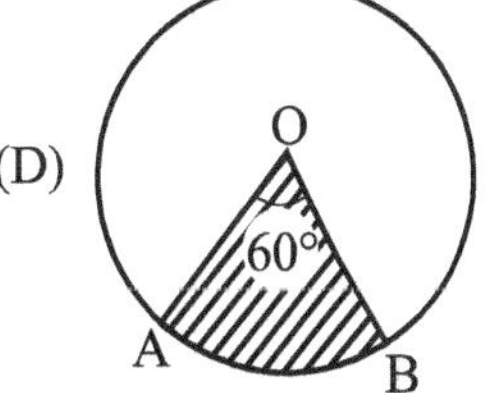

$OB = 14.8$ m.
Area of the shaded region = ?

Fill in the Blanks

DIRECTIONS : *Complete the following statements with an appropriate word / term to be filled in the blank space(s).*

54. A sector of a circle is called a .... sector if the minor arc of the circle is a part of its boundary.

55. The boundary of a sector consists of an arc of the circle and the two ....

56. The region enclosed by an arc and a chord is called the .... of the circle.

57. Circumference of a circle is ....

58. Area of a circle is ....

59. Length of an arc of a sector of a circle with radius r and angle with degree measure θ is ....

60. The area of a circle is the measurement of the region enclosed by its ....

61. If the area of a circle is $154\ \text{cm}^2$, then its circumference is ....

62. Area of a sector of a circle with radius 6 cm, if angle of the sector is $60°$, is ....

❯ True / False

DIRECTIONS : *Read the following statements and write your answer as true or false.*

63. A segment corresponding a major arc of a circle is known as the major segment.

64. If the boundary of a segment is a minor arc of a circle, then the corresponding segment is called a minor segment.

65. A minor sector has an angle 'θ' subtended at the centre of the circle, whereas a major sector has no angle.

66. The perimeter of a circle is generally known as its circumference.

67. Distance moved by a rotating wheel in one revolution is equal to the circumference of the wheel.

68. In a circle of radius 21 cm, an arc subtends an angle of 60° at the centre, then the length of the arc is 22 cm.

69. If the circumference of a circle is 88 cm, then its radius is 14 cm.

70. The length of an arc of a sector of a circle of radius r units and of centre angle θ is $\dfrac{\theta}{360°} \times \pi r^2$.

71. The length of a rope by which a cow must be tethered in order that it may be able to graze of an area of $616 cm^2$ is 18m.

ANSWER KEY & SOLUTIONS

1. **(d)** Let AB be the chord of circle such that $\angle AOB = 90°$

Let OA = 10 cm

$\therefore$ AB $= 10\sqrt{2}$ cm

Area of minor segment A X B

= Area of the sector AOB − Area of ΔAOB

$= \dfrac{90°}{360°} \times \pi(10)^2 - \dfrac{1}{2} \times 10 \times 10$

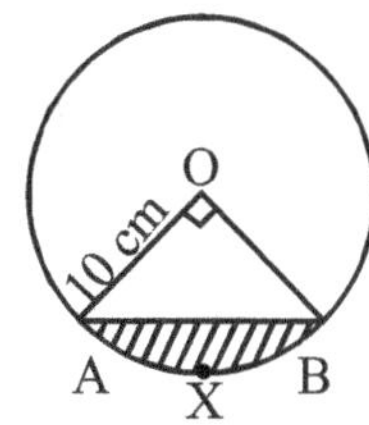

$= 25\pi - 50 = 25 \times 3.14 - 50 = 78.5 - 50 = 28.5$ cm^2.

2. **(a)** Area of the shaded region

$= \dfrac{40°}{360°} \times \dfrac{22}{7} \times (7)^2 - \dfrac{40°}{360°} \times \dfrac{22}{7} \times (3.5)^2$

$= \dfrac{1}{9} \times \dfrac{22}{7} \times (7^2 - 3.5^2) = \dfrac{1}{9} \times \dfrac{22}{7} \times \left(49 - \dfrac{49}{4}\right)$

$= \dfrac{1}{9} \times \dfrac{22}{7} \times \dfrac{49}{4} \times 3 = \dfrac{77}{6}$ cm^2

3. **(b)** We have,

Area of square metal plate = 40 × 40 = 1600 cm^2

Area of each hole $= \pi r^2 = \dfrac{22}{7} \times \left(\dfrac{1}{2}\right)^2 = \dfrac{11}{14}$ cm^2

$\therefore$ Area of 441 holes $= 441 \times \dfrac{11}{14} = 346.5$ cm^2

Hence, area of the remaining square plate

= (1600 − 346.5) = 1253.5 cm^2

4. **(c)** Area of the remaining piece of paper

= Area of trapezium − Area of 2 semi-circles

$= \dfrac{1}{2}(7 + 19) \times 20 - 2 \times \dfrac{1}{2}\pi r^2$

$= \dfrac{1}{2} \times 26 \times 20 - \dfrac{22}{7} \times \dfrac{7}{2} \times \dfrac{7}{2}$

= 260 − 38.5 = 221.5 cm^2

5. **(b)** Diameter of each semi-circle $= \dfrac{42}{3} = 14$ cm

Radius of each semi-circle = 7 cm

Area of 6 semi-circle $= 6 \times \dfrac{\pi r^2}{2} = 3\pi r^2$

$= 3 \times \dfrac{22}{7} \times 7 \times 7 = 462$ cm^2

Area of cloth piece = 42 × 14 = 588 cm^2

Area of the coloured portion = 588 − 462 = 126 cm^2

6. **(b)** Area of rectangle = 28 × 23 = 644 cm^2

Radius of semi-circle = 28 ÷ 2 = 14 cm

Radius of quadrant = 23 − 16 = 7 cm

Area of unshaded region

$= \left(\dfrac{1}{2} \times \dfrac{22}{7} \times 14 \times 14\right) + \left(2 \times \dfrac{1}{4} \times \dfrac{22}{7} \times 7 \times 7\right) = 385$ cm^2

$\therefore$ Shaded area = (644 − 385) = 259 cm^2

7. **(a)** Perimeter of sector = 25 cm

$\Rightarrow 2r + \dfrac{\theta}{360°} \times 2\pi r = 25$

$\Rightarrow 2r + \dfrac{90°}{360°} \times 2 \times \dfrac{22}{7} \times r = 25$

$\Rightarrow 2r + \dfrac{11}{7} r = 25 \Rightarrow \dfrac{25}{7} r = 25 \Rightarrow r = 7$

Area of minor segment $= \left(\dfrac{\pi\theta}{360°} - \dfrac{\sin\theta}{2}\right) r^2$

$= \left(\dfrac{22}{7} \times \dfrac{90°}{360°} - \dfrac{\sin 90°}{2}\right)(7)^2$

$= \left(\dfrac{11}{14} - \dfrac{1}{2}\right) \times 49 = \dfrac{4}{14} \times 49 = 14$ cm^2.

8. **(a)** Let the radii of the two circles be r_1 and r_2, then

$r_1 + r_2 = 15$ (given)   ..... (i)

and $\pi r_1^2 + \pi r_2^2 = 153\pi$ (given)

$\Rightarrow r_1^2 + r_2^2 = 153$ ..... (ii)

On solving, we get

$r_1 = 12,\ r_2 = 3$

Required ratio = 12 : 3 = 4 : 1

9. **(b)** $2\pi r_1 = 503$ and $2\pi r_2 = 437$

$\therefore r_1 = \dfrac{503}{2\pi}$ and $r_2 = \dfrac{437}{2\pi}$

Area of ring $= \pi (r_1 + r_2)(r_1 - r_2)$

$$= \pi \left(\frac{503+437}{2\pi}\right)\left(\frac{503-437}{2\pi}\right)$$

$$= \frac{940}{2}\left(\frac{66}{2\pi}\right) = 235 \times \frac{66}{22} \times 7 = 235 \times 21 = 4935 \text{ sq. cm.}$$

10. (b) $\pi d_1 + \pi d_2 = \pi d \Rightarrow d_1 + d_2 = d$

11. (a) Required area $= \left(7^2 - \frac{1}{4} \times \frac{22}{7} \times 7^2\right) \text{cm}^2$

$$= (49 - 38.5) \text{ cm}^2 = 10.5 \text{ cm}^2$$

12. (a) Let the radii of the outer and inner circles be r_1 and r_2 respectively; we have

Area $= \pi r_1^2 - \pi r_2^2 = \pi(r_1^2 - r_2^2)$

$$= \pi(r_1 - r_2)(r_1 + r_2)$$

$$= \pi(5.7 - 4.3)(5.7 + 4.3) = \pi \times 1.4 \times 10 \text{ sq. cm}$$

$$= 3.1416 \times 14 \text{sq. cm.} = 43.98 \text{ sq. cms.}$$

13. (b) Area of sector $= 240°/360° \times \pi(100)^2 = 20933 \text{ cm}^2$.

Let r be the radius of the new circle, then

$$20933 = \pi r^2 \Rightarrow r = \sqrt{\frac{20933}{\pi}} = 81.6 \text{ cm.}$$

14. (d)   **15. (b)**

16. (c) Joining B to O and C to O

Let the radius of the outer cirlce be r

$\therefore$ perimeter $= 2\pi r$

But $OQ = BC = r$ [diagonals of the square BQCO]

$\therefore$ Perimeter of $ABCD = 4r$.

Hence, ratio $= \dfrac{2\pi r}{4r} = \dfrac{\pi}{2}$

17. (c) Radius of outer concentric circle $= (35 + 7) \text{ m} = 42 \text{ m.}$

Area of path $= \pi (42^2 - 35^2) \text{ m}^2 = \frac{22}{7}(42^2 - 35^2) \text{ m}^2$

18. (c) Perimeter $= \frac{1}{4} \times 2\pi r + 2r$

$$= \left(\frac{1}{2} \times \frac{22}{7} \times 7 + 2 \times 7\right) \text{cm} = 25 \text{ cm}$$

19. (d) $2\pi r = 4\pi \Rightarrow r = 2$

Area $= \pi(2)^2 = 4\pi$

When, $2\pi r = 8\pi$

$\Rightarrow r = 4$

Area $= 16\pi$

20. (b) Let r be the radius of circle, then area $= \pi r^2$

When r is diminished by 10%

then, area $= \pi\left(r - \frac{r}{10}\right)^2 = \pi r^2\left(\frac{81}{100}\right)$

Thus, area is diminished by $\left(1 - \frac{81}{100}\right)\% = 19\%$

21. (b) Perimeter $= \frac{2\pi r}{2} + 2r$

$$= \pi r + 2r$$

$$\Rightarrow (\pi + 2)\, r = 36$$

$$\Rightarrow \left(\frac{36}{7}\right) - r = 36$$

$$\Rightarrow r = 7 \text{ cm}$$

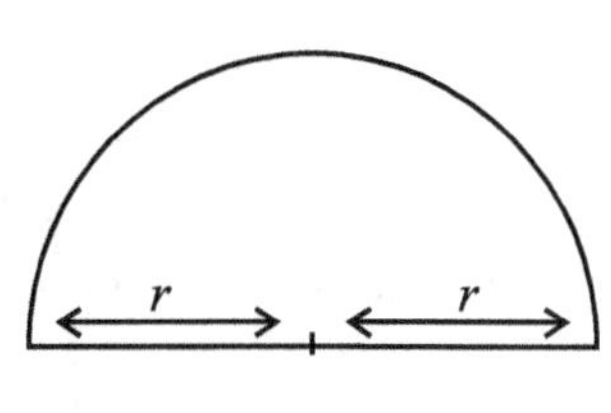

Hence, diameter $= 7 \times 2 = 14 \text{ cm.}$

22. (a) Required area $= \pi\left[(r+d)^2 - r^2\right]$

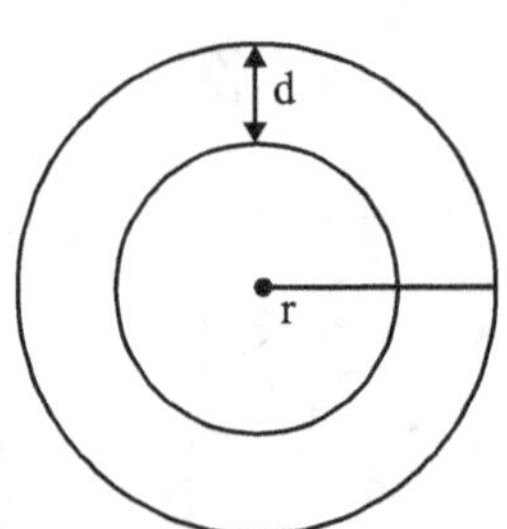

$$= \pi[r^2 + d^2 + 2rd - r^2]$$

$$= \pi[d^2 + 2rd] = \pi d[d + 2r]$$

23. (a)

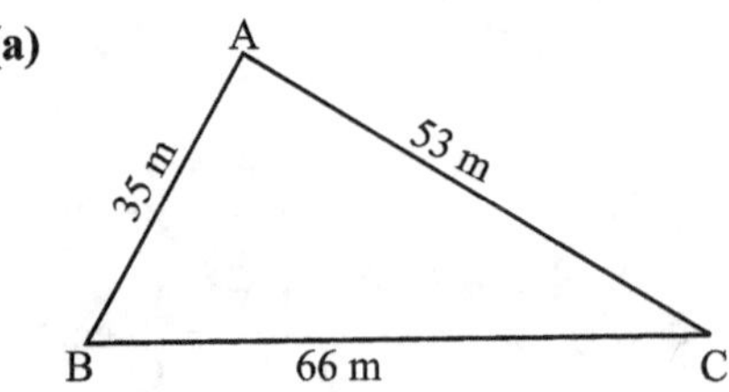

Here, $a = 66 \text{ m}$, $b = 53 \text{ m}$ & $c = 35 \text{ m}$

$$s = \frac{a+b+c}{2} = \frac{66+53+35}{2} = 77\text{m}$$

Area of $\Delta = \sqrt{s(s-a)(s-b)(s-c)}$

So, area of $\Delta = \sqrt{77(11)(24)(42)} = 924$

$\pi r^2 = 2(924)$

$$\Rightarrow r^2 = \frac{2 \times 924 + 7}{22} \Rightarrow r^2 = 588$$

$$\Rightarrow r = 14\sqrt{3} \text{ m}$$

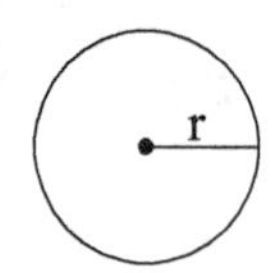

24. (a) Area of square $= 2 \text{ cm}^2$

Side of square $= \sqrt{2} \text{ cm}$

$OP = \dfrac{\sqrt{2}}{2}$ cm, $OQ = x$ cm

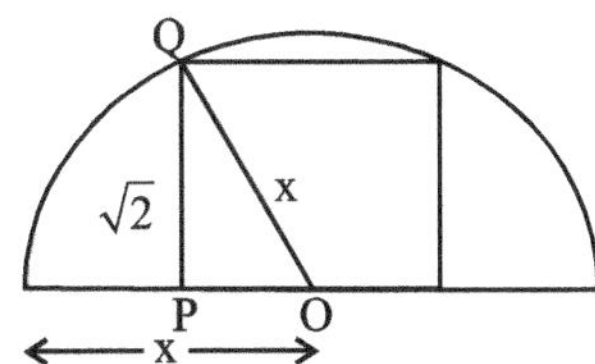

$$\Rightarrow x^2 = \left(\sqrt{2}\right)^2 + \left(\dfrac{\sqrt{2}}{2}\right)^2$$

$$\Rightarrow x^2 = 2 + \dfrac{2}{4}$$

$$\Rightarrow x^2 = \dfrac{5}{2} \Rightarrow x = \sqrt{\dfrac{5}{2}} \text{ cm.}$$

$$AC = 2\sqrt{\dfrac{5}{2}} \text{ cm} \qquad (AC = \text{Diameter})$$

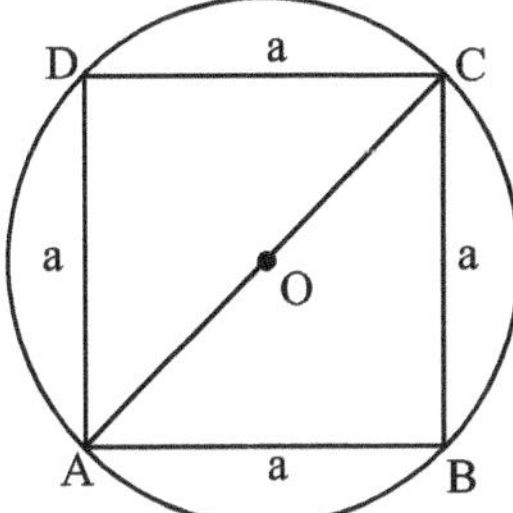

Area of square $= \dfrac{1}{2} \times AC \times BD$

Area of square $= \dfrac{1}{2} \times d_1 \times d_2$

$$= \dfrac{1}{2} \times 2\sqrt{\dfrac{5}{2}} \times 2\sqrt{\dfrac{5}{2}} = 5 \text{ cm}^2$$

25. (c) Given,

Two circle each of radius is 2 and difference between their centre is $2\sqrt{3}$

$$AB = 2\sqrt{3} \Rightarrow AC = \dfrac{1}{2} AB$$

$$AC = \sqrt{3} = CB$$

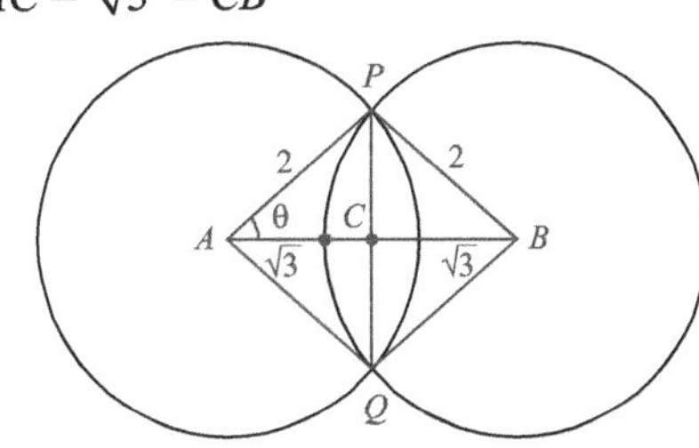

In $\triangle APC$, $\cos\theta = \dfrac{AC}{AP} = \dfrac{\sqrt{3}}{2}$ $(\angle C = 90°)$

$$\Rightarrow \quad \theta = 30°$$

$$\left\{ \dfrac{1}{2} \times d_1 \times d_2 \right\}$$

We know,

Area of common region

$= 2\ (\text{Area of sector} - \text{Area of } \triangle APQ)$

$$= 2\left(\dfrac{60°}{360°} \times \pi(2)^2 - \dfrac{1}{2} \times (2)^2 \times \sin 60° \right)$$

$$= 2\left(\dfrac{4\pi}{6} - \dfrac{4\sqrt{3}}{4} \right)$$

$$= 2\left(\dfrac{2}{3}(3.14) - (1.73) \right)$$

$$= 2\ (2.09 - 1.73) = 2\ (0.36) = 0.72.$$

$\therefore$ Area of region lie between 0.7 and 0.75.

26. (a)

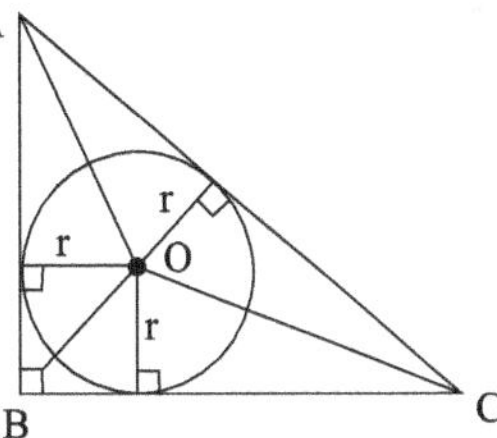

circumference of circle $= 2\pi r$ ...(i)

Area of $\triangle ABC = [\text{ar}(\triangle AOB) + \text{ar}(\triangle BOC) + \text{ar}(\triangle AOC)]$

$$= \dfrac{1}{2} AB \times r + \dfrac{1}{2} \times BC \times r + AC \times r$$

$$= \dfrac{1}{2}\ r\ [AB + BC + AC] = \dfrac{1}{2}\ r \times 7\pi \qquad \text{...(ii)}$$

From (i) and (ii),

$$\dfrac{\text{Circmference of circle}}{\text{Area of triangle}} = \dfrac{2\pi r}{\dfrac{1}{2} r \times 7\pi} = \dfrac{4}{7}$$

27. (b) As 1 radian = 1 degree $\times \dfrac{180°}{\pi}$

$$\therefore \ \dfrac{2\pi}{3} \text{ radian} = \left(\dfrac{2\pi}{3} \times \dfrac{180°}{\pi} \right)$$

$$\therefore \ \text{Time} = \dfrac{120}{6} = 20 \text{ min.}$$

28. (d) Area of the circle $= \pi\left(\dfrac{7}{\sqrt{\pi}} \right)^2 = \dfrac{\pi(49)}{\pi} = 49 \text{ cm}^2.$

Now, consider $\dfrac{154}{\pi} = \dfrac{154 \times 7}{22} = 49 \text{ cm}^2$

29. (c) $\dfrac{\pi r_1^2}{\pi r_2^2} = \dfrac{25}{16}$

$$\Rightarrow \dfrac{r_1}{r_2} = \dfrac{5}{4}$$

$$\Rightarrow \dfrac{2\pi r_1}{2\pi r_2} = \dfrac{5}{4} = \dfrac{5 \times 125}{4 \times 125} = \dfrac{625}{500}$$

30. **(b)** Area $= \dfrac{\theta}{360°} \times \pi r^2 = \dfrac{30°}{360°} \times \pi(7)^2 = \dfrac{49\pi}{12}$

31. **(a)** (a) Area $= \dfrac{\theta}{360°} \times \pi r^2 = \dfrac{60°}{360°} \times \dfrac{22}{7} \times (6)^2 = \dfrac{132}{7}$ cm^2

(b) Area of minor sector $= \dfrac{\theta}{360°} \times \pi r^2$

$= \dfrac{60°}{360°} \times \dfrac{22}{7} \times 14 \times 14 = 102.57$ cm^2

Area of major sector

= Area of circle – Area of minor sector

$= \dfrac{22}{7}(14)^2 - 102.57$

$= 615.44 - 102.57 = 512.87$ cm^2

(c) $\dfrac{C}{A} = \dfrac{2\pi(5)}{\pi(5)^2} = \dfrac{2}{5}$

(d) Given, $\left(\dfrac{\theta}{360°}\right) 2\pi r = 22$

$\therefore$ Area of sector $= \left(\dfrac{\theta}{360°}\right)\pi r^2 = \left(\dfrac{\theta}{360°}\right)\dfrac{\pi r}{2}(2r)$

$= \left(\dfrac{\theta}{360°}\right) 2\pi r \left(\dfrac{r}{2}\right) = \dfrac{22 \times 6}{2} = 66$ cm^2

32. **(d)**

33. **(a)** Justification : Let the radius of the circle be r units.

When $2\pi r = \pi r^2$,   (numerically)

We have, $2r = r^2$, *i.e.* $r = 2$

34. **(a)**   **35. (b)**   **36. (a)**

Sol. **(37-41)**

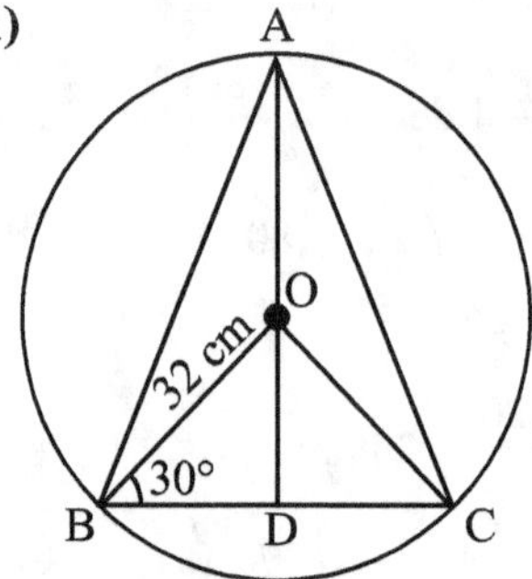

37. **(b)** $\cos 30° = \dfrac{BD}{32}$

$BD = 16\sqrt{3}$ cm.

side $BC = 32\sqrt{3}$ cm

38. **(c)** $AD = \sqrt{AB^2 - BD^2}$

$= \sqrt{(32\sqrt{3})^2 - (16\sqrt{3})^2}$

$= 48$ cm

39. **(b)** Side of square $= 6 \times 7 = 42$ cm.

Area of square $= 42 \times 42 = 1764$ cm^2

40. **(d)** Area of each circular

$= \pi(7)^2 = \dfrac{22}{7} \times 49$

$= 154$ cm^2

41. **(a)** Area of remaining

portion $= 1764 - 9 \times 154 = 378$ cm^2

42. **(b)** Here r = 14 mm

Length of silverwire

$= 2\pi r + 8r$

$= 2 \times \dfrac{22}{7} \times 14 + 8 \times 14$

$= 200$ mm

43. **(c)** Area of each sector

$= \dfrac{1}{8} \times \dfrac{22}{7} \times 14 \times 14 = 77$ mm^2

44. **(d)** Circumference of inner part $= 44$ mm

$\Rightarrow 2 \times \dfrac{22}{7} \times r = 44$

$\Rightarrow r = 7$ mm

outer radius $= 7 + 3 = 10$ mm

outer circumference

$= 2 \times \dfrac{22}{7} \times 10 = 62.86$ mm

45. **(c)** Difference of areas

$= \dfrac{22}{7}(10^2 - 7^2)$

$= 51\,\pi$ mm^2

46. **(c)** Number of revolution

$= \dfrac{\text{Distance}}{\text{Outer circumference}}$

$= \dfrac{80\pi}{20\pi} = 4.$

47. **(a)** Both assertion and reason are correct. Also, reason is the correct explanation of the assertion.

$C = 2 \times \dfrac{22}{7} \times r = 176$

$\Rightarrow r = \dfrac{176 \times 7}{2 \times 22} = 28$ cm.

48. **(a)** Both assertion and reason are correct. Also, reason is the correct explanation of the assertion.

Area of the path $= \pi\left[\left(\dfrac{10}{2}\right)^2 - \left(\dfrac{6}{2}\right)^2\right]$

$= \pi(25 - 9) = 16\pi$

Areas Related to Circles

49. **(d)** Assertion is not correct, but reason is true.

$2\pi r = 22$

$\Rightarrow r = 3.5$ cm

$\therefore$ Area of the circle $= \dfrac{22}{7} \times 3.5 \times 3.5 = 38.5$ cm^2.

50. (A) $\to$ (q); (B) $\to$ (r); (C) $\to$ (p); (D) $\to$ (s)

51. (A) $\to$ (q); (B) $\to$ (r); (C) $\to$ (s); (D) $\to$ (p)

52. (A) $\to$ (t); (B) $\to$ (r); (C) $\to$ (s); (D) $\to$ (p); (E) $\to$ (q)

53. (A) $\to$ (q); (B) $\to$ (p); (C) $\to$ (s); (D) $\to$ (r)

(A) Area of the shaded region

$$= \dfrac{90°}{360°}\pi\left[(26)^2 - (23)^2\right]$$

$$= \dfrac{1}{4} \times \dfrac{22}{7}\left[(26)^2 - (23)^2\right] = 115.5 \approx 115 \text{ m}^2$$

(B) $AB = 2 \times AD = 2 \times 6.5 = 13$ cm

$$BC = \sqrt{(AB)^2 - (AC)^2}$$

$$= \sqrt{(13)^2 - (5)^2} = 12 \text{ cm}$$

Area $(\Delta ABC) = \dfrac{1}{2} \times AC \times BC = \dfrac{1}{2}(5)(12) = 30$ cm^2

$= 0.003$ m^2

(C) $(AC)^2 = (AB)^2 + (BC)^2 = 64 + 36 = 100$

$AC = 10$ cm

Area of the shaded region

= (area of the circle) – (area of the rectangle $ABCD$)

$$= \left[\dfrac{22}{7} \times \left(\dfrac{10}{2}\right)^2\right] - (8 \times 6)$$

$= (78.57 - 48) = 30.57$ cm^2

(D) Area of the shaded region $= \dfrac{60°}{360°} \times \dfrac{22}{7} \times (14.8)^2$

$= 114.7$ m^2

54. minor **55.** radii **56.** segment

57. $2\pi r$. **58.** πr^2 **59.** $\dfrac{\theta}{360°} \times 2\pi r$

60. boundary **61.** 44 cm **62.** 132/7 cm^2

63. True **64.** True **65.** True

66. True **67.** True **68.** True

69. True **70.** False **71.** False

Probability

DIRECTIONS : *This section contains multiple choice questions. Each question has 4 choices (a), (b), (c) and (d) out of which only one is correct.*

1. Two dice are thrown at a time, then find the probability that the difference of the numbers shown on the dice is 1.

   (a) $\dfrac{3}{16}$ (b) $\dfrac{5}{18}$

   (c) $\dfrac{7}{36}$ (d) $\dfrac{7}{18}$

2. A book containing 100 pages is opened at random. Find the probability that a doublet page is found.

   (a) $\dfrac{8}{25}$ (b) $\dfrac{9}{100}$

   (c) $\dfrac{7}{100}$ (d) $\dfrac{11}{100}$

3. When two dice are thrown, find the probability of getting a number always greater than 4 on the second dice.

   (a) $\dfrac{2}{3}$ (b) $\dfrac{1}{3}$

   (c) $\dfrac{3}{5}$ (d) $\dfrac{2}{5}$

4. Two numbers are chosen from 1 to 5. Find the probability for the two numbers to be consecutive.

   (a) $\dfrac{3}{5}$ (b) $\dfrac{2}{5}$

   (c) $\dfrac{4}{5}$ (d) $\dfrac{2}{3}$

5. An unbiased die is rolled twice. Find the probability of getting the sum of two numbers as a prime

   (a) $\dfrac{3}{5}$ (b) $\dfrac{5}{12}$

   (c) $\dfrac{7}{12}$ (d) $\dfrac{4}{5}$

6. Two fair dice are thrown. Find the probability that both dice show different numbers.

   (a) $\dfrac{1}{6}$ (b) $\dfrac{5}{6}$

   (c) $\dfrac{32}{36}$ (d) $\dfrac{29}{36}$

7. A bag contains 40 coins, consisting of ₹2, ₹5 and ₹10 denominations. If a coin is drawn at random, the probability of drawing a ₹2 coin is $\dfrac{5}{8}$. If x number of ₹2 coins are removed from the bag and then a coin is drawn at random, the probability of drawing a ₹2 coin is $\dfrac{1}{2}$. Find the value of x.

   (a) 5 (b) 2
   (c) 10 (d) 8

8. A factory has 120 workers in January, 90 of them are female workers. In February, another 15 male workers were employed. A worker is then picked at random. Calculate the probability of picking a female worker.

   (a) $\dfrac{3}{4}$ (b) $\dfrac{4}{9}$

   (c) $\dfrac{2}{3}$ (d) $\dfrac{1}{2}$

9. A box contains a number of marbles with serial number 18 to 38. A marble is picked at a random. Find the probability that it is a multiple of 3.

   (a) $\dfrac{3}{5}$ (b) $\dfrac{7}{20}$

   (c) $\dfrac{3}{4}$ (d) $\dfrac{1}{3}$

10. One card is drawn from a well shuffled deck of 52 cards.
   I.   The probability that the card will be diamond, is 1/2.
   II. The probability of an ace of heart is 1/52.
   III. The probability of not a heart is 3/4.
   IV. The probability of king or queen is 1/26.
   Which of the statement(s) is/are true?
   (a) I and II
   (b) II and III
   (c) III and IV
   (d) None of these

11. A fair die is thrown once. The probability of getting a composite number less than 5 is
   (a) $\dfrac{1}{3}$
   (b) $\dfrac{1}{6}$
   (c) $\dfrac{2}{3}$
   (d) 0

12. If a letter is chosen at random from the letter of English alphabet, then the probability that it is a letter of the word 'DELHI' is
   (a) $\dfrac{1}{5}$
   (b) $\dfrac{1}{26}$
   (c) $\dfrac{5}{26}$
   (d) $\dfrac{21}{26}$

13. The probability of raining on day 1 is 0.2 and on day 2 is 0.3. The probability of raining on both the days is
   (a) 0.2
   (b) 0.1
   (c) 0.06
   (d) 0.25

14. Which of the following cannot be the probability of an event?
   (a) 2/3
   (b) $-1/5$
   (c) 15%
   (d) 0.7

15. The probability that a two digit number selected at random will be a multiple of '3' and not a multiple of '5' is
   (a) $\dfrac{2}{15}$
   (b) $\dfrac{4}{15}$
   (c) $\dfrac{1}{15}$
   (d) $\dfrac{4}{90}$

16. The probability of getting a number greater than 2 in throwing a die is
   (a) 2/3
   (b) 1/3
   (c) 4/3
   (d) 1/4

17. Out of one digit prime numbers, one number is selected at random. The probability of selecting an even number is
   (a) $\dfrac{1}{2}$
   (b) $\dfrac{1}{4}$
   (c) $\dfrac{4}{9}$
   (d) $\dfrac{2}{5}$

18. A single letter is selected at random from the word "PROBABILITY". The probability that the selected letter is a vowel is
   (a) $\dfrac{2}{11}$
   (b) $\dfrac{3}{11}$
   (c) $\dfrac{4}{11}$
   (d) 0

19. A three digit number is to be formed using the digits 3, 4, 7, 8 and 2 without repetition. The probability that it is an odd number is
   (a) $\dfrac{2}{5}$
   (b) $\dfrac{1}{5}$
   (c) $\dfrac{4}{5}$
   (d) $\dfrac{3}{5}$

20. An urn contains 6 blue and 'a' green balls. If the probability of drawing a green ball is double that of drawing a blue ball, then 'a' is equal to
   (a) 6
   (b) 18
   (c) 24
   (d) 12

21. Two coins are tossed simultaneously. The probability of getting at most one head is
   (a) $\dfrac{1}{4}$
   (b) $\dfrac{1}{2}$
   (c) $\dfrac{3}{4}$
   (d) 1

22. If in a lottery, there are 5 prizes and 20 blanks, then the probability of getting a prize is
   (a) $\dfrac{2}{5}$
   (b) $\dfrac{4}{5}$
   (c) $\dfrac{1}{5}$
   (d) 1

23. Which of the following relationship is the correct ?
   (a) $P(E) + P(\overline{E}) = 1$
   (b) $P(\overline{E}) - P(E) = 1$
   (c) $P(E) = 1 + P(\overline{E})$
   (d) None of these

24. For an event E, $P(E) + P(\overline{E}) = q$, then
   (a) $0 \le q < 1$
   (b) $0 < q \le 1$
   (c) $0 < q < 1$
   (d) None of these

25. A girl calculates that the probability of her winning the first prize in a lottery is 0.08. If 6000 tickets are sold, how many tickets has she bought?
   (a) 40
   (b) 240
   (c) 480
   (d) 750

26. Three - digit numbers formed by using digits 0, 1, 2 and 5 (without repetition) are written on different slips with distinct number on each slip, and put in a bowl. One slip is drawn at random from the bowl. The probability that the slip bears a number divisible by 5 is

(a) $\dfrac{5}{9}$ (b) $\dfrac{4}{9}$

(c) $\dfrac{2}{3}$ (d) $\dfrac{1}{3}$

27. A box contains four cards numbered as 1, 2, 3 and 4 and another box contains four cards numbered as 1, 4, 9 and 16. One card is drawn at random from each box. What is the probability of getting the product of the two numbers so obtained , more than 16?

(a) $\dfrac{5}{8}$ (b) $\dfrac{1}{2}$

(c) $\dfrac{3}{8}$ (d) $\dfrac{1}{4}$

28. From the data (1, 4, 7, 16, 27, 29) if 29 is removed, the probability of getting a prime number is

(a) $\dfrac{1}{2}$ (b) $\dfrac{1}{5}$

(c) $\dfrac{2}{5}$ (d) $\dfrac{1}{3}$

29. A bag contains card numbers 3, 4, 5, 6, 7....27. One card is drawn, then probability of prime number card is

(a) $\dfrac{9}{25}$ (b) $\dfrac{8}{27}$

(c) $\dfrac{8}{25}$ (d) $\dfrac{1}{5}$

30. Two dice are rolled, then probability of getting a total of 9 is

(a) $\dfrac{1}{3}$ (b) $\dfrac{1}{9}$

(c) $\dfrac{9}{10}$ (d) $\dfrac{8}{9}$

31. From a bag containing 100 tickets numbered 1, 2, 3, ..., 100 one ticket is drawn. If the number on this ticket is x, then the probability that $x + \dfrac{1}{x} > 2$ is ......

(a) 0   (b) 0.99

(c) 1   (d) None of these

32. A coin is tossed. Then the probability of getting either head or tail is

(a) 1   (b) $\dfrac{1}{3}$

(c) $\dfrac{1}{2}$ (d) $\dfrac{1}{4}$

33. Two dice are rolled simultaneously. Find the probability that they show different faces.

(a) $\dfrac{3}{4}$ (b) $\dfrac{1}{6}$

(c) $\dfrac{1}{3}$ (d) $\dfrac{5}{6}$

34. A die is thrown once then,

(a) the probability of getting an odd number is $\dfrac{2}{3}$

(b) the probability of getting multiple of 3 is 1/3

(c) the probability of getting a prime number is 2/3

(d) the probability of getting number greater than 5 is 1/3

35. The probability of an event can not be

(a) positive   (b) negative

(c) zero   (d) one

36. If the probability of an event is 0, then it is called a

(a) sure event   (b) certain event

(c) impossible event   (d) none of these

37. Which of the following statement(s) is/are not correct ?

(a) An event which can never happen is called impossible event.

(b) An event which has more than one (favourable) outcomes is called a compound event.

(c) The collection of all possible outcomes of an experiment is called sample space.

(d) None of these

⟫ Case/Passage Based Questions ⟫⟫

DIRECTIONS : *Study the given Case/Passage and answer the following questions.*

Case/Passage-I

On a weekend Rani was playing cards with her family. The deck has 52 cards. If her brother drew one card .

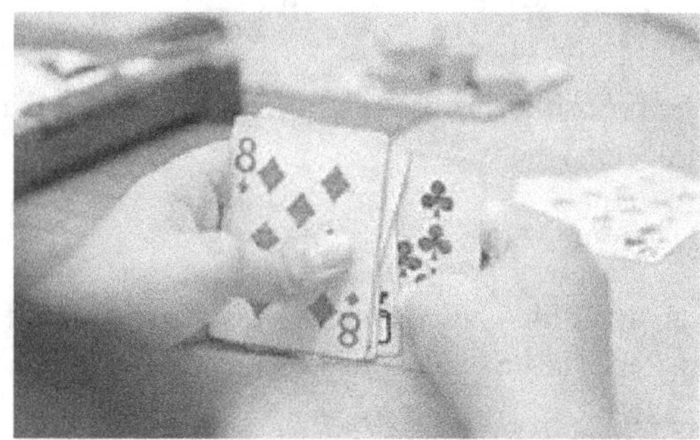

38. Find the probability of getting a king of red colour.

(a) $\dfrac{1}{26}$ (b) $\dfrac{1}{13}$ (c) $\dfrac{1}{52}$ (d) $\dfrac{1}{4}$

39. Find the probability of getting a face card.

(a) $\dfrac{1}{26}$ (b) $\dfrac{1}{13}$ (c) $\dfrac{2}{13}$ (d) $\dfrac{3}{13}$

40. Find the probability of getting a jack of hearts.

(a) $\dfrac{1}{26}$ (b) $\dfrac{1}{52}$ (c) $\dfrac{3}{52}$ (d) $\dfrac{3}{26}$

41. Find the probability of getting a red face card.

(a) $\dfrac{3}{26}$ (b) $\dfrac{1}{13}$ (c) $\dfrac{1}{52}$ (d) $\dfrac{1}{4}$

42. Find the probability of getting a spade.

(a) $\dfrac{1}{26}$ (b) $\dfrac{1}{13}$ (c) $\dfrac{1}{26}$ (d) $\dfrac{1}{4}$

Case/Passage-II

Rahul and Ravi planned to play Business (board game) in which they were supposed to use two dice.

[From CBSE Question Bank-2021]

43. Ravi got first chance to roll the dice. What is the probability that he got the sum of the two numbers appearing on the top face of the dice is 8?

(a) $\dfrac{1}{26}$ (b) $\dfrac{5}{36}$ (c) $\dfrac{1}{18}$ (d) 0

44. Rahul got next chance. What is the probability that he got the sum of the two numbers appearing on the top face of the dice is 13?

(a) 1   (b) $\dfrac{5}{36}$ (c) $\dfrac{1}{18}$ (d) 0

45. Now it was Ravi's turn. He rolled the dice. What is the probability that he got the sum of the two numbers appearing on the top face of the dice is less than or equal to 12 ?

(a) 1   (b) $\dfrac{5}{36}$ (c) $\dfrac{1}{18}$ (d) 0

46. Rahul got next chance. What is the probability that he got the sum of the two numbers appearing on the top face of the dice is equal to 7 ?

(a) $\dfrac{5}{9}$ (b) $\dfrac{5}{36}$ (c) $\dfrac{1}{6}$ (d) 0

47. Now it was Ravi's turn. He rolled the dice. What is the probability that he got the sum of the two numbers appearing on the top face of the dice is greater than 8 ?

(a) 1   (b) $\dfrac{5}{36}$ (c) $\dfrac{1}{18}$ (d) $\dfrac{5}{18}$

Assertion & Reason

DIRECTIONS : *Each of these questions contains an Assertion followed by Reason. Read them carefully and answer the question on the basis of following options. You have to select the one that best describes the two statements.*

(a) If both **Assertion** and **Reason** are **correct** and Reason is the **correct explanation** of Assertion.

(b) If both **Assertion** and **Reason** are correct, but Reason is **not the correct explanation** of Assertion.

(c) If **Assertion** is **correct** but **Reason** is **incorrect**.

(d) If **Assertion** is **incorrect** but **Reason** is **correct**.

48. **Assertion :** If a box contains 5 white, 2 red and 4 black marbles, then the probability of not drawing a white marble from the box is $\dfrac{5}{11}$.

     Reason : $P\left(\overline{E}\right) = 1 - P(E)$, where E is any event.

49. **Assertion :** In rolling a dice, the probability of getting number 8 is zero.

     Reason : Its an impossible event.

50. **Assertion :** An event is very unlikely to happen. Its probability is 0.0001

     Reason : If P(A) denote the probability of an event A, then $0 \le P(A) \le 1$.

51. **Assertion :** If the probability of an event is P then probability of its complementary event will be $1 - P$.

     Reason : When E and $\overline{E}$ are complementary events, then $P(E) + P\left(\overline{E}\right) = 1$

52. **Assertion :** If a die is thrown, the probability of getting a number less than 3 and greater than 2 is zero.

     Reason : Probability of an impossible event is zero.

Match the Following

DIRECTIONS : *Each question contains statements given in two columns which have to be matched. Statements (A, B, C, D,............) in Column-I have to be matched with statements (p, q, r, s,...............) in Column-II.*

53. Match the proposed probability under Column-I with the appropriate written description under column-II :

Column -I	Column-II
(Probability)	(Written Description)
(A) 0.95	(p) An incorrect assignment
(B) 0.02	(q) No chance of happening

(C) –0.3   (r) As much chance of happening as not

(D) 0.5   (s) Very likely to happen

(E) 0   (t) Very little chance of happening

54. Two unbiased coins are tossed simultaneously. Match Column-I with the probabilities given in Column-II.

Column-I		Column-II
(A) The probability of getting one head is	(p)	$\dfrac{3}{4}$
(B) The probability of getting at least one head is	(q)	$\dfrac{1}{4}$
(C) The probability of getting two heads is	(r)	$\dfrac{1}{2}$

Fill in the Blanks

DIRECTIONS : *Complete the following statements with an appropriate word / term to be filled in the blank space(s).*

55. Probability of an event E + Probability of the event 'not E' = ...

56. The probability of an event that cannot happen is .... Such an event is called ....

57. The probability of an event that is certain to happen is .... Such an event is called ....

58. The sum of the probabilities of all the elementary events of an experiment is ....

59. The probability of an event is greater than or equal to .... and less than or equal to ....

60. If P(E) = 0.05, the probability of 'not E' is ....

61. A die is thrown once, the probability of getting a prime number is ....

62. If A is an event of a random experiment, then A^C or $\overline{A}$ or A' is called the ....of the event.

63. A set of events which have no pair in common are called ....

64. An outcome of a random experiment is called an .... event.

True / False

DIRECTIONS : *Read the following statements and write your answer as true or false.*

65. The sum of the probabilities of all the elementary events of an experiment is 1.

66. For any event E, P (E) + P ($\overline{E}$) = 1, where $\overline{E}$ stands for 'not E'. E and $\overline{E}$ are called complementary events.

67. The probability of an event can be greater than 1.

68. If the probability of an event is 1, then it is an impossible event.

69. If A is any event in a sample space, then $P(\overline{A}) = 1 + P(A)$

70. The sum of probabilities of two students getting distinction in their final examinations is 1.2.

71. A bag contains 5 red balls and some blue balls. If the probability of drawing a blue ball is double that of a red ball, the number of blue balls in the bag is 10.

72. A box contains 90 discs which are numbered from 1 to 90. If one disc is drawn at random from the box, the probability that it bears a two-digit number is 0.9

73. An event A associated to a random experiment is said to occur if any one of the elementary events associated to the event A is an outcomes.

74. An event associated to a random experiment is a compound event if it is obtained by combining two or more elementary events associated to the random experiment.

ANSWER KEY & SOLUTIONS

1. (b) $n(S) = 6 \times 6 = 36$

$E = \{(1, 2), (2, 1), (2, 3), (3, 2), (3, 4), (4, 3), (4, 5),$
$(5, 4), (5, 6), (6, 5)\}$

$n(E) = 10$

$\therefore \quad P(E) = \dfrac{n(E)}{n(S)} = \dfrac{10}{36} = \dfrac{5}{18}$

2. (b) $S = \{1, 2, 3, ..., 100\}$

$n(S) = 100$

$E = \{11, 22, 33, 44, 55, 66, 77, 88, 99\}$

$n(E) = 9$

$\therefore \quad P(E) = \dfrac{9}{100}$

3. (b) $n(S) = 6 \times 6 = 36$, $E = \{(1, 5), (2, 5), (3, 5), (4, 5),$
$(5, 5), (6, 5), (1, 6), (2, 6), (3, 6), (4, 6), (5, 6), (6, 6)\}$

$n(E) = 12$

$\therefore \quad P(E) = \dfrac{n(E)}{n(S)} = \dfrac{12}{36} = \dfrac{1}{3}$

4. (b) $E = \{(1, 2), (2, 3), (3, 4), (4, 5)\}$

$n(E) = 4$

$n(S) = 5 \times 2 = 10 \quad \therefore \quad P(E) = \dfrac{n(E)}{n(S)} = \dfrac{4}{10} = \dfrac{2}{5}$

5. (b) The sum of the two numbers lies between 2 and 12. So, the primes are 2, 3, 5, 7, 11.

No. of ways for getting $2 = (1, 1) = 1$

No. of ways of getting $3 = (1, 2), (2, 1) = 2$

No. of ways of getting 5

$= (1, 4), (4, 1), (2, 3), (3, 2) = 4$

No. of ways of getting 7

$= (1, 6), (6, 1), (2, 5), (5, 2), (3, 4), (4, 3) = 6$

No. of ways of getting $11 = (5, 6), (6, 5) = 2$

No. of favourable ways $= 1 + 2 + 4 + 6 + 2 = 15$

No. of exhaustive ways $= 6 \times 6 = 36$

$\therefore \quad$ Probability of getting the sum as a prime

$= \dfrac{15}{36} = \dfrac{5}{12}$

6. (b) $S = \{(1, 1), ..., (1, 6), (2, 1), ..., (2, 6), (3, 1), ..., (3, 6),$
$(4, 1), ..., (4, 6), (5, 1), ..., (5, 6), (6, 1), ..., (6, 6)\}$

$n(S) = 36$

Let E be the event that both dice show different numbers.

$E \{(1, 2), (1, 3),...., (1, 6), (2, 1), (2, 3), (2, 4),...., (2, 6),$
$(3, 1), (3, 2), (3, 4), (3, 5), (3, 6), (4, 1), (4, 2), (4, 3),$
$(4, 5), (4, 6), (5, 1), (5, 2), (5, 3), (5, 4), (5, 6), (6, 1),$
$(6, 2), (6, 3), (6, 4), (4, 5)\}$

$n(E) = 30$

$\therefore \quad P(E) = \dfrac{n(E)}{n(S)} = \dfrac{30}{36} = \dfrac{5}{6}$

7. (c) $n(S) = 40$, let $n(C) = C$

$P(C) = \dfrac{5}{8} \Rightarrow \dfrac{C}{40} = \dfrac{5}{8}$ or $C = 25$

Now, $\dfrac{25 - x}{40 - x} = \dfrac{1}{2} \Rightarrow x = 10$

8. (c) Initial number of workers $= 120$

When 15 male workers are added, then the total number of workers $= 120 + 15 = 135$

Number of female workers $= 90$

$\therefore \quad$ Probability of female workers $= \dfrac{90}{135} = \dfrac{2}{3}$

9. (d) Total number of marbles $= 38 - 18 + 1 = 21$

The multiples of 3 from 18 to 38 are 18, 21, 24, 27, 30, 33, 36.

These are 7 in numbers

$\therefore \quad$ Required probability $= \dfrac{7}{21} = \dfrac{1}{3}$

10. (b) Total number of cards $= 52$

Total number of diamond cards $= 13$

I. $\quad$ P(diamond cards) $= 13/52 = 1/4$

II. $\quad$ P(an ace of heart) $= 1/52$

III. $\quad$ P(not a heart) $= 1 - \dfrac{1}{4} = \dfrac{3}{4}$

IV. $\quad$ P(king or queen) $= \dfrac{4}{52} + \dfrac{4}{52} = \dfrac{8}{52} = \dfrac{2}{13}$

11. **(b)** [**Hint.** The outcomes are 1, 2, 3, 4, 5, 6. Out of these, 4 is the only composite number which is less than 5].

12. **(c)** [**Hint.** The English alphabet has 26 letters in all. The word 'DELHI' has 5 letter, so the number of favourable outcomes = 5.]

13. **(c)** P(raining on both day) = $0.2 \times 0.3 = 0.06$

(Because both independent event)

14. **(b)**

15. **(b)** 24 out of the 90 two digit numbers are divisible by '3' and not by '5'.

The required probability is therefore, $\dfrac{24}{90} = \dfrac{4}{15}$.

16. **(a)** Required probability $= \dfrac{4}{6} = \dfrac{2}{3}$.

17. **(b)** [**Hint.** One digit prime numbers are 2, 3, 5, 7. Out of these numbers, only the number 2 is even.]

18. **(c)** Required probability $= \dfrac{1+2+1}{11} = \dfrac{4}{11}$.

19. **(a)** There are 2 favourable choice (3, 7) for unit place.

$$P = 1 \times 1 \times \dfrac{2}{5} = \dfrac{2}{5}$$

20. **(d)**

21. **(c)** Total outcomes = HH, HT, TH, TT

Favourable outcomes = HT, TH, TT

P(at most one head) $= \dfrac{3}{4}$.

22. **(c)** Required probability $= \dfrac{5}{25} = \dfrac{1}{5}$.

23. **(a)** $P(E) + P(\overline{E}) = 1$

24. **(d)**   **25.** **(c)**

26. **(a)** Total three digit number are : $3 \times 3 \times 2 = 18$

Now, numbers divisible by 5 are :

$2 \times 3 \times 1 + 2 \times 2 \times 1 = 10$

So, probability that the slip bears a number divisible by 5 $= \dfrac{10}{18} = \dfrac{5}{9}$

27. **(c)** Possible products are 1, 4, 9, 16, 2, 8, 18, 32, 3, 12, 27, 48, 4, 16, 36, 64

So, required probability of getting the product of the two numbers so obtained is $\dfrac{6}{16} = \dfrac{3}{8}$

28. **(b)** Probability $= \dfrac{\text{No. of favourable outcomes}}{\text{Total number of outcomes}} = \dfrac{1}{5}$

29. **(c)** Total number of cards = 25

Prime number are 3, 5, 7, 11, 13, 17, 19, 23,

∴ Probability of prime number card $= \dfrac{8}{25}$

30. **(b)** No. of sample space $= 6 \times 6 = 36$

Sum total of 9 = (3, 6), (4, 5), (5, 4), (6, 3)

∴ $P = \dfrac{4}{36} = \dfrac{1}{9}$

31. **(b)** $n(S) = [1, 2, 3, ..., 100] = 100$

∵ $x + \dfrac{1}{x} > 2$

∴ $x^2 + 1 > 2x$

⇒ $x^2 - 2x + 1 > 0$

⇒ $(x - 1)^2 > 0$

$x = [2, 3, ... , 100]$

$n(E) = [2, 3, 4, ..., 100] = 99$

$P(E) = \dfrac{99}{100} = 0.99$

32. **(a)**   **33.** **(d)**

34. **(b)** A die is thrown once therefore, total number of outcomes are {1, 2, 3, 4, 5, 6}

(a) $P(\text{odd number}) = 3/6 = 1/2$

(b) $P(\text{multiple of 3}) = 2/6 = 1/3$

(c) $P(\text{prime number}) = 3/6 = 1/2$

(d) $P(\text{greater than 5}) = 1/6$

35. **(b)** The probability of an event can never be negative.

36. **(c)**

37. **(d)** All the three statements are correct.

38. **(a)** P(king of red colour) $= \dfrac{2}{52} = \dfrac{1}{26}$

39. **(d)** P(getting a face card) $= \dfrac{12}{52} = \dfrac{3}{13}$

40. **(b)** P(getting a jack of hearts) $= \dfrac{1}{52}$

Probability

41. **(a)** P(getting a red face card) $= \dfrac{3}{26}$

42. **(d)** P(getting a spade) $= \dfrac{13}{52} = \dfrac{1}{4}$

43. **(b)** Sum of the two numbers appearing on the top face of dice is 8.

$(2, 6), (3, 5), (4, 4) (5, 3), (6, 2)$

$\therefore$ Required probability $= \dfrac{5}{36}$

44. **(d)** Since, the sum of two numbers appearing on the top face of dice cannot be 13.

So, required probability = 0.

45. **(a)** Since, the pair of number whose sum is less than 0 or equal to 12 in a pair of dice is 36.

$\therefore$ Required probability $= \dfrac{36}{36} = 1$

46. **(c)** Since, the pair of numbers on the top of dice whose sum is 7 are $(1, 6), (2, 5), (3, 4), (4, 3), (5, 2), (6, 1)$

$\therefore$ Required probability $= \dfrac{6}{36} = \dfrac{1}{6}$

47. **(d)** $\dfrac{5}{18}$

48. **(d)** Assertion is not correct, but reason is correct.

$P(\text{white marble}) = \dfrac{5}{5+2+4} = \dfrac{5}{11}.$

$P(\text{not white marble}) = 1 - \dfrac{5}{11} = \dfrac{11-5}{11} = \dfrac{6}{11}.$

49. **(a)** Assertion and Reason both are correct. Also Reason is the correct explanation of the Assertion.

50. **(b)** Assertion and Reason is correct but Reason is not correct explanation for Assertion.

51. **(a)** Both statements are correct and Reason is the correct for Assertion.

52. **(a)** Both statements are correct. Event given in Assertion is an impossible event.

53. $(A) \rightarrow (s); (B) \rightarrow (t); (C) \rightarrow (p); (D) \rightarrow (r); (E) \rightarrow (q)$

54. $(A) \rightarrow (r) ; (B) \rightarrow (p) ; (C) \rightarrow (q)$

Sample space = {HH, HT, TH, TT}

$A : P \text{ (one head)} = \dfrac{2}{4} = \dfrac{1}{2}$

$(\because \text{ favourable event = HT, TH})$

$B : P \text{ (at least one head)} = \dfrac{3}{4}$

$(\because \text{ favourable event = HH, HT, TH})$

$C : P \text{ (two heads)} = \dfrac{1}{4}$ $(\because \text{ favourable event = HH})$

55. 1

56. 0, impossible event

57. 1, sure or certain event

58. 1

59. 0, 1

60. .95

61. 1/2

62. complement

63. mutually exclusive

64. elementary

65. True   **66.** True   **67.** False   **68.** False

69. False   **70.** True   **71.** True   **72.** True

73. True   **74.** True

9 Quadratic Equations

DIRECTIONS : *This section contains multiple choice questions. Each question has 4 choices (a), (b), (c) and (d) out of which ONLY ONE is correct.*

1. If the product of roots of the equation $x^3 - 3x + k = 10$ is -2, then the value of k is

(a) -2 (b) -8

(c) 8 (d) 12

2. If one root of $5x^2 + 13x + k = 0$ be the reciprocal of the other root, then the value of k is

(a) 0 (b) 1

(c) 2 (d) 5

3. If the sum of the roots of a quadratic equation is 6 and their product is 6, the equation is

(a) $x^2 - 6x + 6 = 0$ (b) $x^2 + 6x - 6 = 0$

(c) $x^2 - 6x - 6 = 0$ (d) $x^2 + 6x + 6 = 0$

4. If the equation $x^2 + 2(k+2)x + 9k = 0$ has equal roots, then $k = ?$

(a) 1 or 4 (b) -1 or 4

(c) 1 or -4 (d) -1 or -4

5. If the roots of $5x^2 - kx + 1 = 0$ are real and distinct, then

(a) $-2\sqrt{5} < k < 2\sqrt{5}$

(b) $k > 2\sqrt{5}$ only

(c) $k < -2\sqrt{5}$ only

(d) either $k > 2\sqrt{5}$ or $k < -2\sqrt{5}$

6. If $a - b$, $b - c$ are the roots of $ax^2 + bx + c = 0$, then find the value of $\dfrac{(a-b)(b-c)}{c-a}$

(a) $\dfrac{b}{c}$ (b) $\dfrac{c}{b}$

(c) $\dfrac{ab}{c}$ (d) $\dfrac{bc}{a}$

7. Find the product of the roots of $x^2 + 8x - 16 = 0$

(a) 8 (b) -8

(c) 16 (d) -16

8. If the roots of the equation $ax^2 + bx + c = 0$ are α and β, then the quadratic equation whose roots are $-\alpha$ and $-\beta$ is ______ .

(a) $ax^2 - bx - c = 0$ (b) $ax^2 - bx + c = 0$

(c) $ax^2 + bx - c = 0$ (d) $ax^2 - bx + 2c = 0$

9. If the equation $(1 + m^2)x^2 + (2mc)x + (c^2 - a^2) = 0$ has equal roots, then

(a) $c^2 - a^2 = 1 + m^2$ (b) $c^2 = a^2(1 + m^2)$

(c) $c^2 a^2 = (1 + m^2)$ (d) $c^2 + a^2 = 1 + m^2$

10. Which of the following satisfy the equation $a^2b^2x^2 + b^2x - a^2x - 1 = 0$

(a) $\dfrac{1}{a^2}$ (b) $\dfrac{1}{b^2}$

(c) $\dfrac{-1}{b^2}$ (d) None of these

11. The roots of the quadratic equation $x^2 - 0.04 = 0$ are

(a) ± 0.2 (b) ± 0.02

(c) 0.4 (d) 2

12. One of the two students, while solving a quadratic equation in x, copied the constant term incorrectly and got the roots 3 and 2. The other copied the constant term and coefficient of x^2 correctly as -6 and 1 respectively. The correct roots are

(a) $3, -2$ (b) $-3, 2$

(c) $-6, -1$ (d) $6, -1$

13. The condition for one root of the quadratic equation $ax^2 + bx + c = 0$ to be twice the other, is

(a) $b^2 = 4ac$ (b) $2b^2 = 9ac$

(c) $c^2 = 4a + b^2$ (d) $c^2 = 9a - b^2$

14. If $\left(x-\dfrac{1}{2}\right)^2 - \left(x-\dfrac{3}{2}\right)^2 = x+2$, then $x =$

    (a) 3   (b) 2

    (c) 4   (d) None of these

15. If $x^2 + y^2 = 25$, $xy = 12$, then $x =$

    (a) $\{3, 4\}$ (b) $\{3, -3\}$

    (c) $\{3, 4, -3, -4\}$ (d) $\{-3, -3\}$

16. If $x = \sqrt{7 + 4\sqrt{3}}$, then $x + \dfrac{1}{x} =$

    (a) 4   (b) 6

    (c) 3   (d) 2

17. If the roots of the equation $px^2 + 2qx + r = 0$ and $qx^2 - 2\sqrt{pr}\,x + q = 0$ be real, then

    (a) $p = q$ (b) $q^2 = pr$

    (c) $p^2 = qr$ (d) $r^2 = pq$

18. The equation $2x^2 + 2(p + 1)x + p = 0$, where p is real, always has roots that are

    (a) Equal

    (b) Equal in magnitude but opposite in sign

    (c) Irrational

    (d) Real

19. If the ratio of the roots of the equation $x^2 + bx + c = 0$ is the same as that of $x^2 + qx + r = 0$, then

    (a) $r^2 b = qc^2$ (b) $r^2 c = qb^2$

    (c) $c^2 r = q^2 b$ (d) $b^2 r = q^2 c$

20. The real roots of the equation $x^{2/3} + x^{1/3} - 2 = 0$ are

    (a) 1, 8   (b) $-1, -8$

    (c) $-1, 8$ (d) $1, -8$

21. Which of the following is not a quadratic equation?

    (a) $x^2 - 2x + 2(3 - x) = 0$

    (b) $x(x + 1) + 1 = (x - 2)(x - 5)$

    (c) $(2x - 1)(x - 3) = (x + 5)(x - 1)$

    (d) $x^3 - 4x^2 - x + 1 = (x - 2)^3$

22. If one root of the quadratic equation $ax^2 + bx + c = 0$ is the reciprocal of the other, then

    (a) $b = c$ (b) $a = b$

    (c) $ac = 1$ (d) $a = c$

23. The roots of the equation $x + \dfrac{1}{x} = 3\dfrac{1}{3}$, $x \neq 0$, are

    (a) 3, 1   (b) $3, \dfrac{1}{3}$

    (c) $3, -\dfrac{1}{3}$ (d) $-3, -\dfrac{1}{3}$

24. If the equation $(m^2 + n^2)x^2 - 2(mp + nq)x + p^2 + q^2 = 0$ has equal roots, then

    (a) $mp = nq$ (b) $mq = np$

    (c) $mn = pq$ (d) $mq = \sqrt{np}$

25. Each root of $x^2 - bx + c = 0$ is decreased by 2. The resulting equation is $x^2 - 2x + 1 = 0$, then

    (a) $b = 6, c = 9$ (b) $b = 3, c = 5$

    (c) $b = 2, c = -1$ (d) $b = -4, c = 3$

26. Two distinct polynomials $f(x)$ and $g(x)$ are defined as follows:

$$f(x) = x^2 + ax + 2;\ g(x) = x^2 + 2x + a.$$

If the equations $f(x) = 0$ and $g(x) = 0$ have a common root, then the sum of the roots of the equation $f(x) + g(x) = 0$ is

    (a) $-\dfrac{1}{2}$ (b) 0

    (c) $\dfrac{1}{2}$ (d) 1

27. If α and β are the roots of the quadratic equation $x^2 - 6x - 2 = 0$ and if $a_n = \alpha^n - \beta^n$, then the value of $\dfrac{a_{10} - 2a_8}{2a_9}$ is

    (a) 6.0   (b) 5.2

    (c) 5.0   (d) 3.0

28. Consider the quadratic equation $nx^2 + 7\sqrt{n}\,x + n = 0$, where n is a positive integer. Which of the following statements are necessarily correct?

    I.   For any n, the roots are distinct.

    II. There are infinitely many values of n for which both roots are real.

    III. The product of the roots is necessarily an integer.

    (a) III only   (b) I and III

    (c) II and III   (d) I, II and III

29. Two quadratic equations $x^2 - bx + 6 = 0$ and $x^2 - 6x + c - 0$ have a common root. If the remaining roots of the first and second equations are positive integers and are in the ration 3 : 4 respectively, then the common root is

    (a) 1   (b) 2

    (c) 3   (d) 4

30. The values of k, so that the equations $2x^2 + kx - 5 = 0$ and $x^2 - 3x - 4 = 0$ have one root in common, are

    (a) $3, \dfrac{27}{2}$ (b) $9, \dfrac{27}{4}$

    (c) $-3, \dfrac{-27}{4}$ (d) $3, \dfrac{4}{27}$

31. If $x = \dfrac{3+\sqrt{5}}{2}$ and $y = x^3$, then y satisfies the quadratic equation

(a) $y^2 - 18y + 1 = 0$ (b) $y^2 + 18y + 1 = 0$

(c) $y^2 - 18y - 1 = 0$ (d) $y^2 + 18y - 1 = 0$

32. Let b be a non-zero real number. Suppose the quadratic equation $2x^2 + bx + \dfrac{1}{b} = 0$ has two distinct real roots. Then

(a) $b + \dfrac{1}{b} > \dfrac{5}{2}$ (b) $b + \dfrac{1}{b} < \dfrac{5}{2}$

(c) $b^2 - 3b > -2$ (d) $b^2 + \dfrac{1}{b^2} < 4$

33. If the quadratic equations $2x^2 + 4x + (a+5) = 0$ have equal roots and $(a+4)x^2 + ax - 3b = 0$ have distinct real roots then which of the following is true:

(a) $a = -3, b < \dfrac{3}{4}$ (b) $a = 3, b > \dfrac{3}{4}$

(c) $a = -3, b > -\dfrac{3}{4}$ (d) $a = 3, b < \dfrac{3}{4}$

34. The value of λ such that sum of the squares of the roots of the quadratic equation, $x^2 + (3 - \lambda)x + 2 = \lambda$ has the least value is:

(a) $\dfrac{15}{8}$ (b) 1

(c) $-$ (d) 2

35. If α and β be two roots of the equation $x^2 - 64x + 256 = 0$. Then the value of $\left(\dfrac{\alpha^3}{\beta^5}\right)^{\frac{1}{8}} + \left(\dfrac{\beta^3}{\alpha^5}\right)^{\frac{1}{8}}$ is:

(a) 2 (b) 3

(c) 1 (d) 4

36. Which one of the following is not a quadratic equation?

(a) $(x+2)^2 = 2(x+3)$

(b) $x^2 + 3x = (-1)(1-3x)^2$

(c) $(x+2)(x-1) = x^2 - 2x - 3$

(d) $x^3 - x^2 + 2x + 1 = (x+1)^3$

37. Which constant should be added and subtracted to solve the quadratic equation $4x^2 - \sqrt{3}x - 5 = 0$ by the method of completing the square?

(a) $\dfrac{9}{16}$ (b) $\dfrac{3}{64}$

(c) $\dfrac{3}{4}$ (d) $\dfrac{\sqrt{3}}{4}$

38. Which of the following equations has 2 as a root?

(a) $x^2 - 4x + 5 = 0$

(b) $x^2 + 3x - 12 = 0$

(c) $2x^2 - 7x + 6 = 0$

(d) $3x^2 - 6x - 2 = 0$

39. Values of k for which the quadratic equation $2x^2 - kx + k = 0$ has equal roots is

(a) 0 only   (b) 4 only

(c) 8 only   (d) $0, 8$

40. If α, β are roots of the equation $x^2 - 5x + 6 = 0$, then the equation whose roots are $\alpha + 3$ and $\beta + 3$ is

(a) $2x^2 - 11x + 30 = 0$ (b) $-x^2 + 11x = 0$

(c) $x^2 - 11x + 30 = 0$ (d) $2x^2 - 22x + 40 = 0$

41. If equation $x^2 - (2 + m)x + 1(m^2 - 4m + 4) = 0$ has equal roots, then:

(a) $m = 0$ (b) $m = 6$

(c) $m = 2$ (d) $m = 3$

42. Which of the following equations have no real roots?

(a) $x^2 - 2\sqrt{3}x + 5 = 0$ (b) $2x^2 + 6\sqrt{2} + 8 = 0$

(c) $x^2 - 2\sqrt{3}x - 5 = 0$ (d) $2x^2 - 6\sqrt{2}x - 9 = 0$

43. Two numbers whose sum is 8 and the absolute value of whose difference is 10 are roots of the equation

(a) $x^2 - 8x + 9 = 0$ (b) $x^2 - 8x - 9 = 0$

(c) $x^2 + 8x - 9 = 0$ (d) $-x^2 + 8x + 9 = 0$

44. If α, β are roots of $x^2 + 5x + a = 0$ and $2\alpha + 5\beta = -1$, then

(a) $\alpha = 8$ (b) $\beta = -3$

(c) $\alpha = 9$ (d) $a = -24$

45. The value of p for which the difference between the roots of the equation $x^2 + px + 8 = 0$ is 2, are

(a) 4 (b) 8

(c) 6 (d) -4

46. If the roots of $x^2 + px + 12 = 0$ are in the ratio $1 : 3$, then value(s) of p are

(a) 3 (b) 8

(c) 6 (d) -3

47. Roots of quadratic equation $x^2 - 3x + 2 = 0$ are

(a) 3 (b) -1

(c) 2 (d) 4

48. If $x = 2$ and $x = 3$ are roots of the equation $3x^2 - 2px + 2q = 0$, then

(a) $p = \dfrac{2}{15}$ (b) $p = 15$

(c) $q = 9$ (d) $6p + 2q = 27$

Quadratic Equations

Case/Passage Based Questions

DIRECTIONS : *Study the given Case/Passage and answer the following questions.*

Case/Passage-I

Raj and Ajay are very close friends. Both the families decide to go to Ranikhet by their own cars. Raj's car travels at a speed of x km/h while Ajay's car travels 5 km/h faster than Raj's car. Raj took 4 hours more than Ajay to complete the journey of 400 km.

[From CBSE Question Bank-2021]

49. What will be the distance covered by Ajay's car in two hours?

  (a) $2(x+5)$km   (b) $(x-5)$km

  (c) $2(x+10)$km   (d) $(2x+5)$km

50. Which of the following quadratic equation describe the speed of Raj's car?

  (a) $x^2 - 5x - 500 = 0$ (b) $x^2 + 4x - 400 = 0$

  (c) $x^2 + 5x - 500 = 0$ (d) $x^2 - 4x + 400 = 0$

51. What is the speed of Raj's car?

  (a) 20 km/hour   (b) 15 km/hour

  (c) 25 km/hour   (d) 10 km/hour

52. How much time took Ajay to travel 400 km?

  (a) 20 hour   (b) 40 hour

  (c) 25 hour   (d) 16 hour

Case/Passage-II

The speed of a motor boat is 20 km/hr. For covering the distance of 15 km the boat took 1 hour more for upstream than downstream.   **[From CBSE Question Bank-2021]**

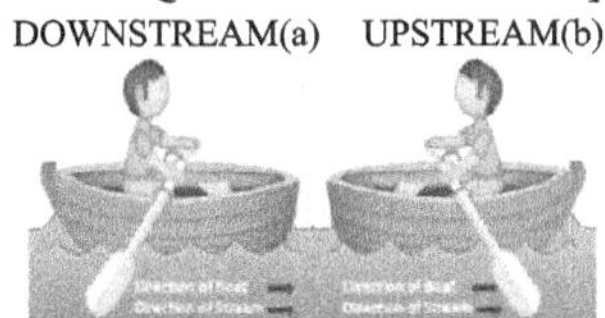

53. Let speed of the stream be x km/hr. then speed of the motorboat in upstream will be

  (a) 20 km/hr   (b) $(20 + x)$ km/hr

  (c) $(20 - x)$ km/hr   (d) 2 km/hr

54. What is the relation between speed ,distance and time?

  (a) speed = (distance)/time   (b) distance = (speed)/time

  (c) time = speed x distance   (d) speed = distance x time

55. Which is the correct quadratic equation for the speed of the current ?

  (a) $x^2 + 30x - 200 = 0$ (b) $x^2 + 20x - 400 = 0$

  (c) $x^2 + 30x - 400 = 0$ (d) $x^2 - 20x - 400 = 0$

56. What is the speed of current ?

  (a) 20 km/hour   (b) 10 km/hour

  (c) 15 km/hour   (d) 25 km/hour

57. How much time boat took in downstream?

  (a) 90 minute   (b) 15 minute

  (c) 30 minute   (d) 45 minute

Assertion & Reason

DIRECTIONS : *Each of these questions contains an Assertion followed by Reason. Read them carefully and answer the question on the basis of following options. You have to select the one that best describes the two statements.*

  (a) If both **Assertion** and **Reason** are **correct** and Reason is the **correct explanation** of Assertion.

  (b) If both **Assertion** and **Reason** are correct, but Reason is **not the correct explanation** of Assertion.

  (c) If **Assertion** is **correct** but **Reason** is **incorrect**.

  (d) If **Assertion** is **incorrect** but **Reason** is **correct**.

58. **Assertion :** If roots of the equation $x^2 - bx + c = 0$ are two consecutive integers, then $b^2 - 4c = 1$.

  Reason : If a, b, c are odd integer then the roots of the equation $4abc\, x^2 + (b^2 - 4ac)\, x - b = 0$ are real and distinct.

59. **Assertion :** $(2x - 1)^2 - 4x^2 + 5 = 0$ is not a quadratic equation.

  Reason : $x = 0, 3$ are the roots of the equation $2x^2 - 6x = 0$.

60. **Assertion :** The equation $9x^2 + 3kx + 4 = 0$ has equal roots for $k = \pm 4$.

  Reason : If discriminant 'D' of a quadratic equation is equal to zero then the roots of equation are real and equal.

61. **Assertion :** $4x^2 - 12x + 9 = 0$ has repeated roots.

  Reason : The quadratic equation $ax^2 + bx + c = 0$ have repeated roots if discriminant $D > 0$.

62. **Assertion :** A quadratic equation $ax^2 + bx + c = 0$, has two distinct real roots, if $b^2 - 4ac > 0$.

  Reason : A quadratic equation can never be solved by using method of completing the squares.

63. **Assertion :** Sum and product of roots of $2x^2 - 3x + 5 = 0$ are $\dfrac{3}{2}$ and $\dfrac{5}{2}$ respectively.

  Reason : If α and β are the roots of $ax^2 + bx + c = 0$, $a \neq 0$, then sum of roots $= \alpha + \beta = -\dfrac{b}{a}$ and product of roots $= \alpha\beta = \dfrac{c}{a}$.

Match the Following

DIRECTIONS : *Each question contains statements given in two columns which have to be matched. Statements (A, B, C, D) in column-I have to be matched with statements (p, q, r, s) in column-II.*

64. Column-II give roots of quadratic equations given in Column-I.

Column-I	Column-II
(A) $6x^2 + x - 12 = 0$	(p) $(-6, 4)$
(B) $8x^2 + 16x + 10 = 202$	(q) $(9, 36)$
(C) $x^2 - 45x + 324 = 0$	(r) $(3, -1/2)$
(D) $2x^2 - 5x - 3 = 0$	(s) $(-3/2, 4/3)$

65.

Column-I	Column-II
(A) $(x-3)(x+4) + 1 = 0$	(p) Forth degree polynomial
(B) $(x+2)^3 = 2x(x^2-1)$	(q) Quadratic equation
(C) $(2x-2)^2 = 4x^2$	(r) Non-quadratic equation
(D) $(2x^2-2)^2 = 3$	(s) Linear equation

66.

Column-I	Column-II
(A) If α, β are roots of $ax^2 + bx + c = 0$, then one of the roots of the equation $ax^2 - bx(x-1) + c(x-1)^2 = 0$	(p) $a < 0, b > 0$
(B) If the roots of $ax^2 + b = 0$ are real, then	(q) real and equal
(C) Roots of $4x^2 - 4x + 1 = 0$	(r) $\dfrac{\beta}{1+\beta}$
(D) Roots of $(x-a)(x-b) + (x-b)(x-c) + (x-c)(x-a) = 0$ are always	(s) Real

Fill in the Blanks

DIRECTIONS : *Complete the following statements with an appropriate word/ term to be filled in the blank space(s).*

67. A quadratic equation in the variable x is of the form $ax^2 + bx + c = 0$, where a, b, c are real numbers and a ......

68. A quadratic equation $ax^2 + bx + c = 0$ has two distinct real roots, if $b^2 - 4ac$ ....

69. The altitude of a right triangle is 7 cm less than its base. If the hypotenuse is 13 cm, the other two sides are ....

70. The equation $ax^2 + bx + c = 0$, $a \neq 0$ has no real roots, if ....

71. The values of k for which the equation $2x^2 + kx + x + 8 = 0$ will have real and equal roots are ....

72. If α, β are roots of the equation $ax^2 + bx + c = 0$, then the quadratic equation whose roots are $a\alpha + b$ and $a\beta + b$ is ....

73. If r, s are roots of $ax^2 + bx + c = 0$, then $\dfrac{1}{r^2} + \dfrac{1}{s^2}$ is ....

74. The quadratic equation whose roots are the sum and difference of the squares of roots of the equation $x^2 - 3x + 2 = 0$ is....

75. If a, b are the roots of $x^2 + x + 1 = 0$, then $a^2 + b^2 = $ ....

76. If α, β are the roots of $x^2 + bx + c = 0$ and $\alpha + h$, $\beta + h$ are the roots of $x^2 + qx + r = 0$, then $h = $ ....

77. A quadratic equation cannot have more than .... roots.

78. Let $ax^2 + bx + c = 0$, where a, b, c are real numbers, $a \neq 0$, be a quadratic equation, then this equation has no real roots if and only if ....

True / False

DIRECTIONS : *Read the following statements and write your answer as true or false.*

79. A quadratic equation cannot be solved by the method of completing the square.

80. If we can factorise $ax^2 + bx + c$, $a \neq 0$, into a product of two linear factors, then the roots of the quadratic equation $ax^2 + bx + c = 0$ can be found by equating each factor to zero.

81. $(x-2)(x+1) = (x-1)(x+3)$ is a quadratic equation.

82. $(x^2 + 3x + 1) = (x-2)^2$ is not a quadratic equation.

83. $x^2 + x - 306 = 0$ represent quadratic equation where product of two consecutive positive integer is 306.

84. The roots of the equation $(x-3)^2 = 3$ are $3 \pm \sqrt{3}$

85. If sum of the roots is 2 and product is 5, then the quadratic equation is $x^2 - 2x + 5 = 0$

86. Sum of the reciprocals of the roots of the equation $x^2 + px + q = 0$ is $1/p$.

87. The nature of roots of equation $x^2 + 2x\sqrt{3} + 3 = 0$ are real and equal.

88. For the expression $ax^2 + 7x + 2$ to be quadratic, the possible values of a are non-zero real numbers.

ANSWER KEY & SOLUTIONS

1. **(c)** Given equation is $x^2 - 3x + (k - 10) = 0$.

∴ Product of roots $= (k - 10)$.

So, $k - 10 = -2 \Rightarrow k = 8$.

2. **(d)** Let the roots be α and $\dfrac{1}{\alpha}$. Then,

product of roots $= \left(\alpha \times \dfrac{1}{\alpha}\right) = 1$.

So, $\dfrac{k}{5} = 1 \Rightarrow k = 5$.

3. **(a)** Required equation is $x^2 - 6x + 6 = 0$.

4. **(a)** Since the roots are equal, we have $D = 0$.

∴ $4(k+2)^2 - 36k = 0 \Rightarrow (k+2)^2 - 9k = 0$

∴ $k^2 - 5k + 4 = 0 \Rightarrow k^2 - 4k - k + 4 = 0$

$\Rightarrow k(k-4) - (k-4) = 0$

$\Rightarrow (k-4)(k-1) = 0 \Rightarrow k = 4$ or $k = 1$.

5. **(d)** The roots of $5x^2 - kx + 1 = 0$ are real and distinct.

∴ $(k^2 - 4 \times 5 \times 1) > 0 \Rightarrow k^2 > 20$

$\Rightarrow k > \sqrt{20}$ or $k < -\sqrt{20} \Rightarrow k > 2\sqrt{5}$ or $k < -2\sqrt{5}$.

6. **(b)** (i) $(a - b)(b - c) = $ product of the roots $= \dfrac{c}{a}$.

(ii) $c - a = -(a - b + b - c) = -$ (sum of the roots)

$= \dfrac{b}{a}$.

7. **(d)** $x^2 + 8x - 16 = 0$

The product of the roots $= \dfrac{c}{a} = -16$.

8. **(b)** Use $x^2 - (\alpha + \beta)x + \alpha\beta = 0$

9. **(b)** Since the equation has two equal roots, $D = 0$

$\Rightarrow (2mc)^2 - 4(1 + m^2)(c^2 - a^2) = 0$

$\Rightarrow 4m^2c^2 - 4c^2 + 4a^2 - 4m^2c^2 + 4m^2a^2 = 0$

$\Rightarrow -4c^2 + 4a^2 + 4m^2a^2 = 0 \Rightarrow 4c^2 = 4a^2 + 4m^2a^2$

$\Rightarrow 4c^2 = 4a^2(1 + m^2) \Rightarrow c^2 = a^2(1 + m^2)$

10. **(b)** $a^2b^2x^2 + b^2x - a^2x - 1 = 0$

$\Rightarrow b^2x(a^2x + 1) - 1(a^2x + 1) = 0$

$\Rightarrow (a^2x + 1)(b^2x - 1) = 0$

$\Rightarrow x = -\dfrac{1}{a^2}, \dfrac{1}{b^2}$

11. **(a)** $x^2 - 0.04 = 0$

$\Rightarrow x^2 = 0.04$

$\Rightarrow x = \pm 0.2$

12. **(d)** Let α, β be the roots of the equation. Then $\alpha + \beta = 5$ and $\alpha\beta = -6$. So, the equation is $x^2 - 5x - 6 = 0$.

The roots of the equation are 6 and -1.

13. **(b)** $\alpha + 2\alpha = -\dfrac{b}{a}$ and $\alpha \times 2\alpha = \dfrac{c}{a} \Rightarrow 3\alpha = -\dfrac{b}{a}$

$\Rightarrow \alpha = -\dfrac{b}{3a}$ and $2\alpha^2 = \dfrac{c}{a} \Rightarrow 2\left(\dfrac{-b}{3a}\right)^2 = \dfrac{c}{a}$

$\Rightarrow \dfrac{2b^2}{9a^2} = \dfrac{c}{a} \Rightarrow 2ab^2 - 9a^2c = 0 \Rightarrow a(2b^2 - 9ac) = 0$

Since $a \neq 0$, ∴ $2b^2 = 9ac$

Hence, the required condition is $2b^2 = 9ac$

14. **(c)** Use options or apply the formula

$a^2 - b^2 = (a - b)(a + b)$, we get $x = 4$

15. **(c)** $x^2 + y^2 = 25$, $xy = 12$

$\Rightarrow x^2 + \left(\dfrac{12}{x}\right)^2 = 25 \Rightarrow x^4 + 144 - 25x^2 = 0$

$\Rightarrow (x^2 - 16)(x^2 - 9) \Rightarrow x^2 = 16$ and $x^2 = 9$

$\Rightarrow x = \pm 4$ and $x = \pm 3$

16. **(a)** We have, $x = \sqrt{7 + 4\sqrt{3}}$

∴ $\dfrac{1}{x} = \dfrac{1}{\sqrt{7 + 4\sqrt{3}}} = \dfrac{\sqrt{7 - 4\sqrt{3}}}{\sqrt{7 + 4\sqrt{3}} \cdot \sqrt{7 - 4\sqrt{3}}} = \sqrt{7 - 4\sqrt{3}}$

∴ $x + \dfrac{1}{x} = \sqrt{7 + 4\sqrt{3}} + \sqrt{7 - 4\sqrt{3}}$

$= (\sqrt{3} + 2) + (2 - \sqrt{3}) = 4$

17. **(b)** Equation $px^2 + 2qx + r = 0$ and $qx^2 - 2\sqrt{pr}\,x + q = 0$ have real roots then from first

$4q^2 - 4pr \geq 0 \Rightarrow q^2 \geq pr$ ... (i)

and from second $4(pr) - 4q^2 \geq 0$ (for real root)

$\Rightarrow pr \geq q^2$ ... (ii)

From (i) and (ii), we get result $q^2 = pr$

18. **(d)** The discriminant of a quadratic equation

$ax^2 + bx + c = 0$ is given by $b^2 - 4ac$.

$a = 2$, $b = 2(p + 1)$ and $c = p$

$b^2 - 4ac = [2(p + 1)]^2 - 4(2p) = 4(p + 1)^2 - 8p$

$= 4[(p + 1)^2 - 2p] = 4[(p^2 + 2p + 1) - 2p] = 4(p^2 + 1)$

For any real value of p, $4(p^2 + 1)$ will always be positive as p^2 cannot be negative for real p.

Hence, the discriminant $b^2 - 4ac$ will always be positive.

When the discriminant is greater than '0' or is positive, then the roots of a quadratic equation will be real.

19. (d) Let 1, 2 be the roots of equations (i), 2 and 4 be the roots of equation (ii).

∴ equations are $x^2 - 3x + 2 = 0$ and $x^2 - 6x + 8 = 0$.

Comparing with $x^2 + bx + c = 0$ and $x^2 + qx + r = 0$, we get $b = -3$, $c = 2$, $q = -6$ and $r = 8$.

Putting these values in the options, we find that option (d) is satisfied.

20. (d) The given equation is $x^{2/3} + x^{1/3} - 2 = 0$

Put $x^{1/3} = y$, then $y^2 + y - 2 = 0$

$\Rightarrow (y - 1)(y + 2) = 0 \Rightarrow y = 1$ or $y = -2$

$\Rightarrow x^{1/3} = 1$ or $x^{1/3} = -2$

∴ $x = (1)^3$ or $x = (-2)^3 = -8$

Hence, the real roots of the given equations are 1, –8.

21. (b) $x(x + 1) + 1 = (x - 2)(x - 5)$

$\Rightarrow x^2 + x + 1 = x^2 - 7x + 10$

$\Rightarrow 8x - 9 = 0$, which is not a quadratic equation.

22. (d) If one root is α, then the other is $\dfrac{1}{\alpha}$

∴ $\alpha \cdot \dfrac{1}{\alpha}$ = product of roots = $\dfrac{c}{a} \Rightarrow 1 = \dfrac{c}{a} \Rightarrow a = c$

23. (b) $x + \dfrac{1}{x} = \dfrac{10}{3} \Rightarrow \dfrac{x^2 + 1}{x} = \dfrac{10}{3} \Rightarrow 3x^2 - 10x + 3 = 0$

$\Rightarrow (x - 3)(3x - 1) = 0 \Rightarrow x = 3, x = \dfrac{1}{3}$

24. (b) '$b^2 = 4ac$'

$\Rightarrow 4(mp + nq)^2 = 4(m^2 + n^2)(p^2 + q^2)$

$\Rightarrow m^2q^2 + n^2p^2 - 2mnpq = 0$

$\Rightarrow (mq - np)^2 = 0 \Rightarrow mq - np = 0.$

25. (a) $\alpha + \beta = b$, $\alpha\beta = c$

Sum of roots of resulting equation = $(\alpha - 2) + (\beta - 2)$

$\Rightarrow (\alpha + \beta - 4) = b - 4$;

Product of roots resulting equation

$= (\alpha - 2)(\beta - 2) = \alpha\beta - 2(\alpha + \beta) + 4$

$= c - 2b + 4$

Now, $2 = b - 4$; $1 = c - 2b + 4$ etc.

26. (c) Given,

$f(x) = x^2 + ax + 2$ and $g(x) = x^2 + 2x + a$

Let α be the common root of $f(x) = 0$ and $g(x) = 0$.

∴ $\alpha^2 + a\alpha + 2 = 0$ ...(i)

and $\alpha^2 + 2\alpha + a = 0$ ...(ii)

Using elimination method,

$\alpha^2 + a\alpha = -2$

and $\alpha^2 + 2\alpha = -a$

$$\underline{\begin{array}{c} - \quad + \qquad + \\ a\alpha - 2\alpha = -2 + a \end{array}}$$

$\Rightarrow \alpha(-2 + a) = -2 + a \Rightarrow \alpha = \dfrac{-2 + a}{-2 + a} = 1$

Substitute value of α in (i) eqn., we get

∴ $-(a + 2) = 1 \Rightarrow a + 2 = -1 \Rightarrow a = -3$

Now $f(x) + g(x) = 0$

∴ $x^2 - 3x + 2 + x^2 + 2x - 3 = 0 \Rightarrow 2x^2 - x - 1 = 0$

So, sum of roots = $\dfrac{1}{2}$

27. (d) $x^2 - 6x - 2 = 0$

α and β are the roots of the above equation.

So, $\alpha^2 - 2 = 6\alpha$

Similarly, $\beta^2 - 2 = 6\beta$

We can see that, $\alpha + \beta = 6$ and $\alpha\beta = -2$

Given: $a_n = \alpha^n - \beta^n$

So, $\dfrac{a_{10} - 2a_8}{2a_9} = \dfrac{\alpha^{10} - \beta^{10} - 2(\alpha^8 - \beta^8)}{2(\alpha^9 - \beta^9)}$

$= \dfrac{\alpha^{10} - \beta^{10} + \alpha\beta(\alpha^8 - \beta^8)}{2(\alpha^9 - \beta^9)}$

$= \dfrac{\alpha^{10} - \alpha^9\beta - (\alpha\beta^9 + \beta^{10})}{2(\alpha^9 - \beta^9)}$

$= \dfrac{\alpha^9(\alpha + \beta) - \beta^9(\alpha - \beta)}{2(\alpha^9 - \beta^9)} = \dfrac{(\alpha + \beta)(\alpha^9 - \beta^9)}{2(\alpha^9 - \beta^9)}$

$= \dfrac{6}{2} = 3$ $(\because a + b = 6)$

28. (b) The given quadratic equation is, $nx^2 + 7\sqrt{n}\ x + n = 0$

Now, the discriminant,

$D = 49n - 4n^2 = n(49 - 4n)$

$D \neq 0$; $\therefore \forall n \in I^+$

$\Rightarrow$ Roots of the quadratic equation are distinct.

For real roots $D \geq 0$

$\Rightarrow n(49 - 4n) \geq 0 \Rightarrow n \leq \dfrac{49}{4}$

So, $n \in \{1, 2, 3, 4, ..., 12\}$

So, x have only finite value.

Product of roots $= \dfrac{n}{n} = 1$

$\Rightarrow$ Products of root is necessarily integer.

Hence, option (b) is correct.

29. **(b)** Let α, β be the roots of $x^2 - bx + 6 = 0$ and α, γ be the roots of $x^2 - 6x + c = 0$

$x^2 - bx + 6 = 0$; $\alpha + \beta = b$, $\alpha + \gamma = 6$

$x^2 - 6x + c = 0$; $\alpha\beta = 6$, $\alpha\gamma = c$

Given, $\dfrac{\beta}{\gamma} = \dfrac{3}{4}$

$\dfrac{\alpha\beta}{\alpha\gamma} = \dfrac{6}{c}$

$\dfrac{\beta}{\gamma} = \dfrac{6}{c} \Rightarrow \dfrac{3}{4} = \dfrac{6}{c} \therefore c = 8$

$\alpha\beta = 6$; $\alpha\gamma = 6$

HCF $(\alpha\beta, \alpha\gamma) = \alpha$

HCF $(6, 8) = 2$

$\alpha = 2$

30. **(c)** Let the common root be t

Then, the equation becomes

$2t^2 + kt - 5 = 0$ ...(i)

$t^2 - 3t - 4 = 0$ ...(ii)

Multiply equation (ii) by 2 and then subtract from equation (i)

$2t^2 + kt - 5 = 0$

$2t^2 - 6t - 8 = 0$

$\underline{\quad -\quad +\quad +\quad\quad\quad\quad}$

$(k + 6)t + 3 = 0$

$t = -\dfrac{3}{k + 6}$

Now, put the value of t in equation (i)

$2\left(\dfrac{-3}{k + 6}\right)^2 + k\left(\dfrac{-3}{k + 6}\right) - 5 = 0$

$\dfrac{18}{(k+6)^2} + \dfrac{-3}{k + 6} - 5 = 0$

$18 - 3k(k + 6) - 5(k + 6)2 = 0$

$18 - 3k2 - 18k - 5k2 - 180 - 60k = 0$

$-8k2 - 78k - 162 = 0$

$8k2 + 78k + 162 = 0$

$4k2 + 39x + 81 = 0$

$4k2 + 27k + 12k + 81 = 0$

$k(4k + 27) + 3(4k + 27) = 0$

$(k + 3)(4k + 27) = 0$

$k = -3, -\dfrac{27}{4}$

31. **(a)** $x = \dfrac{3 + \sqrt{5}}{2}$

$\Rightarrow x^3 = \left(\dfrac{3 + \sqrt{5}}{2}\right)^3 = \dfrac{27 + 5\sqrt{5} + 9\sqrt{5}(3 + \sqrt{5})}{8} = 9 + 4\sqrt{5}$

$\Rightarrow y = x^3 = 9 + 4\sqrt{5}$

$\Rightarrow$ One root is $9 + 4\sqrt{5}$ $\therefore$ other is root $9 - 4\sqrt{5}$

$\therefore$ Sum of roots $= 9 + 4\sqrt{5} + 9 - 4\sqrt{5} = 18$

Product of roots $= (9 + 4\sqrt{5})(9 - 4\sqrt{5}) = 1$

$\therefore$ Required equation is: $y^2 - 18y + 1 = 0$

32. **(c)** $D > 0$ (for real roots)

$\Rightarrow b^2 - 4 \times 2 \times \dfrac{1}{b} > 0 \Rightarrow \dfrac{b^3 - 8}{b} > 0$

$\Rightarrow \dfrac{(b - 2)(b^2 + 2b + 4)}{b} > 0$

$\Rightarrow b \in (-\infty, 0) \cup (2, \infty)$

Clearly options A and B are wrong

Let $f(b) = b^2 - 3b$

range of $f(b)$ when $b \in (-\infty, 0) \cup (2, \infty)$

$= (f(2), \infty) = (-2, \infty)$

$\Rightarrow b^2 - 3b > -2$ is correct

So, $b \in (-\infty, 0) \cup (2, \infty)$ is subset of solution set of $b^2 - 3b + 2 > 0$

Also D is wrong as $b^2 + \dfrac{1}{b^2} \in (0, \infty)$

33. **(c)** (i) For equal roots,

$D = 0 \Rightarrow b^2 - 4ac = 0$

$16 - 8(a + 5) = 0$

$a + 5 = 2$

$a = -3$

(ii) For distinct real roots,

$D > 0 \Rightarrow b^2 - 4ac > 0$

$a^2 + 12b(a + 4) > 0$

$9 + 12b > 0$

$b > -\dfrac{9}{12}$

$b > -\dfrac{3}{4}$

34. (d) The given quadratic equation is

$x^2 + (3 - \lambda)x + 2 = \lambda$

Sum of roots $= \alpha + \beta = \lambda - 3$

Product of roots $= \alpha\beta = 2 - \lambda$

$\alpha^2 + \beta^2 = (\alpha + \beta)^2 - 2\alpha\beta$

$= (\lambda - 3)^2 - 2(2 - \lambda)$

$= \lambda^2 - 4\lambda + 5$

$= (\lambda - 2)^2 + 1$

For least $(\alpha^2 + \beta^2)$, $\lambda = 2$.

35. (a) $\because \alpha + \beta = 64,\ \alpha\beta = 256$

$\dfrac{\alpha^{3/8}}{\beta^{5/8}} + \dfrac{\beta^{3/8}}{\alpha^{5/8}} = \dfrac{\alpha + \beta}{(\alpha\beta)^{5/8}} = \dfrac{64}{(2^8)^{5/8}} = \dfrac{64}{32} = 2$

36. (c) $(x + 2)(x - 1) = x^2 - 2x - 3$

$\Rightarrow \quad x^2 - x + 2x - 2 = x^2 - 2x - 3$

$\Rightarrow \quad x - 2 = -2x - 3 \Rightarrow 3x = -1 \Rightarrow x = \dfrac{-1}{3}$

37. (b) $4x^2 - \sqrt{3}x - 5 = 0$

$\Rightarrow \quad x^2 - \dfrac{\sqrt{3}}{4}x - \dfrac{5}{4} = 0$

$\Rightarrow \quad x^2 - 2 \cdot \dfrac{\sqrt{3}}{8} \cdot x + \left(\dfrac{\sqrt{3}}{8}\right)^2 - \left(\dfrac{\sqrt{3}}{8}\right)^2 - \dfrac{5}{4} = 0$

$\Rightarrow \quad \left(x - \dfrac{\sqrt{3}}{8}\right)^2 - \dfrac{3}{64} - \dfrac{5}{4} = 0 \Rightarrow \left(x - \dfrac{\sqrt{3}}{8}\right)^2 - \dfrac{83}{64} = 0$

Hence, the required constant that should be added and subtracted is $\dfrac{3}{64}$.

38. (c) $2x^2 - 7x + 6 = 2(2)^2 - 7(2) + 6$

$= 8 - 14 + 6 = 14 - 14 = 0$

39. (d) Compare the quadratic equation $2x^2 - kx + k = 0$ with the standard form of quadratic equation

$ax^2 + bx + c = 0;\ a = 2,\ b = -k,\ c = k$

For equal roots, discriminant, $D = 0$

$\Rightarrow \quad b^2 - 4ac = 0 \ \Rightarrow (-k)^2 - 4(2)(k) = 0$

$\Rightarrow \quad k^2 - 8k = 0 \Rightarrow k = 0, 8$

40. (c) Let $\alpha + 3 = x \ \therefore \alpha = x - 3$ (replace x by $x - 3$)

So the required equation

$(x - 3)^2 - 5(x - 3) + 6 = 0$

$\Rightarrow \quad x^2 - 6x + 9 - 5x + 15 + 6 = 0 \Rightarrow x^2 - 11x + 30 = 0$

$(x^2 - 11x + 30) \times 2 = 0 \Rightarrow 2x^2 - 22x + 60 = 0$

41. (b)   **42. (a)**

43. (b) Let the roots be α and β.

$\alpha + \beta = 8,\ |\alpha - \beta| = 10$

$(\alpha - \beta)^2 = 100 \Rightarrow (\alpha + \beta)^2 - 4\alpha\beta = 100 \Rightarrow \alpha\beta = -9$

$\therefore \quad x^2 - 8x - 9 = 0 \Rightarrow (x^2 - 8x - 9) = 0$

or $-(-x^2 + 8x + 9) = 0$

44. (d) Since, α and β are roots of $x^2 + 5x + a = 0$

$\therefore \quad \alpha + \beta = -5$ and $\alpha\beta = a$

Consider $2\alpha + 5\beta = -1$

$\Rightarrow \quad 2\alpha + 5(-5 - \alpha) = -1 \Rightarrow 2\alpha - 25 - 5\alpha = -1$

$\Rightarrow -3\alpha = 24 \Rightarrow \alpha = -8$ and $\beta = -5 + 8 = 3$

Also, $\alpha\beta = (3)(-8) = -24 = a$

45. (c) Let α and β be the roots of $x^2 + px + 8 = 0$

$\Rightarrow \quad \alpha + \beta = -p$ and $\alpha\beta = 8$

$\Rightarrow \quad \alpha(-p - \alpha) = 8 \Rightarrow -p\alpha - \alpha^2 = 8$

$\Rightarrow \quad \alpha^2 + p\alpha + 8 = 0 \qquad \qquad \text{... (i)}$

Also, given $\alpha - \beta = 2$

$\therefore \quad \alpha + \beta = -p$ and $\alpha - \beta = 2$ together gives

$2\alpha = 2 - p \Rightarrow p = 2 - 2\alpha$

Put value of 'p' in equation (i), we get

$\alpha^2 + (2 - 2\alpha)\alpha + 8 = 0 \Rightarrow \alpha^2 + 2\alpha - 2\alpha^2 + 8 = 0$

$\Rightarrow -\alpha^2 + 2\alpha + 8 = 0$

On solving this, we get, $\alpha = -2, 4$

$\therefore \quad p = \pm 6$ (when $\alpha = -2, 4$)

46. (b) Let the roots of the given equation be α and 3α.

Now, $\alpha + 3\alpha = -p$ and $\alpha(3\alpha) = 12$

$\Rightarrow 4\alpha = -p$ and $\alpha^2 = 4 \Rightarrow \alpha = \pm 2$

Now, $4(2) = -p$ and $4(-2) = -p \Rightarrow p = \pm 8$

47. (c) Given equation is

$x^2 - 3x + 2 = 0$

$\Rightarrow \quad x^2 - 2x - x + 2 = 0 \Rightarrow x(x-2) - 1(x-2) = 0$

$\Rightarrow \quad (x-1)(x-2) = 0 \Rightarrow x = 1, 2$

48. **(c)** Since $x = 2$ and $x = 3$ are roots of given equation

$\therefore \quad 3(2)^2 - 2p(2) + 2q = 0$

$\Rightarrow \quad 12 - 4p + 2q = 0 \Rightarrow -2p + q = -6 \quad \dots (i)$

and $\quad 3(3)^2 - 2p(3) + 2q = 0$

$\Rightarrow \quad 27 - 6p + 2q = 0 \Rightarrow -6p + 2q = -27 \quad \dots (ii)$

On solving (i) and (ii), we get

$p = \dfrac{15}{2}$ and $q = -6 + 15 = 9$

49. **(a)** Speed of Ajay's car $= (x + 5)$ km/h.

Distance = Speed × Time $= 2(x + 5)$ km

50. **(c)** $\dfrac{400}{x} - \dfrac{400}{x+5} = 4$

$\Rightarrow x^2 + 5x - 500 = 0$

51. **(a)** $(x + 25)(x - 20) = 0$

$\Rightarrow x = 20$ km/hour

52. **(d)** Speed of Ajay $= x + 5 = 25$ km/h.

Time $= \dfrac{400}{25} = 16$ hours.

53. **(c)** $(20 - x)$ km/hr

54. **(a)** Speed = Distance/Time

55. **(c)** $\dfrac{15}{20-x} - \dfrac{15}{20+x} = 1$

$\Rightarrow x^2 + 30x - 400 = 0$

56. **(b)** $(x - 10)(x + 40) = 0$

$\Rightarrow \quad x = 10$ km/hour

57. **(c)** Speed in downstream $= 20 + 10 = 30$ km/h

Time $= \dfrac{\text{Distance}}{\text{Speed}} = \dfrac{15}{30} = 30$ minutes

58. **(b)** Assertion : Given equation $x^2 - bx + c = 0$

Let α, β be two consecutive roots such that $|\alpha - \beta| = 1$

$\Rightarrow (\alpha + \beta)^2 - 4\alpha\beta = 1 \Rightarrow b^2 - 4c = 1$

Reason : Given equation :

$4abc\, x^2 + (b^2 - 4ac)\, x - b = 0$

$D = (b^2 - 4ac)^2 + 16ab^2c$

$D = (b^2 + 4ac)^2 > 0$

Hence, roots are real and unequal.

59. **(b)** Assertion and Reason both are true statements. But Reason is not the correct explanation.

Assertion : $(2x - 1)^2 - 4x^2 + 5 = 0 \Rightarrow -4x + 6 = 0$

Reason : $2x^2 - 6x = 0 \Rightarrow 2x(x - 3) = 0$

$\Rightarrow x = 0$ and $x = 3$.

60. **(a)** Assertion : $9x^2 + 3kx + 4 = 0$

$\Rightarrow D = b^2 - 4ac = (3k)^2 - 4(9)(4) = 9k^2 - 144$

For equal roots : $D = 0 \Rightarrow 9k^2 = 144$

$\Rightarrow k = \pm\dfrac{12}{3} \Rightarrow k = \pm 4$

61. **(c)** Reason is false.

Assertion : $4x^2 - 12x + 9 = 0$

$\Rightarrow D = b^2 - 4ac = (-12)^2 - 4(4)(9) = 144 - 144 = 0$

$\Rightarrow$ Roots are repeated.

62. **(c)** Assertion is correct. Reason is incorrect.

63. **(a)** Assertion and Reason both are correct and Reason is correct explanation.

Assertion : $2x^2 - 3x + 5 = 0$

$\Rightarrow \alpha + \beta = \dfrac{-b}{a} = \dfrac{-(-3)}{2} = \dfrac{3}{2}$ and $\alpha\beta = \dfrac{c}{a} = \dfrac{5}{2}$

64. (A) → s; (B) → p; (C) → q; (D) → r

(A) $6x^2 + x - 12 = 0$

$6x^2 + 9x - 8x - 12 = 0$

$3x(2x + 3) - 4(2x + 3) = 0$

$(3x - 4)(2x + 3x) = 0$

$x = \dfrac{4}{3}, \dfrac{-3}{2}$

(B) $8x^2 + 16x - 192 = 0$

$8x^2 + 48x - 32x - 192 = 0$

$8x(x + 6) - 32(x + 6) = 0$

$x = 4, -6$

(C) $x^2 - 45x + 324 = 0$

$x^2 - 36x - 9x + 324 = 0$

$x(x - 36) - 9(x - 36) = 0$

$2x(x - 3) + 1(x - 3) = 0$

$x = 9, 36.$

(D) $2x^2 - 5x - 3 = 0$

$2x^2 - 6x + x - 3 = 0$

$x = \dfrac{-1}{2}, 3$

65. (A) → q; (B) → r; (C) → s; (D) → p

66. (A) → (r,); (B) → (p,); (C) → (q) ; (D) → (s)

67. $\neq 0$

68. > 0

69. 5 cm, 12 cm.

70. $b^2 < 4ac$

71. 7 and -9

72. $x^2 - bx + ca = 0$

73. $\dfrac{b^2 - 2ac}{c^2}$

74. $x^2 - 8x + 15 = 0$

75. -1

76. $\dfrac{1}{2}(b - q)$

77. two

78. $b^2 < 4ac$

79. False

80. True

81. False

82. True

83. True

84. True

85. True

86. False

87. True

88. True

10 Arithmetic Progressions

DIRECTIONS: *This section contains multiple choice questions. Each question has 4 choices (a), (b), (c) and (d) out of which only one is correct.*

1. In an A.P. if $a = 5$, $a_n = 81$ and $S_n = 860$, then n is

    (a) 10　　(b) 15　　(c) 20　　(d) 25

2. What is the value of k if $(k + 2)$, $(4k - 6)$ and $(3k - 2)$ are three consecutive terms of an A.P.?

    (a) $k = -3$　(b) $k = 2$　(c) $k = -2$　(d) $k = 3$

3. The first term of an A.P. is 5 and its 100th term is -292. The 50th term of this A.P. will be

    (a) 142　　(b) -142　　(c) 130　　(d) -140

4. If a, b, c are in A.P., then the value of $(a + 2b - c)(2b + c - a)(c + a - b)$ will be

    (a) $4abc$　　　　　　(b) $2abc$

    (c) abc　　　　　　(d) None of these

5. Sum of n terms of the series
    $\sqrt{2} + \sqrt{8} + \sqrt{18} + \sqrt{32} + ...$ is

    (a) $\dfrac{n(n+1)}{2}$　　　　(b) $2n((n+1)$

    (c) $\dfrac{n(n+1)}{\sqrt{2}}$　　　　(d) 1

6. If eight times the 8th term of an A.P. is equal to 12 times the 12th term of the A.P. then its 20th term will be

    (a) -1　　(b) 1　　(c) 0　　(d) 2

7. The 10th term of an AP is 20 and the 19th term is 101. Then, the third term is

    (a) -43　(b) -61　(c) -52　(d) 1

8. Given that the sum of the first 'n' terms of an arithmetic progression is $2n^2 + 3n$, find the 12th term.

    (a) 7^2　　(b) 36　　(c) $\sqrt{625}$　　(d) 56

9. The common difference of the A.P. $\dfrac{1}{p}, \dfrac{1-p}{p}, \dfrac{1-2p}{p}, ...$ is

    (a) 1　　(b) $\dfrac{1}{p}$　　(c) -1　　(d) $-\dfrac{1}{p}$

10. The nth term of the A.P. $a, 3a, 5a, ...$, is
    (a) na　　　　　　(b) $(2n - 1)a$
    (c) $(2n + 1)a$　　　　(d) $2na$

11. If the sum of the series $2 + 5 + 8 + 11 ....$ is 60100, then the number of terms are

    (a) 100　　　　　　(b) 200
    (c) 150　　　　　　(d) 250

12. What is the common difference of four terms in A.P. such that the ratio of the product of the first and fourth term to that of the second and third term is 2 : 3 and the sum of all four terms is 20 ?

    (a) 3　　(b) 1　　(c) 4　　(d) 2

13. There are 60 terms in an A.P. of which the first term is 8 and the last term is 185. The 31st term is

    (a) 56　　(b) 94　　(c) 85　　(d) 98

14. There are four arithmetic means between 2 and -18. The means are
    (a) $-4, -7, -10, -13$　　(b) $1, -4, -7, -10$
    (c) $-2, -5, -9, -13$　　(d) $-2, -6, -10, -14$

15. If the first, second and the last terms of an A.P. are a, b, c respectively, then the sum is

    (a) $\dfrac{(a+b)(a+c-2b)}{2(b-a)}$　　(b) $\dfrac{(b+c)(a+b-2c)}{2(b-a)}$

    (c) $\dfrac{(a+c)(b+c-2a)}{2(b-a)}$　　(d) None of these

16. The sum of 11 terms of an A.P. whose middle term is 30, is
    (a) 320　　　　　　(b) 330
    (c) 340　　　　　　(d) 350

17. The first and last term of an A.P. are a and ℓ respectively. If S is the sum of all the terms of the A.P. and the common difference is $\dfrac{\ell^2 - a^2}{k - (\ell + a)}$, then k is equal to

(a) S (b) $2S$

(c) $3S$ (d) None of these

18. If four numbers in A.P. are such that their sum is 50 and the greatest number is 4 times the least, then the numbers are

(a) 5, 10, 15, 20   (b) 4, 10, 16, 22

(c) 3, 7, 11, 15   (d) None of these

19. Let T_r be the rth term of an A.P. for $r = 1, 2, 3, ...$ If for some positive integers m, n we have, $T_m = \dfrac{1}{n}$ and $T_n = \dfrac{1}{m}$, then T_{mn} equals

(a) $\dfrac{1}{mn}$ (b) $\dfrac{1}{m} + \dfrac{1}{n}$ (c) 1 (d) 0

20. If the sum of the first $2n$ terms of 2, 5, 8, ... is equal to the sum of the first n terms of 57, 59, 61......., then n is equal to

(a) 10   (b) 12   (c) 11   (d) 13

21. The number of terms of the series 5, 7, 9, ... that must be taken in order to have the sum 1020 is

(a) 20   (b) 30   (c) 40   (d) 50

22. If the nth term of an A.P. is $4n + 1$, then the common difference is :

(a) 3   (b) 4   (c) 5   (d) 6

23. If a, b, c, d, e, f are in A.P., then $e - c$ is equal to:

(a) $2(c - a)$ (b) $2(d - c)$

(c) $2(f - d)$ (d) $(d - c)$

24. The number of common terms of the two sequences 17, 21, 25, ..., 417 and 16, 21, 26, ..., 466 is

(a) 19   (b) 20   (c) 21   (d) 91

25. The number of two digit numbers which are divisible by 3 is

(a) 33   (b) 31   (c) 30   (d) 29

26. If the nth term of an A.P. is given by $a_n = 5n - 3$, then the sum of first 10 terms is

(a) 225   (b) 245   (c) 255   (d) 270

27. If $S_1, S_2, S_3, ..., S_r$ are the sum of first n terms of r arithmetic progressions respectively. Whose first terms are 1, 2, 3, ... and whose common differences are 1, 3, 5, ... respectively, then the value of $S_1 + S_2 + S_3 + ... S_r$ is

(a) $\dfrac{(nr-1)(nr+1)}{2}$ (b) $\dfrac{(nr+1)nr}{2}$

(c) $\dfrac{(nr-1)nr}{2}$ (d) $\dfrac{n(nr+1)}{2}$

28. First term of an arithmetic progression is 2. If the sum of its first five terms is equal to one-fourth of the sum of the next five terms, then the sum of its first 30 terms is

(a) 2670   (b) 2610   (c) –2520   (d) –2550

29. The odd natural numbers have been divided in groups as (1, 3) ; (5,7, 9, 11) ; (13, 15, 17, 19, 21, 23), ...

Then the sum of numbers in the 10th group is

(a) 4000   (b) 4003   (c) 4007   (d) 4008

30. Suppose the sum of the first m terms of an arithmetic progression is n and the sum of its first n terms is m, where $m \neq n$. Then, the sum of the first $(m + n)$ terms of the arithmetic progression is

(a) $1 - mn$ (b) $mn - 5$

(c) $-(m + n)$ (d) $m + n$

31. Let $a_n, n \geq 1$, be an arithmetic progression with first term 2 and common difference 4. Let M_n be the average of the first n terms.

Then the sum is $\displaystyle\sum_{n=1}^{10} M_n$

(a) 110   (b) 335   (c) 770   (d) 1100

32. Which of the following represents an A.P. ?

(a) 0.2, 0.4, 0.6, ...   (b) 29, 58, 116....

(c) 15, 45, 135, 405...   (d) 3, 3.5, 4.5, 8.5 ....

33. If $t_n = 6n + 5$, then $t_{n+1} =$

(a) $6(n + 1) + 17$ (b) $6(n - 1) + 11$

(c) $6n + 11$ (d) $6n - 11$

34. Summation of n terms of an A.P. is

(a) $\dfrac{n}{2}(2a + l)$ (b) $\dfrac{n}{2}\left[2a + (n-1)d\right]$

(c) $\dfrac{a(r^n - 1)}{(r - 1)}$ (d) $\dfrac{a(1 - r^n)}{(1 - r)}$

35. $S_n = 54 + 51 + 48 + ... n$ terms $= 513$. Least value of n is

(a) 18   (b) 19

(c) 15   (d) None of these

36. If the nth term of an A.P. be $(2n - 1)$, then the sum of its first n terms will be

(a) $n^2 - 1$ (b) $(n - 1)^2$

(c) $(n - 1)^2 - (2n - 1)$ (d) n^2

37. If $\dfrac{b+c-a}{a}, \dfrac{c+a-b}{b}, \dfrac{a+b-c}{c}$ are in A.P., then which of the following is in A.P.?

(a) a, b, c (b) a^2, b^2, c^2

(c) $\dfrac{1}{a}, \dfrac{1}{b}, \dfrac{1}{c}$ (d) a^3, b^3, c^3

Arithmetic Progressions

Case/Passage Based Questions

DIRECTIONS : *Study the given Case/Passage and answer the following questions.*

Case/Passage-I

India is competitive manufacturing location due to the low cost of manpower and strong technical and engineering capabilities contributing to higher quality production runs. The production of TV sets in a factory increases uniformly by a fixed number every year. It produced 16000 sets in 6th year and 22600 in 9th year.

[From CBSE Question Bank 2021]

Based on the above information, answer the following questions:

38. Find the production during first year.

39. Find the production during 8th year.

40. Find the production during first 3 years.

41. In which year, the production is Rs 29,200.

42. Find the difference of the production during 7th year and 4th year.

Case/Passage-II

Your friend Veer wants to participate in a 200m race. He can currently run that distance in 51 seconds and with each day of practice it takes him 2 seconds less.He wants to do in 31 seconds .

[From CBSE Question Bank 2021]

43. Which of the following terms are in AP for the given situation

    (a) 51,53,55....   (b) 51, 49, 47....

    (c) –51, –53, –55....   (d) 51, 55, 59...

44. What is the minimum number of days he needs to practice till his goal isachieved

    (a) 10   (b) 12   (c) 11   (d) 9

45. Which of the following term is not in the AP of the above given situation

    (a) 41   (b) 30   (c) 37   (d) 39

46. If n^{th} term of an AP is given by $a_n = 2n + 3$ then common difference of an AP is

    (a) 2   (b) 3   (c) 5   (d) 1

47. The value of x, for which 2x, x+ 10, 3x + 2 are three consecutive terms of an AP

    (a) 6   (b) –6   (c) 18   (d) –18

Assertion & Reason

DIRECTIONS : *Each of these questions contains an Assertion followed by Reason. Read them carefully and answer the question on the basis of following options. You have to select the one that best describes the two statements.*

(a) If both **Assertion** and **Reason** are **correct** and Reason is the **correct explanation** of Assertion.

(b) If both **Assertion** and **Reason** are correct, but Reason is **not the correct explanation** of Assertion.

(c) If **Assertion** is **correct** but **Reason** is **incorrect**.

(d) If **Assertion** is **incorrect** but **Reason** is **correct**.

48. **Assertion :** Let the positive numbers a, b, c be in A.P., then $\dfrac{1}{bc}, \dfrac{1}{ac}, \dfrac{1}{ab}$ are also in A.P.

    Reason : If each term of an A.P. is divided by abc, then the resulting sequence is also in A.P.

49. **Assertion :** The sum of the series with the nth term, $t_n = (9 - 5n)$ is (465), when no. of terms $n = 15$.

    Reason : Given series is in A.P. and sum of n terms of an A.P. is $S_n = \dfrac{n}{2}\big[2a + (n-1)d\big]$.

50. **Assertion :** Sum of first 10 terms of the arithmetic progression $- 0.5, - 1.0, - 1.5, \dots\dots\dots\dots$ is 27.5.

    Reason : Sum of n terms of an A.P. is given as $S_n = \dfrac{n}{2}[2a + (n-1)d]$ where a = first term, d = common difference.

51. **Assertion :** Sum of first hundred even natural numbers divisible by 5 is 500.

    Reason : Sum of first n-terms of an A.P. is given by $S_n = \dfrac{n}{2}[a + \ell]$ where ℓ = last term.

52. **Assertion :** If n^{th} term of an A.P. is $7 - 4n$, then its common difference is –4.

    Reason : Common difference of an A.P. is given by $d = a_{n+1} - a_n$.

53. **Assertion :** If S_n is the sum of the first n terms of an A.P., then its nth term a_n is given by $a_n = S_n - S_{n-1}$.

    Reason : The 10th term of the A.P. 5, 8, 11, 14, $\dots\dots\dots$ is 35.

54. **Assertion :** Arithmetic between 8 and 12 is 10.

Reason : Arithmetic between two numbers 'a' and 'b' is given as $\dfrac{a+b}{2}$.

Match the Following

DIRECTIONS : *Each question contains statements given in two columns which have to be matched. Statements (A, B, C, D) in column-I have to be matched with statements (p, q, r, s) in column-II.*

55.

Column -I (A.P.)	Column-II (Common Difference)
(A) $1, \dfrac{3}{2}, 2, \dfrac{5}{2}, \dots$	(p) -4
(B) $\dfrac{1}{3}, \dfrac{5}{3}, \dfrac{9}{3}, \dfrac{13}{3}, \dots$	(q) 0.2
(C) 1.8, 2.0, 2.2, 2.4	(r) $4/3$
(D) 0, -4, -8, -12	(s) $1/2$

56.

Column-I (A.P.)	Column-II (n^{th} term)
(A) 119, 136, 153, 170	(p) $13 - 3n$
(B) 7, 11, 15, 19, ...	(q) $9 - 5n$
(C) 4, -1, -6, -11, ...	(r) $3 + 4n$
(D) 10, 7, 4, 3, ...	(s) $17n + 102$

Fill in the Blanks

DIRECTIONS : *Complete the following statements with an appropriate word / term to be filled in the blank space(s).*

57. 4, 10, 16, 22, ..., ...

58. 1, -1, -3, -5, ..., ...

59. 11th term from last term of an A.P. 10, 7, 4........., -62, is ....

60. In a flower bed, there are 23 rose plants in the first row, 21 in the second, 19 in the third, and so on. There are 5 rose plants in the last row. Number of rows in the flower bed is ....

61. Sum of $1 + 3 + 5 + ... + 1999$ is ....

62. The sum of 8 A.Ms between 3 and 15 is ....

63. The sum of n terms of an A.P. is $4n^2 - n$. The common difference = ...

64. The difference of corresponding terms of two A.P's will be ....

65. Sum of all the integers between 100 and 1000 which are divisible by 7 is ....

True / False

DIRECTIONS : *Read the following statements and write your answer as true or false.*

66. In an AP with first term a and common difference d, the nth term (or the general term) is given by $a_n = a + (n - 1)d$.

67. If ℓ is the last term of the finite AP, say the nth term, then the sum of all terms of the AP is given by :

$$S = \frac{n}{2}(a + \ell)$$

68. The balance money (in ₹) after paying 5% of the total loan of ₹ 1000 every month is 950, 900, 850, 800, . . . 50. represented A.P.

69. 2, 4, 8, 16, ... is not an A.P.

70. 10th term of A.P. 2, 7, 12, ... is 45.

71. 301 is a term of A.P. 5, 11, 17, 23, ...

72. The general form of an A.P. is a, $a + d$, $a + 2d$, $a + 3d$, ...

73. In an Arithmetic progression, the first term is denoted by 'a' and 'd' is called the common difference.

74. If $a_{n+1} - a_n$ = same for all 'n', then the given numbers form an A.P.

75. If S_n of A.P. is $3n^2 + 2n$, then the first term of A.P. is 3.

ANSWER KEY & SOLUTIONS

1. **(c)** $S_n = \dfrac{n}{2}(a + a_n)$

$\Rightarrow 860 = \dfrac{n}{2}(5 + 81)$

$n = 860 \div 43 = 20$

2. **(d)** $(k + 2)$, $(4k - 6)$ and $(3k - 2)$ are in A.P.

$\Rightarrow 4k - 6 - k - 2 = 3k - 2 - 4k + 6$

$\Rightarrow 3k - 8 = -k + 4 \Rightarrow 3k + k = 4 + 8$

$\Rightarrow 4k = 12 \Rightarrow k = \dfrac{12}{4} = 3$

3. **(b)** $a = 5$, $t_{100} = -292$

$t_{100} = 5 + (100 - 1)d$

$\qquad\qquad [\text{using } t_n = a + (n - 1)d]$

$\Rightarrow -292 = 5 + 99d$

$\Rightarrow -292 - 5 = 99d$

$\Rightarrow d = \dfrac{-297}{99} \Rightarrow d = -3$

$\therefore\ t_{50} = 5 + (50 - 1)(-3) = 5 + (-147)$

$= 5 - 147 \Rightarrow t_{50} = -142$

4. **(a)** Let a, b, c are in A.P.

$\therefore\ b - a = c - b \Rightarrow 2b = a + c$

So the given expression becomes

$(a + a + c - c)(a + c + c - a)(2b - b)$

$= (2a)(2c)(b) = 4abc$

5. **(c)** Here, $a_1 = \sqrt{2}$, $a_2 = \sqrt{8} = 2\sqrt{2}$

$\therefore\quad d = 2\sqrt{2} - \sqrt{2} = \sqrt{2}, a = \sqrt{2}$

$S_n = \dfrac{n}{2}\left[2a + (n - 1)d\right]$

$= \dfrac{n}{2}\left[2 \times \sqrt{2} + (n - 1)\sqrt{2}\right] = \dfrac{n(n+1)}{\sqrt{2}}$

6. **(c)** $t_8 = a + 7d$, $t_{12} = a + 11d$

According to question, $8t_8 = 12t_{12}$ (given)

$\Rightarrow\ 8(a + 7d) = 12(a + 11d)$

$\Rightarrow\ 8a + 56d = 12a + 132d$

$\Rightarrow\ 8a - 12a + 56d - 132d = 0$

$\Rightarrow\ -4a - 76d = 0$

$\Rightarrow a + 19d = 0 \qquad\qquad \text{...(i)}$

$\therefore\quad t_{20} = a + 19d = 0$ using (i)

$\therefore\quad t_{20} = 0$

7. **(a)** Given that,

$t_{10} = a + 9d = 20 \qquad\qquad \text{....(i)}$

and $t_{19} = a + 18d = 101 \qquad \text{....(ii)}$

By solving equations (i) and (ii), we get

$a = -61$, $d = 9$

$t^3 = a + 2d = -61 + 2 \times 9 = -43$

8. **(a)** $S_n = 2n^2 + 3n$

$a_n = S_n - S_{n-1}$

$\quad a_{12} = S_{12} - S_{11}$

$= 2(12)^2 + 3(12) - (2(11)^2 + 3(11))$

$= 288 + 36 - (242 + 33) = 288 + 36 - 242 - 33$

$= 46 + 3 = 49 = 7^2$

9. **(c)** $d = \dfrac{1 - p}{p} - \dfrac{1}{p} = \dfrac{1 - p - 1}{p} = \dfrac{-p}{p} = -1$

10. **(b)** $a_n = a + (n - 1)d = a + (n - 1)2a$

$\qquad\qquad\qquad\qquad [\because d = 3a - a = 2a]$

$= a + 2an - 2a = 2an - a = (2n - 1)a$

11. **(b)**

12. **(d)** Take the four terms as $a - 3x$, $a - x$, $a + x$, $a + 3x$

The sum $= 4a = 20 \Rightarrow a = 5$

Also, $3(a^2 - (3x)^2) = 2(a^2 - x^2)$

$\Rightarrow x = 1$

However, the common difference is $2x$ and not x

$\therefore\quad$ When $x = 1$, $d = 2x = 2$

13. **(d)** Let d be the common difference

then 60th term $= 8 + 59d = 185$

$\Rightarrow\ 59d = 177$

$\Rightarrow d = 3$

$\Rightarrow\ $ 31st term $= 8 + 30 \times 3 = 98.$

14. (d) Let the means be X_1, X_2, X_3, X_4 and the common difference be b; then 2, X_1, X_2, X_3, X_4, –18 are in A.P.;

$\Rightarrow \quad -18 = 2 + 5b$

$\Rightarrow \quad 5b = -20$

$\Rightarrow b = -4$

Hence, $X_1 = 2 + b = 2 + (-4) = -2;$

$X_2 = 2 + 2b = 2 - 8 = -6$

$X_3 = 2 + 3b = 2 - 12 = -10;$

$X_4 = 2 + 4b = 2 - 16 = -14$

The required means are –2, –6, –10, –14.

15. (c)

16. (b)

17. (b) We have, $S = \dfrac{n}{2}(a+\ell) \Rightarrow \dfrac{2S}{a+\ell} = n \qquad \ldots(i)$

Also, $\ell = a + (n-1)d \Rightarrow d = \dfrac{\ell-a}{n-1} = \dfrac{\ell-a}{\dfrac{2S}{a+\ell}-1}$

$= \dfrac{\ell^2 - a^2}{2S - (\ell+a)} \qquad \therefore \ k = 2S$

18. (a)

19. (c)

20. (c) Given, $\dfrac{2n}{2}\{2.2 + (2n-1)3\} = \dfrac{n}{2}\{2.57 + (n-1)2\}$

or $\quad 2(6n+1) = 112 + 2n$

or $10n = 110 \ \therefore \ n = 11$

21. (b)

22. (b)

23. (b) Let x be the common difference of the A.P. $a, b, c, d, e, f.$

$\therefore \quad e = a + (5-1)x$

$\qquad [\because a_n = a + (n-1)d]$

$\Rightarrow \quad e = a + 4x \qquad \ldots(i)$

and $c = a + 2x \qquad \ldots(ii)$

$\therefore \quad$ Using equations (i) and (ii), we get

$\qquad e - c = a + 4x - a - 2x$

$\Rightarrow e - c = 2x = 2(d-c).$

24. (b) Common terms will be 21, 41, 61, ...

$21 + (n-1)\,20 \leq 417$

$\Rightarrow n \leq 20.8 \Rightarrow n = 20$

25. (c) Two digit numbers which are divisible by 3 are 12, 15, 18,..., 99;

So, $99 = 12 + (n-1) \times 3.$

26. (b) Putting $n = 1, 10$, we get $a = 2, l = 47$.

$\therefore \quad S_{10} = \dfrac{10}{2}(2+47) = 5 \times 49 = 245.$

27. (b) $S_1 = \dfrac{n}{2}[2(1) + (n-1)(1)]$

$S_2 = \dfrac{n}{2}[2(2) + (n-1)(3)]$

$S_3 = \dfrac{n}{2}[2(3) + (n-1)(5)]$

$\cdots\cdots\cdots\cdots\cdots\cdots\cdots\cdots\cdots$
$\cdots\cdots\cdots\cdots\cdots\cdots\cdots\cdots\cdots$
$\cdots\cdots\cdots\cdots\cdots\cdots\cdots\cdots\cdots$

$S_r = \dfrac{n}{2}[2(r) + (n-1)(2r-1)]$

Adding $S_1, S_2, S_3, \ldots, S_r$, we have

$S_1 + S_2 + \ldots + S_r = \dfrac{n}{2}\left[(2)\dfrac{r(r+1)}{2} + (n-1)\dfrac{r}{2}[1+2r-1]\right]$

$= \dfrac{n}{2}\left[r(r+1) + (n-1)r^2\right]$

$= \dfrac{nr}{2}[r+1+nr-r] = \dfrac{nr}{2}[nr+1]$

28. (d) $a = 2, d = d,$

According to question,

$S_5 = \dfrac{1}{4}(S_{10} - S_5),\ 4S_5 = S_{10} - S_5,\ 5S_5 = S_{10}$

$5\left[\dfrac{5}{2}\{2\times 2 + (5-1)d\}\right] = \dfrac{10}{2}[2\times 2 + (10-1)d]$

$\left\{S_n = \dfrac{n}{2}(2a + (n-1)d)\right\}$

$\Rightarrow \quad 5\times\dfrac{5}{2}(4+4d)\ \dfrac{10}{2}[4+9d]$

$\Rightarrow \quad 20 + 20d = 8 + 18d$

$\Rightarrow \quad d = -6$

$S_{30} = \dfrac{30}{2}[2\times 2 + (30-1)(-6)] = \dfrac{30}{2}[4 + 29\times(-6)]$

$= \dfrac{30}{2}\times(-170) = \dfrac{-5100}{2} = -2550$

29. (a) Since, the general term of sum of odd natural number in the group is $= n\,(2n)^2 = 4n \times n^2 = 4n^3$

Hence, the required sum of numbers in the 10th group $= 4 \times 10^3 = 4000$

30. **(c)** Given, $S_m = n$ and $S_n = m$

$$S_m = \frac{m}{2}[2a + (m-1)d] = n \qquad \text{...(i)}$$

$$S_n = \frac{n}{2}[2a + (n-1)d] = m \qquad \text{...(ii)}$$

On subtracting Eq. (ii) from Eq. (i), we get

$$\frac{(m-n)}{2}2a + [m(m-1) - n(n-1)]\frac{d}{2} = n - m$$

$$(m-n)a + (m-n)(m+n-1)\frac{d}{2} = -(m-n)$$

$$\Rightarrow 2a + (m+n-1)\,d = -2 \qquad [m \neq n]$$

$$\therefore \quad S_{m+n} = \frac{m+n}{2}[(2a + (m+n-1)d]$$

$$= \frac{m+n}{2}(-2) = -(m+n)$$

31. **(a)** $a_1 = 2, d = 4$

$$M_n = \frac{\dfrac{n}{2}[2a_1 + (n-1)d]}{n} = 2(n+1) - 2 = 2n$$

$$\therefore \quad \sum_{n=1}^{10} M_n = 2\sum_{n=1}^{10} n = 110$$

32. **(a)** Since there is a common difference option (a),
$d = 0.4 - 0.2 = 0.6 - 0.4 = 0.2$

33. **(c)** Put $n + 1$ in place of n in $T_n = 6n + 5$

34. **(b)**

35. **(a)** $S_n = 513; \dfrac{n}{2}[2(54) + (n-1)(-3)] = 513$

$$\Rightarrow n(108 - 3n + 3) = 1026$$
$$\Rightarrow n^2 - 37n + 342 = 0$$
$$\Rightarrow n^2 - 19n - 18n + 342 = 0$$
$$\Rightarrow n(n - 19) - 18(n - 19) = 0$$
$$\Rightarrow (n - 18)(n - 19) = 0 \Rightarrow n = 18 \text{ or } n = 19$$

36. **(d)** $t_1 = 2(1) - 1 = 1$
$t_2 = 2(2) - 1 = 3, t_3 = 2(3) - 1 = 5$ and so on.
$\therefore \quad t_1 + t_2 + t_3 + \ldots + t_n = 1 + 3 + 5 + \ldots[2(n) - 1]$

$$= \frac{n}{2}[2 + (n-1)2] = \frac{n}{2}(2 + 2n - 2) = n^2$$

37. **(c)** $\dfrac{b+c-a}{a}, \dfrac{c+a-b}{b}, \dfrac{a+b-c}{c}$ are in A.P.

Adding 2 to each term

$$\frac{b+c-a}{a} + 2, \frac{c+a-b}{b} + 2, \frac{a+b-c}{c} + 2 \text{ are in A.P.}$$

$$\frac{a+b+c}{a}, \frac{a+b+c}{b}, \frac{a+b+c}{c} \text{ are in A.P.}$$

Dividing each term by $(a + b + c)$,

$$\frac{a+b+c}{a(a+b+c)}, \frac{a+b+c}{b(a+b+c)}, \frac{a+b+c}{c(a+b+c)} \text{ are in A.P.}$$

$$\frac{1}{a}, \frac{1}{b}, \frac{1}{c} \text{ are in A.P.}$$

38. Given that
$a_6 = a + 5d = 16000 \qquad \ldots (i)$
$a_9 = a + 8d = 22600 \qquad \ldots (ii)$

$$\underline{\quad - \quad - \quad - \quad}$$

$$-3d = -6600 \Rightarrow d = 2200$$
$$\Rightarrow \quad a = 5000$$

$\therefore \quad$ Production during first year = 5000

39. Production during 8th year is $(a + 7d) = 5000 + 2(2200)$

$$= 20400$$

40. Production during first 3 year = 5000 + 7200 + 9400

$$= 21600$$

41. $5000 + (n - 1)\,2200 = 29200 \Rightarrow n = 12^{th}$ year

42. Difference $= (a + 6d) - (a + 3d) = 3d = 6600$

43. **(b)**

44. **(c)** $a_n = 51 - (n - 1)2 = 31 \Rightarrow n = 11$

45. **(b)** $a_n = 51 - (n - 1)2 = 30 \Rightarrow n = 11.5$ (not possible)

46. **(a)** $d = a_2 - a_1 = [2(2) + 3] - [2(1) + 3] = 2$

47. **(a)** $2(x + 10) = 2x + 3x + 2 \Rightarrow x = 6$

48. **(a)** $\qquad$ **49.** **(d)**

50. **(a)** Both are correct. Reason is the correct reasoning for assertion.

Assertion : $S_{10} = \dfrac{10}{2}[2(-0.5) + (10-1)\,(-0.5)]$

$$= 5[-1 - 4.5] = 5(-5.5) = 27.5$$

51. **(d)** Assertion is incorrect.

Assertion : Even natural numbers divisible by 5 are 10, 20, 30, 40, ...

They form an A.P. with $a = 10, d = 10$

$$S_{100} = \frac{100}{2}[2(10) + 99(10)] = 50500$$

Reason is correct.

52. **(a)** Both are correct. Reason is the correct explanation.

Assertion : $a_n = 7 - 4n$

$d = a_{n+1} - a_n = 7 - 4\,(n+1) - (7 - 4n)$

$= 7 - 4n - 4 - 7 + 4n = -4.$

53. **(c)** Assertion is correct. Reason is incorrect.

$a_{10} = a + 9d = 5 + 9(3) = 5 + 27 = 32.$

54. **(a)** Both are correct and Reason is the correct explanation for the Assertion.

55. (A) → (s); (B) → (r); (C) → (q); (D) → (p)

(A) Common difference $= d = \dfrac{3}{2} - 1 = \dfrac{1}{2}$

(B) $d = \dfrac{5}{3} - \dfrac{1}{3} = \dfrac{4}{3}$

(C) $d = 2 - 1.8 = 0.2$

(D) $d = -4 - 0 = -4.$

56. (A) → (s); (B) → (r); (C) → (q); (D) → (p)

$13 - 3n = 13 - 3(1) = 10$

$9 - 5n = 9 - 5(1) = 4$

$3 + 4n = 3 + 4(1) = 7$

$17n + 102 = 17(1) + 102 = 119$

57. 28, 34

58. −7, −9

59. −32

60. n = 10

61. $\dfrac{1000}{2}[2(1) + (1000 - 1)2]$

62. $72\left[8\left(\dfrac{3+15}{2}\right)\text{etc.}\right]$

63. 11 [$S_2 = 4(2)^2 - 2 \Rightarrow 14$

$\quad\quad S_1 = 4(1)^2 - 1 \Rightarrow 3$ etc.]

64. another A.P.

65. 70336 [Hint : S = 105 + 112 + ... 994 and 105 + (n − 1)7

$\quad$ = 994 ⇒ 105 + 7n − 7 = 994 ⇒ n = 128 etc.]

66. True

67. True

68. True

69. True

70. False

71. False

72. True

73. True

74. True

75. False

First term $= a = a_1 = 3\,(1)^2 + 2(1) = 5$

11 Circles

➤ **Multiple Choice Questions (MCQs)** ———— »»»

DIRECTIONS : *This section contains multiple choice questions. Each question has 4 choices (a), (b), (c) and (d) out of which only one is correct.*

1. Two circles with centres O and P, and radii 8 cm and 4 cm touch each other externally. Find the length of their common tangent QR.

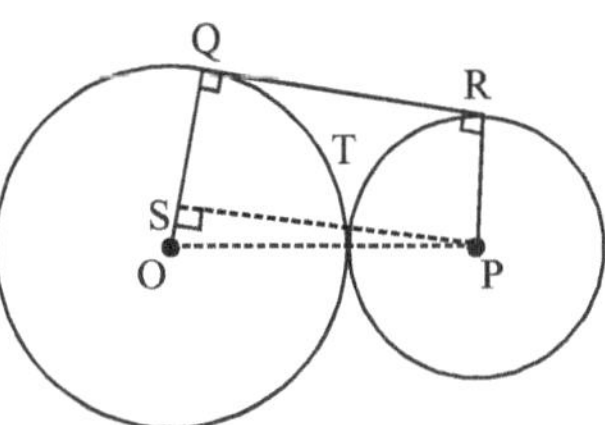

(a) 8 cm   (b) 7 cm   (c) $8\sqrt{2}$ cm   (d) $7\sqrt{3}$ cm

2. Two chords AB and CD of a circle intersect each other at P outside the circle. If AB = 5 cm, BP = 3 cm and PD = 2 cm, find CD.

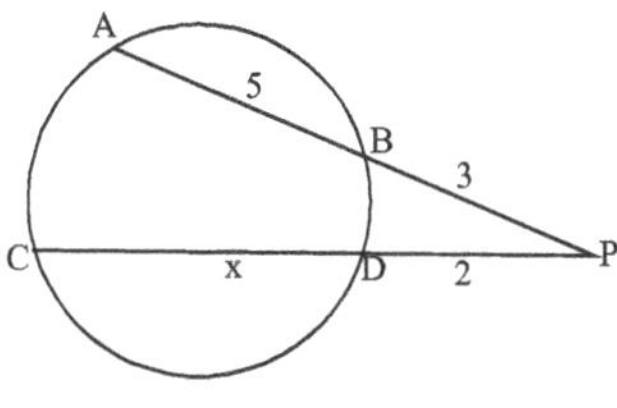

(a) 4 cm   (b) 5 cm   (c) 8 cm   (d) 10 cm

3. A ball is in the rest position against a step PQ. If PQ = 10 cm and QR = 15 cm, then find diameter of the ball.

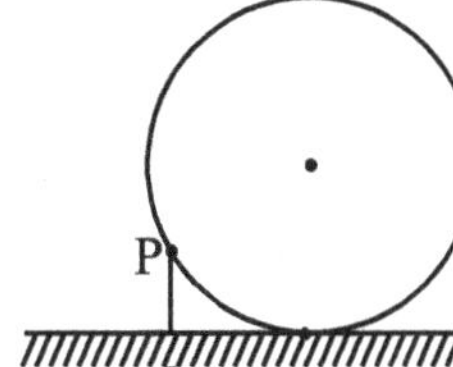

(a) 16 cm

(b) 32.5 cm

(c) 28 cm

(d) 42 cm

4. In the given figure, PA and PB are two tangents to the circle with centre O. If ∠APB = 40°, find ∠AQB and ∠AMB.

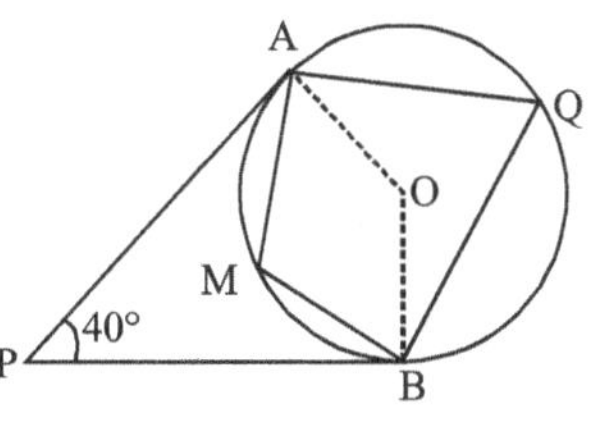

(a) ∠AQB = 70°, ∠AMB = 110°

(b) ∠AQB = 110°, ∠AMB = 70°

(c) ∠AQB = 100°, ∠AMB = 50°

(d) ∠AQB = 60° ∠AMB = 40°

5. A tangent CQ touches a circle with centre O at P. Diameter AB is produced to meet the tangent at C. If ∠ACP = a° and ∠BPC = b°, the relation connecting a and b is

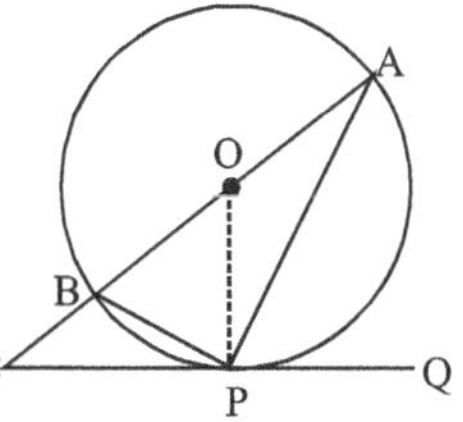

(a) a° + b° = 180°   (b) a° + 2b° = 90°

(c) a° − b° = 60°   (d) 2a° + b° = 100°

6. PQ is a tangent drawn from a point P to a circle with centre O and QOR is a diameter of the circle such that ∠POR = 120°, then ∠OPQ is

(a) 60°   (b) 45°   (c) 30°   (d) 90°

7. If a regular hexagon is inscribed in a circle of radius r, then its perimeter is

(a) $3r$ (b) $6r$ (c) $9r$ (d) $12r$

8. AB and CD are two chords of a circle intersecting at the point P outside the circle. If PA = 12 cm, CD = 7cm and PC = 15 cm, then AB is equal to

(a) 15.5 cm   (b) 4 cm

(c) 8 cm   (d) 10 cm

9. In the figure below (not to scale), AB = CD and $\overline{AB}$ and $\overline{CD}$ are produced to meet at the point p.

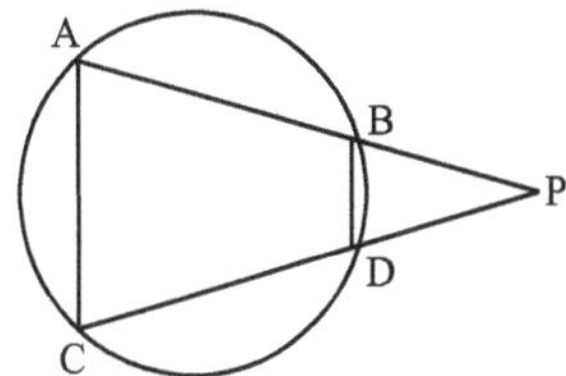

If ∠BAC = 70°, then ∠P is

(a) 30°   (b) 40°   (c) 45°   (d) 50°

10. In the adjoining figure, TP and TQ are the two tangents to a circle with centre O. If $\angle POQ = 110°$, then $\angle PTQ$ is

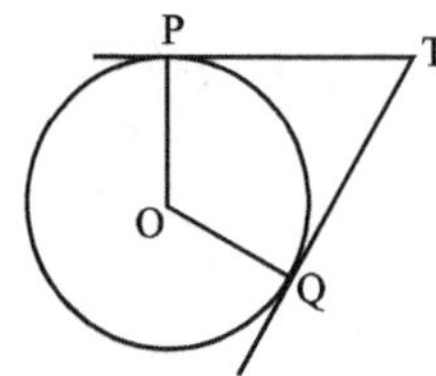

(a) 60° (b) 70° (c) 80° (d) 90°

11. In the diagram below, if l and m are two tangents and AB is a chord making an angle of 60° with the tangent l, then the angle between l and m is

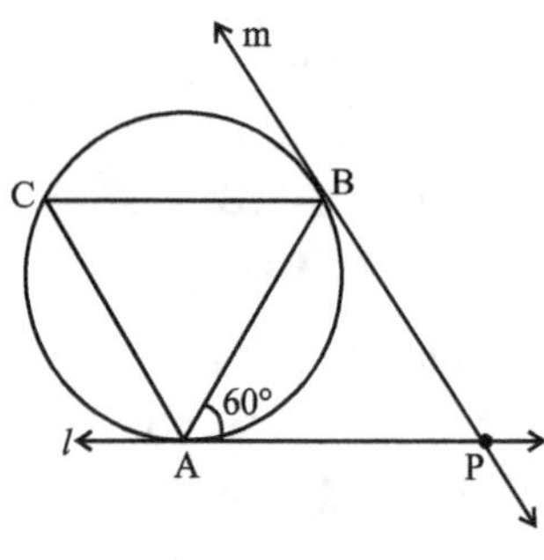

(a) 45° (b) 30° (c) 60° (d) 90°

12. In the diagram, O is the centre of the circle and D, E and F are mid points of AB, BO and OA respectively. If $\angle DEF = 30°$, then $\angle ACB$ is

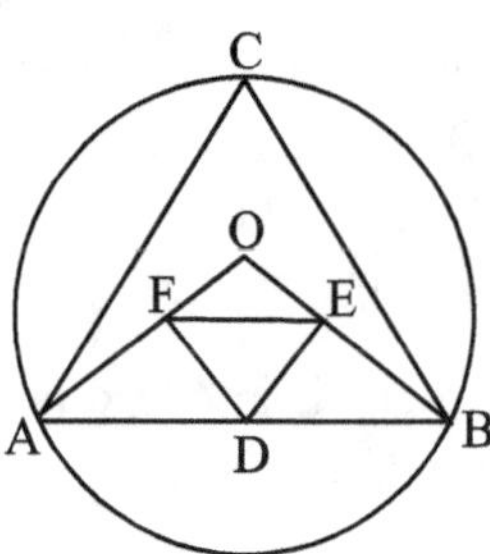

(a) 30° (b) 60° (c) 90° (d) 120°

13. In the below diagram, O is the centre of the circle, AC is the diameter and if $\angle APB = 120°$, then $\angle BQC$ is

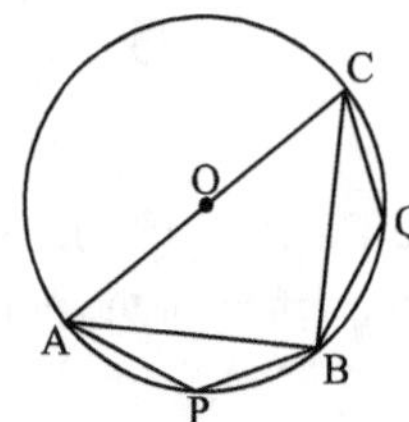

(a) 30° (b) 150° (c) 90° (d) 120°

14. In two concentric circles, if chords are drawn in the outer circle which touch the inner circle, then

(a) all chords are of different lengths.

(b) all chords are of same length.

(c) only parallel chords are of same length.

(d) only perpendicular chords are of same length.

15. Number of tangents to a circle which are parallel to a secant, is

(a) 3 (b) 2 (c) 1 (d) infinite

16. AB and CD are two common tangents to circles which touch each other at a point C. If D lies on AB such that $CD = 4$ cm, then AB is

(a) 12 cm (b) 8 cm (c) 4 cm (d) 6 cm

17. In the figure, $\triangle APB$ is formed by three tangents to the circle with centre O. If $\angle APB = 40°$, then the measure of $\angle BOA$ is

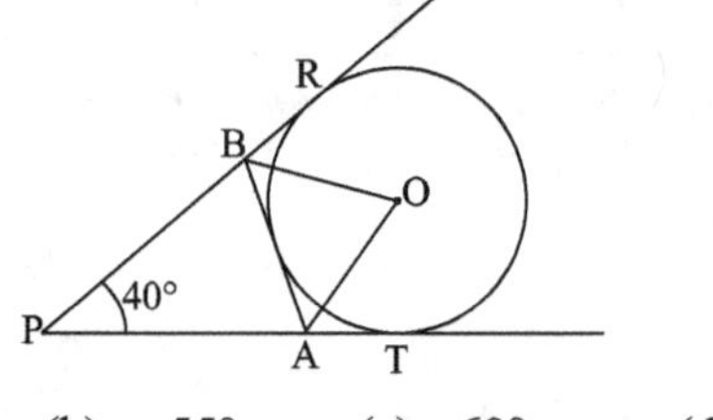

(a) 50° (b) 55° (c) 60° (d) 70°

18. Three circles with radii R_1, R_2 and r touch each other externally as shown in the adjoining figure. If PQ is their common tangent and $R_1 > R_2$, then which of the following relations is correct?

(a) $R_1 - R_2 = r$

(b) $R_1 + R_2 = 2r$

(c) $\dfrac{1}{R_1} + \dfrac{1}{R_2} = \dfrac{1}{r}$

(d) $\dfrac{1}{\sqrt{R_1}} + \dfrac{1}{\sqrt{R_2}} = \dfrac{1}{\sqrt{r}}$

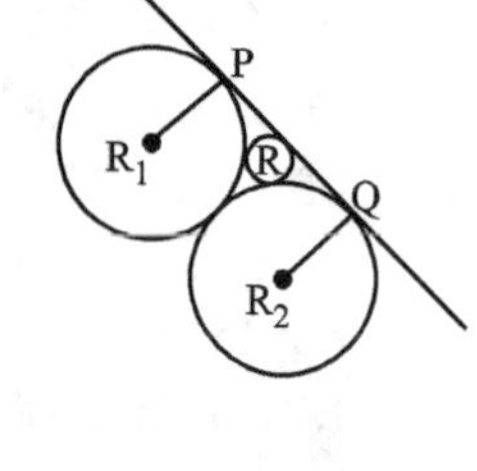

19. Two circles, both of radii a touch each other and each of them touches internally a circle of radius $2a$. Then the radius of the circle which touches all the three circles is

(a) $\dfrac{1}{2}a$ (b) $\dfrac{2}{3}a$ (c) $\dfrac{3}{4}a$ (d) a

20. In the figure, O is the centre of the circle and $OA = CD$, then $\angle CPD$ is

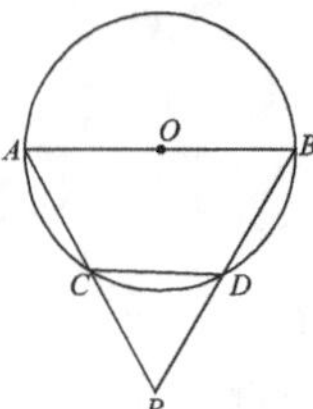

(a) 45° (b) 30° (c) 70° (d) 60°

21. In figure $ABCD$ is a cyclic quadrilateral and $\angle ADC = 80°$, $\angle ACD = 50°$, then $\angle CBD$ is:

Circles

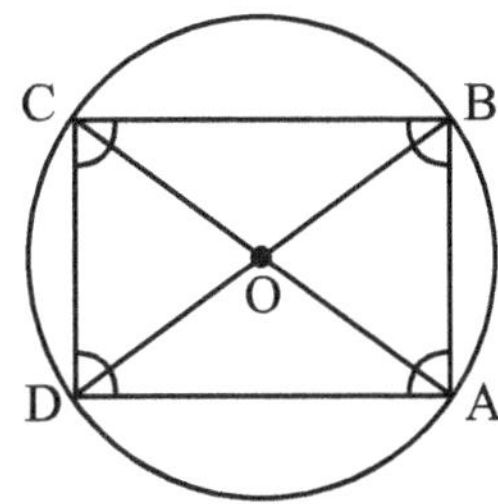

(a) 60°   (b)   130°   (c)   50°   (d) 40°

22. In the given figure, AC is the diameter of the circle. ED ∥ AC, ∠CBE = 65°, then ∠DEC is

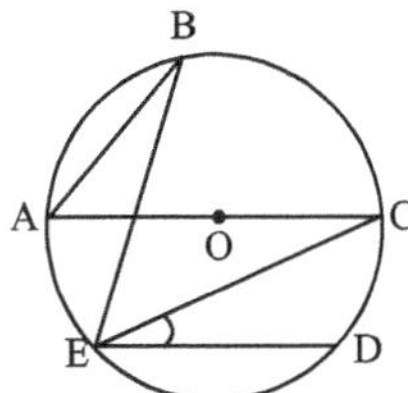

(a) 35°   (b)   25°   (c)   65°   (d) 30°

23. Let *ABCD* be a square of side length 1, and Γ a circle passing through *B* and *C*, and touching *AD*. The radius of Γ is

(a) $\dfrac{3}{8}$ (b) $\dfrac{1}{2}$ (c) $\dfrac{1}{\sqrt{2}}$ (d) $\dfrac{5}{8}$

24. Three circles of radii 1, 2 and 3 units respectively touch each other externally in the plane. The circumradius of the triangle formed by joining the centers of the circles is

(a) 1.5   (b)   2   (c)   2.5   (d) 3

25. Circles A, B and C are externally tangent to each other and internally tangent to circle D. Circles A and B are congruent. Circle C has radius 1 unit and passes through the centre of circle D. Then are radius of circle B is ________ units.

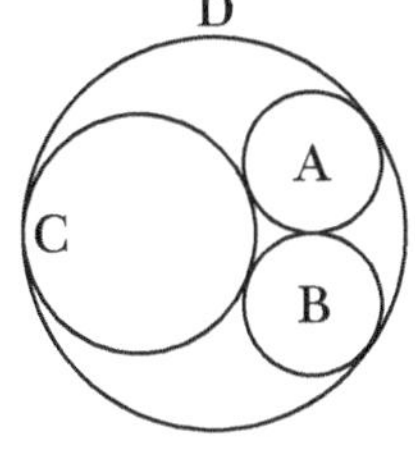

(a) $\dfrac{3}{7}$ (b) $\dfrac{6}{9}$ (c) $\dfrac{8}{9}$ (d) $\dfrac{9}{8}$

26. The length of tangent drawn from a point Q to a circle is 24 cm and distance of Q from the centre of circle is 25 cm. The radius of circle is

(a) 7 cm   (b)   12 cm

(c) 15 cm   (d)   24.5 cm

27. Which of the following is a cyclic quadrilateral?

(a) Rhombus   (b)   Rectangle

(c) Parallelogram   (d)   Trapezium

28. Which of the following is/are not correct?

(a) A secant is a line that intersects a circle in two distinct points.

(b) In a circle, the perpendicular from the centre to a chord bisects the chord.

(c) The point common to a circle and its tangent is called the point of contact.

(d) Adjacent angles of a cyclic quadrilateral are supplementary.

29. Which of the following statement(s) is / are not correct ?

(a) The length of tangent from an external point *P* on circle with centre *O* is always less than *OP*.

(b) The tangent to the circumcircle of an isosceles triangle ABC at *A*, in which *AB* = *AC*, is parallel to *BC*.

(c) If angle between two tangents drawn from a point *P* to a circle of radius 'a' and centre 'O'is 90°, then $OP = a\sqrt{2}$.

(d) None of these

30. Which of the following statement(s) is/are correct?

(a) If a chord *AB* subtends an angle of 60° at the centre of a circle, then angle between the tangents at A and B is also 60°.

(b) The length of tangent from an external point on a circle is always greater than the radius of the circle.

(c) If a number of circle touch a given line segment PQ at a point A, then their centres lie on the perpendicular bisector of *PQ*.

(d) None of these

31. Which of the following statement(s) is/are incorrect?

(a) Angle between the tangent line and the radius at the point of contact is 90°.

(b) A circle can have two parallel tangents atmost.

(c) The distance between two parallel tangents drawn to a circle is equal to twice of radius.

(d) A line intersecting a circle in two points is called a chord.

32. A tangent PQ at a point P of a circle of radius 5 cm meets a line through the centre O at a point Q so that OQ = 12 cm. Length PQ is :

(a) 12 cm   (b)   13 cm

(c) 8.5 cm   (d) $\sqrt{119}$ cm

33. In fig. if TP and TQ are the two tangents to a circle with centre O so that ∠POQ = 110°, then ∠PTQ is equal to

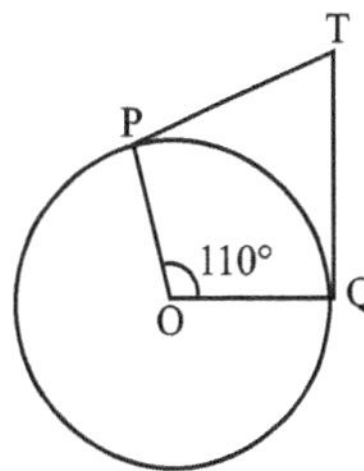

(a) 60°   (b)   70°   (c)   80°   (d)   90°

34. If tangents PA and PB from a point P to a circle with centre O are inclined to each other at an angle of 80°, then ∠POA is equal to

(a) 50°   (b) 60°   (c) 70°   (d) 80°

35. If angle between two radii of a circle is 130°, the angle between the tangents at the ends of the radii is :

(a) 90°   (b) 50°   (c) 70°   (d) 40°

36. In fig. the pair of tangents *AP* and *AQ* drawn from an external point *A* to a circle with centre *O* are perpendicular to each other and length of each tangent is 5 cm.

Then, the radius of the circle is

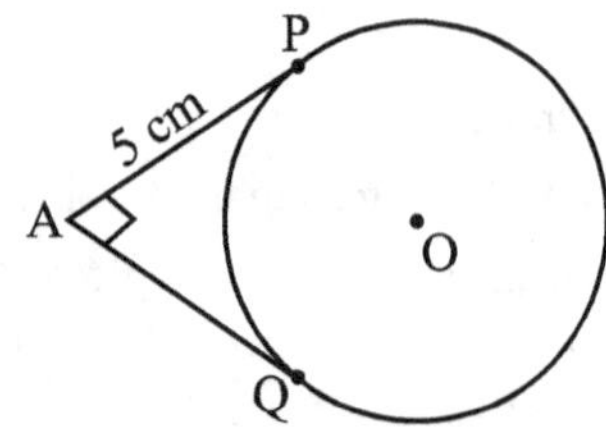

>> **Case/Passage Based Questions** ⟶ ⟩⟩⟩

DIRECTIONS : *Study the given Case/Passage and answer the following questions.*

Case/Passage-I

A Ferris wheel (or a big wheel in the United Kingdom) is an amusement ride consisting of a rotating upright wheel with multiple passenger-carrying components (commonly referred to as passenger cars, cabins, tubs, capsules, gondolas, or pods) attached to the rim in such a way that as the wheel turns, they are kept upright, usually by gravity.

After taking a ride in Ferris wheel, Aarti came out from the crowd and was observing her friends who were enjoying the ride . She was curious about the different angles and measures that the wheel will form. She forms the figure as given below.

[From CBSE Question Bank 2021]

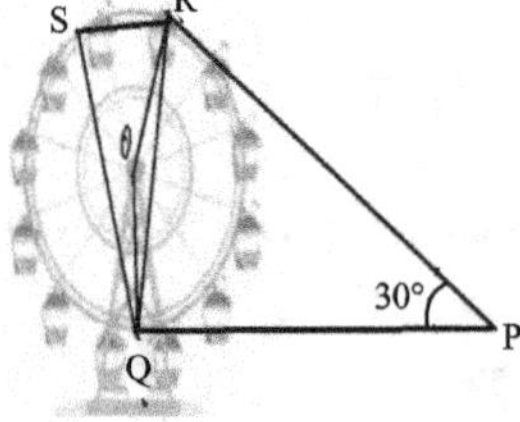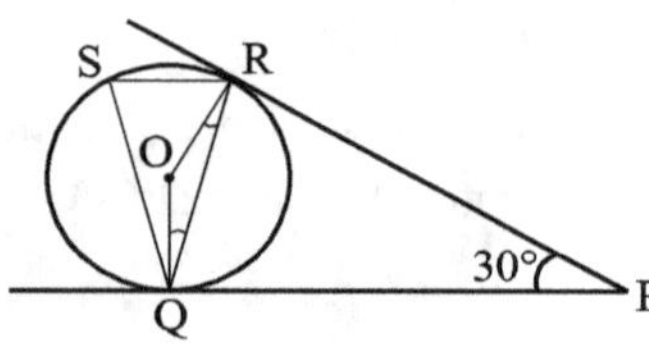

37. In the given figure find ∠ROQ

(a) 60   (b) 100

(c) 150   (d) 90

38. Find ∠RQP

(a) 75   (b) 60

(c) 30   (d) 90

39. Find ∠RSQ

(a) 60   (b) 75

(c) 100   (d) 30

40. Find ∠ORP

(a) 90   (b) 70

(c) 100   (d) 60

Case/Passage-II

Varun has been selected by his School to design logo for Sports Day T-shirts for students and staff . The logo design is as given in the figure and he is working on the fonts and different colours according to the theme.

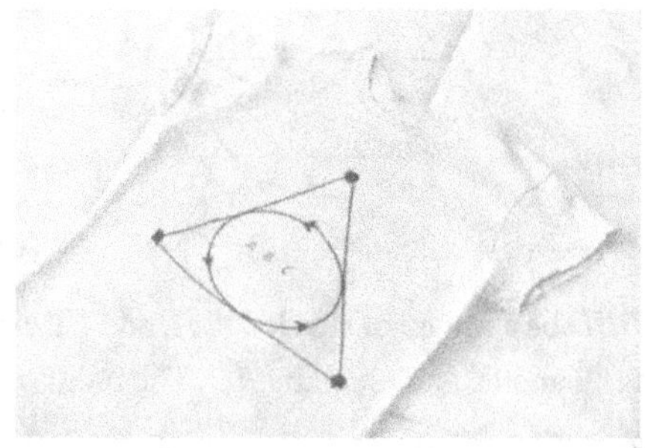

In given figure, a circle with centre O is inscribed in a △ABC, such that it touches the sides AB, BC and CA at points D, E and F respectively. The lengths of sides AB, BC and CA are 12 cm, 8 cm and 10 cm respectively. **[From CBSE Question Bank 2021]**

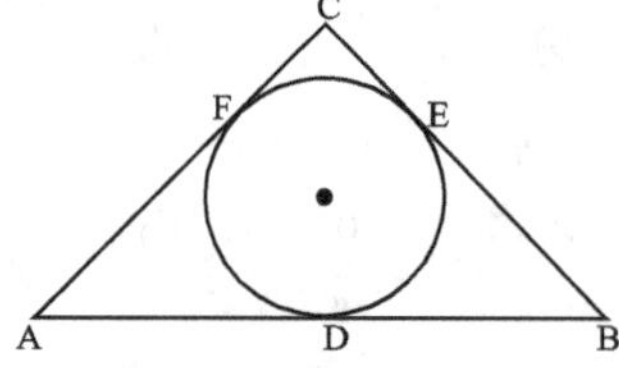

41. Find the length of AD

(a) 7   (b) 8

(c) 5   (d) 9

42. Find the Length of BE

(a) 8   (b) 5

(c) 2   (d) 9

43. Find the length of CF

(a) 9   (b) 5

(c) 2   (d) 3

44. If radius of the circle is 4cm, Find the area of △OAB

(a) 20   (b) 36

(c) 24   (d) 48

45. Find area of △ABC

(a) 50   (b) 60

(c) 100   (d) 90

Assertion & Reason

DIRECTIONS : *Each of these questions contains an Assertion followed by Reason. Read them carefully and answer the question on the basis of following options. You have to select the one that best describes the two statements.*

(a) If both **Assertion** and **Reason** are **correct** and Reason is the **correct explanation** of Assertion.

(b) If both **Assertion** and **Reason** are **correct**, but Reason is **not the correct explanation** of Assertion.

(c) If **Assertion** is **correct** but **Reason** is **incorrect**.

(d) If **Assertion** is **incorrect** but **Reason** is **correct**.

46. **Assertion:** If in a circle, the radius of the circle is 3 cm and distance of a point from the centre of a circle is 5 cm, then length of the tangent will be 4 cm.

Reason: $(\text{hypotenuse})^2 = (\text{base})^2 + (\text{height})^2$

47. **Assertion:** If in a cyclic quadrilateral, one angle is 40°, then the opposite angle is 140°

Reason: Sum of opposite angles in a cyclic quadrilateral is equal to 360°

48. **Assertion:** If length of a tangent from an external point to a circle is 8 cm, then length of the other tangent from the same point is 8 cm.

Reason: length of the tangents drawn from an external point to a circle are equal.

Match the Following

DIRECTIONS : *Each question contains statements given in two columns which have to be matched. Statements (A, B, C, D) in Column-I have to be matched with statements (p, q, r, s) in Column-II.*

49. If AB is a chord of length 6 cm of a circle of radius 5cm, the tangents at A and B intersect at a point X (figure), then match the columns.

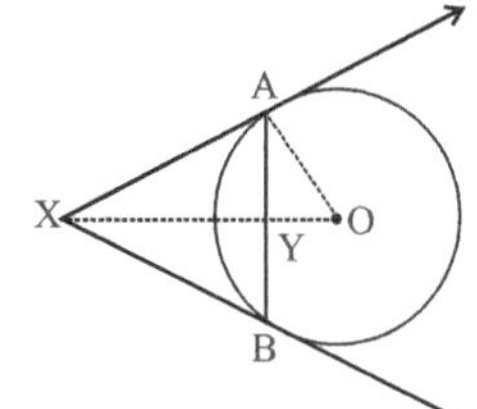

Column-I		Column-II
(A) AY	(p)	4 cm
(B) OY	(q)	3.75 cm
(C) XA	(r)	5 cm
(D) OA	(s)	3 cm

50. If two tangents PA and PB are drawn to a circle with centre O from an external point P (figure), then match the column.

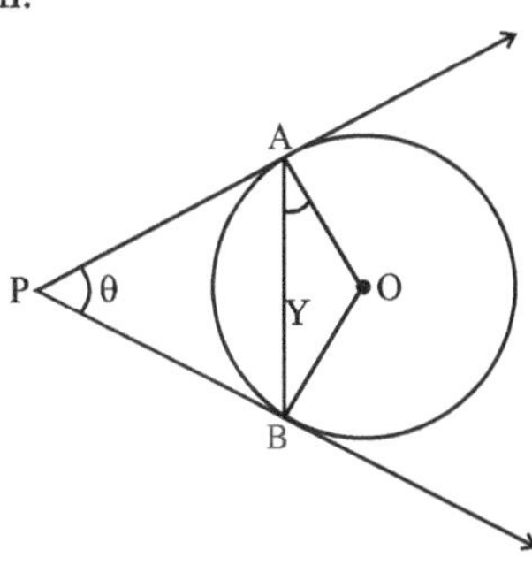

Column-I		Column-II
(A) $\angle$ PAB	(p)	90°
(B) $\angle$ OAP	(q)	$\theta/2$
(C) $\angle$ OAB	(r)	$90° - \dfrac{\theta}{2}$
(D) $\angle$ AOB	(s)	$180° - \theta$

51. If an isosceles $\triangle ABC$ in which $AB = AC = 6$ cm is inscribed in a circle of radius 9 cm, then

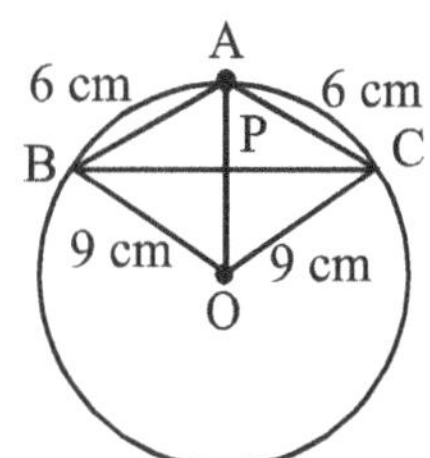

Column-I		Column-II
(A) AP	(p)	$8\sqrt{2}$
(B) CP	(q)	$4\sqrt{2}$
(C) OB	(r)	2
(D) Area of $\triangle ABC$	(s)	9

52. A circle is inscribed in a $\triangle ABC$ having sides $AB = 8$ cm, $BC = 10$ cm and $CA = 12$ cm as shown in figure. Observe the diagram and match the columns.

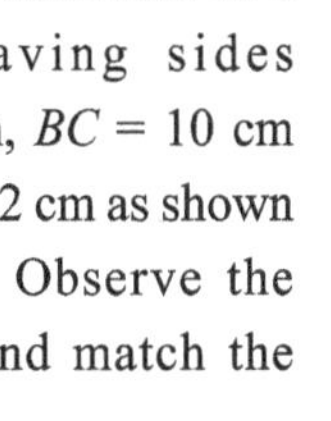

Column-I		Column-II
(A) AD	(p)	15
(B) BE	(q)	7 cm
(C) CF	(r)	3 cm
(D) AD + BE + CF	(s)	5 cm

53.

Column-I Definition	Column-II Term
(A) A line segment which join any two points on a circle.	(p) Secant
(B) A line which intersect the circle in two points.	(q) Tangent
(C) A line that intersects the circle at only one point.	(r) Chord

≫ Fill in the Blanks ————— ≫≫

DIRECTIONS : *Complete the following statements with an appropriate word / term to be filled in the blank space(s).*

54. A tangent to a circle touches it at .... point (s).

55. A line intersecting a circle at two points is called a ....

56. A circle can have .... parallel tangents at the most.

57. The common point of a tangent to a circle and the circle is called ....

58. There is no tangent to a circle passing through a point lying .... the circle.

59. The tangent to a circle is .... to the radius through the point of contact.

60. There are exactly two tangents to a circle passing through a point lying .... the circle.

61. The lengths of the two tangents from an external point to a circle are ....

62. The tangents drawn at the ends of a diameter of a circle are ....

63. In given Fig., the length PB = ... cm.

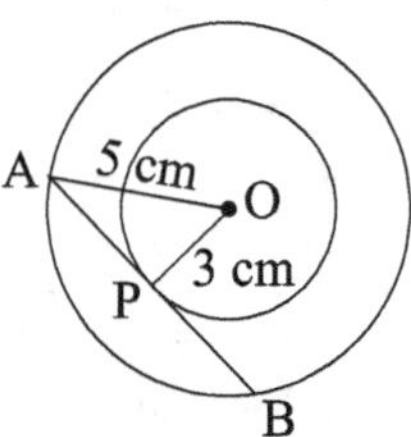

≫ True / False ————— ≫≫

DIRECTIONS : *Read the following statements and write your answer as true or false.*

64. The tangent to a circle is a special case of the secant.

65. The perpendicular at the point of contact to the tangent to a circle does not pass through the centre.

66. A circle can have at the most two parallel tangents.

67. If P is a point on a circle with centre C, then the line drawn through P and perpendicular to CP is the tangent to the circle at the point P.

68. The centre of the circle lies on the bisector of the angle between the two tangents.

69. A tangent to a circle is a line that intersects the circle at only one point.

70. Two equal chords of a circle are always parallel.

71. A line drawn from the centre of a circle to a chord always bisects it.

72. Line joining the centers of two intersecting circles always bisect their common chord.

73. In a circle, two chords PQ and RS bisect each other. Then PRQS is a rectangle.

ANSWER KEY & SOLUTIONS

1. (c) Join O to P and Q. Join P to R. Draw SP ⊥ OQ.

Now SP = QR, as they are opposite sides of rectangle PRQS.

OP = 8 cm + 4 cm = 12 cm; OS = 8 cm − 4 cm = 4 cm

In right triangle POS,

$$SP = \sqrt{OP^2 - OS^2} = \sqrt{12^2 - 4^2} = 8\sqrt{2} \text{ cm}$$

∴ QR = $8\sqrt{2}$ cm

2. (d) Since, two chords AB and CD of the circle are intersecting at P, when produced.

∴ PA . PB = PC.PD

[Each = (length of the tangent from P)^2]

⇒ (AB + PB) . (PB) = (PD + DC) · PD

⇒ (5 + 3) (3) = (2 + x) 2

⇒ 24 = (2 + x) (2) ⇒ 12 = 2 + x

⇒ x = 10 ⇒ CD = 10 cm

3. (b) In right ΔOSP,

OP^2 = PS^2 + OS^2

$r^2 = 225 + (r - 10)^2$

⇒ $r^2 = 225 + r^2 - 20r + 100$

⇒ 20 r = 325 ⇒ 2r = 32.5

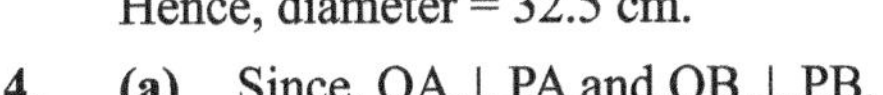

Hence, diameter = 32.5 cm.

4. (a) Since, OA ⊥ PA and OB ⊥ PB,

∴ In quadrilateral AOBP,

⇒ 40° + 90° + 90° + ∠AOB = 360°

⇒ ∠AOB = 140°

Also, ∠AQB = $\frac{1}{2}$ of ∠AOB = 70° and ∠AMB = $\frac{1}{2}$

of reflex ∠AOB = $\frac{1}{2}$ × (360° − 140°) = $\frac{1}{2}$ × 220 = 110°

[∵ The angle subtended by an arc at the centre is double the angle subtended by the arc at any point on the remaining part of the cirlce.]

5. (b) Given, ∠BPC = b° and ∠ACP = a°.

Also, ∠OPA = ∠OAP = b° (Angles in an isosceles triangle OAP, angle in alternate segment.)

∠CPO = 90° ∴ ∠CPA = 90° + b°

In Δ ACP, ∠ACP = 180° − [(b° + 90°) + b°]

⇒ a° + 2b° = 90°

6. (c) Since, PQ is tangent from a point P

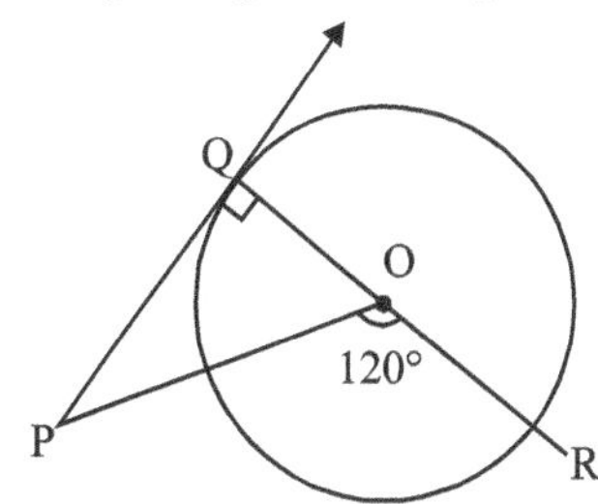

∴ ∠OQP = 90° ⇒ ∠POR = 120°

∴ ∠POR + ∠POQ = 180° [linear pair]

∠POQ = 180° − 120° = 60°

In ΔOPQ

⇒ ∠OPQ + ∠OQP +∠ POQ = 180°

[∵ Sum of angles of Δ = 180°]

∴ ∠OPQ + 90° + 60° = 180° ⇒ ∠OPQ = 30°

7. (b) Side of the regular hexagon inscribed in a circle of radius r is also r, the perimeter is 6r.

8. (a)

9. (b) Exterior angle of a cyclic quadrilateral is equal to its interior opposite angle.

∠BAC = ∠DCA and proceed.

10. (b) [**Hint.** OP ⊥ PT, OQ ⊥ QT.

In quad. OPTQ, ∠POQ + ∠OPT + ∠PTQ + ∠OQT = 360°

⇒ 110° + 90° + ∠PTQ + 90° = 360°

⇒ ∠ PTQ = 70°]

11. (c) Tangents drawn to a circle from an external point are equal.

12. (b) (i) ADEF is a parallelogram.

    (ii) ∠FAD = 30° and ∠OAD = ∠OBA

       (angles opposite to equal sides)

13. (b) (i) APBC is a cyclic quadrilateral.

    (ii) ∠ABC is an angle in a semi circle.

    (iii) ABQC is a cyclic quadrilateral.

14. (b) All chords are of same length.

15. (b) Only two tangents are parallel to a secant.

16. (b) $AD = CD$

and $BD = CD$

$\therefore AB = AD + BD = CD + CD$

$= 2CD = 2 \times 4 = 8$ cm

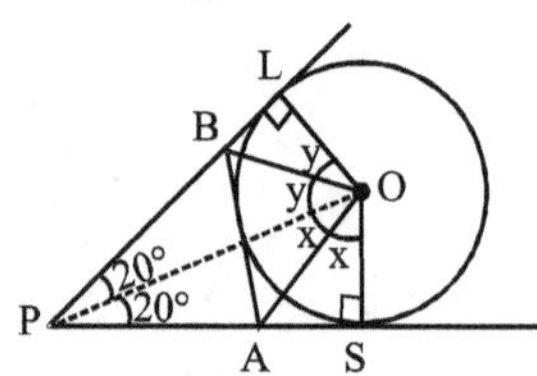

17. (d) We redraw the figure.

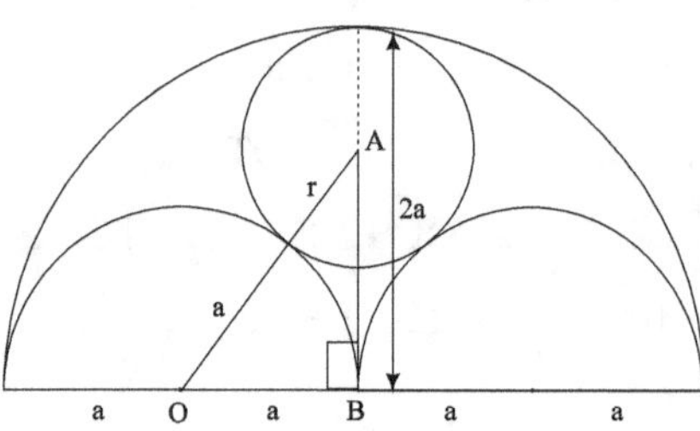

In ΔOPS, using Pythagoras theorem, $\angle POS = 70°$

and In ΔPOL, $\angle POL = 70°$

From figure, $2x + 2y = 140°$

$\angle BOA = x + y = 70°$

18. (d) Here, PQ is the common tangent to the three circles

So, $PR = \sqrt{(R_1 + r)^2 - (R_1 - r)^2} = \sqrt{4R_1 r}$ ...(i)

$RQ = \sqrt{4R_2 r}$ ....(ii) $\qquad PQ = \sqrt{4R_1 R_2}$ ....(iii)

We know that $PQ = PR + RQ$

$\Rightarrow \sqrt{4R_1 R_2} = \sqrt{4R_1 r} + \sqrt{4R_2 r}$ ($\because$ From (i), (ii) and (iii))

$\Rightarrow \sqrt{R_1 R_2} = \sqrt{R_1 r} + \sqrt{R_2 r}$ $\qquad \therefore \dfrac{1}{\sqrt{r}} = \dfrac{1}{\sqrt{R_2}} + \dfrac{1}{\sqrt{R_1}}$

19. (b)

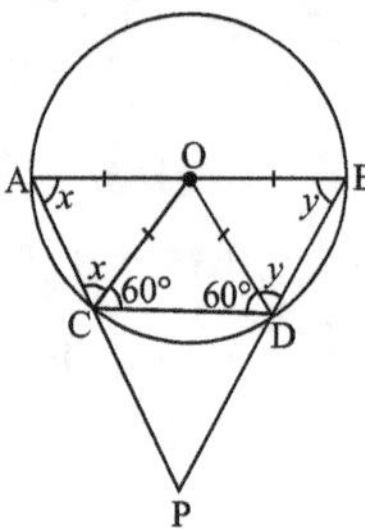

Since, in figure, ΔAOB is a right angled triangle

$\therefore \quad OA^2 = AB^2 + OB^2$

$\Rightarrow \quad (a + r)^2 = (2a - r)^2 + a^2$

$\Rightarrow \quad a^2 + 2ar + r^2 = 4a^2 + r^2 - 4ar + a^2$

$\Rightarrow \quad 6ar = 4a^2 \Rightarrow r = \dfrac{2a}{3}$

20. (d) In the given figure, ODC is equilateral triangle

$\Rightarrow \angle ODC = \angle OCD = 60°$

Now, in quadrilateral $ABCD$

$\Rightarrow x + x + 60° + y + y + 60° = 360°$

$\Rightarrow x + y = 120°$

In ΔABP,

$\angle APB = 180° - (x + y) = 60°$

21. (c) In cyclic quadrilateral ABCD,

$\angle ADC = 80°$ and $\angle ABC = 100°$

($\because$ opposite angles of a cyclic quadrilateral are supplementary)

Now, $\angle ACD = \angle DBA = 50°$

(angles in same segment of a circle are equal).

$\therefore \angle CBD = \angle ABC - \angle ABD = 50°$

22. (b) $\angle ABC = \angle ABE + \angle CBE = 90°$

(angle in a semi circle is a right angle)

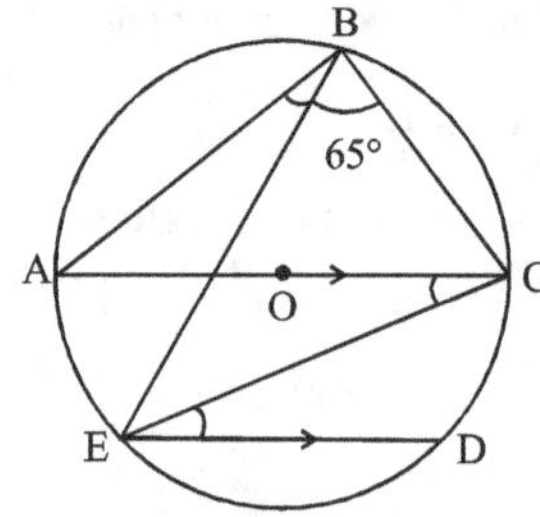

$\Rightarrow \angle ABE = 90° - 65° = 25°$

$\Rightarrow \angle ACE = \angle ABE = 25°$

($\because$ angles in same segment of a circle are equal)

$\Rightarrow \angle ACE = \angle DEC = 25°$

[alternate interior angles are equal]

23. (d) $ABCD$ is a square of sides

$AB = BC = CD = AD = 1$ unit

A circle Γ passing through B and C and touching AD at N, where BC is chord of circle.

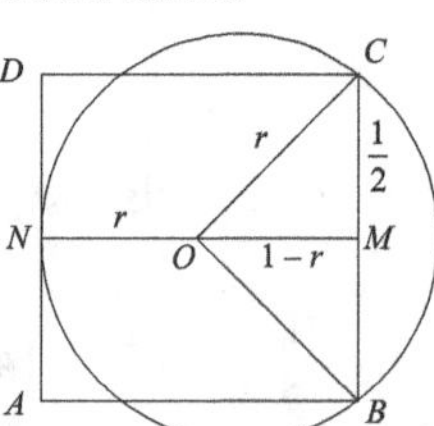

$\therefore \quad OM$ bisects the chord BC

$\therefore \quad CM = MB = \dfrac{1}{2} BC = \dfrac{1}{2}$ $\qquad (\because BC = 1)$

$\Rightarrow \quad OM = MN - ON = 1 - r$

In ΔOMC, $OC^2 = OM^2 + CM^2$

$\Rightarrow \quad r^2 = (1 - r)^2 + \left(\dfrac{1}{2}\right)^2$

$\Rightarrow \quad r^2 = 1 - 2r + r^2 + \dfrac{1}{4} \Rightarrow r = \dfrac{5}{8}$

24. **(c)** Since, radii of circles are 1, 2 and 3 units.

∴ Side of ΔABC are $AB = 5$, $BC = 3$, $AC = 4$

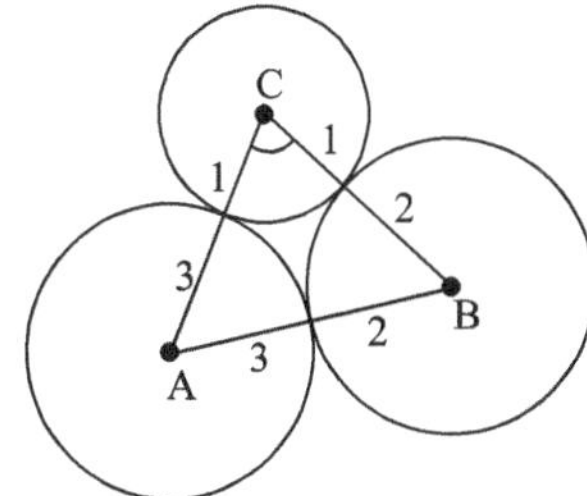

∴ ΔABC is formed a right angled triangle, where AB is hypotenuse of triangle.

Since, circumradius of a right angled triangle is the half of the hypotenuse.

∴ Circumradius $= \dfrac{1}{2} \times AB = \dfrac{1}{2} \times 5 = 2.5$

25. **(c)** In ΔMAN

$(2 - r)^2 = x^2 + r^2$

$\Rightarrow \quad 4 + r^2 - 4r = x^2 + r^2$

$4(1 - r) = x^2 \Rightarrow 4 - 4r = x^2$

$\Rightarrow \quad r = \dfrac{4 - x^2}{4}$

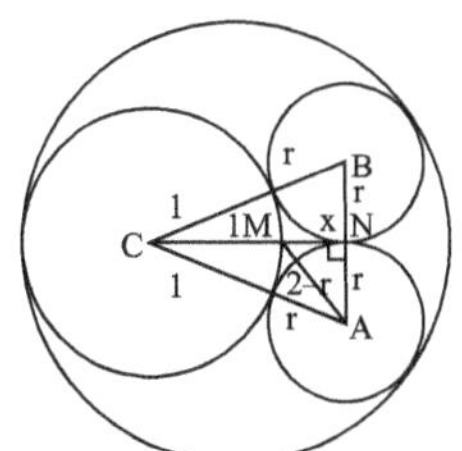

In ΔCAN, $(1 + x)^2 + r^2 = (1 + r)^2$

$1 + x^2 + 2x + r^2 = 1 + r^2 = 2r$

$\Rightarrow \quad x^2 + 2x = 2r \Rightarrow x^2 = 2r - 2x$

$\Rightarrow \quad x^2 = 2\left(\dfrac{4 - x^2}{4}\right) - 2x$

$\Rightarrow x^2 = \dfrac{4 - x^2}{2} - 2x$

$\Rightarrow \quad 2x^2 = 4 - x^2 - 4x \Rightarrow 3x^2 + 4x - 4 = 0$

$\Rightarrow \quad 3x^2 + 6x - 2x - 4 = 0 \Rightarrow 3x(x + 2) - 2(x + 2) = 0$

$\Rightarrow \quad x = \dfrac{2}{3}, x = -2.$

$r = 4 - \dfrac{\left(\dfrac{2}{3}\right)^2}{4} = \dfrac{4 - \dfrac{4}{9}}{4} \Rightarrow \dfrac{36 - 4}{36} = \dfrac{32}{36} \Rightarrow \dfrac{8}{9}.$

26. **(a)** Here, O is the centre of circle.

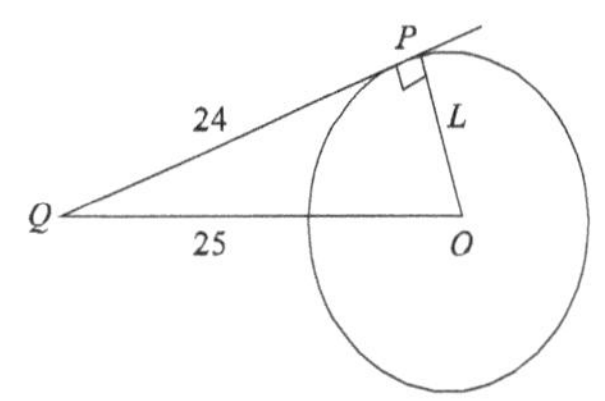

Let r be the radius of circle $r = \sqrt{(25)^2 - (24)^2}$

$= \sqrt{625 - 576} = \sqrt{49}$

$= 7$ cm

27. **(b)**   **28.** **(d)**

29. **(d)** All the three statements are correct.

30. **(d)** All the three statements are false.

31. **(d)**

32. **(d)** O is the centre of the circle. The radius of the circle is 5 cm.

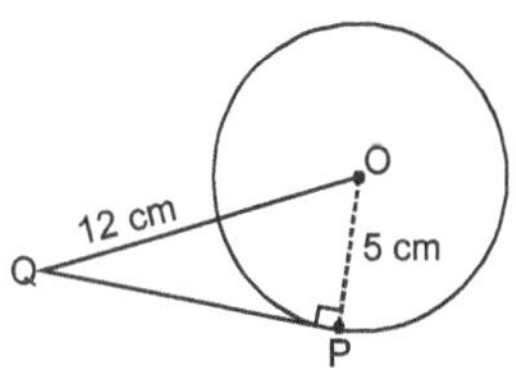

PQ is tangent to the circle at P. Then,

OP = 5 cm and ∠OPQ = 90°.

We are given that OQ = 12 cm.

By Pythagoras Theorem, we have

$PQ^2 = OQ^2 - OP^2 = (12)^2 - (5)^2 = 144 - 25 = 119$

$\Rightarrow \quad PQ = \sqrt{119}$ cm.

33. **(b)** In figure, TPOQ is a quadrilateral.

Here, ∠OPT $=$ ∠OQT $= 90° \Rightarrow$ ∠PTQ $+$ ∠POQ $= 180°$

$\Rightarrow \quad$ ∠PTQ $+ ∠110° = 180° \Rightarrow$ ∠PTQ $= 70°$.

34. **(a)** In figure

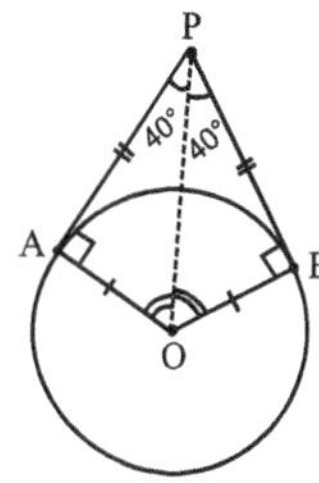

$\Delta OAP \cong \Delta OBP$ (SSS congruence)

$\Rightarrow \quad$ ∠POA $=$ ∠POB $= -$ ∠AOB   ... (i)

Also, ∠AOB $+$ ∠APB $= 180°$

$\Rightarrow \quad \angle AOB + 80° = 180°$

$\Rightarrow \quad \angle AOB = 100° \qquad \text{... (ii)}$

Then, from (i) and (ii),

$$\angle POA = \frac{1}{2} \times 100° = 50°.$$

35. **(b)**

36. **(c)**

37. **(c)** $\because \angle ROQ + \angle RPQ = 180°$

$\Rightarrow \angle ROQ = 180° - 30° = 150°$

38. **(a)** $\because \angle RQP = \angle QRP$

and $\angle RQP + \angle QRP + \angle QPR = 180°$

$\Rightarrow 2\angle RQP = 180° - 30° \Rightarrow \angle RQP = 75°$

39. **(b)** $\angle RSQ = \frac{1}{2}\angle ROQ = \frac{1}{2} \times 150° = 75°$

40. **(a)** $90° \; [\because OR \perp RP]$

Sol. (41-45)

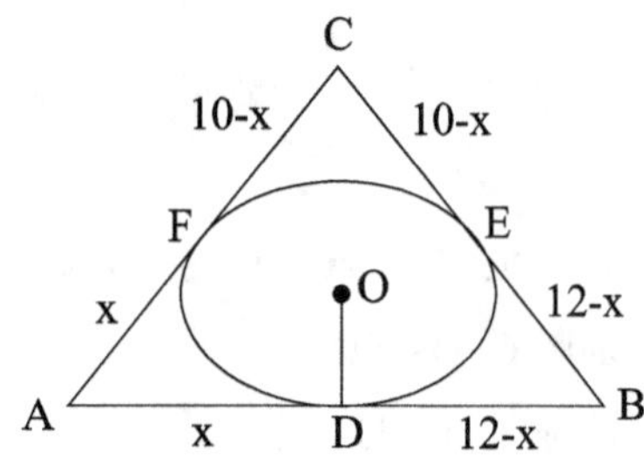

$BC = 10 - x + 12 - x = 8$

$\Rightarrow x = 7.$

41. **(a)** $AD = 7$ cm

42. **(b)** $BE = 12 - x = 12 - 7 = 5$ cm

43. **(d)** $CF = 10 - x = 10 - 7 = 3$ cm

44. **(c)** $Ar \, \Delta OAB = \frac{1}{2} \times AB \times OD$

$= \frac{1}{2} \times 12 \times 4 = 24 \text{ cm}^2$

45. **(b)** $Ar \, \Delta ABC = Ar \, \Delta AOB + Ar \, \Delta OBC + Ar \, \Delta AOC$

$= 24 + \frac{1}{2} \times 8 \times 4 + \frac{1}{2} \times 10 \times 4 = 60 \text{ cm}^2$

46. **(a)** $(OA)^2 = (AB)^2 + (OB)^2$

$AB = \sqrt{25 - 9} = 4$ cm.

Both Assertion and Reason are correct.

Also, Reason is the correct explanation of the Assertion.

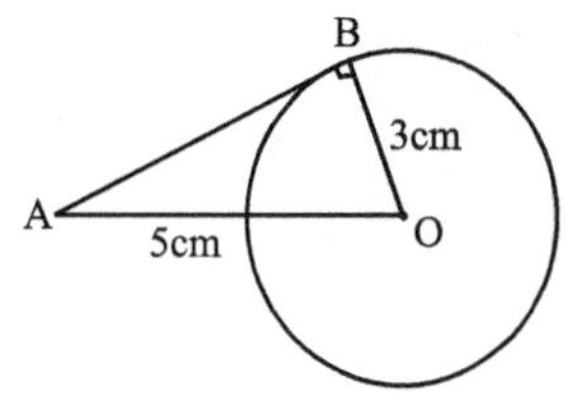

47. **(c)** Angle $+ 40° = 180°$

Angle $= 180° - 40° = 140°.$

48. **(a)**

49. (A) $\rightarrow$ (s); (B) $\rightarrow$ (p); (C) $\rightarrow$ (q); (D) $\rightarrow$ (r)

50. (A) $\rightarrow$ (r); (B) $\rightarrow$ (p); (C) $\rightarrow$ (q); (D) $\rightarrow$ (s)

51. (A) $\rightarrow$ (r); (B) $\rightarrow$ (q); (C) $\rightarrow$ (s); (D) $\rightarrow$ (p)

$OP \perp BC$, Let $AP = x$ cm and $PB = CP = y$ cm

On applying Pythagoras in ΔAPB and ΔOPB, we have

$36 = y^2 + x^2$ and $81 = (9 - x)^2 + y^2$

On solving these, we get, $x = 2$ cm and $y = 4\sqrt{2}$ cm.

Area of $\Delta ABC = \frac{1}{2}(BC \times AP) = \frac{1}{2} \times 8\sqrt{2} \times 2 = 8\sqrt{2}$ cm^2.

52. (A) $\rightarrow$ (s); (B) $\rightarrow$ (r); (C) $\rightarrow$ (q); (D) $\rightarrow$ (p)

$AD = AF = x$ cm, $BD = BE = y$ cm, $CE = CF = z$ cm

($\because$ tangents drawn from an exterior point to a circle are equal in length).

$AB = 8$ cm $\Rightarrow AD + BD = 8 \Rightarrow x + y = 8 \qquad \text{... (i)}$

Similarly, $BE + CE = 10$

$\Rightarrow \quad y + z = 10 \qquad \text{... (ii)}$

and $\quad z + x = 12 \qquad \text{... (iii)}$

Adding equations (i) + (ii) + (iii),

$\Rightarrow \quad x + y + z = 15 \qquad \text{... (iv)}$

Thus, on solving (i), (ii), (iii) and (iv)

we get, $AD = x$ cm $= 5$ cm

$BE = y$ cm $= 3$ cm

$CF = z$ cm $= 7$ cm

53. (A) $\rightarrow$ (r); (B) $\rightarrow$ (p); (C) $\rightarrow$ (q)

54. One

55. Secant

56. Two

57. Point of contact

58. inside

Circles

59. perpendicular

60. outside

61. equal

62. Parallel

63. 4 cm

$$PB = AP = \sqrt{5^2 - 3^2} \qquad (\because OP \perp AB)$$
$$= \sqrt{25 - 9} = 4 \text{ cm}$$

64. True   **65.** False   **66.** True   **67.** True

68. True   **69.** True   **70.** False   **71.** False

72. True   **73.** True

12 Constructions

DIRECTIONS : *This section contains multiple choice questions. Each question has 4 choices (a), (b), (c) and (d) out of which only one is correct.*

1. To draw tangent from an exterior point 'P' to a circle using the centre 'O' of the circle, first we
   (a) join P to O.
   (b) draw tangent from P to the circle.
   (c) draw secant from P which intersects the circle at two points.
   (d) draw perpendicular at P to PO.

2. To divide a line segment AB of any length in the ratio 2 : 5, first draw a ray AX (or BX) making an acute angle with AB. Then, draw 7 arcs intersecting the ray at X_1, X_2, X_3, X_4, X_5, X_6 and X_7 such that $AX_1 = X_1X_2 = X_2X_3 = X_3X_4 = X_4X_5 = X_5X_6 = X_6X_7$. Then join X_7B, then after

   (a) join X_2B
   (b) draw X_2B' parallel to $X_7 B$, which intersects AB at B′.
   (c) join X_5B
   (d) draw perpendicular from X_2 to AB.

3. To draw a pair of tangents to a circle which are inclined to each other at an angle of 45° it is required to draw tangents at end points of those two radii of the circle, the angle between them should be-

   (a) 60°   (b) 90°   (c) 45°   (d) 135°

4. Which is true?

   In order to divide a line segment AB = 6 cm, in the radio 3 : 5, we draw a ray AX making an acute angle ∠BAX. Along AX mark off.... points A_1, A_2, A_3 etc. such that $AA_1 = A_1A_2$ = etc., The number of points is

   (a) 3   (b) 5   (c) 8   (d) 2

5. To divide a line segment *AB* in the ratio 2 : 5, first a ray *AX* is drawn, so that ∠*BAX* is an acute angle and then at equal distance points are marked on the ray *AX* such that the minimum number of these point is
   (a) 2   (b) 5
   (c) 4   (d) 7

6. The sides of a triangle (in cm) are given below. In which case, the construction of triangle is not possible.
   (a) 8, 7, 3   (b) 8, 6, 4
   (c) 8, 4, 4   (d) 7, 6, 5

7. Given a triangle with side $AB = 8$ cm. To get a line segment $AB' = \dfrac{3}{4}$ of *AB*, it is required to divide the line segment *AB* in the ratio
   (a) 3 : 4   (b) 4 : 3
   (c) 1 : 3   (d) 3 : 1

8. To draw a pair of tangents to a circle which are inclined to each other at an angle of 70°, it is required to draw tangents at end points of those two radii of the circle, the angle between them should be
   (a) 110°   (b) 20°
   (c) 90°   (d) 120°

9. To divide a line segment AB in the ratio p : q (p, q are positive integers), draw a ray AX so that ∠BAX is an acute angle and then mark points on ray AX at equal distances such that the minimum number of the points is
   (a) greater of p and q (b) $p + q$
   (c) $p + q - 1$ (d) pq

10. Draw a pair of tangents to a circle which are inclined to each other at an angle of 35°, it is required to draw tangents at the end points of those two radii of the circle, the angle between which is
    (a) 105°   (b) 70°
    (c) 140°   (d) 145°

11. To divide a line segment AB in the ratio 4 : 7, a ray AX is drawn first such that ∠BAX is an acute angle and then points A1, A2, A3, ... are located at equal distance on the ray AX and the point B is joined to
    (a) A_{12} (b) A_{11} (c) A_{10} (d) A_9

❯ Match the Following ━━━ ❯❯❯

DIRECTIONS : *Given below question contains statements given in two columns which have to be matched. Statements (A, B, C, D,....) in Column-I have to be matched with statements (p, q, r, s,....) in Column-II.*

---

12. To draw tangents from an exterior point P to a circle, drawn using a bangle, each step of continue diagram in random order is given in column I and how to draw each steps of continue diagram is written in different random order in column II match the items in two columns.

Column-I	**Column-II**
(A) 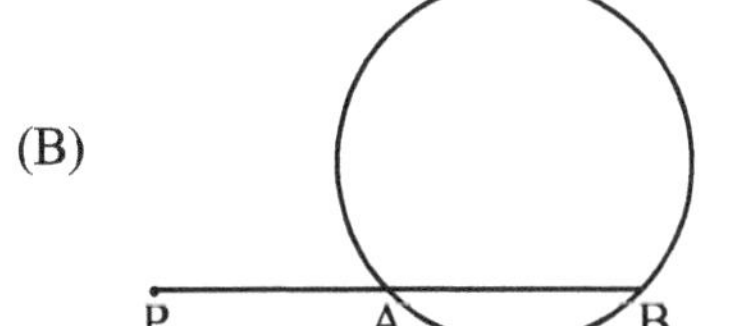	(p) Draw a circle using a bangle
(B) 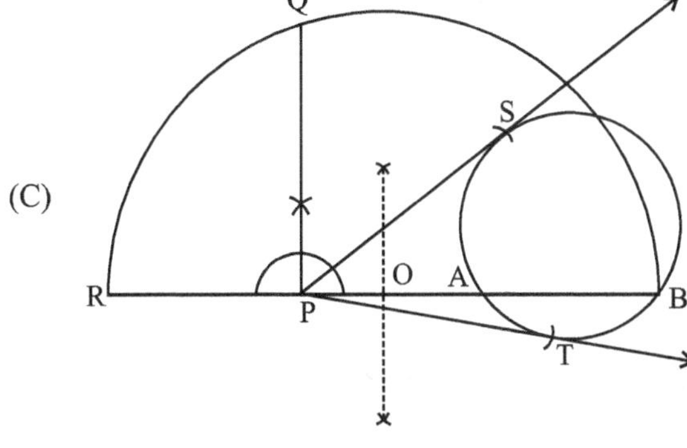	(q) Draw perpendicular bisector of RB, which intersects RB at O.
(C) 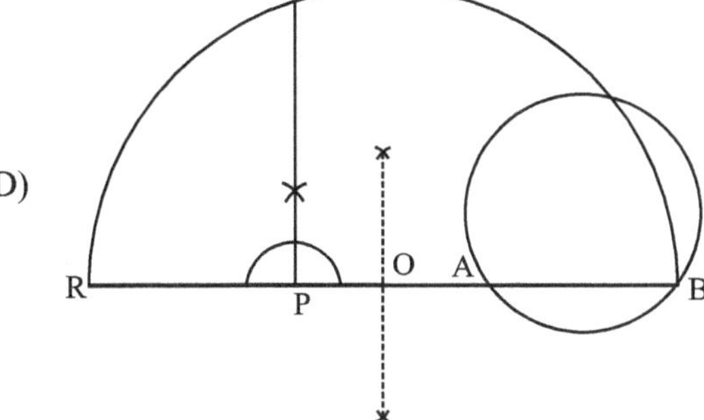	(r) Draw a secant PAB intersecting the circle at A and B.
(D) 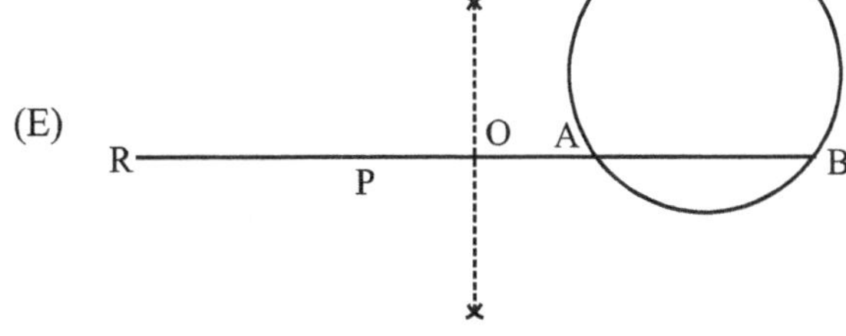	(s) Produce AP to R, such that PA = PR.
(E)	(t) Draw PQ perpendicular to RB at P which intersects the semi-circle drawn with centre O and radius OR at Q.

(F)

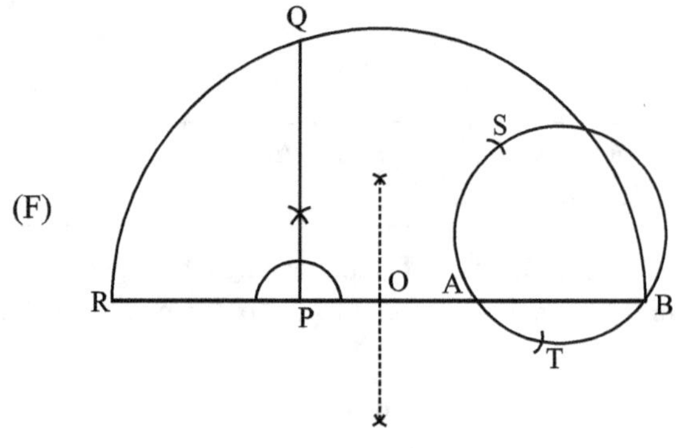

(u) Draw ray PS and PT.

(G)

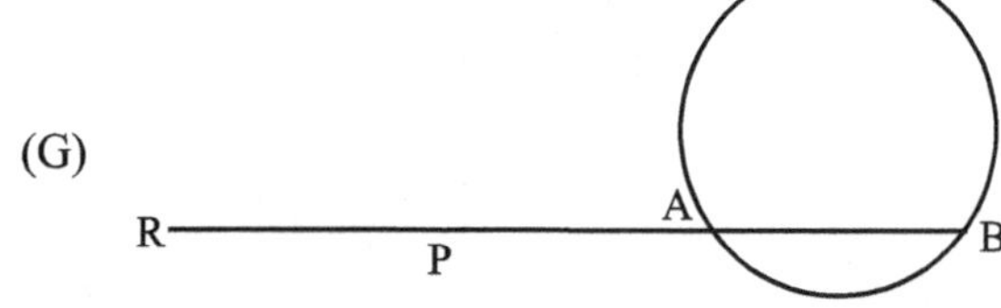

(v) With centre O and radius OB (or OR), draw a semi-circle.

(H)

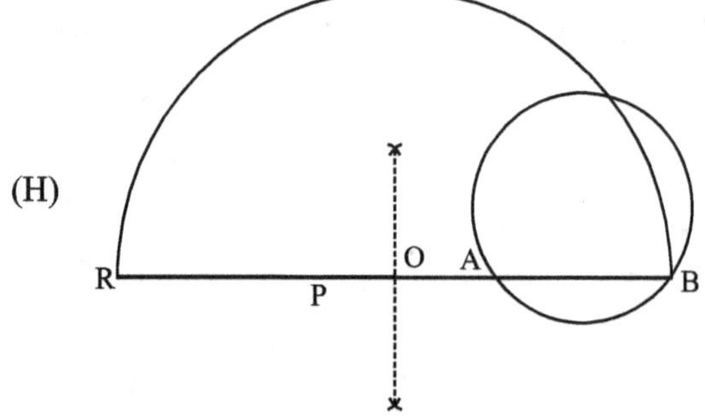

(w) With centre P and radius PQ draw arcs intersecting the circle drawn using the bangle at S and T.

Fill in the Blanks

DIRECTIONS : *Complete the following statements with an appropriate word / term to be filled in the blank space(s).*

13. Two circles are called concentric if both have .... centre and .... radii.

14. To construct a triangle we must know atleast its .... parts.

15. To construct the tangents to a circle from a external point if distance of point from centre of circle is .... radius of circle.

True / False

DIRECTIONS : *Read the following statements and write your answer as true or false.*

16. We can not draw the tangent to a circle at a given point on it, when the centre of the circle is not known.

17. We can draw the tangents to a circle from a point outside it (external point), only when its centre is known.

18. Construction of a triangle is not possible if $AB + BC < AC$.

19. To draw the perpendicular bisector of line segment PQ, we open the compass more than $\frac{1}{2}$ PQ.

ANSWER KEY & SOLUTIONS

1. **(a)** Join P to O

2. **(b)** draw X_2B' parallel to X_7B, which intersects AB at B'.

3. **(d)** Here PA and PB are two tangents inclined at an angle 45°

Then, $x + 90° + 90° + 45° = 360°$
$x + 225° = 360°$
$x = 360° - 225°$
$x = 135°$

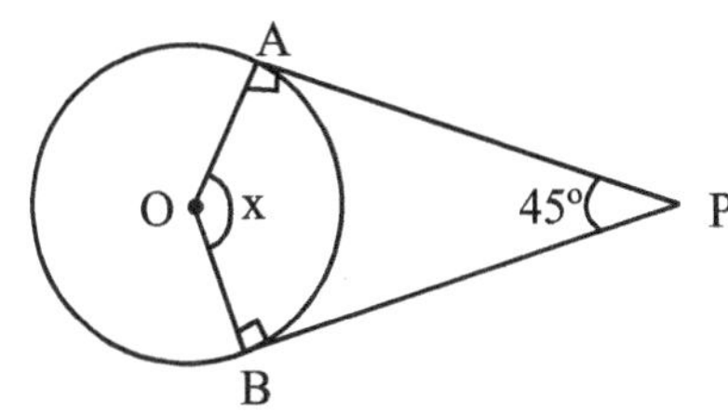

4. **(c)**

5. **(d)** We know that, to divide a line segment AB in the ratio $m : n$, first draw a ray AX which makes an acute $\angle BAX$ then, marked $m + n$ points at equal distance.

Here, $m = 2, n = 5$

∴ Minimum number of these points $= 2 + 5 = 7$

6. **(c)** We know that, in a triangle sum of two sides of triangle is greater than the third side. Here, the sides of triangle given in option (c) does not satisfy this condition. So, with these sides the construction of a triangle is not possible.

7. **(d)**   **8.** **(a)**   **9.** **(b)**

10. **(d)**   **11.** **(b)**

12. (A) → (p); (B) → (r); (C) → (u); (D) → (t); (E) → (q); (F) → (w); (G) → (s); (H) → (v)

13. Same, different

14. Three

15. More than

16. False

17. False

18. True

19. True

13 — Some Applications of Trigonometry

DIRECTIONS : *This section contains multiple choice questions. Each question has 4 choices (a), (b), (c) and (d) out of which only one is correct.*

1. From a point on the ground, the angles of elevation of the bottom and the top of a transmission tower fixed at the top of a 20 m high building are 45° and 60° respectively. Find the height of the tower.

   (a) $20\left(\sqrt{3}-1\right)$ m   (b) $20\sqrt{3}$ m

   (c) 20 m   (d) 40 m

2. From the figure, find the value of $\dfrac{\tan\theta}{\tan\phi}$ and it is given that 'D' be the mid point of BC.

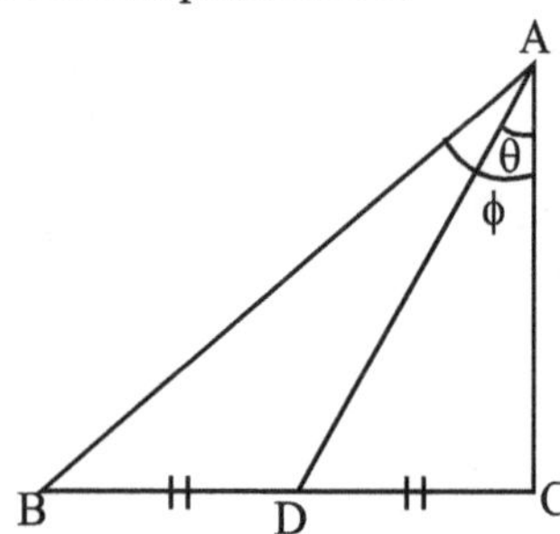

   (a) $\dfrac{3}{4}$ (b) $\dfrac{1}{2}$

   (c) $\dfrac{1}{\sqrt{2}}$ (d) $\dfrac{4}{7}$

3. The angles of elevation of the top of a tower, as seen from two points A and B situated in the same line and at distance x and y respectively. from the foot of the tower, are complementary. Find the height of the tower.

   (a) $\sqrt{x+y}$ (b) $\sqrt{xy}$

   (c) xy (d) $\sqrt{x}+\sqrt{y}$

4. A 15m long ladder placed vertically along a wall broke in such a way that its top touches the ground making an angle of 60° with it. At what height from the ground did the ladder break?

   (a) 7.34 m   (b) 8 m

   (c) 9.46 m   (d) 6.96 m

5. A tree 6 m tall casts a 4 cm long shadow. At the same time, a flag pole casts a shadow 50 m long. How long is the flag pole?

   (a) 75 m   (b) 100 m

   (c) 150 m   (d) 50 m

6. The height of a tower is h and the angle of elevation of the top of the twoer is α. On moving a distance h/2 towards the tower, the angle of elevation becomes β. What is the value of cotα – cotβ?

   (a) $\dfrac{1}{2}$ (b) $\dfrac{2}{3}$

   (c) 1   (d) 2

7. A bridge across a river makes an angle of 45° with the river bank. If the length of the bridge across the river is 150 m, width of the river is

   (a) $75\sqrt{2}$ m   (b) 150 m

   (c) $\dfrac{75}{\sqrt{2}}$ m   (d) 75 m

8. A professor standing on one end of a football field observes the elevation of the top of a flood light tower at an angle of α. He then walks a distance equal to twice the height of the tower and finds that the elevation of the top is now at an angle of 90°– α. What is the value of tanα ?

   (a) $1-\sqrt{2}$ (b) $\sqrt{2}-1$

   (c) $\sqrt{2}$ (d) 1

9. An electrician has a repair an electric fault on a pole of height 5 cm. He has to reach a point 1.3 m below the top of the pole to undertake the repair work. What should

be the length of the ladder that he should use which, when inclined at an angle of 60° to the horizontal, would enable him to reach the required position? Also, how far from the foot of the pole should he place the foot of the ladder?

[Take $\sqrt{3} = 1.73$].

(a) 4.28 m, 2.14 m

(b) 4.28 m, 2.83 m

(c) 4.6 7m, 2.14 m

(d) 3.67 m, 2.14 m

10. An aeroplane when flying at a height of 3125 m from the ground passes vertically below another plane at an instant when the angles of elevation of the two planes from the same point on the ground are 30° and 60° respectively.Find the distance between the two planes at that instant.

(a) 3920 m (b) 6250 m

(c) 5125 m (d) 4444 m

11. In the adjoining figure, the length of *BC* is

(a) $2\sqrt{3}$ cm

(b) $3\sqrt{3}$ cm

(c) $4\sqrt{3}$ cm

(d) 3 cm

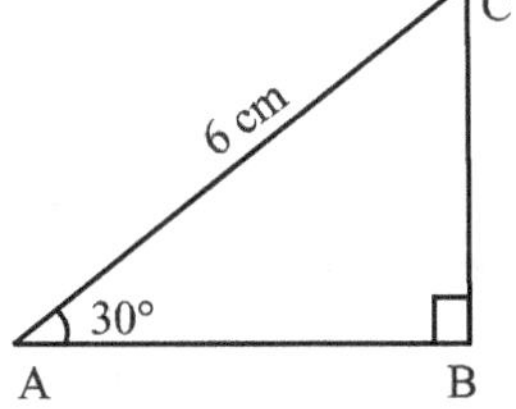

12. If the angle of depression of an object from a 75 m high tower is 30°, then the distance of the object from the tower is

(a) $25\sqrt{3}$ m (b) $50\sqrt{3}$ m

(c) $75\sqrt{3}$ m (d) 150 m

13. The angles of elevation of the top of a tower from two points at distances *m* and *n* metres are complementary. If the two points and the base of the tower are on the same straight line, then the height of the tower is

(a) $\sqrt{mn}$ (b) *mn*

(c) $\dfrac{m}{n}$ (d) None of these

14. If the height and length of the shadow of a man are the same, then the angle of elevation of the sun is

(a) 45° (b) 60°

(c) 90° (d) 120°

15. The height of a tree, if it casts a shadow 15 m long on the level of ground, when the angle of elevation of the sun is 45°, is

(a) 10 m (b) 14 m

(c) 8 m (d) 15 m

16. In the given figure, the positions of the observer and the object are mentioned, the angle of depression is

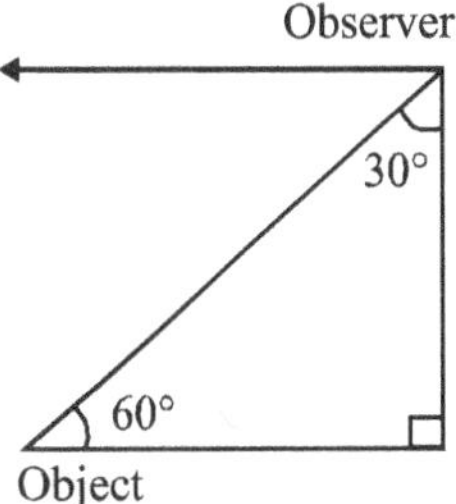

(a) 30° (b) 90°

(c) 60° (d) 45°

17. A person walks towards a tower. Initially when he starts, angle of elevation of the top of tower is 30°. On travelling 20 metres towards the tower, the angle changes to 60°. How much more has he to travel to reach the tower?

(a) $10\sqrt{3}$ metres (b) 10 metres

(c) 20 metres (d) $\dfrac{10}{\sqrt{3}}$ metres

18. ABC is a field in the form of an equilateral triangle. Two vertical poles of heights 45m and 20m are erected at A and B respectively. The angles of elevation of the tops of the two poles from C are complementary to each other. There is a point D on AB such that from it, the angles of elevation of the tops of the two poles are equal.Then AD is equal to –

(a) $17\dfrac{5}{12}$ m (b) $20\dfrac{10}{13}$ m

(c) $20\dfrac{5}{13}$ m (d) $17\dfrac{10}{12}$ m

19. A vertical pole of height 10 metres stands at one corner of a rectangular field. The angle of elevation of its top from the farthest corner is 30°, while that from another corner is 60°. The area (in m^2) of rectangular field is

(a) $\dfrac{200\sqrt{2}}{3}$ (b) $\dfrac{400}{\sqrt{3}}$

(c) $\dfrac{200\sqrt{2}}{\sqrt{3}}$ (d) $\dfrac{400\sqrt{2}}{\sqrt{3}}$

20. From the top of a building of height 'h' meter, the angle of elevation of the top of the tower is 'a' and angle of depression of the foot of the tower is 'b'. The height of the tower is

(a) $\dfrac{h+(\tan\alpha+\tan\beta)}{\tan\beta}$ (b) $\dfrac{h(\tan\alpha+\tan\beta)}{\tan\beta}$

(c) $\dfrac{h\tan(\alpha+\beta)}{\tan\beta}$ (d) $\dfrac{h+\tan(\alpha+\beta)}{\tan\beta}$

21. Which of the following is/are incorrect?

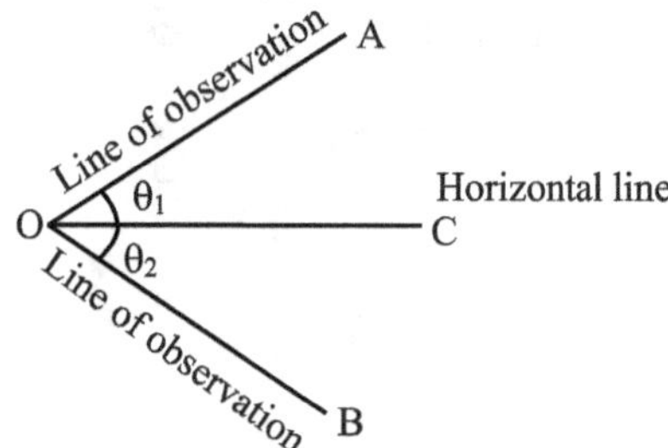

(a) θ_1 is the angle of elevation.

(b) θ_2 is the angle of depression.

(c) The angle of elevation or depression is always measured from horizontal line through the point of observation.

(d) θ_1 and θ_2 are always equal.

22. Which of the following statements are incorrect?

(a) Line of sight is the line drawn from the eyes of the observer to a point in the object where the person is viewing.

(b) Angle of elevation is the angle formed by the line of sight with horizontal through the eyes of observer when the object is above the horizontal level.

(c) Angle of depression is the angle formed by the line of sight with the horizontal when the object is below the horizontal level.

(d) None of these

Case/Passage Based Questions

DIRECTIONS : *Study the given Case/Passage and answer the following questions.*

Case/Passage-I

A group of students of class X visited India Gate on an education trip. The teacher and students had interest in history as well. The teacher narrated that India Gate, official name Delhi Memorial, originally called All-India War Memorial, monumental sandstone arch in New Delhi, dedicated to the troops of British India who died in wars fought between 1914 and 1919. The teacher also said that India Gate, which is located at the eastern end of the Rajpath (formerly called the Kingsway), is about 138 feet (42 metres) in height.

[From CBSE Question Bank 2021]

23. What is the angle of elevation if they are standing at a distance of 42m away from the monument?

(a) 30°   (b) 45°

(c) 60°   (d) 0°

24. They want to see the tower at an angle of 60°. So, they want to know the distance where they should stand and hence find the distance.

(a) 25.24 m   (b) 20.12 m

(c) 42 m   (d) 24.64 m

25. If the altitude of the Sun is at 60°, then the height of the vertical tower that will cast a shadow of length 20 m is

(a) $20\sqrt{3}$ m   (b) $20/\sqrt{3}$ m

(c) $15/\sqrt{3}$ m   (d) $15\sqrt{3}$ m

26. The ratio of the length of a rod and its shadow is 1:1 . The angle of elevation of the Sun is

(a) 30°   (b) 45°

(c) 60°   (d) 90°

27. The angle formed by the line of sight with the horizontal when the object viewd is below the horizontal level is

(a) corresponding angle

(b) angle of elevation

(c) angle of depression

(d) complete angle

Assertion & Reason

DIRECTIONS : *Each of these questions contains an Assertion followed by Reason. Read them carefully and answer the question on the basis of following options. You have to select the one that best describes the two statements.*

(a) If both **Assertion** and **Reason** are **correct** and Reason is the **correct explanation** of Assertion.

(b) If both **Assertion** and **Reason** are correct, but Reason is **not the correct explanation** of Assertion.

(c) If **Assertion** is **correct** but **Reason** is **incorrect**.

(d) If **Assertion** is **incorrect** but **Reason** is **correct**.

28. Assertion :

In the figure,

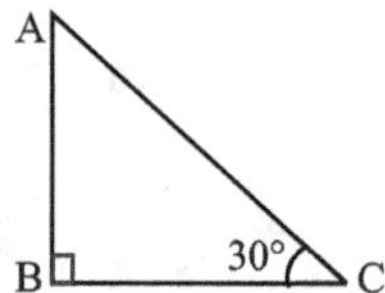

if $BC = 20$ m, then

height AB is 11.56 m.

Reason : $\tan\theta = \dfrac{AB}{BC} = \dfrac{\text{perpendicular}}{\text{base}},$

where θ is the angle $\angle ACB$.

29. **Assertion :** If the length of shadow of a vertical pole is equal to its height, then the angle of elevation of the sun is 45°.

Reason : According to pythagoras theorem, $h^2 = l^2 + b^2$, where h = hypotenuse, l = length and b = base

❯ Match the Following

DIRECTIONS : *Each question contains statements given in two columns which have to be matched. Statements (A, B, C, D) in column-I have to be matched with statements (p, q, r, s) in column-II.*

30. From a window, h metres high above the ground, of a house in a street, the angles of elevation and depression of the top and bottom of another house on the opposite side of the street are α and β respectively, then match the column.

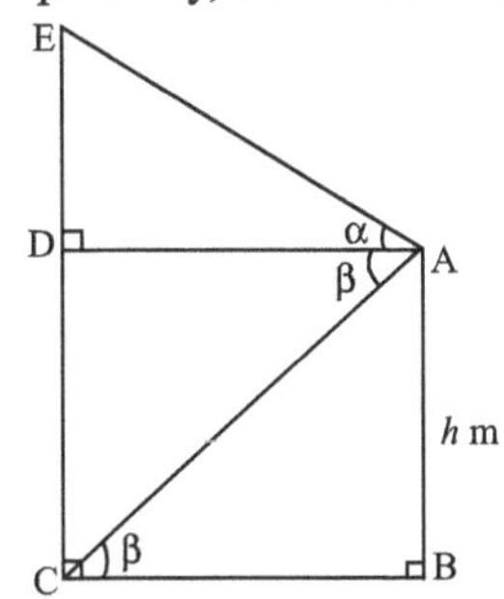

Column-I	Column-II
(A) DB	(p) $h(1 + \tan\alpha \cot\beta)$
(B) DE	(q) $h / \sin\beta$
(C) CE	(r) $h \tan\alpha \cot\beta$
(D) AD	(s) $h \cot\beta$

31.

Column-I	Column-II
(A) 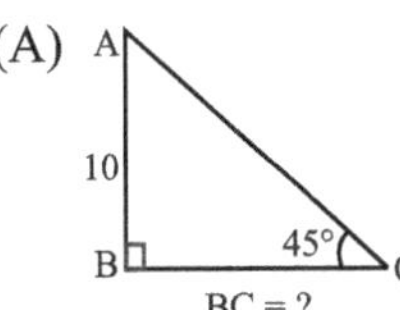 $BC = ?$	(p) $60°$
(B) 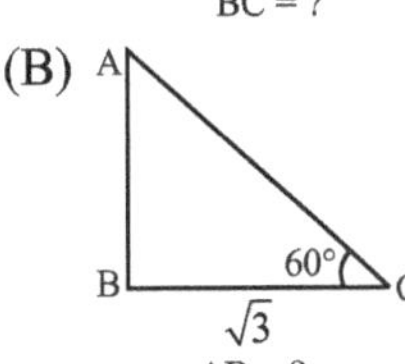 $AB = ?$	(q) 10
(C) 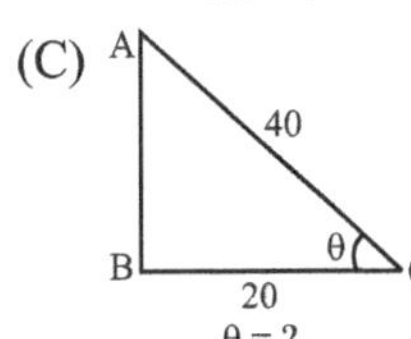 $\theta = ?$	(r) $\dfrac{1}{5}$
(D) 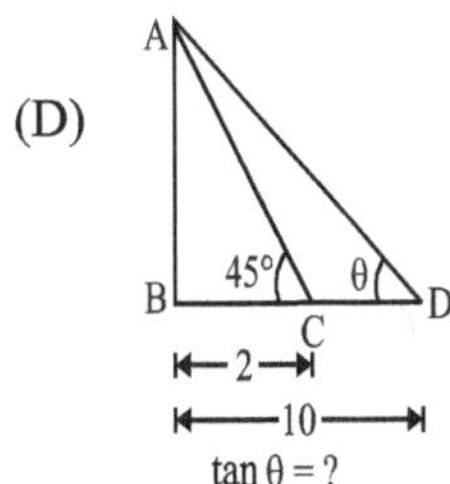 $\tan\theta = ?$	(s) 3

❯ Fill in the Blanks

DIRECTIONS : *Complete the following statements with an appropriate word / term to be filled in the blank space(s).*

32. The .... is the line drawn from the eye of an observer to the point in the object viewed by the observer.

33. The .... of an object viewed, is the angle formed by the line of sight with the horizontal when it is above the horizontal level, i.e., the case when we raise our head to look at the object.

34. The .... of an object viewed, is the angle formed by the line of sight with the horizontal when it is below the horizontal level, i.e., the case when we lower our head to look at the object.

35. In the adjoining figure, the positions of observer and object are marked.

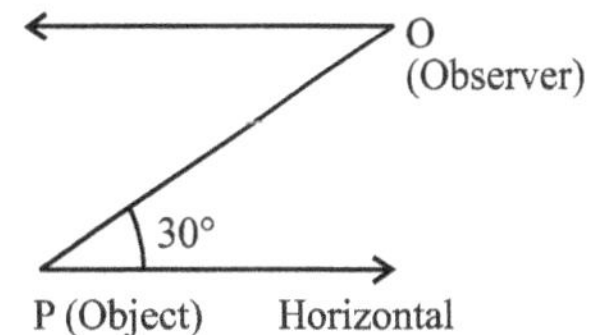

The angle of depression is ....

36. The top of a building from a fixed point is observed at an angle of elevation 60° and the distance from the foot of the building to the point is 100 m. then the height of the building is................

37. In fig. the angles of depressions from the observing positions O_1 and O_2 respectively of the object A are ...., ...

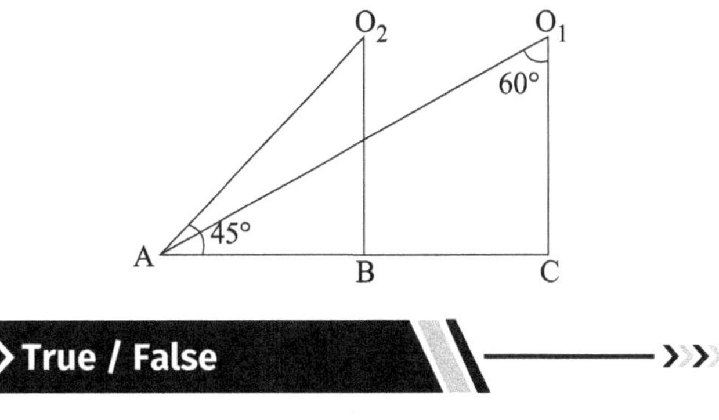

❯ True / False

DIRECTIONS : *Read the following statements and write your answer as true or false.*

A straight highway leads to the foot of a tower of height 50 m. From the top of the tower, the angles of depression of two cars standing on the highway are 30° and 60°. [$\sqrt{3} = 1.73$]

Now, based on the above information, mark the given statements as true or false.

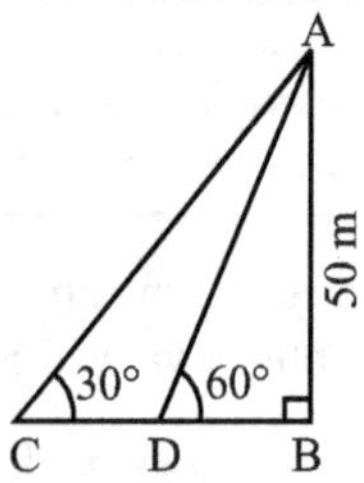

38. Distance between the cars is 57.67 m.

39. First car is at a distance of 38.90 m from the tower.

40. Second car is at a distance of 86.50 m. from the tower.

41. Car at point C is at a distance of 200 m away from the top of the tower.

ANSWER KEY & SOLUTIONS

1. **(a)** Let AB be the building of height 20m and BC be the transmission tower of height h metres.

In $\triangle\, OAB$, $\tan 45° = \dfrac{AB}{OA} \Rightarrow 1 = \dfrac{20}{OA}$

$\Rightarrow OA = 20$ m

In $\triangle OAC$,

$\tan 60° = \dfrac{h+20}{20}$

$\Rightarrow \sqrt{3} = \dfrac{h+20}{20}$

$\Rightarrow h = 20\left(\sqrt{3}-1\right)$ m

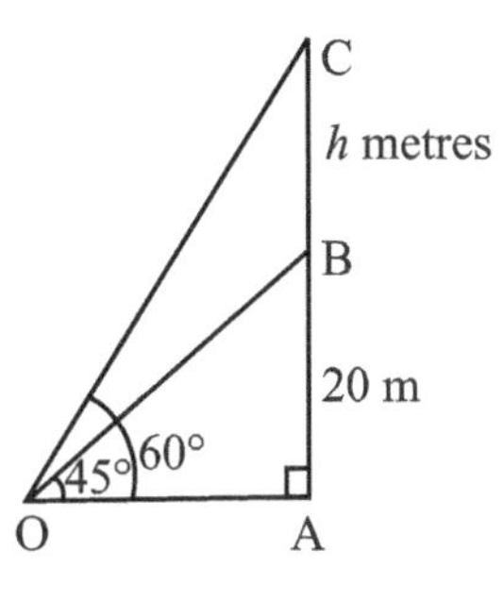

2. **(b)** BD = DC given as D is the mid point of BC.

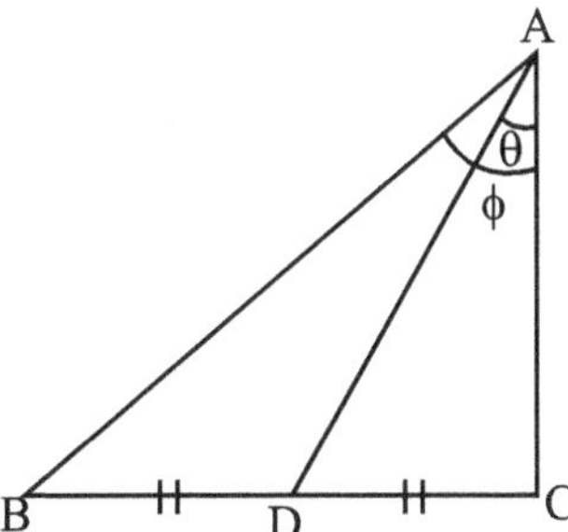

In $\triangle ADC$, $\cot\theta = \dfrac{AC}{CD}$ ... (i)

In $\triangle ABC$, $\cot\phi = \dfrac{AC}{BC}$ ... (ii)

$\therefore \dfrac{\cot\theta}{\cot\phi} = \dfrac{\dfrac{AC}{CD}}{\dfrac{AC}{BC}}$

$= \dfrac{\dfrac{AC}{CD}}{\dfrac{AC}{2CD}}$ $[\because 2CD = BC]$

$\Rightarrow \dfrac{\cot\theta}{\cot\phi} = \dfrac{2}{1}$

$\Rightarrow \dfrac{\tan\theta}{\tan\phi} = \dfrac{1}{2}$

3. **(b)** Let DC be the tower of height 'h' metres.

In rt. $\triangle ACD$, $\tan\theta = \dfrac{h}{x}$ ... (i)

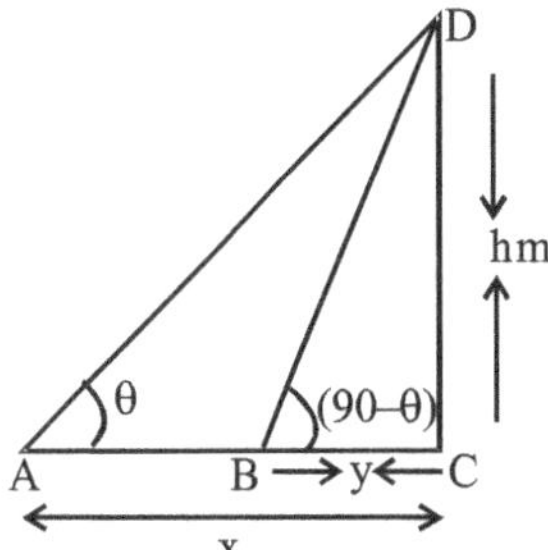

In rt. $\triangle BDC$, $\tan (90 - \theta) = \dfrac{h}{y}$

$\Rightarrow \cot\theta = \dfrac{h}{y}$ ... (ii)

Multiplying (i) by (ii), we get

$\tan\theta \times \cot\theta = \dfrac{h}{x} \times \dfrac{h}{y}$

$\Rightarrow \tan\theta \times \dfrac{1}{\tan\theta} = \dfrac{h^2}{xy}$

$\Rightarrow 1 = \dfrac{h^2}{xy} \Rightarrow h^2 = xy$

$\Rightarrow h = \sqrt{xy}$

4. **(d)**

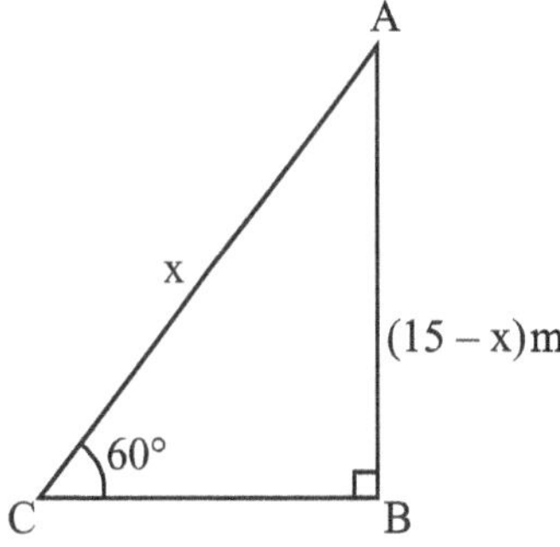

Let the broken part of the ladder, AC = x metres

$\therefore$ length of ladder = AC + AB = 15 m

$\Rightarrow$ x + AB = 15 $\Rightarrow$ AB = (15 – x)m

In $\triangle$ ABC,

$\sin 60° = \dfrac{AB}{AC} = \dfrac{15-x}{x} \Rightarrow \dfrac{\sqrt{3}}{2} = \dfrac{15-x}{x}$

$\Rightarrow \sqrt{3}x = 30 - 2x \Rightarrow x\left(\sqrt{3}+2\right) = 30$

$$\Rightarrow \quad x = \frac{30}{\sqrt{3}+2} = \frac{30\left(2-\sqrt{3}\right)}{(2)^2 - \left(\sqrt{3}\right)^2}$$

$$\Rightarrow \quad x = 30\left(2-\sqrt{3}\right) = 8.04\,\text{m}$$

Hence, AB $= 15 - x = (15 - 8.04)\text{m} = 6.96$ m

5.   (a) Let h be the length of the pole.

By the given condition $\dfrac{6}{4} = \dfrac{h}{50}$

$$\Rightarrow \quad h = \frac{6 \times 50}{4} = 75\text{m}$$

6.   (a) Here, In rt. $\triangle ABD$,

$$\cot\alpha = \frac{BD}{AB} = \frac{\dfrac{h}{2} + BC}{h} \quad ....(i)$$

also, In rt. $\triangle ABC$,

$$\cot\beta = \frac{BC}{AB} = \frac{BC}{h}$$

Now, $\cot\alpha - \cot\beta$

$$= \frac{\dfrac{h}{2} + BC}{h} - \frac{BC}{h} = \frac{1}{2}$$

7.   (a)

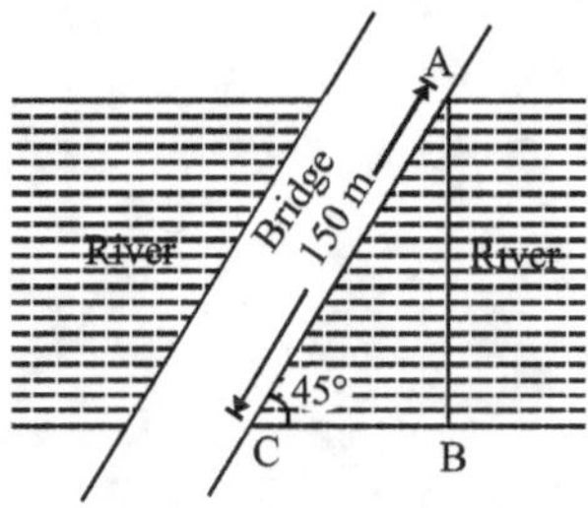

$$\frac{x}{150} = \sin 45° = \frac{1}{\sqrt{2}}$$

$$\Rightarrow \quad x = \frac{150}{\sqrt{2}} \cdot \frac{\sqrt{2}}{\sqrt{2}} = 75\sqrt{2}\ \text{m.}$$

8.   (b) In the following figure,

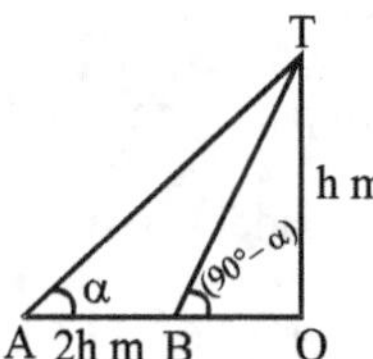

Let OB $= x$ m.

$$\tan\alpha = \frac{h}{2h + x} \qquad ...(i)$$

$$\tan(90° - \alpha) = \frac{h}{x} \Rightarrow x = \tan\alpha \qquad ...(ii)$$

From (i) and (ii)

$$\tan^2\alpha + 2\tan\alpha - 1 = 0$$

$$\therefore \tan\alpha = \sqrt{2} - 1$$

9.   (a) In figure, the electrician is required to reach the point B on the pole AD.

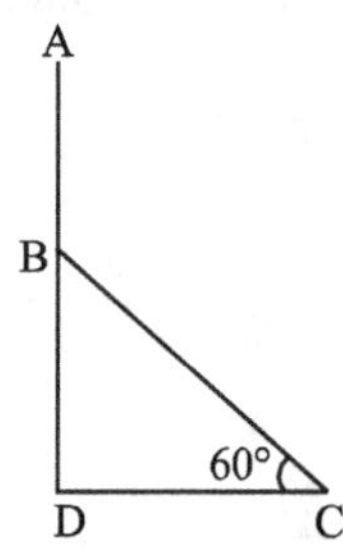

So, BD $= $ AD $-$ AB $= (5 - 1.3)$
$= 3.7$ m

So, $\sin 60° = \dfrac{BD}{BC} \Rightarrow \dfrac{3.7}{BC} = \dfrac{\sqrt{3}}{2}$

$$\therefore BC = \frac{3.7 \times 2}{\sqrt{3}} = 4.28\ \text{m (Approx.)}$$

i.e., the length of the ladder should be 4.28 m

Now, $\dfrac{DC}{BD} = \cot 60° = \dfrac{1}{\sqrt{3}}$

i.e., $DC = \dfrac{3.7}{\sqrt{3}} = 2.14\text{m}\left(\text{Approx}\right)$

Therefore, he should place the foot of the ladder at a distance of 2.14 m from the pole.

10.   (b) Let A_1 and A_2 be the position of the two aeroplanes.

and $A_1 A_2 = x$ m

OM $= y$ m

$$\frac{y}{3125} = \cot 30° = \sqrt{3}$$

$$\Rightarrow \quad y = \sqrt{3} \times 3125$$

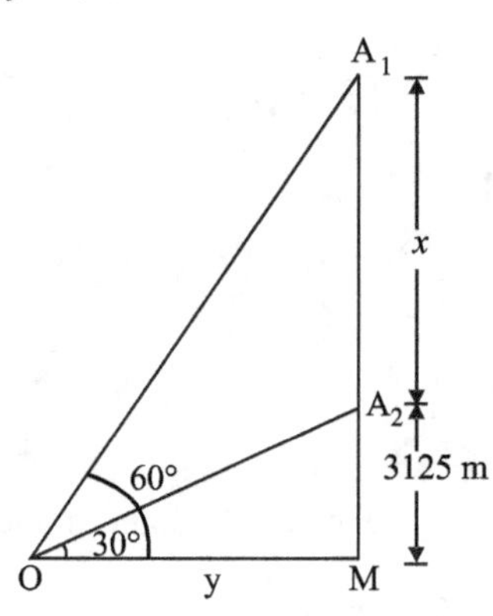

Also, $\dfrac{y}{3125+x} = \cot 60° = \dfrac{1}{\sqrt{3}}$

$\Rightarrow \dfrac{(3125)\sqrt{3}}{3125+x} = \dfrac{1}{\sqrt{3}}$

$\Rightarrow 3125 + x = (3125)\,(3) \Rightarrow x = 6250$ m.

11. **(d) Hint:** $\sin 30° = \dfrac{BC}{AC}$

$\Rightarrow \dfrac{1}{2} = \dfrac{BC}{6} \Rightarrow BC = 3$ cm.

12. **(c) Hint:** $\tan 30° = \dfrac{AB}{OB}$

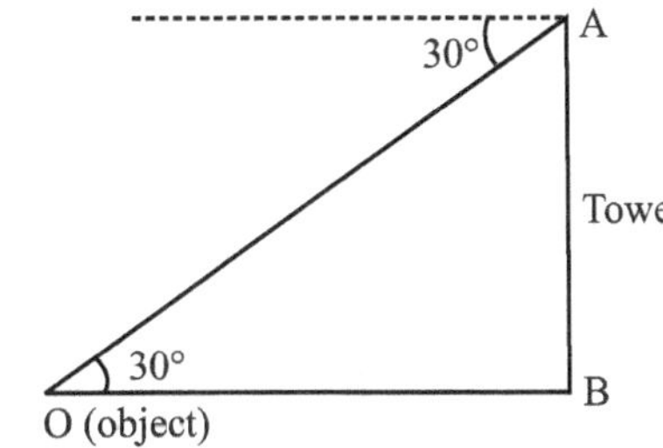

$\Rightarrow \dfrac{1}{\sqrt{3}} = \dfrac{75}{OB}$

$\Rightarrow OB = 75\sqrt{3}$ m

13. **(a)**

14. **(a)** Let AB be the height of a man and BC be the shadow of a man.

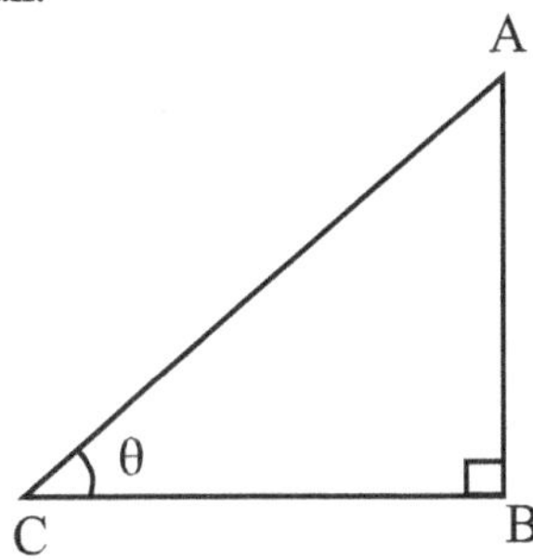

$\therefore AB = BC$

In $\triangle ABC$,

$\tan\theta = \dfrac{AB}{BC} \Rightarrow \dfrac{AB}{AB} = \tan\theta \Rightarrow \tan\theta = 1 \Rightarrow \theta = 45°$

$\Rightarrow \quad \tan\theta = 1 \Rightarrow \theta = 45°$

15. **(d)** Let BC be the tree of height h metre.

Let AB be the shadow of tree.

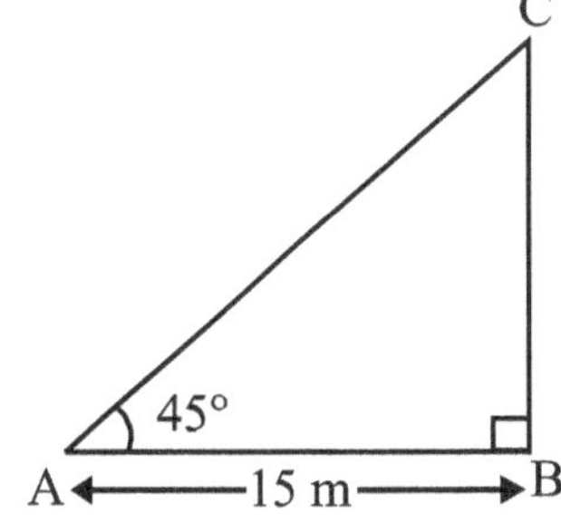

In $\triangle ABC$,

$\dfrac{BC}{BA} = \tan 45°$

$\Rightarrow BC = AB = 15$ m.

16. **(c)** $\angle XCA = \angle CAB = 60°$

Hence, angle of depression $= 60°$

17. **(b)**

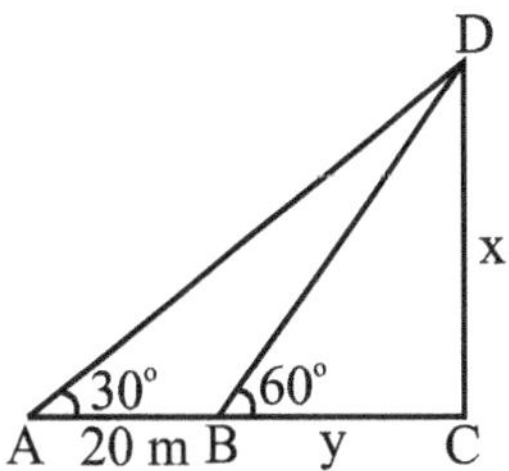

In $\triangle DBC$, $\tan 60° = \dfrac{x}{y} \Rightarrow x = \sqrt{3}y$ ... (i)

In $\triangle ADC$, $\tan 30° = \dfrac{x}{20+y}$

$\Rightarrow \dfrac{1}{\sqrt{3}} = \dfrac{\sqrt{3}y}{20+y}$ ($\because$ From (i))

$\Rightarrow y + 20 = 3y$

$\Rightarrow 2y = 20 \Rightarrow y = 10$ m

18. **(b)**

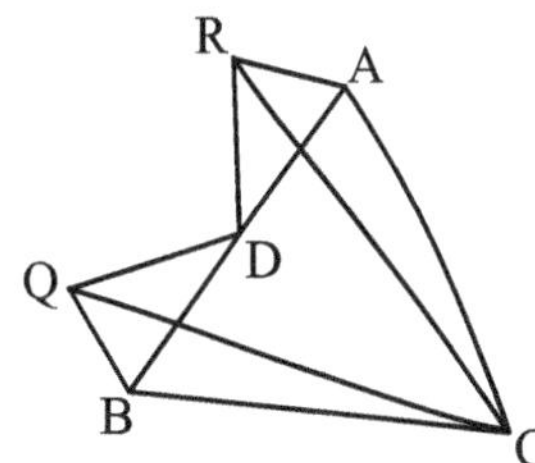

Taking $\triangle ARC$ and $\triangle BQC$

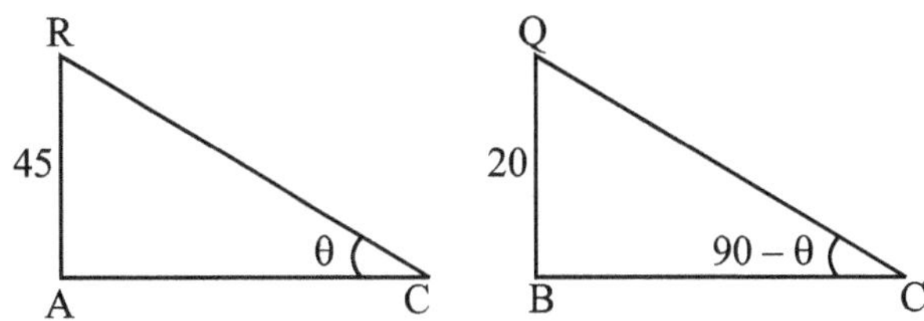

$\tan(90 - \theta) = \cot\theta$

$\dfrac{20}{BC} = \dfrac{AC}{45}$ (let $AC = BC = AB = x$ m)

$x^2 = 900 \Rightarrow x = 30$

Now, in $\Delta\,ARD$ and BQD

$\dfrac{45}{AD} = \dfrac{20}{BD} = \tan\theta \Rightarrow \dfrac{AD}{BD} = \dfrac{9}{4}$

$AD = \dfrac{9}{13} \times 30 = 20\left(\dfrac{10}{13}\right)$ m

19. **(a)** Let $PQRS$ be the rectangular field with length l and width b and RT be the vertical pole.

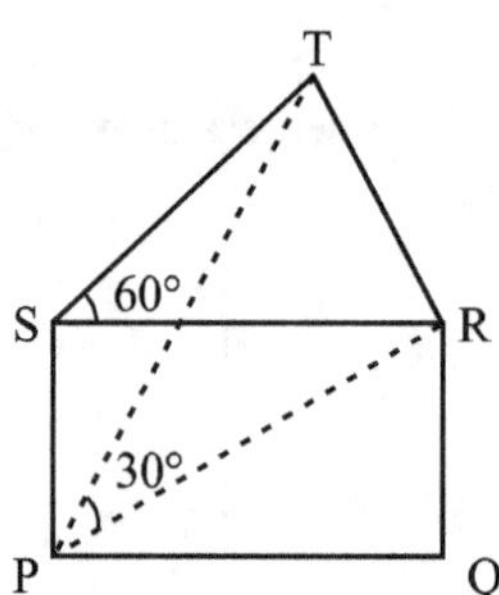

In ΔPRT, $\tan 30° = \dfrac{RT}{PR} \Rightarrow \dfrac{1}{\sqrt{3}} = \dfrac{10}{PR}$

$PR = \sqrt{l^2 + b^2} = 10\sqrt{3}$

$l^2 + b^2 = 100 \times 3 = 300$ ... (i)

In ΔSRT, $\tan 60° = \dfrac{10}{SR}$

$\Rightarrow \quad \sqrt{3} = \dfrac{10}{SR}$

$SR = \dfrac{10}{\sqrt{3}} = l$

$\Rightarrow \quad l^2 = \dfrac{100}{3}$ ... (ii)

Use equation (ii) in (i), then

$b^2 = 300 - \dfrac{100}{3} = \dfrac{800}{3}$

$l^2 b^2 = \dfrac{100}{3} \times \dfrac{800}{3} = \dfrac{80000}{9}$

$\Rightarrow \quad lb = \dfrac{200\sqrt{2}}{3}$

Hence, the required area of rectangular field is

$\dfrac{200\sqrt{2}}{3}$.

20. **(b)** In figure,

$\tan\alpha = \dfrac{y}{x}$ and

$\tan\beta = \dfrac{h}{x}$

$\therefore \quad \dfrac{\tan\alpha}{\tan\beta} = \dfrac{y}{h}$

$h + y = h\left(1 + \dfrac{\tan\alpha}{\tan\beta}\right)$

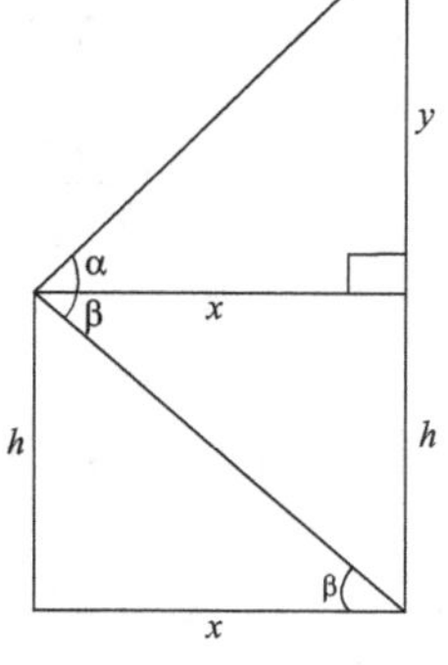

21. **(d)**

22. **(d)** All the statements given in option a, b and c are correct.

23. **(b)**

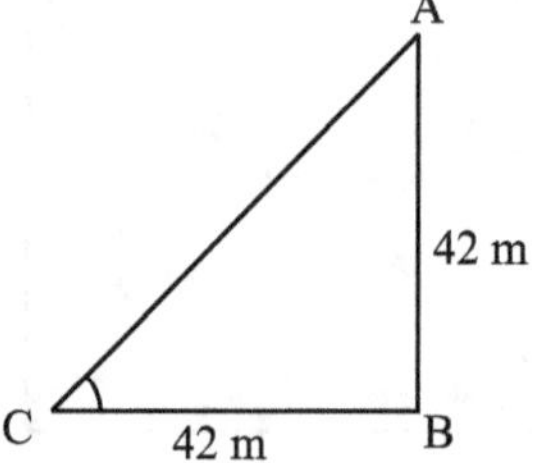

Since h = 42

     d = 42

So $\theta = 45°$

24. **(a)** $\tan 60° = \dfrac{42}{x}$

$x = \dfrac{42}{\sqrt{3}} = \dfrac{42}{3}\sqrt{3} = 14\sqrt{3} = 24.24$ m

25. **(a)**

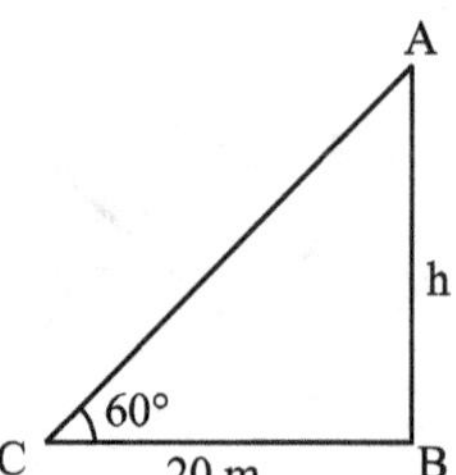

$\tan 60° = \dfrac{h}{20}$

$h = 20\sqrt{3}$ m

26. **(b)**

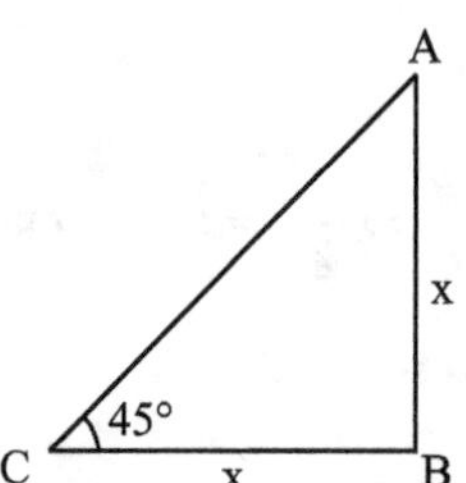

Since ratio of length of a rod : Shadow of rod = 1:1

so Angle = 45°

27. **(a)** Corresponding angle

28. **(a)** Both the assertion and reason are correct, reason is the correct explanation of the assertion.

$$\tan 30° = \frac{AB}{BC} = \frac{AB}{20}$$

$$AB = \frac{1}{\sqrt{3}} \times 20 = \frac{20}{1.73} = 11.56 \text{ m.}$$

29. **(b)** Both assertion and reason are correct, but reason is not the correct explanation of the assertion.

30. **(A)** → q; **(B)** → r; **(C)** → p; **(D)** → s

31. **(A)** → q ; **(B)** → s ; **(C)** → p ; **(D)** → r

(A) $\tan 45° = \dfrac{AB}{BC} \Rightarrow BC = 10$

(B) $\tan 60° = \dfrac{AB}{BC} = \dfrac{AB}{\sqrt{3}} \Rightarrow AB = \sqrt{3} \times \sqrt{3} = 3$

(C) $\cos\theta = \dfrac{20}{40} = \dfrac{1}{2} = \cos 60° \Rightarrow \theta = 60°$

(D) In $\triangle ABC$, $\tan 45° = \dfrac{AB}{BC} \Rightarrow AB = 2$, and

$$\tan\theta = \frac{AB}{BD} = \frac{2}{10} = \frac{1}{5}.$$

32. line of sight

33. angle of elevation

34. angle of depression

35. 30°

36. $100\sqrt{3}$ m

37. [30°, 45°]

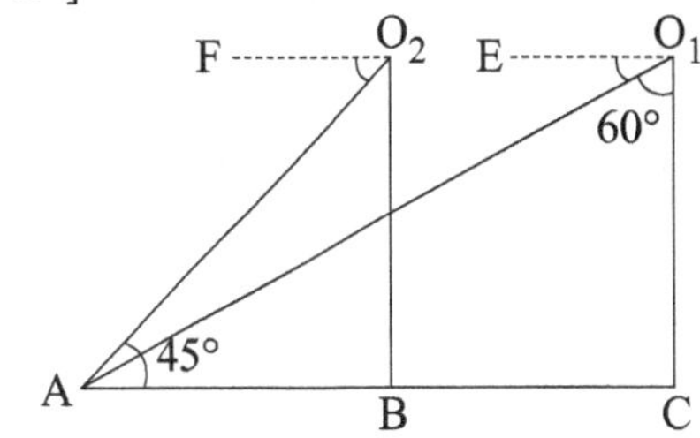

Depression angle at $O_1 = 90° - 60° = 30°$

Depression angle at $O_2 = 45° = \angle BAO_2$

38. True

39. False

40. True

41. False

14 Surface Areas and Volumes

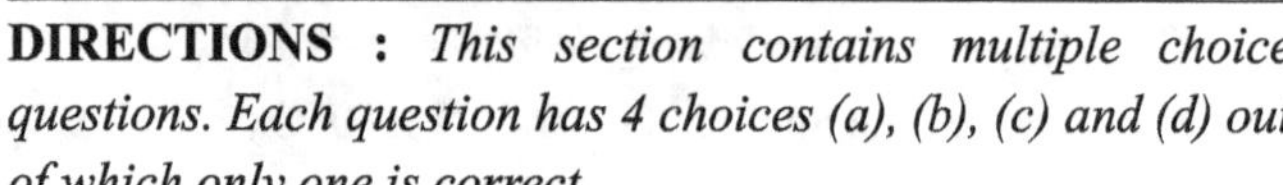

Multiple Choice Questions (MCQs) ———— ≫≫≫

DIRECTIONS : *This section contains multiple choice questions. Each question has 4 choices (a), (b), (c) and (d) out of which only one is correct.*

1. The volume of a cylinder is $448\,\pi$ cm^3 and height 7 cm. Find its lateral surface area and total surface area is
   (a) 253 cm^2 (b) 352 cm^2
   (c) 532 cm^2 (d) 325 cm^2

2. The diameter of a garden roller is 1.4 m, and 2m long. How much area will it cover in 5 revolutions.
   (a) 44 m^2 (b) 140 m^2
   (c) 440 m^2 (d) 220 m^2

3. If a sphere and a cube have equal surface areas, then the ratio of the diameter of the sphere to the edge of the cube is
   (a) $1 : 2$ (b) $2 : 1$
   (c) $\sqrt{\pi} : \sqrt{6}$ (d) $\sqrt{6} : \sqrt{\pi}$

4. The internal and external diameter of a hollow hemispherical vessel are 42 cm and 45.5 cm. respectively. Find its capacity (volume) and also its outer curved surface area.
   (a) 5.27 litres, 3253.25 cm^2
   (b) 5.20 litres, 3253.25 cm^2
   (c) 5.27 litres, 3200.18 cm^2
   (d) 5.27 litres, 3250.25 cm^2

5. If h, c, v are respectively the height, the C.S.A and the volume of a cone, find the value of $3\pi vh^3 - c^2h^2 + 9v^2$
   (a) 1 (b) 2
   (c) 0 (d) 3

6. The diagram shows the parts of a right cylinder. The volume of the cylinder, in cm^3 is

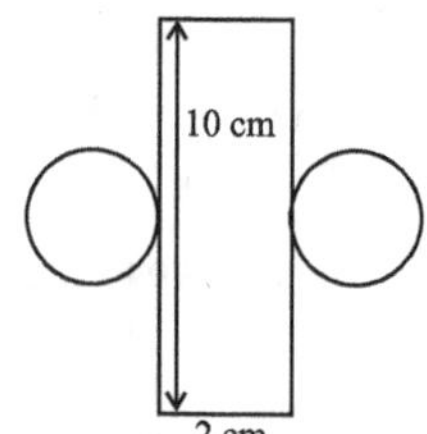

   (a) $\dfrac{20}{\pi}$

   (b) $\dfrac{50}{\pi}$

   (c) $\dfrac{25}{\pi}$

   (d) $40\,\pi$

7. If h be the height and α the semi-vertical angle of a right circular cone, then its volume is given by
   (a) $\dfrac{1}{3}\pi h^3 \tan^2 \alpha$ (b) $\dfrac{1}{3}\pi h^2 \tan^2 \alpha$
   (c) $\dfrac{1}{3}\pi h^2 \tan^3 \alpha$ (d) $\dfrac{1}{3}\pi h^3 \tan^3 \alpha$

8. Cubes A, B, C having edges of 18 cm, 24 cm and 30 cm respectively are melted and moulded into a new cube D. Find the edge of the bigger cube D.
   (a) 32 (b) 28
   (c) 39 (d) 36

9. The height of a conical tent is 14 m and its floor area is 346.5 m^2. The length of canvas, 11m wide, required for it is.
   (a) 490 m (b) 525 m
   (c) 665 m (d) 860 m

10. Three identical cones with base radius r are placed on their bases so that each is touching the other two. The radius of the circle drawn through their vertices is –
    (a) smaller than r
    (b) equal to r
    (c) larger than r
    (d) depends on the height of the cones

11. The diameter of hollow cone is equal to the diameter of a spherical ball. If the ball is placed at the base of the cone, what portion of the ball will be outside the cone?
    (a) 50% (b) less than 50%
    (c) more than 50% (d) 100%

12. A slab of ice 8 inches in length, 11 inches in breadth, and 2 inches thick was melted and resolidified in the form of a rod of 8 inches diameter. The length of such a rod, in inches, is nearest to
    (a) 3   (b) 3.5
    (c) 4   (d) 4.5

13. The base radii of a cone and a cylinder are equal. If their curved surface areas are also equal, then the ratio of the slant height of the cone to the height of the cylinder is
    (a) $2 : 1$ (b) $1 : 2$
    (c) $1 : 3$ (d) $3 : 1$

14. If the perimeter of one face of a cube is 20 cm, then its surface area is
    (a) 120 cm^2 (b) 150 cm^2
    (c) 125 cm^2 (d) 400 cm^2

15. A cube of side 12 cm is painted red on all the faces and then cut into smaller cubes, each of side 3 cm. What is the total number of smaller cubes having none of their faces painted?
    (a) 16   (b) 8
    (c) 12   (d) 24

16. If the diameter of the sphere is doubled, the surface area of the resultant sphere becomes x times that of the original one, then x would be
    (a) 2   (b) 3
    (c) 4   (d) 8

17. If h be the height and α the semi-vertical angle of a right circular cone, then its volume is given by
    (a) $\dfrac{1}{3}\pi h^3 \tan^2 \alpha$ (b) $\dfrac{1}{3}\pi h^2 \tan^2 \alpha$
    (c) $\dfrac{1}{3}\pi h^2 \tan^3 \alpha$ (d) $\dfrac{1}{3}\pi h^3 \tan^3 \alpha$

18. If the radius of the sphere is increased by 100%, the volume of the corresponding sphere is increased by
    (a) 200%   (b) 500%
    (c) 700%   (d) 800%

19. A sphere is melted and half of the melted liquid is used to form 11 identical cubes, whereas the remaining half is used to form 7 identical smaller spheres. The ratio of the side of the cube to the radius of the new small sphere is
    (a) $\left(\dfrac{4}{3}\right)^{1/3}$ (b) $\left(\dfrac{8}{3}\right)^{1/3}$
    (c) $(3)^{1/3}$ (d) 2

20. If a solid of one shape is converted to another, then the volume of the new solid
    (a) remains same   (b) increases
    (c) decreases   (d) can't say

21. In the adjoining figure, the bottom of the glass has a hemispherical raised portion. If the glass is filled with orange juice, the quantity of juice which a person will get is
    (a) $135 \,\pi \text{ cm}^3$
    (b) $117 \,\pi \text{ cm}^3$
    (c) $99 \,\pi \text{ cm}^3$
    (d) $36 \,\pi \text{ cm}^3$

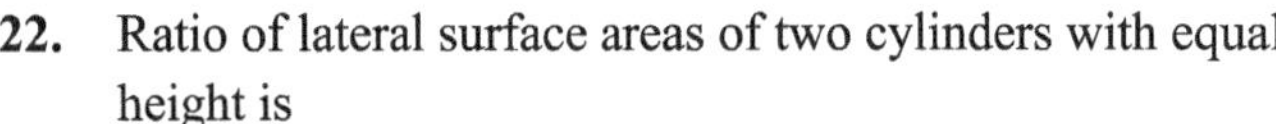

22. Ratio of lateral surface areas of two cylinders with equal height is
    (a) $1 : 2$ (b) $H : h$
    (c) $R : r$ (d) None of these

23. Ratio of volumes of two cylinders with equal height is
    (a) $H : h$ (b) $R : r$
    (c) $R^2 : r^2$ (d) None of these

24. Ratio of volumes of two cones with same radii is
    (a) $h_1 : h_2$ (b) $s_1 : s_2$
    (c) $r_1 : r_2$ (d) None of these

25. Volume of a spherical shell is given by
    (a) $4\pi (R^2 - r^2)$ (b) $\pi (R^3 - r^3)$
    (c) $4\pi (R^3 - r^3)$ (d) $\dfrac{4}{3}\pi (R^3 - r^3)$

26. The volume of a largest sphere that can be cut from cylindrical log of wood of base radius 1m and height 4 m, is
    (a) $\dfrac{16}{3} \neq \text{m}^3$ (b) $\dfrac{8}{3} \neq \text{m}^3$
    (c) $\dfrac{4}{3} \neq \text{m}^3$ (d) $\dfrac{10}{3} \neq \text{m}^3$

27. If four times the sum of the areas of two circular faces of a cylinder of height 8 cm is equal to twice the curve surface area, then diameter of the cylinder is
    (a) 4 cm   (b) 8 cm
    (c) 2 cm   (d) 6 cm

28. A rectangular sheet of paper 40 cm × 22 cm, is rolled to form a hollow cylinder of height 40 cm. The radius of the cylinder (in cm) is
    (a) 3.5   (b) 7
    (c) 80/7   (d) 5

29. A right circular cylinder has its height equal to two times its radius. It is inscribed in a right circular cone having its diameter equal to 10 cm and height 12 cm, and the axes of both the cylinder and the cone coincide. Then, the volume (in cm³) of the cylinder is approximately
    (a) 107.5   (b) 118.6
    (c) 127.5   (d) 128.7

30. If the ratio of volumes of two cubes is 27 : 64, then the ratio of their surface area is:
    (a) 3 : 4
    (b) 4 : 3
    (c) 9 : 16
    (d) 16 : 9

31. Volumes of two spheres are in the ratio 125 : 64. The ratio of their surface areas will be
    (a) 5 : 4
    (b) 25 : 16
    (c) 16 : 25
    (d) 125 : 64

32. A solid metallic block of volume one cubic metre is melted and recast into the form of a rectangular bar of length 9 metres having a square base. If the weight of the block is 90 kg and biggest cube is cut off from the bar, then the weight of the cube is
    (a) $6\dfrac{1}{3}$ kg
    (b) $5\dfrac{2}{3}$ kg
    (c) $4\dfrac{2}{3}$ kg
    (d) $3\dfrac{1}{3}$ kg

33. Consider a cuboid all of whose edges are integers and whose base is a square. Suppose the sum of all its edges is numerically equal to the sum of the areas of all its six faces. Then, the sum of all its edges is
    (a) 12
    (b) 18
    (c) 24
    (d) 36

34. Shyam wants to make a solid brick shape structure from 400 wooden cubes of unit volume each. If the sides of the solid brick have the ratio 1 : 2 : 3, then the maximum number of cubes, which can be used, will be ________.
    (a) 400
    (b) 288
    (c) 300
    (d) 384

35. Sealed bottle containing some water is made up of two cylinders A and B of radius 1.5 cm and 3 cm respectively, as shown in the figure. When the bottle is placed right up on a table, the height of water init is 15 cm, but when placed upside down the height of water is 24 cm. The height of the bottle is

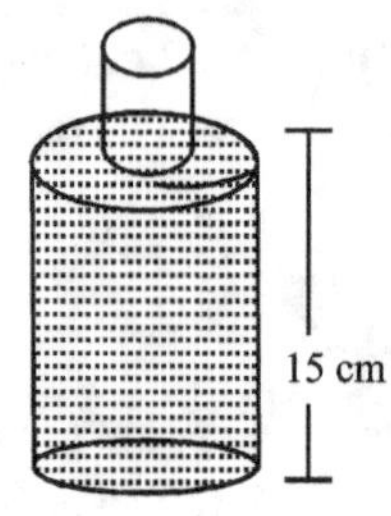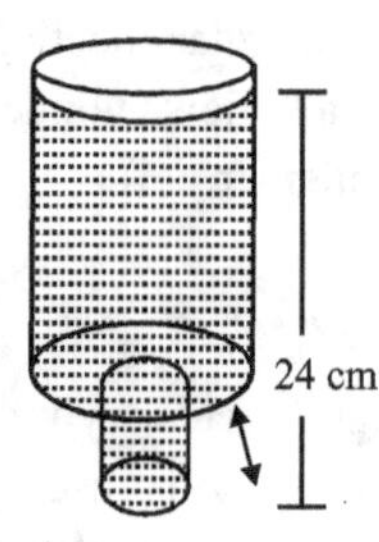

    (a) 25 cm
    (b) 26 cm
    (c) 27 cm
    (d) 28 cm

36. The number of solid cones with integer radius and integer height each having its volume numerically equal to its total surface area is
    (a) 0
    (b) 1
    (c) 2
    (d) infinite

37. A solid metallic cylinder of height 10 cm and diameter 14 cm is melted to make two cones in the proportion of their volumes as 3 : 4, keeping the height 10 cm, what would be the percentage increase in the flat surface area?
    (a) 9
    (b) 16
    (c) 50
    (d) 200

38. Given three cubes with integer side lengths, if the sum of surface areas of three cubes is 498 sq. cm, then the sum of the volumes of the cubes in all possible solutions is
    (a) 731
    (b) 495
    (c) 1226
    (d) None of these

39. Which one of the following is/are incorrect ?
    (a) Total surface area of cuboid is $2(lb + bh + hl)$
    (b) Total surface area of a cube is $4l^2$
    (c) Area of four walls = $2h\,(l + b)$
    (d) Area of four walls = Height × Perimeter of the room

40. A Circular Cylinder can not be separated into
    (a) circular end at the bottom
    (b) curved surface
    (c) circular end at the top
    (d) None of these

41. Which one of the following is / are incorrect ?
    (a) Total surface area of cylinder is $2\pi r^2 + 2\pi rh$.
    (b) Total surface area of a sphere is $4\pi r^2$.
    (c) Total surface area of cone is $\pi r^2 + \pi rl$.
    (d) None of these

42. Which one of the following is/ are made up of combinations of two or more of the basic solids?
    (a) Buildings
    (b) Funnel
    (c) Monuments
    (d) Test-tube

43. Among the following, which one is/are correct?
    (a) The slant height is the longest side of a pyramid.
    (b) The section between the base and a plane parallel to the base of a solid is known as frustum.
    (c) All the surfaces of a cuboid are square.
    (d) For a cylinder, the top, the bottom and the walls of the cylinder determine the total surface area.

44. If a marble of radius 2.1 cm is put into a cylindrical cup full of water of radius 5cm and height 6 cm, then how much water flows out of the cylindrical cup?
    (a) 38.8 cm^3
    (b) 55.4 cm^3
    (c) 19.4 cm^3
    (d) 471.4 cm^3

45. A cubical ice-cream brick of edge 22 cm is to be distributed among some children by filling ice-cream cones of radius 2 cm and height 7 cm upto its brim. How many children will get the ice-cream cones?
   (a) 163   (b) 263   (c) 363   (d) 463

46. The volume of the largest right circular cone that can be cut out from a cube of edge 4.2 cm is
   (a) 9.7 cm^3 (b) 77.6 cm^3
   (c) 58.2 cm^3 (d) 19.4 cm^3

47. If two solid hemispheres of same base radius r are joined together along their bases, then curved surface area of this new solid is
   (a) $4\pi r^2$ (b) $6\pi r^2$ (c) $3\pi r^2$ (d) $8\pi r^2$

48. A right circular cylinder of radius r cm and height h cm ($h > 2r$) just encloses a sphere of diameter
   (a) r cm   (b) $2r$ cm   (c) h cm   (d) $2h$ cm

> **Case/Passage Based Questions** ──── »»»

DIRECTIONS : *Study the given Case/Passage and answer the following questions.*

Case /Passage-I

Adventure camps are the perfect place for the children to practice decision making for themselves without parents and teachers guiding their every move. Some students of a school reached for adventure at Sakleshpur. At the camp, the waiters served some students with a welcome drink in a cylindrical glass and some students in a hemispherical cup whose dimensions are shown below. After that they went for a jungle trek. The jungle trek was enjoyable but tiring. As dusk fell, it was time to take shelter. Each group of four students was given a canvas of area 551m^2. Each group had to make a conical tent to accommodate all the four students. Assuming that all the stitching and wasting incurred while cutting, would amount to 1m^2, the students put the tents. The radius of the tent is 7 m.

[From CBSE Question Bank 2021]

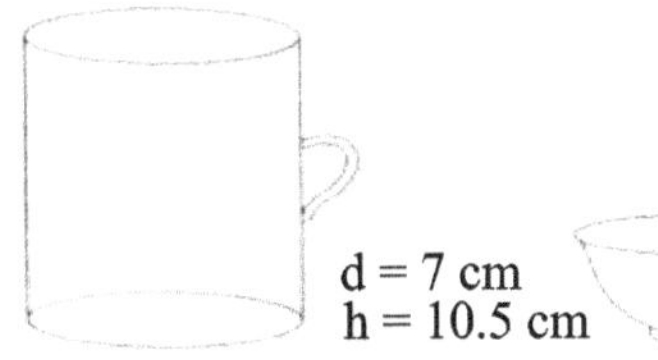

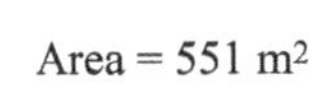

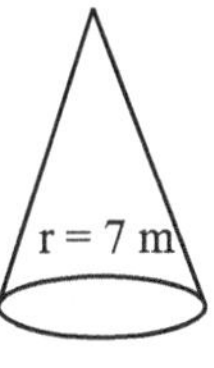

49. The volume of cylindrical cup is
   (a) 295.75cm^3 (b) 7415.5cm^3
   (c) 384.88cm^3 (d) 404.25cm^3

50. The volume of hemispherical cup is
   (a) 179.67cm^3 (b) 89.83 cm^3
   (c) 172.25 cm^3 (d) 210.60 cm^3

51. Which container had more juice and by how much?
   (a) Hemispherical cup, 195 cm^3
   (b) Cylindrical glass, 207 cm^3
   (c) Hemispherical cup, 280.85 cm^3
   (d) Cylindrical glass, 314.42 cm^3

52. The height of the conical tent prepared to accommodate four students is
   (a) 18m   (b) 10m
   (c) 24m   (d) 14m

53. How much space on the ground is occupied by each student in the conicaltent
   (a) 54m^2 (b) 38.5m^2
   (c) 86m^2 (d) 24m^2

Case /Passage-II

[From CBSE Question Bank 2021]

The Great Stupa at Sanchi is one of the oldest stone structures in India, and an important monument of Indian Architecture. It was originally commissioned by the emperor Ashoka in the 3rd century BCE. Its nucleus was a simple hemispherical brick structure built over the relics of the Buddha. .It is a perfect example of combination of solid figures. A big hemispherical dome with a cuboidal structure mounted on it. $\left(\text{Take } \pi = \dfrac{22}{7}\right)$

54. Calculate the volume of the hemispherical dome if the height of the dome is 21 m —
   (a) 19404 cu. m   (b) 2000 cu .m
   (c) 15000 cu. m   (d) 19000 cu. m

55. The formula to find the Volume of Sphere is-

(a) $\frac{2}{3}\pi r^3$　　　　(b) $\frac{4}{3}\pi r^3$

(c) $4\,\pi r^2$　　　　(d) $2\,\pi r^2$

56. The cloth require to cover the hemispherical dome if the radius of its base is14m is

(a) 1222 sq.m

(b) 1232 sq.m

(c) 1200 sq.m

(d) 1400 sq.m

57. The total surface area of the combined figure i.e. hemispherical dome withradius 14m and cuboidal shaped top with dimensions 8m × 6m × 4m is

(a) 1200 sq. m　　　　(b) 1232 sq. m

(c) 1392 sq.m　　　　(d) 1932 sq. m

58. The volume of the cuboidal shaped top is with dimensions mentioned in question 4

(a) 182.45 m³　　　　(b) 282.45 m³

(c) 292m³　　　　(d) 192m³

Case /Passage-III

On a Sunday, your Parents took you to a fair. You could see lot of toys displayed,and you wanted them to buy a RUBIK's cube and strawberry ice-cream for you. Observe the figures and answer the questions-:　　**[From CBSE Question Bank 2021]**

59. The length of the diagonal if each edge measures 6cm is

(a) $3\sqrt{3}$　　　　(b) $3\sqrt{6}$

(c) $\sqrt{12}$　　　　(d) $6\sqrt{3}$

60. Volume of the solid figure if the length of the edge is 7cm is-

(a) 256 cm³　　　　(b) 196 cm³

(c) 343 cm³　　　　(d) 434 cm³

61. What is the curved surface area of hemisphere (ice cream) if the base radiusis 7cm?

(a) 309 cm²　　　　(b) 308 cm²

(c) 803 cm²　　　　(d) 903 cm²

62. Slant height of a cone if the radius is 7cm and the height is 24 cm

(a) 26cm　　　　(b) 25 cm

(c) 52 cm　　　　(d) 62cm

63. The total surface area of cone with hemispherical ice cream is

(a) 858 cm²　　　　(b) 885 cm²

(c) 588 cm²　　　　(d) 855 cm²

 **Assertion & Reason**

DIRECTIONS : *Each of these questions contains an Assertion followed by Reason. Read them carefully and answer the question on the basis of following options. You have to select the one that best describes the two statements.*

(a) If both **Assertion** and **Reason** are **correct** and Reason is the **correct explanation** of Assertion.

(b) If both **Assertion** and **Reason** are correct, but Reason is **not the correct explanation** of Assertion.

(c) If **Assertion** is **correct** but **Reason** is **incorrect**.

(d) If **Assertion** is **incorrect** but **Reason** is **correct**.

64. **Assertion:** Total surface area of the cylinder having radius of the base 14 cm and height 30 cm is 3872 cm².

Reason: If r be the radius and h be the height of the cylinder, then total surface area $= (2\pi rh + 2\pi r^2)$.

65. **Assertion:** If the height of a cone is 24 cm and diameter of the base is 14 cm, then the slant height of the cone is 15 cm.

Reason: If r be the radius and h the slant height of the cone, then slant height $= \sqrt{h^2 + r^2}$.

66. **Assertion:** If the radius of a cone is halved and volume is not changed, then height remains same.

Reason: If the radius of a cone is halved and volume is not changed then height must become four times of the original height.

67. **Assertion:** If a ball is in the shape of a sphere has a surface area of 221.76 cm², then its diameter is 8.4 cm.

Reason: If the radius of the sphere be r, then surface area, $S = 4\pi r^2$, i. e. $r = \frac{1}{2}\sqrt{\dfrac{S}{\pi}}$.

68. **Assertion:** No. of spherical balls that can be made out of a solid cube of lead whose edge is 44 cm, each ball being 4 cm. in diameter, is 2541

Reason : Number of balls $= \dfrac{\text{Volume of one ball}}{\text{volume of lead}}$.

Surface Areas and Volumes

Match the Following

DIRECTIONS : *Each question contains statements given in two columns which have to be matched. Statements (A, B, C, D)in Column-I have to be matched with statements (p, q, r, s) in Column-II.*

69. For figure shown, match the column

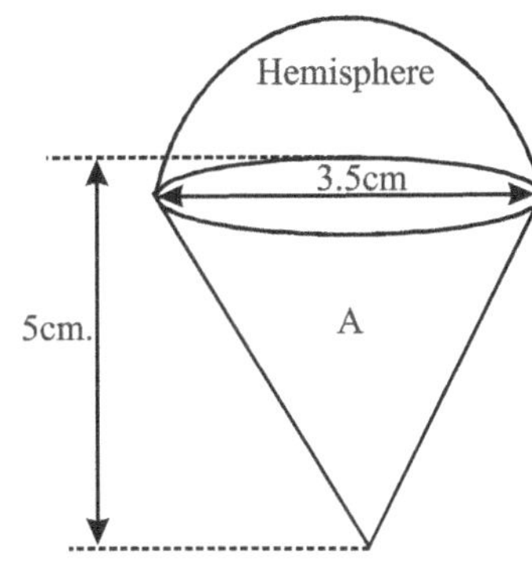

Fig. : Top (Lattu)

Column -I		Column-II	
(A) Curved area of hemisphere		(p)	3.25
(B) Height of cone		(q)	77/4
(C) Slant height of cone		(r)	3.7
(D) Surface area of top		(s)	39.6

70. For a wooden article was made by scooping out a hemisphere from each end of a solid cylinder, as shown in Fig. If the height of the cylinder is 10 cm, and its base is of radius 3.5 cm, match the column.

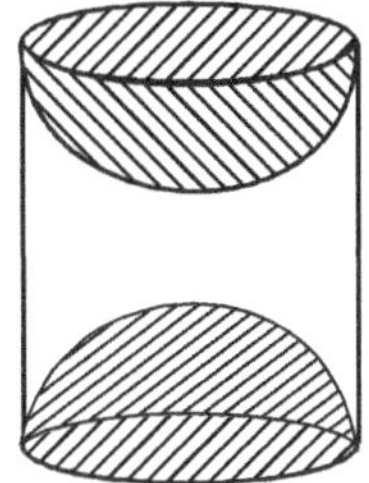

Column-I		Column-II	
(A) Volume of cylinder		(p)	616/3
(B) Volume of scoops		(q)	374
(C) Total surface area		(r)	$122.5\,\pi$
(D) Volume of the article		(s)	$171.5/3\,\pi$

71. From a solid cylinder of height 2.4 cm and diameter 1.4cm a conical cavity of the same height and same diameter is hollowed out then match the column.

Column-I		Column-II	
(A) Area of bottom of cylinder		(p)	10.56
(B) Outer curved surface area		(q)	1.54
(C) Curved area of conical cavity		(r)	5.5
(D) Total surface area		(s)	17.6

72.

Column-I (Object)		Column-II (Shape)	
(A) Dice		(p)	Right circular cone
(B) Road rollers		(q)	Sphere
(C) Ice-cream cone		(r)	Cylinder
(D) Volleyball		(s)	Cube

Fill in the Blanks

DIRECTIONS : *Complete the following statements with an appropriate word / term to be filled in the blank space(s).*

73. The volume of a cube with diagonal d is ....

74. A cube is a special type of ....

75. If the heights of two cylinders are equal and their radii are in the ratio of 7 : 5, then the ratio of their volumes is ....

76. The volume of a solid is the measurement of the portion of the .... occupied by it.

77. If the volume of a cube is 64 cm^3, then its surface area is ....

78. If the volume and the surface area of a solid sphere are numerically equal, then its radius is ....

79. The length of the diagonal of a cube that can be inscribed in a sphere of radius 7.5 cm is ....

True / False

DIRECTIONS : *Read the following statements and write your answer as true or false.*

80. Volume of the solid is measured in cubic units.

81. Area is the length of the boundary of a closed figure.

82. Area is the total surface covered by a closed figure.

83. The volume of sphere of diameter is $\dfrac{\pi d^3}{6}$.

84. The total surface area of a solid cylinder of radius r and height h is $2\pi r (h + r)$.

85. If a right circular cone and a cylinder have equal circles as their base and have equal heights, then the ratio of their volumes is 2 : 3

86. If the base area and the volume of a cone are numerically equal, then its height is 3 units.

87. If the curved surface of a right circular cylinder is 1760 cm^2 and its radius is 21 cm, then its height is $\dfrac{80}{3}$ cm.

88. If the total surface area of a cube is $\dfrac{50}{3}$ m^2, then its side is (5/3) m.

ANSWER KEY & SOLUTIONS

1. **(b)** Volume of cylinder $= \pi r^2 h$

$448\pi = \pi r^2 \times 7$

$\Rightarrow \quad r^2 = \dfrac{448}{7} \quad \Rightarrow \quad r = \sqrt{\dfrac{448}{7}}$

$\Rightarrow r = \sqrt{64} \Rightarrow r = 8$ cm

$\therefore \quad$ L. S. A or C. S. A $= 2\pi r h$

$= 2 \times \dfrac{22}{7} \times 8 \times 7 = 352$ cm^2

2. **(a)** $r = \dfrac{1.4}{2} = 0.7$ m and $h = 2$ m

Area covered $=$ C.S.A $\times$ number of revolutions

$= 2\pi r h \times 5 = 10\pi r h$

$\Rightarrow \quad 10\left(\dfrac{22}{7}\right)(0.7)(2) = 44$ m^2

3. **(d)** Let the diameter of the sphere be d units and the edge of the cube be a units, then

$4\pi\left(\dfrac{d}{2}\right)^2 = 6a^2 \Rightarrow \dfrac{d^2}{a^2} = \dfrac{6}{\pi} \Rightarrow \dfrac{d}{a} = \dfrac{\sqrt{6}}{\sqrt{\pi}}.$

4. **(a)** $R = \dfrac{45.5}{2} = 22.75$ cm , $r = \dfrac{42}{2} = 21$ cm

Capacity (volume)

$= \dfrac{2}{3}\pi\,(\mathrm{R}^3 - \mathrm{r}^3) = \dfrac{2}{3} \times \dfrac{22}{7} \times [(22.75)^3 - (21)^3]$

$= \dfrac{2}{3} \times \dfrac{22}{7} \times 2513.543 = 5266.46$ cm^3

or $\quad = \dfrac{5266.46}{1000}$ lts. $= 5.27$ litres

Outer surface area

$= 2\pi\mathrm{R}^2 = 2 \times \dfrac{22}{7} \times (22.75)^2 = 3253.25$ cm^2

5. **(c)** We know that, $\ell = \sqrt{r^2 + h^2}$,

$v = \dfrac{1}{3}\pi r^2 h\,,\, c = \pi r \ell$

L.H.S. $3\pi v h^3 - c^2 h^2 + 9v^2$

$\Rightarrow \quad 3\pi\left(\dfrac{1}{3}\pi r^2 h\right) h^3 - (\pi r \ell)^2 h^2 + 9\left(\dfrac{1}{3}\pi r^2 h\right)^2$

$\Rightarrow \quad 3\pi\left(\dfrac{1}{3}\pi r^2 h\right) h^3 - \pi^2 r^2 (r^2 + h^2)$

$h^2 + 9 \times \dfrac{1}{9}\pi^2 r^4 h^2 \qquad \left(\because \ \ell = \sqrt{h^2 + r^2}\right)$

$\Rightarrow \quad \pi^2 r^2 h^4 - \pi^2 r^4 h^2 - \pi^2 r^2 h^4 + \pi^2 r^4 h^2 = 0 =$ R.H.S.

6. **(b)** Height of cylinder, $h = 2$ cm

Circumference of base of cylinder $= 10$ cm

$\Rightarrow \quad 2\pi r = 10 \Rightarrow r = \dfrac{5}{\pi}$

Volume of the cylinder $= \pi r^2 h = \pi \times \dfrac{25}{\pi^2} \times 2 = \dfrac{50}{\pi}$

7. **(a)** In right $\triangle$AOB

$\dfrac{\mathrm{OB}}{\mathrm{OA}} = \tan\alpha \Rightarrow \mathrm{OB} = h\tan\alpha$

$\Rightarrow \quad r = h\tan\alpha$

Volume of cone $= \dfrac{1}{3}\pi r^2 h$

$= \dfrac{1}{3}\pi(h\tan\alpha)^2 h\ = \dfrac{1}{3}\pi h^3 \tan^2\alpha$

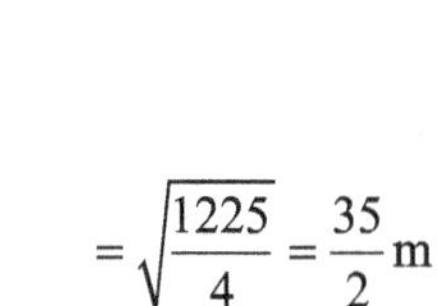

8. **(d)** Volume of $A = 18^3 = 5832$ cm^3

Volume of $B = 24^3 = 13824$ cm^3

Volume of $C = 27000$ cm^3

Total volume A, B and $C = 46656$ cm^3

Now, volume of new cube $D =$ sum of volumes of A, B and C.

Let a be the edge of D.

Then $a^3 = 46656 \Rightarrow a = 36$ cm.

9. **(b)** $\pi r^2 = 346.5 \Rightarrow r^2 = \left(\dfrac{3465}{10} \times \dfrac{7}{22}\right)$

$= \dfrac{441}{4} = \left(\dfrac{21}{2}\right)^2 \Rightarrow r = \dfrac{21}{2}$ m

$l = \sqrt{r^2 + h^2} = \sqrt{\dfrac{441}{4} + (14)^2} \quad = \sqrt{\dfrac{1225}{4}} = \dfrac{35}{2}$ m

Area of canvas

$$= \pi r l = \left(\frac{22}{7} \times \frac{21}{2} \times \frac{35}{2}\right) \text{m}^2 = 577.5 \text{m}^2$$

Length of canvas $= \dfrac{\text{Area}}{\text{Width}} = \dfrac{577.50}{1.1} \text{m} = 525$ m

10. (c) The centres of the bases of the cones form a triangle of side $2r$. The circumference of the circle will be identical to a circle drawn through the vertices of the cones and thus, it will have a radius of $2/\sqrt{3}$ times r, which is greater than r.

11. (c) Though, it is given that diameter of the cone is equal to the diameter of the spherical ball. But the ball will not fit into the cone because of its slant shape. Hence, more than 50% of the portion of the ball will be outside the cone.

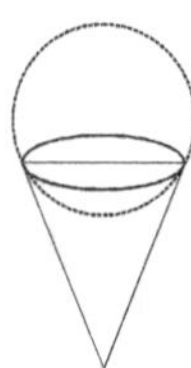

12. (b) Volume of the given ice cuboid $= 8 \times 11 \times 2 = 176$

Let the length of the required rod be ℓ.

$$\therefore \quad \pi \ell \frac{8^2}{4} = 176 \quad \therefore \quad \ell = 3.5 \text{ inches}$$

13. (a) $\pi r \ell = 2\pi r h \Rightarrow \dfrac{\ell}{h} = \dfrac{2}{1}$

14. (b) Edge of cube $= \dfrac{20}{4}$ cm $= 5$ cm,

surface area $= 6 \times 5^2$ cm$^2 = 150$ cm^2

15. (b)

16. (c)

17. (a)

18. (c) When the radius is increased by 100%, the corresponding volume becomes 800% and thus increase is 700%.

19. (b) As per the given conditions,

$$11 a^3 = 7 \times \frac{4}{3} \times \pi \times r^3 \quad \therefore \quad \frac{a}{r} = \left(\frac{8}{3}\right)^{1/3}$$

20. (a)

21. (b) [**Hint.** Quantity of juice

$$= \left(\pi \times 3^2 \times 15 - \frac{2}{3} \pi \times 3^3\right) \text{cm}^3]$$

22. (c) $2\pi R h : 2\pi r h = R : r$

23. (c) $\pi R^2 h : \pi r^2 h = R^2 : r^2$

24. (a) $\dfrac{1}{3} \pi r_1^2 h_1 : \dfrac{1}{3} \pi r_2^2 h_2$

$$\Rightarrow \frac{1}{3} \pi r_1^2 h_1 : \frac{1}{3} \pi r_1^2 h_2 \quad (\because r_1 = r_2)$$

$$\Rightarrow h_1 : h_2$$

25. (d) Volume of spherical shell

$$= \frac{4}{3} \pi R^3 - \frac{4}{3} \pi r^3 = \frac{4}{3} \pi (R^3 - r^3)$$

26. (c) Volume of sphere $= \dfrac{4}{3} \pi r^3 = \dfrac{4}{3} \pi (1)^3$

27. (b)   **28. (a)**

29. (c) Let h be the height and r be the radius of the cylinder.

Given $h = 2r$

Since, $\triangle PSC \sim \triangle AOC$

$\therefore$ By similarity of two triangles, we have

$$\frac{PS}{AO} = \frac{SC}{OC} = \frac{PC}{AC} \Rightarrow \frac{h}{12} = \frac{5-r}{5} = \frac{PC}{AC}$$

$$\Rightarrow \frac{h}{12} = \frac{5-r}{5} \Rightarrow \frac{2r}{12} = \frac{5-r}{5} \Rightarrow 10r = 60 - 12r$$

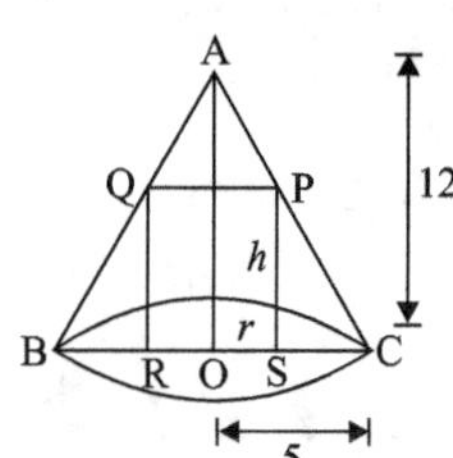

$$\Rightarrow r = \frac{30}{11} \text{ and } h = \frac{60}{11}$$

Volume of cylinder $= \pi r^2 h = \dfrac{22}{7} \left(\dfrac{900}{121}\right) \dfrac{60}{11} \approx 127.50$

30. (c) Let a_1 and a_2 be the sides of two cubes and S_1 and S_2 be the surface area of cubes

$$\therefore \frac{a_1^3}{a_2^3} = \frac{27}{64} \Rightarrow \frac{a_1}{a_2} = \frac{3}{4}, \frac{S_1}{S_2} = \frac{6a_1^2}{6a_2^2} = \frac{9}{16}$$

31. (b) $\dfrac{V_1}{V_2} = \dfrac{125}{64} ; \dfrac{\frac{4}{3} \pi r_1^3}{\frac{4}{3} \pi r_2^3} = \dfrac{125}{64} \Rightarrow \dfrac{r_1}{r_2} = \dfrac{5}{4} ;$

$$\frac{SA_1}{SA_2} = \frac{4\pi r_1^2}{4\pi r_2^2} = \left(\frac{r_1}{r_2}\right)^2 = \frac{25}{16} = 25 : 16.$$

32. (d) Volume of metallic block = 1 m^3 ...(1)

Let the side of the square base be x m

So, volume of the rectangular bar = $x^2 \times 9$ ...(2)

Volume of metallic block = Volume of rectangular bar

So, $9x^2 = 1 \Rightarrow x^2 = \dfrac{1}{9} \Rightarrow x = \dfrac{1}{3}$ m

Side of biggest cube possible = $\dfrac{1}{3}$ m

So, weight of the cube = weight of block $\times \left(\dfrac{1}{3}\right)^3$

$= 90 \times \dfrac{1}{27} = \dfrac{10}{3}\,\text{kg} = 3\dfrac{1}{3}\,\text{kg}$

33. (c) Since, all the edges of cuboid are integers and base is square.

Let the length, breadth and height of cuboid be x, x, y.

Sum of all edges of cuboid = $4x + 4x + 4y$

Sum of area of all faces = $2x^2 + 2xy + 2xy$

Given,

Sum of all edges of cuboid = Sum of area of all faces

$\therefore \quad 4x + 4x + 4y = 2(x^2 + xy + xy)$

$\Rightarrow \quad x^2 + 2xy - 4x - 2y = 0$

$\Rightarrow \quad x^2 + 2x\,(y - 2) - 2y = 0$

$\Rightarrow \quad x = \dfrac{-2(y-2) \pm \sqrt{4(y-2)^2 + 4(2y)}}{2}$

$\Rightarrow \quad x = y - 2 \pm \sqrt{y^2 - 2y + 4}$

Then x is integer, when $y = 2$ $\therefore$ $y = 2, x = 2$

Hence, the required sum of edges of cuboid

$= 8x + 4y = 16 + 8 = 24$

34. (d) Let sides of the solid brick be $x, 2x$ and $3x$.

Volume = Number of bricks = $6x^3$

$6x^3 < 400$

$x^3 < \dfrac{400}{6}$

$x^3 < 66\dfrac{2}{3}$

Number less than 66 which is perfect cube is 64 than volume = $6 \times 64 = 384$ i.e., no. of cube = 384.

35. (c)

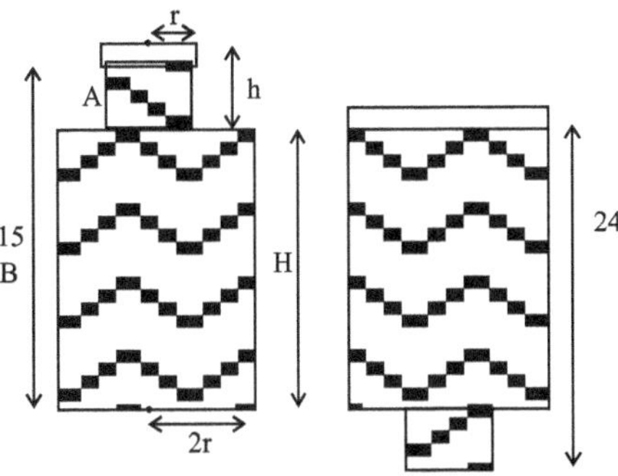

Let the height of cylinder A be h and height of cyilnder B be H. Since, in both the situation, the volume of the water in the bottle remains same, then

$\pi(2r)^2 H + \pi r^2(15 - H) = \pi r^2 h + \pi(2r)^2(24 - h)$

$\pi r^2\,[4H + (15 - H)] = \pi r^2[h + 4(24 - h)]$

$4H + 15 - H = h + 4\,(24 - h)$

$3H + 15 = h + 96 - 4h$

$3H + 15 = 96 - 3h$

$H + 5 = 32 - h$

$H + h = 27$ cm

36. (b) Let height and radius of cone is h and r respectively such that $h, r \in I$

$\because$ Volume of cone = Surface area of cone

$\therefore \quad \dfrac{1}{3}\pi r^2 h = \pi r l + \pi r^2$

$\Rightarrow \quad \dfrac{1}{3}\pi r^2 h = \pi r \sqrt{h^2 + r^2} + \pi r^2$

$\Rightarrow \quad \dfrac{1}{3} r h = \sqrt{h^2 + r^2} + r \qquad [\because r \neq 0]$

$\Rightarrow \quad rh - 3r = 3\sqrt{h^2 + r^2}$

$\Rightarrow \quad r^2 h^2 + 9r^2 - 6hr^2 = 9h^2 + 9r^2$

$\Rightarrow \quad h^2(r^2 - 9) = 6hr^2 \Rightarrow h = \dfrac{6r^2}{r^2 - 9}$

$\Rightarrow \quad h = 6\left(\dfrac{r^2}{r^2 - 9}\right) \quad \Rightarrow \quad h = 6 + \dfrac{54}{r^2 - 9}$

h and r are integers

Here $(r^2 - 9)$ should be factor of 54.

$\therefore \quad r^2 - 9 = 1, 2, 3, 6, 9, 18, 27, 54.$

$\Rightarrow \quad r^2 = 10, 11, 12, 15, 18, 27, 36, 63.$

$\therefore \quad r = 6$ (only possible value)

$\therefore \quad h = 6 + \dfrac{54}{36 - 9} = 6 + 2 = 8 \quad \therefore \quad r = 6, h = 8$

37. (c) Let r_1 and r_2 be the radii of two cones.

Volume of cylinder = Sum of volume of two cones

$$\pi \times 7^2 \times 10 = \frac{\pi}{3} \times 10(r_1^2 + r_2^2)$$

$$\Rightarrow \quad r_1^2 + r_2^2 = 49 \times 3 \qquad \qquad ...(i)$$

$\therefore \quad$ Percentage increase

$$= \frac{\pi r_1^2 + \pi r_2^2 - 2\pi \times 7^2}{2 \times \pi \times 7^2} \times 100 = \frac{r_1^2 + r_2^2 - 2 \times 49}{2 \times 49} \times 100$$

$$= \frac{(49 \times 3 - 49 \times 2)}{49 \times 2} \times 100 \qquad \text{[From (i)]}$$

$$= 50\%$$

38. (c) It is given that $6(x^2 + y^2 + z^2) = 498$, where x, y and z are sides of cubes.

$x^2 + y^2 + z^2 = 83$, for x, y, z to be integer

$x = \sqrt{49}$, $y = \sqrt{25}$, $z = \sqrt{9} \Rightarrow x = 7, y = 5, z = 3$

Now, sum of volumes$= 7^3 + 5^3 + 3^3$

$\Rightarrow \quad 343 + 125 + 27 = 495$

For x, y, z to be integer

$x = \sqrt{81}$, $y = \sqrt{1}$, $z = \sqrt{1} \Rightarrow x = 9, y = 1, z = 1$

Sum of volumes $= 9^3 + 1^3 + 1^3 = 729 + 1 + 1 = 731$

So, total sum of volume of cubes is $(495 + 731)$ 1226.

39. (b) 40. (d) 41. (d) 42. (b) 43. (c)

44. (a) 45. (c) 46. (d) 47. (a) 48. (b)

49. (d) Volume of cylindrical cup $= \pi r^2 h$

$$\frac{22}{7} \times \frac{7}{2} \times \frac{7}{2} \times 10.5 = 404.25 \text{ cm}^3$$

50. (b) Volume of hemispherical cup

$$= \frac{2}{3}\pi r^3 = \frac{3}{2} \times \frac{22}{7} \times \left(\frac{7}{2}\right)^3 = 89.83 \text{ cm}^3$$

51. (d) Cylindrical glass, 314.42 cm^3

52. (c) Curved surface area of cone $= 551 \Rightarrow \pi rl = 441$

$$\Rightarrow \frac{22}{7} \times 7 \times 1 = 551$$

$$\Rightarrow 1 = 25.045$$

$$\therefore \ h = \sqrt{1^2 - r^2} = 24 \text{ m}$$

53. (b) Space occupied by each student $= \dfrac{\pi r^2}{4} = 38.5 \text{ m}^2$

54. (a) Volume of hemispherical dome

$$= \frac{2}{3}\pi r^3 = \frac{2}{3} \times \frac{22}{7} \times 21 \times 21 \times 21 = 19404 \text{ cu. m}$$

55. (b) $\dfrac{4}{3}\pi r^3$

56. (b) Cloth required to cover hemispherical done = curved surface area of hemisphere $= 2\pi r^2 = 1232$ sq. m

57. (c) Surface area of combined figure $= 2\pi r^2 + 2(1 + b)h$
$= 1232 + 2(6 + 4)8 = 1392$ sq. m

58. (d) 192 m^3

59. (d) Length of diagonal $= \sqrt{31^2} = 6\sqrt{3}$

60. (c) Volume of cube $= (\text{side})^3 = 343$ cm^3

61. (b) Curved surface area of hemisphere $= 2\pi r^2 = 308$ cm^2

62. (b) Slant height $= \sqrt{r^2 + h^2} = 25$ cm

63. (a) 858 cm^2

64. (a) Assertion and Reason both are correct and reason is the correct explanation of the assertion .

Total surface area $= 2\pi rh + 2\pi r^2 = 2\pi r(h + r)$

$$= 2 \times \frac{22}{7} \times 14 \ (30 + 14) = 88 \ (44)$$

$$= 3872 \text{ cm}^2$$

65. (d) Assertion is incorrect here, but reason is correct.

Slant height $= \sqrt{(14/2)^2 + (24)^2} = \sqrt{49 + 576}$

$$= \sqrt{625} = 25 \text{ cm}$$

66. (d) Assertion is incorrect and reason is true.

$$\frac{V_1}{V_2} = \frac{(1/3)\pi r^2 h_1}{(1/3)\pi (r/2)^2 h_2} = \frac{4h_1}{h_2}$$

As $\ V_1 = V_2$

$\therefore \quad h_2 = 4h_1$

67. (a) Both assertion and reason are correct and reason is the correct explanation of the assertion.

68. (c) Assertion is correct but reason is not correct.

69. (A) $\to$ (q); (B) $\to$ (p); (C) $\to$ (r); (D) $\to$ (s)

70. (A) $\to$ (r); (B) $\to$ (s); (C) $\to$ (q) ; (D) $\to$ (p)

71. (A) $\to$ (q); (B) $\to$ (p); (C) $\to$ (r); (D) $\to$ (s)

72. (A) $\to$ (s); (B) $\to$ (r); (C) $\to$ (p); (D) $\to$ (q)

73. $\dfrac{d^3}{3\sqrt{3}}$ cb. units.

74.	cuboid	**82.**	True
75.	49 : 25	**83.**	True
76.	space	**84.**	True
77.	96 cm^2	**85.**	False
78.	3 units	**86.**	True
79.	15 cm	**87.**	False
80.	True	**88.**	True
81.	False		

15. Statistics

DIRECTIONS : *This section contains multiple choice questions. Each question has 4 choices (a), (b), (c) and (d) out of which only one is correct.*

1. For the following grouped frequency distribution

Class	3–6	6–9	9–12	12–15	15–18	18–21	21–24
Frequency	2	5	10	23	21	12	3

Consider the following.

(I) Lower limit of model class is 12

(II) Frequency of the class preceding the model class = 10

(III) Mode = 14.6

(IV) Width of the model class is 4

Which of the following is correct?

(a) I and II   (b) II and III

(c) I, II and III   (d) All of these

2. The marks in science of 80 students of class X are given below. Find the mode of these marks obtained by the students in science.

Marks	0–10	10–20	20–30	30–40	40–50
Frequency	3	5	16	12	13
Marks	50–60	60–70	70–80	80–90	90–100
Frequency	20	5	4	1	1

(a) 53.18   (b) 53.25

(c) 52.25   (d) 53

3. There are three sections A, B and C in class X with 25, 40 and 35 students respectively. The average marks obtained by section A, B and C are 70%, 65% and 50% respectively. Find the average marks of entire class X.

(a) 59%   (b) 56%

(c) 63%   (d) 61%

4. The mean weight of a class of 35 students is 45kg. If the weight of a teacher be included, the mean weight increases by 500 grams. Find the weight of the teacher.

(a) 63 kg   (b) 61 kg

(c) 64 kg   (d) 70 kg

5. In the following distribution

Monthly income range (in ₹)	Number of families
Income more than ₹ 10,000	100
Income more than ₹ 13,000	85
Income more than ₹ 16,000	69
Income more than ₹ 19,000	50
Income more than ₹ 22,000	33
Income more than ₹ 25,000	15

the number of families having income range (in ₹) 16000 – 19000 is

(a) 15   (b) 16

(c) 17   (d) 19

6. Find the mean of the following frequency distribution.

Class Interval	0–10	10–20	20–30	30–40	40–50
Frequency	8	12	10	11	9

(a) 25. 3   (b) 25.2

(c) 24   (d) 25.5

7. Calculate the mean of the following frequency distribution:

C. I.	0–80	80–160	160–240	240–320	320–400
Frequency	22	35	44	25	24

(a) 195.5   (b) 198.8

(c) 196.8   (d) 195

8. If the mean of first 'n' odd natural numbers is 'n' itself, what is the value of 'n'?

(a) 2   (b) 3

(c) 1   (d) Any natural number

9. What is the arithmetic mean of 20 fours, 40 fives, 30 sixes and 10 tens?

  (a) 50   (b) 25

  (c) 5.6   (d) 33

10. The mean of discrete observations $y_1, y_2, \ldots\ldots, y_n$ is given by

  (a) $\dfrac{\sum\limits_{i=1}^{n} y_i}{n}$ (b) $\dfrac{\sum\limits_{i=1}^{n} y_i}{\sum\limits_{i=1}^{n} i}$

  (c) $\dfrac{\sum\limits_{i=1}^{n} y_i f_i}{n}$ (d) $\dfrac{\sum\limits_{i=1}^{n} y_i f_i}{\sum\limits_{i=1}^{n} f_i}$

11. If the mean of the numbers $27 + x, 31 + x, 89 + x, 107 + x, 156 + x$ is 82, then the mean of $130 + x, 126 + x, 68 + x, 50 + x, 1 + x$ is

  (a) 75   (b) 157

  (c) 82   (d) 80

12. If the class-intervals are $10 - 19, 20 - 29, 30 - 39, \ldots\ldots\ldots\ldots$, then the upper limit of the first class-interval is

  (a) 19.5   (b) 19

  (c) 20   (d) None of these

13. The numbers 3, 5, 7 and 9 have their respective frequencies $x - 2, x + 2, x - 3$ and $x + 3$. If the arithmetic mean is 6.5, then the value of x is

  (a) 3   (b) 4

  (c) 5   (d) 6

14. The median of a set of 9 distinct observations is 20.5. If each of the largest 4 observation of the set is increased by 2, then the median of the new set

  (a) is increased by 2

  (b) is decreased by 2

  (c) is two times the original median

  (d) remains the same as that of the original set

15. A set of numbers consists of three 4's, five 5's, six 6's, eight 8's and seven 10's. The mode of this set of numbers is

  (a) 6   (b) 7

  (c) 8   (d) 10

16. The mean of a set of 20 observation is 19.3. The mean is reduced by 0.5 when a new observation is added to the set. The new observation is

  (a) 19.8   (b) 8.8

  (c) 9.5   (d) 30.8

17. In a frequency distribution, the mid value of a class is 10 and the width of the class is 6. The lower limit of the class is

  (a) 6   (b) 7   (c) 8   (d) 12

18. If the mean of the observations $x, x + 3, x + 5, x + 7$ and $x + 10$ is 9, then the mean of the last three observations is

  (a) $10\dfrac{1}{3}$ (b) $10\dfrac{2}{3}$

  (c) $11\dfrac{1}{3}$ (d) $11\dfrac{2}{3}$

19. The mean of fifteen different natural numbers is 13. The maximum value for the second largest of these numbers is

  (a) 46   (b) 51   (c) 52   (d) 53

20. For the data $(2, 9, x + 6, 2x + 3, 5, 10, 5)$ if mean is 7, then mode is

  (a) 3   (b) 5   (c) 9   (d) 10

21. The mean of three positive numbers is 10 more than the smallest of the numbers and 15 less than the largest of the three. If the median of the three numbers is 5, then the mean of squares of the numbers is

  (a) $108\dfrac{2}{3}$ (b) $116\dfrac{2}{3}$

  (c) $208\dfrac{1}{3}$ (d) $216\dfrac{2}{3}$

22. Positive integers from 1 to 21 are arranged in 3 groups of 7 integers each, in some particular order. Then the highest possible mean of the medians of these 3 groups is ______

  (a) 16   (b) 12.5

  (c) 11   (d) 14

23. The mean of 5 observation is 15. If the mean of first three observations is 14 and last three observations is 17, then the third observation is :

  (a) 18   (b) 19   (c) 17   (d) 20

24. The mean of a group of eleven consecutive natural numbers is m. What will be the percentage change in the mean when next six consecutive natural numbers are included in the group ?

  (a) $m\%$ (b) $\dfrac{m}{3}\%$ (c) $\dfrac{m}{300}\%$ (d) $\dfrac{300}{m}\%$

25. A 100 mark examination was administered to a class of 50 students. Despite only integer marks being given, the average score of the class was 47.5. Then, the maximum number of students who could get marks more than the class average is

  (a) 25   (b) 35   (c) 45   (d) 49

26. Let $x_1, x_2, ..., x_{11}$ be 11 distinct positive integers. If we replace the largest of these integers by the median of the other 10 integers, then

(a) the median remains the same

(b) the mean increases

(c) the median decreases

(d) the mean remains the same

27. The mean of 15 observations written in some order is 50. If the mean of first eight observations and last eight observations are 48 and 53 respectively, then the eighth observation is

(a) 35   (b) 80   (c) 72   (d) 58

DIRECTIONS : *Study the given Case/Passage and answer the following questions.*

Case/Passage-I

COVID-19 Pandemic

The COVID-19 pandemic, also known as coronavirus pandemic, is an ongoing pandemic of coronavirus disease caused by the transmission of severe acute respiratory syndrome coronavirus 2 (SARS-CoV-2) among humans.

[From CBSE Question Bank 2021]

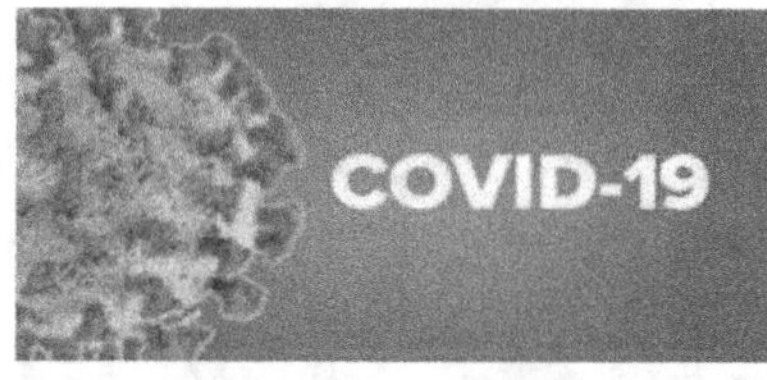

The following tables shows the age distribution of case admitted during a day in two different hospitals

Table 1

Age (in years)	5-15	15-25	25-35	35-45	45-55	55-65
No. of cases	6	11	21	23	14	5

Table 2

Age (in years)	5-15	15-25	25-35	35-45	45-55	55-65
No. of cases	8	16	10	42	24	12

Refer to table 1

28. The average age for which maximum cases occurred is

(a) 32.24   (b) 34.36

(c) 36.82   (d) 42.24

29. The upper limit of modal class is

(a) 15   (b) 25

(c) 35   (d) 45

30. The mean of the given data is

(a) 26.2   (b) 32.4

(c) 33.5   (d) 35.4

Refer to table 2

31. The mode of the given data is

(a) 41.4   (b) 48.2

(c) 55.3   (d) 64.6

32. The median of the given data is

(a) 32.7   (b) 40.2

(c) 42.3   (d) 48.6

Case/Passage-II

COVID-19 Pandemic

Electricity energy consumption is the form of energy consumption that uses electric energy. Global electricity consumption continues to increase faster than world population, leading to an increase in the average amount of electricity consumed per person (per capita electricity consumption).

[From CBSE Question Bank 2021]

Teriff	:	LT. Residential
Type of Supply	:	Single Phase
Meter Reading Date	:	31-11-13
Previous Reading Date	:	31-10-13
Bill Number	:	384750
Connected Load	:	3 kW
Meter Reading	:	65700
Previous Meter Reading	:	65500
Units consumed	:	269

A survey is conducted for 56 families of a Colony A. The following tables gives the weekly consumption of electricity of these families.

Weekly consumption (in units)	0-10	10-20	20-30	30-40	40-50	50-60
No. of families	16	12	18	6	4	0

The similar survey is conducted for 80 families of Colony B and the data is recorded as below:

Weekly consumption (in units)	0-10	10-20	20-30	30-40	40-50	50-60
No. of families	0	5	10	20	40	5

Refer to data received from Colony A

33. The median weekly consumption is

    (a) 12 units   (b) 16 units

    (c) 20 units   (d) None of these

34. The mean weekly consumption is

    (a) 19.64 units   (b) 22.5 units

    (c) 26 units   (d) None of these

35. The modal class of the above data is I

    (a) 0-10   (b) 10-20

    (c) 20-30   (d) 30-40

Refer to data received from Colony B

36. The modal weekly consumption is

    (a) 38.2 units   (b) 43.6 units

    (c) 26 units   (d) 32 units

37. The mean weekly consumption is

    (a) 15.65 units   (b) 32.8 units

    (c) 38.75 units   (d) 48 units

Assertion & Reason

DIRECTIONS : *Each of these questions contains an Assertion followed by Reason. Read them carefully and answer the question on the basis of following options. You have to select the one that best describes the two statements.*

    (a) If both **Assertion** and **Reason** are **correct** and Reason is the **correct explanation** of Assertion.

    (b) If both **Assertion** and **Reason** are correct, but Reason is **not the correct explanation** of Assertion.

    (c) If **Assertion** is **correct** but **Reason** is **incorrect**.

    (d) If **Assertion** is **incorrect** but **Reason** is **correct**.

38. **Assertion :** The arithmetic mean of the following given frequency distribution table is 13.81.

x	4	7	10	13	16	19
f	7	10	15	20	25	30

    Reason : $\bar{x} = \dfrac{\sum f_i x_i}{\sum f_i}$.

39. **Assertion :** If the number of runs scored by 11 players of a cricket team of India are 5, 19, 42, 11, 50, 30, 21, 0, 52, 36, 27 then median is 30.

    Reason : Median $= \left(\dfrac{n+1}{2}\right)^{th}$ value, if n is odd.

40. **Assertion :** If the value of mode and mean is 60 and 66 respectively, then the value of median is 64.

    Reason : Median $= \dfrac{1}{2}$ (mode + 2 mean).

Match the Following

DIRECTIONS : *Each question contains statements given in two columns which have to be matched. Statements (A, B, C, D) in column-I have to be matched with statements (p, q, r, s) in column-II.*

41. The table shows a frequency distribution of the life time of 400 radio tubes tested at a company.

Life time (hours)	Number of tubes	Life time (hours)	Number of tubes
300 – 399	14	800 – 899	62
400 – 499	46	900 – 999	48
500 – 599	58	1000 – 1099	22
600 – 699	76	1100 – 1199	6
700 – 799	68		

Column-II gives data for description given in Column-I, match them correctly.

	Column-I		Column-II
(A)	Upper limit of the fifth class	(p)	100
(B)	Lower limit of the eighth class	(q)	949.5
(C)	Class marks of the seventh class	(r)	1000
(D)	Class interval size	(s)	799

42. Following is the distribution of heights of students in a class and the total number of students is 50.

Height (in cm)	Frequency	Cumulative frequency
150 – 155	12	a
155 – 160	b	25
160 – 165	10	c
165 – 170	d	43
170 – 175	e	48
175 – 180	2	f

With the help of information given match the columns.

Column-I (Unknown)		Column-II (Values)	
(A)	$a =$	(p)	35
(B)	$b =$	(q)	5
(C)	$c =$	(r)	13
(D)	$d =$	(s)	50
(E)	$e =$	(t)	12
(F)	$f =$	(u)	8

43.

	Column-I		Column-I
(A)	The arithmetic mean of a set of observations is obtained by	(p)	Value of the $\left(\dfrac{n+1}{2}\right)^{th}$ observation.
(B)	The value of the observation having maximum frequency is called	(q)	$\dfrac{1}{2}\times$ Value of $\left[\left(\dfrac{n}{2}\right)^{th}+\left(\dfrac{n}{2}+1\right)^{th}\right]$ observations.
(C)	If n is odd, then median is equal to	(r)	Median
(D)	If n is even, then median is equal to	(s)	Mode
(E)	– divides the arranged series (in ascending or descending order) into two equal parts.	(t)	Dividing the sum of the values of observations by the number of observations parts.

44.

	Column-I		Column-II
(A)	Mean of first five prime numbers is	(p)	12
(B)	Mean of all factors of 24 is	(q)	7.5
(C)	Mean of first six multiples of 4 is	(r)	5.6
(D)	If mean of $x-5y$, $x-3y$, $x-y$, $x+y$, $x+3y$ and $x+5y$ is 12, then x is	(s)	14

45. For the following marks distribution of 5 students in an examination, match Column-I with the data given in Column- II.

Class interval	0–10	10–20	20–30	30–40
No. of students	1	3	0	1

Here,

x_k = lower limit of the modal class interval

h = width of the class interval

f_k = frequency of the modal class

f_{k-1} = frequency of the class preceding the modal class

f_{k+1} = frequency of the class succeeding the modal class

Column-I	Column-II
(A) x_k	(p) 3
(B) f_k	(q) 10
(C) f_{k-1}	(r) 0
(D) h	(d) 1

46. For the given frequency distribution, match the Column-I with Column-II.

Class	30–35	35–40	40–45	45–50	50–55	55–60	60–65
Frequency	14	16	18	23	18	8	3

h = width of the class interval

c = cumulative frequency

f = frequency of the class interval to which median belongs

l_1 = lower limit of the median class interval

Column-I	Column-II
(A) f	(p) 45.4
(B) c	(q) 45
(C) l_1	(r) 48
(D) median	(s) 23

▶ Fill in the Blanks ⟫⟫

DIRECTIONS : *Complete the following statements with an appropriate word / term to be filled in the blank space(s).*

47. Median divides the total frequency into .... equal parts.

48. The algebraic sum of the deviations from arithmetic mean is always ....

49. The class mark of a class is 25 and if the upper limit of that class is 40, then its lower limit is ....

50. The mid-value of 20-30 is ....

51. The sum of 12 observations is 600, then their mean is ....

52. In the class interval 35-46, the lower limit is .... and upper limit is ....

53. A class interval of a data has 15 as the lower limit and 25 as the size, then the class mark is ....

54. 0–10, 10–20, 20–30 .... so on are the classes, the lower boundary of the class 20–30 is ....

55. The mid-point of a class interval is called its ....

56. Facts or figures, collected with a definite purpose, are called ....

57. Value of the middle-most observation (s) is called ....

58. The .... is the most frequently occurring observation.

59. 3 median = mode + ... mean

60. To find the mode of a grouped data, the size of the classes is ....

61. On an ogive, point A (say), whose Y- co-ordinate is $\dfrac{n}{2}$ (half of the total observation), has its X-coordinate equal to .... of the data.

62. Two ogives, for the same data intersect at the point P. Then, Y-coordinate of P represents ....

DIRECTIONS : *Read the following statements and write your answer as true or false.*

63. The median for grouped data is formed by using the formula, $\text{Median} = l + \left(\dfrac{\dfrac{n}{2} - cf}{f}\right) \times h$

64. $\text{Class mark} = \dfrac{\text{Upper class limit} + \text{Lower class limit}}{2}$

65. The median of grouped data with unequal class sizes cannot be calculated.

66. The modal value is the value of the variate which divides the total frequency into two equal parts.

67. The mean of x, y, z is y, then $x + z = 2y$

68. 2(Median – Mean) = Mode – Mean.

69. Mean may or may not be the appropriate measure of central tendency.

70. If 16 observations are arranged in ascending order, then median is $\dfrac{(8\text{th observation} + 9\text{th observation})}{2}$

71. Median of 15, 28, 72, 56, 44, 32, 31, 43 and 51 is 43.

72. Mode of 2, 3, 4, 5, 0, 1, 3, 3, 4, 3 is 3.

73. Mean of 41, 39, 48, 52, 46, 62, 54, 40, 96, 52, 98, 49, 42, 52, 60 is 55.4

ANSWER KEY & SOLUTIONS

1.   **(c)**

Class	3–6	6–9	9–12	12–15	15–18	18–21	21–24
f_i	2	5	10	23	21	12	3

Here the maximum frequency is 23 and the corresponding class is 12-15

We have $l = 12$, $h = 13$, $f = 23$, $f_1 = 10$

and $f_2 = 21$

$$\text{Mode} = l + \frac{f - f_1}{2f - f_1 - f_2} \times h$$

$$\Rightarrow \quad \text{Mode} = 12 + \frac{23 - 10}{46 - 10 - 21} \times 3$$

$$\Rightarrow \quad \text{Mode} = 12 + \frac{39}{15} = 14.6$$

2.   **(a)**   The class (50-60) has maximum frequency i.e. 20 therefore this is the modal class.

Lower Limit of the modal class $= l = 50$

Class-Interval $= h = 10$

Frequency of the modal class $= f_i = 20$

Frequency of the class preceding the modal class $= f_0 = 13$

Frequency of the class succeeding the modal class $= f_2 = 5$

$$\text{Mode}, N_0 = 1 + \left(\frac{f_1 - f_0}{2f_1 - f_0 - f_2} \right) \times h$$

$$= 50 + \left(\frac{20 - 13}{2 \times 20 - 13 - 5} \right)$$

$$= 50 + \frac{7}{22} \times 10 = 50 + 3.18 = 53.18$$

3.   **(d)** $n_1 = 25 \quad \overline{x}_1 = 70\%$

$n_2 = 40 \quad \overline{x}_2 = 65\%$

$n_3 = 35 \quad \overline{x}_3 = 50\%$

$$\overline{x} = \frac{n_1 \overline{x}_1 + n_2 \overline{x}_2 + n_3 \overline{x}_3}{n_1 + n_2 + n_3}$$

$$= \frac{(25 \times 70) + (40 \times 65) + (35 \times 50)}{25 + 40 + 35}$$

$$= \frac{1750 + 2600 + 1750}{100} = \frac{6100}{100} = 61\%$$

4.   **(a)**   Let the mean weight of a class of 35 students be $\overline{x}_1$ and that of both students and a teacher be $\overline{x}_2$

Then $\overline{x}_1 = 45$ kg and

$$\overline{x}_2 = 45 + \frac{500}{1000} = 45 + 0.5 = 45.5\,\text{kg}$$

$$\overline{x}_1 = \frac{\Sigma x_1}{n_1}, \quad \overline{x}_2 = \frac{\Sigma x_2}{n_1}$$

$$\Rightarrow 45 = \frac{\Sigma x_1}{35}, \quad 45.5 = \frac{\Sigma x_2}{36}$$

$$\Rightarrow \quad \Sigma x_1 = 1575 \text{ kg}, \quad \Sigma x_2 = 1638 \text{ kg}$$

$\Rightarrow$ Total weight = weight of students + weight of teacher

$\therefore$ Weight of teacher = Total weight – weight of students

$\therefore$ Weight of the teacher $= \Sigma x_2 - \Sigma x_1$

$$= 1638 - 1575 = 63 \text{ kg}$$

5.   **(d)**   Clearly, the number of families having income range (in ₹)

$16000 - 19000 = 69 - 50 = 19.$

6.   **(b)**

C.I.	x_i	f_i	$f_i x_i$
0 – 10	5	8	40
10 – 20	15	12	180
20 – 30	25	10	250
30 – 40	35	11	385
40 – 50	45	9	405
		50	1260

We have $\bar{x} = \dfrac{\Sigma fx}{\Sigma f} = \dfrac{1260}{50} = 25.2$

7. (c) Let $a = 200$

C.I.	f_i	x_i	$d_i = x_i - 200$	$f_i d_i$
0 – 80	22	40	– 160	– 3520
80 – 160	35	120	– 80	– 2800
160 – 240	44	200	0	0
240 – 320	25	280	+80	+2000
320 – 400	24	360	+ 160	+ 3840
	150			– 480

$$\bar{x} = a + \frac{1}{n}\sum_{i=1}^{5} f_i d_i = 200 + \frac{1}{150}(-480)$$

$= 200 - 3.2 = 196.8$

8. (d) First find the sum of first 'n' odd natural numbers

$1 = 1^2$

$1 + 3 = 4 = 2^2$

$1 + 3 + 5 = 9 = 3^2$

$1 + 3 + 5 + \dots + (2n - 1) = n^2.$

$\text{Mean} = \dfrac{\text{Sum of observations}}{n} = \dfrac{n^2}{n} = n$

It is given that the mean is 'n' itself.

$\therefore \quad n = n$

Thus, 'n' is any natural number.

9. (c) $\bar{x} = \dfrac{20(4) + 40(5) + 30(6) + 10(10)}{20 + 40 + 30 + 10}$

$= \dfrac{80 + 200 + 180 + 100}{100} = \dfrac{560}{100} = 5.6$

10. (a)

11. (a) Given,

$82 = \dfrac{(27 + x) + (31 + x) + (89 + x) + (107 + x) + (156 + x)}{5}$

$\Rightarrow \quad 82 \times 5 = 410 + 57 \Rightarrow 410 - 410 = 5x \Rightarrow x = 0$

$\therefore$ Required mean is,

$\bar{x} = \dfrac{130 + x + 126 + x + 68 + x + 50 + x + 1 + x}{5}$

$\bar{x} = \dfrac{375 + 5x}{5} = \dfrac{375 + 0}{5} = \dfrac{375}{5} = 75$

12. (a)   **13. (c)**

14. (d) Since $n = 9$, then middle term $= \left(\dfrac{9+1}{2}\right)^{th} = 5^{th}$ term.

Now, last four observations are increased by 2.

$\because$ The median is 5th observation, which is remains unchanged.

$\therefore$ There will be no change in median.

15. (c) Mode of the data is 8 as it is repeated maximum number of times.

16. (b)

17. (b) Let x be the upper limit and y be the lower limit.

Since, the mid value of the class is 10.

$\therefore \quad \dfrac{x + y}{2} = 10 \Rightarrow x + y = 20 \quad \quad .....(i)$

and $x - y = 6$ (width of the class = 6) $\quad .....(ii)$

By solving equations (i) and (ii), we get $y = 7$.

Hence, lower limit of the class is 7.

18. (c) We know, $\text{Mean} = \dfrac{\text{Sum of all the observations}}{\text{Total no. of observation}}$

$\Rightarrow \quad \text{Mean} = \dfrac{x + x + 3 + x + 5 + x + 7 + x + 10}{5}$

$9 = \dfrac{5x + 25}{5} \Rightarrow x = 4$

So, mean of last three observations i.e; 14, 11 and 9 is

$\dfrac{14 + 11 + 9}{3} = \dfrac{34}{3} = 11\dfrac{1}{3}$

19. (b) Given, $\dfrac{x_1 + \dots + x_{15}}{15} = 13$

$x_1 + x_2 + x_3 + \dots + x_{15} = 15 \times 13 = 195$

In order to set the second largest and largest, first thirteen natural numbers are

$1, 2, 3, 4, 5, 6, 7, 8, 9, 10, 11, 12, 13$

So, $x_{14} + x_{15} = 195 - \dfrac{13 \times 14}{2}$

$\Rightarrow \quad x_{14} + x_{15} = 195 - 91 = 104$

Now, from the options, we have

$x_{14} = 51$ and $x_{15} = 53$

Now, second largest is 51.

20. (c) Mean $= \dfrac{2+9+x+6+2x+3+5+10+5}{7} = 7$

$3x + 40 = 49 \Rightarrow x = 3$

$x + 6 = 9 \Rightarrow 2x + 3 = 9$

Data $(2, 9, 9, 9, 5, 10, 5)$ and Mode $= 9$

21. (d) Let the three numbers be a, b and c such that $a > b > c$

According to the given condition

$\dfrac{a+b+c}{3} = c + 10 = a - 15 = k$

$\Rightarrow \quad c = k - 10$

Also, $a = k + 15$; $b = 5$ ($\because$ Median $= 5$)

We know that, $a + b + c = 3k$

$\Rightarrow \quad k + 15 + 5 + k - 10 = 3k$

$\Rightarrow \quad 10 = k$

Thus, $a = 25$, $b = 5$, $c = 0$

$\therefore \quad$ Mean of squares of the numbers

$= \dfrac{25^2 + 5^2 + 0^2}{3} = \dfrac{650}{3} = 216\dfrac{2}{3}$

22. (d) We need to maximize the median in each group to maximize the average of all median.

Highest possible median is 18 at there should be 3 numbers higher than it in a group of 7.

So we have

$$1 \quad 2 \quad 3 \quad ⑱ \quad 19 \quad 20 \quad 21$$

Similarly, $4 \quad 5 \quad 6 \quad ⑭ \quad 15 \quad 16 \quad 17$

$$7 \quad 8 \quad 9 \quad ⑩ \quad 11 \quad 12 \quad 13$$

Medians are, $\quad 18, 14$ and 10.

Mean $= \dfrac{18 + 14 + 10}{3} = \dfrac{42}{3} = 14$

23. (a) 3rd observation $= (14 \times 3) + (3 \times 17) - (5 \times 15) = 18$

24. (d) Since, the mean of a group of eleven consecutive natural numbers is m, then

$\dfrac{x + x + 1 + \ldots + x + 10}{11} = m$

$11x + 55 = 11\,m$; $x + 5 = m$; $x = m - 5$

Let n be the mean when next six consecutive natural numbers are included in the group then

$\dfrac{x + x + 1 + \ldots.. + x + 16}{17} = n$;

$17x + \dfrac{16 \times 17}{2} = 17n$

$17x + 8 \times 17 = 17\,n$

$m - 5 + 8 = n$

$\Rightarrow n = m + 3$

$\qquad (\because x = m - 5)$

Hence, required percentage change in the mean

$= \dfrac{n - m}{m} \times 100 = \dfrac{m + 3 - m}{m} \times 100 = \dfrac{300}{m}\%$

25. (d) Total number of students $= 50$

Average marks of student $= 47.5$

$\therefore$ Total marks of students $= 50 \times 47.5 = 2375$

Now, the student get integer marks

Hence, for maximum number of students who could get marks more than 47.5,

we will divide total marks by 48.

$\therefore \dfrac{2375}{48} \approx 49$

26. (c) Let $x_1 < x_2 < \ldots < x_{11}$

Median of $x_1, x_2, \ldots, x_{10} = \dfrac{x_5 + x_6}{2}$

Now replace x_{11} by $\dfrac{x_5 + x_6}{2}$ and then arrange in order

So, new set of numbers are

$x_1, x_2, x_3, x_4, x_5, \dfrac{x_5 + x_6}{2}, x_6, x_7, x_8, x_9, x_{10},$

Hence, median is $\dfrac{x_5 + x_6}{2} < x_6$

$\Rightarrow$ median decreases

27. **(d)** Let $x_1, x_2, x_3, ..., x_{15}$ be the no. of observations

$$x_1 + x_2 + x_3 + x_4 + ... + x_8 = 384$$

$$x_8 + x_9 + x_{10} + ... + x_{15} = 424$$

$$x_1 + x_2 + x_3 + ... + x_{15} = 750$$

$$x_1 + x_2 + x_3 + x_4 + x_5 + x_6 + x_7 + x_8 ... + x_{15} = 750$$

$$384 - x_8 + 424 = 750$$

Hence, eighth observation is 58

28. **(c)** Mode $= l + \left(\dfrac{f_1 - f_0}{2f_1 - f_0 - f_2}\right) h = 36.82$

29. **(d)** Modal class = The class with maximum frequency

$$= 35 - 45$$

$\therefore$ Upper limit of modal class = 45

30. **(d)** Mean $= \dfrac{\Sigma f_i x_i}{\Sigma f_i} = \dfrac{2830}{80} = 35.4$

31. **(a)** Mode $= l + \left(\dfrac{f_1 - f_0}{2f_1 - f_0 - f_2}\right) h = 41.4$

32. **(b)** Median $= 1 + \left(\dfrac{\dfrac{n}{2} - Cf}{f}\right) \times h = 40.2$

Weekly consumption	No. of families f_i	Cumulative frequency cf	Class marks x_i	$f_i x_i$
1-10	16	16	5	8
10-20	12	28	15	180
20-30	18	46	25	450
30-40	6	52	35	210
40-50	4	56	45	180
50-60	0	0	55	0
	$\Sigma f_i = 56$			$\Sigma f_i d_i = 110$

33. **(c)** Median $= 1 + \left(\dfrac{\dfrac{n}{2} - cf}{f}\right) h = 20$ units

34. **(a)** Mean $(\bar{x}) = \dfrac{\Sigma f_i x_i}{\Sigma f_i} = 19.64$ units

35. **(c)** Modal class = the class with maximum frequency

$$= 20 - 30$$

36. **(b)** Modal weekly consumption

$$= 1 + \left(\dfrac{f_1 - f_0}{2f_1 - f_0 - f_2}\right) h = 43.6 \text{ units}$$

37. **(c)** Mean weekly consumption

$$= \dfrac{\Sigma f_i x_i}{\Sigma f_i} = \dfrac{3100}{80} = 38.75 \text{ units}$$

38. **(a)** Both assertion and reason are true, reason is the correct explanation of the assertion.

39. **(d)** Arranging the terms in ascending order,

0, 5, 11, 19, 21, 27, 30, 36, 42, 50, 52

median value $= \left(\dfrac{11+1}{2}\right)^{th} = 6^{th}$ value $= 27$

40. **(c)** Median $= \dfrac{1}{3}$ (mode $+ 2$ mean) $= \dfrac{1}{3}(60 + 2 \times 66) = 64$

41. (A) $\rightarrow$ (s); (B) $\rightarrow$ (r); (C) $\rightarrow$ (q); (D) $\rightarrow$ (p)

42. (A) $\rightarrow$ (t); (B) $\rightarrow$ (r); (C) $\rightarrow$ (p); (D) $\rightarrow$ (u); (E) $\rightarrow$ (q); (F) $\rightarrow$ (s)

As we know, cumulative frequency of an interval is equal to the sum of frequency of that interval and of previous intervals.

$\therefore$ $a = 12$

$a + b = 25 \Rightarrow b = 13$ $\qquad (\because a = 12)$

Now, $25 + 10 = c \Rightarrow c = 35$

$c + d = 43 \Rightarrow d = 8$ $\qquad (\because c = 35)$

$43 + e = 48 \Rightarrow e = 5$

and, $f = 48 + 2 = 50$

43. (A) $\rightarrow$ (t); (B) $\rightarrow$ (s); (C) $\rightarrow$ (p); (D) $\rightarrow$ (q); (E) $\rightarrow$ (r)

44. (A) $\rightarrow$ (r); (B) $\rightarrow$ (q); (C) $\rightarrow$ (s); (D) $\rightarrow$ (p)

45. (A) $\rightarrow$ (q); (B) $\rightarrow$ (s); (C) $\rightarrow$ (t); (D) $\rightarrow$ (q)

46. (A) $\rightarrow$ (s); (B) $\rightarrow$ (u); (C) $\rightarrow$ (q); (D) $\rightarrow$ (p)

47. two

48. zero

49. 10

50. 25

51. 50

52. 35, 46	**53.** 27.5	**63.** True	**64.** True
54. 20	**55.** class-mark	**65.** False	**66.** False
56. data	**57.** median	**67.** True	**68.** False
58. mode	**59.** 2	**69.** True	**70.** True
60. uniform	**61.** Median	**71.** True	**72.** True
62. cumulative frequency of the median class.		**73.** True	

www.ingramcontent.com/pod-product-compliance
Lightning Source LLC
Chambersburg PA
CBHW060111120726
48003CB00009B/2594